ZAGAT®

New York City
Gourmet Shopping
& Entertaining
2008

EDITOR
Carol Diuguid

Published and distributed by
Zagat Survey, LLC
4 Columbus Circle
New York, NY 10019
T: 212.977.6000
E: nycgourmetshopping@zagat.com
www.zagat.com

ACKNOWLEDGMENTS

We thank Betsy Andrews, Siobhan Burns, Caren Weiner Campbell, Mikola De Roo, Margot P. Ernst, Lynn Hazlewood, George Louis Jr., Gerard Miller, Bernie Onken, Patty Tang, Alexandria Tara, Miranda Van Gelder and Laura J. Vogel, as well as the following members of our staff: Josh Rogers (assistant editor), Christina Livadiotis (editorial assistant), Sean Beachell, Maryanne Bertollo, Sandy Cheng, Reni Chin, Larry Cohn, Alison Flick, Jeff Freier, Shelley Gallagher, Michelle Golden, Caroline Hatchett, Roy Jacob, Natalie Lebert, Mike Liao, Dave Makulec, Andre Pilette, Becky Ruthenburg, Robert Seixas, Kilolo Strobert, Sharon Yates, Yoji Yamaguchi and Kyle Zolner.

Contents

Ratings & Symbols

	Name	Symbols	Category	Zagat Ratings			
Zagat Top Spot				QUALITY	DISPLAY	SERVICE	COST

Area, Address & Contact

Review, surveyor comments in quotes

				▽ 23	9	13	$15

Z Tim & Nina's ◗ *Seafood*

W 50s | 4 Columbus Circle (8th Ave.), 1/A/B/C/D to 59th St./Columbus Circle | 212-977-6000 | www.zagat.com

Fanatical fish fanciers find that the fastest route to "fairly fared fin fare" is a foray to this "grungy grotto" below Columbus Circle, where the catch is "never more than a day old" and "the price is always net"; still, sensitive shoppers say the "surly staffers should be used as fish-bait"; P.S. check out the "daily East River specials" and Tim and Nina's catering service on the A train.

Ratings

Quality, Display and **Service** are rated on a scale of 0 to 30.

0	-	9	poor to fair
10	-	15	fair to good
16	-	19	good to very good
20	-	25	very good to excellent
26	-	30	extraordinary to perfection
	▽		low response | less reliable

Cost reflects our surveyors' estimate of the price range, indicated as follows:

I	Inexpensive
M	Moderate
E	Expensive
VE	Very Expensive

Symbols

Z	Zagat Top Spot (highest ratings, popularity and importance)
◗	open until 8:30 PM or later
🖃	mail order available via catalog, phone or Web
⊅	no credit cards accepted

About This Survey

Here are the results of our **2008 New York City Gourmet Shopping & Entertaining Survey,** covering 1,758 establishments in New York City, including 357 party sites. In addition, we've added 75 outstanding online sources. Like all our guides, this one is based on the collective opinions of thousands of savvy consumers.

WHO PARTICIPATED: Input from 6,807 avid customers forms the basis for the ratings and reviews in this guide (their comments are shown in quotation marks within the reviews). Of these surveyors, 60% are women, 40% men; the breakdown by age is 12% in their 20s; 28%, 30s; 22%, 40s; 22%, 50s; and 16%, 60s or above. Their collective experience adds up to roughly 655,000 transactions a year. We sincerely thank each of these participants – this book is really "theirs."

HELPFUL LISTS: Whether you're looking for food, flowers, wine or liquor, staff or locations or whether you want to save money or splurge, our lists can help you find exactly the right place. See Best Overall (page 9), Top Ratings (pages 10–18) and Best Buys (page 19). We've also provided 57 handy indexes. And, for the first time ever, we've added an Online Sources section to help guide you to the best Web sites for everything from fresh flowers, fish and meat to candy, baked goods and even hard-to-find party accessories. See Best Overall and Top Quality Ratings (pages 308–309).

ABOUT ZAGAT: This marks our 28th year reporting on the shared experiences of consumers like you. What started in 1979 as a hobby involving 200 of our friends has come a long way. Today we have over 300,000 surveyors and now cover dining, entertaining, golf, hotels, movies, music, nightlife, resorts, shopping, spas, theater and tourist attractions worldwide.

SHARE YOUR OPINION: We invite you to join any of our upcoming surveys – just come to at **zagat.com,** where you can rate and review establishments year-round. Each participant will receive a free copy of the resulting guide when published.

AVAILABILITY: Zagat guides are available in all major bookstores, by subscription at **zagat.com** and for use on a wide range of mobile devices via **Zagat To Go.**

FEEDBACK: There is always room for improvement, thus we invite your comments and suggestions about any aspect of our performance. Just contact us at nycgourmetshopping@zagat.com.

New York, NY
July 19, 2007

Nina and Tim

Nina and Tim Zagat

What's New

New York's gourmet shopping and entertainment scene has continued to flourish since our last Survey, with a whopping 64% of voters reporting spending more on food and entertaining than they did two years ago. They are cooking at home 3.7 times a week, on average, and nearly a third of them say they are entertaining more at home too. Here's what else is happening:

 **A SCENE GROWS IN BROOKLYN:** If the trend continues, the Borough of Churches will soon be known as the Borough of Bakeries: in the past year Park Slope alone has gained three top-flight patisseries, including an impressive new French-Belgian player, Colson, Trois Pommes, opened by a former Union Square Cafe pastry chef, and an offshoot of the Carroll Gardens veteran Sweet Melissa. In Boerum Hill, bespoke bakers Cheryl Kleinman and Ellen Baumwoll joined forces to debut a retail storefront, Betty Bakery, while Cheeks set up shop in Williamsburg and is whipping up American classics using all-natural and local ingredients.

THINKING GREEN: Speaking of natural ingredients, New Yorkers' focus on the wholesomeness and provenance of their food continues to grow, with 82% of surveyors saying they are willing to pay more for food that is organic, locally produced and/or sustainably sourced. Nearly half of them are regular shoppers of the Greenmarket system, and their other options for conscientious buying keep increasing. Examples include Maury Rubin's Bird Bath bakeries, which not only peddle all-organic creations, but boast interiors built exclusively with environmentally sound materials. And Great Performances, one of NYC's top caterers, has acquired its own organic farm Upstate, produce from which is turning up on plates at swish events all over town.

 CUPCAKE WARS: NYC's love affair with the cupcake shows no signs of cooling, so for the first time this year we include a tops-in-genre ranking. It may raise an eyebrow or two that the shop that spawned the craze, Magnolia Bakery, has been supplanted by bakeries opened by former employees, including Sugar Sweet Sunshine on the Lower East Side (No. 1) and Billy's Bakery in Chelsea (No. 4).

SWEET SHAKEUP: The city's seemingly insatiable appetite for high-end chocolates is being fed by a field of boutiques that's stronger than ever, and includes some upstarts to challenge the old guard. The most dramatic example is Kee's Chocolates, a SoHo sliver owned by young French-trained confectioner Kee Ling Tong, which has steadily built a devoted following since opening five years ago, and this year displaced reigning king La Maison du Chocolat as No. 1 for Candy in NYC. Another relative newcomer, Chocolat Michel Cluizel, elbowed out more seasoned veterans to rise to No. 4 in the category. There are also more and more purveyors like Chelsea's Chocolat Moderne and the Flatiron's Vere that have no storefronts but nonetheless have

subscribe to zagat.com

gained national recognition for their high-quality goods sold online, in gourmet outlets and from their factories during specified hours.

MI, OH MY: Stick-to-the-ribs *banh mi* sandwiches, long a staple in the Vietnamese community, seem to be gaining a toehold among mainstream munchers. The classic version features roast pork, cilantro, pickled carrots, cucumber and hot peppers piled high on a crusty baguette, and this year three practitioners made our list of top-rated Sandwich Shops: Bánh Mì Saigon Bakery, Nicky's Vietnamese Sandwiches and Viet-Nam Bánh Mì So #1.

BRIDGE AND TUNNEL: Increasingly the city's Major Gourmet Markets are casting their eyes to the outer boroughs as they chart their expansion plans. In addition to Fairway's gargantuan, wildly popular new outpost in Brooklyn's Red Hook and the more modest – but still welcome – branch of Amish Market in Glendale, Queens, construction is underway on a Whole Foods Market on the fringe of Park Slope, and plans also are moving forward for the city's second Trader Joe's store, to be located in Forest Hills.

ON THE HORIZON: Slated to open soon in TriBeCa is an outpost of the renowned Philadelphia coffee purveyor La Colombe, a retail store/espresso bar that will give NYers a crack at some of the country's best roasted beans (rated No. 1 for Coffee in our Online Sources Survey). A supplier to many of the nation's top restaurants, the company has been running a training school for chefs and other professionals in the old Terminal Warehouse space in West Chelsea. In the works from chef Cesare Casella is Bean Bar, a take-out counter in Grand Central, which will sell Tuscan bean dishes that should be familiar to regulars of his eatery, Maremma, as well as uncooked legumes and other Italian imports. Also set to open in Grand Central is the city's second outpost of a Westchester ice cream mainstay, Blue Pig.

BITCHIN': While surveyors are greatly enamored by NYC's food, wine and entertaining resources, they also find occasional things to fault. When asked what irritated them most, 41% said crowding and lines, 30% cited high prices and 16% pointed to poor service. Hopefully, the purveyors included in this guide will take their customers' complaints to heart.

SURF'S UP: A remarkable 67% of our surveyors report turning to the Internet for their food and entertaining-related needs at least occasionally, thus, for the first time ever this year we conducted a survey of the best gourmet shopping and entertaining re- sources online. We have included reviews covering our surveyors' top 75 picks, along with a number of handy top lists and indexes in the back of the book, starting on page 307.

New York, NY
July 19, 2007

Carol Diuguid

RIVERSIDE PARK
Riverside Dr.
W. 86th St.
Dean & DeLuca
E. 86th St.
UPPER WEST SIDE
American Museum of Natural History
E. 83rd St.
Lobel's Prime Meats
UPPER EAST SIDE
2nd Ave.
1st Ave.
Zabar's
W. 79th St.
Metropolitan Museum of Art
E. 79th St.
West End Ave.
Broadway
La Maison du Chocolat
Citarella
W. 74th St.
Amsterdam Ave.
Columbus Ave.
Levain Bakery
The Lake
William Poll
E. 75th St.
Citarella
W. 72nd St.
West Side Hwy.
Broadway
Central Park West
Payard Pâtisserie & Bistro
E. 72nd St.
CENTRAL PARK
5th Ave.
Madison Ave.
Ito En
Park Ave.
Lexington Ave.
3rd Ave.
E. 69th St.
2nd Ave.
1st Ave.
1/4 mi
W. 66th St.
E. 64th St.

Borgatti's Ravioli & Egg Noodles
N.J.
BRONX
Time Warner Center
Bouchon Bakery
Whole Foods
The Pond
Sherry-Lehmann
E. 61st St.
TriServe
Queensborough Bridge
Absolute Bagels
Citarella
MAN
La Guardia Airport
Columbus Circle
Central Park South
Petrossian Boutique & Cafe
E. 59th St.
E. 57th St.
Top detail
Artopolis Bakery
8th Ave.
Westerly Natural Market
Ave. of the Americas
MIDTOWN
Dessert Delivery / Wine & Roses
Bridge Kitchenware
E. 55th St.
E. 52nd St.
Bottom detail
Lemon Ice King of Corona
Rockefeller Center
La Maison du Chocolat
Lexington Ave.
Pisacane Midtown
Zezé
E. 49th St.
Sahadi's
Two for the Pot
QUEENS
Sullivan St. Bakery
5th
Madison Ave.
E. 47th St.
Grand Central Terminal
Murray's Cheese Shop
United Nations
D'Amico Foods
BROOKLYN
Kennedy International Airport
W. 42nd St.
BRYANT PARK
Penzeys Spices
Coluccio & Sons
Broadway
Original SoupMan
Villabate Pasticceria
New York Public Library
Park Ave.
3rd Ave.
2nd Ave.
1st Ave.
2 mi

Burgundy Wine Company
W. 26th St.
Park Ave. S.
Lexington Ave.
3rd Ave.
2nd Ave.
1st Ave.
FDR Dr.
East River
W. 25th St.
MADISON SQ. PARK
Whole Foods
Ave. of the Americas
Belle Fleur
GRAMERCY PARK
E. 23rd St.
W. 23rd St.
W. 22nd St.
5th Ave.
E. 21st St.
CHELSEA
Moore Brothers Wine Co.
E. 18th St.
10th Ave.
9th Ave.
8th Ave.
7th Ave.
W. 16th St.
Broadway
UNION SQ.
Irving Pl.
E. 14th St.
Amy's Bread
Whole Foods
MEAT-PACKING DIST.
E. 12th St.
Gansevoort St.
Jack's Stir Brew Coffee
EAST VILLAGE
Stonehouse
Hudson St.
Greenwich Ave.
7th Ave. S.
W. 10th St.
Citarella
University Pl.
4th Ave.
E. 10th St.
E. 9th St.
1st Ave.
Ave. A
Ave. B
TOMPKINS SQ. PARK
WEST VILLAGE
Patisserie Claude
WASHINGTON SQ. PARK
3rd Ave.
E. 4th St.
Charles St.
Jones St.
Florence Meat
GREENWICH VILLAGE
Lafayette St.
Whole Foods
Russ & Daughters
Sugar Sweet Sunshine
Colette's Cakes
Barrow St.
Morton St.
Murray's Cheese Shop
Broadway
Bleecker St.
Dean & DeLuca
E. Houston St.
Il Laboratorio del Gelato
Rivington St.
LOWER EAST SIDE
Raffetto's
Sullivan St.
Alessi
Olive's
Greene St.
Prince St.
NOLITA
Delancey St.
Allen St.
Kossar's Bialys
Kee's Chocolates
Spring St.
Dom's Fine Foods
SOHO
Broome St.
Pickle Guys
Grandaisy Bakery
Thompson St.
Grand St.
DiPalo Dairy
LITTLE ITALY
E. Broadway
Hudson St.
Varick St.
Viet-Nam Banh Mi So #1
Canal St.
Bazzini, A.L.
TRIBECA
White St.
Center St.
CHINATOWN
Manhattan Bridge
Hudson River
W. Broadway
Church St.
Leonard St.
Worth St.
Park Row
Madison St.
Henry St.
FDR Dr.
Jay St.
East River
1/4 mi
Korin Japanese Trading Co.
Warren St.
City Hall

Best Overall

Averaging Quality, Display & Service ratings.

<u>28</u> Zezé | *Flowers*
Moore Brothers | *Wines*
Colette's Cakes | *Bakery*

<u>27</u> Lobel's Meats | *Meat*
Richart Design | *Candy*
Belle Fleur | *Flowers*
Ito En | *Coffee/Tea*
Minamoto Kitchoan | *Candy*
Bottlerocket Wine | *Wine*
Petrossian | *Caviar*

<u>26</u> Takashimaya | *Flowers*
Pierre Marcolini | *Candy*
La Maison Chocolat | *Candy*
Vino | *Wines*
Dessert Delivery | *Bakery*
Murray's Cheese | *Cheese*
Sylvia Weinstock | *Bakery*
Nespresso | *Coffee/Tea*
Le Dû's Wines | *Wine*
Artisanal | *Cheese*
East Village Meat | *Meat*
Russ & Daughters | *Smoked Fish*
Sherry-Lehmann | *Wine*
Artopolis Bakery | *Bakery*
LeNell's | *Wines**
Jacques Torres | *Candy*
Staubitz Market | *Meat*

<u>25</u> Abigail Kirsch | *Caterer*
Payard Pâtisserie | *Bakery*
Williams-Sonoma | *Cookware*

Burgundy Wine | *Wine*
Bloom | *Flowers*
Faicco's Pork | *Meat*
DiPalo Dairy | *Cheese*
Lady M | *Bakery*
Italian Wine | *Wine*
Bedford Cheese | *Cheese*
Blue Apron | *Specialty*
Teuscher Chocolates | *Candy*
Manhattan Fruitier | *Specialty*
Crush Wine | *Wine*
Florence Meat | *Meat*
Kee's Chocolates | *Candy*
Morrell | *Wine*
Despaña Foods | *Specialty*
Martine's Chocolates | *Candy*
Red, White & Bubbly | *Wine*
Glorious Food | *Caterer*
Villabate | *Bakery*
Korin Japanese | *Cookware*
Almondine Bakery | *Bakery*
Bouley Bakery | *Bakery*
Biancardi Meats | *Meat*
Vosges | *Candy*
Black Hound | *Bakery*
Financier Pâtisserie | *Bakery*
Bay Ridge Bakery | *Bakery*
Bierkraft | *Beer*
Ariston | *Flowers*

<u>24</u> Calabria Pork | *Meat*

KEY NEWCOMERS

Our take on the most notable new arrivals of the past year. For a full list see the Noteworthy Newcomers index on page 269.

Alessi | *Cookware*
Barbarini Alimentari | *Prepared*
Brooklyn Kitchen | *Cookware*
Cheeks | *Bakery*
Choice Market | *Prepared*
Colson Patisserie | *Bakery*
Formaggio Essex | *Cheese*
Grom | *Ice Cream*

Kidfresh | *Specialty*
Max Brenner | *Candy*
Nespresso Boutique | *Coffee/Tea*
Stonehouse | *Specialty*
Tinto Fino | *Wine*
Tisserie | *Bakery*
Tribeca Treats | *Bakery*
Vestry Wines | *Wine*

* Indicates a tie with property above

Top Quality Ratings

Ratings are to the left of names. Lists exclude places with low votes, unless indicated by a ∇. Major Gourmet Markets are listed by the scores they received for the applicable department.

29
- Colette's Cakes
- Lobel's Meats
- Zezé
- Florence Meat
- Grandaisy Bakery*
- Kee's Chocolates
- Salumeria Biellese
- Burgundy Wine
- DiPalo Dairy
- La Maison Chocolat
- Staubitz Market | Bklyn
- Borgatti's Ravioli | Bx
- Martine's Chocolates
- Moore Brothers
- Sherry-Lehmann

28
- Petrossian
- Dessert Delivery
- Belle Fleur
- Murray's Cheese
- Vino
- Il Laboratorio
- Artisanal
- Russ & Daughters
- Kossar's Bialys
- Ito En

- Korin Japanese*
- Villabate | Bklyn*
- Artopolis Bakery | Qns
- Pierre Marcolini
- Levain Bakery
- Sullivan St. Bakery
- Almondine Bakery | Bklyn
- Calabria Pork | Bx*
- East Village Meat*
- Faicco's Pork | multi
- Takashimaya
- Pisacane
- Bierkraft | Bklyn
- Simchick, L.
- Payard Pâtisserie
- Randazzo's | Bx
- Blue Ribbon Market
- Jacques Torres | multi
- Madonia Bakery | Bx
- Ronnybrook Farms
- Coluccio & Sons | Bklyn
- Richart Design*
- Raffetto's
- Lady M
- Bridge Kitchenware

BY CATEGORY

BAGELS/BIALYS

28
- Kossar's Bialys

26
- Absolute Bagels
- Ess-a-Bagel
- Bagel Oasis | Qns
- Murray's Bagels
- H & H Bagels

25
- Terrace Bagels | Bklyn
- Hot Bialys | Qns

BREAD

29
- Grandaisy Bakery

28
- Sullivan St. Bakery
- Blue Ribbon Market
- Madonia Bakery | Bx

27
- Balthazar Bakery
- Bouley Bakery
- Falai Panetteria
- Addeo's | Bx

CAKES

29
- Colette's Cakes

28
- Dessert Delivery
- Payard Pâtisserie
- Lady M

27
- Soutine
- S&S Cheesecake | Bx

26
- Black Hound
- Sylvia Weinstock

CANDY

29
- Kee's Chocolates
- La Maison Chocolat
- Martine's Chocolates

28
- Pierre Marcolini
- Jacques Torres | multi
- Richart Design
- Minamoto Kitchoan

27
- Teuscher Chocolates

CATERERS/EVENT PLANNERS

26 Abigail Kirsch | *multi*
25 Glorious Food
Blue Smoke
Cleaver Co.
24 Foremost
Great Performances
23 David Burke
Movable Feast | *Bklyn*

CAVIAR/SMOKED FISH

28 Petrossian
Russ & Daughters
Zabar's
27 Barney Greengrass
Murray's Sturgeon
Sable's
26 Caviar Russe
24 Acme Smoked Fish | *Bklyn*

CHEESE/DAIRY

29 DiPalo Dairy
28 Murray's Cheese
Artisanal
Ronnybrook Farms
Zabar's
Joe's Dairy
27 Alleva Dairy
Dean & DeLuca

COFFEE

27 D'Amico Foods | *Bklyn*
Jack's Stir Brew
McNulty's Tea
26 Porto Rico Import
Mudspot
Joe
25 Nespresso Boutique
Sensuous Bean

COOKIES

28 Levain Bakery
27 Patisserie Claude
Stork's Pastry | *Qns*
26 Black Hound
Duane Park
25 City Bakery
Veniero's
24 One Girl Cookies | *Bklyn*

COOKWARE/SUPPLIES

28 Korin Japanese
Bridge Kitchenware
27 Zabar's
Williams-Sonoma
Alessi
Dean & DeLuca
26 Cook's Companion | *Bklyn*
Broadway Panhandler

CUPCAKES

27 Sugar Sweet
26 Amy's Bread
25 Baked | *Bklyn*
Billy's Bakery*
Make My Cake*
24 BabyCakes
Sweet Melissa | *Bklyn*
23 Magnolia Bakery

DELIS/SANDWICHES

(See also Sandwich Shops)
27 Dean & DeLuca
Zabar's
26 William Poll
Agata & Valentina
25 E.A.T.
Whole Foods
24 Katz's Deli
Fairway | *multi*
Manganaro Foods

FLOWERS

29 Zezé
28 Belle Fleur
Takashimaya
27 Ariston
Bloom
26 Dahlia
25 Surroundings
Chelsea Wholesale

GIFT BASKETS

29 Sherry-Lehmann
28 Dessert Delivery
Artisanal
27 Orchard | *Bklyn*
Manhattan Fruitier
26 Black Hound
Wild Edibles
24 Chelsea Baskets

GREENMARKET VENDORS

29 Bulich Mushroom
Violet Hill Farm
Blue Moon Fish
Yuno's Farm
28 Keith's Farm
Coach Dairy Goat
Flying Pigs
Cherry Lane Farms

HEALTH/NATURAL FOODS

- 27 Whole Foods
- 25 Westerly Natural
  - Gary Null's
  - Commodities Natural
  - Fairway | *multi*
- 24 LifeThyme Mkt.
  - Perelandra Natural | *Bklyn*
  - Bell Bates Natural

HERBS/SPICES

- 27 Penzeys Spices
  - Dean & DeLuca
  - Kalustyan's
- 26 Aphrodisia
- 24 Spice Corner
  - Manhattan Fruit Ex.
- 23 Angelica's Herbs
  - Foods of India*

ICE CREAM

- 28 Il Laboratorio
- 27 Lemon Ice King | *Qns*
  - L'Arte del Gelato
- 26 Sant Ambroeus
  - Cones
- 25 Brooklyn Ice Cream | *Bklyn*
  - Ciao Bella Gelato | *multi*
  - Chinatown Ice Cream

MAJOR GOURMET MARKETS

- 27 Zabar's
  - Dean & DeLuca
- 26 Whole Foods
  - Citarella
  - Agata & Valentina
  - Fairway | *multi*
- 25 Eli's Manhattan
  - Eli's Vinegar

MEATS/POULTRY

- 29 Lobel's Meats
  - Florence Meat
  - Salumeria Biellese
  - Staubitz Market | *Bklyn*
- 28 Calabria Pork | *Bx*
  - East Village Meat*
  - Faicco's Pork | *multi*
  - Agata & Valentina

NEWCOMERS (RATED)

- 29 Grandaisy Bakery
- 27 Tribeca Treats▽
  - Alessi
  - Stonehouse

- 26 Formaggio Essex▽
- 25 Nespresso Boutique
- 22 Max Brenner
- 20 Tisserie

NUTS/DRIED FRUITS

- 29 Bazzini, A.L.
- 27 Sahadi's | *Bklyn*
  - Kalustyan's
- 26 Dean & DeLuca
- 25 Zabar's
- 24 Economy Candy
- 23 Sweet Life
- 21 Aji Ichiban

PARTY RENTALS

- 24 TriServe
- 23 Atlas Party Rentals
- 22 Party Rental
- 20 Party Time
  - Props for Today*
- 19 Broadway Famous

PASTAS

- 29 Borgatti's Ravioli | *Bx*
- 28 Raffetto's
- 27 Agata & Valentina
  - Queen Ann Ravioli | *Bklyn*
  - Piemonte Ravioli
- 26 Pastosa Ravioli | *multi*
  - Durso's Pasta | *Qns*
- 25 Ravioli Store

PASTRIES

- 28 Villabate | *Bklyn*
  - Artopolis Bakery | *Qns*
  - Almondine Bakery | *Bklyn*
  - Payard Pâtisserie
- 27 Financier Pâtisserie
  - Bouley Bakery
  - Bouchon Bakery
  - Margot Pâtisserie

PIES/TARTS

- 28 Payard Pâtisserie
- 27 Bouchon Bakery
- 26 Silver Moon
  - La Bergamote
  - Duane Park
- 25 Steve's/Pies | *Bklyn*
  - City Bakery
  - Once Upon A Tart

PREPARED FOODS

- 26 Dean & DeLuca
  - William Poll
  - Remi to Go

Pepe
25 Bottega/Via
Lorenzo & Maria's
Zabar's
E.A.T.

PRODUCE

27 Dean & DeLuca
Whole Foods
26 Greenmarket
Eli's Manhattan
25 Fairway | *multi*
Garden of Eden | *multi*
Greenwich Produce
24 Manhattan Fruit Ex.

SANDWICH SHOPS

(See also Delis/Sandwiches)
25 Olive's
Bánh Mì Saigon
24 'wichcraft
Nicky's Vietnamese | *multi*
23 Carve
Viet-Nam Bánh*
Starwich
22 Tiny's Giant

SEAFOOD

28 Citarella
Pisacane
Randazzo's | *Bx*
27 Consenza's Fish | *Bx*
26 Leonard's
Lobster Place
Wild Edibles
25 Fish Tales | *Bklyn*

SINGULAR FOCUS

27 Pickle Guys (*pickles*)
Stonehouse (*olive oil*)
25 O&CO. (*olive oil*)
23 Dale & Thomas (*popcorn*)

Pickles, Olives (*pickles*)
Rice/Riches (*rice pudding*)

SOUPS

25 Zabar's
E.A.T.
24 Dishes
23 Original SoupMan | *multi*
22 Hale & Hearty | *multi*
Fairway | *multi*
Devon & Blakely
20 Whole Foods

SPECIALTY SHOPS

28 Coluccio & Sons | *Bklyn*
27 Dom's
Blue Apron | *Bklyn*
Bangkok Grocery
Despaña Foods | *multi*
Sahadi's | *Bklyn*
Kalustyan's
26 Titan Foods | *Qns*

TEA

28 Ito En
27 Two for the Pot | *Bklyn*
Tea Box
McNulty's Tea
26 Porto Rico Import
T Salon
25 Harlem Tea
Ten Ren Tea | *multi*

WINES/LIQUOR

29 Burgundy Wine
Moore Brothers
Sherry-Lehmann
28 Vino
Bierkraft | *Bklyn*
27 Morrell
Italian Wine
Le Dû's Wines

BY ETHNIC FOCUS

AMERICAN

26 Two Little Red Hens
Cake Man Raven | *Bklyn*
25 City Bakery
Make My Cake
Eddie's Sweet | *Qns*
Shake Shack
Blue Smoke
24 'wichcraft

CHINESE

25 Ten Ren Tea | *multi*
23 May May
Bayard St. Meat
Flor de Mayo
22 Hong Keung
21 Kam Man Food
Asia Market
20 Hong Kong | *multi*

FRENCH/BELGIAN

29 Burgundy Wine
   La Maison Chocolat
   Martine's Chocolates
28 Pierre Marcolini
   Payard Pâtisserie
   Jacques Torres | multi
   Richart Design
27 Financier Pâtisserie

GERMAN/AUSTRIAN

27 Schaller & Weber
   Stork's Pastry | Qns
26 Oppenheimer Meats
   Duane Park
24 Koglin Hams∇

GREEK/MED.

28 Artopolis Bakery | Qns
26 Titan Foods | Qns
   Poseidon Bakery
25 O&CO.
24 Todaro Brothers
   Mangia
23 Ninth Ave. Int'l
22 Likitsakos

INDIAN/MIDDLE EASTERN

27 Sahadi's | Bklyn
   Kalustyan's
25 Damascus Bread | Bklyn
   D'Vine Taste | Bklyn
24 Spice Corner
23 Chickpea
   Hampton Chutney
   Patel Brothers | Qns

ITALIAN

29 Florence Meat
   Grandaisy Bakery
   Salumeria Biellese
   DiPalo Dairy
   Borgatti's Ravioli | Bx
28 Vino
   Villabate | Bklyn
   Sullivan St. Bakery

JAPANESE

28 Ito En
   Takashimaya
   Minamoto Kitchoan
27 Tea Box
24 Beard Papa Sweets
23 Katagiri
   Sunrise Mart
22 Panya Bakery

JEWISH (KOSHER‡)

28 Russ & Daughters
   Kossar's Bialys‡
27 Fischer Bros.‡
   Pickle Guys‡
   Barney Greengrass
   Murray's Sturgeon‡
26 Oppenheimer Meats
   Orwasher's‡

RUSSIAN/UKRAINIAN

28 East Village Meat
26 Caviar Russe
25 Astoria Meat∇ | Qns
   First Ave. Pierogi∇
24 M & I Foods | Bklyn

BY LOCATION

CHELSEA

29 Salumeria Biellese
   Burgundy Wine
28 Ronnybrook Farms
27 Williams-Sonoma
   Ariston
   L'Arte del Gelato
26 Lobster Place
   T Salon

CHINATOWN/LITTLE ITALY

29 DiPalo Dairy
27 Bangkok Grocery
   Alleva Dairy
   Despaña Foods
   Piemonte Ravioli
25 Ten Ren Tea
   Bánh Mì Saigon
   Chinatown Ice Cream

EAST VILLAGE

28 East Village Meat
26 Stonehouse
   Porto Rico Import
   Black Hound
   Mudspot
   Russo Mozzarella
   Joe
   Pepe

FLATIRON/ UNION SQUARE

29 Moore Brothers
28 Belle Fleur
27 Italian Wine
26 Whole Foods
   Bottlerocket Wine
25 City Bakery
   Union Sq. Wines
   Shake Shack

GARMENT DISTRICT/ HELL'S KITCHEN

28 Artisanal
   Sullivan St. Bakery
27 Dean & DeLuca
   Williams-Sonoma
26 Whole Foods
   Amy's Bread
   H & H Bagels
   Poseidon Bakery

GREENWICH VILLAGE

29 Florence Meat
28 Murray's Cheese
   Faicco's Pork
   Blue Ribbon Market
   Raffetto's
27 Dean & DeLuca
   Jack's Stir Brew
   Patisserie Claude

LOWER EAST SIDE

28 Il Laboratorio
   Russ & Daughters
   Kossar's Bialys
27 Falai Panetteria
   Pickle Guys
   Sugar Sweet
26 Clinton St. Baking
   Whole Foods

MIDTOWN

29 Zezé
   La Maison Chocolat
   Martine's Chocolates
28 Petrossian
   Dessert Delivery
   Pierre Marcolini
   Sullivan St. Bakery
   Takashimaya

MURRAY HILL/GRAMERCY

28 Vino
   Artisanal
27 Manhattan Fruitier

26 Kalustyan's
26 Les Halles
   Wild Edibles
   Ess-a-Bagel
25 Milano Gourmet

SOHO

29 Grandaisy Bakery
   Kee's Chocolates
28 Jacques Torres
   Joe's Dairy
27 Dom's
   Balthazar Bakery
   Dean & DeLuca
   Alessi

TRIBECA/DOWNTOWN

28 Korin Japanese
   Financier Pâtisserie
27 Bouley Bakery
   Dean & DeLuca
26 Sylvia Weinstock
   Chambers Wines
   Leonidas
   Duane Park

UPPER EAST SIDE

29 Lobel's Meats
   La Maison Chocolat
   Martine's Chocolates
   Sherry-Lehmann
28 Ito En
   Payard Pâtisserie
   Lady M
27 Teuscher Chocolates

UPPER WEST SIDE

28 Levain Bakery
27 Soutine
   Fischer Bros.
   Zabar's
   Bouchon Bakery
   Barney Greengrass
   Murray's Sturgeon
   Margot Pâtisserie

WEST VILLAGE

29 Colette's Cakes
27 Le Dû's Wines
   McNulty's Tea
26 Sant Ambroeus
   Li-Lac Chocolates
   Chocolate Bar
   Pepe
24 Integral Yoga

OUTER BOROUGHS

BRONX

29	Borgatti's Ravioli
28	Calabria Pork
	Randazzo's
	Madonia Bakery
27	Vincent's Meat
	S&S Cheesecake
	Addeo's
	Biancardi Meats

BROOKLYN: CARROLL GARDENS/ COBBLE HILL

29	Staubitz Market
27	D'Amico Foods
26	Esposito's Pork
	American Beer
25	Fish Tales
	Court Pastry
	Mazzola Bakery
24	One Girl Cookies

BROOKLYN: HEIGHTS/DUMBO

28	Almondine Bakery
	Jacques Torres
27	Sahadi's
	Two for the Pot
26	Cook's Companion
25	Brooklyn Ice Cream
	Ciao Bella Gelato
	Heights Chateau

BROOKLYN: PARK SLOPE

28	Bierkraft
27	Blue Apron
26	Russo Mozzarella
	Red, White & Bubbly
	Cocoa Bar
	Prospect Wine
25	Chocolate Room
	D'Vine Taste

QUEENS

28	Artopolis Bakery
27	Ottomanelli's Meats
	Despaña Foods
	Lemon Ice King
	Ottomanelli & Sons
	Stork's Pastry
26	Titan Foods
	Pastosa Ravioli

STATEN ISLAND

26	Pastosa Ravioli
	Royal Crown
	Mother Mousse
25	Eggers Ice Cream
24	Bari Pork
	Ralph's Ices
	Sedutto's
23	Original SoupMan

Top Display Ratings

Ratings are to the left of names.

28 Zezé
Richart Design
Takashimaya
Payard Pâtisserie
Colette's Cakes
Bloom
La Maison Chocolat

27 Ito En
Bottlerocket Wine
Minamoto Kitchoan
Belle Fleur
Nespresso Boutique
Petrossian
Williams-Sonoma
Dylan's Candy
Moore Brothers
Pierre Marcolini

26 Sylvia Weinstock
MarieBelle's
Terence Conran
Jacques Torres | *multi*
Black Hound
Artopolis Bakery | *Qns*
Alessi
Lady M
Dean & DeLuca
Abigail Kirsch | *multi*
Teuscher Chocolates
Rice/Riches
Vosges

25 Artisanal
Crush Wine
Financier Pâtisserie
Murray's Cheese
Lobel's Meats
Vino
Crate & Barrel
Discovery Wines
Sant Ambroeus
O&CO.
Glorious Food
Whole Foods
Bouley Bakery
Pescatore
Chocolat Michel
Chocolate Bar
Bouchon Bakery
Blue Apron | *Bklyn*
Wild Edibles
Manhattan Fruitier
East Village Meat

24 Eleni's Cookies
Tea Box
Godiva Chocolatier
Bedford Cheese | *Bklyn*
Bodum
La Bergamote*
Astor Wines
Dessert Delivery
Max Brenner

Top Service Ratings

Ratings are to the left of names.

29 | Moore Brothers

28 | Zezé
Florence Meat

27 | Colette's Cakes
Lobel's Meats
Bottlerocket Wine

26 | Cleaver Co.
Le Dû's Wines
Ottomanelli & Sons | *multi*
Dessert Delivery
Bay Ridge Bakery | *Bklyn*
Dorian's Seafood*
LeNell's | *Bklyn*
Pisacane
Prospect Wine | *Bklyn*

25 | Simchick, L.
Sylvia Weinstock*
Minamoto Kitchoan
Vino
TriServe
Two for the Pot | *Bklyn*
Abigail Kirsch | *multi*
Faicco's Pork | *multi*
D'Vine Taste | *Bklyn*
Nespresso Boutique*
Red, White & Bubbly | *Bklyn*
Richart Design*
Tavalon Tea*
Belle Fleur
Biancardi Meats | *Bx*

Staubitz Market | *Bklyn*
Borgatti's Ravioli | *Bx*
Big Nose Full Body | *Bklyn*
Ito En
Italian Wine
Burgundy Wine
Fish Tales | *Bklyn*
Petrossian
Esposito's Pork | *Bklyn*
Esposito Meat
Murray's Cheese
Sundaes & Cones
Bierkraft | *Bklyn*
Chambers St. Wines
DiPalo Dairy
East Village Meat

24 | Smith & Vine | *Bklyn*
Despaña Foods | *multi*
Glorious Food
Michael-Towne Wines | *Bklyn*
Russ & Daughters
Pierre Marcolini
Bedford Cheese | *Bklyn*
Sherry-Lehmann
Kee's Chocolates
West Side Wine
William Poll*
Oppenheimer Meats
Leonard's
Mister Wright
Slope Cellars | *Bklyn*

Best Buys

In order of Bang for the Buck rating.

1. Moore Brothers
2. Bottlerocket Wine
3. Borgatti's Ravioli | *Bx*
4. Madonia Bakery | *Bx*
5. LeNell's | *Bklyn*
6. Villabate | *Bklyn*
7. Artopolis Bakery | *Qns*
8. Bay Ridge Bakery | *Bklyn*
9. Pickle Guys
10. Delillo Pastry | *Bx*
11. East Village Meat
12. DiPalo Dairy
13. Raffetto's
14. Sugar Sweet
15. Faicco's Pork | *multi*
16. Jack's Stir
17. Eddie's Sweet | *Qns*
18. Red, White & Bubbly | *Bklyn*
19. Sahadi's | *Bklyn*
20. Bangkok Grocery
21. Sundaes & Cones
22. Greenmarket | *multi*
23. Porto Rico Import
24. Skyview Discount | *Bx*
25. Addeo's | *Bx*
26. Penzeys Spices
27. Calabria Pork | *Bx*
28. Prospect Wine | *Bklyn*
29. Murray's Cheese
30. D'Amico Foods | *Bklyn*
31. Java Girl
32. Smith & Vine | *Bklyn*
33. Biancardi Meats | *Bx*
34. Almondine Bakery | *Bklyn*
35. Harlem Tea
36. Vino
37. Dahlia
38. Coluccio & Sons | *Bklyn*
39. Florence Meat
40. Titan Foods | *Qns*
41. Best Cellars
42. Salumeria Biellese
43. Grandaisy Bakery
44. Artuso Pastry | *Bx*
45. Mudspot
46. Esposito's Pork | *Bklyn*
47. Kurowycky Meat
48. Astor Wines
49. Dessert Delivery
50. Greene Grape

OTHER GOOD VALUES

Alleva Dairy
American Beer
Aphrodisia
Bedford Cheese
Bierkraft
Billy's Bakery
Chambers St. Wines
Consenza's Fish
Court Pastry
Damascus Bread
Despaña Foods
D'Vine Taste
Egidio Pastry
Esposito Meat
Financier Pâtisserie
Heights Chateau
Joe
Kossar's Bialys
L'Arte del Gelato
McNulty's Tea
Michael-Towne Wines
Mister Wright
Piemonte Ravioli
PJ Wine
Poseidon Bakery
Queen Ann Ravioli
Randazzo's
Rocco's Pastry
Royal Crown
Russ & Daughters
Staubitz Market
Sullivan St. Bakery
Sweet Life
Teitel Brothers
Terrace Bagels
Trader Joe's
Two for the Pot
Vincent's Meat
Vintage New York
West Side Wine

NYC SOURCES
DIRECTORY

NYC Sources

Abbey Rent-All *Party Rentals*

| - | - | - | I |

Bayside | 203-16 Northern Blvd. (204th St.) | Queens | 718-428-8899 | 800-924-0428 | www.abbeyrent.com

For nearly 50 years, this Bayside rental outfit has been keeping parties going with a full range of tents, canopies, chairs, tables, linens and – summertime hosts, take note – even ice cream carts and portable air conditioners; N.B. delivery rates vary from borough to borough: $150 to the Bronx and Brooklyn, $125 to Manhattan, and $25 to Queens and LI.

☑ Abigail Kirsch *Caterer*

| 26 | 26 | 25 | VE |

Chelsea | 71 W. 23rd St. (6th Ave.) | F/V to 23rd St. | 212-696-4076

Chelsea | Chelsea Piers | Pier 60 (Hudson River & 23rd St.) | C/E to 23rd St. | 212-336-6060

Chelsea | Chelsea Piers Lighthouse | Pier 61 (Hudson River & 23rd St.) | C/E to 23rd St. | 212-336-6144

Bronx | Botanical Garden | 200th St. (Southern Blvd.) | B/D to Fordham Rd. | 718-220-0300

Tarrytown | Tappan Hill | 81 Highland Ave. (bet. Benedict Ave. & Gunpowder Ln.), NY | 914-631-3030
www.abigailkirsch.com

"Everyone should be lucky enough to have an event – or go to one – run by Abigail Kirsch" according to acolytes of this reigning deity of catering and her "wonderful" operation voted NYC's "absolute best"; whether off-site or in one of her "memorable venues", "fabulous food" and "professional", "courteous" service "turn special occasions into something extraordinary", though keep in mind this is "champagne living on a champagne budget."

☑ Absolute Bagels ●⊘ *Bagels*

| 26 | 14 | 20 | I |

W 100s | 2788 Broadway (bet. 107th & 108th Sts.) | 1 to 110th St. | 212-932-2052

"It's the real deal" declare the "students carbo-packing" at this "hole-in-the-wall" near Columbia, which honors the "old-fashioned" "art of bagel-making" with "doughy" hand-rolled "spheres" sporting a "perfect" "crunchy" crust; with an "imaginative" "multitude of toppings" and "cheery" service that ensures the "lines move quickly", it's hailed by "those in-the-know" as the "absolute best" in the area.

Academy Floral Co. ▣ *Flowers*

| 23 | 19 | 23 | M |

W 100s | 2780 Broadway (107th St.) | 1 to 110th St. | 212-222-0771 | 800-231-7592 | www.academyfloral.com

Appreciated as a "classic florist", this "reliable" family-owned blooms biz near Columbia has been making arrangements "for all occasions" for almost a century now; though its specialty is flowers from Holland and South America, often arrayed in signature fish-bowl vessels, they can also produce gift baskets with fruit, candy, plants and balloons.

	QUALITY	DISPLAY	SERVICE	COST

Acker Merrall & Condit Co. ◑▣ *Wine/Liquor*

| 26 | 21 | 22 | E |

W 70s | 160 W. 72nd St. (bet. B'way & Columbus Ave.) | 1/2/3 to 72nd St. | 212-787-1700 | www.ackerstore.com

It's "first-class all the way" at this veteran UWS "wine haven" offering a "good balance of prices" and a great range" of choices, with particular strengths in California Cabernets, Bordeaux, Burgundys and Super Tuscans; add to that a staff that "really knows how to help customers" and its "famed" auctions (live or online), regular tasting events, monthly specials and an "excellent" assortment of single-malts, and it's easy to see why it's "been here for nearly 200 years."

NEW Ackerson, T.B., Wine Merchants *Wine/Liquor*

| - | - | - | M |

Ditmas Pk | 1205 Cortelyou Rd. (Westminster Rd.) | Brooklyn | Q to Cortelyou Rd. | 718-826-6600 | www.tbackersonwine.com

Brooklyn's latest neighborhood-to-watch, Ditmas Park, gets its first wine boutique with the arrival of this slim, husband and wife–run shop, whose attractively arranged inventory is limited but slowly expanding; its labels from around the globe are mostly from small-production vineyards, including some hard-to-find bottlings, with an emphasis on organic, bio-dynamic and kosher selections, many of them priced under $20; N.B. it hosts regular tastings and seminars.

Acme Smoked Fish ⊟ *Caviar/Smoked Fish*

| 24 | 13 | 18 | M |

Greenpoint | 30-56 Gem St. (N. 15th St.) | Brooklyn | G to Nassau Ave. | 718-383-8585 | www.acmesmokedfish.com

"Get to the source" advise afishionados of this "family-owned" Greenpoint wholesaler, which "supplies the best" smoked fish to outlets like Zabar's and Citarella; on Fridays from 8 AM–1 PM anyone can snag "top-flight" lox, Nova, sable, whitefish, herring and sturgeon straight from the on-site smokehouse – if you're willing to "schlep" for "fresher" goods "at bargain-basement prices", "you won't be disappointed."

Addeo's ⊟ *Baked Goods*

| 27 | 18 | 22 | I |

Bronx | 2352 Arthur Ave. (bet. 186th & 187th Sts.) | 2 to Pelham Pkwy. | 718-367-8316 ▣
Bronx | 2372 Hughes Ave. (186th St.) | 2 to Pelham Pkwy. | 718-367-8316

"Old-world products do still exist" sigh supporters of this family-run "step-back-in-time" Arthur Avenue bakery and its nearby offshoot, whose *pane di casa* and other "top-notch" "rustic" loaves continue to make it a "staple" of "the Bronx's Little Italy"; though the staff of life is the thing here, it also bakes biscotti, pepper crackers and "love-'em" seeded breadsticks that could be "NYC's best."

Z Agata & Valentina ◑▣ *Major Gourmet Mkt.*

| 26 | 23 | 20 | E |

E 70s | 1505 First Ave. (79th St.) | 6 to 77th St. | 212-452-0690 | www.agatavalentina.com

Its East Side champions claim this "culinary godsend" "should be the template" for "superior" Italian-style gourmandizing everywhere given its "go-to" status for "flavorful" prepared foods, "excellent" "fresh" pastas, meats "like buttah" from a "fantastic butcher", "wonderful" seafood, "fab cheeses" featuring "unusual choices" and "beautiful" baked goods, all backed by "accommodating" "staffers who know their products"; though the setup's a "congested" "labyrinth" that "can be daunting" "to maneuver", everyone in the area "tolerates it willingly" given that it's a proven "lifesaver" for a "premium" "mangia."

Aji Ichiban ⌨ Candy/Nuts
21 | 20 | 17 | M

Chinatown | 153A Centre St. (Canal St.) | A/C/E to Canal St. | 212-625-8179 ◐
Chinatown | 167 Hester St. (bet. Elizabeth & Mott Sts.) | 6/J/M/N/Q/R/W/Z to Canal St. | 212-925-1133
Chinatown | 17 E. Broadway (Market St.) | F to E. B'way | 212-571-3755 ◐
Chinatown | 37 Mott St. (bet. Bayard & Pell Sts.) | A/C/E to Canal St. | 212-233-7650 ◐
Little Italy | 188 Lafayette St. (Grand St.) | B/D to Grand St. | 212-219-0808
866-833-3888

Like a "Candy Land from the other side of the world", these Chinatown–Little Italy "snack-food boutiques" (links of a Hong Kong chain) boast "a myriad" of "delightful" "bite-size oddities" – "colorful sweets", "excellent, exotic dried fruits", beef jerky, dried fish, etc. – to "feed your taste for adventure"; it's "not cheap", but the stock is "unique" and for those "unidentifiable" items, "free tastings" "make it easier to decide."

Albert's Prime Meats ⌨ Meat/Poultry
26 | 21 | 23 | E

E 60s | 836 Lexington Ave. (bet. 63rd & 64th Sts.) | F to Lexington Ave./ 63rd St. | 212-751-3169 | www.albertandsons.net

"Yeah, baby – let me sink my teeth into one of those rib-eyes" roar carnivores of the "excellent" steaks and other meat, poultry and game (including organic selections) cut with care at this family-owned, 45-year-old UES butcher; some say it's "cheaper to dine out", but those who can stomach the "expensive" tabs swear "you really can taste the difference in every bite"; N.B. it also offers prepared foods.

Ⓩ NEW Alessi ⌨ Cookware
27 | 26 | 20 | E

SoHo | 130 Greene St. (bet. Houston & Prince Sts.) | N/R to Prince St. | 212-941-7300 | www.alessi.com

"Eye candy" abounds at this "cool" "museumlike" SoHo store showcasing Alessi's brand of "well-designed" "high-end" stainless-steel cookware, appliances and "avant-garde" tabletop items from Italy; though some surveyors quip the "esoteric" gadgets work best as an "IQ test", most find the wares "fabulous", "if you can afford them"; P.S. "savor a true cappuccino after shopping" at the in-store branch of Joe coffee bar.

Alice's Tea Cup Coffee/Tea
24 | 23 | 20 | M

W 70s | 102 W. 73rd St. (bet. Amsterdam & Columbus Aves.) | 1/2/3 to 72nd St. | 212-799-3006

(continued)

Alice's Tea Cup, Chapter II *Coffee/Tea*
E 60s | 156 E. 64th St. (bet. Lexington & 3rd Aves.) | 6 to 68th St. |
212-486-9200

Alice's Tea Cup, Chapter III *Coffee/Tea*
NEW **E 80s** | 220 E. 81st St. (bet. 2nd & 3rd Aves.) | 6 to 77th St. |
212-734-4832
www.alicesteacup.com

"A trip to Wonderland" for "discriminating tea lovers", this "super-cute" Upper Westsider (with two East Side sequels) pairs its "count-less" types of "tea-licious" brews with "scrumptious" scones, finger sandwiches and "fairy-tale desserts"; the "whimsical", Lewis Carroll-inspired setting is "popular to a fault" for "mom-and-daughter" confabs or "light lunch with the girlfriends", "intimate bridal showers" or children's parties; P.S. the front shop vends bulk teas, pots, books and more.

Alidoro 🌱 *Deli/Sandwich* ▽ 27 | 18 | 22 | M
SoHo | 105 Sullivan St. (bet. Prince & Spring Sts.) | C/E to Spring St. |
212-334-5179

"Let the maestro do his work and you won't be disappointed" say regulars of this SoHo storefront where the "huge" "quality" sand-wiches with an Italian bent (many featuring fresh mozzarella) are best when "made by the proprietor" and enjoyed on a bench in one of the nearby parks; though a few find "the long waits amongst preten-tious hipsters" hard to bear, most are happy to "tune out" the sur-roundings for what they call "the best in the city, period."

Alleva Dairy ▣ *Cheese/Dairy* 27 | 20 | 23 | M
Little Italy | 188 Grand St. (Mulberry St.) | 6/J/M/N/Q/R/W/Z to
Canal St. | 212-226-7990 | 800-425-5382 | www.allevadairy.com
The "real deal" "for all your Italian cheese" needs, this "family-owned" Little Italy vet (established 1892) is "committed" to supply-ing the "highest quality" in "mouthwatering" mozzarella, ricotta and assorted imports; also featuring a sideline in salami, prosciutto, ol-ive oils and the like, it's a "nice surprise" "that hasn't compromised", with "good prices" to boot.

Z Almondine Bakery 🌱 *Baked Goods* 28 | 23 | 23 | M
Dumbo | 85 Water St. (bet. Dock & Main Sts.) | Brooklyn | A/C to High St. |
718-797-5027 | www.almondinebakery.com
It's "the real stuff" rave Francophiles of this little shop's "superla-tive" French bakery staples – notably the "finest" croissants and baguettes and "jewellike" pastries – considered "the closest thing to Paris" this side of the East River; "master" baker (and Le Bernardin alum) Hervé Poussot is the man behind this operation touted by locals as "one more reason to move to Dumbo."

A Matter of Health ◑▣ *Health Food* 21 | 16 | 19 | M
E 70s | 1478 First Ave. (77th St.) | 6 to 77th St. | 212-288-8280
Really it's a matter of space at this health food store, a "cramped" but much-appreciated source in the underserved neighborhood bor-

QUALITY   DISPLAY   SERVICE   COST

dering Yorkville carrying a "broad selection" of natural products at "reasonable prices"; yes, "crowded shelves" and "narrow aisles" can be claustrophobic, but luckily there's a "friendly" staff you can "ask for what you're looking for."

Ambassador Wines & Spirits ● *Wine/Liquor* | 24 | 18 | 20 | E |

E 50s | 1020 Second Ave. (54th St.) | E/V to Lexington Ave./53rd St. | 212-421-5078 | www.ambassadorwines.com

This "reliable" East Side wine shop "always has a little something tucked away for the experimental customer", with different areas displaying Burgundies, dessert wines, half-bottles and magnums, as well as a "walk-in refrigerated case" holding its "excellent range of sake"; the "helpful" staff "knows its stuff", and regulars can purchase Bordeaux and Burgundy futures with no deposit required.

American Beer Distributing ⌨ *Beer* | 26 | 18 | 23 | M |

Cobble Hill | 256 Court St. (bet. Butler & Kane Sts.) | Brooklyn | F/G to Bergen St. | 718-875-0226 | www.americanbeerbuzz.com

From "cheap" "macro swill" to pricier "exotic brews from far and wide", the beer "flows like bottled water" at this "longtime" Cobble Hill "institution", which also offers snacks and other beverages; the staff "bends over backwards" to help you "shop easily" in the "bare-bones" but "well-organized" 4,000-sq.-ft. space, and it also delivers.

Amish Market ● *Major Gourmet Mkt.* | 23 | 21 | 17 | M |

E 40s | 240 E. 45th St. (bet. 2nd & 3rd Aves.) | 4/5/6/7/S to 42nd St./Grand Central | 212-370-1761

Financial Dist | 53 Park Pl. (bet. Church St. & W. B'way) | 2/3/A/C/E to Park Pl. | 212-608-3863

W 40s | 731 Ninth Ave. (bet. 49th & 50th Sts.) | C/E to 50th St. | 212-245-2360 | 866-264-7449

NEW **Glendale** | 8000 Cooper Ave. (80th St.) | Queens | L/M to Myrtle/Wyckoff Aves. | 718-894-1199

www.amishfinefood.com

Maybe the "name is disingenuous" ("where are the Amish?"), but this "fast, convenient" gourmet grocer quartet is still "good for the soul" given the "bounty" of its "wide array of cheeses", "beautifully displayed produce", "great mix of prepared foods" (including "appetizing" pizza) and extras like "vats of olives"; nonbelievers contend it's "more a wannabe" where "service is often spotty", but it's always "useful in a pinch", especially at the Park Place location, which is among the area's few "reliable" "meal savers."

☑ Amy's Bread *Baked Goods* | 26 | 22 | 20 | M |

Chelsea | Chelsea Mkt. | 75 Ninth Ave. (bet. 15th & 16th Sts.) | A/C/E/L to 14th St./8th Ave. | 212-462-4338

G Village | 250 Bleecker St. (bet. Leroy & Morton Sts.) | A/B/C/D/E/F/V to W. 4th St. | 212-675-7802 ●

W 40s | 672 Ninth Ave. (bet. 46th & 47th Sts.) | C/E to 50th St. | 212-977-2670 ●

www.amysbread.com

Carbophiles "sing the praises" of the "heavenly" "artisan" goods at Amy Scherber's bakery trio, now considered a NYC "classic"; reknowned for its "fantastic" handmade breads (including signatures like the semolina-raisin-fennel), it also traffics in sweets from "out-of-this-world" sticky buns to "awesome cupcakes", as well as "delicious sandwiches" and other "good lunchables" – perfect for "eating at one of the few tables" if you can snag one.

Andrew & Alan's Bakery & Chocolate Factory ▣ *Baked Goods*

| 22 | 22 | 22 | M |

Staten Island | 61 New Dorp Plaza (bet. New Dorp Ln. & Rose Ave.) | 718-667-9696 | www.andrewandalansbakery.com

"If you're ever in Staten Island", supporters suggest you "stop in" at this veteran German-American bakery/chocolate shop and "try any" of the treats, including "old-world" favorites (babka, strudel), special-occasion cakes and chocolate-covered strawberries and pretzels that alone are "worth the trip"; as the "long lines on holidays" attest, it's considered the "closest to homemade you'll find" in these parts.

Angelica's Herbs, Spices & Oils ⊘ *Herbs/Spices*

| 23 | 18 | 20 | M |

E Village | 147 First Ave. (9th St.) | 6 to Astor Pl. | 212-677-1549

"Excellence and temptation abound" in this "treasure trove" of herbs and spices in the East Village, where you might feel a bit "dizzy" to be surrounded by the "earthy, medicinal, exotic, intriguing" selection; the "very informative" staff will help you find what you need, whether it's the ingredients for your own curry powder, or advice on how to cure what ails you.

Annie's *Produce*

| 21 | 17 | 18 | M |

E 80s | 1204 Lexington Ave. (bet. 81st & 82nd Sts.) | 4/5/6 to 86th St. | 212-861-6078
E 80s | 1330 Lexington Ave. (bet. 88th & 89th Sts.) | 4/5/6 to 86th St. | 212-427-8800 ◓

There's "something for everyone" at this East Side duo known for its "good-looking and good-tasting produce" (including organic options at comparatively "lower prices") as well as for its flowers; still, a few naysayers note they "have everything you need – but nothing special"; N.B. the 88th Street location is open 24/7 with free delivery.

Anopoli Ice Cream Parlor ⊘ *Ice Cream*

| - | - | - | I |

Bay Ridge | 6920 Third Ave. (bet. Ovington & Bay Ridge Ave.) | Brooklyn | R to Bay Ridge/95th St. | 718-748-3863

Paying a visit to this 100-year-old ice cream parlor in Bay Ridge is "like going back in time"; you can find all the soda fountain classics, like ice cream floats, malts and banana splits, along with a full diner menu, and there's a "great old-time atmosphere" thanks to the ornate wood trim, large mirrors and friendly service.

Anstice Carroll Catering ⊘ *Caterer/Events*

| ▽ 26 | 26 | 26 | M |

G Village | 622 Greenwich St. (bet. Leroy & Morton Sts.) | 212-242-1498 | www.ansticecarrollcatering.com
By appointment only

Admirers "love working with" this West Village caterer who's "in a class of her own", demonstrating "elegance in performance and spirit" as she coordinates events with the "finest attention to detail"; from the "delicious and beautiful food" to the "flowers, staff, rentals and location", she's "as good as it gets."

Anthony Garden Boutique Ltd. *Flowers* `-  -  -  E`

E 70s | 1027 Lexington Ave. (bet. 73rd & 74th Sts.) | 6 to 77th St. | 212-737-3303

Whether patrons are in pursuit of a landscaped terrace complete with vintage ornaments, flowers in abundance for a "large-scale gala or wedding" or simply a "beautiful, classy arrangement", they'll receive "something appropriate" from this Upper East Side floral boutique; its "creative" owner, trained in the 17th-century style, displays "a discriminating eye for fabulous finds" and pays "attention to the smallest detail" – no wonder he's been "in business for years."

Antony Todd *Flowers* `-  -  -  VE`

E Village | 44 E. 11th St. (bet. B'way & University Pl.) | 4/5/6/L/N/Q/R/W to 14th St./Union Sq. | 212-529-3252 | www.antonytodd.com

There's absolutely "nothing cutesy" about the work of this East Village event designer known for his "edgy, contemporary" mix of "beautiful flowers" and fabrics; big corporate bashes, weddings and private parties all get gussied up in high style, so naturally he comes "highly recommended", but "be prepared to spend a pretty penny" for such sensational work.

Aphrodisia *Herbs/Spices* `26  22  22  M`

G Village | 264 Bleecker St. (bet. 6th & 7th Aves.) | A/B/C/D/E/F/V to W. 4th St. | 212-989-6440 | www.aphrodisiaherbshoppe.com

"Dusty and cluttered but fun", this "warm, sensual shop" that's been on Bleecker since "way back when" is "crammed" full of "every earthly spice" imaginable; there's also "a nice selection of teas, small gifts and jewelry", but it's the "exotic, mystical, intoxicating, bewitching" selection of herbs and seasonings that distinguishes this "excellent gem in the heart of the Village."

Appellation Wine & Spirits ●▣ *Wine/Liquor* `▽ 25  23  25  M`

Chelsea | 156 10th Ave. (bet. 19th & 20th Sts.) | C/E to 23rd St. | 212-741-9474 | www.appellationnyc.com

The "well-chosen" stock at this eco-minded "boutique wine store" in Chelsea is a sign that organic, biodynamic and sustainable wineries are becoming "mainstream", but for the uninitiated there's "personal service" as well as weekly tastings and a handy reference bookcase to help "wine geeks and the curious" explore this "under-represented" market segment; the setup of its "stark", "amazing"-looking space has bottles organized in order from light to full-bodied.

Areo Ristorante *Caterer* `▽ 21  17  17  E`

Bay Ridge | 8424 Third Ave. (85th St.) | Brooklyn | R to 86th St. | 718-238-0079

If you want to spice up your event with "deliciously fresh" traditional Italian fare served by a "friendly" crew (with a side of "Brooklyn attitude") and even entertainment, this popular Bay Ridge restaurant can deliver; it's also possible to hold a party in its 65-seat space, though planners should note that it can get "very noisy."

Ariston Floral Boutique ⊡ Flowers | 27 | 24 | 23 | E |

Chelsea | 110 West 17th St. (bet. 6th & 7th Aves.) | 4/5/6/L/N/Q/R/W to 14th St./Union Sq. | 212-929-4226 | 800-422-2747 | www.aristonflorist.com

NEW **E 40s** | 425 Lexington Ave. (bet. 43rd & 44th Sts.) | 4/5/6/7/S to 42nd St./Grand Central | 212-867-8880 | www.aristonfloralboutique.com

With a new Chelsea location a few blocks from its old Union Square digs and an East Side seedling too, business seems to be flourishing for the "flower experts" at this family-run operation creating bouquets of "exquisite" blooms and providing "excellent service"; surveyors say they can be "creative" or do just "exactly what you want" and the result will be "stunning", albeit with "prices to match."

Arté Around the Corner Baked Goods | 24 | 20 | 20 | M |

W 70s | 274 Columbus Ave. (bet. 72nd & 73rd Sts.) | 1/2/3 to 72nd St. | 212-875-2195 | www.artearoundthecorner.com

Touted as a "hidden treasure" by locals who "love getting their morning espresso and muffin" here, this UWS coffee bar/bakery around the bend from its parent, Arté Cafe, vends "excellent" baked goods, Italian specialty products (including fresh and dried pastas) and prepared foods; there are a few seats, but "cramped quarters" have most placing it in the best-for-takeout category.

Arthur Avenue Caterers Caterer | ▽ 24 | 18 | 20 | M |

Bronx | Arthur Avenue Retail Mkt. | 2344 Arthur Ave. (186th St.) | B/D to Fordham Rd. | 718-295-5033 | 866-272-5264 | www.arthuravenue.com

"For Italian specialties", there's "nothing like" the catering arm of the Arthur Avenue Retail Market, affiliated with the Bronx institution Mike's Deli; providing "primo" homestyle *cucina* for large and small events and even offering mozzarella-making demos, it has catered for the likes of Martin Scorsese, the Mayor of NY and the Yankees.

Artie's Deli ◗⊡ Deli/Sandwich | 21 | 17 | 18 | M |

W 80s | 2290 Broadway (bet. 82nd & 83rd Sts.) | 1 to 79th St. | 212-579-5959 | www.arties.com

"Fantastically fresh", "colossal" sandwiches, matzo ball soup, smoked fish and other kosher-style specialties are "pure comfort" "for the soul" say surveyors smitten with this "solid" "old-fashioned" UWS deli; though some kvetch it's a "pale alternative" to the city's stalwart nosheries, even critics concede "you could do much worse if you're stuck Uptown."

⊠ Artisanal ⊡ Cheese/Dairy | 28 | 25 | 23 | E |

Garment Dist | 500 W. 37th St., 2nd fl. (10th Ave.) | 1/2/3/A/C/E to 34th St./Penn Station | 212-239-1200 | www.artisanalcheese.com

Murray Hill | 2 Park Ave. (32nd St.) | 6 to 33rd St. | 212-532-4033 | www.artisanalbistro.com ◗ 877-797-1200

"If you're a turophile", "paradise" awaits at Terrence Brennan's Murray Hill bistro, where the "bountiful" retail counter is "the ulti-

	QUALITY	DISPLAY	SERVICE	COST

mate" "showcase" of "fragrant", "scary-delicious" fromage in a 250-strong "world-wide assortment" that's stocked on-site in carefully calibrated caves; if the "phenomenal selection" "makes your head spin", a "true-believer staff" of "cheese masters" will assist with "queries and discoveries", helping to justify the "lofty prices"; P.S. the Garment District wholesale/mail-order outlet hosts "very informative" classes toward cheese degrees.

Art of Cooking, The ▣ Cookware — 23 | 21 | 20 | E

W Village | 555 Hudson St. (bet. Perry & W. 11th Sts.) | 1 to Christopher St. | 212-414-4940 | 877-414-4940 | www.artofcookingnyc.com
Would-be chefs do "serious shopping" or just "browse and dream" at this "cute" West Village storefront with an "enticing" selection of "high-quality" kitchenware and gifts curated by an owner with "impeccable taste"; in all, fans find "it's nice to support" this "local store", even if price tags sometimes inspire "double-takes."

☑ Artopolis Bakery ● Baked Goods — 28 | 26 | 23 | M

Astoria | Agora Plaza | 23-18 31st St. (23rd Ave.) | Queens | N/W to Astoria/Ditmars Blvd. | 718-728-8484 | 800-553-2270 | www.artopolis.net
"Transcends" what you'll find in a "neighborhood full of Greek bakeries" rave connoisseurs of this Astoria Hellenic's baked goods touted as some of the "best variety and quality outside of Athens"; its offerings both traditional and with French leanings include "outstanding" pastries and cakes, "peasant" breads and some savories ("go for the tiropites and spanakopites"), all arrayed in a "beautiful" space whose marble-and-lacquered pine fittings were imported from Greece.

Artuso Pastry Shop ● Baked Goods — 26 | 22 | 22 | M

Bronx | 670 E. 187th St. (Cambreleng Ave.) | 2 to Pelham Pkwy. | 718-367-2515 | www.artusopastry.com
A bona fide "neighborhood favorite", this Bronx mainstay boasts a rich "history" (since 1946) to go with its "wonderful" Italian pastries including "fresh, quality" cakes, cookies, cannoli, sfogliatelle and the like; with "Artuso family" members still at the helm, supporters say it's the "ultimate in Arthur Avenue–area" pasticcerias.

A Salt & Battery ● Prepared Food — 22 | 15 | 18 | M

W Village | 112 Greenwich Ave. (bet. 12th & 13th Sts.) | A/C/E/L to 14th St./8th Ave. | 212-691-2713 | www.asaltandbattery.com
"Real-deal" "fresh fish 'n' chips", "done right" and dished up by "helpful, quick-witted" authentic Brit "blokes" make this West Village chippy "a must for Anglophiles", expats or anyone fostering "fantasies of living in the East End"; other "guilty, fattening pleasures" include "wonderful" battered sausage, pasties, pot pie – and "if you're feeling naughty" go for the "deep-fried Mars bar."

Asia Market Specialty Shop — 21 | 12 | 13 | I

Chinatown | 71½ Mulberry St. (bet. Bayard & Canal Sts.) | 6/J/M/N/Q/R/W/Z to Canal St. | 212-962-2020
Your "complete one-stop shop for Asian cooking", this market in Chinatown carries "quality", "reasonably priced herbs, dried

goods", produce, sauces and teas as well as "all the spices for Indonesian, Malaysian and other Southeast Asian" cuisines; despite the "hordes" of shoppers and a "nonexistent staff", it's well "worth a visit."

Astoria Meat Products ⊉ *Meat/Poultry*   ▽ 25 | 19 | 22 | M

Astoria | 35-09 Broadway (bet. 35th & 36th Sts.) | Queens | N/W to B'way | 718-726-5663

This old-fashioned emporium in Astoria specializing in cured and smoked Eastern European meats remains a family-run operation despite the passing of late, lamented owner George Wasyerniuk; it can be counted on not only for its "great selection" of hams, sausages, kielbasa, meatloaf and cold cuts, but also "personal service", "fair prices" and a relaxed shopping experience that "sure beats the frenzy at all-inclusive" butchers.

Astor Wines & Spirits ●▣ *Wine/Liquor*   25 | 24 | 22 | M

NoHo | 399 Lafayette St. (E. 4th St.) | 6 to Astor Pl. | 212-674-7500 | www.astorwines.com

"Bigger and better" than ever in its "snazzy" 11,000-sq.-ft. digs, NoHo's "heavyweight champion of booze" continues to knock out customers with its "mind-boggling array" of liquors, sake and "quality" vinos, both "known and unknown vintages"; "friendly service", "free tastings", a "dog-friendly" setup and a range of choices "to fit all budgets" add up to a "terrific adult candy store"; N.B. the Study at Astor Center, its "upstairs classroom" division, is slated to open in fall 2007.

☒ Atlas Party Rentals *Party Rentals*   23 | 18 | 20 | M

Mt. Vernon | 554 S. Columbus Ave. (Sandford Blvd.), NY | 212-929-8888 | 800-695-6565 | www.partyrenter.com

A "large assortment of rentals" from tents and dance floors to tables, chairs and dishes can be delivered to party-throwers in the five boroughs (and LI, Westchester, and Connecticut) by this two-pronged team, a merger of Atlas and AAA Best Chair Rentals, with showrooms in Mount Vernon, NY, and Westport, CT; respondents cite as points in their favor "reliable" service and decent prices, comparatively speaking, and a willingness to take on last-minute jobs; N.B. $100 minimum order for delivery.

Au Bon Pain *Baked Goods*   16 | 16 | 14 | I

E 40s | 16 E. 44th St. (bet. 5th & Madison Aves.) | 4/5/6/7/S to 42nd St./Grand Central | 212-867-6356
E 40s | 600 Third Ave. (40th St.) | 4/5/6/7/S to 42nd St./Grand Central | 212-370-9823 ●
Financial Dist | 80 Pine St. (Water St.) | 2/3 to Wall St. | 212-952-9007
Garment Dist | Macy's | 151 W. 34th St. (bet. 6th & 7th Aves.) | 1/2/3/A/C/E to 34th St./Penn Station | 212-494-1091 ●
Garment Dist | 420 Fifth Ave. (37th St.) | 7/B/D/F/V to 42nd St./Bryant Park | 212-730-5401 ●
NoHo | 684 Broadway (W. 3rd St.) | A/B/C/D/E/F/V to W. 4th St. | 212-420-1694 ●

(continued)

| | QUALITY | DISPLAY | SERVICE | COST |

(continued)

Au Bon Pain

Union Sq | 73 Fifth Ave. (15th St.) | 4/5/6/L/N/Q/R/W to 14th St./
Union Sq. | 212-242-9836 ◑

W 40s | Newscorp Building | 1211 Sixth Ave. (bet. 47th & 48th Sts.) |
B/D/F/V to 47-50th Sts./Rockefeller Ctr. | 212-840-5093

W 50s | 1251 Sixth Ave. (50th St.) | B/D/F/V to 47-50th Sts./
Rockefeller Ctr. | 212-921-5908 ◑

Downtown | 1 Metrotech Ctr. (Myrtle Ave.) | Brooklyn | A/C/F to
Jay St./Borough Hall | 718-624-9598

800-825-5227 | www.aubonpain.com
Additional locations throughout the NY area

"Nine-to-fivers" and other "on-the-go" types "depend" on this
"ubiquitous" bakery/sandwich shop chain that "serves its purpose"
as a "quick, cheap snack" haven and "lunchtime staple" supplying
muffins, sandwiches, soups and such that are "perfectly acceptable", especially "in a pinch"; just remember that "mass-produced"
quality and "spotty service" are part of the deal – "behind the French
name" is a "typical" "American" "franchise."

Australian Homemade ◑ *Ice Cream*

| 23 | 21 | 21 | M |

E Village | 115 St. Marks Pl. (bet. Ave. A & 1st Ave.) | 6 to Astor Pl. |
212-228-5439 | www.australianhomemade.com

"Ice cream addicts" always "have a g'day" at this East Village purveyor of "super-rich and creamy" concoctions, offering plenty of "interesting flavors", including the popular Belgian chocolate, in "cute,
modern" digs; if you "don't get enough calories" from your cone or
cup, there's also a line of "delicious" chocolates that are almost "too
pretty to eat."

BabyCakes NYC ◑▤ *Baked Goods*

| 24 | 21 | 22 | M |

LES | 248 Broome St. (bet. Ludlow & Orchard Sts.) | F/J/M/Z to
Delancey/Essex Sts. | 212-677-5047 | www.babycakesnyc.com

"Who knew wheat-free, dairy-free could be so delicious?" marvel converts to this "cute", "'50s-ish little" Lower East Side bakery "offering alternatives" for the food-sensitive with its
"delicious" cupcakes, cakes, pastries and other "vegan goodies"
they manage to make without gluten, soy, nuts, refined sugar or
other problem ingredients for the "allergic" and "health-
conscious"; completing the picture is an overall "happy vibe"
that has groupies gushing "I'm in love!"

Bacchus Wine
Made Simple ◑▤ *Wine/Liquor*

| 19 | 21 | 21 | E |

W 70s | 2056 Broadway (bet. 70th & 71st Sts.) | 1/2/3 to 72nd St. |
212-875-1200 | www.bacchusnyc.com

It changed hands recently, but the formula at this "easy-to-
navigate" Upper West Side wine purveyor remains the same – a
focus on "carefully chosen" small-production vineyards, arranged
and displayed according to style/taste categories (juicy, bold, premium, etc.); cynics pan the minimalist approach as a "gimmick", but
most agree it works well for "beginners" and the "indecisive."

	QUALITY	DISPLAY	SERVICE	COST

Back to the Land ❶ *Health Food* — 23 | 21 | 20 | M

Park Slope | 142 Seventh Ave. (bet. Carroll St. & Garfield Pl.) | Brooklyn | F to 7th Ave. | 718-768-5654 | www.backtothelandnaturalfoods.com

Park Slopers who aren't "members of the Food Coop" turn to this "well-stocked" neighborhood "legend" for "high-quality" organic products and health foods; its "thorough" selection makes it "convenient" and the "checkout lines move quickly", but "chichi" price points explain why many "locals call it 'Back to the Bank.'"

Bagel Bob's *Bagels* — 22 | 15 | 18 | I

E 80s | 1638 York Ave. (bet. 86th & 87th Sts.) | 4/5/6 to 86th St. | 212-535-3838

G Village | 51 University Pl. (bet. 9th & 10th Sts.) | R/W to 8th St. | 212-533-2627 ✆
www.bagelbobs.com

"Convenient" outlets for "fresh" bagels, this Yorkville–Greenwich Village twosome "does the trick" for a "cheap carb fix", especially "Mondays from 4 to 7" PM when the "half-price" deal "can't be beat"; the "efficient" "assembly-line" setups may seem like "nothing special", but hey, this could be "the best reason to go to NYU" – "nice job, Bob."

Bagel Buffet ❶ *Bagels* — 17 | 14 | 16 | I

G Village | 406 Sixth Ave. (bet. 8th & 9th Sts.) | A/B/C/D/E/F/V to W. 4th St. | 212-477-0448

After 30 years in business, this 24/7 "Village institution" remains a "cheap" resource for "decent bagels" and deli fare served in "old"-school "cafeteria-style" digs; though it "looks a little tired" and "crusty", it's "always open" for a "quick" day-or-night bite "in the heart of" Downtown.

Bagel Hole ✆ *Bagels* — 22 | 14 | 18 | I

Park Slope | 400 Seventh Ave. (bet. 12th & 13th Sts.) | Brooklyn | F to 7th Ave. | 718-788-4014

"All bagels are not created equal", and the "smaller", "chewy" rounds with a "blistery crust" at this "handy" "Park Slope favorite" earn a hole lotta love from "traditional" types for demonstrating the way they're "supposed to be"; but if the goods "aren't oversized and full of air", neither is the "cramped" space.

Bagel Oasis ❶🖃 *Bagels* — 26 | 15 | 20 | I

Fresh Meadows | 183-12 Horace Harding Expwy. (L.I. Expwy.) | Queens | 718-359-9245 | 888-224-3561 | www.bageloasis.com

The "Hamptons"-bound attest "traffic won't seem so bad" after an "easy stop" at this Fresh Meadows vet (since 1961), which "should be a landmark" given its "amazing" handmade bagels made to "old-fashioned" standards: crisp outside, "heavenly inside" and "baked fresh" "all day and night long"; it's open round the clock, so once "hooked" you'll never have to "pass it without going in."

Bagelry ✆ *Bagels* — 19 | 14 | 15 | I

Murray Hill | 429 Third Ave. (30th St.) | 6 to 33rd St. | 212-679-9845

NYC's lone surviving member of a once-mighty chain, this Murray Hill drop-by "thrives" as a weekend source of "basic bagels with all the fixin's" even if the goods are "a little small" and "clueless" service leads to "endless waits"; skeptics are "not that impressed", but supporters say its rolled holes are "perfectly edible" (if "far from perfect") and ergo it attracts "lots of business."

Bagels & Co. ⌖⬚ *Bagels*   22 | 18 | 18 | I

E 70s | 1428 York Ave. (76th St.) | 6 to 77th St. | 212-717-0505 ◗
W 70s | 393 Amsterdam Ave. (79th St.) | 1 to 79th St. | 212-496-9400 ◗
Hillcrest | 188-02 Union Tpke. (Saul Weprin St.) | Queens | 718-217-7755
www.bagelsandco.com
"If you need kosher", this "traditional" threesome's "big, fluffy bagels" and "delicious" bialys fit the bill, as do the other "reliable" fare and the "efficient" staff; and for company of your own, the catering service offers "good quality" at some of the "cheapest" prices around; N.B. it closes at 3 PM on Friday and all day Saturday.

Bagels on the Square ◗ *Bagels*   21 | 18 | 19 | I

G Village | 7 Carmine St. (bet. Bleecker St. & 6th Ave.) | A/B/C/D/E/F/V to W. 4th St. | 212-691-3041
Put away "enough calories for a week" at this 24/7 Village "staple", where "chewy" bagels "the size of your head" come in a "really unique" range of flavors (like "the French toast one") and slathered with "mounds" of "delicious spreads"; perhaps it's "not for purists", but given the "speedy", "cheerful" service and square deal, "what's not to love?"

Bagelworks, Inc. ◗ *Bagels*   23 | 14 | 18 | I

E 60s | 1229 First Ave. (bet. 66th & 67th Sts.) | 6 to 68th St. | 212-744-6444
It's definitely "not flashy", but Upper Eastsiders "swear by" this "tiny" "neighborhood" joint's "flavorful (and not excessively doughy)" bagels, "made on-premises" and topped with a "toothsome" lineup of "interesting spreads"; despite the "no-frills" space and service "without the hoo-ha", worked-up fans find that "waiting in line" here is "worth your while."

Bagel Zone ⬚ *Bagels*   17 | 16 | 19 | I

E Village | 50 Ave. A (bet. 3rd & 4th Sts.) | F/V to Lower East Side/2nd Ave. | 212-533-9948
"Nice concept" say admirers of this East Village cafe-cum-"antique" shop, which vends "piping hot bagels" along with schmears and sandwiches amid a "curious assortment of Moroccan" wares like "chandeliers and lighting fixtures"; some suggest the vittles are "not the best", but it's run by "great guys" and you might even bag a tasty "pedestal table to go."

Baked ⌖ *Baked Goods*   25 | 21 | 21 | M

Red Hook | 359 Van Brunt St. (bet. Dikeman & Wolcott Sts.) | Brooklyn | F/G to Smith/9th Sts. | 718-222-0345 | www.bakednyc.com
"Delicious" "twists on old American favorites" produced by this Red Hook "hipster" bakery – "homey, delicate", "amazing" cakes and cupcakes, muffins, scones, the "best" brownies – lead many to moon "wish it were in Manhattan"; its "funky" modern digs make a "nice place to sit with your coffee and something sweet" (and there

are also panini and a few other prepared items at lunchtime) – meaning it's perfect for "fortifying yourself" pre-"Fairway."

Baked Ideas ☞ *Baked Goods* — | — | — | M

SoHo | 450 Broadway (bet. Grand & Howard Sts.) | 212-925-9097 | www.bakedideas.com
By appointment only

The likenesses of celebrities and politicians often turn up on the handiworks of SoHo baker/designer Patti Paige, whose whimsical edible specialties include hand-decorated novelty cookies in shapes ranging from George Dubya's pate to a NYC taxicab; not surprisingly, she does a big business in customized edible favors for corporate events and weddings.

Z Balducci's ●☞ *Major Gourmet Mkt.* 25 | 24 | 20 | E

Chelsea | 81 Eighth Ave. (14th St.) | A/C/E/L to 14th St./8th Ave. | 212-741-3700
W 60s | 155 W. 66th St. (bet. Amsterdam Ave. & B'way) | 1 to 66th St./Lincoln Ctr. | 212-653-8320
www.balduccis.com

Maybe "this ain't the old Balducci's", but even nostalgists who miss the defunct Greenwich Village original give the nod to this "beautiful" Chelsea megamart (with a less impressive Lincoln Center–area branch) for its "wealth of" gourmet goods, including a "rich assortment of meats", "well-crafted" prepared foods, "luscious" produce displayed "like art", "delicious" deli, "irresistible" bakery items and "seafood so fresh it'll slap you"; it continues to "tantalize" with imports "you can't find anywhere else" and quality that remains "exceptional in its class", and even those stymied by "wildly expensive" price tags find it "fun to browse"; P.S. the extras Downtown include a coffee bar and "secret seating" upstairs.

Balthazar Bakery ● *Baked Goods* 27 | 24 | 21 | E

SoHo | 80 Spring St. (bet. B'way & Crosby St.) | 6 to Spring St. | 212-965-1785 | www.balthazarny.com

"Voilà – a little bit of Paris when you can't jump on a plane" is the refrain of those who "squeeze" into this wildly "popular", "way-too-crowded" French bakery (sidecar to SoHo's famed brasserie) vending "terrific", "crunchy" baguettes and other "can't-be-beat" breads, "fabulous" croissants and tarts "worth every calorie"; no, this level of "culinary craftsmanship" doesn't come cheap, but then its legions of devotees declare they'd "pay anything" for the "ethereal" goods here.

Banchet Flowers ☞ *Flowers* — | — | — | VE

Meatpacking | 809 Washington St. (bet. Gansevoort & Horatio Sts.) | A/C/E/L to 14th St./8th Ave. | 212-989-1088 | www.banchetflowers.com

Although they're "never too ornate", the "unusual luxury arrangements" from the "talented florists" at this "wonderful" Meatpacking District shop are "meant to impress", note surveyors, who cite its "incredible orchids" – not to mention seriously "expensive" tabs; the

QUALITY DISPLAY SERVICE COST

chic quarters double as an event space for weddings, fashion shows and parties, while the adjacent Flower Bar includes a drinks counter where bouquet buyers can wait for their posies.

B & B Meat Market ⊅ *Meat/Poultry*
-	-	-	E

Williamsburg | 168 Bedford Ave. (bet. N. 7th & 8th Sts.) | Brooklyn | L to Bedford Ave. | 718-388-2811

This family-owned butcher shop has been plying Williamsburg residents with Eastern European sausages and cold cuts since the early 1970s; it's an old-time black and white–tiled market that's also a source for homemade prepared foods such as stuffed cabbage and sauerkraut.

B & E Quality Beverage *Beer*
-	-	-	I

Woodside | 32-31 57th St. (bet. Northern Blvd. & 32nd Ave.) | Queens | G/R/V to Northern Blvd. | 212-243-6812

A veritable "beer paradise", this "wonderful" Woodsider "has it all" when it comes to suds, offering "everything from kegs to hard-to-find microbrews", with a particular emphasis on hard ciders and Belgian, German and English brews; its impressive inventory also includes soft drinks, ice and snacks, presided over by a "pleasant" staff, and there's convenient delivery too – in short, it's a "great source" for "party"-throwers.

☑ Bangkok Center Grocery *Specialty Shop*
27	17	23	I

Chinatown | 104 Mosco St. (bet. Mott & Mulberry Sts.) | 6/J/M/N/Q/R/W/Z to Canal St. | 212-349-1979

Hidden away on a Chinatown backstreet, this "gem" of a market is "small but well-stocked" with "hard-to-find ingredients" – from housemade curry pastes to fresh coconut milk – that will enhance "your Thai dinner at home"; regulars report you "can always rely on them" to dispense "friendly cooking advice" and, really, "where else can you buy fresh kaffir lime leaves?"

Bánh Mì Saigon Bakery ⊅ *Deli/Sandwich*
25	11	16	I

Chinatown | 138-01 Mott St. (bet. Grand & Hester Sts.) | 6/J/M/N/Q/R/W/Z to Canal St. | 212-941-1541

One of the "best-kept secrets in Chinatown", this Vietnamese hideaway at the back of a Mott Street jewelry store sells what supporters say is the "perfect" *bahn mi* sandwich – roast pork, cilantro, pickled carrots, cucumber and hot peppers loaded up on "crusty" French bread – amounting to a "salty, sweet, spicy, crunchy, delicious" meal for "practically pennies"; seating is limited and "ambiance" nil, but its "filling" "quick fixes" always "satisfy"; N.B. it now offers meatball, chicken and veggie options.

NEW Barbarini Alimentari *Prepared Food*
-	-	-	E

Financial Dist | 225 Front St. (bet. Beekman St. & Peck Slip) | 4/5/6/J/M/Z to Brooklyn Bridge/City Hall | 212-227-8890 | www.barbarini.net

"Delicious" Italiana abounds at this "tiny" Financial District "gem" of a deli/cafe, where sandwiches, pastas and other prepared foods share space with pastries and desserts, as well as olive oils, vinegars, cheeses, sauces, jams, coffee and other staples imported from The Boot; there are a few cafe tables for eating on-premises, and it also specializes in catering business lunches and other office affairs.

Bari Pork Store *Meat/Poultry* | 24 | 21 | 22 | M |

Bensonhurst | 6319 18th Ave. (64th St.) | Brooklyn | N to 18th Ave. | 718-837-9773

Borough Park | 7119 18th Ave. (bet. 71st & 72nd Sts.) | Brooklyn | N to 18th Ave. | 718-837-1257

Gravesend | 158 Ave. U (W. 7th St.) | Brooklyn | N to Ave. U | 718-372-6405

Staten Island | 1755 Richmond Rd. (bet. Dogan Hills & Seaver Aves.) | 718-667-7780

www.barigourmet.com

"It's hard to choose" among the housemade Italian sausages and other pig-licious products at these individually owned "real-deal" Italian meat shops in Brooklyn and Staten Island, which also carry imported cured meats and pantry goods; made-on-the-premises mozzarella, *arancini* (fried rice balls) and all manner of antipasti round out the offerings.

Bari Restaurant Equipment *Cookware* | 24 | 15 | 17 | M |

LES | 240 Bowery (bet. Houston & Prince Sts.) | F/V to Lower East Side/2nd Ave. | 212-925-3845 | www.bariequipment.com

"If you aspire to culinary greatness, this is the place" cheer champions of this "crowded" no-frills Lower East Side restaurant supply shop where the inventory spanning "everything *including* the kitchen sink" – from walk-in freezers to old-fashioned ketchup bottles – appeals to pros and amateurs alike; service swings between "down-to-earth" and "not helpful", but the "good" prices make up for any shortcomings.

Z Barney Greengrass *Caviar/Smoked Fish* | 27 | 18 | 19 | E |

W 80s | 541 Amsterdam Ave. (bet. 86th & 87th Sts.) | 1 to 86th St. | 212-724-4707 | www.barneygreengrass.com

"If it's smoked, you want Greengrass" is the word on this West Side "old-world wonder" with a "lofty reputation" as "the most authentic" purveyor of "sturgeon extraordinaire", "sable like butter", "delectable fresh whitefish" and caviar; the "classic" '20s-era setup is a "true NY experience" with "sporadic" service and "chaotic" conditions when the "line outside for brunch" forms on weekends, but "it's been there forever for a reason" and remains "the gold standard" (but just "bring your gold card").

Baskin-Robbins *Ice Cream* | 17 | 15 | 14 | I |

Chelsea | 269 Eighth Ave. (bet. 23rd & 24th Sts.) | C/E to 23rd St. | 212-229-2622

Chelsea | 289 Seventh Ave. (bet. 26th & 27th Sts.) | 1 to 28th St. | 212-229-4799

E 60s | 1225 First Ave. (66th St.) | 6 to 68th St. | 212-734-5465

Flatiron | 536 Sixth Ave. (bet. 14th & 15th Sts.) | F/L/V to 14th St./6th Ave. | 212-727-0444

(continued)

	QUALITY	DISPLAY	SERVICE	COST

(continued)

Baskin-Robbins

Gramercy | 218 E. 14th St. (bet. 2nd & 3rd Aves.) | 4/5/6/L/N/Q/R/W to 14th St./Union Sq. | 212-388-9992

Murray Hill | 302 Fifth Ave. (31st St.) | B/D/F/N/Q/R/V/W to 34th St./Herald Sq. | 212-268-0686

Murray Hill | 601 Second Ave. (33rd St.) | 6 to 33rd St. | 212-532-5003

TriBeCa | 100 Chambers St. (Church St.) | 1/2/3/A/C to Chambers St. | 212-619-1222

TriBeCa | 321 Broadway (bet. Thomas & Worth Sts.) | R/W to City Hall | 212-577-7550

Greenpoint | 892 Manhattan Ave. (Greenpoint Ave.) | Brooklyn | G to Greenpoint Ave. | 718-349-2930

800-859-5339 | www.baskinrobbins.com
Additional locations throughout the NY area

If you've got an "ice cream urge" and don't like the "fancy", "high-butterfat" choices at other places, this "inexpensive", "reliable" "American classic" is "good in a pinch", offering one of the "biggest selection" of flavors around ("more than 31"); the less-enthralled say the "chemical" "aftertaste" and "surly" service aren't so sweet, but parents find it hard to beat their "amazing" cakes when it's time for a birthday party.

Bayard Street Meat Market *Meat/Poultry* | 23 | 17 | 13 | I |
(aka Deluxe Food Market)

Chinatown | 57 Bayard St. (Elizabeth St.) | 6/J/M/N/Q/R/W/Z to Canal St. | 212-619-6206 ☞

Little Italy | 79 Elizabeth St. (bet. Grand & Hester Sts.) | B/D to Grand St. | 212-925-5766 ◐

A bastion of fresh beef, pork, poultry and just about any animal part you can imagine ("*the* place to get duck's tongue"), these Chinatown–Little Italy meat retailers are justly appreciated for their "large variety" and fair prices that "will always beat the supermarket's"; insiders note the shopping experience is even better if "you know Mandarin or Cantonese"; N.B. the vast Elizabeth Street location also features sushi, fish counters as well as pastries, fresh juices and ice cream.

Bay Ridge Bakery *Baked Goods* | 25 | 23 | 26 | M |

Bay Ridge | 7805 Fifth Ave. (78th St.) | Brooklyn | R to 77th St. | 718-238-0014 | www.bayridgebakery.com

"You want great pastries?" – Bay Ridge locals suggest this longtime bake shop turning out "elegant" "European-style" specialties including cakes, pies and tarts, Danish and a few Greek classics like baklava; it's a family-owned operation that's rated among the "best" in the area, with the added appeal of an open kitchen allowing customers to watch the chef in action; N.B. it specializes in wedding and other special-occasion cakes.

⊿ Bazzini, A.L., Co. ▣ *Major Gourmet Mkt.* ▽ | 27 | 20 | 21 | E |

TriBeCa | 339 Greenwich St. (Jay St.) | 1 to Franklin St. | 212-334-1280 | www.bazzininuts.com

It's "well known" that this 1880s-vintage TriBeCa fixture "shines" as an "established" source of "delicious nuts" – the "freshest" "A+

QUALITY · DISPLAY · SERVICE · COST

quality" with "fantastic" choices from almonds to walnuts – but these days it also "comes up big" as an "excellent gourmet shop" where the "very inviting" draws include "fresh produce" and meats, "tasty" prepared foods, "Italian delicacies" like imported pasta and olive oils, and an "excellent assortment" of dried fruits and candy; yes, it's on the "expensive" side, but it's "def worth it" for anyone driven nutty by the area's "sorely lacking" options.

Beacon Wines & Spirits ◑▣ *Wine/Liquor* | 21 | 18 | 16 | M |

W 70s | 2120 Broadway (74th St.) | 1/2/3 to 72nd St. | 212-877-0028 | www.beaconwine.com

A "respectable" purveyor of "fine wines and spirits" located right "across the street from Citarella" and Fairway, this Upper West Side shop boasts a "wide-ranging" selection of "attractively priced" and "easy-to-find" bottles; sure, it lacks "ambiance" and "helpful" staffers can be "hard to find", but "if you know your wines and what you want", "you'll surely find something."

Beard Papa Sweets   *Baked Goods* | 24 | 17 | 20 | I |

E 40s | Cafe Zaiya | 18 E. 41 St. (bet. 5th & Madison Aves.) | 4/5/6/7/S to 42nd St./Grand Central | 212-779-0600

E Village | 740 Broadway (Astor Pl.) | 6 to Astor Pl. | 212-353-8888 ◑

W 70s | 2167 Broadway (bet. 76th & 77th Sts.) | 1/2/3 to 72nd St. | 212-799-3770

W Village | 5 Carmine St. (bet. Bleecker St. & 6th Ave.) | A/B/C/D/E/F/V to W. 4th St. | 212-989-8855 ◑
www.muginohousa.com

Find "little pockets of heaven" within these brightly lit outposts of a Japanese chain "devoted to the cream puff" – "amazingly delicious", "crispy-on-the-outside" cream-filled babies in flavors from "rich vanilla" to "exquisite green tea and chocolate"; addicts "hooked from the very first bite" say its "indulgent" treats "should be classified as a controlled substance", though a skeptical few shrug this "one-trick pony" "doesn't live up to the hype."

Bed Bath & Beyond ◑▣ *Cookware* | 20 | 19 | 15 | M |

Chelsea | 620 Sixth Ave. (bet. 18th & 19th Sts.) | 1 to 18th St. | 212-255-3550

E 60s | 410 E. 61st St. (1st Ave.) | N/R/W to Lexington Ave./59th St. | 646-215-4702

W 60s | 1932 Broadway (Columbus Ave.) | 1 to 66th St./Lincoln Ctr. | 917-441-9391

Canarsie | 459 Gateway Dr. (Fountain Ave.) | Brooklyn | A/C to Euclid Ave. | 718-235-2049

Elmhurst | 72-15 25th Ave. (bet. 73rd & 77nd Sts.) | Queens | G/R/V to Elmhurst Ave. | 718-429-9438

Rego Pk | 96-05 Queens Blvd. (63rd Dr.) | Queens | G/R/V to Woodhaven Blvd. | 718-459-0868

Staten Island | Staten Island Mall | 2795 Richmond Ave. (Platinum Ave.) | 718-982-0071
800-462-3966 | www.bedbathandbeyond.com

"It's all about convenience" at this "reliable" "one-stop" franchise whose kitchen departments boast a "staggering" array of "main-

QUALITY | DISPLAY | SERVICE | COST

stream" pots and pans, utensils, cutlery and appliances, as well as a "limited" selection of "high-end" brands; though it's a "zoo" on weekends and the staffers can be "clueless", its "amazing return policy", "reasonable prices" and frequent "20 percent off coupons in the mail" mean that even those who swear they "hate chain stores" consider it a "necessary evil" for "stocking up" city apartments.

☑ Bedford Cheese Shop ●☑☞ Cheese/Dairy 27 | 24 | 24 | E

Williamsburg | 229 Bedford Ave. (N. 4th St.) | Brooklyn | L to Bedford Ave. | 718-599-7588 | 888-484-3243 | www.bedfordcheeseshop.com
Now in a "lovely" "new space" that "only makes it better", this Williamsburg "pioneer" proves that the "hip can do dairy" with "by far" the neighborhood's "best selection" of "unique cheeses" (150-plus varieties) tended by "knowledgeable" staffers who dole out samples and "make everything sound interesting"; it also "abounds" with "hard-to-find gourmet" goods and bread from leading bakeries, resulting in "really fun" shopping for "expensive" tastes.

Beekman Liquors ●☑ Wine/Liquor 24 | 19 | 24 | M

E 40s | 500 Lexington Ave. (bet. 47th & 48th Sts.) | 4/5/6/7/S to 42nd St./Grand Central | 212-759-5857 | www.beekmanliquors.com
"Packed full" with 3,500 wines (most from California and France) as well as a "wide range of spirits", in particular single-malts, "rare" whiskeys and sake, this "small", "solid" Midtown store near Grand Central is ideal for a "quick pickup"; it's been "around for decades" and "looks it" quip some, but the service still "makes the grade."

Beekman Marketplace ☑☞ Meat/Poultry ▽ 22 | 19 | 22 | M

E 40s | 883 First Ave. (bet. 49th & 50th Sts.) | 6 to 51st St. | 212-755-7756 | www.beekmanmarketplace.com
Since relocating from its original shop on the same block, this Sutton Place butcher and grocer (fka Empire Purveyors) has been expanding its offerings, providing patrons not only with the "finest quality" prime meat, poultry and game, but also breads and pastries, comfort-oriented prepared foods and even a line of gift baskets, all overseen by second-generation owners who provide a wonderful "family touch"; N.B. there are also an in-store cafe and catering services.

Belfiore Meats Meat/Poultry ▽ 25 | 19 | 22 | M

Staten Island | 2500 Victory Blvd. (Willowbrook Rd.) | 718-983-0440
Known to regulars for its "high-quality" "always-fresh" meats, this Italian butcher-cum-specialty foods shop-cum-caterer also purveys prepared foods (roast chicken, roast pork), baked goods and gelato; surveyors say the "expert" service is generally "friendly", if occasionally undercut by a little "Staten Island 'charm.'"

Bell Bates Natural Food Market Health Food 24 | 20 | 20 | M

TriBeCa | 97 Reade St. (bet. Church St. & W. B'way) | 1/2/3/A/C to Chambers St. | 212-267-4300 | www.bellbates.com
"They have everything" at this "Downtown pioneer" of natural foods, offering TriBeCa residents and workers a "wide variety" of "healthy choices", including a "large selection of spices", coffee and other

	QUALITY	DISPLAY	SERVICE	COST

bulk items; service can vary between "knowledgeable" and "indifferent", but the salad bar and prepared foods are always "quite good."

☑ Belle Fleur *Flowers*

	28	27	25	VE

Flatiron | 134 Fifth Ave., 4th fl. (bet. 18th & 19th Sts.) | N/R/W to 23rd St. | 212-254-8703 | www.bellefleurny.com

"The name says it all" at this Flatiron District florist where "exquisite", "chic blooms" arranged by a "mother-daughter duo" that shares a "gorgeous sense of color" result in "flawless", "artful" ensembles; "exceptional one-on-one service" means "lucky recipients are always thrilled", so even though "price tags are high", it's "the perfect way to say 'I love you – and I'm really rich.'"

Ben & Jerry's *Ice Cream*

	24	18	18	M

E 40s | Grand Central Terminal | main concourse (42nd St. & Vanderbilt Ave.) | 4/5/6/7/S to 42nd St./Grand Central | 212-953-1028 ●

E Village | 41 Third Ave. (bet. 9th & 10th Sts.) | 6 to Astor Pl. | 212-995-0109 ●

Garment Dist | Macy's | 151 W. 34th St. (bet. 6th & 7th Aves.) | B/D/F/N/Q/R/V/W to 34th St./Herald Sq. | 212-594-0018 ●

W 40s | 30 Rockefeller Plaza, concourse level (bet. 49th & 50th Sts.) | B/D/F/V to 47-50th Sts./Rockefeller Ctr. | 212-218-7843

W 40s | 680 Eighth Ave. (43rd St.) | A/C/E to 42nd St./Port Authority | 212-221-1001 ●

W 100s | 2722 Broadway (104th St.) | 1 to 103rd St. | 212-866-6237 ● www.benandjerrys.com

"Simply the best" exclaim enthusiasts of this "goofy and wonderful" Vermont-based chain with outposts throughout the city scooping "over-the-top flavors" of "all-natural" ice cream; while some claim it's "too sweet", "too rich" and "long past its prime", most others insist it'll "leave you craving more."

Ben's Kosher Deli ● *Deli/Sandwich*

	21	17	17	M

Garment Dist | 209 W. 38th St. (7th Ave.) | 1/2/3/7/N/Q/R/S/W to 42nd St./Times Sq. | 212-398-2367 🖃

Bayside | Bay Terrace | 211-37 26th Ave. (Bell Blvd.) | Queens | LIRR to Bayside | 718-229-2367

800-344-2367 | www.bensdeli.net

The "monster sammies" made with "amazing" house-cured pastrami and corned beef are more than worth the "artery clog" according to advocates of this "reasonably priced", "old-fashioned" Garment District-Bayside kosher deli duo, whose "flaky knishes" and "can't-miss matzo-ball soup" also "hold their own"; however, a few find it a bit "watered-down" compared to other "Jewish-style" spots – maybe "if the waiters were ruder, it would be perfect."

Berger's On The Go *Deli/Sandwich*
(fka Berger's Delicatessen)

	▽ 21	11	20	M

Murray Hill | 2 E. 39th St. (bet. 5th & Madison Aves.) | 7/B/D/F/V to 42nd St./Bryant Park | 212-719-4173

Last year, this Diamond District deli "favorite" moved to Murray Hill and modernized its offerings, adding more health-conscious and to-go items; early reports are mixed: some say it's a "consistent" contender with "great corned beef" and "fast" service, but others lament it's "not what it used to be."

Berkshire Berries 🖃✈ *Produce* 27 | 22 | 24 | M
See Greenmarket; for more information, call 413-623-5779 or
800-523-7797 | www.berkshireberries.com
Gooseberry and wild blueberry–ginger are among the new flavors offered by this Berkshires-based Greenmarket vendor offering "excellent preserves" made from "ripe and luscious" fruit; loyalists also "love the NYC rooftop honey" (from apiaries atop city buildings) and "the best maple syrup", and note that while the "service is fine", the ratio of "quality to price" is even better.

Berried Treasures ✈ *Produce* 28 | 22 | 24 | M
See Greenmarket; for more information, call 646-391-3162
"Justifiably known for her strawberries", "friendly" nutritionist-turned-farmer Franca Tantillo brings "small, fragrant, flavorful, juicy" specimens from her Catskills farm to grateful NYC Greenmarket shoppers; "in recent years, she's been branching out", growing other types of berries along with a "broad selection of potatoes", several kinds of beans, garlic and shallots – "superior produce" that fans "always" find "worth a try."

Best Cellars *Wine/Liquor* 21 | 24 | 23 | I
E 80s | 1291 Lexington Ave. (87th St.) | 4/5/6 to 86th St. |
212-426-4200 | www.bestcellars.com ●🖃
NEW **W 80s** | 2246 Broadway (bet. 80th & 81st Sts.) | 1 to 79th St. |
212-362-8730
"Always on the cutting edge" with a "fabulous" "rotating selection" and "knowledgeable" staff, this "unintimidating" pair of independently owned vintners "proves cheap wine doesn't have to be bad", and while "experienced oenophiles" may cringe at the categorization of labels by taste ('juicy', 'smooth', 'big', etc.), the system is "accessible" to "novices"; the East Side store offers "frequent" tastings and its stock is available via Fresh Direct, while the Broadway location hosts educational dinners and other programs.

Beth's Farm Kitchen 🖃 *Specialty Shop* 27 | 24 | 26 | M
See Greenmarket; for more information, call 800-331-5267 |
www.bethsfarmkitchen.com
Hudson Valley–based preserves purveyor Beth Linskey buys produce from area farmers to go into her "diverse" assortment of "delectable" jams and jellies, "superb chutneys" and pickles sold at the Greenmarket; regulars rave about "the absolute best" raspberry jam "known to man" and "addictive" red-pepper jelly, and appreciate the "cheery", "informative" booth workers' usage suggestions for the more unusual products; P.S. "beautifully wrapped" gift boxes are "ready for giving year-round."

Better Burger ● *Prepared Food* 19 | 15 | 17 | M
Chelsea | 178 Eighth Ave. (19th St.) | C/E to 23rd St. |
212-989-6688

(continued)

Better Burger

Murray Hill | 561 Third Ave. (37th St.) | 6 to 33rd St. | 212-949-7528
W 40s | 587 Ninth Ave. (bet. 42nd & 43rd Sts.) | A/C/E to 42nd St./
Port Authority | 212-629-6622
www.betterburgernyc.com

When healthy-minded sorts want to "satisfy the burger 'n' fries craving" "without guilt", they say this "earth-conscious" mini-chain is "much appreciated", offering organic "tasty alternatives" ("where else can you get an ostrich burger with air-baked fries and wasabi ketchup?"); fat-free "delicious smoothies" are another plus, though a few who "don't get the hubbub" want to know "better than what?"

NEW Betty Bakery *Baked Goods*

| – | – | – | E |

Boerum Hill | 448 Atlantic Ave. (bet. Bond & Nevins Sts.) | Brooklyn |
A/C/G to Hoyt/Schermerhorn Sts. | 718-246-2402

A joint venture from exclusive wedding-cake crafters Cheryl Kleinman and Ellen Baumwoll (the latter of Bijoux Doux), this new Boerum Hill bakery focuses on cupcakes, "beautiful" petit fours and, yes, full-size cakes; its snug, homey quarters, centered around a pastel-green 1930s-era stove, include a few seats in which to savor the treats, along with coffee and tea poured by a "friendly" crew.

Between the Bread *Caterer*

| 21 | 18 | 18 | M |

W 50s | 145 W. 55th St. (bet. 6th & 7th Aves.) | N/Q/R/W to 57th St. |
212-765-1840 | www.betweenthebread.com

"Business meetings" and "office parties" "look easy" in the hands of this Midtown "corporate-catering" specialist and prepared foods shop that provides a "wonderful variety" of "seasonal" New American fare in "creative presentations"; some pan its offerings as "pedestrian", but many others hail it as a "dependable" option for "no-fuss" planning.

Biancardi Meats ≠ *Meat/Poultry*

| 27 | 23 | 25 | M |

Bronx | 2350 Arthur Ave. (bet. Crescent Ave. & 187th St.) | B/D to
Fordham Rd. | 718-733-4058

This family-owned, Italian-oriented Arthur Avenue butcher has been taking meat "seriously" since 1932 and continues to "reign supreme" with "excellent-quality", "value"-priced cuts of all kinds, as well as sausages and more esoteric offerings (baby goat, game birds, rabbit and more – "just ask and it will appear"); given that "great traditional" places like this are "losing popularity to supermarkets and gourmet shops", far-flung fans say it's more than "worth the trip" to the Bronx.

Z Bierkraft ●◑▭ *Beer*

| 28 | 21 | 25 | M |

Park Slope | 191 Fifth Ave. (bet. Berkeley Pl. & Union St.) | Brooklyn |
M/R to Union St. | 718-230-7600 | www.bierkraft.com

For "one-stop gourmet shopping", regulars recommend this Park Slope beer expert that offers not only a "vast", "well-curated" selection of suds, including drafts you can take home in "reusable growler jugs", but also "tasty" "delights" such as "wonderful" cheeses, "mouthwatering cold cuts", "gift-worthy" condiments, "handmade chocolates" and more; an "approachable" staff will guide you along this "dangerous but delicious route", which is "costly", but hey, still "cheaper than going to Belgium."

Big Apple Florist 🖃 *Flowers* ▽ 24 | 24 | 25 | M

E 40s | 228 E. 45th St. (bet. 2nd & 3rd Aves.) | 4/5/6/7/S to 42nd St./ Grand Central | 212-687-3434 | 800-554-0001 | www.bigapplefloral.com

"Too bad about the deli"-esque name, because this East Midtown florist's "designer-looking" arrangements are "haute level" according to aficionados; the staff is "personable" and willing to design "something custom, even over the phone", resulting in posies that are "pleasing to the eye", and, better still, come "without the big-bucks price tag."

Big Nose Full Body ❶🖃 *Wine/Liquor* 24 | 21 | 25 | M

Park Slope | 382 Seventh Ave. (bet. 11th & 12th Sts.) | Brooklyn | F to 7th Ave. | 718-369-4030 | www.bignosefullbody.com

It's a "pleasure to spend time" at this "wonderful", "quaint" Park Slope shop where oenophiles can sniff out "smart choices" "for every budget" from the "limited", but "interesting" selection of 350 labels, "hand selected by the owner" and "beautifully displayed"; with "knowledgeable service", a "fabulous Web site" and weekly tastings, it's "what a neighborhood wine store should be."

Bijoux Doux Specialty Cakes *Baked Goods* – | – | – | VE

G Village | 304 Mulberry St. (bet. Bleecker & Houston Sts.) | 212-226-0948 🖃🗷
Boerum Hill | 448 Atlantic Ave. (bet. Bond & Nevins Sts.) | Brooklyn | 718-237-2271
www.bijouxdoux.com
By appointment only

"Beautiful, delicious cakes with imaginative designs" distinguish pastry chef Ellen Baumwoll's Village-based boutique bakery, which caters to brides-to-be and high-end party planners; her signature flavors are hazelnut-almond and Valrhona-chocolate, in layers that stack up in "wonderful" designs both classic and contemporary; N.B. Baumwoll often takes appointments at her Boerum Hill atelier, in the same building with Betty Bakery, the retail bake shop she recently opened with fellow gâteau great Cheryl Kleinman.

Billy's Bakery ❶ *Baked Goods* 25 | 23 | 22 | M

Chelsea | 184 Ninth Ave. (bet. 21st & 22nd Sts.) | C/E to 23rd St. | 212-647-9956 | www.billysbakerynyc.com

"Bless Billy!" enthuse admirers of this Chelsea bakery known for its "moist, buttery" cupcakes topped with "to-die-for" icing, as well as for "tasty" full-size cakes, pies and other "homespun" "American-style" sweets, all "beautifully displayed" in "hip" "retro"-'40s digs; the "friendly" counter folk only "add to the sugar high", and while "lines out the door" are not uncommon, at least they're "not as long" as at that higher-profile cupcakery to the south.

	QUALITY	DISPLAY	SERVICE	COST

Bird Bath ◑ *Baked Goods*

| | – | – | – | M |

E Village | 223 First Ave. (13th St.) | 646-722-6565 🖛
NEW **W Village** | 145 Seventh Ave. S. (Charles St.) | 1 to
Christopher St. | 646-722-6570
www.buildagreenbakery.com

The City Bakery's Maury Rubin goes green with this East Village–
West Village pair of eco-conscious bakeries/coffee shops, the interiors of which are made from nontoxic, recyclable, environmentally
sound materials, right down to the counter crew's hemp jackets;
in the cases are cookies, muffins, bear claws and such, whose ingredients are wholesome and all-organic yet manage to maintain
Rubin's trademark decadence.

BJ's Wholesale Club ◑ ◰ *Major Gourmet Mkt.*

| | 17 | 10 | 8 | I |

Starrett City | Gateway Ctr. | 339 Gateway Dr. (Erskine St.) |
Brooklyn | 3 to Van Siclen Ave. | 718-942-2090
College Pt | 137-05 20th Ave. (Whitestone Expwy., exit 15) |
Queens | 718-359-9703
Middle Vill | Metro Mall | 66-26 Metropolitan Ave. (69th St.) |
Queens | M to Middle Vill./Metropolitan Ave. | 718-326-9080
www.bjs.com

For "Super Bowl parties and such" this outer-borough wholesaler
chain is a bonanza of "bargains" sold "in bulk", with "warehouse"
aisles lined with "prepackaged deli items", frozen prepared foods
that make "acceptable side dishes", "cheap bakery products" and
"generic" housewares like "crock pots and snow-cone machines";
conditions are basic and "disorganized" and the "run-of-the-mill"
goods "leave taste in the mind of the beholder", but if you need "5 lbs
of anything" it's "quick and inexpensive" – "what do you expect?"

☒ Black Hound

| | 26 | 26 | 22 | E |

New York ◑ ◰ *Baked Goods*

E Village | 170 Second Ave. (bet. 10th & 11th Sts.) | L to 1st Ave. |
212-979-9505 | 800-344-4417 | www.blackhoundny.com

"Stunning" works of art are as "beautiful to behold as they are delicious
to eat" are the trademark of this "lovely little" East Village bakery
prized for "wicked", "wonderfully rich" cakes – including "mini" versions "perfect for two" – as well as "fancy" cookies, tarts and truffles
sure "to set your diet back centuries"; a "disappointed" minority
claims that the taste of some items "doesn't lives up to" their "perfect looks", but the general consensus is that the goods are generally "top-notch" – and "you pay for it."

Blanc & Rouge ◑ ◰ *Wine/Liquor*

| | – | – | – | M |

Dumbo | 81 Washington St. (bet. Front & York Sts.) | Brooklyn | F to
York St. | 718-858-9463 | www.brwine.com

A "friendly", "quaint secret" in Dumbo, this wine store housed in an
old factory space "isn't huge", stocking some 150 labels, but it still
features a "good selection" of "affordable" and unusual bottles from
the New World (Chile, Argentina, Australia, New Zealand, etc.) as
well as the traditional Burgundies and Bordeaux; it holds weekly
tastings on Wednesday evenings.

	QUALITY	DISPLAY	SERVICE	COST

ⓩ Bloom *Flowers*

27 | 28 | 22 | VE

E 50s | 541 Lexington Ave. (50th St.) | 6 to 51st St. | 212-832-8094 |
www.bloomflowers.com

Its "gorgeous", "work-of-art" arrangements "receive raves from everyone" say customers of this "beautiful" Midtown shop, which offers "not just flowers" but home furnishings and accessories too, meaning "there's plenty to look at while you wait for your creation"; given such "simple" yet "over-the-top" bouquets, its near-"extortionate" prices are "a given", but happily "the blooms last long enough" that most are able to "forget the cost"; N.B. they also offer event-planning and interior design services.

Bloomingdale's Cookware ●◗▣ *Cookware*

24 | 22 | 16 | E

E 50s | 1000 Third Ave. (bet. 59th & 60th Sts.) | 4/5/6 to 59th St./
Lexington Ave. | 212-705-2237 | 800-472-0788 | www.bloomingdales.com

"Watch for sales!" advise insiders of this famed East Side department store's kitchen section, whose "well-organized" selection of "top" "consumer" brands ("All-Clad, Calphalon", etc.) and "terrific" variety of utensils and gadgets are priced on the "high end" but become "bargains" if you can "wait" for a reduction; service runs the gamut from "extremely knowledgeable" to "nonexistent", but still this stalwart wins raves for its wedding registry service and "exquisite gift-wrapping."

ⓩ Blue Apron Foods *Specialty Shop*

27 | 25 | 24 | E

Park Slope | 814 Union St. (7th Ave.) | Brooklyn | B/Q to 7th Ave. |
718-230-3180

"An oasis in the borough", this pint-size Park Slope specialty shop is an epicurean "favorite" for its locally "unparalleled" cheese and charcuterie selection and well-edited lineup of "fine foods", from imported pastas to Jacques Torres chocolates, including some of "the most obscure ingredients, with advice on how to use them"; "knowledgeable" staffers and "lovely displays" "make up for" the "cramped" quarters and "steep prices"; P.S. "too bad the South Slope location closed."

Blue Meadow Flowers *Flowers*

- | - | - | E

E Village | 336 E. 13th St. (bet. 1st & 2nd Aves.) | L to 1st Ave. |
212-979-8618

"Classy, tightly wrapped bouquets with flowers that last for weeks" come in unusual vases and terra-cotta containers at this East Village floral boutique; its "innovative designs" based on classic European and Victorian styles are deemed "just beautiful" and (no surprise) "expensive" too; N.B. open weekdays only.

Blue Moon Fish ⌲ *Seafood*

29 | 20 | 26 | M

See Greenmarket; phone number unavailable | www.bluemoonfish.com

A "Greenmarket staple" since 1987, this North Fork fishmonger has seafood lovers "over the moon" with its "pristine local" offerings that are nearly "as fresh as if you caught them yourself"; the fish comes filleted or whole, or even smoked, and accompanied by "loads of knowledge and suggestions" about how to cook it courtesy of "charming", "skillful" staffers – given the "great vibe" and "fair prices", it's no wonder there are always "long lines" ("get there early before they sell out").

NEW Blue Pig *Ice Cream* — | — | — | M

Brooklyn Heights | 60 Henry St. (bet. Cranberry & Orange Sts.) | Brooklyn | 2/3 to Clark St. | 718-596-6301

The life-size blue pig standing outside the door and teen-friendly tunes on the sound system alert passersby to the presence of this new Brooklyn Heights ice cream shop, whose cases hold a rainbow-hued array of flavors packed with ingredients like cookie dough, sprinkles and M&Ms; a spin-off of a Croton, NY, favorite, it has another location expected to open soon in Grand Central Terminal.

Z Blue Ribbon Market *Baked Goods* 28 | 22 | 23 | E

G Village | 14 Bedford St. (bet. Downing & W. Houston Sts.) | 1 to Houston St. | 212-647-0408 | www.blueribbonrestaurants.com

Acclaimed as a "wonderful addition" to the Bromberg brothers' "empire", this "tiny" Greenwich Village storefront allows fans of the famously "fresh, homey" and "delicious" breads baked in the 150-year-old oven of its nearby restaurant sibling, Blue Ribbon Bakery, to "take them home"; it also sells a small selection of spreads, cheeses, smoked fish, oils and condiments to go with the loaves, as well as "superb" 'toasts' (open-faced sandwiches) and soups, all dispensed by a "friendly" low-key crew.

Blue Smoke Catering *Caterer* 25 | 20 | 23 | E

Chelsea | 640 W. 28th St. (bet. 11th & 12th Aves.) | C/E to 23rd St. | 212-488-1500 | www.bluesmoke.com

For an "alternative party idea", 'cuennoisseurs recommend the catering arm of Danny Meyer's upscale Chelsea smokehouse, which supplies "yummo" "country-style food" including "oh, yeah" barbecue and the "best mac 'n' cheese in the world"; there's also "helpful" pro service whether the event's held at the restaurant, downstairs jazz club or off-site, and while it's true that the fare's mostly "limited to carnivores", c'mon – "who doesn't love good BBQ?"

Blue Water Flowers *Flowers* — | — | — | E

SoHo | 265 Lafayette St. (bet. Prince & Spring Sts.) | 6 to Spring St. | 212-226-0587 | 800-964-7108 | www.bluewaterflowers.com

A striped awning and antique shutters give an old-fashioned feel to this SoHo shop, but the flowers are up-to-the-minute, unusual blooms arranged in ginger jars; those in search of something longer lasting will find orchids planted in ceramic or terra-cotta pots, as well as topiaries of rosemary, myrtle, ivy and azalea, dried-flower wreaths or pomanders; N.B. gourmet gift baskets are also available.

Bodum *Coffee/Tea* 24 | 24 | 20 | M

Meatpacking | 415 W. 14th St. (bet. 9th & 10th Aves.) | A/C/E/L to 14th St./8th Ave. | 212-367-9125 | 800-232-6386 | www.bodumusa.com

"The go-to name" for "coffee and tea paraphernalia", this Meatpacking District branch of the Danish housewares emporium is a bonanza of "nifty kitchen gadgets" that's famed for its "ingenious"

"French press coffeemakers" along with "brilliantly" "stylish" kettles, frothers, mugs and more; with a "neat", "modern" layout harboring a "welcome little" cafe for a cuppa their "quality" java, it bodes well as a "retail experiment done right"; N.B. "don't forget to check" the "back bargain" room for "great sale" items.

Boerum Hill Food Company ❶ *Prepared Food*   – | – | – | M

Boerum Hill | 134 Smith St. (bet. Bergen & Dean Sts.) | Brooklyn | F/G to Bergen St. | 718-222-0140

At this "cozy little" Boerum Hill cafe/prepared foods shop/catering biz (an offshoot of the down-the-block eatery Saul), the homemade lures range from fresh-baked muffins for breakfast to soups and "mac 'n' cheese to die for" for lunch or "monster egg sandwiches" that are "satisfying any time of day"; there's also coffee from Gorilla and sweets like brownie treats, which satisfy those on-the-run as well as those opting to linger in its "pleasant" space.

Bonsignour ❶ *Prepared Food*   ∇ 26 | 18 | 23 | M

W Village | 35 Jane St. (8th Ave.) | A/C/E/L to 14th St./8th Ave. | 212-229-9700

A "friendly, neighborhood kitchen" in the West Village, this "casual", "charming" shop is "a real winner" avow aficionados who mention "the best muffins baked every morning" ("get there while they're still warm") as well as "great salads", "good sandwiches" and diverse daily dinners-to-go like chili, lasagna or jambalaya, best followed by one of the cupcakes and other sweets; some take out just as far as the "appealing bench" outside on the sidewalk.

⛝ Borgatti's Ravioli & Egg Noodles ⇎ *Pasta*   29 | 19 | 25 | I

Bronx | 632 E. 187th St. (bet. Belmont & Hughes Aves.) | B/D to Fordham Rd. | 718-367-3799 | www.borgattis.com

You'd think they'd been "waiting for you all day" given the warm welcomes you get at this 70-year-old pasta purveyor on Arthur Avenue, where buyers can watch the goods being made by the "third generation of Borgattis", a family whose "passion for their product" "comes across" in "superlative fresh" noodles (some "cut to order") and ravioli made with "the most exquisite silken, salty ricotta"; even though the old-time "rolling machines" have been retired, the entire experience is still "wonderfully nostalgic" right down to the "bargain" prices.

Bottega del Vino ❶ ⛝ *Prepared Food*   25 | 21 | 20 | E

E 50s | 7 E. 59th St. (bet. 5th & Madison Aves.) | N/R/W to 5th Ave./ 59th St. | 212-223-3028 | www.bottegadelvinonyc.com

Via Quadronno ❶ ⛝ *Prepared Food*

E 70s | 25 E. 73rd St. (bet. 5th & Madison Aves.) | 6 to 77th St. | 212-650-9880 | www.viaquadronno.com

At this "festive" East Side Italian-style duo, "Euro-types" mingle with "movers and shakers" to nibble "tiny servings of fabulous food", sip "outstanding cappuccino" and stock up on oils, vinegars and coffees; "panini are the real bargain" among the "delicious" if "ultra-expensive" offerings (the Uptown branch is famous for

	QUALITY	DISPLAY	SERVICE	COST

them), while wines (natch) are highlighted at the roomy Midtown spot with its signature risotto Amarone and its own special glassware to sip from or buy.

Bottino *Prepared Food* | 22 | 21 | 18 | M |

Chelsea | 246 10th Ave. (bet. 24th & 25th Sts.) | C/E to 23rd St. | 212-206-6766 | www.bottinonyc.com

The take-out adjunct of the same-name Italian eatery next door, this West Chelsea "gem" is just the place for meals on-the-go, or for snack breaks while gallery-hopping; among the offerings are "a good selection of creative sandwiches and salads" as well as baked-on-premises pies, tarts and cookies, all for "a good price."

☑ Bottlerocket Wine & Spirit *Wine/Liquor* | 26 | 27 | 27 | M |

Flatiron | 5 W. 19th St. (bet. 5th & 6th Aves.) | 1 to 18th St. | 212-929-2323 | www.bottlerocketwine.com

An "innovator" among vintners, this Flatiron shop gets an "A+ in creativity" for the "eye-catching" themed displays for its 365 labels, with such categories as 'takeout' and 'gifts', that are a "godsend" for novices and "fun for the initiated"; "printed descriptions" for each bottle and a "friendly" staff help "make shopping unintimidating and enjoyable" at this "terrific addition to the winescape of Manhattan."

Bottle Shoppe *Wine/Liquor* | - | - | - | M |

Williamsburg | 301 Bedford Ave. (Grand St.) | Brooklyn | L to Bedford Ave. | 718-302-3433

"Italian finds", Australian Shirazes, Argentinean Malbecs and Japanese sake at "fair prices" ($8–$15 a bottle) make this "little" Williamsburg wine store a hit with locals; patrons can sample from the 200 available labels at the weekly free tastings on Friday nights; N.B. a Web site is in the works for 2007.

☑ Bouchon Bakery ● *Baked Goods* | 27 | 25 | 21 | E |

W 60s | Time Warner Ctr. | 10 Columbus Circle, 3rd fl. (bet. 58th & 60th Sts.) | 1/A/B/C/D to 59th St./Columbus Circle | 212-823-9366 | www.bouchonbakery.com

"Perfectly decadent" say the swarms buzzing around Thomas Keller's perpetually packed ("be prepared to wait") French-inspired bakery/take-out counter in the Time Warner Center, adjacent to his casual cafe of the same name, providing "magical" pastries, cakes, cookies, breads and other baked goods as well as "delicious" sandwiches, quiches, salads, soups and even housemade chocolates, all on view in "gorgeous display cases"; neither the sometimes "overwhelmed" staff nor the "high-rent" prices (if "cheap compared to per se" upstairs) dissuade the "masses"; P.S. there's a small seating area for on-the-spot "indulging."

☑ Bouley Bakery & Market *Baked Goods* | 27 | 25 | 22 | E |

TriBeCa | 130 W. Broadway (Duane St.) | 1 to Franklin St. | 212-608-5829 | www.davidbouley.com

You just might "want to move to TriBeCa" after visiting chef David Bouley's tri-level destination for "uniformly superb", "splurge"-worthy French-style baked goods – "heavenly" brick-oven breads, croissants, tarts, macaroons – all "displayed like precious jewelry" on the first floor, along with "excellent sandwiches" and other prepared foods; in the cellar are cheeses, fish, meats, olives, oils and such, while the second story houses the eatery Upstairs.

Bowery Kitchen Supplies 🖃 *Cookware* 22 | 14 | 15 | M

Chelsea | Chelsea Mkt. | 75 Ninth Ave. (bet. 15th & 16th Sts.) | A/C/E/L to 14th St./8th Ave. | 212-376-4982

Bowery Kitchen East 🖃 *Cookware*

NEW **LES** | 5 Rivington St. (Bowery) | F/V to Lower East Side/2nd Ave. | 212-477-8681
www.bowerykitchens.com

A "cook's haven" tucked into the back of Chelsea Market, this "incredibly cluttered" kitchenware shop has earned a rep for being one of the "best" for "hard-to-find items" like "ramekins, small whisks and other strange things" as well as cookware, cutlery, appliances, professional-grade stainless steel work tables and storage racks, all at "reasonable" prices; despite "uneven" service, all agree it's fun for "browsing"; N.B. the LES offshoot opened post-Survey.

Brasil Coffee House 🖃🛇 *Coffee/Tea* 21 | 18 | 21 | I

Murray Hill | Ramada Hotel | 161 Lexington Ave. (bet. 29th & 30th Sts.) | 6 to 28th St. | 212-213-9725 ◐

LIC | LIC Art Ctr. | 44-02 23rd St. (44th Ave.) | Queens | E/V to 23rd St./Ely Ave. | 718-729-2720

LIC | 45-02 23rd St. (45th Ave.) | Queens | E/V to 23rd St./Ely Ave. | 718-729-7424

LIC | 48-19 Vernon Blvd. (49th Ave.) | Queens | 7 to Vernon Blvd. | 718-729-5969 ◐

877-327-2745 | www.brasilcoffeehouse.com

Considered a "change of pace" for a caffeine "boost", this "charming" cafe chainlet dispenses "decent Brazilian coffee" along with "delish" Amazonian nibbles like *coxinha* (chicken croquettes), cheesebread, coconut muffins and other "rare finds"; being "unpretentious" "places to chill", they're somewhat "neglected" but always a "pleasant" "reprieve" from the megachains.

Bread Alone 🖃 *Baked Goods* 27 | 20 | 22 | M

See Greenmarket; for more information, call 845-657-3328 or 800-769-3328 | www.breadalone.com

"Addicts" aver the array of "rich, nutritious", "chewy" whole-grain artisanal loaves – not to mention "delicious muffins", "must" scones and handrolled croissants – from this Ulster County organic bakery is "worth a trip" to the Catskills; fortunately, carbophiles without cars can get their fix at the year-round Greenmarket booth, where "friendly" staffers are anything but crusty.

Bread Stuy 🛇 *Baked Goods* - | - | - | M

Bed-Stuy | 403 Lewis Ave. (Atlantic Ave.) | Brooklyn | A/C to Utica Ave. | 718-771-0633 | www.breadstuy.com

This funky Bed-Stuy bakery/cafe run by a husband-and-wife team is appreciated for its housemade breads (its cheddar loaves are a signature, as are the cracked wheat), red velvet cake and other sweets,

	QUALITY	DISPLAY	SERVICE	COST

as well as panini; its warm, wood-accented space serves as something of a local gathering spot, a venue for kids' art classes and a place for local artists to display their works.

☑ Bridge Kitchenware 🖃 *Cookware*   28 | 16 | 20 | E

E 40s | 711 Third Ave., entry on 45th St. (bet. 44th & 45th Sts.) | 4/5/6/7/S to 42nd St./Grand Central | 212-688-4220 | 800-274-3435 | www.bridgekitchenware.com

This long-lived East Side "Aladdin's cave of culinary wonders" stocks an "intelligent", if "overwhelming", array of "chef-quality" cookware, appliances, barware and pastry equipment (supporters swear: "if they don't have it, it doesn't exist"); it's a "connoisseur's paradise" in spite of sometimes "crotchety" service and prices that can be "a bit high", and even if "it's not the prettiest store", it still "outclasses others by a mile."

Broadway Famous   19 | 17 | 17 | M
Party Rentals *Party Rentals*

Union Sq | 200 Park Ave. S., Suite 1610 (17th St.) | 4/5/6/L/N/Q/R/W to 14th St./Union Sq. | 212-269-2666
Williamsburg | 134 Morgan Ave. (bet. Johnson Ave. & Meserole St.) | Brooklyn | L to Morgan Ave. | 718-821-4000
www.broadwayfamous.com

With a 50,000-sq.-ft. warehouse in Williamsburg and a 3,000-sq.-ft. Union Square showroom, this party-rentals outfit "always has enough in stock", making it a "no-nonsense supplier that always comes through" with tables, chairs, dinnerware and dance floors (though no tents) at "moderate prices"; it has a tendency to be a "very busy place", so the initiated advise it's "best if you know what you want before calling"; N.B. minimum order is $1,000 in December and $250 at other times, with a $25 delivery fee.

Broadway Panhandler 🖃 *Cookware*   26 | 20 | 19 | M

G Village | 65 E. Eighth St. (bet. B'way & University Pl.) | R/W to 8th St. | 212-966-3434 | 866-266-5927 | www.broadwaypanhandler.com

"Long before the chains moved in", cooks counted on this kitchenware "favorite" for its "inspiring", "expansive" assortment of "moderate to upscale" wares including "one of the best selections of Le Creuset in the city", as well as for its "well-informed" staff and "decent prices"; its recent move to the Village has brought it "closer to its Broadway roots", and though nostalgists may say the new digs lack the "charm" of its longtime SoHo space, all agree it remains a "great resource" for both "serious cooks" and amateurs.

Brooklyn Ice Cream Factory ✍ *Ice Cream*   25 | 18 | 20 | M

Dumbo | Fulton Ferry Landing Pier | Old Fulton St. (Water St.) | Brooklyn | A/C to High St. | 718-246-3963 ◑
NEW **Greenpoint** | 97 Commercial St. (Manhattan Ave.) | Brooklyn | G to Greenpoint Ave.

A "purist's delight", this "old-school" Dumbo destination on the Fulton Ferry Pier dishes out eight "classic" and "really, really creamy", "made-on-premises" flavors, "each one a winner", including the "rich, dark" chocolate and "to-die-for" peach; you may have to stand in a "line going out the door", but at least the "spectacular view is free"; N.B. the Greenpoint branch opened post-Survey.

NEW Brooklyn Kitchen ⌐ Cookware
`- | - | - | M`

Williamsburg | 616 Lorimer St. (Metropolitan Ave.) | Brooklyn | L to Lorimer St. | 718-389-2982 | www.thebrooklynkitchen.com

This "adorable" new Williamsburg kitchenware shop has a retro feel owing perhaps to its stock of "vintage Pyrex" and refurbished cast-iron pans that round out its small but solid collection of gadgets and "top-quality" cookware from the likes of Le Creuset and KitchenAid; it's a "much-needed addition to the neighborood" say the converted, who also call service "über-friendly."

Brooklyn Liquors ● Wine/Liquor
`23 | 15 | 19 | I`

Sunset Pk | Costco | 976 Third Ave. (bet. 37th & 38th Sts.) | Brooklyn | D/M/N/R to 36th St. | 718-499-2257 | www.brooklynliquors.com

"Perfect party planning" for a song can be yours at this "friendly" "Costco neighbor under the Gowanus Expressway" in Sunset Park, where you can shop for "discount Dom Perignon", "cheap" "fine wines" and spirits; the choices are "limited", but there's "free parking" and "you can't beat the prices" on its "weekly specials."

Bruno Bakery ●⌐ Baked Goods
`23 | 22 | 18 | M`

G Village | 245 Bleecker St. (bet. 6th & 7th Aves.) | A/B/C/D/E/F/V to W. 4th St. | 212-242-4959

G Village | 506 La Guardia Pl. (bet. Bleecker & Houston Sts.) | B/D/F/V to B'way/Lafayette St. | 212-982-5854

www.pasticceriabruno.com

The "gorgeous" cases at this "busy" "old-time" Village Italian bakery and its NYU-area offshoot are filled with "everything for the sweet tooth" from master baker Biagio Settepani's "wonderful" cakes, biscotti and cannoli to "delicious" gelato; "helpful" service, "fair" prices and espresso bars ensure they're "always worth a stop."

Bruno the King of Ravioli ● Pasta
`24 | 18 | 20 | M`

Gramercy | 282 First Ave. (bet. 16th & 17th Sts.) | L to 1st Ave. | 212-254-2156

Gramercy | 387 Second Ave. (bet. 22nd & 23rd Sts.) | 6 to 23rd St. | 212-685-7666

W 70s | 2204 Broadway (bet. 78th & 79th Sts.) | 1 to 79th St. | 212-580-8150

888-652-7866 | www.brunoravioli.com

With three fiefdoms in Manhattan, this Hoboken-based noodle slinger rewards loyal subjects with "pastas fit for a king" but suited to a "peasant's budget", including a "multitude" of ravioli ("seasonal choices are the best!") and other shapes; there are also sauces and prepared dishes that will "convince anyone you're an Italian chef"; P.S. "stock up and put the rest in the freezer."

Bulich Mushroom Co., Inc. ⊄ Produce
`29 | 23 | 27 | M`

See Greenmarket; for more information, call 518-943-3089

One of the last mushroom growers left in NY State, this third-generation Hudson Valley fungus farmer pops up on Saturdays at the

Greenmarket; surveyors feel "sooo lucky" to get the "incredibly fresh" portabello, crimini, shiitake, oyster and white table varieties, all with "excellent concentrated flavor" ("they smell just like earth"), and are also grateful for the "reasonable" rates and "friendly", "helpful" staffers who let you "choose as small an amount as you desire."

BuonItalia ☑ Specialty Shop   26 | 18 | 16 | M

Chelsea | Chelsea Mkt. | 75 Ninth Ave. (bet. 15th & 16th Sts.) | A/C/E/L to 14th St./8th Ave. | 212-633-9090 | www.buonitalia.com
Offering "every Italian item you could ever need", this specialty grocer "conveniently located in the Chelsea Market" stocks "top-quality" "treasures" – "from Parmesan to black truffles" to a "wonderful supply of pastas" – that include "some interesting imports"; still, a few fret that the "staff seems indifferent" and the goods "overpriced", although they admit shopping here is "definitely cheaper than flying to Italy"; N.B. the back counter and cafe serve prepared foods.

☑ Burgundy   29 | 23 | 25 | E
Wine Company ☑ Wine/Liquor

Chelsea | 143 W. 26th St. (bet. 6th & 7th Aves.) | 1 to 28th St. | 212-691-9092 | 888-898-8448 | www.burgundywinecompany.com
"Focus" has its rewards, as this "brilliant" Chelsea "pro" demonstrates with its "reliable", "top-notch" selection of Rhônes, Oregonians and, "of course", wines from the namesake French region, all shown off by a staff of "enthusiastic" "experts willing to share their knowledge"; the "prices go with the territory", but it's "simply heaven" for "serious buyers", and "regular folk" "will feel welcome" too; P.S. the tastings every day are simply "amazing."

Buttercup Bake Shop Baked Goods   23 | 21 | 20 | M

E 50s | 973 Second Ave. (bet. 51st & 52nd Sts.) | 6 to 51st St. | 212-350-4144 ●
W 70s | 141 W. 72nd St. (bet. Amsterdam & Columbus Aves.) | 1/2/3 to 72nd St. | 212-787-3800
www.buttercupbakeshop.com
This East Side–West Side twosome specializes in "beautiful and delicious" cupcakes crowned with a "colorful" range of "creamy, light" frostings, not to mention "classic" layer cakes, "incredible" banana pudding and other sweet Americana; "friendly" and "kitschy", it gets "pretty packed", especially "around the holidays"; N.B. separately owned.

Butterfield Market ☑ Specialty Shop   23 | 21 | 19 | E

E 70s | 1114 Lexington Ave. (bet. 77th & 78th Sts.) | 6 to 77th St. | 212-288-7800 | www.butterfieldmarket.com
Infused with that "old New York feeling" (it dates to 1915), this "gourmet" grocer on the Upper East Side is a "heaven for the kitchen-challenged", "covering all the bases" with its "wonderful prepared entrees and side dishes", "tasty sandwiches" and "museum-quality produce"; all in all, surveyors are "never disappointed, except when paying the bill" – "this is one expensive market."

NEW Café Grumpy *Coffee/Tea*

▽ 26 | 13 | 19 | M

Chelsea | 224 West 20th St. (bet. 7th & 8th Sts.) | 1 to 18th St. | 212-255-5511

Greenpoint | 193 Meserole Ave. (Diamond St.) | Brooklyn | G to Nassau Ave. | 718-349-7623

www.cafegrumpy.com

Promoting java "snobbery at its finest", these Chelea-Greenpoint cafes "treat coffee like wine", listing "beans by region" on an exotic international menu (new brews are highlighted monthly) and grinding each cup fresh on state-of-the-art "drip" equipment; the "unique" "fix" "might be the best" in town, and with a "knowledgeable staff" also serving sandwiches and "real espresso", even "purists" find nothing to grouse about.

Café Habana To Go ◑▣ *Prepared Food*

24 | 14 | 16 | I

NoLita | 229 Elizabeth St. (bet. Houston & Prince Sts.) | N/R to Prince St. | 212-625-2002 | www.ecoeatery.com

"When the wait's too long" for "delicious" Cuban eats at the NoLita restaurant next door ("and when isn't it?"), fans know "plan B" is takeout from this offshoot, where "curt service is worth putting up with" for "fabulous sandwiches", trademark "amazing" grilled corn, "giant burritos" and other "tasty", "authentic" grub; "prices are easy to digest" too, making it clear "this place sure knows how to do to-go."

Café Indulge ◑▣ *Prepared Food*

▽ 23 | 15 | 17 | I

Murray Hill | 561 Second Ave. (31st St.) | 6 to 33rd St. | 212-252-9750

"The best scones" in the Murray Hill neighborhood emerge from this bakery/cafe say fans, but "they don't last long, so get there early"; salads, wraps and sandwiches suit lunchers, while the popular "delicioso" indulgences (flourless chocolate cake, tiramisu, Napoleons, etc.) even include sugar-free cookies and muffins for calorie counters.

Café Regular ⊘ *Coffee/Tea*

- | - | - | M

Park Slope | 318A 11th St. (bet. 4th & 5th Aves.) | Brooklyn | F/M/R to 4th Ave./9th St. | 718-768-4170

South Slopers "love the European feel" of this "tiny" coffeehouse, an "adorable" retro nook with a Parisian-style marble-top bar and a bench-lined wall where the regular crowd cozies up for "great coffee, espresso and repartee" with the sociable staffers; featuring beans blended by La Colombe and baked goods from the Sullivan Street Bakery, it has its hip clientele gloating "Manhattanites will be jealous."

Cafe Scaramouche ▣ *Baked Goods*

- | - | - | I

Carroll Gardens | 524 Court St. (Huntington St.) | Brooklyn | F/G to Smith/9th Sts. | 718-855-9158 | www.cafescaramouche.com

Homemade cookies (including the signature dulce de leche), tiramisu and other French, Italian and Argentinean-influenced baked items are all showcased within this Carroll Garden emporium whose space evokes the coziness of a living room; aside from catering, the shop also distributes its goods to the likes of Dean & Deluca.

	QUALITY	DISPLAY	SERVICE	COST

Cafe Spice ● *Prepared Food* | 19 | 16 | 17 | M |

E 40s | Grand Central Terminal | dining concourse (42nd St. & Vanderbilt Ave.) | 4/5/6/7/S to 42nd St./Grand Central | 646-227-1300 | www.cafespice.com

"Savory" subcontinental dishes for those on-the-go is the deal at this take-out arm of the Indian mini-chain on Grand Central's dining concourse; the less-than-impressed shrug "unremarkable", but commuters who rely on its convenience call it "quick, easy" and "pretty tasty" – especially given the "food-court" milieu.

Caffé Roma Pastry ⊘ *Baked Goods* | 23 | 21 | 18 | M |

Little Italy | 385 Broome St. (Mulberry St.) | 6/J/M/N/Q/R/W/Z to Canal St. | 212-226-8413

"Low-key" but long on history and "atmosphere", this Little Italy "old-timer" (since 1918) is a guardian of "classic" Italian *dolces* such as "tasty" ricotta cheesecake, cannoli, gelati and tiramisu that are often washed down with a cup of espresso; nostalgists note that tasting the treats here "seems like old times."

Caffe' Simpatico ⌨ *Baked Goods* | ▽ 15 | 19 | 16 | M |

W 50s | 501 W. 57th St. (10th Ave.) | 1/A/B/C/D to 59th St./Columbus Circle | 212-489-7575

Ruthy's Bakery & Cafe ⌨ *Baked Goods*

Chelsea | Chelsea Mkt. | 75 Ninth Ave. (bet. 15th & 16th Sts.) | A/C/E/L to 14th St./8th Ave. | 212-463-8800
Chelsea | Chelsea Piers | Pier 62 (Hudson River & 23rd St.) | C/E to 23rd St. | 212-336-6333
888-729-8800 | www.ruthys.com

Known for "awesome cheesecake" and rugalach, this Chelsea Market bakery/cafe (along with its Chelsea Piers and West Side satellites) also custom-designs specialty and birthday cakes, with everything available for nationwide shipping or Manhattan delivery below 96th Street; it leaves the majority "really delighted", even if a ruthless few report "mediocre" results.

Cake Chef Inc. ⊘ *Baked Goods* | ▽ 22 | 18 | 23 | I |

Staten Island | 957 Jewett Ave. (Victory Blvd.) | 718-448-1290

"The quality" is "unsurpassed" rave reviewers of this Staten Island bake shop beloved for its cakes, pastries and a "cheese crumb ring that's to die for" as well as its collection of vintage cookie jars, which can be bought and filled with "home-baked" treats; one caution: the selection is "small", so "order ahead" because "if you go after 2 PM on a Sunday, you can forget it."

Cakeline *Baked Goods* | - | - | - | E |

Rockaway Bch | 220 Beach 132nd St., Belle Harbor (Rockaway Beach Blvd.) | Queens | 718-634-5063 | www.cakeline.com
By appointment only

Once a pastry chef for über-caterer Glorious Food, Cynthia Peithman now heads her own cakery in Rockaway Beach, turning out custom-crafted multi-tier confections (including her signature Autumn Leaf style) for weddings and other special occasions; customers who "don't mind the cost" can choose from seven flavors of cake and more than two dozen buttercream, ganache and mousse fillings.

Z Cake Man Raven Confectionery ● *Baked Goods*

26 | 15 | 14 | M

Fort Greene | 708 Fulton St. (bet. Oxford St. & Portland Ave.) | Brooklyn | C to Lafayette Ave. | 718-694-2253 | www.cakemanraven.com

The "best red velvet cake this side of the Mason-Dixon" results in "lines out the door" at this unassuming Fort Greene sweets spot run by a South Carolina–bred baker, whose other "moist, rich and tasty" variations include carrot, mocha–peanut butter and pineapple-cream cheese; walk-ins can purchase up to four "mammoth" slices at a time (whole cakes require advance orders), and though some say service "has been lacking recently", most shrug "the product is so good, who cares?"

Z Calabria Pork Store ⌐▢⃥ *Meat/Poultry*

28 | 21 | 24 | M

Bronx | 2338 Arthur Ave. (bet. 183rd & 187th Sts.) | B/D to Fordham Rd. | 718-367-5145

"Pork, pork and more pork" is the deal at this Arthur Avenue Italian deli, where shoppers find aromatic sausages dangling from the ceiling and an "old-fashioned" butcher counter boasting a "fair-priced", porcine-oriented "great selection", manned by a "knowledgeable" crew – all of which "takes you back 40 years"; among its other "delicious" products are housemade mozz and lots of imported goods.

Calandra Cheese Co. ▢⃥ *Cheese/Dairy*

▽ 26 | 18 | 22 | M

Bronx | 2314 Arthur Ave. (bet. Crescent Ave. & 186th St.) | B/D to Fordham Rd. | 718-365-7572

Since 1952, this "simple" Arthur Avenue shop has been a "find" for "authentic Italian cheese", notably its homemade specialties: "creamy mozzarella", "ricotta that melts on your tongue" and the enriched mozz variants scamorza and caciocavallo; add a hoard of imports, "old-world hospitality" and "real value", and "it's a must" on the strip.

Callahan Catering ▢⃥ *Caterer/Events*

- | - | - | VE

Garment Dist | 37 W. 39th St., Suite 406 (bet. 5th & 6th Aves.) | 212-327-1144 | www.callahancatering.com
By appointment only

This "exclusive" off-site caterer based in the Garment District delivers the "best, most creative" party ideas to a well-heeled clientele, which applauds its "gorgeous" food-and-drink offerings that "never cease to entertain the eye"; no task seems too big, be it flying European chefs into the Hamptons or organizing acrobats in tents, and admirers insist it's "worth every penny" – "if you can afford it."

Call Cuisine Caterers *Prepared Food*

24 | 20 | 20 | E

E 50s | 1032 First Ave. (bet. 56th & 57th Sts.) | E/V to Lexington Ave./ 53rd St. | 212-752-7070

"Fabulous takeout" meals from this Sutton Place standby please "older", well-heeled locals "when their chef is off", but regular folk – or "anyone who wants to be praised for cooking they haven't done" – can find a "top-quality" (if "limited") selection of prepared dishes here; though "snooty" "counterhelp" can be annoying, the business, which specializes in hors d'ouevres, has been catering to upmarket clients like the UN since 1980.

Caputo Bakery ▣⊘ *Baked Goods* 23 | 17 | 18 | I

Carroll Gardens | 329 Court St. (bet. Sackett & Union Sts.) | Brooklyn | F/G to Carroll St. | 718-875-6871 | www.caputobakery.com

"Don't miss the lard bread, especially if it's just coming out of the oven" urge regulars who revere this "excellent old-time" Carroll Gardens institution for its "crusty, not mushy" loaves, including "wonderful" semolina, olive, prosciutto, brioche and "seasonal specialties" all at "low prices"; the "teenage counter girls" take their time, so it helps if you "know what you want when you walk in."

Carmine's Takeout ◐ *Prepared Food* 23 | 16 | 18 | M

W 40s | 200 W. 44th St. (bet. 7th & 8th Aves.) | 1/2/3/7/N/Q/R/S/W to 42nd St./Times Sq. | 212-221-0242

W 90s | 2450 Broadway (bet. 90th & 91st Sts.) | 1/2/3 to 96th St. | 212-721-5493

www.carminesnyc.com

"A boon for the harried" and those who "need a red-sauce fix" without the "headache" of a noisy dining room, these adjuncts to the famed West Side eateries offer the same "hearty, delicious" Italian fare for takeout or delivery; though service is on the "slow" side, its portions "gigantic" enough to last "for three days" ("don't even try to eat the whole thing") ensure "lots of bang for the buck" and make it an apt choice when feeding "a crowd."

☑ Carnegie Deli ◐▣⊘ *Deli/Sandwich* 23 | 16 | 15 | E

W 50s | 854 Seventh Ave. (55th St.) | N/Q/R/W to 57th St. | 212-757-2245 | 800-334-5606 | www.carnegiedeli.com

"Blue collars", "blue bloods" and everyone in between come with "mouths open wide" for the "ridiculously" "overstuffed" brisket, corned beef and pastrami sandwiches ("just try to finish one") that are the hallmark of this NYC deli "icon"-cum-"tourist" attraction; no surprise it's perpetually "overrun", while the "delightfully brusque" service seems like it "hasn't changed for generations"; P.S. "you gotta have the cheesecake."

Carol's Cuisine ◐ *Caterer* - | - | - | E

Staten Island | 1571 Richmond Rd. (Four Corners Rd.) | 718-979-5600 | www.carolscafe.com

At her cafe and cooking school in Staten Island, Carol Frazzetta is a "perfectionist" and it shows in her "excellent food" and ability to make celebratory affairs "effortless and beautiful"; whether on the premises of her restaurant or off-site, she "always tries to give an above-board event", which explains why she's "been around for years – and we hope years to come."

Carrot Top Pastries *Baked Goods* 23 | 18 | 20 | I

Washington Hts | 3931 Broadway (bet. 164th & 165th Sts.) | 1/A/C to 168th St./B'way | 212-927-4800 ◐

(continued)

(continued)

Carrot Top Pastries

Washington Hts | 5025 Broadway (214th St.) | 1 to 215th St. |
212-569-1532
www.carrottoppastries.com

The "excellent" namesake cake has made this toothsome twosome
a "neighborhood favorite" in Washington Heights (and a "must-
visit" for "Columbia" types) – but its offerings, all baked at the 165th
Street location, now encompass cheesecake, pies, muffins, cookies
and even breakfast and lunch entrees; "accommodating service" is
the icing on the cake.

Carry On Tea & Sympathy ◑⬛ *Coffee/Tea* | 23 | 20 | 20 | M |

W Village | 110 Greenwich Ave. (bet. 12th & 13th Sts.) | A/C/E/L to
14th St./8th Ave. | 212-989-9735 | ·
www.teaandsympathynewyork.com

"Exiles and Anglophiles alike" are keen on "one-stop shopping" for
"real British" goods like "you'd get in Sainsbury's" at this "teeny"
carry-out store appended to the West Village's Tea & Sympathy;
stocked with "loose teas", condiments, sweets, teapots and heaps
more, it's a "sure bet" for a "proper English" spread that's "authentic" down to the "expat staff's" "lurvely accents"; P.S. they can also
arrange for a "London black cab" to convey catering to your door.

Carve ◑⬛ *Deli/Sandwich* | 23 | 16 | 16 | M |

W 40s | 760 Eighth Ave. (47th St.) | C/E to 50th St. | 212-730-4949
Choice carved-to-order meats help explain why followers find this
shop to be the "best" of its kind in Midtown; yes, seats are sometimes "scarce" and the tabs "expensive", but most maintain it's an
obvious pick when you're seeking something other than "the usual
tuna on rye."

Casa Cupcake *Baked Goods* | 22 | 19 | 19 | M |

W 40s | 545 Ninth Ave. (bet. 40th & 41st Sts.) | A/C/E to 42nd St./
Port Authority | 212-465-1530

Cupcake Cafe *Baked Goods*

Flatiron | Books of Wonder | 18 W. 18th St. (bet. 5th & 6th Aves.) |
1 to 18th St. | 646-307-5878
www.cupcakecafe.com

"Buttercream babes line up" for this Flatiron–Hell's Kitchen duo's
"intensely colored", "piped flower"-adorned cupcakes, "a real wow" at
"office parties" and other festive occasions; "eye-popping custom-
made cakes", "fresh" muffins, pecan pie and doughnuts also please
proponents, even as a "disappointed" minority murmurs the cupcakes'
"taste and texture definitely do not live up to" their "decadent" look;
N.B. the Flatiron offshoot is located inside Books of Wonder.

Casa Della Mozzarella *Cheese/Dairy* | ∇ 29 | 21 | 25 | M |

Bronx | 604 E. 187th St. (Arthur Ave.) | B/D to Fordham Rd. | 718-364-3867
"The best fresh mozzarella" "this side of heaven" is plenty of incen-
tive to "schlep" to this Arthur Avenue stalwart, where patrons can
"watch it being made" before requesting a standard ball or an order

of bocconcini (their "life-altering" mini-mozzes); it's also "a real Bronx deli experience" for "old-time Italian" "staples" including "excellent" "sliced meats" and house-brand olive oil, and everything comes with "the friendliest" "banter" on the side.

Cassinelli Food Products ⊘ Pasta

▽ | 25 | 18 | 22 | M

Astoria | 31-12 23rd Ave. (31st St.) | Queens | N/W to Astoria/Ditmars Blvd. | 718-274-4881

For more than 50 years, this Astoria pasta purveyor has been a favorite among carb connoisseurs thanks to its "better-than-homemade" pastas; the offerings include three types of spinach ravioli alone, a whole line of meat tortellini as well as the usual suspects like fettuccine and linguine, which lauders label "everything you want them to be."

Castle & Pierpont ⊡ Flowers

▽ | 24 | 22 | 21 | VE

Garment Dist | 353 W. 39th St. (bet. 8th & 9th Aves.) | 212-244-8668 | www.castlepierpont.com
By appointment only

The "easy-to-work-with" proprietors at this Garment District floral studio show "great artistic talent in arranging" "the freshest" "exotic flowers" according to smitten surveyors who say the results are "always lovely"; the "fun" staff can also orchestrate details (tableware, lighting, decor) for high-style events ranging from intimate parties to Broadway openings and corporate extravaganzas, whether beneath chandeliered ceilings or in garlanded gazebos.

Catering by Restaurant Associates Caterer

20 | 19 | 20 | E

Garment Dist | 330 Fifth Ave. (bet. 32nd & 33rd sts.) | B/D/F/N/Q/R/V/W to 34th St./Herald Sq. | 212-613-5500 | www.restaurantassociates.com

Arguably the "largest player in town", with exclusive rights to parties at local major venues, including the Guggenheim and Met, this mammoth Garment District–based operation "handles large parties with ease", offering "solid food preparation and presentation"; while some feel this "corporate" giant may have "stretched itself too thin", to many others it's an "institution" and "one of the best values around."

Catering Company, The ⊘ Events

- | - | - | E

Chelsea | 224 W. 29th St. (bet. 7th & 8th Aves.) | C/E to 23rd St. | 212-564-5370 | www.thecateringcompanynyc.com

"Extremely professional" staffers at this hip Chelsea-based caterer are "wonderful to work with" and pull off "perfect events" with "creative" cuisine and "excellent service" for "nonprofits" and "corporate clients" alike, including film and stage premieres, fund-raisers and book launches; it's on the expensive side, but "worth the money" for the "fantastic" "personal attention."

Cato Corner Farm ⊘ Cheese/Dairy

27 | 19 | 24 | E

See Greenmarket; for more information, call 860-537-3884 | www.catocornerfarm.com

"Very popular" for its raw-milk and hormone-free cheeses created by a "dedicated" Colchester, CT, producer, this Greenmarket vendor's "exceptional" artisanal fromages include "breathtakingly lovely cheddar", "tangy blue", "pungent, flavorful" washed-rind 'hooligan' and "earthy" 'womanchego', all dispensed by a "knowledgeable" crew; though there are a few grumbles about "uneven" selection and "high prices", most don't mind given such "glorious" products from a "real family farm."

Caviar Russe ●□ Caviar   26 | 22 | 23 | VE

E 50s | 538 Madison Ave., 2nd fl. (bet. 54th & 55th Sts.) | E/V to 5th Ave./ 53rd St. | 212-980-5908 | 800-692-2842 | www.caviarrusse.com

"Serious caviar lovers" jonesing for a "fix" of "the best Russian product" head for this Midtown restaurant and its "extraordinary selection" of "very fresh" eggs to take out, along with "high-end appetizers" like smoked salmon and foie gras; the "solicitous service", opulent digs and "top-notch" "little touches" like mother-of-pearl spoons and silver tureens on sale will make you "feel like the rich and famous", but "expect to pay the cost."

CBK Cookies □ Baked Goods   ▽ 23 | 22 | 20 | E

E 80s | 337 E. 81st St. (bet. 1st & 2nd Aves.) | 212-794-3383 | www.cbkcookies.com
By appointment only

Befitting this "cute" "hole-in-the-wall" bake shop's Upper East Side milieu, its "pretty" sugar cookies and "top-quality" character birthday cakes are all bespoke; customers who consider Cynthia Bruce Kramer's decorative tins of custom cookies "great for client gifts" or wedding showers willingly place orders and keep the necessary appointments, because walk-ins are destined to depart empty-handed; N.B. all ages can enroll in their amateur cookie-decorating classes.

Ceci-Cela Baked Goods   24 | 19 | 16 | M

Little Italy | 55 Spring St. (bet. Lafayette & Mulberry Sts.) | 6 to Spring St. | 212-274-9179 ●
TriBeCa | 166 Chambers St. (bet. Greenwich St. & W. B'way) | 1/2/3/A/C to Chambers St. | 212-566-8933
www.ceci-celapatisserie.com

"Ooh-la-la", "you can smell the fabulous pastries from down the block" assert amis who love to "grab treats" at these "small" Little Italy–TriBeCa patisseries whose wares include "great almond brioche", pain au chocolat and "the best tarts"; a faction frets that their "French style" extends to "uneven service" ("can't beat this place for a croissant and a snub"); N.B. they also do wedding cakes.

Cellar 72 ●□ Wine/Liquor   ▽ 26 | 26 | 23 | E

E 70s | 1355 Second Ave. (bet. 71st & 72nd Sts.) | 6 to 68th St. | 212-639-9463 | www.cellar72.com

Led by vino expert Guy Goldstein of the Tour de France restaurant group (Nice Matin, Marseille), this "classy" Upper East Side boutique boasts "real sommeliers" who will gladly help a customer choose from the "outstanding" array of 3,000 labels in the "cool wine cellar" that's visible through the glass floor; it's "expensive", but surveyors find the scene a "refreshing change", and a computer to help pair bottles with food is a nice plus.

	QUALITY	DISPLAY	SERVICE	COST

Centovini ●☞ *Wine/Liquor*
▽ 20 | 21 | 20 | E

SoHo | 25 W. Houston St. (Mercer St.) | B/D/F/V to B'way/ Lafayette St. | 212-334-5348 | www.centovinibar.com

All Italian, all the time is the theme of this "beautiful" Fellini-inspired vintner, co-created by the owners of the Gramercy restaurant i Trulli and the design shop Moss; customers may have to "fight the SoHo sidewalk traffic" to get in for a look at its selection of regional bottles (over 100, the name notwithstanding), but afterwards they can reward themselves with a bite and a glass at the equally stylish eatery attached to the store.

Ceriello Fine Foods ☞ *Specialty Shop*
24 | 22 | 20 | E

E 40s | Grand Central Mkt. | Lexington Ave. (43rd St.) | 4/5/6/7/S to 42nd St./Grand Central | 212-972-4266 ●
Douglaston | 4435 Douglaston Pkwy. (Northern Blvd.) | Queens | 718-428-2494
877-613-6637 | www.ceriellofinefoods.com

"It's like a sausage museum!" marvel commuters who "love the convenience" of this Grand Central Market stall stocking "high-quality, consistent" links as well as dry-aged porterhouses, stuffed pork roasts and other "fantastic meats"; you'll "pay a premium for the location", however, so head instead to the Queens original, which is also a "nirvana for Italian foodstuffs."

Certé *Caterer/Events*
- | - | - | M
(fka Lyn's Catering)

W 50s | 20 W. 55th St. (bet. 5th & 6th Aves.) | B/D/F/V to 47-50th Sts./ Rockefeller Ctr. | 212-397-2020 | www.certenyc.com

Although longtime executive chef Edward Sylvia renamed and relocated the former Lyn's Catering one block in Midtown after taking over the reins in 2006, he serves the same familiar global-inspired cuisine for small-scale events in the cafe and larger, off-site affairs; among the neighborhood office set, it's a popular choice for "business lunch deliveries" and "beautiful cookie trays."

Chambers Street Wines ●☞ *Wine/Liquor*
26 | 21 | 25 | M

TriBeCa | 160 Chambers St. (bet. Greenwich St. & W. B'way) | 1/2/ 3/A/C to Chambers St. | 212-227-1434 | www.chambersstwines.com

"Quality" is key at this "terrific" TriBeCa wine shop whose many "treasures" include an "impressive" inventory of small production *vins* (especially from the Loire Valley) offered at modest prices; the "knowledgeable" staffers do their utmost to please, "walking visitors through" the selections and helping them "pick out something great" they might "never have tried otherwise."

Charbonnel et Walker *Candy/Nuts*
22 | 22 | 19 | E

E 40s | Saks Fifth Ave. | 611 Fifth Ave. (bet. 49th & 50th Sts.) | E/V to 5th Ave./53rd St. | 212-940-4024 | www.charbonnel.co.uk

"You'll never eat another M&M" after a stop at this "premium" English confectioner's Saks Fifth Avenue showcase, where Yanks can now indulge in the "finest-quality Mayfair chocolates", notably "sublime"

QUALITY DISPLAY SERVICE COST

truffles, in an attractive cafe/espresso bar setting; add a tasting counter with a conveyor belt showcasing brownies, toffee cupcakes and other "decadent" desserts, and it's enough to get the majority "hooked" even if some shrug the "staid offerings" are "not exciting."

Charles, Sally & Charles Catering ⊄ *Caterer/Events*

| – | – | – | E |

Park Slope | Brooklyn Botanic Garden | 1000 Washington Ave. (Montgomery St.) | Brooklyn | Q to Prospect Park | 718-398-2400 | www.palmhouse.com

As the exclusive caterer for the Brooklyn Botanic Garden, this Park Slope outfit can set your event in a "beautiful" 52-acre "garden oasis" complete with Victorian greenhouse; still, it's the food "better than most restaurants'" and "friendly" staff striving to ensure "every detail is perfect" that really make this planner "something special."

NEW Cheeks ⊄ *Baked Goods*

| – | – | – | I |

Williamsburg | 378 Metropolitan Ave. (bet. Havemeyer & Marcy Sts.) | Brooklyn | L to Bedford Ave. | 718-599-3583

On a heavily trafficked stretch of Metropolitan Avenue, this small Williamsburg newcomer is fast becoming a local standby; owner-baker Melanie Schrimpe takes an artisanal approach, using all-natural and local ingredients to concoct inventively flavored scones and homey "old-fashioned" desserts like red velvet cake with boiled icing, cupcakes, quick breads and cookies.

Cheese of the World *Cheese/Dairy*

| 25 | 21 | 23 | M |

Forest Hills | 71-48 Austin St. (Queens Blvd.) | Queens | E/F/G/R/V to Forest Hills/71st Ave. | 718-263-1933

"Try a taste of something new" at this "amazing" "neighborhood cheese joint" in Forest Hills, whose "tiny" space is chock-a-block with 400-odd "value-adjusted" wheels, including "interesting types" you "can't even find in the city"; with an "energetic staff" that "knows its cheese" and a sideline in "cured meats" and "specialty goods", it's the type of local "landmark" that "makes it difficult to move."

Chef & Company *Caterer/Events*

| ∇ 25 | 25 | 24 | E |

Flatiron | 8 W. 18th St. (bet. 5th & 6th Aves.) | 646-336-1980 | www.chefandco.com
By appointment only

"Their forte is corporate" say businesslike backers of this Flatiron caterer/cafe, commended for its "professional" style and the "creative and chic" twists on International favorites that result in some "amazing" menus; they're equally "accommodating" for workplace gatherings or full-service events at their various venues, though surveyors part company on the cost ("reasonable" vs. "too expensive").

Chelsea Market Baskets ▭ *Specialty Shop*

| 24 | 23 | 21 | E |

Chelsea | Chelsea Mkt. | 75 Ninth Ave. (bet. 15th & 16th Sts.) | A/C/E/L to 14th St./8th Ave. | 212-727-1484 | 888-727-7887 | www.chelseamarketbaskets.com

"It's more than just baskets" at this Chelsea Market "wonderland" where you can "make your own" "customized, specialty gift basket", choosing from an "endless" selection of baby toys, books, "chocolates, cookies, popcorn and all things gourmet" (including "imported goodies" "with a British twist"); in short, this shop has "something for everyone" – and "every budget"; N.B. it does a mostly mail-order business.

Chelsea Wholesale Flower Market 🖼️ Flowers

25 | 21 | 19 | M

Chelsea | Chelsea Mkt. | 75 Ninth Ave. (bet. 15th & 16th Sts.) | A/C/E/L to 14th St./8th Ave. | 212-620-7500 | www.chelseaflowersny.com

"There's always a ruckus" at this popular, "aromatic" "flower heaven" in Chelsea Market, where customers "hand pick" from the "plethora" of plants and cut blooms on display (including "the best assortment" of "cheap orchids that last forever"); timid types should know there's "professional help" if you want it, and even though prices are "not exactly wholesale", it's "hard to beat when you want quantity."

Chelsea Wine Vault ●🖼️ Wine/Liquor

23 | 23 | 22 | M

Chelsea | Chelsea Mkt. | 75 Ninth Ave. (bet. 15th & 16th Sts.) | A/C/E/L to 14th St./8th Ave. | 212-462-4244 | www.chelseawinevault.com

A "willing and able" staff guides vinophiles through this "spacious" cellar-esque wine shop with a "convenient" location inside Chelsea Market and an "eclectic" selection strong on labels from California and France; "fun" tastings and classes and an overall "friendly, unpretentious" vibe have most saying "it's a pleasure to shop" here.

Cherry Lane Farms 🚫 Produce

28 | 24 | 26 | M

See Greenmarket; for more information, call 856-455-7043

Aficionados "wait all year for the fabulous asparagus" at the Greenmarket stall of this second-generation South Jersey farm, whose 30 types of "high-quality", "wonderfully robust produce" also include tomatoes, okra, zucchini, baby lettuces, eggplant, cauliflower and a growing array of herbs; the colorful, fresh vegetables and "service with a smile" make this "one of the nicest stands in the market, from every point of view"; N.B. though the name would suggest otherwise, the only fruit it offers is strawberries.

Cheryl Kleinman Cakes 🚫 Baked Goods

▽ 28 | 25 | 25 | E

Boerum Hill | 448 Atlantic Ave. (bet. Bond & Nevins Sts.) | Brooklyn | 718-237-2271

By appointment only

"Easy to work with" and incorporating designs both traditional and modern, this Boerum Hill baker of special-occasion cakes has patrons pledging undying love for her nuptial creations, which are not only "delicious" ("lemon pound cake every bit as good as they say") but are also "so beautiful" that surveyors "almost want to plan another wedding"; if "expensive for Brooklyn", boosters say it's still "half the price" of its Manhattan "equals"; N.B. there's now a retail shop on the premises called Betty Bakery.

	QUALITY	DISPLAY	SERVICE	COST

Chestnuts in the Tuileries *Flowers* — | — | — | VE

TriBeCa | 55 Van Dam St., Ste. 801 (bet. Hudson & Varick Sts.) |
212-367-8151 | www.chestnutsinthetuileries.com
By appointment only

Inspired by gardens in Paris, floral and special events designer Emily
Weaver (a former City of Lights denizen) brings a dash of Gallic flair
to her TriBeCa studio, producing "unique" tailored arrangements
known for their monochromatic color schemes, textured foliage and
use of rare orchids; though some wilt at the "sky-high prices", the few
surveyors who know her work say she's among the "best in the area."

Chez Laurence Bistro ◐ *Baked Goods* 23 | 20 | 18 | M

Murray Hill | 245 Madison Ave. (38th St.) | 4/5/6/7/S to 42nd St./
Grand Central | 212-683-0284

"Terrific" brioche, croissants, Napoleons and other French classics –
plus holiday specialties like bûche de Noël and gingerbread houses –
attract *amis* to this long-standing Murray Hill patisserie/bistro;
some surveyors detect a soupçon of Gallic "attitude", but that may
dissipate in the wake of an early-2007 change in ownership.

Chickpea ◐ *Prepared Food* 23 | 16 | 17 | I

E Village | 210 E. 14th St. (bet. 2nd & 3rd Aves.) | L to 1st Ave. |
212-228-3445
E Village | 23 Third Ave. (bet. 9th St. & St. Marks Pl.) | 6 to Astor Pl. |
212-254-9511
www.getchickpea.com

"Who knew a chickpea could taste like this?" marvel mavens about
this East Village duo's "authentic" Middle Eastern eats, including
some of the "best falafel" around, hummus that's a "must" and "kosher
and vegetarian options", all at "decent" prices; both "inviting"
branches stay open into the wee hours, and 14th Street delivers.

NEW Chicory Brooklyn *Prepared Food* — | — | — | M

Cobble Hill | 243 Degraw St. (Clinton St.) | Brooklyn | F/G to Carroll St. |
718-797-2121

Already popular in the "takeout-starved community" of Cobble Hill,
this "welcome" newcomer offers "delicious" homey fare like "excellent
fried chicken" and "wonderful scones", all made from scratch, with
bonuses such as homemade chips and "truffle mayo"; "waits" and
"uneven quality" give a few pause, but most agree it "has potential."

Chinatown Ice Cream Factory ◐ ▤ ✂ *Ice Cream* 25 | 15 | 19 | I

Chinatown | 65 Bayard St. (bet. Elizabeth & Mott Sts.) |
6/J/M/N/Q/R/W/Z to Canal St. | 212-608-4170 |
www.chinatownicecreamfactory.com

A "scrumptious selection of exotic Asian flavors" "call out to your
wild side" at this Chinatown ice cream parlor where the "friendly,
helpful" staff is generous with samples, which help you choose between such offerings as the "incredible" lychee and "yummy" black
sesame; although there's "no seating", most agree it's the perfect
spot for a "post–dim sum sweet."

	QUALITY	DISPLAY	SERVICE	COST

Choc-Oh! Lot Plus *Candy/Nuts* ▕ – ▏ – ▏ – ▏ M ▏

Bay Ridge | 7911 Fifth Ave. (bet. 79th & 80th Sts.) | Brooklyn | R to 77th St. | 718-748-2100

With 1,000-plus chocolate molds on sale, this Bay Ridge "supply store for candy-making" provides "all the fixings for chocoholics" to cast their own stash, along with "lots of" other paraphernalia for creating and decorating cakes and confections; and for faster gratification, they also stock ready-made candies, truffles and holiday cookies.

Chocolate Bar ▣ *Candy/Nuts* ▕ 26 ▏ 25 ▏ 22 ▏ E ▏

NEW **W 50s** | Henri Bendel | 712 Fifth Ave., 3rd fl. atrium (56th St.) | F to 57th St. | 212-582-8283

W Village | 48 Eighth Ave. (bet. Horatio & Jane Sts.) | A/C/E/L to 14th St./8th Ave. | 212-366-1541 ◗

www.chocolatebarnyc.com

"Hip" West Villagers confirm this "cute", "creative" coffee nook and "gourmet" candy shop "lives up to its rep" with a "delectable" choice of chocolates, both bars and bonbons; its various flavors of "awesome" hot chocolate add an "intriguing" twist, and though it's "on the expensive side", most agree it's a "sinfully good" way "to splurge"; N.B. an offshoot inside Midtown's famed Henri Bendel department store including a full-service eatery opened post-Survey.

Chocolate Room, The ◗▣ *Candy/Nuts* ▕ 25 ▏ 21 ▏ 21 ▏ M ▏

Park Slope | 86 Fifth Ave. (bet. Baltic & Warren Sts.) | Brooklyn | 2/3 to Bergen St. | 718-783-2900 | www.thechocolateroombrooklyn.com

Now there's room for "indulging" in Park Slope thanks to this "cozy" cafe and sweets boutique, which will "rock your world" with "killer" specialty desserts and a line of "divine" chocolates from renowned confectioner Fritz Knipschildt, not to mention dessert wines and "real-deal" "hot cocoa"; it's a "great" after-dinner drop-by with "a date" ("if you're lucky"), but be forewarned that "the word is out" and the crowds are coming in.

Chocolat Michel Cluizel ▣ *Candy/Nuts* ▕ 25 ▏ 25 ▏ 21 ▏ VE ▏

Gramercy | ABC Carpet & Home | 888 Broadway (19th St.) | N/R to 23rd St. | 212-477-7335 | www.chocolatmichelcluizel.com

An "adult delight" in the midst of ABC Carpet & Home, this French chocolatier's "fantasy" showroom and its "artisanal" bars and bonbons are "a must" for "serious" sweet tooths, who can either "take some home" or do dessert in-store (but save room on the charge card since "they aren't cheap").

Chocolat Moderne ▣ *Candy/Nuts* ▕ – ▏ – ▏ – ▏ E ▏

Chelsea | 27 W. 20th St., Suite 904 (bet. 5th & 6th Aves.) | 212-229-4797 | www.chocolatmoderne.com

By appointment only

Banker-turned-chocolatier Joan Coukos has gained something of a cult following for her dark chocolate–covered bonbons with sophisticated flavorings, sold at outlets around town like the City Bakery and the Chocolate Room (as well as at her Chelsea factory, if you make an appointment first); her intensely flavored creations include

QUALITY | DISPLAY | SERVICE | COST

a line made with traditional Japanese ingredients (shiso, tamari, sesame), as well as filled 'bistro bars' and grapefruit caramels covered in dark chocolate.

NEW Choice Market ⊄ *Prepared Food*

– | – | – | M

Clinton Hill | 318 Lafayette Ave. (Grand Ave.) | Brooklyn | G to Classon Ave. | 718-230-5234

Locals are "wooed" to this new take-out spot, an "amazingly welcome addition" to Clinton Hill providing pastries, pies and other "gorgeous sweets", as well as "excellent" prepared foods like mac 'n' cheese, pasta salads and sandwiches, all at "reasonable prices"; there's an open kitchen to watch the cooks at work, as well as a communal table for on-site snacking – though given that this place is usually "packed", seats may be hard to come by.

Choux Factory *Baked Goods*

23 | 17 | 21 | I

Chelsea | 316 W. 23rd St. (bet. 8th & 9th Aves.) | C/E to 23rd St. | 212-627-4318 ◐

E 40s | 865 First Ave. (bet. 48th & 49th Sts.) | 6 to 51st St. | 212-223-0730

E 80s | 1685 First Ave. (bet. 87th & 88th Sts.) | 4/5/6 to 86th St. | 212-289-2023

Ok, they may be "costly" and "cholesterol-boosting", but otherwise "what's not to like?" wonder worshipers of the "scrumptious" cream-filled pastry puffs in "unique flavors" (green tea, strawberry) turned out by this Japan-based chainlet; there's also "rich, tasty Kona coffee" to go with 'em, poured by a staff that remains "gracious" "no matter how busy" things get.

NEW Christie's Jamaican Patties ⊄ *Prepared Food*

▽ 21 | 14 | 18 | I

Prospect Heights | 387 Flatbush Ave. (Prospect Park) | Brooklyn | Q to 7th Ave. | 718-636-9746

"There's nothing else like" the West Indian–style curries, jerk chicken and other island specialties at this Prospect Heights purveyor where the "coco bread is the best on the planet", and the beef and veggie patties are popular too; the bright yellow digs are "not the most appealing" to some, but most agree the fare's "worth closing your eyes for."

Christopher Norman Chocolates ⊑ *Candy/Nuts*

23 | 23 | 23 | E

Financial Dist | 60 New St. (bet. Beaver St. & Exchange Pl.) | 4/5 to Bowling Green | 212-402-1243 |
www.christophernormanchocolates.com

"A little piece of heaven" "tucked away" in the Financial District, this "modest shop" and chocolate factory is the fiefdom of "artistic" confectioner John Down, who "rivals" "top-tier chocolatiers" with his handmade truffles and bars, notably those sculpted into "amazing" designs; the goods are "expensive" but "hard to resist", and though the store is "worth finding" for the freshest possible product, you can also "get it at Whole Foods" and Dean & DeLuca.

	QUALITY	DISPLAY	SERVICE	COST

Christos Steak House ● *Meat/Poultry*   - | - | - | E

Astoria | 41-08 23rd Ave. (bet. 41st & 42nd Sts.) | Queens | N/W to Astoria/Ditmars Blvd. | 718-726-5195

This two-for-one spot in Astoria – it's both a Greek restaurant and a butcher shop – has been under new ownership since 2006, but continues to gratify carnivores with its selection of prime aged meats, sausages, poultry and game; don't forget to "order early" for that "Easter baby lamb!"

Ciao Bella Gelato ▣ *Ice Cream*   25 | 20 | 18 | M

NEW **E 40s** | Grand Central Terminal | lower level (42nd St. & Vanderbilt Ave.) | 4/5/6/7/S to 42nd St./Grand Central | 212-867-5311 ●

E 90s | 27 E. 92nd St. (bet. 5th & Madison Aves.) | 4/5/6 to 86th St. | 212-831-5555 ●

Financial Dist | World Financial Ctr. | 225 Liberty St. (bet. S. End Ave. & West St.) | 1/2/3/A/C to Chambers St. | 212-786-4707

NoLita | 285 Mott St. (bet. Houston & Prince Sts.) | B/D/F/V to B'way/Lafayette St. | 212-431-3591 ●

Dumbo | Rice | 81 Washington St. (bet. Front & York Sts.) | Brooklyn | F to York St. | 718-222-9880 ●⊟

800-435-2863 | www.ciaobellagelato.com

"Italy must be jealous" of this mini-chain of "sublime", high-end gelaterias given its "rich palette" of "luscious", "incredibly creamy" flavors, including "creative" seasonal specialties and sorbets "saturated with fruit"; while a few sniff that it's "not quite as special as it used to be" (save for the "extraordinary prices"), they're outvoted by those who consider it the "crème de la crème of ice cream."

Cipriani Le Specialità ▣ *Baked Goods*   26 | 24 | 20 | E

E 40s | 110 E. 42nd St. (Lexington Ave.) | 4/5/6/7/S to 42nd St./Grand Central | 212-557-5088 | www.cipriani.com

Gourmets are gleeful about this Grand Central–area bakery/takeout chip off the Cipriani block proffering high-end Italian baked goods and prepared foods including fresh-made breadsticks, pastries and sandwiches; there are also house-label imported comestibles such as olive oils, pastas, sauces and vinegars; P.S. those who feel it's a tad "overpriced" just "wait for the rush hour specials."

☑ Citarella ▣ *Major Gourmet Mkt.*   26 | 23 | 22 | E

E 70s | 1313 Third Ave. (75th St.) | 6 to 77th St. | 212-874-0383 ●

G Village | 424 Sixth Ave. (9th St.) | A/B/C/D/E/F/V to W. 4th St. | 212-874-0383 ●

Harlem | 461 W. 125th St. (bet. Amsterdam & Morningside Aves.) | 1 to 125th St. | 212-874-0383

W 70s | 2135 Broadway (75th St.) | 1/2/3 to 72nd St. | 212-874-0383 ●

866-248-2735 | www.citarella.com

Go "upscale without the attitude" at this famed mini-chain of "one-stop" shops for "the refined gourmet", which "built its reputation" by supplying an "abundant variety" of "impeccable" seafood so "exceptionally fresh" it's practically "still quivering", along with "top-of-the-line meats" from "cheerful" "old-fashioned butchers";

they're also "incredibly helpful" sources of "hearty" prepared foods likened to "edible art", "high-end" deli items, a "super" "array of cheeses", "gorgeous" produce "staples" and "top-drawer" smoked fish and caviar, and though "prices are pretty steep", legions of "happy shoppers" confirm quality is "never an issue."

Z City Bakery *Baked Goods*　　25 | 22 | 18 | E

Flatiron | 3 W. 18th St. (bet. 5th & 6th Aves.) | 1 to 18th St. | 212-366-1414 | www.thecitybakery.com

Maury Rubin's legendary Flatiron bakery/cafeteria specializes in "decadent" sweets "to diet for": "perfect pretzel croissants", "outstanding tarts", "platonic-ideal" cookies, "famously" "unbeatable hot chocolate" and now even a "selection of vegan baked goods"; the "heavenly" prepared foods (including some of the "best mac 'n' cheese in the city") made with "top-notch ingredients" add up to "magic in your mouth" as well, so despite "ditzy help" and "stratospheric prices", it's no surprise this NYC "classic" is "always crowded."

Z Cleaver Company *Caterer/Events*　　25 | 20 | 26 | E

Chelsea | Chelsea Mkt. | 75 Ninth Ave. (bet. 15th & 16th Sts.) | A/C/E/L to 14th St./8th Ave. | 212-741-9174 | www.cleaverco.com

"You had me at first bite" enthuse fans of Mary Cleaver's "high-quality" Chelsea Market caterer, which shows off "brilliant" chops in concocting the "freshest", most "innovative" dishes with a "commitment" to "organic, sustainable suppliers" (including many Greenmarket regulars); covering details from venue to menu, the "imaginative" event planning service features "excellent" "responsive" staffers who "definitely set them apart"; P.S. its seasonal "munchies" are also served at the neighboring eatery The Green Table.

Clinton St.　　26 | 20 | 20 | M
Baking Company ●⊄ *Baked Goods*

LES | 4 Clinton St. (bet. Houston & Stanton Sts.) | F/J/M/Z to Delancey/Essex Sts. | 646-602-6263 | www.clintonstreetbaking.com

"Moist and tender" muffins "as big as a city pothole", "fabulous" scones and "fluffy" biscuits that may be "the best" in town are among the unimpeachable wares of this tiny Lower East Side bakery/cafe; meanwhile, "dinner plate–size" blueberry pancakes and the like draw "multitudes" of "students, hipsters and other Downtown characters" for weekend brunches that "feel so NYC"; P.S. it also offers "wonderful special-order birthday cakes."

Coach Dairy Goat Farm ⊄ *Cheese/Dairy*　　28 | 20 | 24 | M

See Greenmarket; for more information, call 518-398-5325

Blessed is this Dutchess County goat's-milk cheesemaker say surveyors who "go to heaven" when its "superb", "flavorful" artisanal *chèvres* "melt in their mouths"; partisans also praise the "genial sellers" at its Union Square Greenmarket stall, who provide "entertainment value" along with "generous samples", as well as its "exotic, excellent" varieties (peppercorn, with herbs, dill, triple-cream, etc.) that make "great house gifts"; N.B. its products are also available at Zabar's, Dean & DeLuca and other gourmet shops around town.

	QUALITY	DISPLAY	SERVICE	COST

NEW Cobblestone Foods *Specialty Shop* | – | – | – | M |

Carroll Gardens | 199 Court St. (Clinton St.) | Brooklyn | F/G to Bergen St. | 718-222-1661 | www.cobblestonefoods.com

Taking over the former Tuller space, this Cobble Hill specialty shop is small but well-stocked with "delicious" products, including prepared foods, baked goods and a "good selection" of artisanal cheeses; so far, most say it's "maintained the high quality" of its predecessor.

Cocoa Bar ❶ *Candy/Nuts* | 26 | 22 | 19 | M |

NEW LES | 21 Clinton St. (bet. Houston & Stanton Sts.) | F/J/M/Z to Delancey/Essex Sts. | 212-677-7417

Park Slope | 228 Seventh Ave. (bet. 3rd & 4th Sts.) | Brooklyn | F to 7th Ave. | 718-499-4080
www.cocoabarnyc.com

A "comfortable" "place to meet" and "while away" some time, this Park Slope coffee/wine bar's "carefully curated variety" of goodies includes "first-class chocolates" that inspire "delicious" pairings with vino, plus "excellent" desserts, java and hot cocoa; with its "hipster staff", "free Internet access" and "gorgeous" "outdoor seating", it earns its standing as a "neighborhood staple"; N.B. the more expansive LES location opened post-Survey.

Cold Stone Creamery ❶ *Ice Cream* | 20 | 20 | 19 | M |

E 80s | 1651 Second Ave. (bet. 85th & 86th Sts.) | 4/5/6 to 86th St. | 212-249-7085 ▣

G Village | 2 Astor Pl. (bet. B'way & Lafayette St.) | 6 to Astor Pl. | 212-228-4600

W 40s | 253 W. 42nd St. (bet. 7th & 8th Aves.) | 1/2/3/7/N/Q/R/S/W to 42nd St./Times Sq. | 212-398-1882 ▣

Bensonhurst | 1877 86th St. (bet. Bay 20th St. & 19th Ave.) | Brooklyn | D/M to 18th Ave. | 718-232-8269

Downtown | Atlantic Terminal Mall | 139 Flatbush Ave. (Atlantic Ave.) | Brooklyn | D/M/N/R to Pacific St. | 718-230-1562

Astoria | 34-20 Broadway (bet. 34th & 35th Sts.) | Queens | G/R/V to Steinway St. | 718-204-7298

Elmhurst | 88-01 Queens Blvd. (B'way) | Queens | G/R/V to Grand Ave. | 718-760-0800

Fresh Meadows | 176-60 Union Tpke. (Utopia Tpke.) | Queens | E/F to Kew Gardens/Union Tpke. | 718-591-5800
www.coldstonecreamery.com

"Be prepared for sugar coma" at this "kitschy" ice cream chain, where you pick "decadent" add-ins to be "smashed" into "super-creamy" concoctions; while the jaded grumble about paying "a lot of money for some frozen milk" and "annoying" singing servers pandering to "children and tourists", for many the "massive servings" of "sinful" treats are "worth every extra lap to burn off the calories."

⛒ Colette's Cakes ✂ *Baked Goods* | 29 | 28 | 27 | VE |

W Village | 681 Washington St. (bet. Charles & W. 10th Sts.) | 212-366-6530 | www.colettescakes.com
By appointment only

West Village wedding and special-occasion cake baker Colette Peters excels at sculptured, "inventive" and "simply exquisite" multilayer creations that are "almost too pretty to eat" – but happily taste "marvelous"; Peters is sweet with the customers as well ("she sat with us for over an hour"), and while naturally "you pay for" such "unbeatable" quality – voted Tops in this Survey – and service, acolytes attest it's "worth every penny."

Colin Cowie Lifestyle ⇄ *Events* ▽ 28 | 29 | 25 | VE

Flatiron | 80 Fifth Ave., Suite 1004 (bet. 13th & 14th Sts.) | 212-396-9007 | www.colincowie.com
By appointment only

With its "over-the-top" orchestration, this ultra-exclusive Flatiron event planner "puts the wow factor" into "fabulous" fetes produced on the chicest sites (eateries, museums, homes of the rich and famous) for a boldface-name clientele that includes Jerry Seinfeld, John Travolta and Oprah; niceties like theme coordination and fashion design ensure "guests feel like Hollywood royalty", and though impresario Cowie is notoriously "full of himself", "anything you wish for, you will get."

NEW Colson Patisserie *Baked Goods* ▽ 25 | 21 | 22 | M

Park Slope | 374 Ninth St. (6th Ave.) | Brooklyn | F to 7th Ave. | 718-965-6400 | www.colsonpastries.com

Park Slope "needed this place" sigh surveyors smitten with this "small" new "standout", a French-Belgian "patisserie that really deserves its European" descriptor given its expertly rendered, *delicieux* output including "lovely small pastries" ("excellent" financiers, brioche, croissants, etc.), cakes, tarts, housemade gelato and sandwiches; despite its ambitious output, however, the vibe is strictly laid-back "neighborhood place", another reason locals are wishing this "welcome" arrival had "more tables."

⊠ Coluccio & Sons *Specialty Shop* 28 | 21 | 22 | M

Borough Park | 1214 60th St. (New Utrecht Ave.) | Brooklyn | N/B to New Utrecht Ave. | 718-436-6700

"You'll feel like you're in Italy" "the second you walk in" to this "old-school", family-owned "king of Italian specialty products" in Borough Park that "has anything you can imagine" when it comes to "high-quality" imported and local products – cheeses, meat, olives, oils, vinegars and some 80 different kinds of pasta – all at "hard-to-beat prices"; "it's loyal to its customers and its customers are loyal in return."

Columbus Bakery ☾ *Baked Goods* 21 | 19 | 15 | M

W 80s | 474 Columbus Ave. (83rd St.) | 1 to 86th St. | 212-724-6880 | www.arkrestaurants.com

Habitués hail this "casual" Upper Westsider's "tasty" baked goods ("great sticky buns", "excellent breads and Danish"), which now include low-carb loaves and desserts, and there are also prepackaged sandwiches, salads and personal pizzas; although vocal critics claim that the food and "awkward" service "don't hit the high notes", the "hectic" scene speaks for itself – this veteran remains a "neighborhood fave" for a "quick bite or something sweet."

	QUALITY	DISPLAY	SERVICE	COST

Columbus Circle
Wine & Liquor ●⊟ *Wine/Liquor*

22	17	20	M

W 50s | 1780 Broadway (bet. 57th & 58th Sts.) | 1/A/B/C/D to 59th St./ Columbus Circle | 212-247-0764 | www.columbuscirclewine.com

Everyone down to the "cash-register guy knows his wine" at this "welcoming" Columbus Circle wine shop that offers "surprisingly good" selections that are "priced competitively"; right now, it's a bona fide "neighborhood" store – down to the sound of the "Lotto machine" at work – but plans are afoot for a fall 2007 relocation to a larger, sleeker space up the block.

Commodities Natural ● *Health Food*

25	20	19	M

E Village | 165 First Ave. (bet. 10th & 11th Sts.) | L to 1st Ave. | 212-260-2600

"If you know what you want", this "neighborhood health food store" in the East Village is a solid "standby", offering a "very good selection" and a juice bar that's the "perfect place for a healthful snack", all presided over by a "helpful" staff; the "small space" can often get "too crowded", however, and persnickety shoppers complain about its sometimes "unkempt" appearance.

Cones, Ice Cream Artisans ●∌ *Ice Cream*

26	21	21	M

G Village | 272 Bleecker St. (bet. Morton St. & 7th Ave. S.) | 1 to Christopher St. | 212-414-1795

"Even in the dead of winter, there's always a crowd" at this Greenwich Village ice cream shop owned by a pair of Argentinean brothers, where the "creative" flavors are handmade employing the "freshest real ingredients"; the cones can be "pricey", but groupies say it's "worth it" for "pure, rich" ice cream that's "truly a step above", if not "bordering on the sublime."

Confetti Cakes ∌ *Baked Goods*

-	-	-	E

W 80s | 102 W. 87th St. (bet. Amsterdam & Columbus Aves.) | 212-877-9580 | www.confetticakes.com

By appointment only

Former fashionista Elisa Strauss now produces "painstakingly beautiful", made-from-scratch wedding and special-event cakes at her Upper West Side bespoke bakery; among the hand-sculpted shapes and designs she creates are cartoon characters, handbags, yachts, mounted fish and cases of wine, spanning a wide variety of flavors, fillings and icings; N.B. she also teaches private and group classes.

Connecticut Muffin ∌ *Baked Goods*

17	16	17	M

NoLita | 10 Prince St. (bet. Bowery & Elizabeth St.) | N/R to Prince St. | 917-237-1623

Brooklyn Heights | 115 Montague St. (bet. Henry & Hicks Sts.) | Brooklyn | 2/3/4/5/M/N/R/W to Borough Hall/Court St. | 718-875-3912 ●

Fort Greene | 423 Myrtle Ave. (Clinton St.) | Brooklyn | G to Clinton/ Washington Aves. | 718-935-0087

Park Slope | 171 Seventh Ave. (1st St.) | Brooklyn | F to 15th St. | 718-768-2022 ●

(continued)

(continued)

Connecticut Muffin

Park Slope | 206 Prospect Park W. (bet. 15th & 16th Sts.) | Brooklyn | F to 15th St. | 718-965-2067 ◗

This "cute" Brooklyn chain (with an outpost in NoLita) remains a "reliable" "standby" for "neighborhood" types to "chat" over "good-tasting muffins", scones and the like along with cups of "great coffee", all for "very little dough"; still, foes fed up with its "mediocre" output grumble "I wish they'd go back to Connecticut."

Consenza's Fish Market *Seafood*   27 | 21 | 23 | M

Bronx | 2354 Arthur Ave. (186th St.) | B/D to Fordham Rd. | 718-364-8510

"The clams and oysters are begging to be gobbled right up" at this Bronx seafood "favorite" where the *vongole*, *scungilli* and other "amazing" delights are always gloriously "fresh"; run by a third-generation fishmonger and his "helpful" staff, this "old-Italy" veteran is "well worth the trip" to Arthur Avenue; N.B. the oyster bar is located in front of the main market.

Cook's Companion, A *Cookware*   26 | 21 | 23 | M

Brooklyn Heights | 197 Atlantic Ave. (bet. Clinton & Court Sts.) | Brooklyn | 2/3/4/5/M/N/R/W to Borough Hall/Court St. | 718-852-6901

A "well-chosen selection" of pots and pans, "quality knives", cookbooks and other kitchen accessories "from A (All-Clad) to Z (Zyliss)" "pack" this "charming little" Brooklyn Heights shop where "reasonable prices", "helpful salespeople" and "two congenial cats" boost the "charm" factor; it's a "neighborhood asset" according to locals who say it's a "wonderful place to just browse" but essential when those "last-minute entertaining binds" arise.

Corner Bagel Market, The ⊘ *Bagels*   22 | 16 | 20 | I

E 80s | 1324 Lexington Ave. (88th St.) | 4/5/6 to 86th St. | 212-996-0567

"Consistent" quality proves they don't cut corners at this Upper Eastsider, a "favorite local" source for "darned good" housemade bagels that have a "delicious" thin crust but are "not huge and pillowy"; nostalgists claim the results are "almost as good as" the classic rounds of "memory."

NEW Corner Bakery & Cafe *Baked Goods*   - | - | - | E

E 90s | 1645 3rd Ave. (92nd St.) | 6 to 96th St. | 212-860-8060
E 90s | 1659 3rd Ave. (92nd St) | 6 to 96th St. | 212-860-8060

Following an ownership split, these two branches of the former Yura triumvirate have a new name but otherwise produce the same baked goods and prepared foods that have gained it such a passionate following in its Upper East Side neighborhood and beyond; the 1645 Third Avenue location has an attached full-service cafe where the goods can be sampled on-site.

Corrado Bread & Pastry *Baked Goods*   21 | 18 | 18 | M

NEW Chelsea | 161 W. 22nd St. (bet. 6th & 7th Aves.) | 1 to 23rd St. | 212-620-7777

E 40s | Grand Central Mkt. | Lexington Ave. (43rd St.) | 4/5/6/7/S to 42nd St./Grand Central | 212-599-4321 ◗

(continued)

Corrado Bread & Pastry

E 70s | 960 Lexington Ave. (70th St.) | 6 to 68th St. | 212-774-1904

These flour-power brokers gather breads and pastries from the area's finest bakeries "all under one roof" to sell from its Chelsea and UES storefronts (plus a "convenient" stall at Grand Central), saving carb-lovers some steps; the "kudos" that go to their "excellent baguettes", brioches, cakes, muffins, scones and sandwiches are slightly offset by gripes about variable service ("friendly" vs. "brusque") and a feeling among some that prices are "a little high."

Così *Deli/Sandwich* | 18 | 17 | 15 | M |

E 50s | 60 E. 56th St. (bet. Madison & Park Aves.) | 4/5/6 to 59th St./Lexington Ave. | 212-588-1225 ◐

Financial Dist | World Financial Ctr. | 200 Vesey St. (Church St.) | R/W to Cortlandt St. | 212-571-2001

Financial Dist | 55 Broad St. (bet. Beaver & Exchange Sts.) | J/M/Z to Broad St. | 212-344-5000 ◐

Gramercy | 257 Park Ave. S. (21st St.) | 6 to 23rd St. | 212-598-4070 ◐

G Village | 504 Sixth Ave. (13th St.) | F/L/V to 14th St./6th Ave. | 212-462-4188 ◐

G Village | 841 Broadway (13th St.) | 4/5/6/L/N/Q/R/W to 14th St./Union Sq. | 212-614-8544 ◐

Murray Hill | 461 Park Ave. S. (31st St.) | 6 to 33rd St. | 212-634-3467

W 40s | 11 W. 42nd St. (bet. 5th & 6th Aves.) | 1/2/3/7/N/Q/R/S/W to 42nd St./Times Sq. | 212-398-6662 ◐

W 50s | Paramount Plaza | 1633 Broadway (51st St.) | 1 to 50th St. | 212-397-9838 ◐

W 70s | 2160 Broadway (76th St.) | 1 to 79th St. | 212-595-5616 ◐

www.getcosi.com

Additional locations throughout the NY area

"You can't beat" the "delicious", "fresh"-baked flatbread that's "the main event" at this "solid" all-over-town sandwich chain, which many deem all the more "deelish" given its "myriad" healthy options and "reasonable prices"; however, the less-content cite "just-ok" offerings, "spotty" service and not-so-cosi interiors.

Costco Wholesale ◐⌨ *Major Gourmet Mkt.* | 21 | 13 | 10 | I |

Sunset Pk | 976 Third Ave. (bet. 37th & 39th Sts.) | Brooklyn | D/M/N/R to 36th St. | 718-965-7603

Astoria | 32-50 Vernon Blvd. (bet. B'way & 33rd Rd.) | Queens | N/W to B'way | 718-267-3680

Staten Island | 2975 Richmond Ave. (Independence Ave.) | 718-982-9000

800-774-2678 | www.costco.com

"If bigger is better", this warehouse-chain "juggernaut" is "the greatest" at furnishing the "suburban hordes" with "in-bulk" quantities of "well-known brands" at "deep discounts", making it an apt choice for a "lifetime supply" of "surprisingly" "edible" fare like "pre-packed" seafood, "nice fruits and veggies", "cheap meats" ("one package lasts a year") and "everyday baked goods", along with "whole sets" of cookware; "don't expect service", but if you're "feeding a crowd" and "have the space" for storage, "the price is very right."

County Chair

-	-	-	M

Party Rentals *Party Rentals*

Mt. Vernon | 25 Oak St. (West Lincoln Ave.), NY | 914-664-5700 | www.countychair.com

In business since 1934, this Mt. Vernon–based party rentals enterprise makes its "nice assortment" of tents, tables, chairs, grills and countless other wares and furnishings available to the five boroughs and satisfies hosts and hostesses with "usually reliable" "easy-to-deal with" service; in sum, "no complaints here."

Court Pastry Shop ● ⋈ *Baked Goods*

25	19	21	I

Carroll Gardens | 298 Court St. (bet. Degraw & Douglass Sts.) | Brooklyn | F/G to Carroll St. | 718-875-4820

Once you "inhale the wonderful aroma" it's hard to "resist buying one of everything" report regulars at this Carroll Gardens Sicilian institution (since 1948) where the "top-notch" treats include "addictive" cannoli, "delightful" traditional cookies, "excellent ices in the summer" and perhaps the "best biscotti west of Genoa"; its "old-neighborhood feel" and staffers straight "out of *Moonstruck*" give fans even more reason to "love this place."

Cousin John's Bakery ● *Baked Goods*

21	19	20	M

Park Slope | 70 Seventh Ave. (bet. Berkeley & Lincoln Pls.) | Brooklyn | B/Q to 7th Ave. | 718-622-7333

"Still a neighborhood favorite" after nearly 20 years in business, this "funky little" Park Slope bakery turns out "delicious" treats – strawberry shortcake, tarts, croissants, muffins, cookies and the like – as well as "great coffee" to wash it all down; N.B. eat in the open kitchen upstairs and you can watch the bakers at work.

Cozy Soup & Burger ● *Prepared Food*

17	10	14	I

G Village | 739 Broadway (Astor Pl.) | R/W to 8th St. | 212-477-5566

Some of the "biggest", "juiciest" burgers around and a "surprising variety of comfort foods" draw "NYU students" and others to this veteran Village "retreat" that's open 'round the clock; fashionistas fuss that it's "not much to look at", but fans hardly care as long as their "appetite's sated" and the grub's this "cheap."

Crate & Barrel ⌨ *Cookware*

22	25	20	M

E 50s | 650 Madison Ave. (59th St.) | N/R/W to 5th Ave./59th St. | 212-308-0011

NoHo | Cable Building | 611 Broadway (Houston St.) | N/R to Prince St. | 212-308-0011 ●

800-967-6696 | www.crateandbarrel.com

"From soup bowls to nut jars", these "clean-lined" East Side and SoHo chain outposts stock a "vast" selection of "young and zippy" cookware, cutlery, gadgets and accessories, as well as tableware and barware, at "reasonable prices"; while the "enticing" displays are "fun to browse", surveyors split on quality ("excellent" vs. "will only last one season") and the service that some find "knowledgeable" and others wish were "better."

Creative Cakes ✍ *Baked Goods*

–	–	–	E

E 70s | 400 E. 74th St. (bet. 1st & York Aves.) | 6 to 77th St. | 212-794-9811 | www.creativecakesny.com

Since 1979 UES sugarmeister Bill Schutz has been concocting "wonderfully imaginative" custom cakes in two dimensions (personalized magazine covers, Monopoly boards) as well as sculpted 3-D shapes (Yankee Stadium, Madison Square Garden, Louis Vuitton handbags, pinball machines, battleships); only one element never changes: all cakes are chocolate fudge with buttercream icing.

Creative Edge Parties *Caterer*

–	–	–	E

W Village | 110 Barrow St. (bet. Greenwich & Washington Sts.) | 212-741-3000 | www.creativeedgeparties.com
By appointment only

Those keen on this West Village caterer/event planner cite its "amazing" gourmet New American eats, custom-crafted with skill worthy of a fine restaurant to give it the edge in "quality"; the cost is steep but "reasonable" given the expertise (and "great service" from "the nicest" folks), and the results will equally impress small gatherings or casts of thousands.

Crossroads ●▣ *Wine/Liquor*

25	10	22	M

Union Sq | 55 W. 14th St. (bet. 5th & 6th Aves.) | 4/5/6/L/N/Q/R/W to 14th St./Union Sq. | 212-924-3060 | www.crossroadswines.com

Some call this "unpretentious" Union Square store a "lovably cluttered" "treasure trove" of wines, while others disparage the "poor" layout that has "bottles crammed into every nook", creating a "claustrophobic" impasse; either way, "there's quality behind the stacked boxes", and if you can navigate the aisles, you'll find some "incredible buys" – and if you can't, "just ask" the "patient" staff.

Crumbs Bake Shop ● *Baked Goods*

22	21	21	M

E 70s | 1371 Third Ave. (bet. 78th & 79th Sts.) | 6 to 77th St. | 212-794-9800
NEW **G Village** | 37 E. Eighth St. (University Pl.) | R/W to 8th St. | 212-673-1500
W 40s | 43 W. 42nd St. (bet. 5th & 6th Aves.) | 7/B/D/F/V to 42nd St./Bryant Park. | 212-221-1500
W 70s | 321½ Amsterdam Ave. (bet. 75th & 76th Sts.) | 1 to 79th St. | 212-712-9800
www.crumbsbakeshop.com

Best known for its "huge, decadent" specialty cupcakes in "scrumptious" flavors like Oreo, Reese's, red velvet and tiramisu, this rapidly expanding chainlet (including a new branch near NYU) should "please the sweet tooth in anyone" – small wonder you'll often "spot celebrities cheating on their Hollywood diets" here; N.B. all products (e.g. cookies, muffins, brownies and even wedding cakes) are kosher.

▣ Crush Wine Co. ●▣ *Wine/Liquor*

26	25	24	E

E 50s | 153 E. 57th St. (bet. Lexington & 3rd Aves.) | 4/5/6 to 59th St./Lexington Ave. | 212-980-9463 | 877-980-9463 | www.crushwineco.com

It's no mere crush – more like "love at first sight" for novices and "serious" oenophiles who visit this chic Midtown boutique stocking a

	QUALITY	DISPLAY	SERVICE	COST

"fabulous", "diverse" selection of wines mainly from small growers; of course, with 2,500 labels comprised of "everyday drinking" vintages, collectible "rarities" (the latter stored in 'The Cube', the temperature-controlled room at the back of the store) and an "expert" staff, this "one-stop shop" is "easy to get passionate" about.

Cucina & Co. *Prepared Food*

21 | 20 | 16 | M

E 40s | MetLife Bldg. | 200 Park Ave. (45th St.) | 4/5/6/7/S to 42nd St./ Grand Central | 212-682-2700 ◗

Garment Dist | Macy's Cellar | 151 W. 34th St. (bet. 6th & 7th Aves.) | B/D/F/N/Q/R/V/W to 34th St./Herald Sq. | 212-868-2388 ◗

W 40s | 30 Rockefeller Plaza, north concourse level (bet. 49th & 50th Sts.) | B/D/F/V to 47-50th Sts./Rockefeller Ctr. | 212-332-7630
www.patinagroup.com

A "solid bet" for an "above-average lunch" or a bite "before getting on the train home", this trio housed in Macy's, Rockefeller Center and the MetLife Building offers a "variety" of "well-prepared" dishes, including the "best rotisserie chicken", "imaginative salads" and "outstanding cookies"; there's "something for every taste" – and it's "not expensive", either.

Cucina Vivolo ◗ *Prepared Food*

∇ 23 | 17 | 21 | M

E 50s | 222 E. 58th St. (bet. 2nd & 3rd Aves.) | 4/5/6 to 59th St./ Lexington Ave. | 212-308-0222

E 70s | 138 E. 74th St. (bet. Lexington & Park Aves.) | 6 to 77th St. | 212-717-4700
www.vivolonyc.com

Either for "good" Italian takeout or "a light meal", Upper Eastsiders turn to this "nice" cafe duo (spin-offs of the restaurant Vivolo) for "good-size servings" of "dependable" panini at lunch, pastas at dinner and homemade desserts anytime of day; delivery is "prompt", while the "homey ambiance" and "great-deal" prix fixe offerings make it a "favorite hangout" of many.

Dahlia *Flowers*

26 | 22 | 23 | M

E 40s | Grand Central Terminal | dining concourse (42nd St. & Vanderbilt Ave.) | 4/5/6/7/S to 42nd St./Grand Central | 212-697-5090

E 40s | Grand Central Terminal | main concourse (42nd St. & Vanderbilt Ave.) | 4/5/6/7/S to 42nd St./Grand Central | 212-697-5090

W 40s | 30 Rockefeller Ctr., concourse level (bet. 49th & 50th Sts.) | B/D/F/V to 47-50th Sts./Rockefeller Ctr. | 212-247-2288

For flowers that last "so long you start to question if they're real", commuters "hurrying" through Grand Central hit these "convenient" petal purveyors whose "robust bunches" and "cute vases" are perfect for "that quick bouquet"; gilding the lily are the "corner-deli prices" – no wonder it's a "madhouse during the holidays."

Daisy May's BBQ USA *Prepared Food*

24 | 12 | 18 | M

W 40s | 623 11th Ave. (46th St.) | A/C/E to 42nd St./Port Authority | 212-977-1500 | www.daisymaybbq.com

There's "no better cure for the 'cue craving" than this Hell's Kitchen storefront's BBQ rated "worth the trek" to "outer Mongolia"

	QUALITY	DISPLAY	SERVICE	COST

(aka 11th Avenue) – though its "convenient street carts" save Midtown and Wall Street office workers the trip; "portions are generous" and "cheap" and it delivers, so you can "invite the neighbors for a party."

Dale & Thomas Popcorn ◗🔲 *Specialty Shop*

23	20	20	M

W 40s | 1592 Broadway (48th St.) | N/R/W to 49th St. | 212-581-1872
W 70s | 2170 Broadway (bet. 76th & 77th Sts.) | 1 to 79th St. | 212-769-0150
800-679-6677 | www.daleandthomaspopcorn.com

Definitely "not your mother's popcorn", the many "amazing, inventive flavors" featured at these "cute" if "touristy" Times Square and UWS chain outposts are both "exotic" and "delicious", even if regulars recommend "sticking to the basics" (i.e. the "to-die-for kettle corn"); given its "friendly staff" and "generous portions", "the only problem is if you check the calorie count" before diving into the "chocolate-covered popcorn."

Damascus Bread & Pastry 🔲 *Baked Goods*

25	16	22	I

Brooklyn Heights | 195 Atlantic Ave. (bet. Clinton & Court Sts.) | Brooklyn | 2/3/4/5/M/N/R/W to Borough Hall/Court St. | 718-625-7070 | 800-367-7482 | www.damascusbakery.com

A "jewel in the crown of Mideastern Atlantic Avenue", this Brooklyn Heights Syrian bakery turns out "divine" baked "delicacies" from "fresh" flatbreads "in every possible iteration" to "high-quality" pastries ("excellent spinach pies" and some of the "best baklava" going) to dips and spreads; "friendly owners" and evocative "old-school" surroundings make patrons' hearts go pita-pat.

🄩 D'Amico Foods 🔲 *Coffee/Tea*

27	19	23	I

Carroll Gardens | 309 Court St. (bet. Degraw & Sackett Sts.) | Brooklyn | F/G to Carroll St. | 718-875-5403 | 888-814-7979 | www.damicofoods.com

Wake up and "smell the coffee roasting" at this "old-school" Carroll Gardens java merchant, a "real neighborhood" stalwart (since 1948) where an "incredible" selection of beans are toasted daily and scooped straight from the sack to guarantee "the freshest" brews around; it's also an affordable "Italian specialties" grocer and sandwich maker, and locals "love" that "nothing changes" here since it's already "as good as it gets."

Daniel's Bagels ◗ *Bagels*

24	18	18	I

Murray Hill | 569 Third Ave. (bet. 37th & 38th Sts.) | 4/5/6/7/S to 42nd St./Grand Central | 212-972-9733

For "Murray Hillers" and those "on the way to Grand Central", this "busy" "neighborhood fave" is among the few options for "mouthwatering" "homemade" bagels "that still have holes" topped with "yum-o" spreads; the "pallid" surroundings are easily forgiven, but "be prepared" for "long lines" and "lacking" service that make it "unwieldy on weekends."

	QUALITY	DISPLAY	SERVICE	COST

David Beahm Designs *Flowers*   - | - | - | VE
Chelsea | 631 W. 27th St. (bet. 11th & 12th Aves.) | 212-279-1344 | www.davidbeahm.com
By appointment only

"Jaws drop" at the "absolute beauty" of the "artful" bouquets that come out of David Beahm's Chelsea floral studio, where he also designs events and custom celebrations such as Catherine Zeta-Jones' opulent wedding to Michael Douglas; those lacking a superstar's budget can choose à la carte arrangements and still get the "amazing service and attention to detail" that make him "a joy to work with."

David Burke at   23 | 21 | 20 | E
Bloomingdale's *Caterer/Events*
E 50s | Bloomingdale's | 150 E. 59th St. (bet. Lexington & 3rd Aves.) | 4/5/6 to 59th St./Lexington Ave. | 212-705-3800 | www.burkeinthebox.com

The "funky" style of celeb chef David Burke's "busy" New American cafe (located right "inside Bloomie's") extends to its catering arm, which brings his "signature elegance" to an imaginative array of "fresh" and "delish" edibles from hors d'oeuvres to desserts, with a "friendly" team to tend to events either in-store or off-site; doubters say despite "much hoopla" it's "good but not incredible."

David's Bagels ◑✿ *Bagels*   23 | 12 | 18 | I
E Village | 228 First Ave. (bet. 13th & 14th Sts.) | L to 1st Ave. | 212-533-8766
Gramercy | 331 First Ave. (bet. 19th & 20th Sts.) | L to 1st Ave. | 212-780-2308

Boosters boast this "underrated" East Village and Gramercy duo "can rival any" for "exceptional" bagels featuring a "crusty outside" with a "good crunch" and a "fluffy" center that's "not too doughy"; some say the "standard" setups "could use a bit of an upgrade", but given rounds this "cheap" and "reliable", "who wants frills?"

NEW David Stark Design &   - | - | - | VE
Production ✿ *Caterer/Events*
Carroll Gardens | 87 Luquer St. (Clinton St.) | Brooklyn | 718-534-6777 | www.davidstarkdesign.com
By appointment only

Taking the maximal approach to event planning and production, this Carroll Gardens–based studio works on a showstopping scale to reshape whole venues with lighting effects, oversize stage props and wildly creative backdrops while integrating everything from invitation design to floral arrangements; the one-of-a-kind results have secured a high-rolling corporate, media and private clientele as well as institutions like the NYC Opera and MoMA.

David Ziff Cooking ✿ *Caterer*   - | - | - | E
E 90s | 184 E. 93rd St. (bet. Lexington & 3rd Aves.) | 6 to 96th St. | 212-289-6199 | www.davidziffcooking.com

They "make it all so easy" gush admirers of this full-service Upper East Side caterer co-owned by chef David Ziff and Alan Bell, which draws on global gastronomy to cook up "excellent and interesting"

	QUALITY	DISPLAY	SERVICE	COST

menus that "guests rave about"; with a "caring and pleasant" crew to provide "superb service" and attend "to every detail", it's "a great experience from start to finish" that's "worth every penny" of the quite reasonable cost.

☑ Dean & DeLuca 🖃 *Major Gourmet Mkt.* | 27 | 26 | 20 | VE |

E 80s | 1150 Madison Ave. (85th St.) | 4/5/6 to 86th St. | 212-717-0800
Financial Dist | Borders Books & Music | 100 Broadway (Pine St.) | 4/5 to Wall St. | 212-577-2153
G Village | 75 University Pl. (bet. 10th & 11th Sts.) | 4/5/6/L/N/Q/R/W to 14th St./Union Sq. | 212-473-1908 ◗
Murray Hill | Borders Books & Music | 576 Second Ave. (32nd St.) | 6 to 33rd St. | 212-696-1369 ◗
SoHo | 560 Broadway (Prince St.) | N/R to Prince St. | 212-226-6800
W 40s | Paramount Hotel | 235 W. 46th St. (bet. B'way & 8th Ave.) | 1/2/3/7/N/Q/R/S/W to 42nd St./Times Sq. | 212-869-6890 ◗
W 40s | 9 Rockefeller Plaza (49th St.) | B/D/F/V to 47-50th Sts./Rockefeller Ctr. | 212-664-1363 ◗
W 50s | Time Warner Ctr. | 10 Columbus Circle, 2nd fl. (bet. 58th & 60th Sts.) | 1/A/B/C/D to 59th St./Columbus Circle | 212-765-4400 ◗
800-221-7714 | www.deananddeluca.com

"The Tiffany's of gourmet groceries", this ever-"fashionable" "fancy food" chain remains "the benchmark" "for the discriminating" with its "exquisite" presentation of "anything your heart desires" in the way of "museum"-grade produce, "exceptional" prepared foods, "scrumptious" baked goods, an "excellent range" of "rare" and "exciting" cheeses, "imaginative" specialty items, "high-quality spices" "you aren't even sure how to spell" and "fantastic kitchenware"; "top-dollar" prices that some deem "prohibitive" "bordering on the outlandish" mean it's "not practical for everyday", but those who go to "shop selectively" or "just to browse" are in for a "true experience"; N.B. the SoHo and Madison Avenue sites stock the full lineup, with the other outlets limited to coffee, prepared foods and baked goods.

Debauve & Gallais 🖃 *Candy/Nuts* | ▽ 27 | 25 | 26 | VE |

E 60s | 20 E. 69th St. (Madison Ave.) | 6 to 68th St. | 212-734-8880 | www.debauveandgallais.com

Imported "from Paris with love", this "very fine, very French" Upper East Side chocolatier boasts more than two centuries of history in its native land, where it supplied the court at Versailles and still ranks among "the world's best"; the "elegant", chandelier-lit boutique stocks "regal-looking" handmade bonbons and truffles that are undeniably "good enough for kings", but watch out for price tags so "expensive" they'd shock Marie Antoinette.

Delillo Pastry Shop 🖃 *Baked Goods* | 26 | 22 | 23 | I |

Bronx | 606 E. 187th St. (bet. Arthur & Hughes Aves.) | B/D to Fordham Rd. | 718-367-8198

"Some things just never change, thank goodness" sigh smitten surveyors who come to this Bronx institution (since 1925) for the "freshest" "traditional Italian pastries", including "delicious" cannoli that's been handmade by the owner's uncle for the past 40 years; no wonder the "small seating area" can't accommodate the many *amici* seeking to "complete their trip to Arthur Avenue" with "a latte and Napoleon" here.

Deli Masters   21 | 16 | 17 | M
Kosher Deli ◑▣ *Specialty Shop*
Fresh Meadows | 184-02 Horace Harding Expwy. (184th St.) | Queens | 718-353-3030 | www.delimasterskosher.com
Sure, it may have "less flash" than other places, but this circa-1950 Fresh Meadows kosher deli legend is still a "good rest stop if you're stuck on the LIE" thanks to "high-quality" offerings including the "best" pastrami sandwiches; naturally, it's advised to "bring a big appetite."

Delmonico   21 | 19 | 18 | E
Gourmet Food ◑ *Specialty Shop*
E 40s | 375 Lexington Ave. (bet. 41st & 42nd Sts.) | 4/5/6/7/S to 42nd St./Grand Central | 212-661-0150
E 50s | 320 Park Ave. (50th St.) | 6 to 51st St. | 212-317-8777
E 50s | 55 E. 59th St. (bet. Madison & Park Aves.) | 4/5/6 to 59th St./Lexington Ave. | 212-751-5559
Get "in and out fast" with the lunchtime crowd at this Midtown food market threesome, where the "service counters are tops for sandwiches" and the "fresh", "well-monitored" "buffet offerings" are generally "worth" the "high prices"; given the "great variety" and 24/7 accessibility, regulars find them "convenient and better than the delis", "but 'gourmet' is pushing it."

Deluxe Food Market ⊅ *Specialty Shop*   ▽ 21 | 13 | 9 | I
Chinatown | 79 Elizabeth St. (bet. Grand & Hester Sts.) | B/D to Grand St. | 212-925-5766
"You'll find exactly what you want" at this Chinatown market that's a "favorite source" for Asian products (it "has everything") as well as "fresh fish", meats, baked goods, sandwiches and prepared foods; sensitive shoppers report it can be "a bit chaotic", but "superior quality" and "cheap prices" prevail.

DeRobertis Pasticceria &   22 | 21 | 21 | I
Caffe ◑▣ *Baked Goods*
E Village | 176 First Ave. (bet. 10th & 11th Sts.) | L to 1st Ave. | 212-674-7137 | www.derobertiscaffe.com
"Step back in time" to the "days when the East Village had an Italian contingent" at this "old-fashioned", "New Yawky" pastry shop where the "decor is 1923" and the fourth generation of DeRobertises "purveys the treats of yore"; most notable are the "gold-standard" pignoli cookies, "great cannoli", ices and "delicious coffee."

Z Despaña Foods ▣ *Specialty Shop*   27 | 23 | 24 | E
Little Italy | 408 Broome St. (bet. Cleveland Pl. & Lafayette St.) | 6 to Spring St. | 212-219-5050 | www.despananyc.com
Jackson Hts | 86-17 Northern Blvd. (bet. 86th & 87th Sts.) | Queens | 7 to 90th St. | 718-779-4971 | www.despanabrandfoods.com
An "unbelievable resource for Spanish foods", this Jackson Heights import store and its newer Little Italy offshoot are "chock-full" of

	QUALITY	DISPLAY	SERVICE	COST

"amazing" Iberian items, from "delectable sausages" and house-made chorizo to some 55 varieties of cheese and plenty of bottled, jarred and canned imported goods; plus, the staff is "very informative about their products and provide generous samples", making it "a great place to explore and discover new treats"; P.S. "don't miss the sandwiches prepared at the back counter."

⊠ Dessert Delivery ▭ *Baked Goods* | 28 | 24 | 26 | E |

E 50s | 360 E. 55th St. (bet. 1st & 2nd Aves.) | E/V to Lexington Ave./ 53rd St. | 212-838-5411 | www.dessertdeliveryny.com
This little shop in East Midtown "can get anyone off their diet" confide cookie connoisseurs citing a clever and "well-edited" selection of sweet treats the likes of "beautiful" cakes that also taste "really delicious", "apple pie that's about the best there is" and what may be "the city's finest black-and-white cookie"; "first-class" owners oversee the "fast, friendly service", assuring that customers get their just desserts; N.B. the Say It With Flour division makes gift baskets.

De Vino ◖▭ *Wine/Liquor* | ▽ 25 | 24 | 23 | E |

LES | 30 Clinton St. (Stanton St.) | F/J/M/Z to Delancey/Essex Sts. | 212-228-0073 | www.de-vino.com
Owner Gabrio Tosti di Valminuta (who hails from a family of wine-makers) shares his passion for vinos at his small Lower East Side boutique; there's "no attitude, just good service" and primo advice on the "wonderful", well-displayed wines that are mostly Italian in origin.

Devon & Blakely *Prepared Food* | 22 | 20 | 18 | M |

E 40s | 140 E. 45th St. (bet. Lexington & 3rd Aves.) | 4/5/6/7/S to 42nd St./Grand Central | 212-338-0606
E 40s | 250 Park Ave. (bet. 46th & 47th Sts.) | 4/5/6/7/S to 42nd St./ Grand Central | 212-661-0101
E 40s | 461 Fifth Ave. (bet. 40th & 41st Sts.) | 7/B/D/F/V to 42nd St./ Bryant Park | 212-684-4321
E 40s | 780 Third Ave. (49th St.) | 6 to 51st St. | 212-826-0212
E 50s | 650 Fifth Ave., lower level (52nd St.) | B/D/F/V to 47-50th Sts./ Rockefeller Ctr. | 212-489-0990
www.devonandblakely.com
"Freshly made" soups, "amazing" salads and "reliable" sandwiches served up in locations dotted "all over Midtown" make this chain a "convenient" "lunch standby" for many; however, critics warn that service "can be slow", while its "gourmet" aspirations translate to somewhat "steep" tabs.

DiFiore Marquet ◖ *Baked Goods* | - | - | - | E |
(fka Marquet Patisserie)

G Village | 15 E. 12th St. (bet. 5th Ave. & University Pl.) | 4/5/6/L/N/Q/R/W to 14th St./Union Sq. | 212-229-9313
Formerly a branch of Marquet Patisserie, this "comfortable" NYU-area bakery/cafe still offers "great French pastries" (brioche, croissants), breads from Balthazar and other "wonderful" baked goods, but it's now making a name for itself with ambitious prepared foods (think filet mignon and roasted fish), including many dishes with a Brazilian or French twist.

Dimple *Prepared Food* ▽ 22 | 11 | 19 | I

Garment Dist | 11 W. 30th St. (bet. B'way & 5th Ave.) |
B/D/F/N/Q/R/V/W to 34th St./Herald Sq. | 212-643-9464
Jackson Hts | 35-68 73rd St. (bet. 35th & 37th Aves.) | Queens |
7/E/F/G/R/V to 74th St./B'way | 718-458-8144 ●☂

"Delicious" kosher and vegetarian Indian fare are dished out at
the Garment District half of this duo, while the Jackson Heights
outpost also offers non-veggie dishes; both are "fantastically
cheap" and even though there's "no ambiance or decor",
they're "always packed on weekends", serving buffet buffs and
take-out artists alike.

☑ DiPalo Dairy *Cheese/Dairy* 29 | 23 | 25 | M

Little Italy | 200 Grand St. (Mott St.) | 6 to Spring St. |
212-226-1033

A "shrine" to "the gospel of cheese", this "family-run" Little Italy "institution" is "legendary" for its "exhaustive" selection of formaggio,
voted No. 1 in NYC, featuring "unbeatable" "fresh mozzarella" and
ricotta plus a "wide range" of "real Italian" imports from parmigiano
to pecorino; also a source of "old-country" "delights" like pasta and
olive oil, it's operated "with love" by "chatty" "experts" who "won't
rush you" "once your number is up", and though there are often
"long lines", that only confirms it's "one of the greats."

DiPaola Turkeys ☢ *Meat/Poultry* 27 | 16 | 24 | M

See Greenmarket; for more information, call 609-587-9311

It's "all turkey, all the time" at this Hamilton, NJ–based Greenmarket
poultry provider whose devoted fans "gobble up" its "luscious",
"moist" farm-raised birds year-round; "fresh, not frozen", the meat
comes in the form of "superior" tenderloins, breasts and burgers, as
well as "addictive" Italian sausage (try the spicy for a "wild pasta
sauce"); there may be "no deals" here – aside from the "free
samples" – but all agree "you get what you pay for."

Dirty Bird to-go ● *Prepared Food* 20 | 15 | 16 | M

W Village | 204 W. 14th St. (bet. 7th & 8th Aves.) | A/C/E/L to 14th St./
8th Ave. | 212-620-4836 | www.dirtybirdtogo.com

The "soul-satisfying" "free-range chicken is a real treat" at this small
Village takeout dishing up "delicious" brined birds rotisserie-style or
in a "heavenly fried" version, with roasted potatoes, garlic kale,
cornbread, sandwiches and wraps rounding out the menu; "fast, efficient delivery" is a plus, but some "wish the sides were better",
given that "it's not cheap."

Discovery Wines ● *Wine/Liquor* 22 | 25 | 21 | M

E Village | 10 Ave. A (bet. Houston & 2nd Sts.) | F/V to Lower East Side/
2nd Ave. | 212-674-7833 | www.discoverywines.com

Service-with-a-swipe is the hook at this "cool" gallerylike East
Village wine store, whose "high-tech information portals" enable
customers to scan bar-coded picks for pricing, tasting info, food
suggestions and images of vineyards; the kiosks are "entertaining",
but Luddites can always look to "human help" if need be.

Dishes *Prepared Food*

24 | 23 | 17 | E

E 40s | 6 E. 45th St. (bet. 5th & Madison Aves.) | 4/5/6/7/S to 42nd St./ Grand Central | 212-687-5511
E 40s | Grand Central Terminal | dining concourse (42nd St. & Vanderbilt Ave.) | 4/5/6/7/S to 42nd St./Grand Central | 212-808-5511 ●
E 50s | Citigroup Ctr. | 399 Park Ave. (54th St.) | E/V to 5th Ave./ 53rd St. | 212-421-5511
www.dishestogo.com
"When you're on the run" in the Grand Central area, this "upscale" trio is a "convenient" option for "spot-on salads", "wonderful soups" and other "quality lunchtime fare"; "be careful not to take too much" from the "beautifully presented" buffet, however, for everything's a "bit pricey"; N.B. only the dining concourse location is open on weekends.

Doma Cafe & Gallery ● ⊌ *Coffee/Tea*

▽ 25 | 25 | 20 | M

W Village | 17 Perry St. (7th Ave.) | 1/2/3 to 14th St. | 212-929-4339
Every boho hangout "should aspire to" be like this "very West Village" coffeehouse/wine bar, a "relaxed" retreat for "watching the world go by" over "wonderful coffee" and "yummy" "snacks", including pastries, panini, soups and such; it's the favored domain of "screenwriters" and other "loafers" with "laptops", many of whom seem to "live there."

☒ Dom's Fine Foods ▣ *Specialty Shop*

27 | 22 | 19 | M

SoHo | 202 Lafayette St. (bet. Broome & Kenmare Sts.) | 6 to Spring St. | 212-226-1963
Packing "a surprising amount into a small space", this "true Italian" market in SoHo is "worth checking out" for the "spectacular" sandwich counter that makes it a dominant local "lunch stop", along with "great prepared foods" and an "assortment of grocery items" (cheeses, pastas, oils and more) imported from the old country and offered at a "very competitive" cost; and "if you're looking for meat", the "knowledgeable butchers" have the trimming talent to "customize" any cut "to your liking" and pride themselves on their homemade sausage; N.B. in summer 2007 it's relocating to new quarters at 181 Grand St.

☒ Dorian's Seafood Market ▣ *Seafood*

25 | 20 | 26 | E

E 80s | 1580 York Ave. (83rd St.) | 4/5/6 to 86th St. | 212-535-2256
UES denizens were delighted when the "knowledgeable staff" from the dearly departed Rosedale Fishmarket opened this similarly "top-quality" market dealing in "amazingly" "fresh" seafood and prepared items – smoked fish, clam chowder and the like – "delivered with total assurance" (and at no charge, citywide); yes, it's "expensive", but you can expect to "get what you ordered in perfect condition."

☒ Doughnut Plant ▣⊌ *Baked Goods*

26 | 15 | 19 | M

LES | 379 Grand St. (bet. Essex & Norfolk Sts.) | F/J/M/Z to Delancey/Essex Sts. | 212-505-3700 | www.doughnutplant.com
Living up to its name with a "bare-bones" industrial interior and minimal seating, this Lower East Side factory turns out "artisanal

QUALITY DISPLAY SERVICE COST

doughnuts" so "addictive" they "should have a warning label" (think "Homer Simpson's wildest dreams come to life"); the owner's "infectious enthusiasm" for seasonal ingredients inspires "flavors you couldn't imagine" – chestnut, banana pecan, tres leches – and ensures his "high-end" product is "worth the extra dough"; N.B. also sold at specialty markets around NYC.

Downtown Atlantic ❶ *Prepared Food*

| - | - | - | M |

Boerum Hill | 364 Atlantic Ave. (bet. Bond & Hoyt Sts.) | Brooklyn | A/C/G to Hoyt/Schermerhorn Sts. | 718-596-1827 | www.downtownatlantic.com

"You'd never guess there's a world-class bakery hidden in the basement" of this family-owned Boerum Hill restaurant, where pastry chef Fran Sippel's "amazing" cupcakes and other "treats" are "sold from a small counter at the front"; it also serves simple soups, salads and sandwiches to go at lunchtime.

Dual Specialty Store, Inc. ❶ *Herbs/Spices*

| - | - | - | I |

(fka Dowel Quality Products)

E Village | 91 First Ave. (bet. 5th & 6th Sts.) | F/V to Lower East Side/ 2nd Ave. | 212-979-6045

Anything you might need to cook up an Indian feast can be found at this recently redubbed East Village spice heaven, where the "vast selection" of Indian grocery items, dried and preserved fruits, spices and herbs, teas, breads and sweets will thrill any wandering foodie; it's "inexpensive", "the people are friendly" and there's a "terrific beer selection" (over 400 labels) – what more could you ask for?

Duane Park Patisserie *Baked Goods*

| 26 | 17 | 20 | E |

TriBeCa | 179 Duane St. (bet. Greenwich & Hudson Sts.) | 1/2/3/A/C to Chambers St. | 212-274-8447 | 877-274-8447 | www.madelines.net

"A real place in TriBeCa, as opposed to a scene-maker" is the general consensus on this longtime patisserie that pleases patrons with "wonderful" Austrian, French and German specialties spanning "truly magical" cupcakes, "exquisite" pastries, "traditional cookies" and "beautiful, delicious" custom cakes; though service gets mixed reviews ("pleasantly helpful" vs. "rude") and the prices are "expensive", most take it in stride because clearly "much love and expertise goes into the work."

DUB Pies ❶⬛ *Prepared Food*

| ▽ 24 | 15 | 24 | I |

Carroll Gardens | 193 Columbia St. (bet. Degraw & Sackett Sts.) | Brooklyn | F/G to Carroll St. | 646-202-9412 | www.dubpies.com

Traditional Australian and New Zealander "savory pies" "make meat lovers happy" at this West Carroll Gardens (i.e. Navy Yard) takeaway, whose name stands for 'Down Under Bakery' but also names the style of reggae that fills the air; "solid vegetarian" dishes and "sweet dessert pies" are also among the "fantastic cheap eats" on offer.

	QUALITY	DISPLAY	SERVICE	COST

Dumpling Man ● *Prepared Food* | 20 | 16 | 17 | I |

E Village | 100 St. Marks Pl. (bet. Ave. A & 1st Ave.) | L to 1st Ave. | 212-505-2121 | www.dumplingman.com

For "awesomeness in one bite", East Villagers head to this tiny eat-in/takeaway spot where you can watch the kitchen staff's "craftsmanship" in packing the "thin, delicate" wrappers with "inventive" fillings, including a hearty veggie version; even though it's "cheap", purists pooh-pooh it as "yuppie Americanized fusion cuisine" and recommend you "save your money for Chinatown."

Durso's Pasta & Ravioli Co. ▣ *Pasta* | 26 | 20 | 23 | M |

Flushing | 189-01 Crocheron Ave. (Utopia Pkwy.) | Queens | 7 to Flushing-Main St. | 718-358-1311 | www.dursos.com

"Phenomenal pastas" and "great sauces to go with them" earn endorsements from shoppers at this Flushing specialty-foods store with an Italian accent, which also serves more than 50 kinds of prepared dishes, fresh meat and poultry, lotsa bakery items, imported treats and an extensive selection of cheeses – "lines are long at times" but it's "worth it."

❷ D'Vine Taste ● *Specialty Shop* | 25 | 21 | 25 | M |

Park Slope | 150 Seventh Ave. (bet. Carroll St. & Garfield Pl.) | Brooklyn | 2/3 to Grand Army Plaza | 718-369-9548

The "fabulous selection of cheeses, olives", spreads and other "gourmet groceries" keeps Park Slope residents coming back to this Middle Eastern specialty store whose bifurcated space also houses "interesting, delicious prepared foods" including sandwiches at lunchtime; the housemade "fig cakes are addictive" here, as are the "well-stocked" shelves, affordable prices and "friendly, warm and genuinely helpful service."

❷ Dylan's Candy Bar ●▣ *Candy/Nuts* | 21 | 27 | 17 | E |

E 60s | 1011 Third Ave. (60th St.) | N/R/W to Lexington Ave./59th St. | 646-735-0078 | www.dylanscandybar.com

A "cornucopia of candies", this "fantastical" East Side "playground" "for ages 10–110" offers its "bazillion" varieties of sweets (including "vintage stuff" like Dubble Bubble and Dots) in an "eye-popping", "two-level" setting complete with a coffee/ice cream bar; sure, it's a "bedlam" of "tourists and tweens" and the "inflated prices" will bust your "entire piggy bank", but "just try to resist" "the fun factor"; P.S. it's also "nirvana" "for children's parties."

Dynasty Supermarket ● *Specialty Shop* | 19 | 13 | 12 | I |

Chinatown | 68 Elizabeth St. (Hester St.) | 6/J/M/N/Q/R/W/Z to Canal St. | 212-966-4943 | www.dynastysuper.qpg.com

Considered the "mother of all Manhattan Asian markets", this Chinatown superstore is "about as authentic as it gets", offering an "incredible selection" of "live fish, octopi and eels" plus meats, produce, condiments, rice and "every comestible possible in dessicated form"; "there's even a sushi bar, jewelry store" and herbal medicine counter, so although "service is nonexistent", shoppers "keep coming back for the incredible bargains."

	QUALITY	DISPLAY	SERVICE	COST

Eagle Provisions *Meat/Poultry*

| 24 | 13 | 19 | M |

Park Slope | 628 Fifth Ave. (18th St.) | Brooklyn | M/R to Prospect Ave. | 718-499-0026

The "incredible aroma of kielbasa" will have you "salivating" upon entry to this enormous (14,000-sq.-ft.) Park Slope food market, a "terrific" resource for house-smoked meats and other "authentic" Polish specialties as well as "great gourmet products" from all over ("surprisingly good lox"); perhaps most "impressive" is the "massive" beer selection comprising 1,000 labels, "imported and microbrew."

Earthmatters ● *Health Food*

| ▽ 21 | 15 | 12 | M |

LES | 177 Ludlow St. (bet. Houston & Stanton Sts.) | F/V to Lower East Side/ 2nd Ave. | 212-475-4180 | www.earthmatters.com

A healthful oasis on the Lower East Side, this organic market and cafe has a large patio and lounge where (mainly vegetarian) home-made snacks and sandwiches are served, along with organic wines or beers; while it boasts a large selection of teas, most rely on it more as a source for wholesome prepared foods than as a place to "shop for groceries."

East Coast Beer Co. *Beer*

| - | - | - | M |

Sunset Pk | 316 37th St. (bet. 3rd & 4th Aves.) | Brooklyn | R/V to Steinway St. | 718-788-8000

Suds for all seasons and from all regions is the specialty of this "awe-some" Brooklyn brew expert; it's a haul to Sunset Park, to be sure, but it's "worth the trip" on account of the "huge selection" (700 va-rieties) that's genuinely "international", plus, the eclectic stock is reasonably priced.

East Side Bagel ● *Bagels*

| 21 | 16 | 19 | I |

E 70s | 1496 First Ave. (78th St.) | 6 to 77th St. | 212-794-1403

Upper Eastsiders salute this "simple" local shop for the "huge and delicious bagels" that lead a lineup of "brunch essentials" including sandwiches, salads and housemade black-and-white cookies; hold-outs shrug it's "only so-so", but those in the market for "old-fashioned" "value" "can't complain."

East Village Cheese Store ⇌ *Cheese/Dairy*

| 22 | 17 | 19 | I |

E Village | 40 Third Ave. (bet. 9th & 10th Sts.) | 6 to Astor Pl. | 212-477-2601

"How do they do it?" wonder "bargain"-hunters at this "busy" East Village retailer, loaded "wall to wall" with "cheese, wonderful cheese" at "unbelievably low" prices (check out those "$2.99 spe-cials"), along with spreads, cold cuts and breads; it's "nothing fancy" and "freshness can be hit-or-miss", but "if you know what's good" and "need to stock up", "there's no better" deal; P.S. it's "cash only."

NEW East Village Ice Cream ●⇌ *Ice Cream*

| - | - | - | M |

E Village | 218 Avenue B (bet. 13th & 14th Sts.) | L to 1st Ave. | 212-673-6030

A veteran of the Brooklyn Ice Cream Factory has opened this tiny, mango-hued East Village parlor peddling handmade, small-batch scoops that come in an ever-changing array of flavors – though en-

during favorites like vanilla-chocolate-chunk and pistachio are usually on hand; there are jars of toppings on the counter to complete
the treat, as well as a few seats in which to savor it.

Z East Village   28 | 25 | 25 | M
Meat Market ⬛ _Meat/Poultry_
E Village | 139 Second Ave. (bet. 9th St. & St. Marks Pl.) | L to 1st Ave. |
212-228-5590
Admirers of this "old-school" East Village meat market "in the
classic East European/Polish tradition" "hope it never changes"
given that the house-smoked hams, "beautiful" cold cuts and
sausages ("the best kielbasa") and fresh meats on display can
"provoke drooling on sight"; moderate prices and "old-fashioned,
personal service" at the counter are the crowning touches.

Z E.A.T. ◑⬛ _Prepared Food_   25 | 21 | 17 | VE
E 80s | 1064 Madison Ave. (bet. 80th & 81st Sts.) | 4/5/6 to 86th St. |
212-772-0022 | www.elizabar.com
"Everything is delicious" at Eli Zabar's Upper East Side cafe–cum-
prepared foods shop, from the "fabulous crusty breads" to the
"fresh", "high-quality" sandwiches, soups and varied hot dishes; the
scene can be "chaotic" and the service "grumpy", and while your
chances of spotting "famous people" aren't bad, you're more likely
to "see stars when you get the bill."

Eckerton Hill Farm ⬛ _Produce_   26 | 23 | 23 | E
See Greenmarket; for more information, call 610-562-2591
"The godfather of heirloom tomatoes" since 1996, Greenmarket
stalwart Tim Stark also harvests "exceptionally good peppers of all
sizes and heat gradients" in late summer from his bucolic
Pennsylvania farm; these two "superlative" crops are proffered in
"interesting and unusual" varieties, along with colorful clusters of
"wonderful fresh flowers" to "make you smile."

Economy Candy ⬛ _Candy/Nuts_   24 | 17 | 18 | I
LES | 108 Rivington St. (bet. Essex & Ludlow Sts.) | F/J/M/Z to
Delancey/Essex Sts. | 212-254-1531 | 800-352-4544 |
www.economycandy.com
"You name it, they have it" at this "Lower East Side landmark" where
"every inch" of the "old-school" space is "crammed full" with "every
imaginable" candy, both "retro and modern", as well as nuts and
dried fruits, offered individually or in "bulk" "at rock-bottom prices";
it's a "time warp to sweeter" days where your "inner child" can re-
discover the "classics" ("keep digging, you'll find it"), and despite
"cluttered" conditions, penny-pinchers and nostalgists alike will
think they "went to heaven."

Eddie's Sweet Shop ◑⬛ _Ice Cream_   25 | 24 | 22 | I
Forest Hills | 105-29 Metropolitan Ave. (72nd Rd.) | Queens | E/F/G/R/V to
Forest Hills/71st Ave. | 718-520-8514
"Go for nostalgia's sake" but stay for the "heavenly" ice cream at
this "vintage" Forest Hills "throwback" where the "fresh whipped
cream" and "unbelievable" hot fudge make for a mean sundae; while

the "old-time parlor" setting, complete with "counter", "tin ceilings" and "tall glasses", is a "blast from the past", it's the "homemade" frozen stuff that is "not to be missed."

Egg Custard King Café ⊄ *Baked Goods* | - | - | - | I |
Chinatown | 76 Mott St. (bet. Canal & Bayard Sts.) | J/M/Z to Canal St. | 212-226-8208

Since opening in 2005, this unpretentious Chinatown shop has gained a fervent following for its flaky-crusted egg custard tarts, which are available in an array of flavors beyond the classic (honeydew, strawberry, almond, etc.) and priced affordably enough to easily become a daily habit; beyond the eponymous specialty, it purveys other Asian pastries as well as buns and Hong Kong–style 'cafe food' such as sandwiches, noodles, rice dishes and chicken wings.

Eggers Ice Cream Parlor ●⊄ *Ice Cream* | 25 | 19 | 21 | M |
Staten Island | 1194 Forest Ave. (bet. Jewett Ave. & Manor Rd.) | 718-981-2110
Staten Island | 7437 Amboy Rd. (Yetman Ave.) | 718-605-9335

The "old-fashioned creamy treats", including "the best hot fudge, hands down", on top of "always fresh-tasting" ice cream, are "off the charts" at this "classic" ice cream parlor on Staten Island, which also boasts a nostalgia-inducing candy selection; cakes and pies are made on the premises, and it's available for birthday parties; N.B. the Forest Avenue location is independently owned.

Egidio Pastry Shop ▭ *Baked Goods* | 24 | 23 | 22 | M |
Bronx | 622 E. 187th St. (Hughes Ave.) | 2 to Pelham Pkwy. | 718-295-6077 | www.egidiopastryshop.com

"Visit the old country" without leaving the city at this "real-deal" Bronx pasticceria (since 1912) where owner-baker Carmela Lucciola whips up "mouthwatering" "traditional Italian pastries" ("full-size or miniature"), "the best biscotti", "great cappuccino" and summertime ices; N.B. wedding cakes and gingerbread houses are also specialties.

Eileen's Special Cheesecake ●▭ *Baked Goods* | 26 | 18 | 19 | M |
NoLita | 17 Cleveland Pl. (bet. Centre & Kenmare Sts.) | 6 to Spring St. | 212-966-5585 | 800-521-2253 | www.eileenscheesecake.com

This NoLita "old-timer" still specializes in "creamy", "dreamy" cheesecakes "so light" a person could almost "eat an entire 10-inch cake" report respondents who rhapsodize about the "blissful" array of sizes and "innovative flavors" (two new ones: mango and dulce de leche) that make for a "smashing smorgasbord"; despite occasional "crankiness", service is "generally good"; N.B. low-carb and sugar-free versions available.

Eisenberg's Sandwich Shop *Deli/Sandwich* | 20 | 13 | 18 | I |
Flatiron | 174 Fifth Ave. (bet. 22nd & 23rd Sts.) | N/R/W to 23rd St. | 212-675-5096 | www.eisenbergsnyc.com

Serving up "the real deal" since 1929, this "glorious NY institution" "takes you back in time" with its "overstuffed sandwiches" ("try the

chopped liver" or "to-die-for tuna" salad) and "great egg creams";
although some say the "vintage" Flatiron setting "has seen better
days", most consider that to be "a nostalgic virtue."

Eleni's Cookies ▣ *Baked Goods* — 22 | 24 | 20 | E

Chelsea | Chelsea Mkt. | 75 Ninth Ave. (bet. 15th & 16th Sts.) |
A/C/E/L to 14th St./8th Ave. | 212-255-7990 | 888.435.3647 |
www.elenis.com

"The crème de la crème of illustrated cookies" may well be this
Chelsea Market storefront's "elaborate" "little works of art" customizable "for every conceivable occasion and theme" (e.g. "actor-face
cookies for your Oscar party"); while some say the confections "look
better than they taste", most maintain the "amazing workmanship"
and "original presentation" make these "truly special" (if "pricey")
gifts; N.B. there are now cupcakes, cakes and candy by the pound.

☑ Eli's Manhattan ◕▣ *MajorGourmet Mkt.* — 25 | 24 | 16 | VE

E 80s | 1411 Third Ave. (80th St.) | 4/5/6 to 86th St. | 212-717-8100 |
www.elizabar.com

A "great comfort" to Upper Eastsiders, Eli Zabar's "fabulous" "allaround" gourmet market ensures "young professional" types stay
well fed on "outstanding" breads and baked goods ("always a
crowd-pleaser"), a "wide-ranging selection" of "beautiful" cheeses,
"awe-inspiring" specialty items, "picturesque produce" of "exceptional quality", "superior" prepared foods featuring a "wall of soups"
and a "rather small" but "incredible" meat and seafood department;
of course, "excellence has its price" and with tabs tailored to "hedgefund owners" mean regular folk must "choose wisely" here.

Eli's Vinegar Factory ◕▣ *Major Gourmet Mkt.* — 25 | 21 | 16 | VE

E 90s | 431 E. 91st St. (bet. 1st & York Aves.) | 4/5/6 to 86th St. |
212-987-0885 | www.elizabar.com

It's so far over on the East Side you might think you "somehow left
the island", but the intrepid can "count on" Eli Zabar's original
emporium for "anything gourmet", starting with "bountiful",
"always-fresh" produce that "looks like it should be in a gallery" and
following through with "beautiful" "crusty breads" and "first-rate"
prepared foods, cheeses, meat, seafood and specialty items; even if
the "extreme" pricing strikes some as "way out of whack", it's always a "likable" place to splurge on a "special dinner" or a "once-ina-while treat."

Elizabeth Ryan Floral Design *Flowers* — ▽ 28 | 24 | 26 | E

E Village | 411 E. Ninth St. (bet. Ave. A & 1st Ave.) | L to 1st Ave. |
212-995-1111 | 800-260-1486 | www.erflowers.com

"What an eye" Elizabeth Ryan has declare devotees of the "spectacular, unusual flowers" arranged in "fabulous containers" that
emerge from her East Village emporium; the "finished products are
so glorious" they "always draw high praise" and help make any celebration or "party a smash success"; N.B. tablecloths and lighting
are also available.

	QUALITY	DISPLAY	SERVICE	COST

Emack & Bolio's ● *Ice Cream* | 25 | 18 | 20 | M |

E 80s | 1564 First Ave. (bet. 81st & 82nd Sts.) | 4/5/6 to 86th St. |
212-734-0105 🖶

SoHo | 73 W. Houston St. (W. B'way) | 1 to Houston St. | 212-533-5610

W 70s | 389 Amsterdam Ave. (bet. 78th & 79th Sts.) | 1 to 79th St. |
212-362-2747 🖶

www.emackandbolios.com

Even rabid Sox haters are "so glad" this "creative" mini-chain "made its way from Boston" given its "awesome array" of "decadent", "well-crafted" ice cream in an array of "totally addictive" flavors; cynics find it "vastly overrated" and "too expensive", but for most its "spoonable magic" is "worth the calories and the price."

Embassy Wines & Spirits ●▣ *Wine/Liquor*   ∇ 19 | 16 | 15 | E |

E 60s | 796 Lexington Ave. (bet. 61st & 62nd Sts.) | N/R/W to
Lexington Ave./59th St. | 212-838-6551 |
www.embassywinesandspirits.com

True to its name, this East Side store displays wines and liquors from around the globe, including 100 kosher vintages; it's "convenient" for busy shoppers who "need something quickly", and the 'bargain basement' yields some nice windfalls (all wines there are under $10), otherwise, some gripe that it caters to those "who don't care what they pay."

Empire Coffee & Tea Co. ▣ *Coffee/Tea* | 23 | 19 | 22 | M |

W 40s | 568 Ninth Ave. (bet. 41st & 42nd Sts.) | 1/2/3/7/N/Q/R/S/W to
42nd St./Times Sq. | 212-268-1220 | 800-262-5908 |
www.empirecoffeetea.com

"Ask and they'll probably have it" at this "old-style" (circa 1908) Hell's Kitchen shop, a "funky little" space chock-full of "wonderful" fresh-roasted coffees and "interesting teas" as well as cookies, candies and paraphernalia like grinders, coffeemakers and kettles; it's a somewhat "hidden" resource, but the "sweet", "dedicated" service gets a "thumbs-up" and "you can't beat the prices."

Empire Market *Meat/Poultry* | - | - | - | M |

College Pt | 14-26 College Point Blvd. (bet. 14th Ave. & 14th Rd.) |
Queens | 718-359-0209 | www.empire-market.com

This tin-ceilinged German meat-and-poultry shop in College Point, a fourth-generation family business that dates from the 1850s, proves that what's old can be new again with its lineup of all-natural, organic, no-nitrate meats, including a broad selection of items prepped in their own smokehouse (bacon, knockwurst, kielbasa and 10 kinds of chicken sausage); in sum, this is a "place you can trust."

Esposito Meat Market *Meat/Poultry* | 25 | 19 | 25 | M |

Garment Dist | 500 Ninth Ave. (38th St.) | A/C/E to 42nd St./
Port Authority | 212-279-3298

For the "best pork and sausage" dispensed with a side of "old-Italian-NY" atmosphere, take a "highly recommended" visit to this West 30s butcher shop, a third-generation family business purveying the "freshest meats" and game (including venison, quail and

	QUALITY	DISPLAY	SERVICE	COST

rabbit); customers appreciate the "expertise" of its "old-school" staffers, who also happen to be "very friendly."

Esposito's Pork Store ⌁ *Meat/Poultry*   26 21 25 M

Carroll Gardens | 357 Court St. (bet. President & Union Sts.) | Brooklyn | F/G to Carroll St. | 718-875-6863

One of the last "holdouts" in gentrified Carroll Gardens, this third-generation Italian meat market has been supplying Brooklynites with "outstanding pork products" since 1971; it's especially known for its "vast assortment" of house-cured and dried sausages (salami, hot and sweet soppresata, pepperoni), but it also offers imports like prosciutto as well as made-on-premises mozz and prepared foods like arancini, lasagna and sandwiches.

Ess-a-Bagel ◐▤ *Bagels*   26 17 18 I

E 50s | 831 Third Ave. (bet. 50th & 51st Sts.) | 6 to 51st St. | 212-980-1010
Gramercy | 359 First Ave. (21st St.) | 6 to 23rd St. | 212-260-2252
www.ess-a-bagel.com

"Nothing beats" these Eastsiders for "hilariously huge" bagels that "can double as flotation devices" but still achieve a "blend of chewiness and crustiness" that's "among the best" and "heartiest" in town; only the "joshing" "countermen are fresher" than the "loads of spreads", making this a "ritual" dose of "moxie" "you can only get in the Big Apple", complete with "madhouse" conditions on weekends.

Evelyn's Hand-Dipped Chocolates ▤ *Candy/Nuts*   25 20 22 M

Financial Dist | 4 John St. (bet. B'way & Nassau St.) | A/C to B'way/Nassau | 212-267-5170

Dipping since 1963, this "tiny shop" is a "Wall Street standby" for "handmade (really) chocolates" that are "always fresh" and "just the right amount of sweet"; "simply" "fabulous" goods at prices "less expensive than the big names" make it a "mecca" "around the holidays", and for followers it's a pleasure "to see Evelyn there" any time.

Fabiane's Cafe & Pastry ◐⌁ *Baked Goods*   - - - M

Williamsburg | 142 N. Fifth St. (Bedford Ave.) | Brooklyn | L to Bedford Ave. | 718-218-9632

At this wee Williamsburger, a French Culinary Institute–trained chef offers a mix of Brazilian, French and American fare, much of it organic; the menu ranges from "delicious desserts" and baked goods (the "best" croissants, passion-fruit mousse, vegan tofu-almond-pistachio cake, etc.) to prepared salads and chicken pot pie; now that the cafe also serves wine and beer, it's tempting to settle in at a table for some "hipster-watching."

⌁ Faicco's Pork Store *Meat/Poultry*   28 23 25 M

G Village | 260 Bleecker St. (bet. 6th & 7th Aves.) | A/B/C/D/E/F/V to W. 4th St. | 212-243-1974
Bay Ridge | 6511 11th Ave. (bet. 65th & 66th Sts.) | Brooklyn | N to Fort Hamilton Pkwy. | 718-236-0119

Specializing in "all parts of the pig but the oink", these traditional Italian meat markets/salumerias and their offerings including "hard-to-find cuts" are the "real deal", as is its "wonderful selection" of "housemade sausages" (fresh as well as dried and cured); there's also fresh mozzarella, housemade sauces, oils, vinegars and other imported comestibles, all rung up by "friendly" counter folk; N.B. the Village branch is the original (circa 1940), while the Bay Ridge sibling is newer and bigger.

🛛 Fairway ● *Major Gourmet Mkt.* 26 | 19 | 17 | M
Harlem | 2328 12th Ave. (bet. 132nd & 133rd Sts.) | 1 to 125th St. | 212-234-3883
W 70s | 2127 Broadway (74th St.) | 1/2/3 to 72nd St. | 212-595-1888
Red Hook | 480-500 Van Brunt St. (Reed St.) | Brooklyn | F/G to Smith/9th Sts. | 718-694-6868
www.fairwaymarket.com
All that "your heart desires" from "staples" "to the exotic" awaits "under one rooftop" at this "competitively priced" UWS gourmet market "workhorse" and its "gargantuan" Harlem and Red Hook outposts; it's a "consummate" shopping "experience" with an "encyclopedic" selection of "beautifully presented" produce, a "cornucopia" of "sublime" smoked fish, a "terrific cheese counter" tended by "well-informed" folks, a "great choice of organic" goods, "hard-to-beat" specialty items ("they've got it somewhere"), "yummy" prepared foods and a "diverse fresh selection" of seafood and "perfectly aged prime beef"; sure, "navigating" the "hectic" "scrum" "is an acquired skill", but those whose perseverance is "rewarded" confirm this is "the way to go."

Falai Panetteria ●▣ *Baked Goods* 27 | 21 | 21 | M
LES | 79 Clinton St. (bet. Delancey & Rivington Sts.) | F/J/M/Z to Delancey/Essex Sts. | 212-777-8956 | www.falainyc.com
Pastry chef–turned-restaurateur Iacopo Falai opened this "tiny", sunlit Lower East Side panettria/cafe to purvey his "excruciatingly fresh and subtly flavored breads" and "fantastic pastries"; among the "wonderful" sweets on display are cream-filled Italian doughnuts, almond croissants, fruit tarts, and cocoa-dusted nuts and raisins, while savories span *salumi*, homemade pastas and hot panini.

Family Store, The *Specialty Shop* - | - | - | M
Bay Ridge | 6905 Third Ave. (bet. Ovington Ave. & 69th St.) | Brooklyn | R to Bay Ridge Ave. | 718-748-0207
Living up to its name, this "quaint shop" in Bay Ridge is run by a "friendly" family that "goes out of its way to make you feel welcome" as you browse the store's "authentic" selection of dry goods and "homemade" Middle Eastern and Mediterranean prepared foods; the "delicious" items "vary daily", so "whether you're cooking or letting them do it", this is a "wonderful" option.

Famous Wines & Spirits ▣ *Wine/Liquor* ▽ 22 | 17 | 23 | M
Financial Dist | 40 Exchange Pl. (William St.) | 2/3 to Wall St. | 212-422-4743 | www.famouswines.com
"Convenience is the key to the success" of this "friendly" family-run "sleeper" of a wine shop in the Financial District that proves

	QUALITY	DISPLAY	SERVICE	COST

"reliable vintages" can be found in "unexpected locations"; its "excellent" inventory – and "free tastings every Friday" evening – is a surefire investment for the stockbroker-heavy clientele.

F&B *Prepared Food*

20	17	17	I

Chelsea | 269 W. 23rd St. (bet. 7th & 8th Aves.) | C/E to 23rd St. | 646-486-4441 ●

E 50s | 150 E. 52nd St. (bet. Lexington & 3rd Aves.) | 6 to 51st St. | 212-421-8600

www.gudtfood.com

"Hot dogs with flair" are the main attraction of these "cool" cafe/takeaway twins in Chelsea and the East 50s where Danish franks and brockwurst with "spectacular toppings" make for "wonderful combos", the smoked tofu dog is "veggie heaven" and the frites should trigger an "addiction alert"; N.B. Midtown offers WiFi hook-up.

Fat Witch Bakery ▣ *Baked Goods*

25	21	21	M

Chelsea | Chelsea Mkt. | 75 Ninth Ave. (bet. 15th & 16th Sts.) | A/C/E/L to 14th St./8th Ave. | 212-807-1335 | 888-419-4824 | www.fatwitch.com

"Moist", "fudgey", "seriously dangerous brownies" in a variety of flavors (caramel, cherry, cappuccino) cast a spell on Muggles seeking "chocolate fixes" at this Chelsea Market shop, while waistwatchers opt for the three-bite Witch Babies so as not to "eat too many and fall off the broomstick"; yes, prices may be "a bit steep", but "go later in the afternoon" for "goodies at a discount."

Fay Da Bakery ⌀ *Baked Goods*

19	17	13	I

Chinatown | 191 Center St. (Hester St.) | 6/J/M/N/Q/R/W/Z to Canal St. | 212-966-8934

Chinatown | 82 Elizabeth St. (bet. Grand & Hester Sts.) | B/D to Grand St. | 212-966-8206

Chinatown | 83 Mott St. (Canal St.) | 6/J/M/N/Q/R/W/Z to Canal St. | 212-791-3884

Elmhurst | 86-12 Justice Ave. (B'way) | Queens | B/V to Grand Ave./Newton | 718-205-5835

Flushing | 37-11 Main St. (37th Ave.) | Queens | 7 to Flushing-Main St. | 718-888-9890

Flushing | 41-60 Main St. (Sanford Ave.) | Queens | 7 to Flushing-Main St. | 718-886-4568

Flushing | 46-15 Kissena Blvd. (Juniper Ave.) | Queens | 718-353-0730

www.fayda.com

This Chinese bakery chain satisfies with "fresh" delights from "the best" steamed buns to the "lightest, spongiest cakes", some with "fresh fruit and cream" (a "nice change" from "rich" European desserts), and other "delicacies" "tonged out of the bins by the staff"; service that's "not too attentive" and "no-nonsense" environs don't deter regulars, who confess they "always wind up with bags and bags."

Feast & Fêtes ⌀ *Caterer*

▽ 27	27	26	VE

E 60s | 20 E. 76th St. (bet. 5th & Madison Aves.) | 212-737-2224 | www.danielnyc.com

By appointment only

It's no surprise that this Upper East Side outfit "knows how to do upscale events" since it's the catering arm of *très* tony eatery Daniel, with chef Daniel Boulud and event planner Jean-Christophe Le Picart heading off-premises to take any fete "over the top"; they match the same "superb" fare served in the restaurant with "impeccable service" that's just as "impressive", and though the pedigree comes "at a cost", fat wallets call it "surprisingly affordable for the quality."

Fellan Florist Flora Galleria ▭ *Flowers* ▽ | 24 | 23 | 26 | E |

E 60s | 1243 Second Ave. (65th St.) | 6 to 68th St. | 212-421-3567 | 800-335-5267 | www.fellan.com

"Superior service" is a signature of this "reliable" family-owned Upper East Side florist that's been serving the carriage trade for 80 years; "absolutely fresh flowers" imported from around the world "tell the story" of their continued popularity, and if it's a gift basket that's needed, those are available too.

Fermented Grapes ◑▭ *Wine/Liquor* | 22 | 21 | 24 | M |

Prospect Heights | 651 Vanderbilt Ave. (bet. Park & Prospect Pls.) | Brooklyn | 2/3 to Grand Army Plaza | 718-230-3216 | www.fermentedgrapes.net

You "can't go wrong with any bottle" here vouch Prospect Heights vinophiles of this "neighborhood" wine shop whose "quality-over-quantity" approach results in a "limited but interesting" selection; its "helpful", "down-to-earth" staff and "frequent" tastings with "generous pours" have locals toasting it as a "favorite."

Ferrara Cafe ◑▭ *Baked Goods* | 22 | 23 | 18 | M |

Little Italy | 195 Grand St. (bet. Mott & Mulberry Sts.) | 6/J/M/N/Q/R/W/Z to Canal St. | 212-226-6150 | 800-533-6910 | www.ferraracafe.com

"You can smell it blocks away" so fans can't resist a stop at this Little Italy "landmark" offering "nearly every" "old-fashioned" Italian sweet imaginable – "consistently fresh" pastries from "delicious" Napoleons and cannoli to "don't-miss" lobster tails and tiramisu "that never goes wrong" – plus "sodas in every flavor" and "great gelato"; more modern touches are the "tourist lines and high prices", as well as a few gripes that its confections with a "commercial" feel are "more hype than hypnotic."

Fifth Avenue Chocolatiere ▭ *Candy/Nuts* | 20 | 17 | 20 | E |

E 40s | 693 Third Ave. (bet. 43rd & 44th Sts.) | 4/5/6/7/S to 42nd St./Grand Central | 212-935-5454

E 50s | 969 Third Ave. (bet. 57th & 58th Sts.) | 4/5/6 to 59th St./Lexington Ave. | 212-230-0065

NEW **Financial Dist** | 1 NY Plaza (Broad & Water Sts.) | 4/5/6 to 63rd St. | 212-514-8426

800-958-8474 | www.1800chocolate.net

For more than 30 years, this East Side chocolate bastion (with new outposts in the East 40s and the Financial District) has been enticing with its "soft, melty" truffles and other all-kosher confections; "fun novelty shapes" are a specialty – think "vampire-bat lollipops" at Halloween, baby bottles for a new arrival, etc. – and they can be customized for parties and office events.

	QUALITY	DISPLAY	SERVICE	COST

Fifth Avenue Epicure ● *Prepared Food* ▽ 19 | 21 | 20 | M

Flatiron | 144 Fifth Ave. (bet. 19th & 20th Sts.) | N/R/W to 23rd St. | 212-929-3399

When "home-cooked meals without the hassle" are needed, this Flatiron prepared foods shop is a "popular" option offering a "wide selection" of goods that includes the "best soup" (10 varieties) and "nicely displayed" baked-in-house brownies, pastries and more; even better, it's "not too expensive, despite the neighborhood."

NEW Fika ⌐ *Coffee/Tea* ▽ 22 | 16 | 21 | M

W 50s | 41 W. 58th St. (bet. 5th & 6th Aves.) | N/Q/R/W to 57th St. | 212-832-0022 | www.fikanyc.com

"Still a relative secret", this Midtown espresso bar/cafe is a "little Scandinavian" surprise specializing in "amazing coffee" imported from Sweden ("who knew?") along with "delicious" sweet "treats" and a sandwich board featuring gravlax and Swedish meatballs; the streamlined space is too compact for kicking back, but it beats a "trek out to Ikea" for your next lingonberry fix.

Financier Pâtisserie *Baked Goods* 27 | 25 | 21 | E

Financial Dist | Winter Garden | 3-4 World Financial Ctr. (Vesey St.) | 1/2/3/A/C to Chambers St. | 212-786-3220

Financial Dist | 35 Cedar St. (bet. Pearl & William Sts.) | 2/3 to Wall St. | 212-952-3838 ●

Financial Dist | 62 Stone St. (bet. Mill Ln. & William St.) | 2/3 to Wall St. | 212-344-5600 ●

www.financierpastries.com

Wall Streeters are sweet on this threesome of Financial District patisseries boasting an "amazing selection" of "impeccable" Parisian confections so "gorgeous" it almost "seems wrong to eat them"; among the "delicious delights" are well-known favorites (croissants, éclairs, Napoleons) "done to perfection" plus some "hard-to-find" specialties, a growing menu of savories and "incredible coffee"; prices called "steep" by some are justifiable to others "given the high quality."

Fine & Schapiro ● *Deli/Sandwich* 20 | 15 | 17 | M

W 70s | 138 W. 72nd St. (bet. B'way & Columbus Ave.) | 1/2/3 to 72nd St. | 212-877-2874 | www.fineandschapiro.com

Noshers crown this "convenient" UWS "old-time deli" (celebrating its 80th year) as a "jewel for kosher dining" thanks to its "large menu" of "fresh, fabulous" "overstuffed sandwiches" and other "classic" offerings that mark it as "one of a dying breed"; maybe "the surroundings are tired" and service is with "an attitude", but it's a treasured "survivor" nonetheless.

Fireman Hospitality Group *Caterer* - | - | - | E

W 50s | 888 7th Ave., Suite 203 (bet. 56th & 57th Sts.) | N/Q/R/W to 57th St. | 212-265-0100 | www.thefiremangroup.com

"Have a party" at one of the restaurants in Shelly Fireman's Midtown empire via their on-site catering service, whose "helpful" staff draws on ample experience to arrange food and service for up to

1,000 attendees at venues like the Redeye Grill's Sky Room and the Trattoria dell'Arte's Il Naso Room; it's favored by a corporate clientele of accounting, brokerage and law firms that can dig into deep pockets to settle the tab.

First Avenue Wines & Spirits ● *Wine/Liquor* | 23 | 19 | 23 | M |

Gramercy | 383 First Ave. (bet. 22nd & 23rd Sts.) | 6 to 23rd St. | 212-673-3600

Oenophiles make a run on the "great buys" at this family-owned Gramercy wine shop that stocks "name brands" along with lesser-known labels, including strong showings in California boutique wines as well as producers from Australia, New Zealand and Long Island, all presided over by staffers brimming with "helpful information"; the back room, with its "excellent assortment of fine" vintages, helps bear out the store's reputation as an "out-of-the-way" "gem."

First Ave. Pierogi & | ∇ 25 | 13 | 19 | I |
Deli Co. ⊟ *Prepared Food*

E Village | 130 First Ave. (bet. 7th St. & St. Marks Pl.) | L to 1st Ave. | 212-420-9690

"Pierogi and blintz heaven" awaits at this East Village deli that, in addition to the "fantastic" namesake, dishes out "stuffed cabbage, barley mushroom soup" and other stick-to-your-ribs "Ukrainian specialties" deemed "well-worth a trip Downtown"; just ignore the "Soviet-era setting" advise apparatchiks, and focus instead on the "bang for the buck."

Fischer Bros. & Leslie ▭⊟ *Meat/Poultry* | 27 | 19 | 22 | VE |

W 70s | 230 W. 72nd St. (bet. B'way & West End Ave.) | 1/2/3 to 72nd St. | 212-787-1715 | www.fischerbros.com

The "Tiffany's" of glatt butchers is how devotees describe this meat shop/deli that "serves an important Upper West Side niche" with its kosher meats ranked among "the best in the city", as well as its "great" prepared foods; it doesn't take credit cards, so, given the premium pricing, you may want to "cash your paycheck" first; N.B. there's weekly delivery service to Connecticut and New Jersey, as well as the Hamptons in summertime.

Fish Tales *Seafood* | 25 | 22 | 25 | M |

Cobble Hill | 191A Court St. (bet. Bergen & Wyckoff Sts.) | Brooklyn | F/G to Bergen St. | 718-246-1346 | www.fishtalesonline.com

"It's like the fishing boat is docked in front" of this "small", "outstanding" Cobble Hill market where the "first-class" catches "from the briny deep" are "so fresh" and the staff "super-helpful" and "knowledgeable"; it also offers a "nice selection" of "ready-to-eat specialties", along with "free lemons" and recipes – but just "go early", because the "top-quality" offerings are "limited."

Floralies *Flowers* | ∇ 26 | 23 | 24 | E |

E 50s | 122 E. 55th St. (bet. Lexington & Park Aves.) | E/V to Lexington Ave./53rd St. | 212-755-3990 | www.floraliesinc.com

Swank clients like Cartier and Le Bernardin attest to the success of this Murray Hill florist, where owner Kostas creates "unusual" arrangements that are "elegant and stunning without being over-the-top"; he's been in business for nearly a quarter-century now, bringing his "reliably beautiful" touch to parties, weddings and big corporate bashes alike.

Flor de Mayo ● *Prepared Food* | 23 | 14 | 18 | I |

W 80s | 484 Amsterdam Ave. (bet. 83rd & 84th Sts.) | 1 to 86th St. | 212-787-3388

W 100s | 2651 Broadway (101st St.) | 1 to 103rd St. | 212-595-2525

"Moist", "tender" rotisserie chicken is the "flavorful" favorite at these "no-frills" Upper West Side takeouts serving an "interesting" array of Peruvian, Chinese and Cuban fare, though while everything's "well cooked", many just "stick with the Latin food"; it all comes "for a song" and the service is "friendly."

☑ Florence Meat Market ☑ *Meat/Poultry* | 29 | 19 | 28 | M |

G Village | 5 Jones St. (bet. Bleecker & W. 4th Sts.) | 1 to Christopher St. | 212-242-6531

Satisfied surveyors consider this "old-time" (circa 1936), sawdust-sprinkled Village butcher among the "best and nicest in the business", known for "exceptional quality", "unparalleled service" ("they trim, season and tie up a roast to perfection") and "some terrific bargains" – especially on "their famous Newport steak" – along with more "pricey cuts" and game too; "if you need to rustle up an amazing dinner, start here"; N.B. call ahead and pre-order – you may be spared a long "wait."

Flowers by Reuven *Flowers* | - | - | - | E |

Garment Dist | 255 West 36th St., 2nd fl. (bet. 7th & 8th Sts.) | 212-564-4740 | www.flowersbyreuven.net
By appointment only

Now ensconced in a brand new second-floor Garment District studio, floral and event designer Reuven and his staff continue to create the tailor-made arrangements and displays for weddings and dinner parties that have garnered them rave reviews for three decades now; you simply "can't go wrong" according to admirers – who include a sprinkling of celebs and actors – especially given the relatively "fair prices."

Flowers of the World ☑ *Flowers* | ▽ 28 | 29 | 24 | VE |

Financial Dist | 80 Pine St. (bet. Pearl & Water Sts.) | 2/3 to Wall St. | 212-425-2234

W 50s | 150 W. 55th St. (bet. 6th & 7th Aves.) | N/Q/R/W to 57th St. | 212-582-1850

800-582-0428 | www.flowersoftheworld.com

"Walk by and see" the "truly divine displays" of "superb" flowers in the windows of this "innovative" Financial District bloomery and its West 50s offshoot, known for their "breathtaking arrangements"; those who droop over the "insane prices" perk up at the thought of ready-to-go "inexpensive mini-bouquets that are a lifesaver" for the forgetful.

	QUALITY	DISPLAY	SERVICE	COST

Flying Pigs Farm 📧 Meat/Poultry | 28 | 19 | 25 | E |

See Greenmarket; for more information, call 518-854-3844 |
www.flyingpigsfarm.com

Pigs do fly – off the shelves of a Greenmarket booth – in the form of
"consistently outstanding pork" from this upstate farm; among the
"high-quality, natural" "porcine products" are "flavorful" roasts, bacon and sausage ("love the smoked shanks", "superb liverwurst")
while poultry lovers crow FPF's chickens and eggs are "the best
they've ever eaten"; the wares are "certainly not cheap", but "approachable employees" can provide "great recipes" along with the
meat; N.B. open seasonally.

Fong Inn Too Inc. ◐⇩ Specialty Shop | - | - | - | I |

Chinatown | 46 Mott St. (bet. Bayard & Pell Sts.) | 6/J/M/N/Q/R/W/Z to
Canal St. | 212-962-5196

Talk about specialization: this Chinatown food shop sells only 27
products, including "excellent bean curd", soy milk, "fresh rice noodles", "fried taro cakes" and egg roll skins, all at "cheap" prices and
"made on-site"; it's mainly a restaurant supplier, which might explain the sometimes "nonexistent service."

Food Emporium ◐ Major Gourmet Mkt. | 16 | 14 | 12 | M |

E 50s | 405 E. 59th St. (1st Ave.) | 4/5/6 to 59th St./Lexington Ave. |
212-752-5836

E 50s | 969 Second Ave. (51st St.) | 6 to 51st St. | 212-593-2224

E 60s | 1175 Third Ave. (68th St.) | 6 to 68th St. | 212-249-6778

E 80s | 1450 Third Ave. (82nd St.) | 4/5/6 to 86th St. | 212-628-1125

Murray Hill | 200 E. 32nd St. (3rd Ave.) | 6 to 33rd St. | 212-686-0260

TriBeCa | 316 Greenwich St. (Duane St.) | 1 to Franklin St. |
212-766-4598

Union Sq | 10 Union Sq. E. (14th St.) | 4/5/6/L/N/Q/R/W to 14th St./
Union Sq. | 212-353-3840

W 40s | 452 W. 43rd St. (bet. 9th & 10th Aves.) | A/C/E to 42nd St./
Port Authority | 212-714-1414

W 60s | 2008 Broadway (68th St.) | 1/2/3 to 66th St./Lincoln Ctr. |
212-787-0012

W 90s | 2430 Broadway (90th St.) | 1/2/3 to 96th St. | 212-873-4031
www.thefoodemporium.com
Additional locations throughout the NY area

"If the cupboard is bare", this Manhattan-wide franchise serves as
an "all-purpose" "convenience" stocked with a "utilitarian selection" of "standard supermarket" goods; there are efforts afoot for
this chain to go more "gourmet", with the more "upscale"
Bridgemarket emporium below the Queensboro Bridge leading the
way, but fulminating foes still feel they "leave much to be desired"
and come off as "pricey for fairly basic stuff."

Food For Thought Prepared Food | - | - | - | M |

Chelsea | 130 W. 25th St. (bet. 6th & 7th Aves.) | F/V to 23rd St. |
212-929-4689 | www.foodforthoughtnyc.com

Whether it's for a wedding, cocktail party or corporate gala, this
"easy to work with" event planner/caterer is the choice for those
looking for an affordable option; the 7,000-sq.-ft. Chelsea head-

quarters showcases a cafe and tasting room where potential clients can peruse the possibilities.

Foods of India *Herbs/Spices* | 23 | 16 | 17 | I |

Murray Hill | 121 Lexington Ave. (bet. 28th & 29th Sts.) | 6 to 28th St. | 212-683-4419

Chances are you'll find "something wonderful that you have never tried before" at this Murray Hill spice emporium that's a "must-visit" if you're cooking Indian food at home; it's a "very inexpensive" source of a "more than impressive" variety of curry pastes and powders, and "always worth a look" if you're a fan of South Asian flavors.

Foragers Market ▣ *Specialty Shop* | - | - | - | E |

Dumbo | 56 Adams St. (Front St.) | Brooklyn | F to York St. | 718-801-8400 | www.foragersmarket.com

A "well-edited" selection "makes it a pleasure to shop" at this Dumbo market whose "gourmet" goodies – everything from artisanal cheeses and charcuterie to produce and sandwiches – are in keeping with the store's mantra of 'Seasonal, Regional, Organic'; it also strives to be as green as possible in its packaging and operations, so although some dismiss it as "trendy", others say it's a "splendid" choice.

Foremost Caterers ⊄ *Caterer* | 24 | 22 | 22 | VE |

Moonachie | 65 Anderson Ave. (Romeo St.), NJ | 201-664-2465 | www.foremostcaterers.com

For "strictly" glatt kosher catering, consensus calls this firm "the absolute best" at providing "interesting ideas" and food so "fine" you may not "believe that it's kosher"; it's considered "reliable" for events of "any size", from personal gatherings to large-scale dos at Lincoln Center or the United Nations, and boasts a "top-shelf staff" so "attentive" it's "like having your mother plan the party – without the baggage."

NEW Formaggio Essex *Cheese/Dairy*   ▽ | 26 | 22 | 22 | E |

LES | Essex Street Market | 120 Essex St. (bet. Delancey & Rivington Sts.) | 212-982-8200 | www.formaggio-kitchen.com

"The best of Cambridge comes to NYC" via this Essex Street Market arrival, an offshoot of a beloved Boston institution whose "cramped" stall is "easy to miss but worth looking for" given its "small but fantastic" lineup of cheeses, plus "fabulous" salumi, condiments and sandwiches; it's already gained an enthusiastic following, thanks in part to its "friendly", "knowledgeable" staffers – and the "amazing samples" they hand out.

Fortunato Bros. ◗▣⊄ *Baked Goods* | 25 | 23 | 19 | M |

Williamsburg | 289 Manhattan Ave. (Devoe St.) | Brooklyn | L to Graham Ave. | 718-387-2281

A "homey" holdover from pre-hipster days, this "full-service" Italian bakery/sidewalk cafe in Williamsburg can supply "everything your sweet tooth ever desired", ranging from a "nice selection of miniature pastries" and "always-fresh" cookies (the pignoli are "tops") to "heavenly" ricotta cheesecake, spumoni and gelato; order coffee to "give you a boost" and help stave off the sugar shock.

Franchia ● *Coffee/Tea* | 24 | 23 | 22 | M |

Murray Hill | 12 Park Ave. (bet. 34th & 35th Sts.) | 6 to 33rd St. | 212-213-1001 | www.franchia.com

A "serene" scene in Murray Hill, this "exotic Korean tearoom" and "healthy" restaurant is a "Zen-like" retreat serving a profusion of "unusual and delectable" teas (wild green, white, oolong, herbal, et al.) in "lovely" surroundings that mix modern simplicity with a regal ceiling mural and other ornate elements; its gift shop vends loose leaves and accessories like ceramic teasets, and the "cozy" top floor is available for bridal showers and other private affairs.

Frank's *Meat/Poultry* | 24 | 19 | 21 | E |

Chelsea | Chelsea Market | 75 Ninth Ave. (bet. 15th & 16th Sts.) | A/C/E/L to 14th St./8th Ave. | 212-242-1234 | www.franksnyc.com

Fresh, choice cuts of meat are on tempting "display for passersby" at this Chelsea Market retail/wholesale butcher, which takes its name from its parent, the Italian steakhouse in the Meatpacking District; the "endearingly grumpy" counter crew prompts surveyors to quip "the meat is tender, the service is not" while conceding that nevertheless they'll "cut or grind just how you like it."

Frank's Gourmet Market *Specialty Shop* | ▽ 21 | 18 | 17 | M |

Washington Hts | 807 W. 187th St. (bet. Cabrini Blvd. & Ft. Washington) | A to 190th St. | 212-795-2929

This Washington Heights grocery got its start as "a neighborhood butcher shop" nearly 60 years ago and it's since "mushroomed" into a 6,000-sq.-ft. "gourmet" market that retains a "homey atmosphere" to go with its "decent selection" of fish, meats, cheeses and produce as well as a variety of prepared foods; all agree it's convenient "for those who live way Uptown", but opinions diverge when it comes to the prices (moderate vs. "outrageous").

Fraser-Morris Fine Foods *Prepared Food* | – | – | – | VE |

Carroll Gardens | 191 Columbia St. (bet. Degraw & Sackett Sts.) | Brooklyn | F/G to Carroll St. | 718-643-3507

In business since 1947, this bakery/caterer relocated from the Upper East Side to an out-of-the-way corner of Carroll Gardens a few years back, and continues to produce the brownies, muffins, pies, rugalach and such that go into the gift baskets that are its specialty; it also turns out sandwiches and the like, all made on-premises, and patrons can unwind in the cafe area offering a few seats.

Fresco by Scotto on the Go *Prepared Food* | 24 | 19 | 19 | E |

E 50s | 40 E. 52nd St. (bet. Madison & Park Aves.) | E/V to 5th Ave./ 53rd St. | 212-754-2700 | www.frescobyscotto.com

"Media" and "finance" types favor this family-operated Midtown take-out wing of next-door Fresco by Scotto, a provider of "excellent", "gourmet" Italiana, from salads and sandwiches to signature grilled pizzas; it's the "perfect" (albeit "pricey") quick-lunch option, plus partisans praise it as a "first-rate" caterer.

	QUALITY	DISPLAY	SERVICE	COST

Fresh Bites ◗ *Prepared Food* — | - | - | I

W 50s | 1394 Sixth Ave. (57th St.) | N/Q/R/W to 57th St. |
212-245-3327
"Fair" prices and "filling" sandwiches, salads, smoothies and ready-to-heat entrees make this tiny Midtown take-out joint a staple come lunch hour; it's a convenient weekday option for office workers wanting a "quick bite before a stroll through Central Park."

Z Fresh Direct *Major Gourmet Mkt.* — 23 | 14 | 21 | M

LIC | 23-30 Borden Ave. (23rd Ave.) | Queens | 7 to Vernon Blvd. |
866-283-7374 | www.freshdirect.com
A "godsend" for "convenience", this Queens-based "online grocer" allows shoppers to browse its "pain-free" Web site and order an array of "surprisingly high-quality" gourmet goods for "prompt delivery" with "a click of a mouse", offered at "amazing overall value"; customers can count on the "freshest" selection of produce, deli items, "first-rate" "artisanal cheeses", "fabulous" "ready-to-bake breads", "restaurant-quality" prepared foods ("pretend you cooked"), and "reliably" "excellent cuts of meat" and seafood; now that its "growing pains" are "rapidly improving" the "addicted" declare it "sure beats schlepping."

Friend of a Farmer ◗ *Baked Goods* — 21 | 19 | 18 | M

Gramercy | 77 Irving Pl. (bet. 18th & 19th Sts.) | 4/5/6/L/N/Q/R/W to 14th St./Union Sq. | 212-477-2188
Among the "wholesome" baked goods at this Gramercy Park "faux farmhouse" are "tasty muffins and pies" and "hearty scones and cakes" that seemingly "just came out of mom's oven", plus "fresh", "reliable" breads ("excellent honey whole wheat") that'll "cure what ails ya"; the less-impressed cite "overpriced" wares and call this farmer "no friend of mine", but "long waits" prove he's plenty popular.

Gail Watson Custom Cakes ▤ *Baked Goods* — | - | - | VE

Garment Dist | 335 W. 38th St., 11th fl. (8th Ave.) | 212-967-9167 |
877-867-5088 | www.gailwatsoncake.com
By appointment only
Garment District–based wedding cake baker Gail Watson turns out elaborately crafted gâteaux decorated not only with the usual sugar flowers but also with candy sea shells, marzipan and fresh fruits; she's recently extended her offerings to include bridal favors too (e.g. monogrammed cookies, custom candy trays, cast-sugar boxes holding jordan almonds); N.B. for those tying the knot outside of the NYC area, Watson sells 'cake kits' with instructions and tools to pass along to your local baker.

Garden, The *Specialty Shop* ▽ 24 | 21 | 21 | M

Greenpoint | 921 Manhattan Ave. (Kent St.) | Brooklyn | G to Greenpoint Ave. | 718-389-6448 | www.thegardenfoodmarket.com
"A veritable oasis" in Greenpoint, this "organic market" "offers a nice range of upscale natural" products (the beer selection is a particular strength) as well as "scrumptious bakery items" and "tasty"

prepared foods; "Manhattan expats" aver "you can find almost anything here", meaning there's really "no need to go to the city."

Garden of Eden
Gourmet Market ●☑ *Major Gourmet Mkt.*

| 24 | 23 | 19 | E |

Chelsea | 162 W. 23rd St. (bet. 6th & 7th Aves.) | 1 to 23rd St. | 212-675-6300

Union Sq | 7 E. 14th St. (bet. 5th Ave. & University Pl.) | 4/5/6/L/ N/Q/R/W to 14th St./Union Sq. | 212-255-4200

W 100s | 2780 Broadway (107th St.) | 1 to 110th St. | 212-222-7300

Brooklyn Heights | 180 Montague St. (bet. Clinton & Court Sts.) | Brooklyn | 2/3/4/5/M/N/R/W to Borough Hall/Court St. | 718-222-1515

www.edengourmet.com

Paradise if you "want to avoid crowds", this gourmet market foursome fits "everything you need" in the way of "higher-end" goods into its "fairly small shops", harboring a "pretty display" of "above-average" baked goods, a cheese section with "lots of imports", "reliably high-quality produce", "exceptional" meat and poultry and an "amazing selection of hard-to-find" specialty items ("if they don't have it, you don't need it"); despite "high prices", their status as "local favorites" keeps them "hanging in there against the big boys."

Garnet Wines & Liquors ●☑ *Wine/Liquor*

| 24 | 16 | 18 | M |

E 60s | 929 Lexington Ave. (bet. 68th & 69th Sts.) | 6 to 68th St. | 212-772-3211 | www.garnetwine.com

Still the ruby standard for "super prices" on "high- and low-end items" "from around the world", this "well-stocked" Upper East Side "staple" is often "crowded" with bargain-hunters looking for (and finding) the latest and greatest in scotches, champagne and French and Italian wines; one caveat: the staffers, while "knowledgeable", are sometimes "on the brusque side."

Gary Null's Uptown
Whole Foods ● *Health Food*

| 25 | 23 | 21 | E |

(aka Gary Null's Uptown Foods)

W 80s | 2421 Broadway (89th St.) | 1 to 86th St. | 212-874-4000 | www.garysmarketplace.com

Not to be confused with the superstar natural supermarket chain, this more modest but still "wonderful" Upper West Side health-fooder is an "independent" market with a hands-on owner, "knowledgeable" staff and an "abundant variety" of products; still, there are some complaints about the "budget-taxing" prices, "narrow aisles" and "cramped" conditions, not to mention produce whose quality "varies."

Gauchas Empanadas ⊘ *Prepared Food*

| ∇ 25 | 16 | 19 | I |

E 90s | 1748 First Ave. (bet. 90th & 91st Sts.) | 4/5/6 to 86th St. | 212-360-6400

Beloved for its namesake "flaky" "pockets of goodness", this Yorkville shop (with 20 seats) is also applauded for its assortment of Argentinean prepared foods including "flavorful" steaks; this "next best thing to a trip to South America" also has plans in the works for an online store vending Latin American products.

	QUALITY	DISPLAY	SERVICE	COST

Gimme! Coffee 🖿⊄ *Coffee/Tea* ▽ 27 | 22 | 24 | I

Williamsburg | 495 Lorimer St. (bet. Grand & Powers Sts.) | Brooklyn |
L to Lorimer St. | 718-388-7771 | www.gimmecoffee.com

"Plenty of Williamsburg hipsters" caffeinate at this "simple yet excellent coffee shop", the loftlike urban outpost of an Upstate
college-town chain that air-roasts its own beans to give you joe "of
outstanding quality" in a "great variety of blends"; they also decant
"really strong espresso" topped with "cool" crema filigree, and their
global selection is available online in one- or five-pound bags.

Giorgione 508 ◗🖿 *Deli/Sandwich* - | - | - | M

G Village | 508 Greenwich St. (bet. Canal & Spring Sts.) | C/E to
Spring St. | 212-219-2444

Set in a yet-to-be-nicknamed neighborhood between Hudson Street
and the Holland Tunnel, this hip trattoria – an offshoot of owner
Giorgio DeLuca's Italian eatery around the corner – features a small
front gourmet provisions shop showcasing imported and locally
sourced baked goods; other high-end offerings include loose-leaf
teas, oils and vinegars, organic eggs, dried fruit, smoked fish and almost two dozen types of cheese, as well as prepared sandwiches
ideal for carryout.

Glaser's Bake Shop ⊄ *Baked Goods* 21 | 16 | 21 | I

E 80s | 1670 First Ave. (bet. 87th & 88th Sts.) | 4/5/6 to 86th St. |
212-289-2562 | www.glasersbakeshop.com

"Old Yorkville lives" at this "no-frills" "time capsule", "family-run"
since 1902 and still boasting "original tile floors and wooden display
cases" brimming with Mitteleuropean desserts that "don't break the
bank"; "loyal customers" love what they consider NYC's "best black-
and-whites", as well as "delicious rolls", "great Danish", butter
cookies and "wonderful" apple turnovers" – and find the staff's
"warm" welcomes as "comforting" as the "baked treats."

Glazier Group on Location *Caterer* - | - | - | E

G Village | Twenty Four Fifth | 24 Fifth Ave. (bet. 8th & 9th Sts.) | R/W to
8th St. | 212-505-8000
Seaport | Bridgewaters | 11 Fulton St. (bet. East River Piers &
Seaport Plaza) | 2/3 to Fulton St. | 212-608-7400
www.theglaziergroup.com

As a "sizable" "player" in the "field of restaurant-backed catering",
this Downtown outfit produces "beautifully done" events at eateries
like the Strip House and Michael Jordan's The Steak House, as well
as major venues like Bridgewaters and Twenty Four Fifth; matching
up stylish spaces, pro service and classic American cuisine, it's considered by those in-the-know as "one of the best" in its "niche."

🇿 Glorious Food *Caterer* 25 | 25 | 24 | VE

E 70s | 504 E. 74th St. (bet. East River & York Ave.) | 6 to 77th St. |
212-628-2320 | www.gloriousfood.com

"They'll go over the top for you" at this "premier" UES caterer, which
"knows every trick in the book" about "making an event special", from
"elegant" and "tasty" cuisine to "the fanciest" presentation ("they're

not called 'glorious' for nothing"); the "superb" staff includes "the best-looking waiters in town" and leaves "no detail overlooked", whether the occasion's a "dinner for 12" or a mega institutional affair, so though most "wouldn't call it a bargain", "you get what you pay for."

Godiva Chocolatier ⌨ *Candy/Nuts* | 22 | 24 | 20 | E |

E 40s | Grand Central Terminal | main concourse (42nd St. & Vanderbilt Ave.) | 4/5/6/7/S to 42nd St./Grand Central | 212-808-0276
E 50s | 560 Lexington Ave. (bet. 50th & 51st Sts.) | 6 to 51st St. | 212-980-9810
E 60s | 793 Madison Ave. (67th St.) | 6 to 68th St. | 212-249-9444
Financial Dist | 21 Fulton St. (South St.) | J/M/Z to Fulton St. | 212-571-6965 ●
Financial Dist | 33 Maiden Ln. (Nassau St.) | J/M/Z to Fulton St. | 212-809-8990
W 40s | 1460 Broadway (bet. 41st & 42nd Sts.) | 1/2/3/7/N/Q/R/S/W to 42nd St./Times Sq. | 212-840-6758
W 40s | 30 Rockefeller Plaza, concourse level (bet. 49th & 50th Sts.) | B/D/F/V to 47-50th Sts./Rockefeller Ctr. | 212-246-0346
W 50s | Shops at Columbus Circle | 10 Columbus Circle (bet. 58th & 60th Sts.) | 1/A/B/C/D to 59th St./Columbus Circle | 212-823-9462 ●
W 50s | 52 W. 50th St. (bet. 5th & 6th Aves.) | B/D/F/V to 47-50th Sts./Rockefeller Ctr. | 212-399-1875
W 70s | 245 Columbus Ave. (bet. 71st & 72nd Sts.) | B/C to 72nd St. | 212-787-5804 ●
800-946-3482 | www.godiva.com
Additional locations throughout the NY area

This bonbon behemoth's "reliable", "verrry smooth" morsels packed in that trademark "fancy gold box" guaranteed to "light up faces" make it a "popular" "favorite" among "mass-market" contenders; however, the less-impressed call it the "Campbell's Soup of Belgian chocolate", citing "waxy", "too-sweet" output that doesn't measure up to the city's burgeoning "boutique" producers', but even critics concede the "convenience" of its ubiquitous "golden storefronts" is hard to beat when "you need a quick gift."

Golden Fung Wong
Bakery Shop ●⊄ *Baked Goods* | 18 | 12 | 14 | I |

Chinatown | 41 Mott St. (Pell St.) | 6/J/M/N/Q/R/W/Z to Canal St. | 212-267-4037

"Traditional Chinese wedding pastries", "delicious BBQ pork buns", "airy sponge cakes", mooncakes and – yes – fortune cookies have made this small Chinatown bakery a "longtime staple" for its loyal fan base; however, trendier types would like to see the "old-style" setting get an "upgrade."

Good & Plenty To Go *Prepared Food* | 22 | 19 | 19 | M |

W 40s | 410 W. 43rd St. (bet. 9th & 10th Aves.) | A/C/E to 42nd St./Port Authority | 212-268-4385

"The name says it all" at this "friendly", "tiny" Theater District take-out shop in the Manhattan Plaza complex, where regulars fight "maddening crowds" at lunch for the likes of bourbon-glazed ham, jambalaya, peanut-butter brownies and plenty of other "reliably good" comfort dishes; overall, it's a "real standout – if you can find it."

Gorilla Coffee ●◑ ▣ *Coffee/Tea* | 24 | 17 | 19 | I |

Park Slope | 97 Fifth Ave. (Park Pl.) | Brooklyn | 2/3 to Bergen St. | 718-230-3243 | www.gorillacoffee.com

"Ggrrrrrr": if you're "looking for a robust brew", this Park Slope "neighborhood hang" doesn't monkey around as it supplies "rich, organic Fair Trade coffee" (house-roasted "in small batches") and "nuclear-powered espresso", matched with ape-pealing baked goods; the "cool employees" and "funky, relaxed" vibe are a "perfect fit" for the "requisite Brooklyn hipsters" in residence, who'd "die without" "a jolt" to "start off the day."

Gorzynski Ornery Farm ⌗ *Produce* | 27 | 22 | 27 | M |

See Greenmarket; for more information, call 845-252-7570

"As good as it gets" – "from arugula" to "root veggies" – is how exuberant herbivores describe the goods from this "quintessential Greenmarket stand", where the "tremendously wide range" of "100-percent organic" produce is overseen by "genius" Upstate farmer John Gorzynski ("no 'ornery' guy"), who can always advise you on "how to cook the weird vegetable you're waving" around; the offerings "may seem expensive" but for the "taste and freshness" they're "well-worth the price."

Gotham Gardens ▣ *Flowers* | ▽ 24 | 25 | 23 | E |

W 70s | 325 Amsterdam Ave. (bet. 75th & 76th Sts.) | 1/2/3 to 72nd St. | 212-877-8908 | www.gothamgardens.com

"Otherworldly" is how Upper Westsiders describe the "exquisite", "excitingly different arrangements" that "often incorporate the unexpected" at this "dependable" floral boutique; exotic plants plus "a selection of unusual objects" like imported vases, potpourri, candles, soaps and such help "make it a favorite" for gift-buyers, while brides-to-be and party-throwers can enlist full-service decor design.

Gotham Wines & Liquors ●▣ *Wine/Liquor* | 22 | 17 | 18 | M |

W 90s | 2517 Broadway (94th St.) | 1/2/3 to 96th St. | 212-932-0990 | www.gothamwines.com

"Prices that can't be beat" keep "bargain-hunters" and others "coming back" to this Upper West Side "neighborhood" wine stop that's extolled for its offerings in the under-$15 range, as well as for its "great" variety (some 300) of kosher wines; backers believe the "inventory is worth" putting up with the somewhat "insular" service; P.S. "get on the mailing list for additional discounts."

Gourmet Garage ● *Major Gourmet Mkt.* | 20 | 17 | 15 | M |

E 60s | 301 E. 64th St. (bet. 1st & 2nd Aves.) | F to Lexington Ave./ 63rd St. | 212-535-6271

E 90s | 1245 Park Ave. (96th St.) | 6 to 96th St. | 212-348-5850

G Village | 117 Seventh Ave. S. (bet. Christopher & W. 10th Sts.) | 1 to Christopher St. | 212-699-5980

(continued)

(continued)

Gourmet Garage

SoHo | 453 Broome St. (Mercer St.) | 6 to Spring St. |
212-941-5850

W 90s | 2567 Broadway (96th St.) | 1/2/3 to 96th St. |
212-663-0656

www.gourmetgarage.com

Shoppers "in a hurry" who pull in to this "solid" mini-chain discover a "less-crowded alternative" that "hits on the major categories" of "gourmet goodies" with its "interesting selection" of cheeses, "decent baked goods", "healthy" prepared foods, "creative" deli counter and even "surprisingly good coffee"; but in spite of "generally" "high quality", naysayers are "not impressed" with what they consider a "limited" lineup that "certainly isn't cheap."

Grab Specialty Foods *Specialty Shop*   – | – | – | E

Park Slope | 438 Seventh Ave. (bet. 14th & 15th Sts.) | Brooklyn | F to 7th Ave. | 718-369-7595

In the space that briefly housed an outpost of Blue Apron Foods, this bite-size shop is "much-needed" in its somewhat underserved corner of Park Slope, supplying the locals with artisanal cheeses and charcuterie, baked goods (including loaves from Amy's Bread and cupcakes from Baked), produce and bottled and jarred items like vinegars, oils and jams; it's also a good choice for picking up a gift (think: cheese boards, knives, picnic supplies), and they will also put together custom baskets.

Grace's Marketplace ●▣ *Major Gourmet Mkt.* 24 | 20 | 18 | VE

E 70s | 1237 Third Ave. (71st St.) | 6 to 68th St. | 212-737-0600 |
www.gracesmarketplace.com

Lucky "locals" who "don't want to travel" "could happily spend all day" at this "friendly" Eastsider, "one of the original NYC gourmet markets" and still a "winner" whose "narrow aisles" are graced with "basically everything you could possibly need", including "highly praised" baked goods, "fresh produce", "prime meats", a "wide selection" of cheeses and "top-notch" deli items and prepared foods ("who needs to cook?"); a few fret that it's "expensive" and "too cramped for comfort", but consensus says the "excellent quality", "convenience" and "eternally cheerful service" are "totally worth it."

Gracious Home ▣ *Cookware*   25 | 18 | 19 | E

E 70s | 1217-1220 Third Ave. (70th St.) | 6 to 68th St. |
212-517-6300

W 60s | 1992 Broadway (67th St.) | 1 to 66th St./Lincoln Ctr. |
212-231-7800 ●

800-338-7809 | www.gracioushome.com

"A NYC institution", this "dependable" duo is an Uptown "favorite" for its kitchen sections' "amazing array" of cookware, appliances, utensils and accessories, "basic" to "high-end", all at "un-gracious" prices that have some warning "better get a second mortgage"; service from the "knowledgeable" staff can be "spotty", and its "narrow aisles" try some surveyors' patience, but nonetheless it remains a

	QUALITY	DISPLAY	SERVICE	COST

"favorite" "one-stop" source "for almost anything"; N.B. they now charge $6.50 for delivery.

Gracious Thyme Catering *Caterer*

	–	–	–	E

Harlem | 2191 Third Ave. (bet. 119th & 120th Sts.) | 6 to 116th St. | 212-873-1965 | www.graciousthyme.com

Classic French cuisine inspires the "elegant array of dishes" from this Harlem-based "full-service caterer" and off-site event planner, whose "superb food" is "presented beautifully" enough to do justice to a reception at the Whitney or a U.N. state dinner; also "a delight" is the "extremely gracious staff", which goes all-out to turn festivities of any size into a "wonderful" thyme.

Gramercy Fish *Seafood*

	24	20	22	E

Gramercy | 383 Second Ave. (bet. 22nd & 23rd Sts.) | 6 to 23rd St. | 212-213-5557

There's "always a catch" at this "terrific" Gramercy fishmonger, but of the "flavorful, succulent" variety – i.e. "sparklingly fresh" seafood and "homemade" prepared dishes; "accoutrements such as sauces and produce" and a "helpful" staff are other reasons it's a "go-to" for locals, who agree that "for a tiny place, it delivers" – but "at a high price."

NEW Grandaisy Bakery *Baked Goods*

	29	21	20	M

SoHo | 73 Sullivan St. (bet. Broome & Spring Sts.) | C/E to Spring St. | 212-334-9435 | www.grandaisybakery.com

It goes by a new name after a recent ownership split, but otherwise "nothing's changed" at this "small" SoHo Italian bakery (formerly the original branch of Sullivan St. Bakery), whose "to-die-for" artisanal breads are voted "the best in the city"; some say "pane pugliese and filore are the two best loaves", but it's hard to pick favorites among its "unforgettable" offerings from flatbreads and focaccialike pizzas to panini and sweets; given such "fresh, wonderful" goods, no one minds much if the service "can be lacking" and the decor's "nothing fancy."

Grande Harvest Wines ● *Wine/Liquor*

	23	21	21	E

E 40s | Grand Central Terminal | main concourse (42nd St. & Vanderbilt Ave.) | 4/5/6/7/S to 42nd St./Grand Central | 212-682-5855 | www.ghwines.com

Commuters browse the "attractive displays" then "grab a bottle" before boarding at this Grand Central wine boutique that's an on-the-go oenophile's "delight" given its "limited but decent" selections from France and California as well as its strong showing of single-malt scotches; the staff "impresses", but know that the "handy" location translates to "expensive" prices.

Grand Wine & Liquor ●⌨ *Wine/Liquor*

	▽ 25	17	17	I

Astoria | 30-05 31st St. (30th Ave.) | Queens | N/W to 30th Ave. | 718-728-2520 | www.grandwl.com

"If you can't find it here, it's probably discontinued or doesn't exist" say fans of this "great" Astoria source of unusual wines from Greece, Eastern Europe, Asia and even Peru; low prices and proximity to the N train compensate nonlocals who make the trek to Queens; N.B. they deliver to Manhattan on Saturday mornings.

	QUALITY	DISPLAY	SERVICE	COST

Great Performances *Caterer*

| 24 | 23 | 22 | VE |

SoHo | 304 Hudson St. (Spring St.) | C/E to Spring St. | 212-727-2424 | www.greatperformances.com

A "very professional" performer after nearly 30 years in the business, this SoHo caterer/event planner is "one of the best" at staging indoor or outdoor affairs – often on an epic scale – with "attentive" service and "fantastic food"; it boasts in-house contracts with the Asia Society, BAM, Sotheby's and numerous other notables, though a few razz the "commercial" style of so "big an operation"; P.S. it now has its own organic farm upstate, intended to supply pristine produce to be used in its "fabulous" fare.

Greene Grape, The ● *Wine/Liquor*

| 24 | 23 | 24 | M |

Financial Dist | 55 Liberty St. (bet. B'way & Nassau St.) | J/M/Z to Fulton St. | 212-406-9463
Fort Greene | 765 Fulton St. (bet. S. Oxford & S. Portland Sts.) | Brooklyn | C to Lafayette Ave. | 718-797-9463
www.greenegrape.com

These separately owned wine sources are run by "committed" staffers who impart advice on the "outstanding" examples of low-production labels; the larger Fort Greene original is "great", while lower Manhattanites rate the Financial District spot a "godsend" in a neighborhood "bereft of similar shops"; partisans can pick up some "incredible" boutique spirits at either location.

⬛ Greenmarket *Produce*

| 26 | 23 | 23 | M |

E 40s | Dag Hammarskjold Plaza | 2nd Ave. & 47th St. | Wed., Year-round
E 80s | St. Stephens | E. 82nd St. bet. 1st. & York Aves. | Sat., July–Nov.
E 90s | 92nd St. | 1st Ave. bet. 92nd & 93rd Sts. | Sun., July–Nov.
E 90s | Mt. Sinai Hospital | E. 99th St. bet. Madison & Park Aves. | Fri., July–Nov.
E Village | St. Mark's Church | 2nd Ave. & 10th St. | Tues., June–Dec.
E Village | Tompkins Sq. | Ave. A & 7th St. | Sun., Year-round
Financial Dist | Bowling Green | Battery Pl. & B'way | Tues./Thu., Year-round
Financial Dist | Downtown Path | Church & Vesey Sts. | Tues./Thurs., April–Dec.
Harlem | Harlem Hospital | Lenox Ave. bet 136th & 137th Sts. | Thurs., July–Nov.
Murray Hill | 2nd Ave. & 33rd St. | Sat., June–Dec.
TriBeCa | City Hall Park | B'way bet. Chambers & Warren Sts.
TriBeCa | Greenwich St. bet. Chambers & Duane Sts. | Wed., Apr.–Dec.; Sat., Year-round
Union Sq | Union Sq. | B'way & 17th St. | Mon./Wed./Fri./Sat., Year-round
Inwood | Isham St. bet. Cooper St. & Seaman Ave. | Sat., Year-round
Washington Hts | 175th St. | B'way & 175th St. | Thurs.; June–Nov.
W 50s | Rockefeller Ctr. | 50th St. & Rockefeller Plaza | Thur./Fri./Sat., July–Aug.
W 50s | 57th St. | 57th St. & 9th Ave. | Wed., Apr.–Dec.; Sat., Year-round
W 60s | Tucker Sq. | Columbus Ave. & 66th St. | Thurs./Sat., Year-round

(continued)

Greenmarket

W 70s | 77th St. | Columbus Ave. & 77th St. | Sun., Year-round

W 90s | 97th St. | Columbus Ave. & 97th St. | Fri., Year-round

W 100s | Columbia | B'way bet. 114th & 115th Sts. | Thurs./Sun., Year-round

W 100s | Stranger's Gate | Central Park W. & 106th St. | Sat., July–Nov.

W Village | Abingdon Sq. | Hudson & 12th Sts. | Sat., Year-round

Bronx | Poe Park | Grand Concourse & 192nd St. | Tues., July–Nov.

Bronx | Bronx Borough Hall | Grand Concourse bet. 156th & 158th Sts. | Tues., July–Nov.

Bronx | Lincoln Hospital | Morris Ave. & 148th St. | Tues./Fri., July–Nov.

Borough Park | 14th Ave. bet. 49th & 50th Sts. | Brooklyn | Thurs., July–Nov.

Downtown | Borough Hall | Court & Montague Sts. | Brooklyn | Tues./Sat., Year-round; Thurs., Apr.–Dec.

Flatbush | P.S. 139 Schoolyard | Beverly & Cortelyou Rds. | Brooklyn | Sat., June–Nov.

Fort Greene | Fort Greene Park | Washington Park bet. Dekalb Ave. & Willoughby St. | Brooklyn | Sat., Year-round

Greenpoint | McCarren Park | Driggs Ave. & Lorimer St. | Brooklyn | Sat., Year-round

Park Slope | Grand Army Plaza | Prospect Park, NW entrance | Brooklyn | Sat., Year-round

Sunset Pk | 4th Ave. bet. 59th & 60th Sts. | Brooklyn | Sat., July–Nov.

Williamsburg | B'way & Havemeyer St. | Brooklyn | Thurs., July–Nov.

Windsor Terr | 15th St. & Prospect Park W. | Brooklyn | Wed., May–Oct.

Astoria | 31st Ave. bet. 12th & 14th Sts. | Queens | Wed., July–Nov.

Glendale | Atlas Park | Cooper Ave. & 80th St. | Queens | Sat., June–Nov.

Jackson Hts | 34th Ave. bet. 77th & 78th Sts. | Queens | Sun., May–Nov.

LIC | 48th Ave. & Vernon Blvd. | Queens | Sat., May–Nov.

Staten Island | St. George at Borough Hall | Hyatt & St. Mark's Sts. | Sat., May–Nov. (inside parking lot)

212-788-7476 | www.cenyc.org

"One of the best things to have happened in NYC", this "wonderful" network of markets throughout the five boroughs ("Union Square is the biggest") gives top chefs, gourmands and the "think-globally, eat-locally" set the chance to select from "flowers and fruits piled high" plus regional produce "picked that day" – all the "finest, from farmer to consumer" – as well as "fresh" meats, seafood, cheese, baked goods, jams and other "seasonal goodies"; indeed, it's a veritable "feast for the eyes and palate" – "what would NYers do without it?"

Greenwich Produce ❷ *Produce*

| 25 | 23 | 20 | E |

E 40s | Grand Central Mkt. | Lexington Ave. (43rd St.) | 4/5/6/7/S to 42nd St./Grand Central | 212-490-4444

With an "extra-convenient" location in two booths at opposite ends of Grand Central Market, this produce purveyor "makes waiting for the train a pleasure" as you "pick up last-minute fruit and vegetable needs" or restock your pantry with "gourmet items" like dried nuts, mushrooms and edible flowers; sure, "prices can be high, but the quality lives up to what you pay."

NEW Grom ● *Ice Cream* — | — | — | E

W 70s | 2165 Broadway (bet. 76th & 77th Sts.) | 1 to 79th St. | 646-290-7233 | www.grom.it

Newly opened on the Upper West Side, this first U.S. branch of an Italian chain already has lines out the door for its artisanal gelati, sorbets and granitas made on the premises with all-natural, highest-quality ingredients, including lemons imported from Sicily and pistachios from the Piedmont; regulars more accustomed to the likes of Baskin-Robbins may raise an eyebrow at its prices – cones top out at $9 for an extra-large – but then those 31 flavors never included seasonal fruits or chips made from Ecuadorian chocolate.

G.S. Food Market ⊄ *Seafood* ▽ 19 | 18 | 13 | M

Chinatown | 250 Grand St. (Chrystie St.) | B/D to Grand St. | 212-274-0990

'G.S.' could stand for "good selection" at this Chinatown grocery/seafood market stocking unusual fruits and veggies – durians to mangosteens – an array of fresh and frozen fin fare, noodles, sauces and sundries that make its aisles "so much fun to walk through"; prices that "beat the supermarkets" are another reason most conclude it's "worth the visit", notwithstanding the staff's limited English.

Güllüoglu ▣ *Baked Goods* — | — | — | I

Sheepshead Bay | 1985 Coney Island Ave. (bet. Ave. P & Kings Hwy.) | Brooklyn | B/Q to Kings Hwy. | 718-645-1822 | www.gulluogluusa.com

Straight out of Istanbul comes this homey-looking Sheepshead Bay branch of a 130-year-old Turkish dessert company, which specializes in honey-drenched baklava in its many shapes and permutations (with or without cream, walnuts, etc.); there are also savory treats like filo layered with spinach or kashkaval cheese, poppy-seed pastries and, naturally, thick Turkish coffee (by the cup only).

Guy & Gallard *Coffee/Tea* 20 | 17 | 17 | M

Garment Dist | 1001 Sixth Ave. (bet. 37th & 38th Sts.) | 1/2/3/A/C/E to 34th St./Penn Station | 212-730-0010

Garment Dist | 245 W. 38th St. (bet. 7th & 8th Aves.) | A/C/E to 42nd St./Port Authority | 212-302-7588

Garment Dist | 339 Seventh Ave. (29th St.) | 1 to 28th St. | 212-279-7373

Garment Dist | 469 Seventh Ave. (bet. 35th & 36th Sts.) | 1/2/3/A/C/E to 34th St./Penn Station | 212-695-0006

Murray Hill | 120 E. 34th St. (Lexington Ave.) | 6 to 33rd St. | 212-684-3898 ●

Murray Hill | 180 Madison Ave. (34th St.) | 6 to 33rd St. | 212-725-2392

Murray Hill | 475 Park Ave. S. (bet. 31st & 32nd Sts.) | 6 to 33rd St. | 212-447-5282

www.guyandgallard.com

Granted, "there are better" coffees and teas in town, but this local chain is always there for a "quick" "caffeine jolt" if you're "grabbing early-morning" joe "to go", and it follows through with "light lunch" fare like sandwiches, salads, bagels and baked goods; naysayers are galled at the "movie-theater prices", but most maintain these guys "can definitely compete."

	QUALITY	DISPLAY	SERVICE	COST

Häagen Dazs ● *Ice Cream* | 24 | 18 | 17 | M |

Chinatown | 53½ Mott St. (Bayard St.) | A/C/E to Canal St. | 212-571-1970 ⊟

E 60s | 1188 First Ave. (bet. 64th & 65th Sts.) | 6 to 68th St. | 212-288-5200

Garment Dist | Penn Station | 110 Penn Plaza (32nd St.) | 1/2/3/A/C/E to 34th St./Penn Station | 212-630-0321 ⊟

NoHo | 655 Broadway (bet. Bleecker & Bond Sts.) | B/D/F/V to B'way/Lafayette St. | 212-260-8490

Seaport | South St. Seaport | 89 South St. (Fulton St.) | 2/3 to Fulton St. | 212-587-5335

W 60s | 187 Columbus Ave. (bet. 68th & 69th Sts.) | 1 to 66th St./ Lincoln Ctr. | 212-787-0265

W 70s | 263 Amsterdam Ave. (72nd St.) | 1/2/3 to 72nd St. | 212-787-7165

W 100s | 2905 Broadway (113th St.) | 1 to 116th St. | 212-662-5265

www.haagendazs.com

A "delicious and reliable standby", this national chain's "classic", "rich" ice cream comes in "sinfully decadent" flavors that are "packed with luscious calories"; wallet-watchers, miffed by "small portions" and "not-so-friendly" service, point out that "you can buy a pint cheaper at the supermarket", but for many it's "always a treat" on a "summer day in the hot city."

Haas Company Inc. ▣ *Cookware* | - | - | - | M |

Chelsea | 11 W. 25th St. (5th Ave.) | R/W to 23rd St. | 212-242-2044

The few surveyors who know it "love" this Chelsea cookware store favored by "professional chefs", which specializes in hard-to-find items as well as products by All-Clad, Kyocera and Epicurean; it's a "great place to browse" for "bargains", but just remember it's closed on weekends.

Hale & Hearty Soups ⊟ *Soup* | 22 | 17 | 17 | M |

Chelsea | Chelsea Mkt. | 75 Ninth Ave. (bet. 15th & 16th Sts.) | A/C/E/L to 14th St./8th Ave. | 212-255-2400

E 40s | 22 E. 47th St. (bet. 5th & Madison Aves.) | 4/5/6/7/S to 42nd St./Grand Central | 212-557-1900

E 40s | 466 Lexington Ave. (45th St.) | 4/5/6/7/S to 42nd St./ Grand Central | 212-599-7220

E 40s | 685 Third Ave. (bet. 43rd & 44th Sts.) | 4/5/6/7/S to 42nd St./ Grand Central | 212-681-6460

E 60s | 849 Lexington Ave. (bet. 64th & 65th Sts.) | 6 to 68th St. | 212-517-7600

Garment Dist | 462 Seventh Ave. (35th St.) | 1/2/3/A/C/E to 34th St./ Penn Station | 212-971-0605

W 40s | 49 W. 42nd St. (bet. 5th & 6th Aves.) | 7/B/D/F/V to 42nd St./ Bryant Park | 212-575-9090

W 50s | 30 Rockefeller Plaza, dining concourse (bet. 49th & 50th Sts.) | B/D/F/V to 47-50th Sts./Rockefeller Ctr. | 212-265-2117

W 50s | 55 W. 56th St. (bet. 5th & 6th Aves.) | N/Q/R/W to 57th St. | 212-245-9200

(continued)

(continued)
Hale & Hearty Soups

Brooklyn Heights | 32 Court St. (Remsen St.) | Brooklyn |
2/3/4/5/M/N/R/W to Borough Hall/Court St. | 718-596-5600
www.haleandhearty.com
Additional locations throughout the NY area

"Take stock" of the "wide variety" of "enticing" soups that "rotate often" at this "reliable" if "pricey" chain that also earns souperlatives for "fresh" salads and "unique sandwiches"; those with special diets laud the "handy ingredients lists", and, despite the "boot camp–style queue system and yelling staff", it's the "favorite stop" of many "on a cold, wintry day."

Hampton Chutney Company ● *Prepared Food*

23 | 18 | 19 | M

SoHo | 68 Prince St. (bet. Crosby & Lafayette Sts.) | C/E to Spring St. |
212-226-9996
W 80s | 464 Amsterdam Ave. (bet. 82nd & 83rd Sts.) | 1 to 86th St. |
212-362-5050
www.hamptonchutney.com

"Completely delicious" dosas and trademark housemade chutneys mean seats "are hard to come by" at this twosome serving "tasty" "spins" on traditional Indian offerings along with more authentic examples; "models flock" to the SoHo outpost, while the UWS site tends to be "overrun with children" thanks to the store's kiddie corner.

Han Ah Reum Market ● *Specialty Shop*

22 | 13 | 11 | M

Garment Dist | 25 W. 32nd St. (bet. 5th & 6th Aves.) | B/D/F/N/Q/R/V/W to 34th St./Herald Sq. | 212-695-3283 🖃
Flushing | 141-40 Northern Blvd. (Bowne St.) | Queens | 7 to Flushing-Main St. | 718-358-0700
Flushing | 156-40 Northern Blvd. (Roosevelt Ave.) | Queens | 7 to Flushing-Main St. | 718-888-0005
Flushing | 29-02 Union St. (29th Ave.) | Queens | 7 to Flushing-Main St. | 718-445-5656
www.hanahreum.com

"There's something for everyone" at this quartet of Korean specialty markets (one in the Garment District and three in Flushing) where "just walking through" the "endless array of products, logically arranged" – it's "tops for fish", "fresh fruits and veggies" – is enough to "inspire a non-cook to start"; it's "not always user-friendly" but the "prices are right."

H & H Bagels ●∌ *Bagels*

26 | 15 | 17 | M

W 40s | 639 W. 46th St. (12th Ave.) | A/C/E to 42nd St./Port Authority |
212-595-8000
W 80s | 2239 Broadway (80th St.) | 1 to 79th St. | 212-595-8003
800-692-2435 | www.hhbagels.com

"Iconic bagels" earn these West Side "mainstays" their "well-deserved" rep as a "benchmark" for "fat", "perfectly crafted" rings with "just the right consistency" to be "addictive", served "hot from the ovens" "round the clock"; despite "sparse shops" with "no seating" and "DIY toppings", the multitudes gladly "pony up" "premium prices" (approaching "a buck" a pop) 'cause this is what "makes living in NYC a privilege"; P.S. to avoid "frustrating lines" hit the 46th Street outpost, an "easy" hop "off the West Side Highway."

H & H Midtown Bagels East ●▤ *Bagels* | 25 | 17 | 19 | I |

E 80s | 1551 Second Ave. (bet. 80th & 81st Sts.) | 4/5/6 to 86th St. | 212-734-7441 | www.hhmidtownbagelseast.com

"Off-the-hook" bagels – "big and chewy" but "crisp on the outside" – are dispensed by a "friendly" crew at this 24/7 eatery/caterer, which, as the "sign out front states", has no tie to its crosstown competitor; it's a "madhouse on weekends" and some say prices are "through the roof" for the genre, but most don't mind much given its spheres rated among "the best on the UES."

Harlem Tea Room *Coffee/Tea* | 25 | 23 | 23 | M |

Harlem | 1793 Madison Ave. (bet. E. 117th & 118th Sts.) | 6 to 116 St. | 212-348-3471 | www.harlemtearoom.com

"You'll want to stay all day" at this petite tearoom, a "low-profile" "gem in Harlem" where the plush drapes and "classy" copper-top bar create a "warm vibe" for enjoying an intriguing international choice of stepped brews, with "mouthwatering" cakes and tarts on the side; to confirm it's "a real find", check out the "wonderful" spread of scones, sandwiches and desserts during Saturday afternoon's "high tea."

Harlem Vintage ●◷▤ *Wine/Liquor* | ▽ 28 | 29 | 26 | M |

Harlem | 2235 Frederick Douglass Blvd. (bet. 120th & 121st Sts.) | A/B/C/D to 125th St. | 212-866-9463 | www.harlemvintage.com

"Well worth the trip Uptown", this "superior" Harlem "jewel" of a wine shop spotlights its selections in a "lovely room" and boasts a "knowledgeable" staff and "fabulous" Saturday tastings; small producers (as well as labels by vintners of color) are its specialty, and the offerings are so "wonderful", even if it had "neighborhood competition", most would still consider it "not to be missed."

Hawthorne Valley Farm *Produce* | 28 | 23 | 25 | M |

See Greenmarket; for more information, call 518-672-7500 ext. 250

There's "no need to venture into Whole Foods" when this Greenmarket stall (by way of a community-supported farm in Columbia County) offers its own array of "excellent" organic and biodynamic foods, from "fresh produce" to "great dairy products" – particularly the "luscious yogurt" – grass-fed beef and pork and baked goods that are tasty, if "a little hippie-ish"; don't overlook the eight different kinds of sauerkraut and other fermented delights – their "version of kimchi is fun."

Health & Harmony ●◷▤ *Health Food* | ▽ 26 | 20 | 22 | M |

W Village | 470 Hudson St. (bet. Barrow & Grove Sts.) | 1 to Christopher St. | 212-691-3036

It might be small, but this West Village health shop has an "excellent selection of healthy foods of all types", including vegan options, sugar-free baked goods and Atkins fare, though the produce section is "somewhat limited"; the "attentive" and "helpful" staff – including the resident dietician – can guide you through the "wide variety of products", some of which can be hard to find elsewhere.

Health Nuts ●🖙 Health Food   21 | 14 | 18 | M

E 40s | 835 Second Ave. (bet. 44th & 45th Sts.) | 4/5/6/7/S to 42nd St./ Grand Central | 212-490-2979

E 60s | 1208 Second Ave. (bet. 63rd & 64th Sts.) | F to Lexington Ave./63rd St. | 212-593-0116

W 70s | 2141 Broadway (bet. 75th & 76th Sts.) | 1/2/3 to 72nd St. | 212-724-1972

W 90s | 2611 Broadway (bet. 98th & 99th Sts.) | 1/2/3 to 96th St. | 212-678-0054

Bayside | Bay Terrace | 211-35 26th Ave. (Bell Blvd.) | Queens | 718-225-8164

"Just be careful you don't knock something over" in this chain of stuffed-to-the-gills health food markets, where you "can always find what you need", even if it means digging through some "confusing" displays; while some feel "produce is not its forte", most find it a "reliable" source for "competitively priced" "healthy dry goods."

Heights Chateau ● Wine/Liquor   25 | 24 | 23 | M

Brooklyn Heights | 123 Atlantic Ave. (bet. Clinton & Henry Sts.) | Brooklyn | 2/3/4/5/M/N/R/W to Borough Hall/Court St. | 718-330-0963 | www.heightschateau.com

Brooklyn Heights wine enthusiasts find it easy to "treasure" this "neighborhood" standby whose "spirited" staff dispenses "wonderful advice" on any of its 2,000 labels (plus a bountiful array of tequilas and single-malt scotches); not only can you expect to walk away with the "perfect" bottle "to suit your budget", but their case discounts can make for "real bargains."

Heights Prime Meats 🖙 Meat/Poultry   ▽ 24 | 15 | 21 | E

Brooklyn Heights | 59 Clark St. (bet. Henry & Hicks Sts.) | Brooklyn | 2/3 to Clark St. | 718-237-0133

Locals rely on this recently renovated Brooklyn Heights butcher and deli for a variety of fresh and aged prime meats, poultry (including some organic birds) and sausages, as well as prepared offerings like hot rotisserie chicken and "tasty sandwiches"; overall, "you'll find what you need" and the quality's "good across the board", so most are willing to stomach the "$$$" prices.

Hendricks Wine & Liquors ● Wine/   - | - | - | M
Liquor

Bay Ridge | 7624 Third Ave. (77th St.) | Brooklyn | R to 77th St. | 718-748-1690

Since 1935, this Bay Ridge boozery has offered a "great selection" of traditional liquors, with a focus on whiskeys, cognacs, bourbons and vodkas; for serious oenophiles, its "friendly" owner scouts out hard-to-find wines and boutique vintages, with a more general focus on bottles from LI and NY State, Greece, Spain, Australia and South America – 3,000 labels in all, even though the "store's not very big."

	QUALITY	DISPLAY	SERVICE	COST

Hershey's Times Square ◐ ▱ *Candy/Nuts*

	–	–	–	M

W 40s | 1593 Broadway (48th St.) | N/R/W to 49th St. | 212-581-9100 | 800-454-7737 | www.hersheys.com

On a scale that befits an American icon, this Hershey Co. outlet sports a 215-ft.-tall, Vegas-like facade (the largest in Times Square) whose high-watt signage features 3-D props, steam machines and neon; inside, not surprisingly there are more than a few tourists snapping up T-shirts and souvenirs, but amid all of the flash there is also a wide array of chocolate on sale, including some gift presentations not seen elsewhere.

Hinsch's ⌀ *Ice Cream*

	22	20	22	I

Bay Ridge | 8518 Fifth Ave. (bet. 85th & 86th Sts.) | Brooklyn | R to 86th St. | 718-748-2854

"Old Brooklyn at its most authentic", this "absolute classic" of a parlor is a Bay Ridge "landmark" serving up the "freshest" ice cream in 16 flavors, "homemade" chocolates and "the best egg creams"; the "very special" ambiance and "sweet, helpful" staff make it a "great family place" and a must-stop for those who are nostalgic for the "malt shops of yore."

Holland Court
Meat & Fish Market ▱ *Meat/Seafood*

	▽ 24	19	18	E

E 90s | 1423 Lexington Ave. (93rd St.) | 6 to 96th St. | 212-289-8330

An Upper East Side "standby" for more than a half-century, this small, old-time butcher shop/fish market is a "good neighborhood" purveyor of "quality" seafood and fresh, cut-to-order meats (including cold cuts, sausage and other charcuterie), as well as cheeses and other delicatessen fare; the selection is somewhat "limited", however, and it can be "pricey."

Hong Keung
Seafood & Meat Market *Seafood*

	22	15	15	I

Chinatown | 75 Mulberry St. (bet. Bayard & Canal Sts.) | 6/J/M/N/Q/R/W/Z to Canal St. | 212-571-1445

Although the fin fare is sold without fanfare outside this unassuming Chinatown storefront, the "quality" seafood "is literally swimming" and the prices "can't be beat"; Chinese sauces, noodles, dried mushrooms and other imported dry goods are also available, and while the staff speaks mostly Cantonese, the fish are labeled in English, so if all else fails, pointing usually works.

Hong Kong Supermarket *Specialty Shop*

	20	14	11	I

Chinatown | 109 E. Broadway (Pike St.) | F to E. B'way | 212-227-3388
Sunset Pk | 60-23 Eighth Ave. (61st St.) | Brooklyn | N to 8th Ave. | 718-438-2288 ◐
Elmhurst | 82-02 45th Ave. (B'way) | Queens | G/R/V to Elmhurst Ave. | 718-651-3838 ◐
Flushing | 37-11 Main St. (bet. 37th & 38th Aves.) | Queens | 7 to Flushing-Main St. | 718-539-6868 ◐

"Chock-full of every single Asian product you can imagine and some that you can't", this market mini-chain "carries all the essentials" for

QUALITY DISPLAY SERVICE COST

Eastern cooking plus "quality meats, vegetables", seafood, "condiments, nuts and all manner of scary, pickled things"; plus, "you can't beat the price", although you can expect a "chaotic", "no-frills" setup.

Hot & Crusty ● *Baked Goods* | 15 | 15 | 15 | I |

E 40s | Grand Central Terminal | main concourse (42nd St. & Vanderbilt Ave.) | 4/5/6/7/S to 42nd St./Grand Central | 212-687-6054
E 60s | 1201 Second Ave. (63rd St.) | F to Lexington Ave./63rd St. | 212-753-2542
E 80s | 1276 Lexington Ave. (bet. 86th & 87th Sts.) | 4/5/6 to 86th St. | 212-426-2111
Garment Dist | Penn Station | Seventh Ave. (32nd St.) | 1/2/3/A/C/E to 34th St./Penn Station | 212-279-6450
W 80s | 2387 Broadway (bet. 87th & 88th Sts.) | 1 to 86th St. | 212-496-0632 ⊄
W 100s | 2720 Broadway (bet. 104th & 105th Sts.) | 1 to 103rd St. | 212-666-4900
www.hotandcrusty.com
"When you're hungry, they're around" shrug surveyors about this "unfortunately named" chain "catering to the masses" with "run-of-the-mill" baked goods, sandwiches and soups, fodder for "quick", inexpensive breakfasts or lunches on the go; "boring" it may be, but "when you're running for the train" it's hard to beat.

Hot Bialys ⊄ *Bagels* | 25 | 15 | 18 | I |

Kew Gdns | 116-63 Queens Blvd. (78th Ave.) | Queens | E/F to Kew Gardens/Union Tpke. | 718-544-0900
"Now *that's* a bialy" rave reviewers of this "unassuming" Kew Gardens veteran's "delicious" eponymous product – they're "huge and come in many varieties" – and "the bagels are good too"; the "lack of decor" may be a turnoff for some, but connoisseurs willing to "travel 15 miles" don't give it a second thought because this is "the real thing."

Hudson Yards Catering *Caterer/Events* | ▽ 24 | 21 | 22 | E |

Chelsea | Hudson Yards | 640 W. 28th St., 8th fl. (bet. 11th & 12th Aves.) | 212-488-1500 | www.hycnyc.com
By appointment only
Linked to restaurateur Danny Meyer's dominion (Union Square Cafe, Gramercy Tavern, The Modern and more), this "up-and-coming" West Chelsea caterer takes a chef-driven tack to supply globe-spanning cuisines matched with top-flight service; it's warehouselike HQ can accommodate guests in a private dining area (The Hudson Room) or a massive contiguous events space (The Tunnel at the Waterfront), and it continues to shore up its relationships with a host of off-site corporate clients.

Hungarian Pastry Shop ●⊄ *Baked Goods* | 22 | 18 | 18 | I |

W 100s | 1030 Amsterdam Ave. (111th St.) | 1 to 110th St. | 212-866-4230
"Many a Columbia student wouldn't have graduated" without the "mile-high pastries", "top-notch hamentaschen", "heated poppy seed strudel" and "crisp, buttery butterflies" washed down with "unlimited cups of coffee" at this "charming" Morningside Heights

Hungarian bakery/cafe, "a neighborhood icon for decades"; still, many maintain the eats are "secondary" to the "relaxed" old-world vibe ("Nietzsche would love it").

Hung Chong Import ⊘ *Cookware* | 19 | 13 | 13 | I |

Chinatown | 14 Bowery (bet. Doyers & Pell Sts.) | 6/J/M/N/Q/R/W/Z to Canal St. | 212-349-3392

"Budget-minded" chefs in search of woks, cleavers, bamboo steamers and other "authentic" Asian implements and dishware (like restaurant-style floral serving platters and chopsticks) hit this Chinatown kitchenware shop with an "old NYC" feel where the "awesome selection" overcomes less-than-impressive service and looks; thrifty types tout the sale table on the street "where you can sometimes also buy jade or socks."

Iavarone Bros. ⊟ *Prepared Food* | 25 | 24 | 22 | M |

Maspeth | 6900 Grand Ave. (69th St.) | Queens | 718-639-3623
Middle Vill | 75-12 Metropolitan Ave. (75th St.) | Queens | M to Middle Vill./Metropolitan Ave. | 718-326-0510
www.ibfoods.com

When you need a "homemade dinner you don't have to make", these family-run Italian specialty shops in Queens supply patrons with a "great variety" of prepared foods, as well as "on-the-mark" items "you can't always find in the city", including cheeses, pastas and more; a "great butcher counter" featuring housemade sausages (fresh and dry-cured) is another draw, closely followed by the "gracious service" that keeps you "coming back."

Ideal Cheese ⊟ *Cheese/Dairy* | 27 | 21 | 23 | E |

E 50s | 942 First Ave. (52nd St.) | 6 to 51st St. | 212-688-7579 | 800-382-0109 | www.idealcheese.com

A "popular place" in Sutton Place, this "high-grade cheesemonger" is "sure to entice" with its "wide variety" of "excellent" fromages "from around the world", presented with "ample tasting opportunities" by a team that's "most informed" ("if a bit snooty"); it's also "ideal" for spreads, oils and charcuterie, so expect "to go home with a bagful of goodies."

☑ Il Laboratorio del Gelato ⊟⊘ *Ice Cream* | 28 | 19 | 20 | E |

LES | 95 Orchard St. (Broome & Delancy Sts.) | F/J/M/Z to Delancey/Essex Sts. | 212-343-9922 | www.laboratoriodelgelato.com

"Fantasies do come true" at this LES "shrine to frozen confections", voted No. 1 for Ice Cream in this Survey, where the "irresistible" gelato is "ambrosia" to devotees; while some find it "ridiculously expensive", virtually all agree the "fantastic, imaginative flavors" "ranging from rich to subtle" are "simply the best" and well "worth the trek Downtown", "the wait on line" and "every penny" spent.

Indiana Market & Catering *Caterer* | ∇ 26 | 25 | 27 | M |

W 80s | 333 W. 39th St., Suite 404 (bet. 8th & 9th Aves.) | 1 to 86th St. | 212-736-3531 | www.indiananyc.com

"Meticulous" "attention to detail" marks this "top-notch" UWS caterer/event planner, whose "simpatico staff" is "able to flex to special needs" as they organize off-site events "from inception through execution", covering everything from venue hunting to arranging for flowers and musicians; "innovative" "culinary treats" help "transform any location into a dream party", and they top off the "enthusiastic" performance with "amazing bang for the buck."

Indian Bread Co. ◑ *Prepared Food* | 21 | 13 | 17 | I |

G Village | 194 Bleecker St. (bet. MacDougal St. & 6th Ave.) | A/B/C/D/E/F/V to W. 4th St. | 212-228-1909 | www.indianbreadco.com
Equally "quick" and "yummy" are the meals turned out in this Village Indian take-out/delivery champ whose "tasty" range of stuffed flatbreads, 'naanwiches' (the "perfect analogue to panini"), soups and other inexpensive "delights" suit on-the-go fans just fine; what's more, heat-seekers can get the goods "spiced up."

Integral Yoga Natural Foods ◑ *Health Food* | 24 | 17 | 19 | M |

W Village | 229 W. 13th St. (bet. 7th & 8th Aves.) | 1/2/3 to 14th St. | 212-243-2642 | 800-343-1735 | www.integralyoganaturalfoods.com
"Bulk buyers" get "a warm and fuzzy feeling" at this West Village health food market offering a "solid" selection of "high-quality" "loose grains, nuts", "whole spices" and more, as well as "hard-to-find" produce, prepared foods, vitamins and beauty products; though the space is "cramped", a "meditative" atmosphere prevails, thanks in part to the "relaxed, helpful" staffers, many of whom seem to have just come from a "yoga session" in the attached studio.

International Poultry Co. ◑ *Prepared Food* | - | - | - | M |

E 50s | 983 First Ave. (54th St.) | E/V to Lexington Ave./53rd St. | 212-750-1100
Should you need some fowl, look no further than this East Side poultry place that specializes in a variety of fried and roast bird dishes including chicken, duck and turkey, with "rich noodle pudding" and other "terrific" accompaniments that have indulgers clucking approval; N.B. it specializes in office catering.

In Vino Veritas ◐ *Wine/Liquor* | ∇ 25 | 22 | 22 | M |

E 70s | 1375 First Ave. (74th St.) | 6 to 77th St. | 212-288-0100
It's true: having occupied its spot since the repeal of Prohibition, this "cute" Upper Eastsider is one of NYC's oldest wine and liquor stores, still decked out in vintage decor featuring original stained-glass windows, Murano lamps and cast-iron grapes; comprising its "well-edited" yet "eclectic" inventory are roughly 1,200 Italian vintages, more than a few "bargains" among them, and there's a "helpful" staff on hand to offer suggestions.

Is Wine ◑ *Wine/Liquor* | - | - | - | M |

G Village | 24 West 8th St. (bet. 5th Ave. & MacDougal St.) | R/W to 8th St. | 212-254-7800 | www.is-wine.com
Relocated last year from its former East Village home to a "handsome" new "Adirondack lodge"-like store in NYU country, this quirky wine merchant continues to focus on boutique bottlings and "unique" hard-to-find vintages, most of them imports; a personable

owner introduces these "unknown gems" ("many under $20") to the public via seasonal wine classes at Cooper Union and at Saturday afternoon tastings at the store.

Italian Food Center *Specialty Shop* | 22 | 18 | 20 | M |

Little Italy | 186 Grand St. (Mulberry St.) | 6/J/M/N/Q/R/W/Z to Canal St. | 212-925-2954

"An authentic, local-NYC experience" for more than 60 years, this Little Italy deli and specialty foods market is "an old favorite", offering "fantastic sandwiches" (made with "wonderful" house-baked breads) and other "fresh prepared foods" at "quite good" prices; in addition to hefty heros that "taste like heaven", it also stocks "all the Italian staples", including "lots of imported" items.

☑ Italian Wine Merchants ▤ *Wine/Liquor* | 27 | 24 | 25 | E |

Union Sq | 108 E. 16th St. (bet. Irving Pl. & Union Sq. E.) | 4/5/6/L/N/Q/R/W to 14th St./Union Sq. | 212-473-2323 | www.italianwinemerchant.com

Restaurateur Joe Bastianich's "expertise shines through" at this Union Square "haven for the wine-obsessed" (co-owned with Mario Batali), which deals only in producers from The Boot, offering a "tremendous selection" of "top-flight" "standards" as well as "hard-to-find" "gems"; it's curated by a staff so "knowledgeable and passionate" you could "get your PhD in *vino Italiano*" just shopping here, and while it's "quite a treat" for "collectors" and novices too, there are a few grumbles about "paying restaurant prices at the liquor store" ("mamma mia, that's expensive").

☑ Ito En ▤ *Coffee/Tea* | 28 | 27 | 25 | E |

E 60s | 822 Madison Ave. (69th St.) | 6 to 68th St. | 212-988-7111 | www.itoen.com

Ranking as the "best tea emporium in NYC", this Upper East Side "sanctuary" "has no peers" in its "superb selection" of "authentic" Japanese, Chinese and Indian leaves "both traditional" and "exotic", packaged and "treated as works of art" in a "so-civilized" "boutique" space that's also stocked with "one-of-a-kind" "accoutrements"; run by one of Japan's "premier producers" and staffed by "sophisticated" sorts who "can make neophytes experts", it's "very expensive" but "worth it" to steep in "tea as spirituality."

☑ Jack's Stir Brew Coffee ▤⊟ *Coffee/Tea* | 27 | 23 | 23 | M |

G Village | 138 W. 10th St. (bet. Greenwich Ave. & Waverly Pl.) | 1 to Christopher St. | 212-929-0821
NEW **Seaport** | 222 Front St. (bet. Beekman St. & Peck Slip) | A/C to Fulton St. | 212-227-7631
www.cupajack.com

"Crunchy" types "could live at" this ultra-"cozy" Village coffeehouse, which showcases "awesome" "organic" java of the shade-grown, Fair Trade variety plus "funky teas" and baked goods including chocolate chip cookies so addictive they "should be illegal"; its "quaint" digs and "service with a smile" all but revive the Beat scene, and the new Seaport site may be even more "mellow and welcoming."

		QUALITY	DISPLAY	SERVICE	COST

Z Jacques Torres Chocolate ▭ *Candy/Nuts* | 28 | 26 | 23 | E
SoHo | 350 Hudson St. (King St.) | 1 to Houston St. | 212-414-2462
Dumbo | 66 Water St. (bet. Dock & Main Sts.) | Brooklyn | A/C to High St. | 718-875-9772
www.mrchocolate.com
Follow "pied piper of chocolate" Jacques Torres to one of his "chic", *"Willy Wonka"*–worthy factories/shops – either the "quaint" Dumbo original or the "larger", sleeker West SoHo offshoot – for trademark "ooh-la-la" hot chocolate and "ecstasy-inducing" confections "handmade on the spot"; the "extensive", "delightfully" displayed selection includes treats ranging from "highbrow" "modern truffles" to "fun" chocolate-covered cornflakes and a parade of novelty shapes, ensuring "there's always something new" to sample here.

Jahn's Ice Cream Parlor & Restaurant 🍦 *Ice Cream* | 20 | 20 | 19 | M
Richmond Hill | 117-03 Hillside Ave. (Myrtle Ave.) | Queens | J/Z to 121st St. | 718-847-2800
This "old-fashioned soda fountain" (since 1897) in Richmond Hill offers a big scoop of "nostalgia" to go with its ice cream concoctions, and aficionados insist "you haven't lived until you try" its gut-busting "kitchen sink" sundae ("bring a lot of friends" to take this one on); while it may have become "a little tattered" over the decades, it's still a "one-of-a-kind experience" that brings back the "good old days."

JAS Mart 🍴 *Specialty Shop* | 21 | 16 | 16 | M
E Village | 35 St. Marks Pl. (bet. 2nd & 3rd Aves.) | 6 to Astor Pl. | 212-420-6370
Flatiron | 34 E. 23rd St. (bet. Madison & Park Aves.) | 6 to 23rd St. | 212-387-8721
W 100s | 2847 Broadway (bet. 110th & 111th Sts.) | 1 to 110th St. | 212-866-4780
"You walk into Tokyo" when you enter one of these "small" but "well-stocked" shops that carry "all the specialties from the Land of the Rising Sun" ("from soba to rice to wild candy" options) at "hard-to-beat prices"; there's even "ready-to-eat sushi and edamame" plus plenty of "interesting" spices and ingredients to "make your Japanese meal look and taste fabulous."

Java Girl *Coffee/Tea* | 24 | 23 | 23 | M
E 60s | 348 E. 66th St. (bet. 1st & 2nd Aves.) | 6 to 68th St. | 212-737-3490
Sink into "a comfy seat" at this "cute", "eclectic" East Side coffee shop, a "warm little" "place to sip" "quality brews" and munch French pastries with the "neighborhood regulars" who brag it "buries the chains"; it's also a "welcome" chance to browse for "creative bric-a-brac" or pick up some "premium beans and teas" to go.

Jefferson Market 🍴 *Major Gourmet Mkt.* | ▽ 26 | 20 | 25 | E
G Village | 450 Sixth Ave. (bet. 10th & 11th Sts.) | A/B/C/D/E/F/V to W. 4th St. | 212-533-3377
It "doesn't fancy itself too cool", but this Greenwich Village gourmet market has "managed to stick around since 1929" and still aims to

"satisfy" with a mix of "staples" and "upscale treats"; highlights include "fresh", "delicious" prepared foods that are "more in the nature of comfort" fare and above all an "old-fashioned butcher" where the "very accommodating" countermen will "hook you up" with the "best-quality meat."

Jeffrey's on Essex *Meat/Poultry*   - | - | - | M

LES | Essex St. Market | 120 Essex St. (bet. Delancey & Rivington Sts.) | F/J/M/Z to Delancey/Essex Sts. | 212-475-6521 | www.jeffreysonessex.com
Regulars of this LES meat and poultry counter inside the Essex Street Market advise "always ask for" proprietor and fourth-generation butcher Jeffrey Ruhalter, who "knows exactly what he's doing" and has a "sense of humor"; the result is a side of "education" and "entertainment" to go with his well-priced, "excellent-quality" meats – dry-aged beef, plus various cuts of lamb and pork – and ready-to-cook 'Dinner by Jeffrey' dishes; N.B. catering is a sideline.

jesGORDON ⊄ *Flowers*   - | - | - | VE

Garment Dist | 242 W. 30th St., Suite 1004 (bet. 7th & 8th Aves.) | 212-229-2165 | www.jesgordon.com
By appointment only
With a client list that runs the gamut from Sarah Jessica Parker to Woody Allen, Target to Nissan, Garment District floral and event designer Jes Gordon's style also spans the spectrum from "beautiful flowers" arranged in "slightly edgy, contemporary displays" to simple vines cascading under a canvas ceiling; and, if you really "want to spend a fortune", she crafts opulent, old world–style towering arrangements to beautify a wedding or corporate do.

Jim and Andy's ⊄ *Produce*   - | - | - | I

Cobble Hill | 208 Court St. (Warren St.) | Brooklyn | F/G to Bergen St. | 718-522-6034
At this "small", "old-school neighborhood" produce outfit in Cobble Hill, "there's more stuff than you'd ever think possible", from everyday varieties to "occasional great finds" like "fancy radicchio" and "beautiful endive"; make no mistake: this shop's "friendly" "father-and-son" owners "know their" vegetables and fruits.

Jinil Au Chocolat ▭ *Candy/Nuts*   - | - | - | E

Midwood | 1371 Coney Island Ave. (bet. Aves. J & K) | Brooklyn | Q to Ave. J | 718-758-0199 | 800-645-4645
This Midwood chocolate stop, an offshoot of the LI original, "does wonders" with kosher chocolate, peddling an extensive selection that includes covered fruits and a cavalcade of whimsical shapes (chocolate chess sets, cell phones, etc.); it also specializes in overflowing gift baskets for life occasions from 'newborn' to 'shiva.'

Jive Turkey ◑ *Prepared Food*   ∇ 23 | 20 | 21 | M

Clinton Hill | 441 Myrtle Ave. (bet. Clinton & Waverly Aves.) | Brooklyn | G to Clinton/Washington Aves. | 718-797-1688 | www.thejiveturkey.com
Your family may "fight over the leftovers" after they've tasted the "juicy turkeys" that turn up "every which way" (including the house specialty, deep-fried) at this Clinton Hill storefront; it

also vends "easy" ready-to-bake birds paired with lots of "fixin's'" as well as house-baked sweets like honey-pecan pie and brownies to chase them.

Joe ⌀ *Coffee/Tea* — 26 | 20 | 22 | M

E Village | 9 E. 13th St. (bet. 5th Ave. & University Pl.) | 4/5/6/L/N/Q/R/W to 14th St./Union Sq. | 212-924-7400 | www.joeheartofcoffee.com
G Village | 141 Waverly Pl. (6th Ave.) | A/B/C/D/E/F/V to W. 4th St. | 212-924-6750 | www.joeheartofcoffee.com
NEW SoHo | Alessi store | 130 Greene St. (bet. Houston & Prince Sts.) | N/R to Prince St. | 212-941-7330

"Joe knows joe" sums up these coffeehouse "favorites", which bring a "little piece of Seattle" to the East and West Villages via "classic indie-style" setups where "superb" (and "strong") Fair Trade java is poured "with heart" by "top-notch" baristas in "quaint" boho surroundings; they're "experts at the art" of latte and cappuccino, and Wavery Place sporadically serves Amy Sedaris' "to-die-for" cupcakes; N.B. they've recently opened a mod coffee bar in SoHo's Alessi design store.

☑ Joe's Dairy ⌀ *Cheese/Dairy* — 28 | 14 | 23 | I

SoHo | 156 Sullivan St. (bet. W. Houston & Prince Sts.) | 1 to Houston St. | 212-677-8780

The "undisputed" "best smoked mozzarella" going is the pride of this "quaint" SoHo old-timer, whose cheese is famed for its "smooth-as-silk" texture and "heavenly" "homemade" freshness ("get it when it's still warm"); the rest of this "tiny", "very Italian" shop's offerings are "limited", but it's "a must-visit" for "authenticity" that's also "very reasonably priced."

JoMart Chocolates ▣ *Candy/Nuts* — 24 | 20 | 21 | M

Marine Pk | 2917 Ave. R (bet. E. 29th St. & Nostrand Ave.) | Brooklyn | Q to Ave. U | 718-375-1277 | 800-471-1277 | www.jomartchocolates.com

Now a third-generation family business, this 60-plus-year-old Marine Park chocolatier produces "awesome" confections at prices that won't break the bank; party-throwers appreciate its assortment of molded favors that can suit just about any event, and if what you're looking for isn't on display, they'll make it custom.

Jonathan Flowers *Flowers* — - | - | - | E

W 50s | 36 W. 56th St. (bet. 5th & 6th Aves.) | 212-586-8414
By appointment only

"Jonathan is a creative genius!" rave reviewers of this West 50s florist/event planning outfit whose proprietor "will do exactly what you want, only better" using "the most amazing flowers" and a selection of original props like masks and feathers; better still, he'll "work with your budget" to create an event to be remembered.

Jordan's Lobster Dock *Seafood* — 23 | 13 | 17 | M

Sheepshead Bay | 1 Harkness Ave. (Belt Pkwy. & Knapp St.) | Brooklyn | 718-934-6300 | www.jordanslobsterdock.com

As "close to a Maine lobster shack" as you'll find in Brooklyn, this "no-frills" Sheepshead Bay "staple" is known for "snappy service" and "fresh", "moderately priced" crustaceans that you can have pre-pared "to order" or buy live "to cook at home"; it may be the "7-11 of seafood" (i.e. "convenience shopping" and "no atmosphere"), but nonetheless for fans "it's tops."

Juan Valdez Café *Coffee/Tea* | 22 | 19 | 18 | I |

NEW **E 40s** | 480 Lexington Ave. (47th St.) | 4/5/6/7/S to 42nd St./Grand Central | 212-871-6107

E 50s | 140 E. 57th St. (bet. Lexington & 3rd Aves.) | 4/5/6 to 59th St./Lexington Ave. | 917-289-0981

W 40s | 1451 Broadway (41st St.) | 1/2/3/7/N/Q/R/S/W to 42nd St./Times Sq. | 212-871-7515 ◐
www.juanvaldez.com

"A famous name" that proves Columbia's National Federation of Coffee Growers can do "more than just exporting", these local links of a Bogota-based coffee bar chain dispense "rich, dark" Fair Trade *café* that's "guaranteed to keep you up all day"; also boasting Columbian pastries, "refreshing" sunny environs and "good prices", they may have the mule power to "challenge Starbucks."

Jubilee Marketplace *Major Gourmet Mkt.* | 21 | 19 | 15 | M |

Financial Dist | 99 John St. (bet. Cliff & Gold Sts.) | 2/3 to Fulton St. | 212-233-0808 ◐

NEW **SoHo** | 447 Broadway (bet. Grand & Howard Sts.) | 6/J/M/N/Q/R/W/Z to Canal St. | 212-966-6100

W 60s | Trump Place | 180 Riverside Blvd. (bet. 68th & 69th Sts.) | 1/2/3 to 72nd St. | 212-877-6000 ◐

Deemed "decent grocery" stops, this gourmet market trio is "well-stocked" with "varied and reasonably priced" produce, health foods, a "creative variety of prepared foods" and "quite good" meats and seafood; a less-than-jubilant few feel the offerings "could be bet-ter", but even they say they're "worth trying" as "convenient" op-tions in underserved areas, which "definitely get extra points" for staying "open 24/7."

Junior's Restaurant ◐▣ *Baked Goods* | 23 | 18 | 17 | M |

E 40s | Grand Central Terminal | dining concourse (42nd St. & Vanderbilt Ave.) | 4/5/6/7/S to 42nd St./Grand Central | 212-983-5257

E 40s | Grand Central Terminal | main concourse (42nd St. & Vanderbilt Ave.) | 4/5/6/7/S to 42nd St./Grand Central | 212-692-9800

W 40s | Shubert Alley | 1515 Broadway (45th St.) | 1/2/3/7/N/Q/R/S/W to 42nd St./Times Sq. | 212-302-2000

Downtown | 386 Flatbush Ave. Ext. (DeKalb Ave.) | Brooklyn | 2/3 to Grand Army Plaza | 718-852-5257

800-958-6467 | www.juniorscheesecake.com

The "heavy, creamy", "gold-standard" "classic NY-style" cheesecake at this Downtown Brooklyn "landmark" (with offshoots in Grand Central and the Theater District's Shubert Alley) is still "better than sex" according to connoisseurs; however, there are grumbles that the prices are starting to get "out of line", and as for the "glorified diner fare", surveyors say "skip" it and "eat a full slice of cake instead."

	QUALITY	DISPLAY	SERVICE	COST

Z Kalustyan's ▣ *Specialty Shop* — 27 | 20 | 19 | M

Gramercy | 123 Lexington Ave. (bet. 28th & 29th Sts.) | 6 to 28th St. | 212-685-3451 | www.kalustyans.com

A "huge selection of fresh spices" anchors the "mind-boggling" trove of "hard-to-find" "goodies" at this mostly Indian and Mideastern "mecca" in Gramercy, which stocks everything from "excellent" nuts, dried fruits, rice, beans and teas to "wonderful frozen canapés", fresh flatbreads and cookware; it's a favorite of "adventurous chefs" seeking "fair" prices, but its "narrow" aisles also appeal to novices who "eavesdrop on the great recipes people are shopping for", then afterwards "sate their hunger" at the moderately priced upstairs cafe.

Kam Man Food Products, Inc. ●▣ *Specialty Shop* — 21 | 14 | 10 | I

Chinatown | 200 Canal St. (Mulberry St.) | 6/J/M/N/Q/R/W/Z to Canal St. | 212-571-0330

"Where else can you find plates and bowls for $5 that look like they belong in MoMA" but at this "Chinatown institution" that's "stuffed to the gills" with "Asian foods" – "great teas", "exotic" dry goods, sweets and prepared dishes like barbecued duck – not to mention a basement collection of dishes and cookware that "keeps improving"; this "grotty" spot is strictly "do-it-yourself", though, as the "staff doesn't always speak English."

K & D Wines & Spirits ●▣ *Wine/Liquor* — 24 | 21 | 22 | M

E 90s | 1366 Madison Ave. (bet. 95th & 96th Sts.) | 6 to 96th St. | 212-289-1818 | www.kdwine.com

The "global" 4,000-label wine inventory at this Carnegie Hill "staple" includes a "fairly extensive selection at all price points", from "solid everyday bottles" to "interesting red Bordeaux" and "chateau" bottlings; though "informed", "affable" employees will "help you find what you want", customers who care to learn more can attend happy-hour tastings on Thursdays and Fridays; N.B. free delivery throughout Manhattan for any purchase.

Katagiri ▣ *Specialty Shop* — 23 | 16 | 16 | E

E 50s | 224 E. 59th St. (bet. 2nd & 3rd Aves.) | 4/5/6 to 59th St./ Lexington Ave. | 212-755-3566 | www.katagiri.com

"Delightfully out of place" for a full century now, the "only Japanese supermarket on the Upper East Side" packs loads of "hard-to-find" grocery items into its "tiny" space; "you'll pay a bit more" than at other spots, but you can grab "tasty sushi to go" while shopping, and it's "a lifesaver when you can't get Downtown for sprouts, soy, veggies, spices" and other staples.

Katrina Parris Flowers ▣ *Flowers* — - | - | - | M

Harlem | 1844 Adam Clayton Powell Jr. Blvd. (bet. 111th & 112th Sts.) | 212.222.7030 | www.katrinaparrisflowers.com

By appointment only

A simple, elegant philosophy informs the artful, high-end creations at Katrina Parris and Mark Pinn's Uptown floral emporium, a studio space designed with an eye toward the modern; aside from catering to clients such as President Clinton, Deutsche Bank and Swarovski, this florist offers online services, along with arrangements for weddings and other special events.

Z Katz's Delicatessen ◐ ▣ *Deli/Sandwich* | 24 | 16 | 16 | M |

LES | 205 E. Houston St. (Ludlow St.) | F/V to Lower East Side/2nd Ave. | 212-254-2246 | 800-446-8364 | www.katzdeli.com

"The food is so tasty at this classic" kosher-style deli (circa 1888) that it's definitely "worth the schlep to the Lower East Side" for what many agree is the "best corned beef and pastrami on earth" "piled high" on "huge sandwiches" that "can feed two people" – thus making "the cost in dollars and calories a bit more reasonable"; if you don't mind the "lack of ambiance", "long queues" or "cranky-waiter bit", it makes for a "fun madhouse."

Z Kee's Chocolates *Candy/Nuts* | 29 | 22 | 24 | E |

SoHo | 80 Thompson St. (bet. Broome & Spring Sts.) | C/E to Spring St. | 212-334-3284 | www.keeschocolates.com

"OMG!" rave reviewers of the "divine", "creative" chocolates "made by hand on the premises" at this tiny, "hidden-away" SoHo shop – this year voted tops in NYC for Candy – that's owned and run by "master of flavors" Kee Ling Tong, whose "exotic" fillings, many reflecting an Asian influence, are deemed "unforgettable"; "exquisite" product aside, the vibe is "unpretentious" and the staff "a pleasure to talk to", so "treat yourself" – "it's worth every penny", but just "get there early" because they sometimes start "running out" of choices later in the day.

Keith's Farm ⊟ *Produce* | 28 | 25 | 25 | M |

See Greenmarket; for more information, call 845-856-4955

"Go for the garlic" – "it's the best in the city and maybe anywhere" – but the rest of the organic vegetables and herbs are also "sublime" at this Greenmarket farm stall run by farmer-turned-author Keith Stewart, an "intelligent and thoughtful grower" based in Orange County, NY, whose conversations with customers over the veggie bins can be "one of the greatest things about the market"; "prices are high" but "totally fair" given the quality and "friendly" staff.

NEW Kidfresh *Specialty Shop* | - | - | - | E |

E 80s | 1628 Second Ave. (bet. 84th & 85th Sts.) | 4/5/6 to 86th St. | 212-861-1141 | www.kidfresh.com

"Boy, do these guys know their racket" admire visitors to this new "lazy mom's" dream market on the UES created specially for guppy-size gourmands, who drop their all-natural meals-to-go (animal-shaped sandwiches, chicken tenders with strawberry ketchup) and other healthy edibles into carts scaled just for them; the in-store cafe's juggling chef and ice cream bar are obvious crowd-pleasers, as are the cooking classes for young 'uns offered in a teaching 'kid-chen', so the only drawback is that parents "gotta have large wallets" to bring their little people here.

	QUALITY	DISPLAY	SERVICE	COST

Klatch Coffee Bar ⊅ *Coffee/Tea*

| – | – | – | I |

Financial Dist | 9 Maiden Ln. (bet. B'way & Nassau St.) | J/M/Z to Fulton St. | 212-227-7276

One of the Financial District's more "appreciated" "signs of life", this coffee bar–cum-gallery is a "little" "oasis" that gives "way Downtown types" access to coffee from Porto Rico, "delicious teas" from T Salon and "tasty" breads and baked goods from Balthazar, the Little Pie Company and other foodie faves; the "cool room" features a revolving art display, and they even weave in knitting classes on Thursday evenings.

Koglin Royal Hams ◐☑ *Meat/Poultry*

| ▽ 24 | 21 | 19 | E |

E 40s | Grand Central Mkt. | Lexington Ave. (43rd St.) | 4/5/6/7/S to 42nd St./Grand Central | 212-499-0725 | www.koglinroyalhams.com

When a "German meat craving" hits, this Euro-style charcuterie stand in Grand Central "is the perfect cure", boasting a selection of great wursts ("their frankfurters will be the star of your next barbecue") and other "long-forgotten treats" reminiscent of "once-booming Yorkville"; there are also specialties representing the rest of Europe (e.g. Italian prosciutto), as well as prepared side dishes like macaroni salad.

☑ Korin Japanese Trading Corp. ☑ *Cookware*

| 28 | 23 | 23 | E |

TriBeCa | 57 Warren St. (bet. Church St. & W. B'way) | 1/2/3/A/C to Chambers St. | 212-587-7021 | 800-626-2172 | www.korin.com

Slicing and dicing are elevated to an "art" at this "jewel of a store" in TriBeCa (rated No.1 in NYC for Cookware & Supplies), a veritable "sanctuary" of "high-quality" Japanese wares, including a "fantastic" assortment of traditional "handcrafted" knives that are priced up into the thousands; if the variety seems "overwhelming", rely on the "expert" staff to "guide you through with aplomb."

☑ Kossar's Bialys ☑⊅ *Bagels*

| 28 | 15 | 18 | I |

LES | 367 Grand St. (bet. Essex & Norfolk Sts.) | F/J/M/Z to Delancey/Essex Sts. | 212-473-4810 | 877-424-2597 | www.kossarsbialys.com

The reigning "king of the bialy world", this "landmark" (once again voted No. 1 in its category) still turns out the same "little floury clouds of love" it's been known for since1935, standing as a slice of "living history" on the "now-hip Lower East Side"; it definitely "isn't fancy-schmancy", but its namesake goods are roundly voted "worth the schlep", especially "when hot out of the oven" – and "don't forget" it also vends "old-school bagels", bulkas and pletzels.

Krispy Kreme Doughnuts ◑ *Baked Goods*

| 19 | 16 | 15 | I |

E 80s | 1497 Third Ave. (bet. 84th & 85th Sts.) | 4/5/6 to 86th St. | 212-879-9111

Garment Dist | Penn Station | Seventh Ave. (32nd St.) | 1/2/3/A/C/E to 34th St./Penn Station | 212-947-7175

www.krispykreme.com

"Its red ['Hot Doughnuts'] light shines to us like a beacon" admi⸱ "addicts" of this national chain – now only in Penn Station and or the Upper East Side – where "right before your eyes" conveyor belts "churn" out "sinful", "pillowy", "melt-in-your-mouth" doughnuts; though many maintain that the goods are "sugar overkill", even critics admit their "tasty, greasy", "sweet" goodness can help "soften hangover" woes.

La Bagel Delight *Bagels* | 23 | 17 | 22 | I |
Brooklyn Heights | 90 Court St. (bet. Livingston & Schermerhorn Sts.) | Brooklyn | A/C/F to Jay St./Borough Hall | 718-522-0520
Dumbo | 104 Front St. (Adams St.) | Brooklyn | F to York St. | 718-625-2235
Park Slope | 122 Seventh Ave. (bet. Carroll & President Sts.) | Brooklyn | B/Q to 7th Ave. | 718-398-9529
Park Slope | 252 Seventh Ave. (5th St.) | Brooklyn | F to 7th Ave. | 718-768-6107
www.labageldelight.com
"Everything a bagel should be" says it all about the "chewy, savory" hand-rolled goods turned out at this Brooklyn chain "favorite"; it's also an unpretentious source for solid salads and sandwiches, with "fast", "friendly" service that lox up fans far and wide.

La Bergamote *Baked Goods* | 26 | 24 | 20 | E |
Chelsea | 169 Ninth Ave. (20th St.) | C/E to 23rd St. | 212-627-9010
For "a taste of Paris on Ninth Avenue", *vaux un detour* to this Chelsea corner patisserie whose "impressive-looking" display cases are stocked with "works of art" from "the best croissants", brioches and Danish to "must-try" tarts and handmade truffles; it's a perfect "place to relax with coffee and real French" treats, even if service is *un peu* "uptight", so no surprise it's "extremely popular" – expect "lines out the door" at prime times.

Ladybird Bakery *Baked Goods* | - | - | - | M |
(fka Two Little Red Hens)
Park Slope | 1112 Eighth Ave. (bet. 11th & 12th Sts.) | Brooklyn | F to 7th Ave. | 718-499-8108 | www.twolittleredhens.com
Its owners have parted company and this tiny original branch of Two Little Red Hens has taken on a new name, but much to the relief of its faithful Park Slope following, it's still producing the same homespun, high-quality baked goods for which it has long been known; as ever, it's most appreciated for its artfully decorated cakes and cupcakes, stars of many a birthday party around the borough.

☑ Lady M Cake Boutique ⬜ *Baked Goods* | 28 | 26 | 22 | VE |
E 70s | 41 E. 78th St. (bet. Madison & Park Aves.) | 6 to 77th St. | 212-452-2222 | www.ladymconfections.com
"Combining Japanese aesthetics with French technique", this "austere" Upper East Side "high-end patisserie" is a vision of "heavenly white chic", whose "decadent" "must-try" specialty is the mille crêpes cake (featuring impossibly "creamy and light" layers interspersed with custard), but also notable are the petits choux and chocolate sponge cake with caramel mousse; while customers should "be prepared to drop a bundle", enthusiasts M-phasize it's "worth every single penny."

	QUALITY	DISPLAY	SERVICE	COST

Lafayette French
Pastry Bakers ●⊘✄ *Baked Goods*

| | 21 | 18 | 18 | M |

G Village | 26 Greenwich Ave. (bet. Charles & W. 10th Sts.) | A/B/C/D/E/F/V to W. 4th St. | 212-242-7580

You'll "gain weight just walking in" to this "good old" French bakery in Greenwich Village, an *ancien* source of "classic treats" like "delicious" crème brûlée, croissants, mille-feuille and possibly the "last surviving charlotte russe"; it's all such a "comfort" that regulars happily "overlook the occasional" service quirks.

La Guli ☒ *Baked Goods*

| | ▽ 24 | 25 | 22 | I |

Astoria | 29-15 Ditmars Blvd. (bet. 29th & 31st Sts.) | Queens | N/W to Astoria/Ditmars Blvd. | 718-728-5612

This "classic old-style Italian neighborhood bakery" (circa 1937) "can't be beat" according to adoring Astorians who adore its "fresh and delicious" baked goods ("excellent pignoli nut cookies and sfogliatelle", the 'pregnant cannoli'), gelati and ices; just as customers "who have moved away" still "come back for the treats", the "original owners" recently bought back this family business, and locals are hoping they'll restore all of its "original pizzazz."

☑ La Maison du Chocolat ☒ *Candy/Nuts*

| | 29 | 28 | 23 | VE |

E 70s | 1018 Madison Ave. (bet. 78th & 79th Sts.) | 6 to 77th St. | 212-744-7117

W 40s | 30 Rockefeller Plaza, concourse level (bet. 49th & 50th Sts.) | B/D/F/V to 47-50th Sts./Rockefeller Ctr. | 212-265-9404

800-988-5632 | www.lamaisonduchocolat.com

Just about "the best this side of Paris – or heaven" is the word on the "superb" truffles and other "fragrant, intense", "subtly flavored" chocolates imported from France and offered in "jewel"-worthy displays and packaging at this "ultra-high-end" Madison Avenue boutique and its Rock Center offshoot; it's the "Rolls-Royce" of bonbons – with "awe"-inspiring prices to match – though there are a few grumbles about service that, while "knowledgeable and efficient", can be "frosty" at times; P.S. "try the hot chocolate!" (both stores have tearooms), and check out the tastings and classes.

Lamarca ✄ *Cheese/Dairy*

| | ▽ 26 | 17 | 20 | M |

Gramercy | 161 E. 22nd St. (3rd Ave.) | 6 to 23rd St. | 212-673-7920

"Your cheese palate" "will be rewarded" at this Gramercy shop/trattoria, which makes its mark with the "wonderful", "very fresh" fromages aged on-premises in owner Joe Lamarca's subterranean cave; it also carries a "cherce" lineup of "specialty items" to take out (including baked goods, pastas and "amazing soups"), leaving loyalists with only one lament: it's "closed on weekends."

Landmark Wine & Sake ● *Wine/Liquor*

| | ▽ 25 | 21 | 25 | M |

Chelsea | 167 W. 23rd St. (bet. 6th & 7th Aves.) | 1 to 23rd St. | 212-242-2323 | www.landmarkwinesake.com

This Chelsea wine merchant offers what may well be "the largest sake stash in Manhattan" (some 300 labels) as well as a strong showing of soju (200) and an eccentric, "beautifully edited" selection of wines including Argentinean, French, Spanish and California producers; "affable", "expert" employees who "know their stuff and are willing to share" and a store layout featuring "user-friendly displays" plus a tasting bar for sampling the wares add up to copasetic experiences here.

L'Arte del Gelato *Ice Cream*

27 | 21 | 24 | M

Chelsea | Chelsea Market | 75 Ninth Ave. (bet. 15th & 16th Sts.) | A/C/E/L to 14th St./8th Ave. | 212-366-0570 | www.lartedelgelato.com

The gelato hits the "top of the charts" at this Chelsea Market stand where classics such as "heavenly" chocolate share space with "wild" daily changing flavors, and regulars recommend "torta anything" (upscale ice cream cakes) for parties; the "friendly" service includes "free samples", but cognoscenti caution "if you don't buy once you try, you'll get looks colder than the treats behind the glass."

Lassen & Hennigs ● *Caterer*

∇ 22 | 21 | 23 | M

Brooklyn Heights | 114 Montague St. (bet. Henry & Hicks Sts.) | Brooklyn | 2/3/4/5/M/N/R/W to Borough Hall/Court St. | 718-875-6272 | www.lassencatering.com

Treat your gathering to "everything from soup to nuts" from this "neighborhood deli", a Brooklyn "Heights tradition" since 1949 that's gone "inexorably upscale" and now industriously handles "catering for business and parties"; specializing in "excellent" "homemade" baked goods and prepared foods, they reliably put together platters that matter.

Lassi ● *Prepared Food*

∇ 21 | 13 | 20 | M

G Village | 28 Greenwich Ave. (bet. Charles & W. 10th Sts.) | 1 to Christopher St. | 212-675-2688 | www.lassinyc.com

"Authentic" dals, "carefully prepared" curries, parathas, namesake yogurt drinks and other traditional Indian items are the hallmark of this Village eatery owned by a former Union Square Cafe pastry chef; stick with takeout "unless you want to sit at a narrow counter" – this sliver of a storefront is only six-ft. wide.

La Tropezienne ▣◢ *Baked Goods*

- | - | - | I

Harlem | 2131 First Ave. (bet. 109th & 110th Sts.) | 6 to 110th St. | 212-860-5324

A "great little secret" in East Harlem, this cheerful French bakery pleases its local following with an array of breads, croissants, Danish, turnovers, pastries (éclairs, fruit or ganache tarts) and even hand-painted animal cookies; it's also possible to pick up sandwiches, salads and quiches – best taken to go, since the small cafe area seats only 10 people.

Leaf & Bean ▣ *Coffee/Tea*

23 | 21 | 22 | M

Park Slope | 83 Seventh Ave. (bet. Berkeley Pl. & Union St.) | Brooklyn | B/Q to 7th Ave. | 718-638-5791 | 888-811-5282 | www.leafnbean.com

Park Slopers liken this "very special" "neighborhood" "staple" to a "savvy" "country store" that stocks an "impressive" selection of "wonderful coffees and teas", focusing on organic and Fair Trade blends; the shelves are "cluttered" with an "eclectic" mix of bean-related "accessories", "cool kitchen gadgets" and "kitschy" "decorative items", with an amiable and "informative" crew on hand to "help navigate" the wares.

NEW Leapfrog Caterers *Caterer*
▕ - ▏ - ▏ - ▏ E ▏

Flatiron | 5 E. 20th St. (bet. B'way & 5th Ave.) | 212-460-9100 | www.leapfrogcaterers.com
By appointment only

Chef Cyril Renaud ventures into catering with this new Flatiron-based business offering clients distinctive modern Bretagne cooking backed by a 1,000-strong wine list that draws on the resources of his restaurant, Fleur de Sel; services are provided for cocktail receptions, dinner parties and other events large and small.

☑ Le Dû's Wines ●☰ *Wine/Liquor*
▕ 27 ▏ 24 ▏ 26 ▏ E ▏

W Village | 600 Washington St. (bet. Leroy & Morton Sts.) | 1 to Houston St. | 212-924-6999 | www.leduwines.com

"You could walk into this store blindfolded and walk out with a winning wine every time" rave regulars of this spacious West Village "oasis" owned by Jean-Luc Le Dû, onetime sommelier at Restaurant Daniel; he "picks the best of the best" (including some "really original standouts") from "quality producers" and his staff "couldn't be more helpful" to the neophyte, while weekly in-store tastings are rated "way above average" – as are most prices.

Lee Sims Chocolates ☰ *Candy/Nuts*
▕ - ▏ - ▏ - ▏ M ▏

Staten Island | 1909 Victory Blvd. (bet. Jewett Ave. & Manor Rd.) | 718-448-9276 | 800-540-4887 | www.lschocolates.com

"The quality is always there" say surveyors sweet on this SI chocolate purveyor that's a "must-stop for holiday treats" and other specialty confections; its quaint quarters are "a pleasure" to visit, thanks in no small part to the "helpful" staffers and wallet-amenable prices.

Le Marais ☰ *Meat/Poultry*
▕ 26 ▏ 21 ▏ 19 ▏ E ▏

W 40s | 150 W. 46th St. (bet. 6th & 7th Aves.) | B/D/F/V to 47-50th Sts./Rockefeller Ctr. | 212-869-0900 | www.lemarais.net

Sharing quarters with the Theater District French brasserie of the same name, this glatt kosher butcher has enthusiasts praising its "beautiful display" of meats (lamb, poultry and game) plus sausages, pâtés and such, insisting "if you didn't know they were kosher" you'd never guess; the "expensive" tabs seem to be justified by "first-rate quality" – but at these prices, can't they "at least smile"?

☑ Lemon Ice King of Corona ●≠ *Ice Cream*
▕ 27 ▏ 15 ▏ 18 ▏ I ▏

Corona | Corona Park | 52-02 108th St. (Corona & 52nd Aves.) | Queens | 7 to 103rd St. | 718-699-5133 | www.thelemonicekingofcorona.com

"Long live the King" chant the fervent fans of this Corona "treasure", where "nuttin' – I mean nothing – beats" the namesake lemon Italian ice, though there are a "zillion" other flavors to choose from too, all fabulous enough to make it "worth the wait", especially on a "hot summer night"; "may it be there forever."

	QUALITY	DISPLAY	SERVICE	COST

☑ LeNell's Ltd.: a Wine & Spirit Boutique ●◐▣ Wine/Liquor

27 | 24 | 26 | M

Red Hook | 416 Van Brunt St. (bet. Coffey & Van Dyke Sts.) | Brooklyn | F/G to Smith/9th Sts. | 718-360-0838 | 877-667-6627 | www.lenells.com

In her quirky Red Hook grape-and-grain shop, Southern gal LeNell Smothers "emphasizes quality over snob appeal" as she "educates" "cocktail geeks" and others about "boutique wines" and lesser-known spirits (highlights include the extensive stock of small-cask bourbons, American whiskeys and a "wide selection of bitters"); aptly, the "funky" shop has a shabby-chic country-store ambiance, enhanced by "laid-back", "friendly" service.

Lenny's Bagels ▱ Bagels

23 | 16 | 19 | I

W 90s | 2601 Broadway (bet. 98th & 99th Sts.) | 1/2/3 to 96th St. | 212-222-0410

"Lots of varieties", including some "unusual" ones (e.g. chocolate-raisin), distinguish this Upper West Side fixture dealing in "tasty" bagels; ok, maybe its quarters "leave something to be desired" and service can "disappoint", but nonetheless carb cronies "can't resist" – especially given the bargain pricing that includes deals like "buy 12, and get another six free."

Leonard's ▣ Seafood

26 | 23 | 24 | E

E 70s | 1385 Third Ave. (bet. 78th & 79th Sts.) | 6 to 77th St. | 212-744-2600 | www.leonardsmarket.citysearch.com

Since 1910, locals have relied on this "family-run" Yorkville "staple" for "impeccable" fresh seafood and meats "cut to your precise order", as well as an impressive array of smoked fish, caviar and game birds; it "doesn't come cheap", but most agree that the "high quality" and "personalized" service are "worth it."

Leonidas ▣ Candy/Nuts

26 | 24 | 23 | E

E 50s | 485 Madison Ave. (bet. 51st & 52nd Sts.) | E/V to 5th Ave./53rd St. | 212-980-2608

Financial Dist | 120 Broadway (Thames St.) | J/M/Z to Broad St. | 212-766-6100

Financial Dist | 3 Hanover Sq. (Pearl & William Sts.) | 2/3 to Wall St. | 212-422-9600

Financial Dist | 74 Trinity Pl. (bet. Rector & Thames Sts.) | 1 to Rector St. | 212-233-1111

800-900-2462 | www.leonidas-chocolate.com

"Flown fresh from Belgium", the "silky" chocolates on sale at these "friendly, Euro-feeling" shops almost make it impossible to go "mass-market" again, especially when the "incredible" goods come at a relatively "fair price" for the upscale genre; the Downtown outposts share space with Manon Cafe espresso bars, where you'll "get a free" bonbon "with your perfect cappuccino" – in sum, *"très magnifique."*

Le Pain Quotidien Baked Goods

24 | 23 | 18 | M

E 60s | 833 Lexington Ave. (bet. 63rd & 64th Sts.) | F to Lexington Ave./63rd St. | 212-755-5810

E 70s | 252 E. 77th St. (bet. 2nd & 3rd Aves.) | 6 to 77th St. | 212-249-8600

(continued)

(continued)

Le Pain Quotidien

E 80s | 1131 Madison Ave. (bet. 84th & 85th Sts.) | 4/5/6 to 86th St. | 212-327-4900

G Village | 10 Fifth Ave. (8th St.) | R/W to 8th St. | 212-253-2324

SoHo | 100 Grand St. (Mercer St.) | 6/J/M/N/Q/R/W/Z to Canal St. | 212-625-9009

Union Sq | 38 E. 19th St. (bet. B'way & Park Ave. S.) | 4/5/6/L/N/Q/R/W to 14th St./Union Sq. | 212-673-7900

W 50s | 922 Seventh Ave. (bet. 58th & 59th Sts.) | N/Q/R/W to 57th St. | 212-757-0775 ◑

W 60s | 60 W. 65th St. (bet. B'way & CPW) | 1 to 66th St./Lincoln Ctr. | 212-721-4001

W 70s | 50 W. 72nd St. (bet. Columbus Ave. & CPW) | B/C to 72nd St. | 212-712-9700

W 80s | 494 Amsterdam Ave. (84th St.) | 1 to 86th St. | 212-877-1200
www.painquotidien.com
Additional locations throughout the NY area

There's nothing quotidian about the "impressive" blend of "Euro style" and "substance" at these "awesome" Belgian bakeries/cafes, where "high-quality" "organic ingredients" yield "exceptional" "hearty breads" ("some of the best baguettes outside of Paris") and pastries, plus "scrumptious" sandwiches, salads and soups; the "provincial" settings with "communal farm tables" lend a "convivial" feel, and while the cost "can be steep" "for a chain", most maintain the only pain here is "spotty" service.

NEW Le Petit Prince *Baked Goods*

`-` | `-` | `-` | `M`

Astoria | 33-09 Broadway (33rd St.) | Queens | N/W to 30th Ave. | 718-777-3040

Bringing real-deal French bakery fare to the realm of baklava, this Astoria newcomer purveys a fine lineup of homemade treats including bona fide baguettes, pies, pastries and (but of course) "the best croissants" in the area; the petite cafe setting is cozily welcoming, and a visit won't set you back too many francs.

L'Epicerie *Specialty Shop*

`-` | `-` | `-` | `E`

Fort Greene | 270 Vanderbilt Ave. (DeKalb Ave.) | Brooklyn | G to Clinton/Washington Aves. | 718-636-1200

"Hits the mark with love and care" say supporters of this friendly "little French market" in Fort Greene, whose "limited, select" mostly organic offerings include charcuterie, cheeses, produce, meat, seafood and beyond; when you need a meal to go, there are sandwiches (made with bread from Blue Ribbon Bakery and Amy's) as well as prepared dishes like coq au vin.

Les Halles Market *Meat/Poultry*

`26` | `23` | `20` | `E`

Gramercy | 411 Park Ave. S. (bet. 28th & 29th Sts.) | 6 to 28th St. | 212-679-4111 | www.leshalles.net

"French-style cuts, rich and red" are the main attraction at this butcher beside the famed Gramercy brasserie, closely followed by the meaty "'nasty bits' Anthony Bourdain is always talking about", and it's also a "great resource" for "incredible bread", Paris-worthy desserts and other Gallic goodies; given its proximity, you can either "try the meat" next door "before you buy", or "order, have a bite in the restaurant and pick up on the way out."

Leske's *Baked Goods* ▽ 23 | 18 | 19 | I

Bay Ridge | 7612 Fifth Ave. (bet. 76th & 77th Sts.) | Brooklyn | R to 77th St. | 718-680-2323

A "specialty Scandinavian" bakery that's "been around for years", this "Bay Ridge landmark" puts "old-fashioned" "quality" into a repertoire that includes "all the favorites", from Danishes and black-and-white cookies to "out-of-this-world" rye bread; its loyal clientele claims the "classic treats" are nearly "a magical experience."

🔁 Levain Bakery 🖥️🛇 *Baked Goods* 28 | 18 | 22 | E

W 70s | 167 W. 74th St. (bet. Amsterdam & Columbus Aves.) | 1/2/3 to 72nd St. | 212-874-6080 | 877-453-8246 | www.levainbakery.com

"Cookies will never be the same" after a taste of the "delectable", "softball-size" batter-bombs at this "tiny" Upper West Side bakery, where the "moist and thick" chocolate chip version is "chewy" "decadence defined" – whether to "satiate your sweet tooth" or supply your "last meal"; they also do "off-the-hook" breads, scones and pizzas, and though it's "not the cheapest", most agree it's "worth saving up for", especially since the "nice folks" in charge donate each day's unsold output to charity.

LifeThyme Natural Market ⏺ *Health Food* 24 | 19 | 18 | M

G Village | 410 Sixth Ave. (bet. 8th & 9th Sts.) | A/B/C/D/E/F/V to W. 4th St. | 212-420-9099 | www.lifethymemarket.com

"Not the usual natural market", this Greenwich Villager offers a "dazzling array" of "healthy staples" and "hard-to-find items", as well as an "upstairs beauty emporium", "excellent raw foods selection", "delicious" prepared foods and "sinful" vegan desserts, plus one of the "best juice bars in Manhattan"; things can get "hectic" in its "cramped", overstuffed space, but the staff is usually "helpful."

Likitsakos ⏺ *Produce* 22 | 18 | 15 | M

E 80s | 1174 Lexington Ave. (bet. 80th & 81st Sts.) | 6 to 77th St. | 212-535-4300

Upper Eastsiders praise this "wonderful" gourmet food store for its "consistent produce" but suggest that the "beautifully presented" "Greek specialty items" – "fantastic dips" ("to-die-for taramasalata"), "homemade yogurt", spanakopita – are what really "keep this market packed"; "extras" like "fresh herbs", baked goods and cheese at "reasonable prices" also help to compensate for "cramped" quarters.

Li-Lac Chocolates 🖥️ *Candy/Nuts* 26 | 23 | 23 | E

E 40s | Grand Central Mkt. | Lexington Ave. (43rd St.) | 4/5/6/7/S to 42nd St./Grand Central | 212-370-4866 ⏺

W Village | 40 Eighth Ave. (Jane St.) | A/B/C/D/E/F/V to W. 4th St. | 212-924-2280

866-898-2462 | www.li-lacchocolates.com

Long before "high-quality chocolate was fashionable", this "old-school" "favorite" was producing "irresistible" "American-style" confections and thrilling gift-givers with its "amazing" molded shapes; some say this "old friend" "lost some of its charm" when it moved away from its "original Christopher Street" digs, and note that the city's "newer highbrow" purveyors offer "stiff competition" in its price range, but for most it remains a sweet tooth's "fantasy come true"; N.B. commuters appreciate the Grand Central outpost.

Lindt Chocolate Shop 🖳 Candy/Nuts | – | – | – | E |

E 40s | 367 Madison Ave. (45th St.) | 7 to 5th Ave. | 212-286-1970
W 50s | 692 Fifth Ave. (54th St.) | E/V to 53rd St. | 212-582-3047
www.lindt.com

Located on prime Midtown shopping blocks, these twin outposts of the Swiss chocolate giant carry the company's full line of chocolates, from Lindor truffles to every imaginable kind of bar; they also stock some Italian hard candies and jellies, and offer online ordering as well.

Lioni Latticini Mozzarella Company Cheese/Dairy | ▽ 29 | 17 | 21 | I |

Bensonhurst | 7803 15th Ave. (bet. 78th & 79th Sts.) | Brooklyn | D/M to 79th St. | 718-232-1411

"You want mozzarella, you go here" urge boosters of this Bensonhurst specialty goods and sandwich shop, where the "melt-in-your-mouth" mutz and "fresh" ricotta are delivered direct from their Jersey factory (and other cheeses are imported from The Boot itself); it's also lionized for its "yummy" pastas, Italian desserts and a "mind-boggling" list of 150 "massive" heroes, each christened with a "celebrity" name.

Liqueteria ● Soup | ▽ 19 | 16 | 17 | M |

E Village | 170 Second Ave. (11th St.) | L to 3rd Ave. | 212-358-0300

While this longtime "healthnik haven" in the East Village is popular for its "wonderful choices" of organic juices and smoothies and wheat-free baked goods, "if you love soups, say no more" – except maybe "mm-mm good"; just ignore the noise from the blenders and grab a seat at the counter.

Little Pie Company 🖳 Baked Goods | 24 | 19 | 18 | M |

E 40s | Grand Central Terminal | dining concourse (42nd St. & Vanderbilt Ave.) | 4/5/6/7/S to 42nd St./Grand Central | 212-983-3538 ◐
Meatpacking | 407 W. 14th St. (bet. 9th & 10th Aves.) | A/C/E/L to 14th St./8th Ave. | 212-414-2324
W 40s | 424 W. 43rd St. (bet. 9th & 10th Aves.) | A/C/E to 42nd St./Port Authority | 212-736-4780
www.littlepiecompany.com

"One bite and you're hooked" on the "heaven-sent" pies from this Theater District bakery (with its Grand Central and Meatpacking District offshoots), the "all-time winner" for "perfect crusts" and "scrumptious" fillings at a "fair" price; with an "unparalleled" sour cream–apple-walnut variety that's an "irresistible" temptation to "break your diet", it's a "first choice" "for holidays" ("order in advance" on Thanksgiving), and solo sweet tooths "have to love" the "individual-size" option.

	QUALITY	DISPLAY	SERVICE	COST

LMD Floral Events Interiors *Flowers* | - | - | - | VE |

E Village | 437 E. 12th St. (bet. Ave. A & 1st Ave.) | L to 1st Ave. |
212-614-2734 | www.lmdfloral.com

"I wouldn't use anyone else" aver acolytes of this "inventive" East
Village florist/event designer that takes old-fashioned flowers
(e.g. black irises) and presents them in handmade or vintage containers; although "imaginative young" owner Lewis Miller and his
team are equipped to handle high-budget events too.

☑ Lobel's Prime Meats 🕮 *Meat/Poultry* | 29 | 25 | 27 | VE |

E 80s | 1096 Madison Ave. (bet. 82nd & 83rd Sts.) | 4/5/6 to 86th St. |
212-737-1373 | www.lobels.com

Voted No. 1 in its category in NYC, this fifth-generation family-run
business on the Upper East Side is "the Rolls-Royce of butchers" –
"the Cartier", the "Tiffany's" – supplying "absolutely, positively the
best meat you will every buy" "anywhere on the planet", "from the
hot dogs to the Châteaubriand"; "bloody high" prices are "part of
the legend", but the consensus is that the "remarkable variety and
quality" make it all worthwhile, so go ahead – "sell the kid, buy a
steak"; N.B. prepared foods and online ordering are added bonuses.

Lobster Place 🕮 *Seafood* | 26 | 23 | 22 | M |

Chelsea | Chelsea Mkt. | 75 Ninth Ave. (bet. 15th & 16th Sts.) | A/C/E/L to
14th St./8th Ave. | 212-255-5672
G Village | 252 Bleecker St. (bet. 6th & 7th Aves.) | A/B/C/D/E/F/V to
W. 4th St. | 212-352-8063
www.lobsterplace.com

One of the city's biggest seafood suppliers, this wholesale/retail pair
in the Village and Chelsea Market is a "paradise" for piscophiles,
stocking an "impressive selection" of "super-fresh" offerings from the
sea, including, yes, "da best" lobsters, as well as a "wonderful treasure
chest" of prepared dishes; add "helpful" service and "reasonable"
prices and it's easy to see why many consider it "worth a special trip."

L'Olivier 🕮 *Flowers* | ▽ 29 | 29 | 25 | VE |

Chelsea | 213 W. 14th St. (7th Ave.) | A/C/E/L to 14th St./8th Ave. |
212-255-2828
E 70s | 19 E. 76th St. (bet. 5th & Madison Aves.) | 6 to 77th St. |
212-774-7676
www.lolivier.com

A delivery of an "exquisite", "exotic arrangement" from Olivier
Giugni's UES floral shop will have your co-workers saying "wow" – just
before they "swoon with jealousy"; using a sculptural, orchid-centered
signature look, they "make masterpieces" here, some of which can be
found in NYC's toniest eateries; yes, such envy-producing *fleurs*
come at couture prices; N.B. their Chelsea seedling focuses on events.

Lorenzo & Maria's Kitchen *Prepared Food* | 25 | 24 | 21 | VE |

E 80s | 1418 Third Ave. (bet. 80th & 81st Sts.) | 4/5/6 to 86th St. |
212-794-1080

At this high-end Yorkville take-out/catering "staple" (since 1978),
the gorgeous window display showcases prepared offerings that

range from meat and fish dishes to cakes, cookies and tarts; no doubt, frugal fans "save it for special occasions", but even though it's "very expensive", the consensus is the goods "are the best you can buy."

NEW Lorimer Street Meat Market ⊖ *Meat/Poultry*

- | - | - | M

Williamsburg | 620 Lorimer St. (Skillman Ave.) | Brooklyn | L to Lorimer St. | 718-389-2691

Ensconced in brand-new "across-the-street" quarters, this meat butcher and deli in Williamsburg continues to supply the same old-school Italian aged beef, seasonal game, sausages and prepared foods (lasagna, chicken parm, sandwiches) for which it's known; "friendly, eager-to-serve" staffers help ensure it's holding its own in a neighborhood "undergoing lots of great changes."

Lung Moon Bakery ⊖ *Baked Goods*

19 | 16 | 14 | I

Chinatown | 83 Mulberry St. (bet. Bayard & Canal Sts.) | 6/J/M/N/Q/R/W/Z to Canal St. | 212-349-4945

Purists who "crave the old-style" Chinese goodies are likely to land at this veteran Chinatown bakery, a "cornerstone" for "great pastries" ("especially" the "gorgeous moon cakes") with "just the right texture" to make you long for Hong Kong; mandarins also moon over the pork buns, custard pie, bean cakes and "seasonal" items like bubble tea in the summer.

Luscious Food ● *Prepared Food*

- | - | - | M

Park Slope | 59 Fifth Ave. (bet. Bergen St. & St. Marks Ave.) | Brooklyn | 2/3 to Bergen St. | 718-398-5800 | www.lusciousbrooklyn.com

This Park Slope gourmet-to-go storefront run by two caterers is a neighborhood source for "tasty" comfort fare – mac 'n' cheese, meatloaf and sandwiches built on Royal Crown bakery bread – as well as packaged items such as olive oils, pasta sauces and teas; there are a few seats for on-site munching, but most get it to go.

Macy's Cellar ● ▭ *Cookware*

21 | 18 | 12 | M

Garment Dist | 151 W. 34th St. (bet. 6th & 7th Aves.) | 1/2/3/A/C/E to 34th St./Penn Station | 212-695-4400 | 800-456-2297 | www.macys.com

"Load up on basics" at this "chaotic" department store basement where "everything you need for the kitchen" – from cookware and cutlery to appliances and gadgets – is offered "in many trendy brands" all "in one place" and at "moderate prices" to boot; the goods get downright "cheap" on "sale days", but be warned that those can be a "jungle", with "nonexistent service" fueling the "aggravation", meaning you may end up paying for the "deals" with a "headache."

NEW Madison *Baked Goods*

- | - | - | E

E 90s | 1292 Madison Ave. (bet. 91st & 92nd Sts.) | 6 to 96th St. | 212-860-1598

Formerly known as Yura, this Upper East Side bakery changed names recently after a split in ownership; the only location that remains in the hands of baker-caterer extraordinaire Yura Mohr, it continues to turn out the same high-level cakes and pastries, as well as prepared foods, for which it has long been beloved in the neighborhood.

	QUALITY	DISPLAY	SERVICE	COST

⊿ Madonia Bakery 🚫 *Baked Goods* 28 | 20 | 23 | I

Bronx | 2348 Arthur Ave. (187th St.) | B/D to Fordham Rd. | 718-295-5573

An "Arthur Avenue favorite" "for many decades", this ultra-"authentic" Italian bakery is "known for" "wonderful" "specialty" breads that "can't be surpassed", with upper-crust honors going to the "excellent" olive and prosciutto loaves; add a "nice selection" of cannoli and cookies and "lots of help when needed" and it's "worth the drive" not to "miss out."

Maggie Moo's ⬤ *Ice Cream* 21 | 19 | 19 | M

E 70s | 1437 Second Ave. (bet. 74th & 75th Sts.) | 6 to 77th St. | 212-472-6249

Park Slope | 183 Seventh Ave. (bet. 1st & 2nd Sts.) | Brooklyn | F to 7th Ave. | 718-788-3900

Bayside | 3933 Bell Blvd. (bet. 39th & 40th Aves.) | Queens | 718-229-0229
www.maggiemoos.com

Families on the UES, Park Slope and Bayside have "tons of fun" at these "excellent" ice cream shops where you choose from an eclectic range of goodies to be mixed into "creamy and dense ice cream" to make your own "innovative flavors"; the "very friendly staff" "really caters to kids", who also love the special-occasion cakes.

⊿ Magnolia Bakery ⬤ *Baked Goods* 23 | 20 | 17 | M

W Village | 401 Bleecker St. (W. 11th St.) | 1 to Christopher St. | 212-462-2572

A "serious" "sugar rush" awaits at this "legendary" West Village bakery, a "tiny" shop "reminiscent of yesteryear" that "earns its reputation" with a "swoon"-worthy selection of "sinful" cupcakes topped with "obscenely good" "butter icing", along with "unsung stars" like "must-have" banana pudding; it's "annoying" to "fight off the tourists" and abide a "snooty" staff, but "lines out the door" prove that this "sweet" "taste of Americana" is an enduring "crowd-pleaser."

Magnolia Flowers & Events *Flowers* ∇ 26 | 26 | 26 | E

W Village | 436 Hudson St. (bet. Leroy & Morton Sts.) | 1 to Houston St. | 212-243-7302 | www.magnoliaflowersandevents.com

"Outstanding flowers" from across the globe form the basis for the "fantastically beautiful arrangements" at this West Village florist that's "never a disappointment" to its celeb clientele; though "worth the $$$", they're also adept "at taking a price point and creating a very memorable" piece, making them "perfect for any celebration" – or budget; N.B. gifts and pre-made displays are available at their Bryant Park kiosk, open April–December.

Make My Cake *Baked Goods* 25 | 18 | 18 | M

Harlem | 121 St. Nicholas Ave. (116th St.) | 2/3 to 116th St. | 212-932-0833 🚫

Harlem | 2380 Adam Clayton Powell Blvd. (139th St.) | B/C to 135th St. | 212-234-2344
www.makemycake.com

"Just like grandma's" is the word on the Southern specialties from these Harlem bakeries, home to the "out-of-this-world" likes of red

QUALITY DISPLAY SERVICE COST

velvet cake, sweet potato cheesecake, "light, fluffy cupcakes" and a butter-cream number that'll "melt in your mouth"; whether for birthdays, weddings or catering, a visit is sure to make your day; N.B. the St. Nicholas Avenue original is a sit-down cafe while the adjunct farther Uptown is retail only.

M & I International Foods ☻ *Specialty Shop* | 24 | 23 | 13 | M |

Brighton Bch | 249 Brighton Beach Ave. (bet. Brighton 1st & Brighton 2nd Sts.) | Brooklyn | B/Q to Brighton Bch. | 718-615-1011

It's the "Russian Zabar's" rave reviewers of this big, bi-level Eastern European market that's a "bright spot in Brighton Beach" thanks to its "huge selection" spanning fresh meat and sausages, smoked fish and caviar, cheeses, imported comestibles, "delicious" prepared dishes – from chicken Kiev to pierogi and blintzes – as well as breads, cakes and other bakery items; still, keep in mind that some of its Slavic staples may "require an adventurous palate" – and a "translator" for the Cyrillic-challenged; P.S. it gets "crowded on weekends."

Mandler's: The Original Sausage Co. ☻🖃 *Prepared Food* | 22 | 15 | 17 | M |

NEW **Garment Dist** | 601 Eighth Ave. (bet. 39th & 40th Sts.) | A/C/E to 42nd St./Port Authority | 212-244-4777

Union Sq | 26 E. 17th St. (bet. B'way & 5th Ave.) | 4/5/6/L/N/Q/R/W to 14th St./Union Sq. | 212-255-8999

www.mandlers.com

The "high-quality" Euro sausages are made "in so many delectable ways" (from chorizo to chicken to andouille) at these Midtown/ Union Square links houses that also please with their "variety" of mustards and breakfasts-all-day meals; "fast" delivery and online ordering turn the duo into real wieners.

Manganaro Foods *Deli/Sandwich* | 24 | 19 | 19 | M |

Garment Dist | 488 Ninth Ave. (bet. 37th & 38th Sts.) | A/C/E to 42nd St./Port Authority | 212-563-5331 | 800-472-5264 | www.manganarofoods.com

"A little slice of Italy" in the shadow of the Port Authority, this grocery store/caterer/cafe "with an old-world look" is "like eating in mama's kitchen, assuming mama really knew how to cook"; the counter staff may "need to smile more", but most admit the reason you come to this "irreplaceable institution" is for "top-quality food", including "fresh meats and cheeses" and "killer sandwiches."

Manganaro's Hero Boy ☻ *Deli/Sandwich* | 21 | 15 | 16 | M |

Garment Dist | 494 Ninth Ave. (bet. 37th & 38th Sts.) | A/C/E to 42nd St./Port Authority | 212-947-7325 | www.manganarosheroboy.com

There's "nothing like a hero, boy, to get your juices flowing" fawn fans of this "authentic" Midtown Italian deli that's been a "standby" for over 50 years for its "terrific" selection of 40-odd sandwiches ("they set the bar for six-ft.-long" babies) at "very fair prices"; though critics claim it's "nothing special", others insist it's perfect "pre–Madison Square Garden" or after a softball game; N.B. closed Sundays July–August.

Mangia *Prepared Food*

24	23	17	E

E 40s | 16 E. 48th St. (bet. 5th & Madison Aves.) | B/D/F/V to 47-50th Sts./ Rockefeller Ctr. | 212-754-7600

Financial Dist | Trump Bldg. | 40 Wall St. (bet. Broad & Pine Sts.) | 2/3 to Wall St. | 212-425-4040 ◑

Flatiron | 22 W. 23rd St. (bet. 5th & 6th Aves.) | N/R/W to 23rd St. | 212-647-0200 ◑

W 50s | 50 W. 57th St. (bet. 5th & 6th Aves.) | N/Q/R/W to 57th St. | 212-582-5882

www.mangiatogo.com

"Every possible food one could crave" lures lunchtime hordes to this quartet of prepared foods factories featuring "amazing" salad bars, "tasty" sandwiches and panini, pizzas and a "wonderful" array of seafood and meat dishes (cold and hot) as well as "delish" pastries; the "ridiculously expensive" tabs may be fit for "bankers", but even lowly desk jockeys pony up because the "reliable" goods are "absolutely delicious"; N.B. it specializes in office catering.

Manhattan Espresso Cafe *Coffee/Tea*

21	19	19	M

E 40s | 146 E. 49th St. (bet. Lexington & 3rd Aves.) | 6 to 51st St. | 212-832-3010 | www.manhattanespressocafe.com

Midtown's tourists and desk jockeys refuel on the fly at this "total gem" of an espresso bar, a five-seater cubbyhole whose Illy brand Italian coffee makes for an always-flavorful shot or cuppa; they also dole out crêpes, croissants, pastries and sandwiches, "but space is limited" so plan for an express stop when the cappuccino craving strikes.

Manhattan Fruit Exchange ⊘ *Produce*

24	21	16	I

Chelsea | Chelsea Mkt. | 75 Ninth Ave. (bet. 15th & 16th Sts.) | A/C/E/L to 14th St./8th Ave. | 212-989-2444 | www.manhattanfruitexchange.com

"Filled with attractive, exotic treasures" this Chelsea Market produce peddler is a veritable "cornucopia" of "impeccable" fruits and veggies including slews of seasonal standouts like "terrific mushrooms" and "baby vegetables galore" plus "quality nuts", candy, coffee and juices as well as "lots of fresh and dried herbs"; its "reasonable prices" help explain why it's "always bustling"; P.S. the "only beef" is that it's "cash-only."

☑ Manhattan Fruitier ▣ *Specialty Shop*

27	25	24	E

Gramercy | 105 E. 29th St. (bet. Lexington & Park Aves.) | 6 to 28th St. | 212-686-0404 | www.manhattanfruitier.com

"Discriminating" present-givers looking to "impress" find baskets brimming with "exotic fruits" "almost too lovely to eat" and other delicacies at this Gramercy Park specialist whose "stellar" compositions "should be in the dictionary next to the words 'classy gift'"; the assortments include "quality" chocolates, dried fruits, artisanal cheeses, caviar and assorted other "luscious" "temptations" that can be purchased in the store or through the "reliable online ordering and delivery" system – but know that while they're "oh-so-pretty", they're also "oh-so-pricey."

	QUALITY	DISPLAY	SERVICE	COST

Manley's Wines & Spirits ● *Wine/Liquor*   ▽ 22 | 18 | 21 | M

W Village | 35 Eighth Ave. (bet. 12th & 13th Sts.) | A/C/E/L to 14th St./ 8th Ave. | 212-242-3712

"Wonderfully local", with an "attentive staff" and small-town vibe, this West Village veteran (since 1934) proffers affordable everyday wines and a full line of spirits, along with glassware by Stieglau, Divino and Riedel; stop by during the holiday season for some "model-train action" on tracks suspended near the ceiling.

Manna Catering *Caterer*   - | - | - | E

TriBeCa | 24 Harrison St. (bet. Greenwich & Hudson Sts.) | 1 to Franklin St. | 212-966-3449 | www.mannacatering.com

Known for "haute kosher cuisine" so "delish" it seems heaven sent, this TriBeCa caterer is a sensation for off-site occasions that's done divine work for the likes of Steven Spielberg and Ronald Perelman; with exotic presentations and worldly influences extending from the Mideast to the Far East, this is a nosh that "grandma never made."

Mansoura ▣ *Baked Goods*   - | - | - | M

Midwood | 515 Kings Hwy. (bet. E. 2nd & 3rd Sts.) | Brooklyn | F to Kings Hwy. | 718-645-7977 | www.mansoura.com

"It's the real thing" agree effendis at this Midwood bakery, whose Sephardic kosher specialties are an all-but-unique taste of the Middle East and Mediterranean; "great pastries and candies" are highlights of a lineup that also includes confections and hors d'oeuvres, and gift tins and catering platters present a range of appetizing samples.

Marché Madison *Prepared Food*   20 | 18 | 15 | VE

E 50s | 36 E. 58th St. (bet. Madison & Park Aves.) | N/R/W to 5th Ave./ 59th St. | 212-355-3366

E 70s | 931 Madison Ave. (74th St.) | 6 to 77th St. | 212-794-3360 ●

On-the-go Eastsiders march over to this "chichi" pair that vends a "good" variety of "fresh" fruits, veggies and prepared foods that regulars say "make your mouth water"; but alas, mad shoppers maul "overpriced", "ok" products sold by "sullen servers."

Margaret Braun Cakes & Sugar Objects ⊘ *Baked Goods*   - | - | - | VE

W Village | 33 Bank St. (W. 4th St.) | A/B/C/D/E/F/V to W. 4th St. | 212-929-1582 | www.margaretbraun.com

By appointment only

"Art that tastes delicious" is the métier of exclusive baker Margaret Braun, whose cakes are elaborate creations on fanciful themes, lovingly crafted with baroque details that make each one "a rare thing indeed"; she's the Rembrandt of weddings and special occasions, with a sideline in sugar sculptures that sometimes show up in movies.

Margaret Palca Bakes *Baked Goods*   - | - | - | I

Carroll Gardens | 191 Columbia St. (bet. Degraw & Sackett Sts.) | Brooklyn | 718-802-9771 | www.margaretpalcabakes.com

Rolling "the best" "buttery rugalach" around, pastry chef Margaret Palca's Carroll Gardens bake shop is a modest setup with a "friendly local vibe" where dessert devotees will also find "delicious" "home-made" cakes, pies, brownies and "cookies almost too beautiful to eat"; plus the ovens turn out the "amazing" bread and rolls that bolster their first-rate sandwiches to go.

Margot Pâtisserie *Baked Goods*

27	21	22	M

W 70s | 2109 Broadway (74th St.) | 1/2/3 to 72nd St. | 212-721-0076
Francophiles nominate this West Side "hideaway" as the "perfect" patisserie since its "outstanding" pastries, tarts, cakes and baguette sandwiches are sure to make you "feel like you're back in Paris"; it's something of a "neighborhood" "secret" thanks to an "easy-to-miss" locale, and the expats "sipping coffee and eating croissants" are inclined to plead "don't tell."

☑ MarieBelle's Fine Treats & Chocolates ▣ *Candy/Nuts*

26	26	21	E

SoHo | 484 Broome St. (bet. W. B'way & Wooster St.) | 1/A/C/E to Canal St. | 212-925-6999 | 866-925-8800 | www.mariebelle.com
It's "an experience" just visiting Maribel Lieberman's "stylish" SoHo chocolate boutique, a favorite among "fashionistas" for its trademark silkscreen-patterned bonbons, "delicious little works of art" that "taste as good as they look"; equally "lovely" packaging ensures they make "delightful gifts", leading most to overlook the "pricey" tabs and occasionally "self-important" service; P.S. "stop by the tea room" in back for some "divine" chile-spiked Aztec hot chocolate.

Marlow & Sons ● *Specialty Shop*

-	-	-	M

Williamsburg | 81 Broadway (Berry St.) | Brooklyn | L to Bedford Ave. | 718-384-1441 | www.marlowandsons.com
It's business in the front, party in the back at this Williamsburg grocery shop, from the owners of nearby Diner, where you enter into a small gourmet store and proceed to a rear oyster-and-wine bar; it's a prized "neighborhood resource" for quality comestibles from biodynamic dairy products, farmstead cheeses and pasture-raised meats to small-batch honeys, imported oils and vinegars; N.B. the eatery recently expanded its menu and seating area.

Marquet Patisserie *Baked Goods*

24	21	19	M

Boerum Hill | 221 Court St. (Warren St.) | Brooklyn | F/G to Bergen St. | 718-855-1289
Fort Greene | 680 Fulton St. (S. Portland St.) | Brooklyn | G to Fulton St. | 718-596-2018 ✝
Croissant connoisseurs tip their berets to "the light touch" at these separately owned Boerum Hill and Fort Greene bakeries, where the "excellent" "French pastries", tarts and cakes confirm the value of "attention paid to details"; they also market take-out lunches, and most "don't mind the prices" – it's still "cheaper than a ticket to Paris."

Martha's Country Bakery *Baked Goods*

-	-	-	M

Astoria | 3621 Ditmars Blvd. (bet. 36th & 37th Sts.) | Queens | N/W to Astoria/Ditmars Blvd. | 718-545-9737
The "absolute best aroma" greets walkers-in at this Astoria bakery/cafe, a cupcake specialist that also displays a "fresh" array of full-

size cakes, sweet and savory pies, fruit tarts and more to give even "particular palates" something to "rave about"; a sandwich menu is now available, and the front-porchy quarters have been expanded with more seating.

Martin Bros.
Wines & Spirits ●▣ *Wine/Liquor* | 21 | 18 | 23 | M |

W 100s | 2781 Broadway (107th St.) | 1 to 110th St. | 212-222-8218 | www.martinbrotherswine.com

Upper Westsiders toast the "unpretentious, approachable" yet "knowledgeable" staffers who make this small shop near Columbia a "great neighborhood resource" for the inquisitive imbiber ("I went from a scotch greenhorn to a learned individual after a lesson from the proprietor"); its "carefully selected" stock includes not only "everyday" wines but also a "superb selection of high-dollar Cabernets" and more than 150 single-malt whiskeys.

Ⓩ Martine's Chocolates ▣ *Candy/Nuts* | 29 | 24 | 22 | VE |

E 50s | Bloomingdale's | 1000 Third Ave., 6th fl. (59th St.) | 4/5/6 to 59th St./Lexington Ave. | 212-705-2347 ●
E 80s | 400 E. 82nd St. (bet. 1st & York Aves.) | 4/5/6 to 86th St. | 212-744-6289
www.martineschocolates.com

"Truly freshly made" chocolates – you can "actually see them" being prepared on premises – lure cacao-nnoisseurs to this "sweet asset" on the East Side, whose original Bloomie's location makes the perfect "shoppers' pit stop"; beyond its signature "amazing, rich" filled chocolates, there are novelty offerings "in every shape possible" (think "baseballs and Statues of Liberty") – though naturally such "high quality" comes at a steep price.

Martin's Pretzels ▣ *Baked Goods* | 27 | 18 | 24 | I |

See Greenmarket; for more information, call 315-628-4927 | www.martinspretzels.com

It's a "must for pretzel mavens" say snackers who swear by the hand-rolled, "perfectly crisped and salted" specimens cranked out by this year-round Greenmarket stalwart; the lineup includes whole pretzels, "bags of pieces" ("go for those broken ones!") and a "wonderful" whole-wheat version for the health-conscious, so "take a sample and see for yourself" – they're "great to munch on" as you stroll around "the rest of the market."

Mary's Dairy ●⇄ *Ice Cream* | 24 | 22 | 20 | M |

E Village | 158 First Ave. (bet. 9th & 10th Sts.) | L to 1st Ave. | 212-254-5004
G Village | 171 W. Fourth St. (bet. 6th & 7th Aves.) | A/B/C/D/E/F/V to W. 4th St. | 212-242-6874
www.marysdairynyc.com

Ice cream goes the "hip and trendy" route at this crosstown pair of "friendly, funky" Village spots, where locals hang out on the benches savoring the "seriously delectable" (and "a little overpriced") flavors like Vahlrona chocolate or pistachio halvah; those watching their waistlines praise the no-fat, low-calorie Likety Lite option.

	QUALITY	DISPLAY	SERVICE	COST

Masturbakers *Baked Goods* ▽ 22 | 19 | 23 | M

E Village | Old Devil Moon | 511 E. 12th St. (bet. Aves. A & B) | L to 1st Ave. | 212-475-0476 | www.masturbakers.com

When the occasion calls for "witty" "X-rated confections", this East Village custom baker gets down and dirty with "yummy" "porno cakes" that "surprisingly taste just like mom's"; the graphic goodies are "perfect for bachelor/ette parties", but they'll turn even the tamest get-together into "an orgasmic experience" – however, if you're a soft-core sort, nonexplicit versions are also available.

Mauzone *Prepared Food* 22 | 16 | 18 | M

Flushing | 72-30 Main St. (bet. 72nd & 73rd Aves.) | Queens | 7 to Flushing-Main St. | 718-261-7723 | www.mauzonemarketplace.com

An "outstanding range" of "reasonably" priced food such as "delicious" fried chicken, kugel and all sorts of "homemade" sides send patrons back to this glatt kosher take-out champ in Flushing; N.B. the stores close early on Fridays and all day Saturdays.

Max & Mina's Homemade Inc. ◗⇎ *Ice Cream* ▽ 25 | 21 | 24 | I

Flushing | 71-26 Main St. (bet. 71st Rd. & 72nd Ave.) | Queens | 7 to Flushing-Main St. | 718-793-8629

If you've ever had a craving for housemade ice cream flavored with lox, horseradish or red wine, this Queens-based kosher parlor with a penchant for wacky concoctions "is your place" (perhaps not surprisingly, the original founder, Max, was a dairy-loving biochemist with an experimental edge); less-adventuresome eaters needn't fret, because tamer flavors are available too; N.B. closes early on Friday and reopens Saturday after sundown.

NEW Max Brenner, Chocolate by the Bald Man ▤ *Candy/Nuts* 22 | 24 | 18 | E

E Village | 141 2nd Ave. (9th St.) | N/R/W to 8th St. | 212-388-0030
Union Sq | 841 Broadway (bet. 13th & 14th Sts.) | 4/5/6/L/N/Q/R/W to 14th St./Union Sq. | 212-388-0030
www.maxbrenner.com

One look at the "chocolate pipes running across the ceiling" and it's clear that "Willy Wonka has landed in NYC" at this Union Square outpost of an Israeli-born, "over-the-top" chain of chocolate-themed shops/cafes known for its "inventive" sweets (e.g. chocolate pizza) to make the "blood sugar soar"; "brunch is a zoo", and some consider the offerings overly "expensive" – particularly when you factor in "erratic service" and "screaming kids" – but still diehards declare "I don't care if my hair does fall out"; N.B. there's also a smaller East Village branch.

Maya Schaper Cheese & Antiques ▤ *Cheese/Dairy* ▽ 22 | 23 | 22 | E

W 60s | 106 W. 69th St. (bet. B'way & Columbus Ave.) | 1 to 66th St./Lincoln Ctr. | 212-873-2100

Sure, it's a "strange juxtaposition", but this "quirky" Upper West Side "gem" may make you a "believer" with its "beautiful" sales display of "quaint" kitchen curios side-by-side with "fabulous" fromages, leading to "great finds" both edible and collectible; the antiques run from cheese trays to cookware and cutlery, and though the "selection could be bigger", "friendly service" ensures it's always a pleasure to "browse."

☑ May May ⌨ Specialty Shop   23 | 16 | 19 | I

Chinatown | 35 Pell St. (bet. Bowery & Mott St.) | 6/J/M/N/Q/R/W/Z to Canal St. | 212-267-0733 | www.maymayfood.com

"A NYC classic" for over 40 years, this Chinatown bakery is the "frozen dim sum depot" of choice for party-throwers and others; "flaky pork buns", "fantastic sticky rice pouches" and dumplings with all manner of "fillings to choose from" are "well worth the trip" to Pell Street, as are holiday "sweets" like moon cakes and what some call "the best egg tarts in town."

Mazur's Marketplace & Restaurant   Meat/Poultry   20 | 17 | 18 | E

Douglaston | 254-51 Horace Harding Blvd. (Little Neck Pkwy.) | Queens | 718-428-5000 | www.mazursmarketplace.com

This full-service glatt kosher food market in Queens can be counted on for a "great selection" of edibles ("just ask if you don't see it"), including "excellent quality" butcher items, rotisserie birds, take-out prepared dishes, challah and other baked goods, fresh and smoked fish and now sushi; catering and a next-door restaurant are part of the package; N.B. closes early on Friday and all day Saturday.

Mazzola Bakery ⊘ Baked Goods   25 | 18 | 19 | I

Carroll Gardens | 192 Union St. (Henry St.) | Brooklyn | F/G to Carroll St. | 718-643-1719

The "bread is heaven" at this '20s-era Carroll Gardens "neighborhood bakery", a "pre-gentrification holdover" celebrated for dispensing a "delicious" assortment of specialty loaves (notably the prosciutto-packed lard variety) in an "amazingly warm environment"; and if you don't live by bread alone, they also vend "wonderful baked goods" and "excellent java."

McAdam Buy Rite ⚫⌨ Wine/Liquor   ▽ 22 | 14 | 19 | M

Gramercy | 398 Third Ave. (bet. 28th & 29th Sts.) | 6 to 28th St. | 212-679-1224 | www.americaswineshop.com

The staff at this veteran Gramercy Park wine discounter can help you locate a particular Long Island wine (it carries more than 210), but it also stocks selections from the expected regions (California, France, Australia) for more mainstream shoppers; regulars recommend it as a place to "find the best prices on workhorse" bottles (e.g. "cases of white for the office party"), but say it pays to go in "knowing what you want."

McCabe's Wines & Spirits ⚫ Wine/Liquor   19 | 16 | 19 | M

E 70s | 1347 Third Ave. (77th St.) | 6 to 77th St. | 212-737-0790

At this "decent neighborhood store" on the Upper East Side, plentiful kosher wines (some 300), share the cellar with French, Australian and a growing number of German vintages, along with boutique bottlings from California; those who prefer the hard stuff can get lots of single-malts and small-batch bourbons at "fair prices", so although service gets mixed reviews, this place is "always busy."

McNulty's Tea & Coffee Co. ◐ ▭ *Coffee/Tea* | 27 | 22 | 23 | M |

W Village | 109 Christopher St. (bet. Bleecker & Hudson Sts.) | 1 to Christopher St. | 212-242-5351 | 800-356-5200 | www.mcnultys.com
"No one can call it trendy", but you "can't do better" for "all things good to brew" than this "old-time" (circa 1895) West Village purveyor of "fine coffees and teas", where the "superb" assortment of "exotic" blends is so wide-ranging it's "hard to pick just one"; count on "courteous" "guidance" from in-house "experts" in a milieu so "atmospheric" that "just a whiff is enough" for a "caffeine fix."

Mediterranean Foods ◐ ▭ *Specialty Shop* | ▽ 26 | 22 | 21 | I |

Astoria | 23-18 31st St. (bet. 23rd & 24th Aves.) | Queens | N/W to Astoria/Ditmars Blvd. | 718-721-0221
Astoria | 30-12 34th St. (30th Ave.) | Queens | N/W to 30th Ave. | 718-728-6166
The "best place for a taste of Greece" outside of the Peloponnesus is this "outstanding" Astoria market duo where the "excellent selection" comes at "bargain" prices and is presided over by a "helpful and friendly" crew; "love the choices of olives" and oil, "yogurt, orzo, spices, nuts, candies" and "other essentials" say surveyors who sigh "so many fetas, so little time."

Melange ◐ *Prepared Food* | 21 | 15 | 19 | I |

E 60s | 1188 First Ave. (bet. 64th & 65th Sts.) | 6 to 68th St. | 212-249-3743
E 60s | 1277 First Ave. (bet. 68th & 69th Sts.) | 6 to 68th St. | 212-535-7773
Best known for its "yummy" Middle Eastern "treats", this East Side prepared-food twosome has "everything you need" by way of "healthy", "gourmet" fare, whether it's hummus, falafel or the "best" halvah, all sold at a "great" price; rounding out the endorsement is a "friendly" staff always "willing to offer advice."

Metro Party Rentals *Party Rentals* | - | - | - | M |

Paterson | 188 Lafayette St. (bet. Rosa Parks Ave. & 16th St.), NJ | 973-684-4144 | 800-234-2011 | www.metropartyrentals.com
Though based in northern New Jersey, this rental enterprise serves all of the tri-state area, catering to commercial and private party-throwers and keeping them well-supplied with tables, chairs and china, not to mention customized tents and dance floors; N.B. $200 minimum charge for delivery to Manhattan.

Michael George *Flowers* | ▽ 25 | 25 | 20 | E |

E 40s | 5 Tudor City Pl. (41st St.) | 212-883-0304 | www.mgflowers.com
By appointment only
In business for over three decades, this Tudor City florist-to-the-stars boasts a "fashion"-friendly client list including boldface names such as Tom Ford and Tommy Hilfiger; it also plans chic events, but its real "magic" can be found in its minimalist arrangements – how does it "get those tulips to stand that way"?

	QUALITY	DISPLAY	SERVICE	COST

Michael-Towne
Wines & Spirits ◐ *Wine/Liquor*

| 24 | 24 | 24 | M |

Brooklyn Heights | 73 Clark St. (Henry St.) | Brooklyn | 2/3 to Clark St. | 718-875-3667

"Serving the wine snob and the peppermint-schnapps crowd with equal care", this "convenient", "pleasant and reliable" Brooklyn Heights shop offers a "wide-ranging" selection of vintages from all over the world, plus "top-shelf liquors" (especially bourbon and single-malts) and sake; "extremely helpful" service and "reasonable pricing" enhanced by generous by-the-case discounts make this "handsome" contender that much more attractive.

Michelle's Kitchen 🖃 *Prepared Food*

| 18 | 17 | 17 | M |

E 90s | 1614 Third Ave. (bet. 90th & 91st Sts.) | 4/5/6 to 86th St. | 212-996-0012 | www.michelleskitchen.com

Although its hors d'oeuvres turn up at a number of off-site events, this Yorkville French-Belgian caterer also runs a "pleasant" prepared foods shop where locals "stop by on their way home" for "upscale" sandwiches and other "homestyle" prepared dishes; critics say the offerings are "hit-or-miss", but few would argue with a place offering "quick" to-go meals in an "underserved neighborhood."

Migliorelli Farm ⊘ *Produce*

| 26 | 23 | 22 | I |

See Greenmarket; for more information, call 845-757-3276

"One of the foundations" of the Greenmarket, this "go-to vendor" for fresh fruit and vegetables hauls its "lovely variety of produce", including "especially good greens" that are always "fresh and flavorful", from Tivoli, NY, year-round and is one of the "hardy few" still at Union Square in winter; the gilding on the lettuce leaf is that it's also one of the more "reasonably priced" stalls around.

Miho Kosuda Ltd. *Flowers*

| – | – | – | VE |

E 40s | 310 E. 44th St. (bet. 1st & 2nd Aves.) | 212-922-9122

By appointment only

This chic East Side florist and event planner uses only "the lushest roses and peonies" in pieces that have long attracted a celeb clientele (Manolo Blahnik, among others); the eponymous owner creates posies that are "simple, elegant" and exhibit "just a dash of individual style", generally utilizing only one type of flower in a rainbow of hues.

Milano Gourmet *Prepared Food*

| 25 | 21 | 21 | M |

E 80s | 1582 Third Ave. (89th St.) | 4/5/6 to 86th St. | 212-996-6681 ◐
Murray Hill | 14 E. 34th St. (bet. 5th & Madison Aves.) | 6 to 33rd St. | 212-532-1177
W 100s | 2892 Broadway (bet. 112th & 113th Sts.) | 1 to 110th St. | 212-665-9500 ◐
www.milanogourmet.com

With "great" sandwiches, the "best" cold cuts and "delicious" pastas and salads, it's no wonder the "devoted clientele" can't get enough of the Italian-accented dishes sold at these East Side–West Side markets; plus, all those "helpful" folks inside make the experience all the more "*bellissimo*."

Milk & Cookies ◐ ▭ *Baked Goods* | 24 | 22 | 21 | M |

W Village | 19 Commerce St. (bet. Bedford St. & 7th Ave.) | 1 to Christopher St. | 212-243-1640 | www.milkandcookiesbakery.com

"Pick your own dough and mix-ins" and have "custom cookies" "made fresh to order" at this "cute" West Village bakery, which will whip up an "mm-mm good" batch in about eight minutes and serve 'em with milk from Ronnybrook Farms Dairy; they also sell pre-made cookies and bars along with ice cream sandwiches and shakes, so though the selection's "simple", "kids" at heart "can't resist."

Mille Fiori *Flowers* | – | – | – | E |

Chelsea | 227 W. 29th St., 2nd fl. (bet. 7th & 8th Aves.) | 212-714-2202 | www.millefioriflowers.com
By appointment only

"Recipients are always thrilled" to sign for a delivery from this Chelsea floral shop that sources "gorgeous flowers" – the Japanese peony is among their signature blooms – "made even more beautiful by their arrangements"; it specializes in weddings and corporate events, but no matter the occasion, you can expect "exquisite work" that's "worth the somewhat high prices."

🄩 Minamoto Kitchoan ▭ *Candy/Nuts* | 28 | 27 | 25 | E |

W 40s | Swiss Center Bldg. | 608 Fifth Ave. (49th St.) | B/D/F/V to 47-50th Sts./Rockefeller Ctr. | 212-489-3747 | www.kitchoan.com

This "serene" Japanese confectionary in Midtown is "the closest you can get to Tokyo" without hopping a JAL flight, proffering "beautifully displayed", Japanese wagashi ("traditional" tea sweets) carefully crafted to resemble "perfect little pieces of art"; such "exquisite" creations make "lovely" and "unusual gifts" – thanks particularly to a staff that "takes great care in packaging" – but as some say these "dainty", costly delights are "an acquired taste", just be sure "the recipient knows how special they are."

Mister Wright ● *Wine/Liquor* | 24 | 20 | 24 | M |

E 80s | 1593 Third Ave. (bet. 89th & 90th Sts.) | 4/5/6 to 86th St. | 212-722-4564

"You can't go wrong at Mister Wright" aver admirers of this "no-attitude" Yorkville establishment where there's lots of "open space to browse" the global "variety" of "wines for the common man", though some say the layout can be "a little hard to navigate"; oenophiles "on a budget" appreciate "passionate", "helpful" staffers who "treat you with the same respect" whether you're spending "$5 or $500", toasting this longtime staple as a neighborhood "favorite."

Mondel Chocolates ▭ *Candy/Nuts* | 22 | 19 | 20 | M |

W 100s | 2913 Broadway (114th St.) | 1 to 116th St. | 212-864-2111 | www.mondelchocolates.com

This "old-school" "neighborhood candy joint" in Morningside Heights has supplied the Columbia crowd with quality chocolates and other sweets since the 1940s ("they've been using dark chocolate for decades"), and happily retains its "charming", "unpretentious" atmosphere; a few find its output "uninspired" and shrug the appeal must be "a nostalgia thing", but they're outvoted by boosters who say this "treasure" "should be given landmark protection."

Montague St. Bagels ●☺ *Bagels* | 22 | 14 | 18 | I |

Brooklyn Heights | 108 Montague St. (bet. Henry & Hicks Sts.) | Brooklyn | 2/3/4/5/M/N/R/W to Borough Hall/Court St. | 718-237-2512

"Huge" (think "nuclear-size") bagels "hot" from the oven are the high point at this "reliable" Brooklyn Heights deli/take-out specialist that's also a standby for "surprisingly good" sandwiches, wraps and such; factor in "cheap" pricing and "24-hour" availability, and to many it's "as good as it gets" in the area.

☒ Moore Brothers | 29 | 27 | 29 | M |
Wine Co. ●☺ *Wine/Liquor*

Flatiron | 33 E. 20th St. (bet. B'way & Park Ave. S.) | 6 to 23rd St. | 212-375-1575 | 866-986-6673 | www.moorebrothers.com

"Welcome to NY" – this recent Philadelphia-area import is voted No. 1 for Service in this Survey (and second for Quality in its category), an "elegant", bi-level, 4,000-sq.-ft. "refrigerated" Flatironer whose "limited" but "outstanding" selection of artisanal European wines from "small", independent producers are offered at "reasonable" rates; owners Greg and David Moore "take responsibility" once the bottles "leave the winery" and ensure they're "imported and stored at the right temperature", while in the shop "exceptionally knowledgeable" staffers "go out of their way to inform"; N.B. there are frequent tastings and classes.

☒ Morrell & Co. ☺ *Wine/Liquor* | 27 | 24 | 24 | E |

W 40s | 1 Rockefeller Plaza (bet. 5th & 6th Aves.) | B/D/F/V to 47-50th Sts./Rockefeller Ctr. | 212-688-9370 | 800-969-4637 | www.morrellwine.com

It's "my Midtown sommelier" coo cognoscenti who cram this "tiny" but "elegant" Rock Center retailer filled floor-to-ceiling with a "fantastic selection" of hard-to-find wines and "top-notch" spirits; enthusiasts appreciate the staff's "outstanding knowledge" – not to mention the "informative courses" and "educational catalogs" – while acknowledging hefty tabs ("you pay for what you get"); still, a minority mutters that the "high-end" inventory is matched by "high-end attitude"; N.B. new services include wedding registration, consignment and the sale of futures online.

☒ Morrell Wine Xchange ●☺ *Wine/Liquor* | 26 | 24 | 23 | E |

E 60s | 1035 Third Ave. (bet. 61st & 62nd Sts.) | N/R/W to Lexington Ave./59th St. | 212-832-1144 | www.morrellwinexchange.com

"Any purchase is a winner" at this "small, refined", "reliable" Eastsider (no longer affiliated with Rockefeller Center's Morrell & Co.) known for its "great" imported champagne, Cabernet and Chardonnay – though it has increased its stock of lesser-known California boutique vintages and "might just have that bottle you can't find anywhere else"; its staffers are "accommodating" "even to customers with little expertise", which makes up for prices that, not surprisingly, "aren't cheap."

	QUALITY	DISPLAY	SERVICE	COST

Morrone Bakery ⊄ *Baked Goods* — — — I

Harlem | 324 E. 116th St. (bet. 1st & 2nd Aves.) | 6 to 116th St. |
212-722-2972

Once ubiquitous, Italian bakeries are now scarce in East Harlem, but
this unsung stalwart's brick oven still produces an impressive variety
of breads both familiar and "unusual", including loaves chock-full of
olives or prosciutto; family-owned since 1956, it keeps locals loyal
the old-fashioned way: "wonderful" quality for only a little dough.

Mother Mousse ▭ *Baked Goods* 26 21 23 M

Staten Island | 2175 Hylan Blvd. (bet. Lincoln & Midland Aves.) |
718-987-4242
Staten Island | 3767 Victory Blvd. (Travis Ave.) | 718-983-8366
www.mamamousse.com

Staten Islanders "insist" the mother of all "homemade mousses" is the
"creamy" variety (in numerous "rich" flavors) that this bakery duet
layers into their "top-notch" "triple-decker" cakes and other "fantastic" desserts, guaranteeing "a really special treat" for birthdays,
weddings or any occasion; "presentation is top-of-the-line", and
"nice gift baskets" offer a sampling of their cookies and other treats.

Mother's Bake Shop ⊄ *Baked Goods* 21 20 21 I

Bronx | 548 W. 235th St. (Johnson Ave.) | 1 to 231st St. | 718-796-5676

"Mother never disappoints" say supporters of this "landmark"
Jewish bakery in Riverdale, for more than a half-century a
"dependable" source of "total comfort" classics like "divine" black-
and-white cookies, the "world's best babka" and a plethora of "old-
fashioned" cakes and pastries; "neighborhood" know-it-alls add the
breads and sandwiches are a true "taste of home" too.

Mount Carmel ▽ 26 20 24 M
Wine & Spirits ◐▭ *Wine/Liquor*

Bronx | 612 E. 187th St. (bet. Arthur & Hughes Aves.) | B/D to
Fordham Rd. | 718-367-7833 | www.mountcarmelwines.com

"A real find off Arthur Avenue", this Bronx dealer boasts one of
NYC's most "extensive selections of Italian wines", including lots of
lesser-known *vini* and "specialty spirits" (including a "one-of-a-
kind" lineup of grappas); "friendly staffers" provide "wonderful
service" – especially during Saturday afternoon tastings – so although it makes for a "long trip" for fans from other boroughs, it's a
"favorite destination"; N.B. a move to new across-the-street quarters
is in the works.

Movable Feast, The *Caterer* 23 22 22 E

Park Slope | 284 Prospect Park W. (bet. 17th & 18th Sts.) | Brooklyn |
212-227-7755 | www.mfcatering.com
By appointment only

For festivities "done right", this "very experienced" Park Slope
caterer/event planner has a knack for moving "out of the box" to
personalize "all types of" affairs with a "comforting" start-to-finish
competence that's "a dream come true"; from "memorable", "ele-
gantly presented" food to "professional" service, Brooklynites boast

it's a "class act" that's also "an amazing value"; N.B. it's the in-house caterer for Prospect Park venues including the Boathouse, Audubon Center and Picnic House.

Mrs. Field's Cookies ●▣ *Baked Goods* | 18 | 15 | 15 | M |

Garment Dist | 1 Herald Sq. (bet. 33rd & 34th Sts.) | B/D/F/N/Q/R/V/W to 34th St./Herald Sq. | 212-967-1716
Seaport | South St. Seaport | Pier 17 (Fulton St.) | 2/3 to Fulton St. | 212-587-5335
W 40s | Port Authority | 625 Eighth Ave. (bet. 40th & 41st Sts.) | A/C/E to 42nd St./Port Authority | 212-695-1186
Elmhurst | Queens Place Mall | 8801 Queens Blvd. (bet. 55th & 56th Aves.) | Queens | G/R/V to Grand Ave. | 718-699-0780
www.mrsfields.com

Feedback is all over the field on this "very commercial" mega-chain, with advocates still "warm and fuzzy" on the "freshly baked", "melty" cookies but others "unimpressed" by "cloyingly sweet", "mass-produced" merchandise at "steep" prices; regardless, it's "time-tested" for a "quick" "sugar high" "on the run" – even if many have "no problem jogging past."

m2m *Specialty Shop* | 18 | 15 | 13 | I |

E Village | 55 Third Ave. (11th St.) | 6 to Astor Pl. | 212-353-2698
W 100s | 2935 Broadway (114th St.) | 1 to 110th St. | 212-280-4600 ●

At this "handy" East Village Japanese-Korean "deli-on-steroids" (with a smaller Morningside Heights outpost), "fresh sushi" and other "decent", priced-right prepared foods are joined by a "wide variety of Asian packaged goods" including sauces, condiments and some "hard-to-find ingredients", plus plenty of crunchy-salty "snack staples"; there are also cooking implements, gadgets and small appliances like rice cookers, making it the perfect "pop-in" when "you don't have time to go to Chinatown."

Mudspot ●▣⊐ *Coffee/Tea* | 26 | 19 | 22 | I |

E Village | 307 E. Ninth St. (2nd Ave.) | 6 to Astor Pl. | 212-228-9074 | www.mudnyc.com

Java junkies who flock to the mobile Mudtruck parked on Astor Place can fuel up on the same "explosively strong" brew at this "laid-back" coffeehouse, a model of "East Village hipness" defined by "cozy", brick-lined quarters and "too-cool" service; besides a "serious" "cup o' joe", it proffers "delish" munchies ranging from baked goods to panini and fajitas, so something's sure to hit the spot.

Mule *Coffee/Tea* | - | - | - | I |

Park Slope | 67 Fourth Ave. (bet. Bergen St. & St. Marks Pl.) | Brooklyn | D/M/N/R to Pacific St. | 718-398-6700 | www.mulecafe.com

Kick back in comfort at this "warm" Park Slope cafe, a "Fourth Avenue pioneer" that lends some style to an up-and-coming stretch and makes a handsome hangout for "very smooth" house-roasted coffee, organic teas and "high-quality" Italianate eats including baked goods and "great soups and sandwiches"; among its attractions are "reasonable prices" and a "back porch area", and the wine bar is now open nightly.

	QUALITY	DISPLAY	SERVICE	COST

Murray's Bagels ● *Bagels*   26 | 20 | 20 | I

Chelsea | 242 Eighth Ave. (bet. 22nd & 23rd Sts.) | C/E to 23rd St. | 646-638-1335

G Village | 500 Sixth Ave. (bet. 12th & 13th Sts.) | F/L/V to 14th St./ 6th Ave. | 212-462-2830

www.murraysbagels.com

The "golden" ratio of "crispy" outside to "chewy" inside has devotees declaring this Chelsea–Greenwich Village twosome's "heavenly", "generously sized", "malty" bagels some of the "best in town" – "no question about it"; there are a few grumbles that they "don't toast", but few grouse about the "abundance" of "fresh spreads" and "quick-moving" staff that keeps the "lines" of noshers moving.

Z Murray's Cheese   28 | 25 | 25 | E
Shop ⊡ *Cheese/Dairy*

E 40s | Grand Central Mkt. | Lexington Ave. (43rd St.) | 4/5/6/7/S to 42nd St./Grand Central | 212-922-1540 ●

G Village | 254 Bleecker St. (Cornelia St.) | A/B/C/D/E/F/V to W. 4th St. | 212-243-3289

888-692-4339 | www.murrayscheese.com

Widely considered "the gold standard of cheese in NY", this Village "wonderland" boasts an "astounding" assortment of "premium" "artisanal and seasonal" fromages "from all over the map", with "congenial" "experts" on staff dispensing advice and taste tests; it also offers an array of "accoutrements" and "tasty" prepared foods, and its "spacious" digs include "caves under the store" plus classrooms offering "a cheese education"; P.S. the small "Grand Central outpost is a godsend" for the 'burbs-bound, albeit with less exotic choices.

Murray's Sturgeon ⊡ *Caviar/Smoked Fish*   27 | 19 | 22 | E

W 80s | 2429 Broadway (bet. 89th & 90th Sts.) | 1/2/3 to 96th St. | 212-724-2650 | www.murrayssturgeon.com

Fans of "fresh smoked fish" laud this "tiny" Upper West Side "nosh heaven" for its "sublime" Nova, sturgeon and pickled herring, all sliced "to perfection" by "neighborly" countermen who "know their stuff"; it's also an "institution" for "top-notch" deli-style "Jewish staples", with "homey" "throwback" surroundings dating to 1946 that prove it's "the real deal" – so "what more could you ask?"

Myers of Keswick ⊡ *Specialty Shop*   23 | 21 | 22 | M

W Village | 634 Hudson St. (bet. Horatio & Jane Sts.) | A/C/E/L to 14th St./8th Ave. | 212-691-4194 | www.myersofkeswick.com

"Mushy peas, marmite and Molly the cat" (the store's mascot) await "homesick" Brits at this bonny "haunt" located in an Anglophilic corner of the West Village, which is "crowded as London's tube" with "old faves" that remind one there'll "always be an England"; "expats, there really is a place for treacle" in NYC, plus "fresh bangers and Scotch eggs", "great pork pies", "prawn cocktail crisps", "Bird's custard" and "all of the other 'beastly muck' from across the pond."

	QUALITY	DISPLAY	SERVICE	COST

My Most Favorite Food ●☑ *Baked Goods*   21 | 21 | 18 | E
(fka My Most Favorite Dessert Co.)

W 40s | 120 W. 45th St. (bet. B'way & 6th Ave.) | 1/2/3/7/N/Q/R/S/W to 42nd St./Times Sq. | 212-997-5130

"Well, certainly one of them" concur fans of the "top-notch" kosher desserts (pareve and dairy) retailed at this Midtown eatery/bakery, featuring a "fresh" selection of "decadent" cakes along with all the preferred pastries, pies, cookies and breads; it's admired for "fantastic" "quality", though the bottom line reveals this is a "pricey option."

Myzel Chocolates ☑ *Candy/Nuts*   - | - | - | E

W 50s | 140 W. 55th St. (bet. 6th & 7th Aves.) | N/Q/R/W to 57th St. | 212-245-4233 | www.myzels.com

"Although tiny", this Midtown sweet spot near City Center manages to cram in a sizable array of mass-market chocolates, truffles, cookies, licorice and other crowd-pleasers; satisfied surveyors appreciate that the proprietor "will go beyond the call of duty" when it comes to creating special packages and baskets.

Naidre's ●⊘ *Coffee/Tea*   22 | 20 | 20 | M

Carroll Gardens | 502 Henry St. (Sackett St.) | Brooklyn | F/G to Carroll St. | 718-596-3400
Park Slope | 384 Seventh Ave. (bet. 11th & 12th Sts.) | Brooklyn | F to 7th Ave. | 718-965-7585
www.naidres.com

"Neighborhood" necessities in Park Slope and Carroll Gardens, this "friendly" coffeehouse/cafe couple plies "robust" java along with organic tea, smoothies and a home-cooking menu that offers "a lot of alternatives", from fresh pastries and breakfast fare to stout sandwiches and refreshing "vegetarian options"; the casual quarters provide some "spartan" seating, and their to-go trade is brisk.

Nancy's–Wines For Food ●☑ *Wine/Liquor*   24 | 22 | 23 | M

W 70s | 313 Columbus Ave. (bet. 74th & 75th Sts.) | B/C to 72nd St. | 212-877-4040 | www.nancyswines.com

The "devoted following" of Nancy Maniscalco's "terrific" Upper West Side shop applauds her "concept" of emphasizing "food-friendly" vintages "geared to drinking every day"; they also appreciate "personalized" advice on pairings from "enthusiastic salespeople", and report that among the "offbeat selections" – including Mitteleuropean choices (gruner veltliners, Rieslings, boutique champagnes), seasonal rosés, armagnacs and sakes – are some "real finds at reasonable prices."

Napoli Bakery ⊘ *Baked Goods*   - | - | - | I

Williamsburg | 616 Metropolitan Ave. (bet. Leonard & Lorimer Sts.) | Brooklyn | G/L to Metropolitan Ave./Lorimer St. | 718-384-6945

All-Italian and "all good", this mom-and-pop bakery is an enclave of "old-school charm" in "hipster" Williamsburg that keeps its brick oven burning to supply a generous selection of "excellent" breads and focaccia; "fresh" loaves are its sole claim to fame, however, so expect a sparse stock otherwise.

| | QUALITY | DISPLAY | SERVICE | COST |

Natural Frontier ● *Health Food* — 24 | 17 | 18 | M

E 80s | 1424 Third Ave. (bet. 80th & 81st Sts.) | 6 to 77th St. | 212-794-0922
Gramercy | 266 Third Ave. (bet. 21st & 22nd Sts.) | 6 to 23rd St. |
212-228-9133

On the Upper East Side and Gramercy Park frontiers, these natural food shops are "convenient" options for "quality" "basic health fare", and some "things you can't find elsewhere", happily at "reasonable prices"; a "knowledgeable", if "aloof", staff can guide you through the "tight aisles", and for those on the go, there's also an "organic" juice bar, salad bar and "delicious" prepared foods.

Naturally Delicious *Caterer/Events* — - | - | - | E

Carroll Gardens | 487 Court St. (bet. Huntington & Nelson Sts.) |
Brooklyn | F/G to Smith/9th Sts. | 718-237-3727 |
www.naturallydelicious.com

Co-owner Loren Michelle got her start as a chef in eateries like the legendary Quilted Giraffe, so naturally the eats from this Carroll Gardens caterer/event planner are "yum"-inducing and "served up in beautiful presentations"; the "accommodating" staff will handle details from venue selection to photography and music with boutique flair, though critics charge the "follow-through" can be "expensive and a bit haughty."

Nature's Gifts ● *Health Food* — 21 | 18 | 17 | M

E 80s | 1297 Lexington Ave. (bet. 87th & 88th Sts.) | 4/5/6 to 86th St. |
212-289-6283
E 80s | 320 E. 86th St. (bet. 1st & 2nd Aves.) | 4/5/6 to 86th St. |
212-734-8298

Upper Eastsiders head to this pair of "tiny" health food locations for "fresh and delicious" prepared foods, including Greek specialties such as moussaka, spanakopita and housemade yogurt, as well as a new line of unusual baked goods like banana-pomegranate bread; there's also a great selection of cheeses, olive oils and olives.

Z NEW Nespresso Boutique *Coffee/Tea* — 25 | 27 | 25 | E

E 60s | 761 Madison Ave. (65 St.) | 6 to 68th St. | 800-562-1465 |
www.nespresso.com

"Take a break between Hermès and Armani" at this "stylish" new East Side boutique for upmarket caffeine fiends, the local branch of an international outfit that packages its own "perfect espressos" in "fancy" "capsules" designed for brewing by its "incredible" high-tech coffeemakers; the gourmet javas and "Rolls-Royce"-caliber machines are "sold at the site" by "hands-on" staffers, though some will settle for just a "chic" cup since that alone's "expensive" enough.

Neuchatel Chocolates ▣ *Candy/Nuts* — 24 | 23 | 21 | VE

E 50s | Park Ave. Plaza | 55 E. 52nd St. (bet. Madison & Park Aves.) | E/V to 5th Ave./53rd St. | 212-759-1388 | 800-597-0759 |
www.neuchatelchocolates.com

A "great choice for Swiss chocolates", this quiet East Side player on the city's bonbon scene impresses with "the best truffles" and other "luscious" bites that are as "delicious" as they are "attractive"; the prices are way "expensive", but for such "mmm"-quality goods, most say it's "worth it"; N.B. the Financial District branch has closed.

Neuhaus Chocolate Boutique 🖃 Candy/Nuts | 25 | 23 | 22 | E |

E 40s | Grand Central Terminal | main concourse (42nd St. & Vanderbilt Ave.) | 4/5/6/7/S to 42nd St./Grand Central | 212-972-3740
E 50s | 569 Lexington Ave. (bet. 50th & 51st Sts.) | 6 to 51st St. | 212-593-0848
W 70s | 2151 Broadway (bet. 75th & 76th Sts.) | 1 to 72nd St. | 212-712-2112
www.neuhaus.be

"Belgian know-how does it again" at these "fabulous" offshoots of the Brussels-based chocolate chain, where the "high-end" truffles and other "wonderful" confections in"gorgeous displays" can easily become an "expensive" "weakness"; free samples and choose-your-own gift assortments are pluses, but what some consider an increasingly "commercial" feel and occasionally "slow" service are not.

Neuman's Caterer | ▽ 25 | 23 | 22 | E |
(fka Neuman & Bogdonoff)

LES | 173 Chrystie St. (bet. Delancey & Rivington Sts.) | F/V to Lower East Side/2nd Ave. | 212-228-2444 | www.caterernyc.com
Paul Neuman's a solo act since the buyout of his former partner Stacy Bogdonoff, but this Lower East Side caterer/event planner still "does a spectacular job" at delivering "everything you ask for and much more" in the way of "fabulous" seasonal spreads and "wonderful" off-site setups; admirers attest "you can't go wrong" with their handling of "all types of parties", and they "don't charge ridiculous prices, although they could."

New Beef King 🖃🖘 Meat/Poultry | - | - | - | M |

Chinatown | 89 Bayard St. (bet. Mott & Mulberry Sts.) | 6/J/M/N/Q/R/W/Z to Canal St. | 212-233-6612 | www.newbeefking.com
"Beef jerky, Chinese-style" is the specialty of this single-minded Chinatowner, where you won't find fresh meat, just owner Robert Yee's 10 different styles of "dried and cured" beef and pork, based on an old family recipe rooted in Hong Kong; initiates say the results are "juicy morsels" of "flavorful jerky heaven."

New Green Pea ◑ Produce | ▽ 23 | 20 | 19 | M |

Brooklyn Heights | 181 Atlantic Ave. (bet. Clinton & Court Sts.) | Brooklyn | 2/3/4/5/M/N/R/W to Borough Hall/Court St. | 718-596-4624
Bedecked with old-fashioned carts for the fruits and veggies, this "archetype" lives up to its name, supplying Brooklyn Heights residents with "fresh", "high-quality" greens as well as a "wide selection" of condiments, herbs, dried fruits and nuts; given its "reasonable prices", it's "the sort of greengrocer every neighborhood should have."

Newman & Leventhal 🖘 Caterer | - | - | - | VE |

W 80s | 45 W. 81st St. (bet. Columbus Ave. & CPW) | 212-362-9400
By appointment only
If your event "has to be kosher", "one of the top" caterers in town is this "longtime" (circa 1908) Upper West Side outfit, recognized as

"true professionals" at providing "beautifully presented" feasts whether traditional or contemporary, indoors or outdoors, private or corporate; maybe their style's "a bit old-fashioned" – very up-to-date prices notwithstanding – but satisfied customers "cannot recommend them enough."

New Star Fish ⊜ Seafood | - | - | - | M |

LES | Essex Street Market | 120 Essex St. (bet. Delancey & Rivington Sts.) | F/J/M/Z to Delancey/Essex Sts. | 212-475-8365

Tucked into one of the small food stalls in the LES's increasingly busy Essex Street Market, this nautical wholesaler-retailer carries a wide range of fish (some 20 varieties on average) and shellfish, priced according to the market; the staff will cut and clean your purchase to order, but it won't take your plastic, so bring cash.

New York Beverage Beer | - | - | - | M |

Bronx | 515 Bruckner Blvd. (bet. Austin Pl. & 149th St.) | 6 to 149th St. | 212-831-4000 | www.newyorkbeverage.com

The drinkables distributed by this Bronx beverage house aren't limited to alcohol – more than half the company's business is water, soda and juice – but for those who do want a belt with a buzz, it also stocks 300 labels of beer (domestic, German, Belgian, English and Mexican), sold by the keg or by the case, and there's hard cider too.

New York Cake & Baking Distributor ▭ Cookware | 24 | 13 | 12 | M |

Flatiron | 56 W. 22nd St. (bet. 5th & 6th Aves.) | F/V to 23rd St. | 212-675-2253 | www.nycake.com

This Flatiron shop stocks "everything for the sweet kitchen" from cake-decorating supplies like food coloring, gum paste and sprinkles to cookie cutters, pans "in any shape", doilies and "beautiful dragées" and decorations that "pique the imagination" of "amateurs" and "professionals" alike; on the downside are a "surly" staff and a "jumbled" interior that "needs a major face-lift."

New York Wine Exchange ◑▭ Wine/Liquor | ▽ 23 | 21 | 20 | E |

Financial Dist | 9 Broadway (bet. Battery Pl. & Morris St.) | 4/5 to Bowling Green | 212-422-2222 | www.nywineexchange.com

Bankers and accountants are often in the red thanks to this pricey Financial District wine dealer near the Stock Exchange, whose "great selection" emphasizes California Cabernets and Merlots, ports (some 200) and a growing inventory of Hungarian whites and bottles from Uruguay, Portugal and Israel; "location, location, location" is a selling point too – way "south of Houston" this may be one of your "best" options; N.B. a full line of liquor is also available.

New York Wine Warehouse ▭ Wine/Liquor | - | - | - | M |

LIC | 8-05 43rd Ave. (Vernon Blvd.) | Queens | E/V to 23rd St./Ely Ave. | 718-784-8776 | www.nywines.com

If you "need a '63 Fonseca port on the fly, they've got it" declare devotees of this LIC vintner, an "extraordinary secret resource" that will "sell, deal, auction, store, catalog and deliver" wines for knowledge-able oenophiles; its 10,000 labels (including a deep selection of Burgundies) make it a favorite of collectors, who can now order not only by phone or fax but also via the company's Web site.

Nicky's Vietnamese Sandwiches *Deli/Sandwich*

24 | 13 | 20 | I

E Village | 150 E. Second St. (Ave. A) | F/V to Lower East Side/2nd Ave. | 212-388-1088 ●🕀

NEW Boerum Hill | 311 Atlantic Ave. (bet. Hoyt & Smith Sts.) | Brooklyn | A/C/G to Hoyt/Schermerhorn Sts. | 718-855-8838

This "tiny, cheerful" East Villager (with a new outpost in Boerum Hill) specializes in "delicate iterations of the wonderful Vietnamese *banh-mi*" sandwiches: filled with a choice of chicken or pork liver pâté plus "lightly pickled veggies", they pack "a symphony of flavor"; "perfect for a snack", the "cheap" goods also make "quite a tasty bargain."

Ninth Avenue International 🖃 *Specialty Shop*

23 | 18 | 20 | I

W 40s | 543 Ninth Ave. (bet. 40th & 41st Sts.) | A/C/E to 42nd St./Port Authority | 212-279-1000

"The smell alone makes you want to buy spices you've never even heard of", so it's a good thing you can procure them "by the pound" at this "adventure" of a Med mart in Hell's Kitchen; "extraordinary discoveries lurk" beyond the seasonings as well, including everything from "olives and cheese" to "various pickled vegetables" and spreads including what some consider "the best taramasalata in NYC."

Ninth Street Espresso 🕀 *Coffee/Tea*

∇ 28 | 17 | 22 | I

E Village | 700 E. Ninth St. (Ave. C) | L to 1st Ave. | 212-358-9225

NEW Union Sq | Classic Stage Company | 136 E. 13th St. (bet. 3rd & 4th Aves.) | L to 3rd Ave. | 212-228-2930 ●
www.ninthstreetespresso.com

Among "the few real" caffeine craftsmen, this "funky" East Villager combines Northern Italian inspiration with beans from artisan roaster Counter Culture Coffee to produce "excellent" espresso and variants like "true cappuccino" and "mind-blowing macchiato"; throw in baked goods from Tisserie and service from "hip" folks "who care", and "there's no point" in settling for less; N.B. offshoots include a new lobby bar at Union Square's Classic Stage Company and a forthcoming Chelsea Market stall.

Nordic Delicacies 🖃 *Specialty Shop*

∇ 28 | 18 | 23 | M

Bay Ridge | 6909 Third Ave. (bet. Bay Ridge & Ovington Aves.) | Brooklyn | R to Bay Ridge Ave. | 718-748-1874 | 800-346-6734 | www.nordicdeli.com

"One of a kind, from a bygone era" (the 1980s, actually), this "small" twentysomething "Norsk delight" "caters to the remaining Scandinavians" in Bay Ridge with "delicacies they remember from childhood"; there's "not a lot to choose from" if you're hankering for something from the Southern hemisphere, but Nordic "deli items" like pickled herring and cheeses, as well as the "canned fish, jams and sweaters", are all of "the highest quality" at prices you can afjord.

#1 Farmers Market ❶ *Produce* · 23 | 19 | 19 | M

E 50s | 1095 Second Ave. (bet. 57th & 58th Sts.) | 4/5/6 to 59th St./
Lexington Ave. | 212-688-2618
E 70s | 1458 Second Ave. (76th St.) | 6 to 77th St. | 212-396-2626
You "never know what you're going to find" at this "crowded" 24/7
Upper East Side duo where the fruits and vegetables are "always
beautiful" and the cheese, olives, spreads, flowers, cookies and kosher items equally "fresh"; although a few feel that "better deals can
be found" elsewhere, the markets' round-the-clock hours trump all:
"'convenient' is the word."

Nusbaum & Wu Bakery ❶ *Baked Goods* · 18 | 17 | 15 | M

W 100s | 2897 Broadway (113th St.) | 1 to 110th St. | 212-280-5344
Cookie buffs claim the signature black-and-whites are "a revelation"
at this Columbia-area bakery/cafe, which otherwise woos the "students" with its "prime location" and "fair" assortment of bagels,
sandwiches and deli goods; local consensus calls it "nothing amazing, but convenient" if you can "survive the crowds."

O&CO. 🖃 *Specialty Shop* · 25 | 25 | 22 | E

E 40s | Grand Central Terminal | main concourse (42nd St. &
Vanderbilt Ave.) | 4/5/6/7/S to 42nd St./Grand Central | 212-973-1472
G Village | 249 Bleecker St. (bet. 6th & 7th Aves.) | A/B/C/D/E/F/V to
W. 4th St. | 646-230-8373
877-828-6620 | www.oliviersandco.com
"The green lemon olive oil makes your socks roll up and down" – and
that's a good thing at this paean to the juice of the pitted fruit in
Grand Central Station and Greenwich Village; an "amazing array" of
"gorgeously packaged" "regional and infused" olive oil ("and anything made with it" or used to serve it) "tempts" "commuters" to
stop in and get "educated" by "knowledgeable salespeople"; the
quality is "incomparable", but, alas, so are the markups at this "olive
oil lover's version of a wine tasting bar."

⛾ Olive's *Deli/Sandwich* · 25 | 19 | 18 | M

SoHo | 120 Prince St. (bet. Greene & Wooster Sts.) | N/R to Prince St. |
212-941-0111 | www.olivesnyc.com
A perfect quick lunch "stop in SoHo", this tiny storefront is known
for its "addictive", super-"fresh" Med-inflected sandwiches, as well
as "excellent soups", salads, scones and such, offered in appealingly
"substantial portions"; it draws a "trendy crowd" – after all, "the Mac
store is across the street" – despite its lack of seating and sometimes "slow service"; N.B. you can order online for local deliveries.

Olivier Cheng Catering & Events ✍ *Caterer* · ▽ 22 | 26 | 26 | VE

TriBeCa | 12-16 Vestry St. (Hudson St.) | 212-625-3151 | www.ocnyc.com
By appointment only
"Olivier is an artist" coo fans of the chef and co-owner of this top-
shelf TriBeCa caterer/event planner, whose superior "aesthetic
sense" informs chic stagings and "sophisticated" Asian-influenced
cuisine ("no rubber chicken here") while the staff's "strong feeling

for flow" ensures events large and small "run smoothly"; though designer-label "pricey", it's got all the style "money can buy" and routinely sews up business with clients like Gucci and Chanel.

Olivino Wines *Wine/Liquor*
| - | - | - | M |

Fort Greene | 905 Fulton St. (Clinton Ave.) | Brooklyn | G to Clinton/Washington Aves. | 718-857-7952 | www.olivinowines.com
Fort Greene's vino "connoisseurs" go to this "small", olive-green boutique to explore Katrine Pollari's "highly personal, sometimes eccentric" stock of some 350 wines; along with her signature entries from Portugal, Lebanon and South Africa, Pollari pursues unusual varietals from Germany and Austria, and will occasionally host tastings to introduce her finds (check the Web site for dates and times).

Once Upon A Tart . . . *Baked Goods*
| 25 | 22 | 19 | M |

SoHo | 135 Sullivan St. (bet. Houston & Prince Sts.) | C/E to Spring St. | 212-387-8869 | www.onceuponatart.com
Those craving "classic tarts" both sweet and savory "can't resist" the "delish" selection at this "quaint" SoHo bakery/cafe, a "welcoming" "gem" that also turns out "must-have pastries", scones, cakes and cookies and "excels at sandwiches"; with a "helpful staff" to take custom orders for events and "a few tables" on hand "for those needing instant gratification", it leaves the majority happy ever after.

One Girl Cookies *Baked Goods*
| 24 | 23 | 22 | E |

Cobble Hill | 68 Dean St. (bet. Brooklyn Bridge Blvd. & Smith St.) | Brooklyn | F/G to Bergen St. | 212-675-4996 | www.onegirlcookies.com
The "delightful" "morsels" of "yumminess" are just "the right size" for a "girlie" treat at this Cobble Hill bakery/espresso bar, which packs "high quality" into its "tiny", "aesthetically pleasing" cookies and offers them in a "warm and inviting" space; the "unsurpassed" "attention to detail" extends to their "beautifully designed" gift boxes and event favors, which come so "artfully packaged" you may even forget the "hefty prices."

131 Fish Market *Seafood*
| 24 | 17 | 17 | M |

Chinatown | 131 Mott St. (bet. Grand & Hester Sts.) | 6/J/M/N/Q/R/W/Z to Canal St. | 212-925-0970
"Just about every type" of seafood – fish, lobster, crab, prawn, squid, octopus, even sea cucumber – can be found at this "awesome" Chinatown fishmonger where the "consistent" selection comes "at a moderate cost" that "always beats the supermarkets"; those in-the-know recommend "go early" to get the freshest catch.

Oppenheimer Meats, Inc. *Meat/Poultry*
| 26 | 18 | 24 | E |

W 90s | 2606 Broadway (bet. 98th & 99th Sts.) | 1/2/3 to 96th St. | 212-662-0246 | www.oppenheimermeats.com
A "neighborhood winner" since the 1950s, this UWS butcher comes through with "memory-making" prime meats and other "quality" selections, including poultry, veal, pork, lamb, game, sausages and even a small fish selection; notalgists note the "terrific", amiable counter folk take you "back to the good old days" when "service really meant something."

	QUALITY	DISPLAY	SERVICE	COST

Orchard, The *Specialty Shop*

| 27 | 23 | 22 | E |

Midwood | 1367 Coney Island Ave. (bet. Ave. J & Cary Ct.) | Brooklyn | Q to Ave. J | 718-377-1799 | 800-222-0240 | www.orchardfruit.com

Want "the best produce in Brooklyn"? – order delivery from "the gold standard" of Midwood, this kosher shop "famous for their baskets", which are "beautifully" brimming with smoked fish, chocolates, nuts and "fruit, fruit and more fruit"; yes, they deliver, but you might have to tip double because their "platters are so heavy, two people need to carry them."

Oren's Daily Roast ▣ *Coffee/Tea*

| 24 | 19 | 21 | M |

E 40s | Grand Central Mkt. | Lexington Ave. (43rd St.) | 4/5/6/7/S to 42nd St./Grand Central | 212-338-0014 ◗
E 40s | Grand Central Terminal | main concourse (42nd St. & Vanderbilt Ave.) | 4/5/6/7/S to 42nd St./Grand Central | 212-953-1028 ◗
E 50s | 33 E. 58th St. (bet. Madison & Park Aves.) | 4/5/6 to 59th St./Lexington Ave. | 212-838-3345
E 70s | 1144 Lexington Ave. (bet. 79th & 80th Sts.) | 6 to 77th St. | 212-472-6830
E 70s | 985 Lexington Ave. (71st St.) | 6 to 68th St. | 212-717-3907
E 80s | 1574 First Ave. (bet. 81st & 82nd Sts.) | 6 to 77th St. | 212-737-2690
G Village | 31 Waverly Pl. (bet. Greene St. & University Pl.) | A/B/C/D/E/F/V to W. 4th St. | 212-420-5958
Murray Hill | 434 Third Ave. (bet. 30th & 31st Sts.) | 6 to 28th St. | 212-779-1241
W 100s | 2882 Broadway (bet. 112th & 113th Sts.) | 1 to 110th St. | 212-749-8779 ◗
888-348-5400 | www.orensdailyroast.com

"Never far away when you're jonesing" for a "reliable cup", this "worthy" "local" franchise pours "flavorful" coffee that's "freshly roasted" every weekday at its Jersey facility and "impeccably brewed" by "sweet slacker" staffers; they vend 50 blends by the pound and stock H&H bagels, Donut Planet 'nuts and baked goods from Balthazar, ensuring "you're set for the morning" and giving the megachains "a run for their money."

◪ Original SoupMan *Soup*

| 23 | 16 | 15 | M |

E 40s | 4 E. 42nd St. (bet. 5th & Madison Aves.) | 4/5/6/7/S to 42nd St./Grand Central | 212-599-5900 ◗
E 40s | 708 Third Ave. (45th St.) | 4/5/6/7/S to 42nd St./Grand Central | 212-490-8980
E 50s | 672 Lexington Ave. (56th St.) | E/V to Lexington Ave./53rd St. | 212-355-2521 ◗
E 70s | 1369 Third Ave. (78th St.) | 6 to 77th St. | 212-879-9707 ◗
NEW Financial Dist | 110 Pearl St. (Hanover Sq.) | 2/3 to Wall St. | 212-968-7687
Financial Dist | 97 Trinity Pl. (bet. Cedar & Thames Sts.) | 1 to Rector St. | 212-566-7400
NEW Harlem | 414 Lenox Ave. (bet. 130th & 131st Sts.) | 1 to 125th St. | 212-926-7687 ⌷

(continued)

(continued)

Original SoupMan

W 50s | Rockefeller Ctr. | 37 W. 48th St. (bet. 5th & 6th Aves.) | B/D/F/V to 47-50th Sts./Rockefeller Ctr. | 212-582-7400 ●

NEW **Staten Island** | 2345 Richmond Ave. (Norme Ave.) | 718-477-7687

www.originalsoupman.com

"Legendary" 'Soup Nazi' of *Seinfeld* fame, Al Yeganeh, may forever be a cultural "mascot", but his signature dish is "no joke" say devotees of his "divine" chicken chile and "to-die-for" seafood bisques; cynics claim "franchising ruined" his product, and yet the lines at all locations remain "long" – most agree it's "still darn good soup."

Orwasher's Bakery 🖃🖗 *Baked Goods*   26 | 19 | 21 | M

E 70s | 308 E. 78th St. (bet. 1st & 2nd Aves.) | 6 to 77th St. | 212-288-6569 | www.orwashers.com

"One of the best" "old-time bakeries", this Upper East Side "original" (founded in 1916) "can't be beat" for "traditional Jewish" loaves and rolls that epitomize what kosher bread "is supposed to be", served up "fresh" and "with a smile"; "stop by for the rye" and "you'll know" why such "great stuff" is "hard not to eat before you get home."

Oslo Coffee Company 🖗 *Coffee/Tea*   - | - | - | I

Williamsburg | 133B Roebling St. (Metropolitan Ave.) | Brooklyn | L to Bedford Ave. | 718-782-0332

NEW **Williamsburg** | 328 Bedford Ave. (bet. 2nd & 3rd Sts.) | Brooklyn | L to Bedford Ave. | 718-930-9520

www.oslocoffee.com

Though its name's Nordic the inspiration skews Italian at this Williamsburg java hut (and its new coffee-bar offshoot), which fires up an in-house roaster to produce "awesome espresso drinks" like latte and macchiatto that "hit the spot every time"; with "prompt and polite service" whether you're power boosting "on the way to work" or picking up beans by the pound, it's a "top" contender for "best coffee in the 'Burg."

Otafuku ●🖗 *Prepared Food*   ▽ 19 | 9 | 14 | I

E Village | 236 E. Ninth St. (bet. 2nd & 3rd Aves.) | L to 3rd Ave. | 212-353-8503

The menu may be brief, but the taste is big ("yum, yum") at this "tiny" East Villager offering just two "authentic" Japanese "street-food" snacks, takoyaki (an octopus croquette) and okonomiyaki (pancakes with shredded cabbage and a choice of shellfish or meat); it's a "popular" stop for nibbles on the fly, where "you can't beat the prices."

☑ Ottomanelli & Sons 🖃 *Meat/Poultry*   27 | 21 | 26 | E

G Village | 285 Bleecker St. (bet. Jones St. & 7th Ave. S.) | 1 to Christopher St. | 212-675-4217

Woodside | 61-05 Woodside Ave. (61st St.) | Queens | 7 to 61st St. | 718-651-5544

Home to possibly the "most personable butchers in the city", these Italian "gems" owned by separate branches of the Ottomanelli clan are the kind of "classic butcher shops" where the counter staff "knows its customers by name" and offers a "fabulous" selection of "highest-quality" prime meats, including dry-aged beef, housemade sausages and an array of game (everything from kangaroo to quail); the fact that "prices are within reason" makes legions of longtime customers all the more loyal; N.B. the Woodside branch has a line of kosher organic meats.

Ottomanelli Brothers ▣ *Meat/Poultry* | 24 | 18 | 23 | E |

E 80s | 1549 York Ave. (82nd St.) | 4/5/6 to 86th St. | 212-772-7900 | www.ottomanellibros.com

W 70s | 395 Amsterdam Ave. (79th St.) | 1 to 79th St. | 212-496-1049

This "old-school" Upper East Side butcher and its separately owned crosstown cousin keep carnivores happy with "top-quality" cuts, including prime meats, poultry and game, alongside "excellent" Italian-accented prepared foods (baked ziti, lasagna); factor in "excellent-value" (though still not cheap) prices and "knowledgeable, helpful" service, and surveyors ask "how can you go wrong?"; N.B. the York Avenue location offers online ordering.

☑ Ottomanelli's Prime Meats ▣ ✍ *Meat/Poultry* | 27 | 19 | 22 | E |

Flushing | 190-21 Union Tpke. (bet. 189th & 190th Sts.) | Queens | 718-468-2000

"The quality is high, high, high" at this Flushing "neighborhood butcher" that sells everything from ground beef yielding "juicy, succulent burgers" ("you'll never go back to the supermarket" kind) to Kobe beef, alligator, pheasant and other "great" game; "excellent" prepared foods, including Italian specialties, are also on hand, and dispensed by a "friendly" staff.

Our Daily Bread *Baked Goods* | 26 | 21 | 22 | M |

See Greenmarket; for more information, call 518-392-9852

Bread bingers "can't make a bad choice" when selecting from the "wide, unusual selection" of "fresh, tasty" loaves – from challah and cranberry pecan sourdough to sunflower millet flax – baked by this Greenmarket vendor based in Chatham, NJ; also eliciting a collective "mmm" are its "delicious fruit scones" and "fab cookies."

Out of the Kitchen ● *Prepared Food* | - | - | - | M |

W Village | 420 Hudson St. (Leroy St.) | 1/2/3 to Houston St. | 212-242-0399 | www.outofthekitchenonline.com

A wide array of freshly made soups, salads and sandwiches, not to mention "scrumptious" sweets (the cupcakes are the "best") get folks off the sidewalk and into this West Village catering/take-out shop; N.B. the store recently moved into a larger space across the street.

Ovando *Flowers* | - | - | - | VE |

W Village | 337 Bleecker St. (bet. Christopher & W. 10th Sts.) | 1 to Christopher St. | 212-924-7848 | www.ovandony.com

With a "unique" aesthetic among NYC's floral shops, this West Village store sports an all-black decor scheme that allows its colorful blooms to be the star of the show ("if you want drama, they win the Tony"); clients also "love" the outfit's "innovative designs" (a European–South American fusion of styles often featuring orchids and cacti), which are admittedly "for the chic set", i.e. those that can appreciate both the arrangement's charm and price tag.

Ozzie's Coffee ◐ ▭ *Coffee/Tea*

19 | 16 | 16 | M

Park Slope | 249 Fifth Ave. (Garfield Pl.) | Brooklyn | M/R to Union St. | 718-768-6868
Park Slope | 57 Seventh Ave. (Lincoln Pl.) | Brooklyn | B/Q to 7th Ave. | 718-398-6695
www.ozziescoffee.com

Maybe they're "no big deal", but for Park Slopers seeking a stressless "place to stop" for house-roasted coffee and "snacks" this twosome awaits with a "decent" chalkboard-menu lineup delivered by a "hip staff"; the going is "very relaxed (including the service sometimes)" and the overall quality's "simply ok", but if "you have hours to kill" they're eazzy "alternatives" that also retail beans and loose teas.

Paffenroth Gardens ⊄ *Produce*

28 | 26 | 25 | I

See Greenmarket; for more information, call 845-258-2539

All of the produce is "fabulous" here but "superior root vegetables" ("man, those parsnips!") are the true pay dirt at this Greenmarket stand – even the potatoes actually "have taste" exclaim fans; given the farm stall's specialty, it's perhaps not surprising that service (overseen by Upstate grower Alex Paffenroth) is incredibly down-to-earth – they're "friendly" enough to make "customers feel as if they were part of a small town."

Paneantico Bakery & Café ◐ *Baked Goods*

26 | 22 | 19 | M

Bay Ridge | 9124 Third Ave. (92nd St.) | Brooklyn | R to Bay Ridge Ave./ 95th St. | 718-680-2347 | www.newyorkitalianmarket.com

Bread heads "travel for" the "gourmet" "brick-oven" loaves at this Bay Ridge Italian bakery/cafe from the Royal Crown Pastry Shop team, but it's also "noted" for pastries, the "freshest, tastiest" "specialty foods" and its bountiful sandwich board; besides being a "top-quality" "to-go" outlet, it's a "friendly" "neighborhood place" to kick back with a primo "cup of joe."

Pane d'Italia ▭ ⊄ *Baked Goods*

- | - | - | I

Whitestone | 20-04 Utopia Pkwy. (20th Ave.) | Queens | 7 to Flushing-Main St. | 718-423-6260

The staff of life for scores of restaurants around the city emerges from the ovens of this Whitestone Italian bakery, whose 20-plus artisanal breads run the gamut from traditional panella and Tuscan to loaves loaded with broccoli rabe and prosciutto; it also wins the endorsement of walk-in customers who pick up their own from the front retail store.

Panya Bakery ◐⊄ *Baked Goods*

22 | 19 | 20 | I

E Village | 10 Stuyvesant St. (9th St.) | 6 to Astor Pl. | 212-777-1930

This "sweet little" East Villager crams its "tiny" shopfront space with "quality" "Japanese baked goods" like green-tea cake and ti-ramisu, "cute" "pastries with interesting fillings" (including some "funky" savory items) and "fabulous" "fluffy" bread; the staff is "friendly and fast", and cognoscenti confirm the offerings taste "as delicious as they look, which is saying a lot."

Papa Pasquale Ravioli & Pasta Co. *Pasta* ▽ 26 | 18 | 21 | M

Bensonhurst | 7817 15th Ave. (bet. 78th & 79th Sts.) | Brooklyn | D/M to 79th St. | 718-232-1798

"For the Italian in all of us", this family-owned Bensonhurst pasta purveyor is a "must-try" according to surveyors citing the "amazing four-cheese and lobster ravioli" as standouts; manicotti, stuffed shells and such join a wide assortment of olive oils, vinegars and other imported condiments in the grocery storefront, while the "dee-lish" pastas are produced in a mini-factory in back.

Paramount Caviar ▣ *Caviar* - | - | - | E

LIC | 38-15 24th St. (bet. 38th & 39th Aves.) | Queens | N/W to 39th Ave. | 718-786-7747 | 800-992-2842 | www.paramountcaviar.com

It's "*the* destination" for "great caviar" enthuse eggheads about this Long Island City entrepôt, a distributor to such big names as Le Bernardin and Grace's Marketplace, whose premium stock is available to walk-ins in the adjacent showroom; owners Hossain and Amy Aimani are "nice people" who also carry gourmet goodies like foie gras and smoked fish, so "if you have the time" it's worth the hike (though they'll deliver if you call or order online).

Parisi Bakery ⊘ *Baked Goods* 23 | 16 | 21 | I

NoLita | 198 Mott St. (bet. Kenmare & Spring Sts.) | 6 to Spring St. | 212-226-6378

"Prosciutto bread straight from heaven" is one of the blessings at this long-running (since 1910) NoLita Italian bakery, a vendor of authentic homemade loaves to numerous area eateries; Frank Sinatra once was a regular, and nowadays its "great value" on sandwiches (e.g. meatball, chicken parmigiana, "the best cold cuts") keeps it way above par for takeout.

Park Avenue Liquor Shop ▣ *Wine/Liquor* 26 | 19 | 22 | E

E 40s | 292 Madison Ave. (bet. 40th & 41st Sts.) | 4/5/6/7/S to 42nd St./Grand Central | 212-685-2442 | www.parkaveliquor.com

This venerable Midtown wine-and-liquor purveyor focuses on "excellent" "niche items", stocking "one of Gotham's deepest single-malt selections" (some 400 labels), including "whiskies you thought you'd never find", plus "rare infused spirits" and a "top-notch" showing of "interesting" old vintages (especially Burgundies and Bordeaux); however, wallet-watchers note its prices may place it in the "millionaires-only" category.

Park East Kosher
Butchers & Fine Foods ▣ *Meat/Poultry* 26 | 17 | 19 | VE

E 80s | 1623 Second Ave. (bet. 84th & 85th Sts.) | 4/5/6 to 86th St. | 212-737-9800 | www.parkeastkosher.com

Yes, "it may cost you an arm and a leg" just to buy "a rib" at this glatt kosher butcher/specialty market on the Upper East Side, but regulars swear its "cramped, bustling" store "is the place to shop" for the "highest-quality" meats, poultry and game, not to mention seafood and "tons" of prepared foods and other "goodies" to "fill your pantry, fridge and freezer"; just remember to "up the limit on your card before any visit"; N.B. it keeps Sabbath hours.

Park Natural and Organic *Health Food* | – | – | – | M |
Carroll Gardens | 350 Court St. (Union St.) | Brooklyn | F/G to Carroll St. | 718-802-1652 | www.parknatural.com

Appreciated as a generously sized health food shop in Carroll Gardens, this bright and spiffy market stocks a plentiful array of fresh veggies and fruits, a wide range of dairy and soy products, lots of natural and organic groceries and just about any vitamin, mineral, herb or supplement you can think of; a recently added deli section makes it a good lunch option as well.

Party Rental Ltd. *Party Rentals* | 22 | 20 | 22 | E |
Chelsea | 261 Fifth Ave., 16th fl. (29th St.) | 888-774-4776
Bridgehampton | 5 Tradesman Path (Butter Ln.), NY | 631-537-4477
Teterboro | 275 North St. (Green St.), NJ | 201-727-4700
888-774-4776 | www.partyrentalltd.com
By appointment only

This party rental giant is the largest of its kind in the NYC area, making their familiar truck logo – a pink hippo – all the more apt, and it has a selection to match, drawing from 200,000 sq.-ft. of warehouse space to offer more than 500 styles of linens and some 65,000 chairs ("they have everything" – except tents); dealings are "professional" but be prepared for an "expensive" bill at the end of it all, with a $500 minimum in peak season (April–June; September–December) and $350 the rest of the year.

Party Time *Party Rentals* | 20 | 9 | 14 | M |
Elmhurst | 82-33 Queens Blvd. (bet. 51st Ave. & Van Loon St.) | Queens | F to Roosevelt Ave. | 212-682-8838 | 877-865-1122 | www.partytimeofcourse.com

A veteran in the party rental biz, this Queens-based operation has been stocking equipment for celebrations since 1935 and continues to offer everything from tables and tents to hot dog carts and ice cream wagons; however, extended track record aside, a few critics complain that service can be iffy.

Pasanella & Son, Vintners ● *Wine/Liquor* | – | – | – | E |
Seaport | 115 South St. (bet. Beekman St. & Peck Slip) | 2/3 to Fulton St. | 212-233-8383 | www.pasanellaandson.com

Set in a former fishmonger's store dating from 1839 and now boasting a 1967 Ferrari parked in the middle of the sales floor, this "great Seaport wine shop" isn't exactly a run-of-the-mill neighborhood boozery; instead, its "quaint and beautiful" space houses a "well-chosen but limited selection" of "pricey" bottles, almost a third of which are Italian, along with vino-related accoutrements (glassware, books, vintage accessories) plus recipes that suggest interesting pairings.

	QUALITY	DISPLAY	SERVICE	COST

▣ Pastosa Ravioli ▤ *Pasta*   26 | 20 | 21 | M

Bronx | 3812 E. Tremont Ave. (Lamport Pl.) | 718-822-2800
Bensonhurst | 7425 New Utrecht Ave. (75th St.) | Brooklyn | D/M to 71st St. | 718-236-9615
Mill Basin | 5223 Ave. N. (E. 53rd St.) | Brooklyn | 718-258-1002
Ozone Pk | 132-10 Cross Bay Blvd. (Sutter Ave.) | Queens | A to Liberty Ave. | 718-835-6240
Staten Island | 1076 Richmond Rd. (Columbus Ave.) | 718-667-2194
Staten Island | 3817 Richmond Ave. (Wilson Ave.) | 718-356-4600
Staten Island | 764 Forest Ave. (B'way) | 718-420-9000
800-727-8672 | www.pastosa.com

"Why cook, when you can go" to one of these separately owned "traditional" Italian "pasta palaces" wonder devoted customers who line up for the "best ravioli and manicotti" "made fresh" and "excellent sauces" to go with them, plus "delicious cold cuts" and "even salads to take out"; it "only gets better than this in your nonna's kitchen", so, given the relatively "cheap prices", you may as well "buy lots and freeze some"; P.S. the Forest Avenue branch specializes in cheeses, offering more than 250 varieties.

Pastrami Factory ● *Deli/Sandwich*   22 | 18 | 17 | M

Gramercy | 333 E. 23rd St. (bet. 1st & 2nd Aves.) | 6 to 23rd St. | 212-689-8090

Just the thought of this Gramercy deli "makes you feel hungry" given that, as you would expect from the name, it has "very good pastrami" (along with "great" knishes, chopped liver and the like), plus some Italian-accented dishes like eggplant parmigiana; however, a kvetching contingent claims it's "overpriced", while offering underwhelming service.

Pastrami Queen ● *Deli/Sandwich*   21 | 13 | 15 | M

E 70s | 1125 Lexington Ave. (bet. 78th & 79th Sts.) | 6 to 77th St. | 212-734-1500 | www.pastramiqueen.com

For an "excellent sandwich without all the hubbub" of other lauded delis, head to this UES classic where the kosher fare is "not cheap, but is worth the price" for "heaping" portions packed with "lots of flavor" – "remember what pastrami used to taste like?"; still, those who object to the "less-than-glamorous" setting and look back nostalgically to the Pastrami King, its former incarnation in Queens.

Patel Brothers ●◐▤ *Specialty Shop*   23 | 17 | 13 | I

Flushing | 42-92 Main St. (bet. Blossom & Cherry Aves.) | Queens | 7 to Flushing-Main St. | 718-661-1112
Jackson Hts | 37-27 74th St. (Northern Blvd.) | Queens | E/V to Roosevelt Ave. | 718-898-3445
www.patelbrothersusa.com

"A mainstay of the large South Asian community in Jackson Heights" (with a sister shop in Flushing), this is an "indispensible" stop for "authentic Indian and Pakistani stuff" – at "bargain basement prices"; with its "dizzying array of spices, chutneys and specialty pickles", as well as "basmati rice", "yogurts, dahls" and "indescribably shaped vegetables" ("fresh, very fresh!"), "the store could be in Delhi."

Z Patisserie Claude *Baked Goods* | 27 | 19 | 19 | M |

G Village | 187 W. Fourth St. (bet. 6th & 7th Aves.) | A/B/C/D/E/F/V to W. 4th St. | 212-255-5911

"If you can survive" Claude's "big-time" "Parisian hauteur" at this "true French bakery" in the Village, "your palate will be enriched" by "perfect" croissants that "bring tears to your eyes"; after 25 years, the "small" but "excellent" selection of "stunning" pastries and cookies shows that this baker may be "mercurial", but he has "hands of gold."

Z Payard
Pâtisserie & Bistro ● □ *Baked Goods* | 28 | 28 | 21 | VE |

E 70s | 1032 Lexington Ave. (bet. 73rd & 74th Sts.) | 6 to 77th St. | 212-717-5252 | 877-972-9273 | www.payard.com

"Ooh-la-la", this "world-class", "oh-so-French" Upper Eastsider is "the Louvre" of "edible art", where the *magnifique* pastries, cakes and chocolates, not to mention ice cream, are "exquisitely" "hand-crafted" for "a sugar rush like no other"; all that "froufrou" "indulgence" is "hard on the wallet" but equally "hard to pass up", so "mortgage the co-op" and go; P.S. "ladies who lunch" congregate over light bites in the neighboring cafe or a full menu in the back bistro, while Tastings by Payard provides catering.

PE & DD Seafood *Seafood* | 28 | 23 | 28 | M |

See Greenmarket; phone number unavailable

"Catch them early" and you'll "go home with the best" "amazing-quality" fresh seafood "caught that morning off of Long Island" and trucked to the Greenmarket, making for a "pristine" selection running the gamut from various "whole fish" to "clams, mussels, oysters and scallops" to "more exotic items like eel and sea urchin"; owner Phil Karlin, a 30-year fisherman, has netted an enthusiastic school of supporters with his "knowledgeable" and "friendly" service.

Z Penzeys Spices ● □ *Herbs/Spices* | 27 | 23 | 23 | M |

E 40s | Grand Central Mkt. | Lexington Ave. (43rd St.) | 4/5/6/7/S to 42nd St./Grand Central | 212-972-2777 | 800-741-7787 | www.penzeys.com

"Marco Polo would be proud" to see the "wonderful selection" of the "best, freshest spices and herbs" around at this Grand Central outpost of a beloved national chain, where the scents can be "intoxicating", and so can the "unbeatable" prices and quality; "so many spices, so little time to cook" sigh the fans of this "small but substantial" shop where the "knowledgeable" staff can offer tips on how to use the "unusual" and "fantastic" spice blends and rubs; N.B. there's even greater variety through its catalog/Web ordering business.

Pepe Giallo To Go ● *Prepared Food* | 26 | 15 | 17 | I |

Chelsea | 253 10th Ave. (bet. 24th & 25th Sts.) | C/E to 23rd St. | 212-242-6055

Pepe Rosso Caffe *Prepared Food*

E 40s | Grand Central Terminal | dining concourse (42nd St. & Vanderbilt Ave.) | 4/5/6/7/S to 42nd St./Grand Central | 212-867-6054
NEW **E Village** | 127 Ave. C (8th St.) | L to 1st Ave. | 212-529-7747 ●

(continued)

Pepe Rosso To Go ● *Prepared Food*

SoHo | 149 Sullivan St. (bet. Houston & Prince Sts.) | A/B/C/D/E/F/V to
W. 4th St. | 212-677-4555

Pepe Verde To Go ●⊘⊟ *Prepared Food*

W Village | 559 Hudson St. (bet. Perry & W. 11th Sts.) | A/C/E/L to
14th St./8th Ave. | 212-255-2221

These popular Italian storefronts prove that the "freshest" pastas
can emerge from the "tiniest spaces" (they make even a "studio
apartment feel big"); overall, they "can't be beat", especially when
picking up a "quick" take-home meal "on-the-go", with "unbelievably"
reasonable prices as the clincher.

Perelandra Natural
Food Center ● *Health Food*

| 24 | 20 | 19 | M |

Brooklyn Heights | 175 Remsen St. (bet. Clinton & Court Sts.) | Brooklyn |
2/3/4/5/M/N/R/W to Borough Hall/Court St. | 718-855-6068 |
www.perelandranatural.com

This "natural foods palace" of Brooklyn Heights has "fabulous,
healthy" takeout, a "fantastic variety" of frozen goods and the "best
bulk section around", not to mention "knowledgeable vitamin-
counter help"; it can be "difficult to maneuver" the "cramped, tall
aisles", but it's still a "very pleasant place to shop", and the
smoothies, sandwiches and salads make it "a fun place for lunch" too.

Pescatore Seafood ●◗⊟ *Seafood*

| 25 | 25 | 22 | E |

E 40s | Grand Central Mkt. | Lexington Ave. (43rd St.) | 4/5/6/7/S to
42nd St./Grand Central | 212-557-4466 | www.pescatoreny.com

The "extensive" selection of both raw and "creative" prepared fin
fare at this "friendly" Grand Central booth "looks so good and tastes
the same way", and commuters in need of "dinner supplies" after work
appreciate its "convenience"; "helpful" service is another plus, and
while it's "expensive", the "specials make it very affordable."

Petak's *Prepared Food*

| 23 | 20 | 19 | E |

E 80s | 1246 Madison Ave. (bet. 89th & 90th Sts.) | 4/5/6 to 86th St. |
212-722-7711

Upper Eastsiders have grown accustomed to this "upscale" source
for prepared foods thanks to its range of "consistent" offerings
(from sandwiches to sushi) that supporters appreciate for their
"high quality"; however, the less-impressed say they'd rather bypass
what they see as "routine" fare served by staffers with "attitude."

Pete Milano's Discount Wine &
Liquor Supermarket *Wine/Liquor*

| - | - | - | M |

Staten Island | 1441 Forest Ave. (Marianne St.) | 718-447-2888

With 4,000 sq. ft., this Staten Islander has room to display its "excellent selection" of 4,000 vintages, including a newly expanded
roster of reds from Spain and Argentina, plus bottlings from New
Zealand and South Africa; customers can get a 10 percent case discount (even for mixed selections), while "average drinkers" seeking
spirits will find a lineup stressing single-malts, bourbons and vodkas.

	QUALITY	DISPLAY	SERVICE	COST

Peter's Market ⬚ *Specialty Shop* | − | − | − | M |

Bayside | 33-35 Francis Lewis Blvd. (bet. 33rd & 34th Aves.) | Queens | 718-463-4141 | www.petersmarketny.com

Four 'greats' equal near-"perfection" – as in "great service, great quality, great prices" and "great creativity" – at this Italian-style specialty shop in Bayside; Manhattanites must take the LIRR to get there, but intrepid gourmets who venture out find prime meats, cheeses, pastas, sauces and – "thank God" say locals – "endless" elegant prepared dishes, like espresso-and-anisette demi-glace pork tenderloin; N.B. it's also one of the top caterers in the borough.

Petite Abeille ◗ *Prepared Food* | 22 | 19 | 19 | M |

Flatiron | 44 W. 17th St. (bet. 5th & 6th Aves.) | F/V to 6th Ave. | 212-604-9350

Gramercy | 401 E. 20th St. (bet. Ave. A & 1st Ave.) | 6 to 23rd St. | 212-727-1505

TriBeCa | 134 W. Broadway (bet. Duane & Reade Sts.) | 1/A/C/E to Canal St. | 212-791-1360

W Village | 466 Hudson St. (Barrow St.) | 1 to Christopher St. | 212-741-6479 ⊋
www.petiteabeille.com

"Cute as the name", this 'little-bee' quartet of "European cafes" is a popular lunchtime stop for "excellent-value" Belgian-accented soups, salads, sandwiches and pastries; though there is seating, overly "cozy" conditions at some branches have regulars opting for takeout.

☑ Petrossian Boutique & Cafe ⬚ *Caviar/Smoked Fish* | 28 | 27 | 25 | VE |

W 50s | 911 Seventh Ave. (bet. 57th & 58th Sts.) | N/Q/R/W to 57th St. | 212-245-2217 | 800-828-9241 | www.petrossian.com

The "Tiffany's of caviar", this "luxe" market/cafe near Carnegie Hall, an adjunct of the posh French-Continental restaurant, is the "ne plus ultra" for "all things roe" as well as "glorious" smoked fish, foie gras and "creative" housemade pastries and chocolates; "impeccable" service and "indulgent" atmospherics are de rigueur, and though it's all "absurdly priced", anyone prepared to "max out" their plastic will find this one's in a "class of its own."

Philip's Candy Shop ⊋ *Candy/Nuts* | − | − | − | I |

Staten Island | 8 Barrett Ave. (Forest Ave.) | 718-981-0062

Although this confectioner moved to Staten Island in 2001 after 70 years in Coney Island, it still hearkens back to the "glory days" of old-school amusement-park treats, with its dreamy selection of cotton candy, caramel apples, candied popcorn, "excellent fudge" and more, all made from scratch.

Piazza Mercato ⬚ *Meat/Poultry* | − | − | − | M |

Bay Ridge | 9204 Third Ave. (92nd St.) | Brooklyn | R to Bay Ridge Ave./95th St. | 718-513-0071 | www.piazzamercato.biz

Most surveyors have yet to discover this Bay Ridge Italian specialty foods shop from the folks behind Royal Crown, but the few who know it praise its "wonderful" selection of house-cured sausages and meats (e.g. cappicolla, prosciutto), recently expanded cheese selection – some of which can be seen dangling from the ceiling – and broad array of old-fashioned Boot-centric prepared dishes.

Pick a Bagel ● *Bagels* | 20 | 18 | 18 | I |

E 70s | 1101 Lexington Ave. (77th St.) | 6 to 77th St. | 212-517-6590
E 70s | 1473 Second Ave. (bet. 76th & 77th Sts.) | 6 to 77th St. | 212-717-4662
Financial Dist | 102 North End Ave. (West Side Hwy.) | 1/2/3/A/C to Chambers St. | 212-786-9200
Gramercy | 297 Third Ave. (bet. 22nd & 23rd Sts.) | 6 to 23rd St. | 212-686-1414
W 50s | 200 W. 57th St. (7th Ave.) | N/Q/R/W to 57th St. | 212-957-5151
www.pickabageltogo.com

Its "wide variety" of offerings – including the "amazing selection of spreads and toppings" that can add up to a "real meal" – is just one reason fans flock to this bagel quintet for "doughy", "life preserver"-size orbs that sate big appetites; the less-impressed detect "no particular pizzazz" here, but even skeptics concede it's "convenient" for a "quick carb fix."

☑ Pickle Guys, The ▣ *Specialty Shop* | 27 | 18 | 23 | I |

LES | 49 Essex St. (bet. Grand & Hester Sts.) | B/D to Grand St. | 212-656-9739 | www.pickleguys.com

"These guys seem to have eclipsed Gus" marvel longtime brine-lovers of this descendant of a "Lower East Side icon", where "one of the joys of living in NYC" is a peck of "pickles like your bubby used to make", served "straight out of the barrel" with "old-style humor"; from "full sours" and "snappy half-sours to horseradish-infused" varieties, these "fresh and flavorful" puppies will "shock a bland palate"; P.S. also "try the pickled tomatoes and celery" – "and don't forget the kraut"; closed Saturdays.

Pickles, Olives Etc. ▣ *Specialty Shop* | 23 | 19 | 22 | M |

E 80s | 1647 First Ave. (86th St.) | 4/5/6 to 86th St. | 212-717-8966 | www.picklesandolives.com

Cuke aficionados find heaven in a half-sour and divinity in a kosher dill at this "pickle-lover's paradise", though at 20 varieties strong, it's also an "olive-lover's orgasmatron"; and given other offerings like "roasted eggplant salad with a delicious smoky flavor", regulars rate it a "wonderland" that's the perfect stop on your way to an UES dinner party ("bring something to your hosts other than wine").

Pie by the Pound ● *Prepared Food* | 20 | 18 | 16 | M |

E 80s | 1542 Second Ave. (bet. 80th & 81st Sts.) | 6 to 77th St. | 212-517-5017
E Village | 124 Fourth Ave. (bet. 12th & 13th Sts.) | 4/5/6/L/N/Q/R/W to 14th St./Union Sq. | 212-475-4977
www.piebythepound.com

The pizzas are "nothing like the heavy, old-school NYC" pies aver experts who've tasted the "tasty", "unique", thin-crust samplings cut up and dished out by this Downtown-Uptown duo that vends its offerings, as the name states, by the pound; while the pies may be somewhat "pricier" than the competition, the myriad options (over 40 varieties) help compensate.

Piemonte Ravioli *Pasta* | 27 | 19 | 22 | M |

Little Italy | 190 Grand St. (bet. Mott & Mulberry Sts.) | B/D to Grand St. | 212-226-0475 | www.piemonteravioli.com

"So many shapes, so many fillings, so little time!" lament loyalists of this veteran pasta shop that's deemed "worth a special trip to Little Italy"; in the biz since 1920, it offers "the best selection", including "real-deal" "fresh", "flavorful" ravioli varieties "from pumpkin to lobster" that will "make anyone look like a master chef"; there are also chocolates and other comestibles imported from the old country.

Z Pierre Marcolini ⬛ *Candy/Nuts* | 28 | 27 | 24 | VE |

E 50s | 485 Park Ave. (58th St.) | 4/5/6 to 59th St./Lexington Ave. | 212-755-5150 | www.marcolinichocolatier.com

"Just when you thought NYC didn't need another fancy chocolatier", along came this East Side Belgian "class act" and its "phenomenal", "mmm" chocolates in "gorgeous flavors" and connoisseur-conscious formulations (e.g. "fantastic single-origin" bonbons that "provide insight into chocolate *terroir*"); yes, they're "beyond expensive", but when looking to splurge or give a gift "perfect for any occasion", most find it "well worth" the outlay to sample "Brussels' best – on Park Avenue."

pinkberry ● *Ice Cream* | - | - | - | M |

Chelsea | 170 Eighth Ave. (bet. 18th & 19th Sts.) | A/C/E/L to 14th St. | 212-488-2510

E 80s | 1577 Second Ave. (82nd St.) | 4/5/6 to 86th St. | 212-861-0574

Garment Dist | 7 W. 32nd St. (bet. 5th & 6th Aves.) | B/D/F/N/Q/R/V/W to 34th St./Herald Sq. | 212-695-9631

www.pinkberry.com

With three Manhattan locations and counting, this burgeoning frozen yogurt chain, wildly popular in its home town of LA – where it's affectionately known as 'Crackberry' – may be reinventing the genre with its product that actually tastes like yogurt, offered in just two flavors, plain or green tea, and topped with the likes of fresh fruit, granola and chocolate chips; there are also smoothies and shaved ice, all dispensed in modern, style-conscious digs that feel a long way from the TCBY of yore.

Pino Prime Meats ⊘ *Meat/Poultry* | ▽ 27 | 20 | 24 | M |

SoHo | 149 Sullivan St. (bet. Houston & Prince Sts.) | C/E to Spring St. | 212-475-8134

"Simply terrific" is how surveyors describe this small "old-time" family butcher in SoHo "that goes the extra mile", whether serving up prime meats, housemade sausages, salami or wild boar ("they have every cut here"); if the "excellent quality" and "reasonable prices" weren't enticement enough, how could "you not love" a place where "opera is always on the radio" and owner Pino Cinquemani "is bantering in Italian with customers"?

	QUALITY	DISPLAY	SERVICE	COST

☑ Pisacane Midtown *Seafood* — 28 | 19 | 26 | E

E 50s | 940 First Ave. (bet. 51st & 52nd Sts.) | 6 to 51st St. | 212-752-7560
A "devoted clientele" has "such faith" in this "reliable", family-run fishmonger on the East Side that many "just ask what is fresh", and the staff "never advises wrong"; a "traditional" kind of place selling both raw and prepared offerings, it "caters to the wealthy", but hey, "these guys know their fish", and sometimes, you really do "get what you pay for."

Piu Bello ● *Ice Cream* — 21 | 19 | 17 | M

Forest Hills | 70-09 Austin St. (67th Dr.) | Queens | E/F/G/R/V to Forest Hills/71st Ave. | 718-268-4400 | www.piubellogelato.com
"There's no need to go to Manhattan" for the cafe experience provided by this Forest Hills "staple" that makes you feel like "you're in Little Italy" given its Boot-erific menu of baked goods, coffee and "wonderful" gelato "in a huge array of flavors"; however, given the service that's "not very cheery or attentive", some find it best to grab your goodies "to go."

P.J. Bernstein ● *Deli/Sandwich* — 19 | 13 | 17 | M

E 70s | 1215 Third Ave. (bet. 70th & 71st Sts.) | 6 to 68th St. | 212-879-0914 | www.nydelicaterer.com
"In the [era] of dwindling delis", this "local place" on the UES is "still a standout" – even if "it ain't Katz's" – for "standard sandwiches" as well as "remarkably good borscht", chicken soup and matzo balls (it isn't strictly kosher); yes, it can feel "crowded" and "overwhelmed" at times, but "what it lacks in service, it makes up for in taste."

PJ Wine ●◨ *Wine/Liquor* — 27 | 17 | 20 | I

Inwood | 4898 Broadway (bet. 204th & 207th Sts.) | A to 207th St. | 212-567-5500 | www.pjwine.com
Oenophiles "in-the-know" toast the "tremendous selection" at this "warehouse-size" Inwood "find", a "supermarketlike" setup where the aisles are stocked with an "unmatched" array of wines (especially Spanish vintages) and "brand-name liquors" priced for serious "value"; for those who "don't want to hoof it" Uptown, they have a "user-friendly Web site" loaded with special "features" and deliver gratis "for orders over $100."

Plaza Flowers *Flowers* — - | - | - | VE

E 60s | 944 Lexington Ave. (69th St.) | 6 to 68th St. | 212-472-7565
"Beautiful work but very expensive" seems to be the consensus on this French-style Upper East Side florist featuring *pavé*-style arrangements in which blooms are set close and level so as to seem like one; still, though "the flowers in the windows always look gorgeous", their prices can be prohibitive.

Polux Fleuriste ◨ *Flowers* — - | - | - | M

NoLita | 248 Mott St. (bet. Houston & Prince Sts.) | 6 to Spring St. | 212-219-9646
This quaint NoLita florist will have you humming *La vie en rose* as you appreciate owner Anouchka Levy's French-style arrangements: wild

and natural, with herbs and vines scattered among the blooms; the shop also plans events and is a source for other gift items: pashmina shawls, aromatherapy, candles and teas as well as a line of semiprecious jewelry.

Porto Rico Importing Co. ▤ *Coffee/Tea*   26 | 22 | 22 | I

E Village | 40½ St. Marks Pl. (bet. 1st & 2nd Aves.) | N/R to 8th St. | 212-533-1982
G Village | 201 Bleecker St. (bet. MacDougal St. & 6th Ave.) | A/B/C/D/E/F/V to W. 4th St. | 212-477-5421 ◗
SoHo | 107 Thompson St. (bet. Prince & Spring Sts.) | C/E to Spring St. | 212-966-5758
800-453-5908 | www.portorico.com

"Legions of loyal" "coffeephiles in-the-know" "worship" this 1907-vintage Village "emporium" and its sibs for their 140 "glorious" javas ("exotic", "organic and Fair Trade" types included), all "roasted to perfection" and laid out in "sacks of beans" in a "buzzing" "bazaar setting" overseen by a "spacey" but "congenial crew"; the "huge variety of teas" and "unbelievably" "gentle prices" also win support, especially since they "could charge for the smell" alone.

Poseidon Bakery *Baked Goods*   26 | 17 | 23 | I

W 40s | 629 Ninth Ave. (bet. 44th & 45th Sts.) | A/C/E to 42nd St./Port Authority | 212-757-6173

They "hand-roll their phyllo" dough "the way grandmother used to" at this "old-time" (circa 1952) Greek bakery in Hell's Kitchen, the "real deal" for "finger-lickingly sweet" pastries and "savory treats" like the "best spinach pie" around; Hellenists insist the "kind service" makes the "super-fresh" specialties "that much better" – "may they never change!"

NEW Pour *Wine/Liquor*   ▽ 21 | 25 | 25 | M

W 70s | 321 Amsterdam Ave. (75th St.) | 1/2/3 to 72nd St. | 212-501-7687 | www.pourwines.com

"Very helpful" for the dinner party set, this snug new Upper West Side wine shop aims to instruct on "pairings with food", providing each vintage with a notecard that gives info on matching cuisine categories (reinforced by a color-coded tag affixed to the bottle); suppourters "love the concept" and the "offbeat" labels, even if snobs sniff at the "gimmicky" approach; P.S. its "knowledgeable" team hosts tastings Tuesday–Saturday at the bar in back.

Pozzo Pastry Shop *Baked Goods*   21 | 19 | 22 | I

W 40s | 690 Ninth Ave. (bet. 47th & 48th Sts.) | C/E to 50th St. | 212-265-7530 | www.pozzopastry.com

"High quality" at "non-Manhattan prices" is the hallmark of this "old-fashioned" Hell's Kitchen bakery, a "reliable" supplier of special-occasion cakes (the "rum-soaked birthday" version is a "classic") that's pozzitively "the place to go" "for parties"; it's "nothing fancy or pretentious", but it provides the neighborhood with Italian pastries and cookies at "bargain" rates – "bless 'em."

	QUALITY	DISPLAY	SERVICE	COST

Premier Cru *Wine/Liquor*   ▽ 24 | 23 | 23 | E

E 80s | 1200 Madison Ave. (bet. 87th & 88th Sts.) | 4/5/6 to 86th St. | 212-534-6709 | www.premiercruwine.com

After more than doubling its dimensions, this "lovely neighborhood" wine-and-liquor boutique continues its crusade to bring first-class vinos and personalized service to its corner of the UES; its 1,200-label inventory showcases prime picks from vintners in Burgundy and California, and if some suggest it's "a little overpriced", discerning buyers are bound to encounter some "inexpensive gems" too.

Press 195 *Deli/Sandwich*   ▽ 25 | 18 | 18 | I

Park Slope | 195 Fifth Ave. (bet. Sackett & Union Sts.) | Brooklyn | M/R to Union St. | 718-857-1950

Bayside | 40-11 Bell Blvd. (40th Ave.) | Queens | 718-281-1950
www.press195.com

Luring locals with "the longest list of panini options" some "have ever seen", this duo in Park Slope and Bayside boasts "delicious, sometimes inventive" pressed sandwiches plus "nice salads", a "friendly staff" and a wealth of outdoor seating at both locations; the only catch: you have to be "willing to wait."

Pret A Manger *Deli/Sandwich*   21 | 20 | 18 | M

E 40s | 205 E. 42nd St. (3rd Ave.) | 4/5/6/7/S to 42nd St./Grand Central | 212-867-1905

E 40s | 287 Madison Ave. (bet. 40th & 41st Sts.) | 4/5/6/7/S to 42nd St./Grand Central | 212-867-0400

E 50s | 400 Park Ave. (54th St.) | E/V to Lexington Ave./53rd St. | 212-207-4101

E 50s | 630 Lexington Ave. (54th St.) | E/V to Lexington Ave./53rd St. | 646-497-0510

Financial Dist | 60 Broad St. (bet. Beaver St. & Exchange Pl.) | 2/3 to Wall St. | 212-825-8825

Garment Dist | 530 Seventh Ave. (bet. 38th & 39th Sts.) | 1/2/3/7/N/Q/R/S/W to 42nd St./Times Sq. | 646-728-0750

W 40s | 11 W. 42nd St. (bet. 5th & 6th Aves.) | 7/B/D/F/V to 42nd St./Bryant Park | 212-997-5520

W 40s | 30 Rockefeller Plaza, concourse level (bet. 49th & 50th Sts.) | B/D/F/V to 47-50th Sts./Rockefeller Ctr. | 212-246-6944

W 50s | 135 W. 50th St. (bet. 6th & 7th Aves.) | 1 to 50th St. | 212-489-6458

W 50s | 1350 Sixth Ave. (55th St.) | N/Q/R/W to 57th St. | 212-307-6100
866-328-7738 | www.pret.com
Additional locations throughout the NY area

"The best British invasion since the Beatles", this U.K.-based chain serves up "wholesome" sandwiches and salads that are a welcome "change from the norm"; "gracious" counter folk and "crisp, clean" setups add to the experience, and while a few lament the "London prices", most say the rates are "reasonable" given the "quality."

Props for Today *Party Rentals*   20 | 22 | 23 | E

Garment Dist | 330 W. 34th St. (bet. 8th & 9th Aves.) | 1/2/3/A/C/E to 34th St./Penn Station | 212-244-9600 | www.propsfortoday.com

Loaded with sophisticated, movie set–worthy furniture and "tons of playful props" suited to elaborate parties (with themes ranging from

"Art Deco" to "Raj Period" to "Carnival"), this rental vendor draws most of its clients from TV, film and other media companies but also opens its 100,000-sq.-ft. Garment District warehouse to civilians; all agree service is "extremely helpful" – and that you'll need a movie star's salary to cover the "expensive" tab.

☑ Prospect Wine Shop ◑ ⌐ *Wine/Liquor* | 26 | 22 | 26 | M |

Park Slope | 322 Seventh Ave. (bet. 8th & 9th Sts.) | Brooklyn | F to 7th Ave. | 718-768-1232 | www.prospectwine.com
Stocked floor-to-ceiling with a "tremendous" 1,500-strong wine selection, this Park Sloper is an "interesting" prospect for special vintages from old-world growers, premium sakes and "many organic" and biodynamic options; "fair pricing" and a "passionate staff eager to help" with "advice" and "pairing ideas" make it a "great neighborhood shop", and on seasonal Saturday afternoons "wonderful" tastings convene in the garden out back.

Puff & Pao *Coffee/Tea* | - | - | - | M |

G Village | 105 Christopher St. (bet. Bleecker & Hudson Sts.) | 1 to Christopher St. | 212-633-7833 | www.puffandpao.com
"Your taste buds will thank you" for a stop at this Greenwich Village bakery/cafe, a "rare find" for two "homemade" delicacies: profiteroles piped to order with flavored creams and "delicious", "gluten-free" *pao de queijo* (Brazilian cheese bread), sold as mini *paolitos* with baked-in boosters like chorizo, jalapeños or fig and walnut; the latter can be McMuffinized with salad stuffing or breakfast fixings, and the "solid" coffee menu's a pao-erful "bonus."

Pumpkins Organic Market *Specialty Shop* | ▽ 26 | 23 | 21 | E |

Park Slope | 1302 Eighth Ave. (bet. 13th & 14th Sts.) | Brooklyn | F to 7th Ave. | 718-499-8539 | www.pumpkinsorganicmarket.com
"Surely in past decades groceries like this were common" say surveyors of this Park Sloper, a "lovely" if "limited" source of things "to buy for a picnic lunch": "fresh artisanal breads, real heavy whipping cream", "vegan chocolate cookies to die for", locally sourced produce and other "interesting organic foods", all "served with a smile"; even hard-core Manhattanites admit "it rates a trip across the river."

Quality House ⌐ *Wine/Liquor* | ▽ 27 | 21 | 27 | E |

Murray Hill | 2 Park Ave. (bet. 32nd & 33rd Sts.) | 6 to 33rd St. | 212-532-2944 | www.qualityhousewines.com
After "three generations" in the biz, this "high-end" Murray Hill vino shop "serves clients well" with its encyclopedic French inventory, as well as stock from Italy, Germany and Australia; its owner "knows more about wine" than most and carries labels "you can't find" elsewhere, so though it can get "pricey", all agree "quality reigns here."

Quattro's
Game & Poultry Farm ⌐ *Meat/Poultry* | 26 | 19 | 23 | M |

See Greenmarket; for more information, call 845-635-2018
Fans who flock to this Dutchess County farm's Union Square Greenmarket stall on Saturdays cluck over its "superb" poultry se-

	QUALITY	DISPLAY	SERVICE	COST

lections, from the "best free-range chicken" to pheasant, duck and hertiage holiday birds (don't forget to "special-order" "your Thanksgiving turkey and Christmas goose"), not to mention smoked varieties and sausage; loyal customers "quail at the thought of buying birds anywhere else."

Queen Ann Ravioli *Pasta*

| 27 | 19 | 22 | I |

Bensonhurst | 7205 18th Ave. (bet. 72nd & 73rd Sts.) | Brooklyn | N to 18th Ave. | 718-256-1061

Some of the "best homemade pasta in Brooklyn" comes from this longtime "favorite" that inspires loyalists to make "the trek" to Bensonhurst, though its raviolis and other filled "great shapes" are available "in Italian markets all over the city"; it also vends sauces (meat, puttanesca or marinara), fresh mozz, prepared foods like eggplant rollatini and lasagna as well as olive oils and vinegars.

☑ Raffetto's ⇆ *Pasta*

| 28 | 20 | 24 | I |

G Village | 144 W. Houston St. (bet. MacDougal & Sullivan Sts.) | A/B/C/D/E/F/V to W. 4th St. | 212-777-1261

"Wonderful", "crazy-fresh" pasta "cut to order on amazing jangly old machines" is what this "family-owned" Greenwich Village "institution" has been turning out for more than 100 years – and surveyors say "bless them for keeping" up the tradition; in addition to its "heavenly" ravioli and myriad other pasta varieties, it also offers "sauces, cheeses and other tasty ingredients for Italian dishes", as well as a line of prepared foods like lasagna and baked ziti, all at the "world's-best-bargain" prices; P.S. there are even a few more "contemporary" offerings – "chocolate fettuccini" anyone?

Rainbo's Fish at
Essex St. Market ⇆ *Seafood*

| - | - | - | I |

LES | Essex Street Market | 120 Essex St. (bet. Delancey & Rivington Sts.) | F/J/M/Z to Delancey/Essex Sts. | 212-982-8585

This veteran seafood stall in the LES's Essex Street Market offers a respectable showing of fresh everyday choices, all at "great prices"; there's limited counter seating and a juice bar annex that serves muffins and such in the morning, and has become something of a local favorite at lunchtime for its grilled fish and sardine sandwiches.

Ralph's Famous
Italian Ices ◑⇆ *Ice Cream*

| 24 | 14 | 18 | I |

Bayside | 214-15 41st Ave. (Bell Blvd.) | Queens | 718-428-4578
Floral Pk | 264-21 Union Tpke. (bet. 264th & 265th Sts.) | Queens | 718-343-8724
Forest Hills | 73-04 Austin St. (Ascan Ave.) | Queens | E/F/G/R/V to Forest Hills/71st Ave. | 718-263-8816
Whitestone | 12-48 Clintonville St. (12th Rd.) | Queens | 7 to Flushing-Main St. | 718-746-1456
Staten Island | 4212 Hylan Blvd. (bet. Armstrong & Robinson Aves.) | 718-605-5052
Staten Island | 501 Port Richmond Ave. (Catherine St.) | 718-273-3675

(continued)

(continued)

Ralph's Famous Italian Ices

Staten Island | 6272 Amboy Rd. (Bloomingdale Rd.) | 718-605-8133
www.ralphsices.com

"Summer wouldn't feel like summer" without a trip to the original 1949 branch of this Staten Island institution – or one of its ever-multiplying offspring – where "people flock" to enjoy "the best Italian ices" in the warm-weather months and the "line spills out to the street"; there are "so many flavors" (even no-sugar options for dieters) you'll "want to try them all", so "buy pints for home" while you're at it.

❷ Randazzo's Seafood *Seafood* | 28 | 21 | 24 | M |

Bronx | 2327 Arthur Ave. (bet. 183rd & 187th Sts.) | B/D to Fordham Rd. | 718-367-4139

Seafood "from all over the world" at "a fraction" of Manhattan prices, "freshness" you "can always count on" and "service with a smile" – "what's not to like?" about this "Arthur Avenue institution" that "continues to be fabulous"; if you're "looking for the unusual", such as baccalà, anchovies and other Italian specialties, "this should be where you're headed"; P.S. "try the clams at the raw bar outside."

Ravioli Store 🖃 *Pasta* | 25 | 19 | 21 | M |

SoHo | 75 Sullivan St. (bet. Broome & Spring Sts.) | C/E to Spring St. | 212-925-1737 | www.raviolistore.com

Despite the fact that its business is mostly wholesale, a "nice neighborhood feeling" pervades this SoHo pasta shop, where the owner is "always coming up with new" artisanal offerings, and boosters brag the "innovative", "delicious fillings" like Cajun crawfish or sweet potato–fig are "so good by themselves" you may not need sauce; imported condiments and ready-to-heat lasagna and other prepared foods packed by a "kind staff" complete the picture.

Ready to Eat ◕ *Prepared Food* | ▽ 21 | 21 | 24 | M |

W Village | 525 Hudson St. (bet. Charles & W. 10th Sts.) | 1 to Christopher St. | 212-229-1013 | www.readytoeat.net

Classic American cooking is the forte of this "affordable" Village prepared-foods shop/caterer whose "well-packed" offerings come in handy when cooking at home isn't an option; cornbread and cranberry–stuffed turkey breasts, meatloaf and carrot–cream cheesecake are popular choices, and can be eaten on-site in a small seating area.

Really Cool Foods ◕ *Prepared Food* | 21 | 24 | 21 | E |

E 60s | 1059 Third Ave. (bet. 62nd & 63rd Sts.) | F to Lexington Ave./ 63rd St. | 212-605-0900

"Letting the wannabe chef look like he can cook", this "bright, shiny" East Side storefront offers prepackaged, "mostly organic" meal components (complete with recipe cards) that make culinary capers "so easy"; though all the work is "done for you" and meals can be "customized", most agree that "really cool equals really expensive" – it may be "cheaper to go out"; N.B. some offerings are now sold at Gourmet Garage stores.

	QUALITY	DISPLAY	SERVICE	COST

Rebecca Cole Design *Flowers* — | — | — | E

Garment Dist | 247 W. 30th St. (bet. 7th & 8th Aves.) | 212-216-9492 | www.colecreates.com

The Today Show's "fun" gardening editor is the eponymous "color wizard" behind this recently relocated Garment District florist that enlivens special events and indoor gardens with its "breathtaking designs"; even jaded sorts who've "seen many flower arrangements" agree this pricey shop "does fabulous work" ("given only four hours notice, they came through").

Red Jacket Orchards ⌨ *Produce* 27 | 19 | 22 | M

See Greenmarket; for more information, call 315-781-2749 or 800-828-9410 | www.redjacketorchards.com

Hard-core "apple addicts" get their fix at this Finger Lakes orchard's Greenmarket stall, where the "delicious apples" in the crisp-weather months rotate to "fabulous" apricots, plums, peaches and other stone fruits in summer, and there are also pies, tarts and "dangerous" cider doughnuts, all at "very fair prices"; still, it may be most beloved for its "best-on-the-planet" juices, ciders and nectars (which are also available via Fresh Direct, Fairway, Whole Foods and other markets).

☑ Red, White & Bubbly ●⌨ *Wine/Liquor* 26 | 24 | 25 | M

Park Slope | 211-213 Fifth Ave. (bet. President & Union Sts.) | Brooklyn | M/R to Union St. | 718-636-9463 | www.redwhiteandbubbly.com

Wine lovers "would consider moving to Park Slope just to be closer" to this "wonderful shop", a "favorite" for its "attractive" layout (with a temperature-controlled room for the finer vintages), "reasonable" cost and staff of "bubbly", "no-attitude" "enthusiasts"; the frequent tastings feature "some good stuff", and owner Darrin Siegfried offers "amazingly reliable" monthly picks for 'Discovery Wines', 'Best Buys' and '4-pack' specials; N.B. their on-site classes range from Wine 101 to Advanced.

Remi to Go *Prepared Food* 26 | 19 | 19 | E

W 50s | 145 W. 53rd St. (bet. 6th & 7th Aves.) | N/Q/R/W to 57th St. | 212-581-7115 | www.remi.citysearch.com

Now under new ownership, this Midtown prepared foods/catering shop still features the same "top-notch pastas, salads" and other Italian specialties as can be found at its adjacent (but much more expensive) sister restaurant, Remi; in fact, area suits insist it's "one of the best places for a take-out lunch" around; N.B. it expanded its seating during a recent redo.

Renny & Reed *Flowers* — | — | — | VE

E 50s | 505 Park Ave. (bet. 59th & 60th Sts.) | 4/5/6 to 59th St./Lexington Ave. | 212-288-7000 | www.rennyandreed.com

Specializing in the proper English-garden style of arrangements, this tony, family-run florist in Midtown "never disappoints", delivering "creative, lovely", "beautiful bouquets" that have some supporters insisting it's among "the best NY has" to offer; if you can "describe it, they'll produce it", as they have for area hotels (including the

	QUALITY	DISPLAY	SERVICE	COST

Essex House and Four Seasons) and, on occasion, for events at the White House.

☑ Rice to Riches ● ▣ *Baked Goods*

23	26	21	M

NoLita | 37 Spring St. (bet. Mott & Mulberry Sts.) | 6 to Spring St. | 212-274-0008 | www.ricetoriches.com

The "Baskin-Robbins" of "gourmet rice pudding", this "upbeat" NoLita shop specializes in just this one dessert, bringing "new pizzazz" to a heretofore humble dish with its "rich", "super-creamy" version offered in "flavors you never dared to dream of" (mascarpone with cherries, chocolate hazelnut, cheesecake, etc.) and served in "UFO-like snap-lid containers"; the "bright", "futuristic space" is a "nirvana" to "converts" who consider its "unique" concept "totally unexpected" but "brilliant" ("when are they going to franchise?").

Richard Salome Flowers ▣ *Flowers*

-	-	-	VE

E 70s | 1034 Lexington Ave. (bet. 73rd & 74th Sts.) | 6 to 77th St. | 212-988-2933 | 800-578-2621 | www.richardsalomeflowers.com

Bloom boosters say "the flowers are always fresh" at this Upper East Side florist and event planner that "never disappoints" with its "amazing displays", all nestled in unique containers from around the world; it's pricey, but surveyors insist its cut arrangements and hand-painted silk blooms "are worth every penny."

☑ Richart
Design et Chocolat ▣ *Candy/Nuts*

28	28	25	VE

E 50s | 7 E. 55th St. (bet. 5th & Madison Aves.) | N/R/W to 5th Ave./59th St. | 212-371-9369 | 888-742-4278 | www.richart.com

This chichi Midtown French chocolate boutique elicits oohs and aahs for its artistic morsels so "beautiful" in design, if there were a Museum of Chocolate, they'd be in the "permanent collection"; they're also a "treat for the taste buds", with "innovative" fillings that make this house a leader in the "esoteric flavor department", ensuring that its "expensive little bites" rarely fail to "make a statement" – one that says either "I love you dearly" or "I have more money than sense."

Risotteria ● *Prepared Food*

23	16	20	M

G Village | 270 Bleecker St. (Morton St.) | 1 to Christopher St. | 212-924-6664 | www.risotteria.com

"If you like risotto, you'll love" this sliver of a Greenwich Village eatery/take-out shop and its many "addictively delicious" varieties of the made-to-order signature dish; however, surveyors note there's "much more" to be had here, including "excellent" pizza, salads and panini, and "those with food allergies" give it "a gold star" for its gluten-free lineup.

Rita's Ices ● *Ice Cream*

21	14	19	I

Staten Island | Greenridge Plaza Shopping Ctr. | 3285D Richmond Ave. (Arthur Kill Rd.) | 718-227-7860 | www.ritasice.com

"Awesomely cool" and "a kick in the butt for old Italian ice" peddlers is the verdict on this Pennsylvania import in Staten Island that specializes in "totally addictive" "classic summer treats" in a "large variety of flavors", with fantastically fruity ones getting frequent shout-outs and even the sugar-free variety earning full marks ("yummy"); N.B. open April–September.

Robbins Wolfe Eventeurs *Caterer* ▽ 26 | 20 | 22 | VE

Meatpacking | 521 West St. (bet. Gansevoort & Horatio Sts.) | 212-924-6500 | www.robbinswolfe.com
By appointment only

A "fave of UESers and Hamptonites" and other gentry, this ultra-upmarket caterer/event planner (with offices in the Meatpacking District, Locust Valley and the Hamptons) does the full-service monte on a grand scale, handling everything from invites to entertainment to theme decor for smart-set clients like Julliard and the Rubin Museum; the food and drink is predictably top-tier, but "you pay for the quality" and wolves in the fold growl it's "overrated."

Robert Isabell ⊉ *Flowers* ▽ 27 | 26 | 24 | VE

Meatpacking | 410 W. 13th St. (bet. 9th Ave. & Washington St.) | 212-645-7767
By appointment only

"When name-dropping matters", this "wonderful" florist and event planner in the Meatpacking District delivers with "inventive, lavish, showstopping" productions (including "stylish weddings") that you and "your friends will always remember"; plus, the eponymous owner "knows his flowers" too – "everything he does is tasteful" – so when you need an arrangement, this shop is "tops."

Rocco's Pastry Shop ◑ ▣ *Baked Goods* 25 | 23 | 20 | M

G Village | 243 Bleecker St. (bet. Carmine & Leroy Sts.) | A/B/C/D/E/F/V to W. 4th St. | 212-242-6031 | www.roccospastry.com

Those "looking for an authentic Italian" pastry-and-coffee "fix" should look no further than this "cheerful" Greenwich Village bakery/cafe, a "sinful" "sweetfest" that's "often crowded" with natives and "tourists" alike; besides the signature "freshly made cannoli" ("stuffed to order"), highlights of the "huge selection" include "yummy" sfogliatelle and "real" gelato and ices for summer, and enthusiasts who "love all of it" can always "load up" at a "reasonable price."

Rohrs, M. ◑ ▣ *Coffee/Tea* 24 | 18 | 22 | M

E 80s | 303 E. 85th St. (bet. 1st & 2nd Aves.) | 4/5/6 to 86th St. | 212-396-4456 | 888-772-7647 | www.rohrs.com

It claims "a long history" dating to 1896, and this Upper East Side "gem" remains a roaring success as a "quality purveyor" of "smooth" house-roasted coffee in "lots of different" specialty blends, along with a profusion of "wonderful" teas; the goods are available online, but its homespun charm is "totally worth a trip" and in true "old-time" style "a daily dose doesn't break the bank."

Ronaldo Maia *Flowers* – | – | – | VE

E 90s | 1143 Park Ave. (bet. 91st & 92nd Sts.) | 6 to 96th St. | 212-288-1049

This Upper East Side florist attracts an upscale clientele that's simply "thrilled" with the shop's customized arrangements of "lovely and unusual flowers" (no catalogs or mail order here); it also has a way with topiaries and sells a streamlined selection of small gift items, but as with the pricey blooms, you'll "pay dearly."

Ron Ben-Israel Cakes *Baked Goods*   ▽ 25 | 25 | 24 | VE

SoHo | 42 Greene St., 5th fl. (bet. Broome & Grand Sts.) | 212-625-3369 | www.weddingcakes.com
By appointment only

"Charmer" Ron Ben-Israel's "very high-end" SoHo custom bakery specializes in "heavenly" wedding cakes bedizened with "unbelievably real-looking sugar flowers", which may seem "too beautiful to eat" but taste "divine" every time; it's a "rare opportunity" to commission handiwork that's featured in magazine spreads, but if the gâteaux are guaranteed to be "dazzling", "the prices are too."

☒ Ronnybrook Farms Dairy ⌿ *Cheese/Dairy*   28 | 18 | 23 | M

Chelsea | Chelsea Mkt. | 75 Ninth Ave. (bet. 15th & 16th Sts.) | A/C/E/L to 14th St./8th Ave. | 212-741-6455 | 800-772-6455 | www.ronnybrook.com

If there were an Olympic category for "all-around best dairy", this "wonderful family-run" farm would have to win, udders down, for its ultrafresh line of milk, cream, butter, yogurt and "ice cream flavors found nowhere else", all offered at its Chelsea Market storefront as well as at the Greenmarket and in gourmet stores citywide; surveyors moo in favor of its "old-fashioned bottles" and declare its relatively "pricey" goods "worth every penny" – and "every fat gram."

Rootstock & Quade *Flowers*   - | - | - | E

Park Slope | 297 Seventh Ave. (bet. 7th & 8th Sts.) | Brooklyn | F to 7th Ave. | 718-788-8355 | www.rootstockquade.com

"Lovely arrangements and quality flowers" are the deal at this custom-only Park Slope florist that appeals to clients like the Brooklyn Museum of Art with its monochromatic signature style; it also sells herbs and other plants, containers and garden furniture, puts on seasonal lectures and offers "fabulous" event design services.

Rosa Rosa *Flowers*   ▽ 21 | 18 | 19 | M

E 60s | 831A Lexington Ave. (bet. 63rd & 64th Sts.) | F to Lexington Ave./ 63rd St. | 212-935-4706 | www.rosarosaflowers.com

The name of this Upper East Side florist says it all: it specializes in "great deals on roses" that "always look beautiful and last longer", perhaps because the shop receives flower shipments six days a week; it's recently added orchids to its repertoire, but acolytes admit "you don't come here for fantastic floral displays, you come here for nice arrangements at nice prices."

Rosenthal Wine Merchant *Wine/Liquor*   ▽ 28 | 20 | 27 | E

E 80s | 318 E. 84th St. (bet. 1st & 2nd Aves.) | 4/5/6 to 86th St. | 212-249-6650

A vino vendor "of the old school", this Upper Eastsider is a showroom for "hand-picked gems" from 80 "lesser-known" "small vintners", limited to estate-bottled French, Italian and California wines imported by Neal Rosenthal (who is not associated with the store);

they "don't sell anything they don't know intimately", so a visit's sure to be "interesting" if "no bargain"; N.B. tastings are held Saturdays from 4–6 PM.

⊠ Royal Crown Pastry Shop *Baked Goods* | 26 | 21 | 21 | M |

Bensonhurst | 6308 14th Ave. (bet. 63rd & 64th Sts.) | Brooklyn | D/M/N to New Utrecht Ave./62nd St. | 718-234-3208 ✇
Bensonhurst | 6512 14th Ave. (bet. 65th & 66th Sts.) | Brooklyn | D/M/N to New Utrecht Ave./62nd St. | 718-234-1002 ✇
Staten Island | 1350 Hylan Blvd. (Old Town Rd.) | 718-668-0284 ◐
www.newyorkitalianmarket.com

"This is what bread should taste like" declare loyal subjects at these "brick-oven" Italian bakeries, where "classic" "crunchy" loaves "rule" and the "specialty" varieties like fig-and-walnut or chocolate rank among "the best" to be had; other crowning achievements include an "outstanding" "assortment" of pastries and "some great sandwiches" at the cafe-equipped Staten Island branch.

Royal Wine Merchants ▣ *Wine/Liquor* | – | – | – | M |

Gramercy | 25 Waterside Plaza, 2nd fl. (25th St.) | 6 to 23rd st. | 212-689-4855 | www.royalwinemerchants.com

The connoisseur is king at this citadel of oenophilia on the East River's edge (behind Bellevue Hospital Center), a French and Italian specialist that caters to the insider with meticulously chosen wines, including fine and rare vintages stored in a climate-controlled 'cellar' room; buyers in the market for a 1900 Margaux or 1961 Petrus should expect top-tier prices, but on request they fax out notices of "closeouts and specials" that can be "great for bargains."

Ruben's Empanadas *Prepared Food* | 20 | 13 | 18 | I |

E Village | 122 First Ave. (bet. 7th St. & St. Marks Pl.) | L to 1st Ave. | 212-979-0172 ◐
Financial Dist | 77 Pearl St. (bet. Broad St. & Hanover Sq.) | 2/3 to Wall St. | 212-361-6323
SoHo | 505 Broome St. (W. B'way) | C/E to Spring St. | 212-334-3351 ◐
Seaport | South St. Seaport | 64 Fulton St. (bet. Cliff & Gold Sts.) | 2/3 to Fulton St. | 212-962-5330

An "absolute favorite" of Downtown lunchers, this storefront mini-chain churns out "incredibly authentic" South American–style "pockets of flavor" popular enough to require getting there "right at noon before the line is out the door"; given that it serves such "awesome" "handheld food at reasonable prices", it's "no accident they've been in business for over 30 years."

Ruby et Violette *Baked Goods* | ▽ 26 | 23 | 23 | E |

W 50s | 457 W. 50th St. (bet. 9th & 10th Aves.) | C/E to 50th St. | 212-582-6720 | 877-353-9099 | www.rubyetviolette.com

"The Cartier" of chocolate-chunk cookies, this way West Side gourmet baker puts premium imported ingredients into every "delicious" doughy delight and offers "creative variations" infused with dozens of "fantastical" flavorings like champagne, espresso bean, jasmine and Key lime; the "recently changed" ownership now vends brownies and blondies and "still delivers" "the best" quality, but these are "cookies for grown-ups" so expect a suitably adult "price tag."

☑ Russ & Daughters ▣ Smoked Fish | 28 | 24 | 24 | E |

LES | 179 E. Houston St. (bet. Allen & Orchard Sts.) | F/V to Lower East Side/2nd Ave. | 212-475-4880 | 800-787-7229 | www.russanddaughters.com

Smoked fish like "your grandparents would remember" leads the "vaunted" lineup at this "old-world" Jewish deli "treasure" on the Lower East Side, offering "one-stop shopping" for "unbeatable" lox, sable, whitefish, caviar and "everything else" that makes for a "happy nosher"; it's also "the real deal" for "goodies" like rugalach, halvah and babka, not to mention "jewel"-like dried fruits and candy, and as for the tab, most shrug "you gotta pay" for "greatness."

Russo Mozzarella & Pasta Cheese/Dairy | 26 | 17 | 21 | M |

E Village | 344 E. 11th St. (bet. 1st & 2nd Aves.) | L to 1st Ave. | 212-254-7452

Park Slope | 363 Seventh Ave. (bet. 10th & 11th Sts.) | Brooklyn | F to 7th Ave. | 718-369-2874

Rustle up "your own Italian feast" with one stop at this near-centenarian East Villager, a "neighborhood destination" that's known for "excellent", "super-fresh mozzarella" but "satisfies" with "more than just cheese" given its "real-deal" pastas, sauces and meats; the Park Slope offshoot adds housemade prepared foods, breads and desserts to the mix, and it also caters.

Sable's Smoked Fish ▣ Caviar/Smoked Fish | 27 | 19 | 22 | E |

E 70s | 1489 Second Ave. (bet. 77th & 78th Sts.) | 6 to 77th St. | 212-249-6177 | www.sablesnyc.com

"These guys know their smoked fish" boast Upper East Side admirers of this "cramped" shop, where an able team "wins raves" for "succulent" salmon, sturgeon and caviar that'll "melt in your mouth" (and don't miss the "outstanding" lobster salad); the "solicitous countermen" are "generous" with "free taste tests" to "whet your appetite", and though "you pay a premium", it "never fails" "for top quality."

☑ Sahadi's Specialty Shop | 27 | 20 | 22 | I |

Brooklyn Heights | 187 Atlantic Ave. (bet. Clinton & Court Sts.) | Brooklyn | 2/3/4/5/M/N/R/W to Borough Hall/Court St. | 718-624-4550 | www.sahadis.com

"It's worth a trip to the County of Kings" (even on "elbow-to-elbow" weekends) to feast like a sultan on the Mideastern "gold mine" at this "phenomenal" Brooklyn Heights food "bazaar"; the "displays are not high-tech" and you gotta "run to grab a number ticket", but amid the "controlled chaos" you'll find "all sorts of goodies hidden in every corner": "vast selections" of high-quality prepared foods, cheese, chocolates, olives, teas, spices, dried fruits and nuts, rice, grains and beans, coffee, "vinegars and oils" and more – and "all at rock-bottom prices."

	QUALITY	DISPLAY	SERVICE	COST

Sal & Dom's *Baked Goods* ▽ 28 | 23 | 24 | M

Bronx | 1108 Allerton Ave. (Laconia Ave.) | 5 to Pelham Pkwy. | 718-515-3344 | www.salanddoms.com

"Everything Italian" and sweet seems to show up at this "standby" bakery in the Bronx's Williamsbridge area, where the "freshest" pastries, biscotti and cakes ensure "just the smell" "adds an inch to your waistline"; seasonal specialties make it "hands-down popular" "on the holidays", with the locals lining up come Christmas for their marzipan, struffoli and pastiera.

Salsa Caterers *Caterer/Events* - | - | - | M

Bronx | 4006 Third Ave. (174th St.) | 718-716-2020 | www.salsacaterers.com

Spice up any event with Latin, Caribbean or soul food done "to perfection" courtesy of this Bronx caterer/event planner, which ranks with "the very best" at delivering "down-home taste" in "ample" quantities with "top-notch" service and presentation; tending to a mix of private and corporate clients in their banquet rooms or select off-site venues, they're also "magicians" with "your budget", so "definitely" "go for it."

☑ Salumeria Biellese ⌧ *Meat/Poultry* 29 | 18 | 24 | M

Chelsea | 376-378 Eighth Ave. (29th St.) | 1/2/3/A/C/E to 34th St./ Penn Station | 212-736-7376 | www.salumeriabiellese.com

This second-generation Chelsea salumeria brings out "the Italian in everyone" with its "mind-boggling" array of "super-duper sausages" (some 40 varieties) and "wonderful cured meats", both "house-made" and imported, which it supplies to the public as well as to restaurants the likes of Daniel Boulud's and Thomas Keller's; its "reasonable prices" and appealing "slice-of-the-past" milieu are other reasons to "love" this place; N.B. sells sandwiches and other prepared foods too.

Samascott Orchards *Produce* 27 | 20 | 21 | M

See Greenmarket; for more information, call 518-758-7224 | www.samascott.com

"You'll never eat a Red Delicious from the corner deli again" after sampling the "amazing assortment" of heirloom apples that are the specialty of this Kinderhook orchard's Greenmarket stand; its fruits' "endless variety" (e.g. the "juiciest" Yellow Newton Pippins) and "peerless" quality make it a standout, and it doesn't hurt that there are also "bubbling hot cider" and "mmm" doughnuts to "keep you warm" while you make your picks.

S&S Cheesecake ⌧⊅ *Baked Goods* 27 | 12 | 19 | M

Bronx | 222 W. 238th St. (bet. Bailey Ave. & B'way) | 1 to 238th St. | 718-549-3888

"There is no better cheesecake" declare dessert-cart cognoscenti who "dare you to resist" the "creamy", "incredibly smooth texture" of this Bronx bakery's output, which continues to "wow" as the "hands-down" "finest" available; the quality justifies "a schlep" to the frill-free "warehouse" outlet (open Monday–Friday till 3 PM), but it's also "easy enough to find around town" at classy eateries like Morton's or The Palm.

Sandwich Planet ◗ *Deli/Sandwich* ∇ 25 | 14 | 21 | M

Garment Dist | 534 Ninth Ave. (bet. 39th & 40th Sts.) | A/C/E to 42nd St./Port Authority | 212-273-9768 | www.sandwichplanet.com

If "brilliant sandwiches made to order" send you into outer space, head to this Garment District shop that "rewards patrons" with so many "offbeat" options (over 100) that some surveyors just "don't know how they do it all in such a tiny place"; given its diminutive size, many say delivery or takeout is the "best option during lunch hour"; P.S. the "only problem: no liquor license."

Sant Ambroeus ◗ *Ice Cream* 26 | 25 | 21 | E

E 70s | 1000 Madison Ave. (77th St.) | 6 to 77th St. | 212-570-2211
W Village | 259 W. Fourth St. (Perry St.) | 1 to Christopher St. | 212-604-9254
www.santambroeus.com

"'Sheer ambrosia' would be a better name" declare devotees who swoon over this "high-end" Uptown-Downtown duo's espresso, gelato and other "real-deal" Italian "goodies" "fresh and delicious" enough to have you thinking you're on a "trip to Milan" (complete with "expensive" prices); Upper Eastsiders are "delighted" the original location reopened a few years back, reporting its redone (but still "teeny tiny") digs are "much more appealing" now.

Sarabeth's ▣ *Baked Goods* 24 | 22 | 19 | E

Chelsea | Chelsea Mkt. | 75 Ninth Ave. (bet. 15th & 16th Sts.) | A/C/E/L to 14th St./8th Ave. | 212-989-2424
E 70s | Whitney Museum | 945 Madison Ave. (75th St.) | 6 to 77th St. | 212-570-3670
E 90s | 1295 Madison Ave. (bet. 92nd & 93rd Sts.) | 6 to 96th St. | 212-410-7335 ◗
W 80s | 423 Amsterdam Ave. (bet. 80th & 81st Sts.) | 1 to 79th St. | 212-496-6280 ◗
800-773-7378 | www.sarabeth.com

Many "well-maintained" urbanites confess they're "fools for" these "charming" bakeries and "brunch musts", which turn out the "freshly" minted likes of "scrumptious" scones, "marvelous muffins" and other "goodies" best paired with their "luscious" "homemade jams"; the picturesque "country kitchen" setups are a bit "precious" atmospherically (and pricewise), but "the whole world knows" they're "special" so "get on line early to beat the crowd" on Sunday mornings.

Sarge's Deli ◗▣ *Deli/Sandwich* 21 | 15 | 16 | M

Murray Hill | 548 Third Ave. (bet. 36th & 37th Sts.) | 6 to 33rd St. | 212-679-0442 | www.sargesdeli.com

"Sarge keeps his stripes!" decree devotees of this Murray Hill deli "gem" that hits the spot with "huge sandwiches", "24/7 breakfasts" and "chicken noodle soup when you're not feeling so great", all "at reasonable prices"; there's "no problem finding a table" here, and those in-the-know advise "don't come for the interior, come for the vast menu" – better yet, take advantage of its "huge delivery area."

NYC SOURCES

	QUALITY	DISPLAY	SERVICE	COST

Savino's Quality Pasta �⃠ *Pasta* — | — | — | I

Williamsburg | 111 Conselyea St. (bet. Leonard St. & Manhattan Ave.) | Brooklyn | L to Lorimer St. | 718-388-2038

This unpretentious pasta purveyor in Williamsburg is run by a multigenerational crew of Savino family members, who produce fresh noodles like fettuccini and pappardelle as well as frozen filled varieties, including nine kinds of ravioli, stuffed shells and manicotti; offered alongside are ready-to-go housemade pesto or marinara sauce, as well as a small selection of dried pastas, oils and vinegars.

Saxelby Cheesemongers *Cheese/Dairy* ▽ 28 | 22 | 27 | M

LES | 120 Essex St. (bet. Delancey & Rivington Sts.) | F/J/M/Z to Delancey/Essex Sts. | 212-228-8204 | www.saxelbycheese.com

"Many a new cheese lover will emerge" from this "boutique"-like Essex Street Market stall, which honors "the finest in American-made", "small-farm" fromages with its 30-plus "artisanal" offerings ("expect the unusual here") paired with "fresh-baked breads" from Sullivan Street Bakery; owner Anne Saxelby is a "sweetheart" with an "infectious" "passion for her product", so "it's impossible to leave without something."

⚏ Schaller & Weber ▭ *Meat/Poultry* 27 | 22 | 23 | M

E 80s | 1654 Second Ave. (bet. 85th & 86th Sts.) | 4/5/6 to 86th St. | 212-879-3047 | 800-847-4115 | www.schallerweber.com

"Blessedly unchanged" and "still the best", this "last bastion" of "Germanic sausages" and "other Teutonic specialties" in Yorkville has long been known for its "jaw-dropping" selection of meats, wursts and hard-to-find imported delicacies that will have almost anyone "salivating like one of Pavlov's dogs"; even better, the "old-world charm" extends to the "landmark"-worthy setting and "helpful" staff.

Scharffen Berger Chocolate Maker ▭ *Candy/Nuts* 26 | 21 | 21 | E

W 80s | 473 Amsterdam Ave. (bet. 82nd & 83rd Sts.) | 1 to 86th St. | 212-362-9734 | www.scharffenberger.com

Since this "pretty little" store landed on the UWS, "elite chocolate eaters" have been thrilled to "finally" have an outlet of the San Francisco chocolate producer "America can be proud of"; its "stunning baking products" with "to-die-for high cacao content" make for "recipes that explode with taste" ("this is the chocolate to eat, cook with and rub all over!"), and there are also bonbons and drinking options, considered by most to be "worth" the "boutique" prices.

Schatzie's Prime Meats *Meat/Poultry* 25 | 17 | 22 | E

E 80s | 1200 Madison Ave. (bet. 87th & 88th Sts.) | 4/5/6 to 86th St. | 212-410-1555

Regulars of this UES butcher say it's worth going in "just to meet" "friendly, warm, welcoming" owner Tony Schatzie, but the main attraction is his selection of prime meats, poultry and game, any of which he's happy to custom-prepare for a customer; naturally such "quality" offerings and personal service don't come cheap, but "quick delivery and house accounts" sweeten the deal.

	QUALITY	DISPLAY	SERVICE	COST

Schick's Bakery ☒ *Baked Goods* · 20 | 14 | 14 | M

Borough Park | 4710 16th Ave. (bet. 47th & 48th Sts.) | Brooklyn | F to Ditmas Ave. | 718-436-8020 | www.schicksbakery.com

"Where else would one get cakes for Passover?" wonder faithful followers of this "traditional kosher bakery" in Borough Park, an "old standby" for a "large variety" of "heaven-blessed" bounty like mousse cakes, rugalach, krakovsky (cashew brittle) and fancy cookies; "it's all good" "even if you don't have to eat kosher", and Manhattanites can find their products stocked at Zabar's, Fairway and other markets.

Sea Breeze *Seafood* · 23 | 17 | 20 | I

W 40s | 541 Ninth Ave. (40th St.) | A/C/E to 42nd St./Port Authority | 212-563-7537

A "large and tempting display" of "fresh-out-of-the-water" seafood is the catch at this third-generation family seafood market in Hells Kitchen, where "bargain" prices mean you "won't break the bank"; just ignore the "dated, slippery locale" and make sure you "hose your shoes off" before heading home.

Sea Grape Wine Shop ◖☒ *Wine/Liquor* · ▽ 23 | 20 | 26 | M

W Village | 512 Hudson St. (bet. Christopher & W. 10th Sts.) | 1 to Christopher St. | 212-463-7688 | www.seagrapewines.com

"What a great wine shop!" cheer champions of this wee West Villager, known on the "neighborhood" grapevine for stocking "excellent" choices "from around the world", embracing many "lesser-known vineyards" from Languedoc to South Africa; the "very friendly" team is ever "willing to help" with "knowledgeable" suggestions, and the focus on labels under $10 is "always a pleasant" incentive to drift in.

Seaport Flowers *Flowers* · - | - | - | E

Brooklyn Heights | 214 Hicks St. (bet. Montague & Remsen Sts.) | Brooklyn | 2/3/4/5/M/N/R/W to Borough Hall/Court St. | 718-858-6443 | www.seaportflowers.com

"The height of perfection in Brooklyn Heights", this "boutique florist" and event planner produces "artful arrangements" (laced with unique ingredients like artichokes, berries and grapes) that devotees describe as "simply ethereal" and "supremely fresh"; "talented" owner Amy Gardella "is a joy to work with" as is the "wonderful staff", but surveyors are split on price – relatively "affordable" vs. "big bucks."

Sebastians
Catering & Special Events *Caterer* · - | - | - | M

E 50s | 875 Third Ave. (bet. 52nd & 53rd Sts.) | 212-832-3880 | www.sebastians.com
By appointment only

The local branch of a Boston firm, this off-premises caterer specializes in corporate klatches and product launches for clients like Microsoft, Morgan Stanley and Pfizer, serving variations on American fare at prices accounts payable will appreciate; it also provides full event services at sites around town (including in-house at the Museum of the City of New York), and a take-out counter at its East Side HQ offers a sandwich-centric preview of the goods.

Second Helpings ● *Prepared Food* | - | - | - | M |

Park Slope | 448 Ninth St. (7th Ave.) | Brooklyn | F to 7th Ave. | 718-965-1925 | www.secondhelpings.com

At this "health-oriented" Park Slope prepared foods shop, the emphasis is on a rotating variety of natural, mostly organic sandwiches, soups and other offerings that don't scrimp on "seasonings and creativity"; there are some meat and fish dishes on offer, but "amazing veggie" specialties (e.g. "wonderful vegan stews") are its forte, ensuring that this is "no boring health-food place."

Sedutto's ●⇱ *Ice Cream* | 24 | 16 | 18 | M |

E 70s | 1498A First Ave. (bet. 78th & 79th Sts.) | 6 to 77th St. | 212-879-9557

Staten Island | 314 New Dorp Ln. (Clawson St.) | 718-351-3344

"Unassuming, ungimmicky and unbelievably great" is how diehards describe this separately owned UES–Staten Island pair of ice cream "standbys" and their "simple flavors, large portions" and "*delizioso*" "rich and super-creamy" premium product; admirers only "wish there were more locations around the city."

Sensuous Bean, The ▣ *Coffee/Tea* | 25 | 21 | 23 | M |

W 70s | 66 W. 70th St. (bet. Columbus Ave. & CPW) | B/C to 72nd St. | 212-724-7725 | 800-238-6845 | www.sensuousbean.com

"Refreshingly quaint", this longtime Upper Westsider is a "tiny joint" "stuffed" with an "amazing" assortment of 150 "first-class coffees" both "native and imported", plus a 100-strong selection of teas highlighting many "unusual" artisanal leaves; the "charming" staffers offer "advice for the novice", and sensualists can throw in some gourmet chocolates or sweet stuff from Villabate.

September Wines & Spirits ● *Wine/Liquor* | - | - | - | M |

LES | 100 Stanton St. (Ludlow St.) | F/V to Lower East Side/2nd Ave. | 212-388-0770 | www.septemberwines.com

A "very eclectic mix" marks this boutique wine seller on the Lower East Side, a specialist in vintages from family-run, green-leaning producers in up-and-coming regions like Slovenia, Mexico, Morocco, Lebanon and Brazil; it holds tastings Thursday–Saturday nights, and it's also "the perfect place to pick up a bottle" en route to an international "BYOB meal"; N.B. private tastings for the home or office can also be arranged.

Serena Bass Inc. *Caterer* | - | - | - | VE |

Meatpacking | 404 W. 13th St. (bet. 9th Ave. & Washington St.) | A/C/E/L to 14th St./8th Ave. | 212-727-2257 | www.serenabass.com

Soirees don't get more "stylish" than those coordinated by this off-site caterer and event planner based in the Meatpacking District, which matches the "great presentation" of author/owner Serena Bass' "delicious" theme-driven menus with made-to-order setups that showcase "chic" decorating and floral design; its longstanding

	QUALITY	DISPLAY	SERVICE	COST

cachet attracts a client base comprising a who's who of the fashion world, though to dissenters it's all an "expensive" dose of "pretense."

Settepani ☒ *Baked Goods* ∇ 23 | 26 | 20 | M

Harlem | 196 Lenox Ave. (120th St.) | 2/3 to 125th St. | 917-492-4806
Williamsburg | 602 Lorimer St. (bet. Conselyea St. & Skillman Ave.) |
Brooklyn | G/L to Metropolitan Ave./Lorimer St. | 718-349-6524
www.settepani.com

Supporters set store by these "authentic" Italian bakeries for a "wide selection of breads" (old-fashioned casaereccio, focaccia, Pullman sandwich loaves) and "exquisite" dolci such as mousse cakes, pastries and fruit tarts; the Williamsburg flagship caters to the take-out trade while the Harlem spin-off is a full-service "godsend" even if it's "not for those in a hurry."

7th Avenue
Wine & Liquor Co. ◗ *Wine/Liquor* ∇ 20 | 19 | 17 | M

Park Slope | 88 Seventh Ave. (bet. Berkeley Pl. & Union St.) | Brooklyn |
2/3 to Grand Army Plaza | 718-399-3300 | www.seventhavenuewine.com
There's "no snobbery" at this Park Slope vintner, just an "eclectic" assortment of wines, with especially strong representation from Spain and South America, as well as concentration of bourbons and single-malts; free delivery and tastings Mondays–Thursdays are additional draws, however, "if you're looking for a bargain, keep walking."

71 Irving Place
Coffee & Tea Bar ☒ *Coffee/Tea* 22 | 20 | 19 | M

Gramercy | 71 Irving Pl. (bet. 18th & 19th Sts.) | 4/5/6/L/N/Q/R/W to 14th St./Union Sq. | 212-995-5252 | www.irvingfarm.com
Dubbed the "anti-Starbucks", this Gramercy "neighborhood cafe holdout" is the "perfect pit stop for a refuel" of "quality" house-roasted coffee that's a "non-bitter" winner by the cup or by the pound; its "other tempting goodies" ("breakfast snacks", panini, "tasty sweets") "do not disappoint", so it's no surprise the "folksy", "living room"-like premises are "perennially packed."

S. Feldman Housewares ☒ *Cookware* 23 | 15 | 22 | E

E 90s | 1304 Madison Ave. (bet. 92nd & 93rd Sts.) | 4/5/6 to 86th St. |
212-289-7367 | 800-359-8558
This "solid" Upper East Side longtimer with the feel of an "old-fashioned hardware store stocked with luxury items" services the neighborhood with cookware and tabletop items at prices in step with its "well-heeled" client base; service is "helpful", and though its "crammed" quarters can be hard to navigate, for most it's still a "treat to browse."

Shake Shack ◗ *Prepared Food* 25 | 15 | 15 | I

Flatiron | Madison Square Park (Madison Ave. & 23rd St.) | N/R/W to 23rd St. | 212-889-6600 | www.shakeshack.com
At this fast-food stand boasting "an unbeatable location" in Madison Square Park, restaurateur Danny Meyer's "Missouri heritage shows": lunchers wash down "astonishingly tasty", "juicy burgers" "Chicago-style dawgs" and "to-die-for french fries" with "amazing

St. Louis–style frozen custards (as well as beer or wine) – "brave" the "insane lines" because it's "absolutely worth the wait."

Shakoor's Sweet Tooth *Baked Goods*
— | — | — | M

Bed-Stuy | 305 Halsey St. (bet. Marcus Garvey Blvd. & Throop Ave.) | Brooklyn | 718-574-2580 | www.shakoorssweettooth.com

"Unbeatable" sweet potato cheesecake headlines a roster of "many desserts" at this Bed-Stuy bakery, whose traditional Southern slant and "imaginative recipes" do proud by Dixie favorites like red velvet cake, puddings, pies and cobbler; it's also worth giving it a shake for event catering and weddings (complete with down-home prepared foods).

Shawn's Fine Wines & Spirits ●▣ *Wine/Liquor*
▽ 24 | 20 | 21 | M

Park Slope | 141 Seventh Ave. (bet. Carroll St. & Garfield Pl.) | Brooklyn | 2/3 to Grand Army Plaza | 718-622-7947 | www.wineaccess.com/store/shawns/

Loyal locals "like the atmosphere" at this 35-year Park Slope stalwart, whose "dark and woody interior" is the perfect accompaniment for a 1,000-strong wine lineup that's "packed with good choices" at an affordable cost; with fortes in French, Italian and Californian labels and a "very helpful" staff to point out esoteric options, its regulars report they "never bought a bad bottle" here.

☑ Sherry-Lehmann ▣ *Wine/Liquor*
29 | 24 | 24 | E

E 60s | 679 Madison Ave. (bet. 61st & 62nd Sts.) | N/R/W to 5th Ave./59th St. | 212-838-7500 | www.sherry-lehmann.com

"Still the standard-bearer", this "classic" East Side "mecca for wine enthusiasts" maintains a "staggering inventory" ("particularly" the "amazing stock of Bordeaux") that's hailed for its "impeccable quality" and "competitive" cost "in all price ranges"; "service second to none" has the "consummate knowledge" to assist everyone from the "upper crust to the regular Joe", though the "awesome" variety – extending to glassware and accessories – is more fully revealed via "catalog or Web"; N.B. plans are in motion to relocate to roomier quarters at 505 Park Avenue in late summer 2007.

Silver Moon Bakery *Baked Goods*
26 | 21 | 20 | M

W 100s | 2740 Broadway (105th St.) | 1 to 103rd St. | 212-866-4717 | www.silvermoonbakery.com

The Upper West Side gets "upped a notch" by this "darling" French bakery, a "popular" stop for "killer" artisanal breads (including brioche and the "ever-fresh baguettes") plus "outstanding" "sweet treats" likes cakes and tarts; most agree it's "worth it to pay extra" for the "highest quality", and the "daunting" "weekend lines" prove it's "much needed in the neighborhood."

☑ Simchick, L. *Meat/Poultry*
28 | 19 | 25 | E

E 50s | 944 First Ave. (52nd St.) | 6 to 51st St. | 212-888-2299

An "old-school place" where countermen "tell you how to prepare the meat you're buying" and then "ask how it turned out when you return", this East Side butcher purveys "outstanding" prime cuts "worthy of the most demanding eaters" as well as ready-to-cook offerings like marinated steaks and meatloaf; no matter what you order, "you get what you pay for" – "and that's a lot."

NEW Sip Fine Wine ⊘ *Wine/Liquor* ▽ 27 | 27 | 24 | M
Park Slope | 67 Fifth Ave. (bet. Prospect & St. Marks Pls.) | Brooklyn | 2/3 to Bergen St. | 718-638-6105 | www.sipfinewine.com
A "welcome addition" to Park Slope, this "down-to-earth" little wine shop features a "well-chosen", "well-priced" selection with a "focus on lesser-known" vintages from small producers around the globe, concentrating on Spain, France, Italy and California; the "courteous staff" is "not snobby in the least" but it "really knows its stuff", and "educational" sipping's on offer at the "weekly tastings" (Saturdays from 4–7 PM).

67 Wines & Spirits ⊘🖃 *Wine/Liquor* 25 | 20 | 21 | M
W 60s | 179 Columbus Ave. (68th St.) | 1 to 66th St./Lincoln Ctr. | 212-724-6767 | 888-671-6767 | www.67wine.com
There's "nothing to whine about" at this "lively" wine store on the Upper West Side boasting a "fantastic" inventory of "wines from around the world" (10,000-plus labels) at "reasonable" prices; you have to "squeeze through the aisles" of its two-story space, but "terrific tastings" on weekends, "cheerful" "connoisseurs" on staff, an "unbeatable" delivery policy and an informative Web site make it many an oenophile's "mainstay."

Skyview Discount Wines & Liquors ⊘🖃 *Wine/Liquor* 26 | 19 | 24 | I
Bronx | Skyview Shopping Ctr. | 5681 Riverdale Ave. (259th St.) | 1 to 231st St. | 718-601-8222 | www.skyviewwines.com
Observant oenophiles will find "much to choose from" at this Bronx "kosher wine nirvana", where a 500-label international inventory (including champagnes) boasts the "best assortment and prices" around and choice vintages always go "on sale for the holidays"; they also stock sakes and a full line of spirits, and Manhattanites can save themselves a schlep with the free delivery service (for orders over $100).

Slavin, M. & Sons Ltd. *Seafood* 23 | 13 | 16 | M
Brownsville | 31 Belmont Ave. (Thatford Ave.) | Brooklyn | 3 to Sutter Ave. | 718-495-2800 | www.mslavin.com
"Fish doesn't get any fresher" than the fin fare from this seafood wholesaler that "supplies many restaurants" via its familiar fleet of trucks seen all over town; although its nearly century-old family business has evolved into a mega-operation with an online catalog boasting some 4,000 items, it still custom-cuts orders at its Brownsville plant, where it sells its products retail.

Slope Cellars ⊘ *Wine/Liquor* 24 | 21 | 24 | M
Park Slope | 436 Seventh Ave. (bet. 14th & 15th Sts.) | Brooklyn | F to 7th Ave. | 718-369-7307 | www.slopecellars.com
"Deservedly popular" among "connoisseurs and novices alike", this Park Slope wine seller "serves the neighborhood well" with an "ex

cellent" assortment color-coded by price, including some very "decent" deals in the under-$10 'Cheap and Tasty' category; they're "always eager to help" with "atypical" picks "without being overbearing" and sponsor a "fun frequent buyer program" (purchase 12 bottles and the next one's 99¢) as well as biweekly tastings.

Smith & Vine ◐ *Wine/Liquor* | 23 | 22 | 24 | M |
Cobble Hill | 268 Smith St. (bet. Degraw & Sackett Sts.) | Brooklyn | F/G to Carroll St. | 718-243-2864 | www.smithandvine.com

"Boutique but not expensive", this "charming" Smith Street vintner stocks a "fairly small" but "choice selection" of wines ranging from the high-end to numerous "surprisingly delicious" options on the "$10-and-under table"; overseen by "the friendliest" owners who are "always ready" with "smart" suggestions, it's newly sited in "a larger space" ("thank goodness") and now provides pairing ideas "for their cheese store", Stinky Bklyn, "just across the street."

Snack ◐ *Prepared Food* | ▽ 27 | 13 | 16 | M |
SoHo | 105 Thompson St. (bet. Prince & Spring Sts.) | C/E to Spring St. | 212-925-1040

Snack Taverna ◐ *Prepared Food*
W Village | 63 Bedford St. (Morton St.) | 1 to Houston St. | 212-929-3499

This "great hidden gem in SoHo" is known for its homemade Greek dishes including moussaka, lamb stew and savory pies, as well as sandwiches, soups and salads, which are all available for takeout or delivery; its bigger, more ambitious West Village sibling, Snack Taverna, is also an option when cooking at home isn't in the cards.

SoHo Wines & Spirits *Wine/Liquor* | ▽ 21 | 20 | 20 | E |
SoHo | 461 W. Broadway (bet. Houston & Prince Sts.) | N/R to Prince St. | 212-777-4332 | www.sohowines.com

"If you're in a pinch" "and need a quick bottle", this airy SoHo wine-and-liquor merchant is a safe "local bet"; the minimalist, galleryesque space showcases 1,000 vinos (Spain and Italy being strong suits) plus some "excellent" single-malts, and though the going can get "expensive", most maintain "you get what you pay for."

Something Different
Party Rental *Party Rentals* | - | - | - | M |
Paterson | 107-117 Pennsylvania Ave. (Iowa Ave.), NJ | 212-772-0516 | www.somethingdifferentparty.com
By appointment only

Since coming under new management in recent years, this party rental company has opened a new Manhattan showroom that can double as a reception space and has substantially broadened its inventory to offer hip, modern tabletop wares and a full range of event furnishings, including tents, portable bars and some 100,000 chairs; it's also emphasizing high-tech service (delivery trucks are equipped with GPS) to satisfy corporate and private clients and handle last-minute assignments when needed.

	QUALITY	DISPLAY	SERVICE	COST

Something Sweet ● *Baked Goods* — ▽ 23 | 21 | 25 | M

E Village | 177 First Ave. (11th St.) | L to 1st Ave. | 212-533-9986
Though little-known outside the neighborhood, this sweet little East Village bakery boasts a broad selection of "really fresh" cakes (standard and mousse), pies, tarts and pastries that would "wow" 'em in Paree; it's a modest operation that's unlikely to be crowded, but the "homemade taste" is really something.

☒ Soutine *Baked Goods* — 27 | 19 | 23 | E

W 70s | 104 W. 70th St. (bet. B'way & Columbus Ave.) | 1/2/3 to 72nd St. | 212-496-1450 | 888-806-2253 | www.soutine.com
It flies slightly "under the radar", but Upper Westsiders know this "small" bakery as a "rare treat" for "divine" tarte Tatin, pies and "traditional pastries" whose "sublime" "taste and texture" is an "indulgence" that's "worth the trip" from anywhere; the "excellent" staff will also arrange "outstanding specialty cakes" "made to order" for birthdays and weddings (or hors d'oeuvres), and "they deliver locally" too.

Special Attention *Caterer* — - | - | - | M

LES | 325 E. Houston St. (bet. Aves. B & C) | F/V to Lower East Side/2nd Ave. | 212-477-4805 | www.special-attention.com
"Individualized" service proves this Lower East Side caterer's more than just a name as it "reliably" supplies "choice" menus flaunting the "quality and presentation" "guests always rave about", particularly with its Pan-Asian hors d'oeuvres; for off-premises events either "business or personal", it rises "up to and above expectations" to ensure any affair will be "most special"; N.B. for hassle-free hosting, they'll also deliver appetizer trays to your door.

Spice Corner ● *Herbs/Spices* — 24 | 18 | 17 | I

Gramercy | 135 Lexington Ave. (29th St.) | 6 to 28th St. | 212-689-5182
Indian food lovers swoon as soon as they walk into this friendly, modest Indian grocery store in Gramercy Park, thanks to its heady aroma of cinnamon, cardamom, myriad curry blends, peppercorns – "if it's a spice, they have it"; also cramming the shelves are staples like beans, grains, chutneys and cookware, as well as an impressive selection of Indian sweets, all overseen by a friendly staff.

Spoonbread Inc. ● *Caterer* — ▽ 23 | 18 | 22 | M

Harlem | 366 W. 110th St. (bet. Columbus & Manhattan Aves.) | B/C to 110th St. | 212-865-0700
Harlem | 547 Lenox Ave. (bet. 137th & 138th Sts.) | 2/3 to 135th St. | 212-690-3100
www.spoonbreadinc.com
"Norma Jean [Darden] knows Southern food" testify faithful followers of this Harlem caterer, where the spread's "always fresh and delicious" whether you hanker for down-home delights like fried chicken, catfish and collards or "interesting" variations that give the cookin' a global spin; with "top-notch" service either off-site or at the soul fooders Miss Mamie's and Miss Maude's (not to mention a client base spanning Russell Simmons to Jazz at Lincoln Center), it can claim more than a spoonful of "hype."

	QUALITY	DISPLAY	SERVICE	COST

Spruce 🖃 *Flowers* ▽ 27 | 27 | 24 | E

Chelsea | 222 Eighth Ave. (bet. 21st & 22nd Sts.) | C/E to 23rd St. | 212-206-1025 | www.spruceup.com

Putting the "focus on the flowers themselves", this Chelsea florist and event planner will "make [you] want to splurge" on one of its "gorgeous, minimalist arrangements", including owner Gaige Clark's signature, a rose 'hedge' housed in a handmade crate; a "wonderful staff" adds to the charm, and if you find that the "sleek, clean" creations are "too expensive" for a personal purchase, note that they also "make for excellent gifts."

Stage Deli ●🖃 *Deli/Sandwich* 21 | 17 | 17 | E

W 50s | 834 Seventh Ave. (bet. 53rd & 54th Sts.) | 1 to 50th St. | 212-245-7850 | 800-782-4369 | www.stagedeli.com

The legends live on - as menu items - at this Midtown deli that's been delivering "sky-high sandwiches" ("bring a big appetite" for the "wonderful pastrami and corned beef") and "sublime cheesecake" since the 1930s; though some call it "a tourist trap", others favor it for its "first-rate people-watching" and "great service" - "just remember that quality food takes time" (and money - "it's pricey").

Starbucks Coffee ●🖃 *Coffee/Tea* 18 | 18 | 17 | E

Chinatown | 241 Canal St. (Centre St.) | 6/J/M/N/Q/R/W/Z to Canal St. | 212-219-2725

E 70s | 1117 Lexington Ave. (78th St.) | 6 to 77th St. | 212-517-8476
E 90s | 1642 Third Ave. (92nd St.) | 6 to 96th St. | 212-360-0425
E Village | 13-25 Astor Pl. (Lafayette St.) | 6 to Astor Pl. | 212-982-3563
E Village | 141-143 Second Ave. (9th St.) | 6 to Astor Pl. | 212-780-0024
Harlem | 77 W. 125th St. (Lenox Ave.) | 2/3 to 125th St. | 917-492-2454
Murray Hill | 585 Second Ave. (32nd St.) | 6 to 33rd St. | 212-684-1299
SoHo | 150 Varick St. (Spring St.) | C/E to Spring St. | 646-230-9816
W 40s | 682 Ninth Ave. (47th St.) | C/E to 50th St. | 212-397-2288
W 60s | 152-154 Columbus Ave. (67th St.) | 1 to 66th St./Lincoln Ctr. | 212-721-0470
800-782-7282 | www.starbucks.com
Additional locations throughout the NY area

"How did we live without them?"; the chainzilla whose "supercharged coffee" "for the masses" sustains "global domination" still stirs up nonstop debate: backers "never tire of" an "efficient" "pick-me-up" "without risk" while contras "carp about" "too-acidic" brews "for too many bucks", but either way "you can always count on" its "omnipresence" for "easy" "Web surfing and gawking."

Starwich *Deli/Sandwich* 23 | 17 | 18 | M

E 50s | 153 E. 53rd St. (bet. Lexington & 3rd Aves.) | E/V to 5th Ave./53rd St. | 212-371-7772
NEW **E 70s** | 1055 Lexington Ave. (75th St.) | 6 to 77th St. | 212-585-0788 ●
Financial Dist | 63 Wall St. (bet. Pearl & William Sts.) | 2/3 to Wall St. | 212-809-3200 ●
Garment Dist | 72 W. 38th St. (bet. 5th & 6th Aves.) | B/D/F/N/Q/R/V/W to 34th St./Herald Sq. | 212-302-7775

(continued)

(continued)

Starwich

W 40s | 525 W. 42nd St. (bet. 10th & 11th Aves.) | A/C/E to 42nd St./
Port Authority | 212-736-9170 ●
866-942-4864 | www.starwich.com

"Superior sandwiches" are the stars at this mini-galaxy of "upscale"
'wicheries where patrons pick from more than 100 "top-notch" ingredients; skeptics wonder whether its "killer" product is "worth the
big bucks" – yes, all those "choices" can "lead to overspending" –
but the attractive eating areas and free WiFi access help balance the
scales; N.B. they also do a big office catering business.

☑ Staubitz Market *Meat/Poultry*   29 | 23 | 25 | E

Cobble Hill | 222 Court St. (bet. Baltic & Warren Sts.) | Brooklyn | F/G to
Bergen St. | 718-624-0014 | www.staubitz.com

"Old-world service and charm" permeate this Cobble Hill meat market, which has been in business since 1917 and is still known for its
"first-rate" "hand-cut and -trimmed" prime beef and the "best specialty game meats" like pheasant, venison and wild boar; "expensive" prices mean it's more of a "special-occasion" source for many,
but most don't mind because "superb quality" has its price – there's
good "reason this butcher is still around"; P.S. "avoid on days approaching Christmas" unless you're "prepared to wait on line."

Steve's Authentic   25 | 10 | 18 | M
Key Lime Pies *Baked Goods*

Red Hook | Pier 41 | 204-207 Van Dyke St. (bet. Conover & Ferris Sts.) |
Brooklyn | F/G to Smith/9th Sts. | 718-858-5333 | 888-450-5463 |
www.stevesauthentic.com

"A sliver of Key West in Red Hook", Steve Tarpin's single-item "niche"
operation is "the gold standard for Key lime pie", attaining "tart and
delicious" perfection with fresh-squeezed limes and a buttery graham
cracker crust; the goods can be had at the main "warehouse" space
(which also vends chocolate-coated "frozen pie pops"), delivered
around town in a '50s panel truck or available at Zabar's and Citarella.

Stinky Bklyn *Cheese/Dairy*   ▽ 28 | 22 | 25 | M

Cobble Hill | 261 Smith St. (Degraw St.) | Brooklyn | F/G to Carroll St. |
718-522-7425 | www.stinkybklyn.com

Its moniker reflects a "pungent" "sense of humor", but this "high-
style" fromagerie in Cobble Hill is serious when it comes to its "small
but well-chosen" inventory of "wonderful" cheeses, tended by "hip"
but "neighborly" types who are "always ready with a taste" and "creative" "wine pairing" suggestions from the "sister store", Smith &
Vine, across the street; the "prices are reasonable", and it's also worth
sniffing out for its charcuterie, as well as its classes and seminars.

Stokes Farm *Produce*   27 | 21 | 25 | M

See Greenmarket; for more information, call 201-768-3931 |
www.stokesfarm.com

"Excellent fresh produce" "locally grown" (in Bergen County, NJ) is the
story behind this Greenmarket steady – one of the original farmers in

the system from 30 years back – known especially for "beautiful big herb plants" that become herb wreaths at the holidays and a "nice mix of standard and heirloom" tomatoes; the produce bins are presided over by Ron Binaghi, "the friendly, funny emcee-owner-grocer."

Z NEW Stonehouse California Olive Oil 🖃 *Specialty Shop* | 27 | 22 | 23 | E |

E Village | 273 E. 10th St. (1st Ave.) | L to 1st Ave. | 212-358-8700 | www.stonehouseoliveoil.com

At the tasting bar of this East Village outlet for a California olive grove, "you can sample the oils with bread and make a choice" from among the "delicious" selection, including flavored options like "to-die-for Persian lime" and blood orange–infused; "their bottles are beautiful enough for a collection", but don't leave them on your shelf – "they encourage you to bring them back for refills."

Stonekelly Events & Florals *Flowers* | ▽ 25 | 24 | 19 | VE |

W 50s | 736 11th Ave. (bet. 51st & 52nd Sts.) | C/E to 50th St. | 212-245-6611 | www.stonekelly.com

Specializing in event design, this West 50s florist is "always on the money", producing "unusual work" that combines "high-quality" blooms with "flair galore" to achieve an experience that's "not your usual staid affair"; yes, it's "expensive, but it won't disappoint" – unless you factor in service ("the flowers were beautiful, but the staff drove us crazy").

Z Stork's Pastry Shop *Baked Goods* | 27 | 22 | 21 | M |

Whitestone | 12-42 150th St. (12th Rd.) | Queens | 7 to Flushing-Main St. | 718-767-9220

Giving Whitestone's sweet tooths a leg to stand on since "back in the day", this "old-school" German bakery and chocolate shop is the "real" thing for "marvelous" cookies, truffles and pastries that provide a "taste of childhood" with "no compromise in quality"; also a nest of "excellent breads" that "bring tears to" traditionalist's eyes, it's a "local" "favorite" that's always "worth the trip over the bridge."

Streit's Matzo Co. 🖉 *Baked Goods* | 25 | 13 | 16 | I |

LES | 148-154 Rivington St. (bet. Clinton & Suffolk Sts.) | F/J/M/Z to Delancey/Essex Sts. | 212-475-7000 | www.streitsmatzos.com

"*The* place to come for matzos" is this "old-world" Lower East Side factory, a "hole-in-the-wall" outlet and Passover "institution" that's famed for its assortment of kosher wafers with "no leavening ever" as well as "related products" like noodles and farfel; in business since 1925 and "still the same", it's the "best and least expensive" way to procure the "brand of choice" "right after it's made" – "how can you go wrong?"

NEW Subtle Tea 🖃 *Coffee/Tea* | - | - | - | M |

Murray Hill | 121 Madison Ave. (30th St.) | 6 to 28th St. | 212-481-4713 | www.subtleteastore.com

"Tea experts" brew with nuance at this "cute" Murray Hill newcomer, which "will put a cheery buzz in your day" with 40 "delicious" steeped pours (creative "combination blends" among them) accompanied by scones, sandwiches and cookies; the staff's ever "ready to help" "the non-connoisseur", and the modern layout's roomy enough for a communal table plus a retail display of teapots, cups, loose leaves and bath and body sundries.

SugarHill Java & Tea ⊅ *Coffee/Tea* | - | - | - | I |

Harlem | 344 W. 145th St. (St. Nicholas Ave.) | A/B/C/D to 145th St. | 212-281-3010

"Good for the neighborhood" is the word on this "cozy" Harlem coffeehouse, a "friendly" red-brick "haven" for gourmet java and artisanal tea infusions backed up by baked goods like Make My Cake's red velvet masterwork; other attractions include tea parties for young misses, candle-making classes on Mondays and, for the less motivated, just "a moment to relax."

☑ Sugar Sweet Sunshine ● *Baked Goods* | 27 | 21 | 22 | I |

LES | 126 Rivington St. (bet. Essex & Norfolk Sts.) | F/J/M/Z to Delancey/Essex Sts. | 212-995-1960 | www.sugarsweetsunshine.com

Specializing in "superior cupcakes" rated tops in the genre – no mean feat in "cupcake-crazed" NYC – this "cute" Lower East Side bakery/cafe "warms you" with a "comfy" "place to sit" while sampling its trademark "little pieces of heaven" and "numerous other" "addictive" desserts like "moist cakes", cookies and bars; with a "laid-back" vibe that's as "unpretentious" as the goods are "completely fresh", it definitely hits the "sweet spot."

Sui Cheong Meat Market *Meat/Poultry* ▽ | 20 | 19 | 18 | I |

Chinatown | 89 Mulberry St. (Canal St.) | 6/J/M/N/Q/R/W/Z to Canal St. | 212-267-0350

Given its location, it's not surprising this C-town meat market is loaded with "all the cuts for Chinese cooking" including flank steak and pork belly (and ears and brains) in addition to such house specialties as "fine-quality roast pig and soy-sauce chickens" – you even get to see "homemade won tons" prepared before your eyes; never mind that the premises could possibly use an "upgrade."

☑ Sullivan Street Bakery *Baked Goods* | 28 | 20 | 22 | M |

W 40s | 533 W. 47th St. (bet. 10th & 11th Aves.) | C/E to 50th St. | 212-265-5580 | www.sullivanstreetbakery.com

Though its original location "on Sullivan Street" is now separately owned, groupies of bread "genius" Jim Lahey can still go to the "Hell's Kitchen outpost" of this Italian bakery "mecca" and find the same "distinctive" loaves in all the "crusty, earthy" glory that makes many call them "the best, bar none"; it remains a "standard-bearer" for "classic" pane Pugliese and "slabs" of "Roman-style pizza", and if the "off-the-path location" is "a pain", it's "worth the effort" to acquire the goods that grace "many high-end" eateries and gourmet markets.

Sundaes & Cones ● *Ice Cream* | 25 | 22 | 25 | M |

E Village | 95 E. 10th St. (bet. 3rd & 4th Aves.) | 6 to Astor Pl. | 212-979-9398

Black sesame, wasabi, corn – "do these sound like ice cream flavors?" ask frequenters of this "cute" little East Village spot where a "fantastic fusion" of "great-tasting" "exotic" ingredients (and some "regular" ones to please purists) is the deal; what's more: the scoop size is "generous" and the quality "amazing."

Sunrise Mart ◑ *Specialty Shop* | 23 | 18 | 17 | M |

E Village | 4 Stuyvesant St., 2nd fl. (3rd Ave. & 9th St.) | 6 to Astor Pl. | 212-598-3040

SoHo | 494 Broome St. (bet. W. B'way & Wooster St.) | C/E to Spring St. | 212-219-0033

"For all things Japanese", head to these "authentic" markets that feel "just like Tokyo", down to the "tight but well-stocked quarters" (the SoHo branch is "easy to navigate" compared to the "tiny" East Village original); the duo offers "a marvelous assortment" of "hard-to-find" products and ingredients plus sushi, bento boxes and other "tasty snacks."

Superior Confections 🖃 *Candy/Nuts* | - | - | - | I |

Staten Island | 1150 South Ave. (Lois Ln.) | 718-698-3300 | 800-698-3302 | www.superiorchocolatier.com

This third-generation family chocolate business moved to new digs in 2004 but continues to be Staten Islanders' "place to go" for "specialty chocolate for any holiday" and a downright "must-visit for Easter", given its "gigantic" selection of molded shapes; an added bonus: the factory "is a fun place to visit" when kids are in tow.

Sur La Table 🖃 *Cookware* | 26 | 24 | 21 | E |

SoHo | 75 Spring St. (bet. Crosby & Lafayette Sts.) | 6 to Spring St. | 212-966-3375 | www.surlatable.com

"A veritable playground for those who cook" say those enamored of this Seattle chain's "gorgeous" SoHo outpost with a "serious" selection of pots and pans, dishes, "unusual utensils", "hard-to-find gagets" and imported foods; a few quibble that "better deals can be had elsewhere", still, it's hard to "leave without something in hand."

Surroundings 🖃 *Flowers* | 25 | 24 | 23 | VE |

W 70s | 224 W. 79th St. (bet. Amsterdam Ave. & B'way) | 1 to 79th St. | 212-580-8982 | 800-567-7007 | www.surroundingsflowers.com

At this "elegant" veteran florist on the Upper West Side, the "beautiful, lush", "to-die-for flower arrangements" ("perfect to send to the boss or a friend") are accompanied by "gracious, warm", "lovely service" – there's even a horticulturist on staff; most agree, however, that the shop's "really special" designs come at prices that are "on the high side."

Susan Holland & Co. Inc. *Caterer* | - | - | - | VE |

Flatiron | 142 Fifth Ave., 4th fl. (bet. 19th & 20th Sts.) | 212-807-8892 | www.susanholland.com
By appointment only

Combining "interesting" ideas with "absolute dedication to making every detail perfect", this Flatiron caterer/event planner is a master at stunning ambient strokes that lend any venue a major touch of class; they provide "outstanding" food as well as full services from location scouting to lighting, decor and entertainment, and though "so much excellence" is "expensive", the star-studded clientele couldn't be more appreciative.

Sutton Wine Shop ◑🖃 Wine/Liquor ▽ 22 | 18 | 21 | E

E 50s | 403 E. 57th St. (1st Ave.) | 4/5/6 to 59th St./Lexington Ave. | 212-755-6626 | 888-369-9463

"Old-time neighborhood" appeal defines this Sutton Place vino vendor, which "stocks everything" in its tiny digs, from a 2,000-bottle inventory that's notable for Italian wines to specialty items like glassware; maybe "you can get a better deal elsewhere", but at least a staff that "waits on you hand and foot" are part of the package.

Sweet Atelier ⊘ Baked Goods – | – | – | E

E 80s | 245 E. 80th St. (bet. 2nd & 3rd Aves.) | 6 to 77th St. | 718-986-7374 | www.sweetatelier.com

To celebrate any event in colorful style, first consult baker par excellence Alexandra Zohn at her UES atelier, where lavish artistry goes into customizing cakes, cookies and cupcakes to the theme of your choice; often based on well-known characters and logos, the vibrant designs are a surefire hit for birthdays and bridal showers, and on-site baking classes teach groups of all ages how to turn on the flour power.

Sweet Life, The 🖃 Candy/Nuts 23 | 21 | 24 | M

LES | 63 Hester St. (Ludlow St.) | F to E. B'way | 212-598-0092 | 800-692-6887 | www.sweetlifeny.com

"Get lost in all things candy" at this Lower East Side "delight of a little store" where the "fabulous selection" of gummies, jelly beans and "long-lost" candies, imports including dried fruits, nuts, chocolates, honeys and syrups, a "huge block of halvah that sits in the corner" and anything else "you could want that's sweet" is supplied at "mostly fair prices"; still, a minority contends the "quality has declined" since the ownership changed a few years back.

Sweet Melissa Patisserie Baked Goods 24 | 22 | 20 | E

Cobble Hill | 276 Court St. (bet. Butler & Douglass Sts.) | Brooklyn | F/G to Bergen St. | 718-855-3410 ◑

NEW **Park Slope** | 175 Seventh Ave. (bet. 1st & 2nd Sts.) | Brooklyn | F to 7th Ave. | 718-502-9153 www.sweetmelissapatisserie.com

"How sweet it is!" enthuse admirers of Melissa Murphy's "cozy" Cobble Hill patisserie and its "beautiful" new Park Slope spin-off, where the "decadent", "freshly baked" French-American pastries and cakes can "compete with any fancy Manhattan" joint for "consistently high" standards (and prices); there's also a "light" cafe menu and "afternoon tea service" where the "ladies gather", and both sites boast "lovely" "back gardens" for "a true escape"; N.B. they excel at wedding and other special-occasion cakes.

NEW Swich Deli/Sandwich ▽ 23 | 27 | 24 | E

Chelsea | 104 Eighth Ave. (15th St.) | A/C/E/L to 14th St./8th Ave. | 212-488-4800 | www.swichpressed.com

With a "very Chelsea look" - sleek, "modern" and apple-green - to draw in passersby, this new panini peddler is already full at lunchtime with locals lining up for "quick" made-to-order pressed sandwiches stuffed with "quality" ingredients, like house-roasted meats and vegetables; carb-counters appreciate the option to switch ingredients from sandwich to salad.

☒ Sylvia Weinstock Cakes ⬛️⌑ *Baked Goods*

26 | 26 | 25 | VE

TriBeCa | 273 Church St. (Franklin St.) | 212-925-6698 |
www.sylviaweinstock.com
By appointment only

"If you can dream it, Sylvia can bake it" is the promise at this "charming" TriBeCa custom baker, a designer of "spectacular" "gourmet" cakes for weddings and other occasions whose "one-of-a-kind" masterpieces are "a marvel to look at" and taste "as delicious as they are beautiful"; predictably, the craftsmanship is "off-the-charts expensive", but doesn't "every bride" "deserve the very best"?

Sympathy for the Kettle ◑⬛️ *Coffee/Tea*

▽ 27 | 22 | 23 | M

E Village | 109 St. Marks Pl. (bet. Ave. A & 1st Ave.) | 6 to Astor Pl. | 212-979-1650 | www.sympathyforthekettle.com

Sympathizers delight in the "adorable atmosphere" of this "darling little" pink and chocolate–trimmed tea shop in the East Village; serious tea shoppers – both walk-in and online – applaud the "excellent selection" of "high-quality" house-blended teas (many of them organic and Fair Trade) and accoutrements, while the "exotic" beverage menu and pastries to go with make it a hit with lounging "laptop loners."

TableToppers ⬛️ *Party Rentals*

- | - | - | E

Stamford | 7 Shady Ln. (High Ridge Rd.), CT | 203-329-9977
By appointment only

Table linen rentals and party planning are the forte of this upmarket enterprise headquartered in Connecticut; there's a "great selection" of linens (including custom-made options) that can be shipped anywhere – and the "knowledgeable" sales staff appeals to corporate and individual clients alike.

Tai Pan Bakery Inc. ◑⌑ *Baked Goods*

19 | 17 | 13 | I

Chinatown | 194 Canal St. (bet. Mott & Mulberry Sts.) | 6/J/M/N/Q/R/W/Z to Canal St. | 212-732-2222
Flushing | 37-25 Main St. (bet. 37th & 38th Aves.) | Queens | 7 to Flushing-Main St. | 718-461-8668
Flushing | 42-05B Main St. (Maple St.) | Queens | 7 to Flushing-Main St. | 718-460-8787
888-919-8282

An "unbelievable selection" awaits at these "chaotic" Flushing and Chinatown bakery "favorites", which present a panoply of "double-yummy" pastries "both sweet and savory" along with "freshly baked buns", sandwiches, cakes and plenty more; maybe they're "madhouses" with "lousy service" and "waits in line", but the "unbeatable" prices make for a "poor man's heaven."

	QUALITY	DISPLAY	SERVICE	COST

☑ Takashimaya
Floral Boutique *Flowers*

| 28 | 28 | 23 | VE |

E 50s | Takashimaya | 693 Fifth Ave., 6th fl. (bet. 55th & 56th Sts.) | E/V to 5th Ave./53rd St. | 212-350-0111

"Make a statement" with an "exotic", "exquisite" custom floral arrangement from this "Japanese eden" set within the eponymous Fifth Avenue department store; it's a "lovely place to linger and look" (the "hushed setting" is "almost museumlike") at "amazing", "unusual blooms" of "transporting beauty", but although the "presentation is suitably Zen", the prices are "totally indulgent."

Tal Bagels *Bagels*

| 23 | 19 | 18 | M |

E 50s | 977 First Ave. (54th St.) | E/V to Lexington Ave./53rd St. | 212-753-9080 ◑⇺

E 80s | 1228 Lexington Ave. (83rd St.) | 4/5/6 to 86th St. | 212-717-2080 ⇺

E 80s | 333 E. 86th St. (bet. 1st & 2nd Aves.) | 4/5/6 to 86th St. | 212-427-6811 ◑⇺

W 90s | 2446 Broadway (bet. 90th & 91st Sts.) | 1/2/3 to 96th St. | 212-712-0171 ◑

"Chewy", "yeasty" rounds and a "terrific" "spread selection" add up to "bagel bliss" for boosters of this "old school"–style quartet that's also appreciated for its "wonderful lox" dispensed by "gifted slicers who work with surgical precision"; though the goods come with "high prices", "quick-as-a-wink" service compensates.

Tamarind Tea Room ◑ *Coffee/Tea*

| - | - | - | M |

Flatiron | 41 E. 22nd St. (Park Ave. S.) | N/R/W to 23rd St. | 212-674-7400 | www.tamarinde22.com

A small, well-edited selection of "exotic teas" makes for a "lovely" experience at this "cozy" tearoom in the Flatiron District; while the Indian "snacks and sweets" prepared by the "fabulous chefs" at the same-named "sister restaurant next door" can provide "an interesting alternative to the traditional afternoon tea", some of the usual accompaniments are offered, including fruit tarts and pound cake.

Tan My My ⇺ *Seafood*

| ▽ 22 | 16 | 13 | I |

Chinatown | 253-249 Grand St. (bet. Bowery & Chrystie St.) | B/D to Grand St. | 212-966-7837

Considered a "good-value champion" offering some of the "freshest" fish in town, this Chinatown seafood emporium stands out from the competition by offering some "fancy stuff that no one else carries" – which can "drive up the bill" warn wallet-watchers; meats and produce are also on offer.

Tanoreen *Prepared Food*

| - | - | - | I |

Bay Ridge | 7704 Third Ave. (77th St.) | Brooklyn | R to 77th St. | 718-748-5600 | www.tanoreen.com

For "tasty Mediterranean food" that you can "eat in or take home", head to this "really cheap" Bay Ridge restaurant/caterer serving up a variety of appetizers and entrees featuring eggplant plus "amazing lamb", kebabs, salads, rice and stuffed grape leaves; those in-the-know advise "don't leave without trying the hummus" – and then "buy extra to eat throughout the week."

Tarallucci e Vino ● *Baked Goods*   ∇ 24 | 22 | 20 | M

E Village | 163 First Ave. (10th St.) | L to 1st Ave. | 212-388-1190

Flatiron | 15 E. 18th St. (bet. B'way & 5th Ave.) | 4/5/6/L/N/Q/R/W to 14th St./Union Sq. | 212-228-5400

www.tarallucievino.net

Discerning shoppers salute these "authentic Italian" bakery/cafes for their "fresh", "wonderful coffee and pastries" and equally "delicious" panini, not to mention their rainbow of gelato varieties; the "East Village original" is "a bit more down home" and retail-oriented, while the flashier Flatiron offshoot is an eatery/enoteca that's always a stylish stop for light fare and "a great glass of wine."

Target ●◗▭ *Cookware*   17 | 15 | 11 | I

Bronx | 40 W. 225th St. (I-87) | 1 to 225th St./Marble Hill | 718-733-7199

Prospect Heights | Atlantic Terminal Mall | 139 Flatbush Ave. (Atlantic Ave.) | Brooklyn | D/M/N/R to Pacific St. | 718-290-1109

Starrett City | Gateway Ctr. | 519 Gateway Dr. (Erskine St.) | Brooklyn | 718-235-6032

College Pt | 135-05 20th Ave. (Whitestone Expwy., exit 15) | Queens | 718-661-4346

Elmhurst | 8801 Queens Blvd. (55th Ave.) | Queens | G/R/V to Grand Ave. | 718-760-5656

800-440-0680 | www.target.com

"If only they had one in Manhattan" sigh city-dwellers who still "schlep" to the outer-borough outposts of this "nifty" "big-box" re-tailer for "quirky", "well-designed" kitchen supplies that are not only "stylish", but "a great value" to boot; a jaded few maintain that its "limited stock", only "passable service" and "lines, lines, lines" "do not make for pleasant shopping experiences."

Tarzian West *Cookware*   22 | 15 | 18 | M

Park Slope | 194 Seventh Ave. (2nd St.) | Brooklyn | F to 7th Ave. | 718-788-4213

"Absolutely packed with kitchen goodness" (as well as Brooklynites "with strollers") this Park Slope standby makes the most of its "small" space by crowding in "almost too much merchandise" from pots and pans to appliances and gadgets; though some call it "over-priced", with service "that leaves a lot to be desired", it's still "con-venient", and besides, it's "the only game in the neighborhood."

Tastebud's Natural Foods *Health Food*   - | - | - | M

Staten Island | 1807 Hylan Blvd. (Buel Ave.) | 718-351-8693

The main point of attraction at this diminutive health food store is that it's "one of the few natural shops on Staten Island", but none-theless hyperbolic shoppers applaud its selection of wheat-and gluten-free products as the "best in all of NYC"; there's also an or-ganic juice bar and a respectable selection of vegan foods.

	QUALITY	DISPLAY	SERVICE	COST

Taste Caterers ⊄ *Caterer* ▽ 22 | 26 | 22 | E

W Village | 113 Horatio St. (bet. Washington & West Sts.) |
212-255-8571 | www.tastecaterers.com
By appointment only

Good taste marks the boutique talents of this West Village caterer
and event planner, an off-site specialist known for "elegant displays"
of "exquisite" Eclectic eats from a creative kitchen that favors seasonal ingredients and gourmet flourishes; with "courteous servers"
and an "accommodating" staff to handle venue prep and logistics,
it's "worth every penny" for quality suited to heads of state, museums and bigwig fashion designers.

Tastings by Payard *Caterer/Events* ▽ 27 | 24 | 23 | VE

E 70s | 1032 Lexington Ave. (bet. 73rd & 74th Sts.) | 212-744-4422 |
www.tastingsnyc.com
By appointment only

Connoisseurs claim you "can't get nicer French catering" than at this
affiliate of the East Side patisserie powerhouse Payard, which takes
its signature elegance off-premises with "great displays" of haute
bistro fare and "amazing" dessert spreads showcasing "the most
gorgeous and delicious" cakes and pastries; its full-service planners
tailor events on an intimate scale, and the effect's as decorous as it
is dearly priced.

☑ Tavalon Tea Bar ● *Coffee/Tea* 24 | 22 | 25 | M

Union Sq | 22 E. 14th St. (bet. 5th Ave. & Union Square W.) |
4/5/6/L/N/Q/R/W to 14th St./Union Sq. | 212-807-7027 |
www.tavalon.com

Union Square "insanity" is "offset wonderfully" at this bright,
"white" sliver of a tea bar soundtracked by "funky DJs spinning all
day"; its "friendly" staff is on a mission to "bring tea to the hip" – or the
"trendtea", if you will – hawking designer accessories (Eva Solo teapots, mouth-blown glass tumblers) and offering "samples of most of
their blends" (35 and counting), not to mention free weekly classes.

Tazza *Baked Goods* - | - | - | I

Brooklyn Heights | 311 Henry St. (Atlantic Ave.) | Brooklyn |
2/3/4/5/M/N/R/W to Borough Hall/Court St. | 718-243-0487 |
www.tazzabklyn.com

"Much-needed" in the "neighborhood", this Italian cafe/wine bar in
Brooklyn Heights brings on "quality drink and food" in the form of
baked goods, panini, quiche and vinos by the glass or bottle; it also
vends breads imported from the Sullivan Street Bakery and other
top-notch outfits, though the yupscale types noshing and sipping in
the "comfortable" digs prefer to "maintain the calm vibe"
("shhh . . . don't tell").

Tea Box, The *Coffee/Tea* 27 | 24 | 22 | E

E 50s | Takashimaya | 693 Fifth Ave., lower level (bet. 54th & 55th Sts.) |
E/V to 5th Ave./53rd St. | 212-350-0100 | 800-753-2038

"Hidden" in the basement of Takashimaya, Midtown's "swanky"
Japanese department store, is this "wonderful" tea shop proffering

some 40 varieties of "high-quality" loose leaves (green, black and herbal), plus "superb accoutrements", presented in "rarefied" displays; the adjacent "Zen-like" tearoom makes a "lovely" "getaway from the Fifth Avenue bustle", but just keep in mind that the "exquisite" afternoon tea here requires more than a little "dough."

Tea Lounge ◐ *Coffee/Tea* `21` `19` `19` `M`

NEW Cobble Hill | 254 Court St. (Kane St.) | Brooklyn | F/G to Bergen St. | 718-624-5683 ⊄

Park Slope | 350 Seventh Ave. (10th St.) | Brooklyn | F to 7th Ave. | 718-768-4966 ⊄

Park Slope | 837 Union St. (bet. 6th & 7th Aves.) | Brooklyn | B/Q to 7th Ave. | 718-789-2762

www.tealoungeny.com

Stroller-pushers and other "fans of the leafy brew" flock to this Park Slope tea-house twosome (and its new Cobble Hill outpost) with a "bohemian graduate-student feel", where loungers sip and surf free WiFi, "people-watch" or just "curl up" on the "ratty-but-comfy sofas and read" into the wee hours; beyond the deep "selection of teas" and "ok" coffee, there's also a full bar – and "with all those screaming kids" you just may "need a drink."

Teitel Brothers ▣ *Specialty Shop* `26` `18` `21` `I`

Bronx | 2372 Arthur Ave. (E. 186th St.) | B/D to Fordham Rd. | 718-733-9400 | 800-850-7055 | www.teitelbros.com

This "landmark store in Bronx's Little Italy" is "worth the trip to Arthur Avenue" for "great deals" on imported "delicacies from the old country", most notably its "fabulous cheeses", olive oils, cured meats and sausages; sure, it's "no-frills" with a "very straightforward staff", but for many that's just "part of its charm."

Tempo Presto ⊄ *Deli/Sandwich* ▽ `23` `18` `19` `M`

NEW **Park Slope** | 210 Seventh Ave. (3rd St.) | Brooklyn | F to 7th Ave. | 718-369-5885 ◐

Park Slope | 254 Fifth Ave. (bet. Carroll St. & Garfield Pl.) | Brooklyn | M/R to Union St. | 718-636-8899

www.tempobrooklyn.com

Offering Park Slopers "something a little special for takeout", this next-door take-out/catering arm of the Mediterranean eatery Tempo has recently been joined by a second outlet on Seventh Avenue; the highlights here are "excellent twists on the usual panini" and non-pressed sandwiches (the TBLT is "a favorite"), as well as "housemade" gelato and baked goodies that range from cupcakes to wedding cakes.

⒵ Ten Ren `25` `19` `19` `M`
Tea & Ginseng Co. ▣ *Coffee/Tea*

Chinatown | 75 Mott St. (bet. Bayard & Canal Sts.) | 6/J/M/N/Q/R/W/Z to Canal St. | 212-349-2286 | 800-292-2049

Chinatown | 79 Mott St. (bet. Bayard & Canal Sts.) | 6/J/M/N/Q/R/W/Z to Canal St. | 212-732-7178 ◐⊄

SoHo | 138 Lafayette St. (Howard St.) | 6/J/M/N/Q/R/W/Z to Canal St. | 212-343-8098

(continued)

(continued)

Ten Ren Tea & Ginseng Co.

Sunset Pk | 5817 Eighth Ave. (bet. 58th & 59th Sts.) | Brooklyn | N to 8th Ave. | 718-853-0660
Elmhurst | 83-28 Broadway (Dongan Ave.) | Queens | R to Elmhurst Ave. | 718-205-0861
Flushing | 135-18 Roosevelt Ave. (bet. Main & Prince Sts.) | Queens | 7 to Flushing-Main St. | 718-461-9305
www.tenrenusa.com

It's "heaven for tea lovers" at this "must-stop" Chinatown vet (75 Mott Street) known for its "excellent selection" of "premium" leaves imported from Taiwan and China, as well as elegant tea sets and accessories, though the "frosty" staff presiding over it all is deemed less than divine; prices range from "medium to outta-site expensive" "depending on quality", but even the most rarefied blend is way "cheaper than a trip to Shanghai"; N.B. all other locations are bubble tea bars dispensing tapioca pearl drinks and snacks.

Tentation Potel & Chabot
Special Events Catering *Caterer/Events*

∇ 22 | 24 | 19 | VE

Garment Dist | 524 W. 34th St. (bet. 10th & 11th Aves.) | 212-564-7530 | www.tentation.net
By appointment only

"They have the cachet" to stay in demand at this Garment District-based caterer/event planner, a branch of the august Parisian firm Potel & Chabot with ample off-site experience at crafting modern menus synched with "beautiful displays" in the grandest settings; it's "pricey" but "a class act all the way", though some are tempted to add that the "customer-service skills" "could use more polish."

☑ Terence Conran Shop ▣ *Cookware*

25 | 26 | 19 | E

E 50s | Bridgemarket, The | 407 E. 59th St. (1st Ave.) | 4/5/6 to 59th St./Lexington Ave. | 212-755-9079 | www.conranusa.com

"If you love modern", Sir Terence Conran's "beautiful" emporium of "unusual, luxurious" housewares is "utopia" with "stylish" imported finds that are "not always practical" though they sure "look good"; if some find it "overpriced", its setting – a bilevel "glass oasis" at the foot of the Queensboro Bridge – makes it a "delight" just to "window shop."

Terhune Orchards ⊟ *Produce*

27 | 22 | 25 | M

See Greenmarket; phone number unavailable

At this Greenmarket fruit stand "you watch the seasons" go "from peaches and apricots to pears and apples", all arriving from its Upstate orchard in Salt Point; it's "the real deal in freshness" according to fruit fans who also cite "pies, pies, pies" as a draw, and say that some items may be "costly", but the "excellent" products are "worth it" – especially given the "service with extra cheer."

Terrace Bagels ◗⊟ *Bagels*

25 | 18 | 22 | I

Windsor Terr | 224 Prospect Park W. (Windsor Pl.) | Brooklyn | F to 15th St. | 718-768-3943

Some of the "best bagels in Brooklyn" come from this Windsor Terrace storefront whose "fresh", "cooked-the-right-way" rounds are "the kind you can eat plain and not think twice about it"; "terrific" service offsets the "crowded" conditions and "waits" on weekends.

Terranova Bakery ⊄ *Baked Goods* | 26 | 15 | 20 | I |

Bronx | 691 E. 187th St. (bet. Beaumont & Cambreleng Aves.) | B/D to Fordham Rd. | 718-733-3827

If "Arthur Avenue is the best choice for Italian" "staples", one of the strip's standouts is this bakery "throwback" and its "fresh and authentic" output, especially "hearty rustic" breads like the "wonderful" *pane di casa*; given other fortes like focaccia and housemade pasta, fans of the quality and prices advise "if you're in the neighborhood" "make a beeline" for it.

☑ Teuscher Chocolates of Switzerland ▭ *Candy/Nuts* | 27 | 26 | 22 | VE |

E 40s | 620 Fifth Ave. (bet. 49th & 50th Sts.) | B/D/F/V to 47-50th Sts./Rockefeller Ctr. | 212-246-4416
E 60s | 25 E. 61st St. (bet. Madison & Park Aves.) | N/R/W to 5th Ave./59th St. | 212-751-8482
800-554-0924 | www.teuscher-newyork.com

"Just the name makes one's mouth water" say devotees of this "elegant" East Side pair of Swiss chocolate boutiques, who rave most about the "dreamy", "heavenly" champagne truffles that you can eat and then "die happy"; the price suggests these "outrageously good" confections and their "gorgeous packaging" "flew first class from Geneva", but don't expect top-flight service from the "haughty" staff.

Thalia Kitchen ● *Prepared Food* | 21 | 18 | 20 | M |

W 50s | 828 Eighth Ave. (50th St.) | C/E to 50th St. | 212-399-4443 | www.restaurantthalia.com

For "fresh, memorable" entrees, "well-prepared sandwiches", "high-quality salads" and "rather tasty" baked goods and desserts, head to this Theater District take-out storefront located around the corner from parent eatery Thalia; yes, it's tiny – "blink and you'll miss it" – but it's "worth" seeking out en route to a Broadway show.

Thomas Preti Caterers ⊄ *Caterer* | ▽ 23 | 25 | 22 | E |

LIC | 38-03 24th St. (bet. 38th & 39th Aves.) | Queens | 212-764-3188 | www.thomaspreti.com
By appointment only

With its combo of "down-to-earth" flexibility and "top restaurant quality", this off-premises caterer/event planner based in Long Island City goes "beyond expectations" in furnishing "delicious" food and "friendly service", whether for private gatherings or big-box galas; "amazing attention" goes into Preti-fying both cuisine and backdrop to suit the occasion, so count on a performance guests "will complement for years."

3-Corner Field Farm ▭ *Cheese/Dairy* | 27 | 22 | 25 | E |

See Greenmarket; for more information, call 518-854-9695 | www.dairysheepfarm.com

"Sheep's-milk yogurt and excellent merguez" are only two of the "extensive" uses this Adirondacks farm dedicated to 'the complete sheep' finds for its "well-cared-for" hormone- and drug-free live-stock: "succulent lamb", "amazing mutton", half a dozen "terrific" cheeses and even yarn, sheepskin and pet food; the "gracious", "dedicated" owners provide "cheerful service", and as for the "high prices", surveyors say the "quality" makes up for" 'em.

3 Guys from Brooklyn ● Produce

| 23 | 19 | 15 | I |

Bay Ridge | 6502 Ft. Hamilton Pkwy. (65th St.) | Brooklyn | N to Fort Hamilton Pkwy. | 718-748-8340

"Who'da thunk" a "fabulous smorgasbord of fruits and vegetables" ("some quite unusual") could be found "in the heart of Brooklyn", but this "dirt-cheap" Bay Ridge market proves it's possible; happily it's open 24/7, but "steel your nerves" on weekends when "the place gets overwhelmed" with seekers of "produce bargains" considered some of the "best the city."

NEW Three Tarts ▣ Baked Goods

| ▽ 22 | 21 | 21 | M |

Chelsea | 164 Ninth Ave. (20th St.) | C/E to 23rd St. | 212-462-4392 | www.3tarts.com

"Bite-sized pieces of ecstasy" await at this "little sweets" boutique in Chelsea, which does a "delicious" job with the eponymous "nib-bles" ("a must-taste") as well as an uncommon lineup of truffles, parfaits (sold in optional stemware), petits fours and more; also a gift shop tarted up with ceramics, housewares and artisanal honeys, it's "a bit pricey" but "definitely worth" a "stop to get something for the road."

Times Square Bagels ● Bagels

| 19 | 15 | 17 | M |

W 40s | 200 W. 44th St. (bet. B'way & 8th Ave.) | 1/2/3/7/N/Q/R/S/W to 42nd St./Times Sq. | 212-997-7300

Amid the "hustle and bustle" of Times Square resides this handy "pit stop" for "light, fluffy bagels and bialys on the go; while it gets demerits for relatively hefty tabs (chalk it up to the "tourist-trap" locale), regulars rate the "flavorful" offerings more than "worth it" – "long lines" notwithstanding.

NEW Tinto Fino Wine/Liquor

| - | - | - | M |

E Village | 85 First Ave. (bet. 5th & 6th Sts.) | L to 1st Ave. | 212-254-0850

Named for (and scarcely larger than) a premium grape of Spain, this new East Village wine "boutique" from a co-owner of the eatery Tía Pol aims to catch a rising trend by specializing in Spanish imports, offering a multiregional overview spanning familiar Riojas to a novel spotlight on sherries; but the "string-bean" space holds only 150 *botellas*, leading partialists to pray they can "build up their selec-tions" and find "room to display more."

Tiny's Giant Sandwich Shop ●⌀ Deli/Sandwich

| 22 | 18 | 20 | I |

LES | 129 Rivington St. (bet. Essex & Norfolk Sts.) | F/J/M/Z to Delancey/Essex Sts. | 212-982-1690 | www.tinysgiant.com

Space is certainly tiny (just 175 sq.-ft.), but "the tastes are big" at this Lower Eastsider turning out a "staggering variety" of "giant" sandwiches, "generous salads" and such; just as the name covers the spectrum, so do the offerings from hot roast beef for carnivores to Big Mack Daddy veggie burgers for the meat-averse.

NEW Tisserie ⬛ Baked Goods | 20 | 22 | 16 | M

Union Sq | 857 Broadway (E. 17th St.) | 4/5/6/L/N/R/Q/W to 14th St./ Union Sq. | 212-463-0850 | www.tisserie.com

Run by a Paris-trained Venezuelan chef and his brother, this recently arrived "large and bustling" Union Square patisserie/cafe showcases a "wide range" of "decadent" French pastries and desserts that incorporate some "super" "Latin variations" like "out-of-this-world" dulce de leche and "intense" South American chocolate; also serving up sandwiches, "great quiche" and even "vegan soups", it's "a godsend" for the area even if the crowds make the going "kind of slow."

ⓩ Titan Foods ◑⬛ Specialty Shop | 26 | 22 | 20 | I

Astoria | 2556 31st St. (bet. Astoria Blvd. & 28th Ave.) | Queens | N/W to 30th Ave. | 718-626-7771 | www.titanfood.com

When you can't "afford a flight to Athens", this "granddaddy of Greek supermarkets" in Astoria is "the next best thing", offering an array of specialties and "imported items", including "delicious cheeses", "to-die-for olives" and "exceptional baked goods", all at "the best prices"; if the "authentic products" aren't enough to make you feel like you're "back in the homeland", there's "even Greek music" on the sound system.

Todaro Brothers ◑⬛ Specialty Shop | 24 | 21 | 21 | E

Murray Hill | 555 Second Ave. (bet. 30th & 31st Sts.) | 6 to 33rd St. | 212-532-0633 | 877-472-2767 | www.todarobros.com

Murray Hill residents "depend on" this family-owned "blast from the past", an "old-world Italian" gourmet store stocking an "excellent selection of fresh fruits, vegetables, meats, cheeses", fish, pastas and olive oils as well as "wonderful prepared foods" and sandwiches, all "squeezed into a relatively small space"; plus, there's a "friendly" staff that "knows exactly what it's talking about"; P.S. claustrophobes are advised to "avoid Sunday afternoons."

Tops Wines & Spirits ◑ Wine/Liquor | ▽ 23 | 15 | 21 | I

Marine Pk | 2816 Ave. U (E. 28th St.) | Brooklyn | Q to Ave. U | 718-648-7590 | www.topswines.com

This "popular" Marine Park grape-and-grain store is considered tops on its turf for a "wide range of wines", unsurprising given the "huge" stock of 4,000 labels that spans price points "from cheap to very expensive" and highlights a "large selection of kosher" and Australian vintages; for those who need an assist with the wares, owner "Jeff's recommendations" are "very helpful."

ⓩ Trader Joe's ◑ Major Gourmet Mkt. | 24 | 19 | 21 | I

Union Sq | 142 E. 14th St. (bet. 3rd & 4th Aves.) | 4/5/6/L/N/Q/R/W to 14th St./Union Sq. | 212-529-4612 | www.traderjoes.com

"Finally", Manhattanites "can afford to eat better" thanks to this "happening" Union Square gourmet grocer, a link in a "cheery" Cali-based chain that "beats the pants off of ritzier competitors" with an "interesting selection" that offers "lots of organic, natural choices" (including "excellent house" labels that taste "better than name brands"), all at "really fair prices"; trading in the "well-displayed" likes of "reliable" produce, "wonderful frozen meals" with "ethnic" twists, "excellent meats", "fantastic" cheeses and much more, it's "truly all it's cracked up to be" as a "mecca" the multitudes "can't resist", resulting in prime-time "lines longer than the Nile" and widespread appeals for "more locations, please!"

Trader Joe's Wine Shop *Wine/Liquor* | 19 | 19 | 20 | I |

Union Sq | 138 E. 14th St. (bet. Irving Pl. & Union Sq. E.) | 4/5/6/L/N/Q/R/W to 14th St./Union Sq. | 212-529-6326 | www.traderjoes.com

A "lifesaver for the budget-conscious", this Union Square megamart's "welcome" vino annex is "perfect for stocking up" on a "serviceable selection" of "very decent" vintages (with "the occasional jewel" thrown in) at "unbeatable prices", typified by the celebrated "two-buck chuck", which goes for $2.99; snoots scoff at oenology "for beginners" that's "cheap for a reason", but it's "handy" "for a quick fix" and where else can you "walk away with a case" and still "feel rich"?

NEW Tribeca Treats ▭ *Baked Goods* | ▽ 27 | 25 | 25 | M |

TriBeCa | 94 Reade St. (bet. Church St. & W. B'way) | 1/2/3/A/C to Chambers St. | 212-571-0500 | www.tribecatreats.com

Newly arrived in TriBeCa, this "stylish" bakery treats its patrons to a "fantastic" confection selection including cookies, "handmade" chocolates "to die for" and many flavors of "amazing" cakes in sizes ranging from "beautiful cupcakes" on up; it already has a rep as a "reliable" place to indulge or "pick up a gift", with the "sweetest" staff standing by to "make you feel welcome"; N.B. they also take orders for wedding and birthday packages.

Tribeca Wine Merchants ▭ *Wine/Liquor* | 23 | 19 | 20 | E |

TriBeCa | 40 Hudson St. (bet. Duane & Thomas Sts.) | 1/2/3/A/C to Chambers St. | 212-393-1400 | www.tribecawine.com

An "up-and-comer" on the TriBeCa scene, this boutique's wines tend to "eclectic", carefully curated choices showcasing "harder-to-find varieties", with a concentration on Burgundies and smaller vineyards in California and Oregon; it may seem "a bit expensive" to "unfortunates who eschewed Wall Street" careers, but there's a value-oriented $10–$20 rack too; N.B. check their Web site for "great" weekly tastings.

Z TriServe ▭ *Party Rentals* | 24 | 22 | 25 | M |

E 60s | 770 Lexington Ave., 12th fl. (bet. 60th & 61st Sts.) | 718-822-1930 | www.triservepartyrentals.com
By appointment only

Party-throwers rave about this East Side rental outfit, which manages to showcase the "best" ("frequently updated") styles around, whether for furniture, flatware, linens or tents, much of it stored in a Bronx warehouse that's open to drop-ins; it's also known for "knowledgeable", "top-notch" service on all fronts – "even the truckers are good"; N.B. plans to move its showroom are in the works for fall 2007.

NEW Trois Pommes Patisserie ⊘ *Baked Goods*

-　-　-　E

Park Slope | 260 Fifth Ave. (bet. Carroll St. & Garfield Pl.) | Brooklyn | M/R to Union St. | 718-230-3119

A former Union Square Cafe pastry chef has opened this new patisserie along Park Slope's Fifth Avenue strip, where she whips up cakes, pies and such in a neighborhood that suddenly seems awash in high-caliber baked goods; the charming space has a few seats for on-site snacking, as well as an open kitchen that allows patrons to watch the magic happen.

Truffette ⌨ *Specialty Shop*

-　-　-　E

E Village | 104 Ave. B (bet. 6th & 7th Sts.) | 6 to Astor Pl. | 212-505-5813 | www.sos-chefs.com

Discerning foodies depend on this East Village gourmet store that supplies some of the city's top restaurants with all manner of luxury imported and domestic foodstuffs like imported oils, vanilla beans, flavored salts and other exotic products and spices; to top it all off, it also features "potentially the best mushrooms in town", including year-round and seasonal choices.

Trunzo Bros. ⌨ *Specialty Shop*

∇ 25　20　21　M

Bensonhurst | 6802 18th Ave. (68th St.) | Brooklyn | N to 18th Ave. | 718-331-2111 | www.trunzobros.com

For over 30 years, this Bensonhurst market has been the place "to go in the neighborhood" for "meat, pastas, produce, sandwiches", breads and housemade sausages and mozzarella, along with imported "Italian specialties" like cheeses, olive oils and sweets; so whether you're assembling an indulgent gift basket or arranging a catered lunch, this is "a great place."

T Salon *Coffee/Tea*

26　24　21　E

Chelsea | Chelsea Arts Bldg. | 134 W. 26th St., 4th fl. (bet. 6th & 7th Aves.) | 1 to 28th St. | 212-358-0506 ⌨

NEW **Chelsea** | Chelsea Market | 459 W. 15th St. (10th Ave.) | A/C/E/L to 14th St./8th Ave. | 212-243-2259 | 888-358-0506⌨

NEW **SoHo** | Te Casan | 382 W. Broadway (Broome St.) | C/E to Spring St. | 212-584-8000

www.tsalon.com

"Thank god it's back" cry relieved "tea snobs" now that this "relaxing" alternative to "the usual coffee bars" has returned, thanks to owner Miriam Novalle (she "has raised sipping tea to an art form") and her "knowledgeable help" who allow you to "sample and smell" their "amazing selection" of over 400 "unusual" blends; in addition to its fourth-floor Asian-inspired digs in the Chelsea Arts Building and an outpost inside SoHo's Te Casan shop, a brand-new 2,000-sq.-ft. flagship, featuring retail, restaurant and bar areas, has opened inside Chelsea Market.

	QUALITY	DISPLAY	SERVICE	COST

Tuck Shop *Prepared Food*

| − | − | − | I |

E Village | 68 E. First St. (bet. 1st & 2nd Aves.) | F/V to Lower East Side/2nd Ave. | 212-979-5200 ◗
W 40s | 250 W. 49th St (bet. B'way & 8th Ave.) | 1 to 50th St. | 212-757-8481
www.tuckshopnyc.com

Anyone craving "a touch of Australia in the East Village" (or in Midtown) can tuck into a "perfect bite on-the-go" at this bakery pair proffering "authentic meat pies" – ranging from "classic" ground beef to more modern varieties – and "other Aussie treats" such as beer and wine; N.B. they also do catering and feature a selection of groceries from Down Under.

Tuscan Square *Prepared Food*

| 22 | 22 | 16 | E |

W 50s | 16 W. 51st St. (bet. 5th & 6th Aves.) | B/D/F/V to 47-50th Sts./Rockefeller Ctr. | 212-977-7777

This Midtown prepared-foods market (located in "pretty, cozy" Tuscan-inspired digs beneath its parent restaurant) offers "decent" pastas, entrees, sandwiches and soups plus virtually "everything for the Italian farmhouse kitchen", including spice packets and imported vinegars; admirers say they "wouldn't mind visiting often" – if not for the "ridiculously expensive" prices.

☑ Two for the Pot ✄ *Coffee/Tea*

| 27 | 20 | 25 | M |

Brooklyn Heights | 200 Clinton St. (bet. Atlantic Ave. & Pacific St.) | Brooklyn | 2/3/4/5/M/N/R/W to Borough Hall/Court St. | 718-855-8173

"You never know what treat you'll find" among the jars, tins and boxes steeply stacked in this old-fashioned Brooklyn Heights emporium, from a "wide range of coffees" and "unusual teas" to herbs and spices, pantry items and equipment; the "genial owner" "loves his store and it shows" in the "knowledgeable", "wonderfully friendly" service and the "well-chosen" stock – he really does "seem to have everything" – just "look around and ask lots of questions."

☑ Two Little Red Hens *Baked Goods*

| 26 | 22 | 22 | E |

E 80s | 1652 Second Ave. (bet. 85th & 86th Sts.) | 4/5/6 to 86th St. | 212-452-0476 | www.twolittleredhens.com

"Cure any sweet craving" at this Upper East Side bakery/cafe, a "favorite local" "pit stop" for "killer" specialties like the "feather-light" cakes and cupcakes ("a gift from the gods"), "first-rate" tarts and other "habit-forming" goodies; the "homey" quarters and "lovely staff" have "small-town" charm, and though some cluck it "could be cheaper", there's "no substitute" for "perfection"; N.B. the original branch in Park Slope now operates under the name Lady Bird Bakery.

202 to Go ◗ *Baked Goods*

| 22 | 18 | 19 | M |

Chelsea | 202, Chelsea Mkt. | 75 Ninth Ave. (bet. 15th & 16th Sts.) | A/C/E/L to 14th St./8th Ave. | 646-638-1173 | www.nicolefarhi.com

"If you're gonna eat things you probably shouldn't, this is the place to do it" say sweet tooths of the "delicious" scones, muffins, cookies and such on offer at this back espresso bar/take-out counter inside Chelsea Market's Nicole Farhi boutique, though there are also savory selections like panini, soup, salads and a pasta or risotto of the day; P.S. those in-the-know go between 2–4 PM and "snag goodies at half price."

Umanoff & Parsons ⊽ *Baked Goods*

| 24 | 12 | 17 | M |

TriBeCa | 467 Greenwich St. (bet. Debrosses & Watts Sts.) | 1/A/C/E to Canal St. | 212-219-2240 | www.umanoffparsons.com

Its status as a wholesaler to upscale restaurants proves "you can't go wrong" with this TriBeCa bakery's "wide array" of "wonderful" (and kosher) cakes, pies and tarts, "true works of art" featuring the likes of "the best mud cake ever"; with everything sold over the counter right "in their factory", it's "not the easiest shopping" but the "excellent value" is "well worth" "the hassle"; P.S. later this year "they're moving from their longtime digs" to 121st Street and Park Avenue.

Uncle Louie G ●⊽ *Ice Cream*

| 20 | 14 | 17 | I |

W 80s | 2259 Broadway (bet. 80th & 81st Sts.) | 1 to 79th St. | 212-721-2818
Bronx | 3760 E. Tremont Ave. (Randall Ave.) | 718-822-1492
Park Slope | 321 Seventh Ave. (bet. 8th & 9th Sts.) | Brooklyn | F to 7th Ave. | 718-965-4237
Park Slope | 741 Union St. (bet. 5th & 6th Aves.) | Brooklyn | M/R to Union St. | 718-623-6668
Prospect Heights | 157 Prospect Park SW (bet. Seeley & Vanderbilt Sts.) | Brooklyn | F to Fort Hamilton Pkwy. | 718-438-9282
Astoria | 38-02 Broadway (38th St.) | Queens | G/R/V to Steinway St. | 718-728-4454
Forest Hills | 72-73 Austin St. (67th Dr.) | Queens | E/F/G/R/V to Forest Hills/71st Ave. | 718-897-7855
Howard Bch | 158-08 Cross Bay Blvd. (158th Ave.) | Queens | A to Howard Bch./JFK Airport | 718-677-9551
Kew Gdns | 68-46 Main St. (68th Dr.) | Queens | 718-544-7256
Staten Island | 15 Brower Ct. (Giffords Ln.) | 718-605-0056
www.unclelouieg.com

On a hot summer day in Gotham "you can't argue with Louie G's", nothing-fancy franchises scooping "sure-to-please", all-kosher ices and ice creams throughout the five boroughs ("they're just good, they don't have to be cool"); "success speaks for itself", as evidenced by the "long lines", although some surveyors are wary of those "Day-Glo colors" and find the flavors "entirely too artificial"; N.B. closed in winter.

Union Market ●▣ *Major Gourmet Mkt.*

| ▽ 26 | 23 | 23 | M |

Park Slope | 754-756 Union St. (6th Ave.) | Brooklyn | 2/3 to Grand Army Plaza | 718-230-5152 | www.unionmarket.com

It's "perfect for Park Slope" say neighbors of this gourmet market stocking "some really delicious finds", including "breads from the best bakeries", an "amazing cheese section", a "wide selection of specialty items" and prepared foods, "beautiful meat and fish" and "quality produce" that makes it the "place to shop in the summer"; "beautifully laid out" and overseen by "very helpful" staffers, it unites "yuppie" types into a "steady" clientele.

Union Square
Wines & Spirits ◑▣ *Wine/Liquor*   `25` `23` `21` `E`
Union Sq | 140 Fourth Ave. (13th St.) | 4/5/6/L/N/Q/R/W to 14th St./
Union Sq. | 212-675-8100 | www.unionsquarewines.com

An "old standby" in a "tremendous new space", this Union Square temple of oenophilia now augments it "fabulous variety" of vinos with a roomy bar for tastings with the "innovation of the year": a "high-tech" "enomatic" "tasting apparatus" that allows "savvy sippers" to sample among 50 bottles using a refillable "wine card"; with a "courteous" and "trustworthy" staff and "frequent sales and specials" to help quell gripes about "inflated prices", it's "a winner" that "should be a tourist attraction."

United Meat Market   *Meat/Poultry*   `-` `-` `-` `M`
Windsor Terr | 219 Prospect Park W. (bet. 16th St. & Windsor Pl.) |
Brooklyn | F to 15th St. | 718-768-7227

An "out-of-the-way gem" and "a godsend in the land of vanishing butcher shops", this Italian-accented Windsor Terrace meat and specialty foods shop offers a range of fresh beef, pork, chicken and game spanning the spectrum from "everyday" to "specialty cut"; there are also imported vinegars and oils, cheeses, salumi and a host of prepared traditional dishes (lasagnas, roast chickens, "meatballs in sauce") that locals call the "answer to takeout."

UN Wine Exchange ◑▣ *Wine/Liquor*   `-` `-` `-` `M`
E 40s | 885 First Ave. (bet. 49th & 50th Sts.) | 6 to 51st St. | 212-829-7200
Sited two blocks from the U.N., this offshoot of the New York Wine Exchange clan is packed to the rafters with a cellarlike showing of wines, offering a diplomatic choice of 4,000 labels traversing the range from California Cabernets to small producers in Australia, Chile, Italy and Spain; it also deserves recognition for its generous tasting schedule (Monday–Saturday from 5-8 PM).

Urban Organic ◑ *Produce*   ▽ `22` `8` `17` `M`
Park Slope | 240 Sixth St. (bet. 3rd & 4th Aves.) | Brooklyn | 718-499-4321 |
www.urbanorganic.com
By appointment only

The name may sound like an oxymoron, but this "fabulous" Park Slope outfit appeals to busy urbanites with the convenience of weekly or bi-weekly "home-delivered organic fruits and veggies" plus breads, spices, dairy and soy products; it can be "pricey", however, and some say service "has its ups and downs"; N.B. there's a $25 lifetime membership fee.

Uva Wines ◑ *Wine/Liquor*   `-` `-` `-` `M`
Williamsburg | Bedford Mini-Mall | 218 Bedford Ave. (N. 5th St.) |
Brooklyn | L to Bedford Ave. | 718-963-3939 | www.uvawines.com
Spike your vino shopping "with a dollop of hip" at this Williamsburg shop, whose "small" size belies a "high-quality" lineup of expertly picked vintages (organics and biodynamics from global sources among them) that may be the "yuppiest wine selection in the 'Burg"; expect a "helpful" "slacker" staff and under-$20 pricing that prom-

ises "an outstanding bottle for not a lot of money"; N.B. tastings are held Wednesdays and Saturdays.

Varsano's ▭ *Candy/Nuts* — | — | — | M

G Village | 172 W. Fourth St. (bet. 6th & 7th Aves.) | A/B/C/D/E/F/V to W. 4th St. | 212-352-1171 | 800-414-4718 | www.varsanos.com
The recent move across the street to more visible digs has been a good thing according to surveyors who say this little-known "find" of a candy emporium in the West Village is "getting better and better"; its fresh selection of handmade chocolates, caramel-smothered pretzel rods, s'mores, chocolate-covered potato chips and other decadent delights present so many choices, the "patient service" offered by the counter-folk is all the more welcome.

Veniero's ◑▭ *Baked Goods* 25 | 22 | 19 | M

E Village | 342 E. 11th St. (bet. 1st & 2nd Aves.) | L to 1st Ave. | 212-674-7070 | www.venieropastry.com
"You'll want one of everything" from the "mouthwatering display" of "classic Italian pastries" at this "legendary" East Village bakery, a survivor from "bygone days" (established 1894) that still "will wow you" with an "endless" selection of "delectable desserts" like "luscious" cannoli and "cheesecakes made to perfection"; the "touristy" milieu "can get hectic" and "the lines can be interminable", but given such "irresistible" quality at "moderate prices", traditionalists insist "you gotta go."

Vere ▭ *Candy/Nuts* — | — | — | E

Flatiron | 12 W. 27th St., 6th fl. (B'way) | N/R to 28th St. | 866-410-8373 | www.veregoods.com
Chocolate for those who don't like it too sweet is the forte of this high-end confectioner that uses no refined sugar in its bars, bonbons, truffles and brownies, making them instead with fructose and agave nectar, as well as organic, Fair Trade, 75-percent-cacao chocolate; while it has no storefront, it opens its Flatiron factory to retail shoppers on Fridays, when free samples are given out.

NEW Vestry Wines ◑▭ *Wine/Liquor* — | — | — | M

TriBeCa | 65 Vestry St. (Washington St.) | 1 to Canal St. | 212-810-2899 | www.vestrywines.com
Birch wood frames the modern interior of this new way-West TriBeCa wine store, lending warmth to the attractive space and inspiring lingering amid its selection of some 400 labels, the bulk of which are from small producers in California, France and Italy; the accomplished staff is equally welcoming, and, perhaps best of all, offers daily tastings at the bar; N.B. customers can rate wines, take notes and track purchases on the store's Web site.

Vesuvio Bakery *Prepared Food* 23 | 19 | 19 | M

SoHo | 160 Prince St. (bet. Thompson St. & W. B'way) | N/R to Prince St. | 212-925-8248
"Step back in time" at this "old-world" Italian bakery, a SoHo "treasure" that's "retained its charm" (and its 1920s-era facade) despite renovations a few years back; although it offers the same "wonder-

ful" breads, biscotti and pastries, it's "expanded the options to include lovely sandwiches", salads and other "treats"; the only downside: it "can run out of popular items."

Viet-Nam Bánh Mì So #1 ⊘ *Deli/Sandwich* | 23 | 9 | 15 | I |

Chinatown | 369 Broome St. (Mott St.) | 6/J/M/N/Q/R/W/Z to Canal St. | 212-219-8341

"Makes you grateful you live in NYC" say surveyors of this recently renovated Vietnamese deli in Chinatown specializing in "truly superb" and "totally cheap" *banh mi* sandwiches "cheerfully" prepared with "fresh ingredients"; whether you opt for pork, chicken or vegan varieties, regulars advise: "get it spicy – with peppers" and wash it down with fresh sugarcane juice or an iced coffee with condensed milk.

Z Villabate | 28 | 24 | 22 | M |
Pasticceria & Bakery ◑ *Baked Goods*

Bensonhurst | 7117 18th Ave. (bet. 71st & 72nd Sts.) | Brooklyn | N to 18th Ave. | 718-331-8430 | www.villabate.net

Behold "the Italian baker's art" in its "colorful" glory at this "quintessential Brooklyn bakery" in Bensonhurst, where the display cases present a "gorgeous" abundance of the "wonderful pastries and cakes" that "Sicilian dreams" are made of, including "extraordinary cassata", marzipan and rice balls crafted to "perfection" (and "don't forget the cannoli"); "traditional" breads and summertime gelati further confirm it's "the best bet around", so "be prepared for long lines during the holidays."

Vincent's Meat Market ▣ *Meat/Poultry* | 27 | 21 | 23 | M |

Bronx | 2374 Arthur Ave. (bet. E. 186th & 187th Sts.) | B/D to Fordham Rd. | 718-295-9048

"Yeah, Bronx!" – "Vincent's is the tops" crow champions of this circa-1954 Arthur Avenue Italian butcher shop, where the meaty goods (baby lambs among them) hang in the window and the plentiful offerings include prime beef, housemade sausages, chicken and veal rollatini and lots of game; while you're at this "culinary destination" you can also grab imported pastas, cheese and dry goods.

Z Vino ◑▣ *Wine/Liquor* | 28 | 25 | 25 | E |

Gramercy | 121 E. 27th St. (bet. Lexington & Park Aves.) | 6 to 28th St. | 212-725-6516 | www.vinosite.com

Take "a tour of the wine regions of Italy" at this Gramercy store devoted to producers from The Boot, where the "lovely" stock (70 percent of it poured at the companion eatery, I Trulli) is "well-grouped" geographically and tended by staffers who "know their stuff"; it features "little-known" finds plus numerous "aperitivos and digestivos", and is a "must-stop" even if pricing skews "a touch high"; P.S. "don't miss its wine classes" and weekend tastings.

VinoVino ◑ *Wine/Liquor* | ▽ 25 | 21 | 21 | E |

TriBeCa | 211 W. Broadway (bet. Franklin & White Sts.) | 1 to Franklin St. | 212-925-8510 | www.vinovino.net

Oenophiles in-the-know "love love" this tasteful TriBeCa two-in-one, a lofty space that unites a Euro-style enoteca with a glassed-off retail display of some 250 "great wines" "matched with knowledge-able service", with a focus on smaller Spanish and Italian estate growers; the wine bar offers a chance to sample the wares by the glass, and tastings are held Thursday through Saturday evenings; P.S. it's "good for private parties" too.

Vintage New York ●◗▣ *Wine/Liquor* `23` `24` `24` `M`

SoHo | 482 Broome St. (Wooster St.) | 1/A/C/E to Canal St. | 212-226-9463
W 90s | 2492 Broadway (bet. 92nd & 93rd Sts.) | 1/2/3 to 96th St. | 212-721-9999
www.vintagenewyork.com

Out to prove Eastern labels can "rival the highly touted Californians", this SoHo–Upper West Side duo showcases a "terrific selection" of solely "Empire State wines", with "virtually every NY State vineyard represented", from "all over the Finger Lakes, Hudson Valley and the North Fork of Long Island"; you also "gotta love the tasting bars" (sample five vinos for $10) and array of choc-olates, artisanal cheeses and other comestibles, which likewise originate in-state.

Violet Hill Farm *Meat/Poultry* `29` `19` `29` `E`

See Greenmarket; for more information, call 845-439-8040 | vilothillarabians.tripod.com/violethillfarm

"Great goat, heavenly hens and beautiful bacon" are among the standouts at this Sullivan County farm's Greenmarket stall consid-ered one of the "best-of-class in so many categories": "heirloom" pork that's "the platonic ideal of porkiness", "amazing lamb", "great" chicken and rabbits, "many varieties of sausages" and pos-sibly the "best eggs in the market"; to top it all off, staffers are "in-credibly knowledgeable" and will "tailor their advice to how adventurous you are feeling" – so go ahead, "taste the difference."

☑ Vosges Haut Chocolat ▣ *Candy/Nuts* `26` `26` `22` `E`

SoHo | 132 Spring St. (bet. Greene & Wooster Sts.) | C/E to Spring St. | 212-625-2929 | 888-301-9366 | www.vosgeschocolate.com

"The finest choco-centric adventure in NY" is how hip chocolate-lovers sum up this "fabulous – and fabulously expensive" SoHo bou-tique that has earned a reputation for its bonbons boasting "wild twists of flavor" like curry and horseradish as well as for its "beauti-ful purple packaging" and "gorgeous" environs; traditionalist sneer "it's trying too hard" and, needless to say, it's "not a place for people who like Hershey's"; N.B. an UES location is in the works.

VSF *Flowers* ▽ `29` `27` `25` `VE`

W Village | 204 W. 10th St. (bet. Bleecker & W. 4th Sts.) | 1 to Christopher St. | 212-206-7236 | www.vsfnyc.com

"Outstanding in every way", this "spectacular" floral shop in the West Village is the source for "unusual blooms" brought together in arrangements that are "always fabulous, never stilted"; they call their look 'Flemish-garden style', which translates to "universally appealing" products perfect for events or for sending "to favorite clients"; the only drawback seems to be pricing levels that mean its blooms are as expensive "as they are lovely."

Warehouse Wines & Spirits ● *Wine/Liquor* | 22 | 15 | 18 | I |

G Village | 735 Broadway (bet. 8th St. & Waverly Pl.) | R/W to 8th St. | 212-982-7770

"Looks like a warehouse, costs like a warehouse" is the lowdown on this "massive" Village resource for the "everyday drinker", where it's "worth braving the crowds" to score "some incredible buys" on wines ("if you know what you want" and "choose carefully") as well as "brand liquors"; downsides include "minimal service" and packs of party-hearty "college students", but "the financially strapped" will "typically save a few bucks."

Z Westerly Natural Market ●◐▤ *Health Food* | 25 | 17 | 20 | M |

W 50s | 913 Eighth Ave. (bet. 54th & 55th Sts.) | 1/A/B/C/D to 59th St./Columbus Circle | 212-586-5262 | www.westerlynaturalmarket.com

Attention all "granolaheads": this "awesome" Hell's Kitchen health food oasis is "a wonderland of natural foods", with "top-notch organic" fruits and vegetables, a "great bulk-foods section" and myriad grocery items stocked to the ceiling; the service is "warm and welcoming" and its "newly renovated" space is "clean and bright" (though the "very tight aisles" remain "cramped" as ever), while prices are "surprisingly reasonable", especially for office workers looking for "delicious" healthy lunches" from the well-priced back prepared foods area.

Westside Market ●◐▤ *Major Gourmet Mkt.* ▽ | 21 | 19 | 17 | M |

W 70s | 2171 Broadway (bet. 76th & 77th Sts.) | 1/2/3 to 79th St. | 212-595-2536

Chelsea | 77 Seventh Ave. (bet. 15th & 14th Sts.) | 1/2/3 to 14th St. | 212-807-7771

Though "nothing fancy", this longtime gourmet-market fixture is a "real Upper West Side sleeper" that joins with its Chelsea offshoot to offer "all the basics" "for a fair price", including "fresh" produce, "excellent" prepared foods and a "surprisingly wide variety" of cheeses, specialty items, dry goods, deli and more; it's "better than your average" "neighborhood spot", and the original's 24/7 availability makes it a welcome "after-hours alternative" (the Chelsea store closes at midnight).

West Side Wine *Wine/Liquor* | 24 | 23 | 24 | M |

W 80s | 481 Columbus Ave. (83rd St.) | 1 to 86th St. | 212-874-2900 | www.westsidewine.com

Overseen by "well-traveled" owner Andy Besch ("author of *The Wine Guy*"), this "charming" Upper Westsider boasts "one of the best selections of moderately priced" bottles around (mixed with some "premium" picks), all "displayed properly" and tended by a "superb" staff; it aims to make "interesting" sipping affordable, and neophytes who "don't know the difference between a Cabernet and a cabaret" can "trust them" for "lots of great tips."

	QUALITY	DISPLAY	SERVICE	COST

Whole Earth Bakery ●◐⇗ *Baked Goods* | − | − | − | M |

E Village | 130 St. Marks Pl. (bet. Ave. A & 1st Ave.) | 6 to Astor Pl. | 212-677-7597

Proof that "wholesome" fare can be "great tasting too", this congenial little East Village bakery and juice bar is a vegetarian/vegan haven whose organic output includes pastries, brownies and flourless cakes; savories like tofu pizzas, quiche and sandwiches also figure, and their made-to-order wedding cakes will get any marriage off to a healthy start.

☑ Whole Foods | 26 | 25 | 21 | E |
Market ●▣ *Major Gourmet Mkt.*

Chelsea | 250 Seventh Ave. (24th St.) | 1 to 23rd St. | 212-924-5969
NEW **LES** | 95 E. Houston St. (Bowery) | F/V to Lower East Side/2nd Ave. | 212-420-1320 | 888-746-7936
Union Sq | 40 E. 14th St, (bet. B'way & University Pl.) | 4/5/6/L/N/Q/R/W to 14th St./Union Sq. | 212-673-5388
W 50s | Shops at Columbus Circle | 10 Columbus Circle (bet. 58th & 60th Sts.) | 1/A/B/C/D to 59th St./Columbus Circle | 212-823-9600 | 888-746-7936
www.wholefoodsmarket.com

We'd be "wholly lost without them" say New Yorkers who "can't remember life without" these "bright", "well-organized" "shopping arenas", branches of a Texas franchise whose Chelsea flagship and "overwhelming" Columbus Circle and Union Square sites are hailed as the "ultimate" "all-in-one" "health and natural food" sources, featuring "lip-smacking" baked goods, a "sensational display" of "super-fresh" produce, a "dizzying" "smorgasbord" of prepared foods, tons of "interesting" coffees, "incredible" "upscale" cheeses, "wonderful organic meats and poultry" and "stunning seafood"; in sum, it's just about the "best game in town"; N.B. the Lower East Side store opened post-Survey and includes a full-service eatery, Rustica Minardi.

'wichcraft *Deli/Sandwich* | 24 | 19 | 18 | E |

Chelsea | 269 Eleventh Ave. (bet. 27th & 28th Sts.) | C/E to 23rd St. | 212-780-0577
NEW **E 40s** | 555 Fifth Ave. (bet. 45th & 46th Sts.) | B/D/F/V to 47-50th Sts./Rockefeller Ctr. | 212-780-0577
NEW **Flatiron** | 11 E. 20th St. (bet. B'way & 5th Ave.) | 4/5/6/L/N/Q/R/W to 14th St./Union Sq. | 212-780-0577 ●
G Village | 60 E. Eighth St. (Mercer St.) | R/W to 8th St. | 212-780-0577
NEW **Murray Hill** | Equinox | 1 Park Ave. S. (33rd St.) | 6 to 33rd St. | 212-780-0577 ●
NEW **SoHo** | Plus One Fitness Clinic | 106 Crosby St. (Prince St.) | N/R to Prince St. | 212-780-0577
TriBeCa | 397 Greenwich St. (Beach St.) | 1 to Franklin St. | 212-780-0577 ●
W 40s | Bryant Park | Sixth Ave. (bet. 40th & 42nd Sts.) | 7/B/D/F/V to 42nd St./Bryant Park | 212-780-0577
866-942-4272 | www.wichcraftnyc.com

"Genius" Tom Colicchio (of Craft and *Top Chef* fame) casts his spell ever-wider with the proliferating branches of this chain dispensing "ridiculously good" sandwiches along with "delicious soups and salads" and sweets including "unbelievable cupcakes"; its stripped-down digs (most with seating) "feel very of-the-moment" while service is "courteous", but "the sun may set while you wait in line" – and "geez, those prices."

Wild Edibles ●▣ *Seafood* | 26 | 25 | 22 | E |

E 40s | Grand Central Mkt. | Lexington Ave. (43rd St.) | 4/5/6/7/S to 42nd St./Grand Central | 212-687-4255
Murray Hill | 535 Third Ave. (bet. 35th & 36th Sts.) | 6 to 33rd St. | 212-213-8552
www.wildedibles.com

"If the fish were any fresher, it would be in the ocean" gush groupies of this "superb", "high-end" East Side pair that's "got it all" – a "wide selection" of "usual and unusual catches" "nicely displayed", a "wonderful" staff and "tasty", "well-prepared" dishes; it's "wildly expensive", but many are "willing to pay" for the "excellent quality."

William Greenberg Jr. Desserts ▣ *Baked Goods* | 25 | 20 | 20 | VE |

E 80s | 1100 Madison Ave. (bet. 82nd & 83rd Sts.) | 4/5/6 to 86th St. | 212-744-0304 | 800-255-8278 | www.wmgreenbergdesserts.com

"Blow your budget and your diet" at this "benchmark" Jewish bakery, an "Upper East Side tradition" dating back to 1946 for "old-fashioned" "treats" so "hard to resist" they deserve their own "support group", including such standouts as "the ultimate" schnecken, babka, "black-and-whites" and "special-occasion cakes"; though you'll need to "take out a mortgage" to pay, this is "quality you can't get at a lower price" even if some sense a "slide" "since the Greenberg family sold."

▨ William Poll ▣ *Prepared Food* | 26 | 23 | 24 | VE |

E 70s | 1051 Lexington Ave. (75th St.) | 6 to 77th St. | 212-288-0501 | 800-951-7655 | www.williampoll.com

"When you want to make that special impression", try this "top-of-the-line" prepared-foods shop that's been a "dependably dependable" Upper East Side "mainstay" for two generations courtesy of its "exquisite offerings" – from the sandwiches and house-smoked fish to the "amazing" homemade chips and dips; add in "always impeccable service" and "the prices seem almost reasonable."

Williamson Calvert ⊘ *Caterer* | - | - | - | VE |

Prospect Heights | 150 St. Marks Ave. (Carlton Ave.) | Brooklyn | B/Q to 7th Ave. | 718-956-5633 | www.williamsoncalvert.com

Missoni, MoMA and Annie Leibovitz are just a few of the high-profile clients who've secured the catering and event-planning services of this high-end, Brooklyn-based outfit favored by big guns in the arts, entertainment and publishing fields; chef Bryan Calvert provides a range of market-driven New American menu options, while partner and veteran producer Deborah Williamson oversees all areas of event production.

NYC SOURCES

	QUALITY	DISPLAY	SERVICE	COST

Z Williams-Sonoma 🖃 *Cookware* — 27 | 27 | 23 | E

Chelsea | 110 Seventh Ave. (bet. 16th & 17th Sts.) | 1 to 18th St. | 212-633-2203

E 50s | 121 E. 59th St. (bet. Lexington & Park Aves.) | 4/5/6 to 59th St./Lexington Ave. | 917-369-1131

E 80s | 1175 Madison Ave. (86th St.) | 4/5/6 to 86th St. | 212-289-6832

W 50s | Shops at Columbus Circle | 10 Columbus Circle (bet. 58th & 60th Sts.) | 1/A/B/C/D to 59th St./Columbus Circle | 212-823-9750 ❶ 800-541-2233 | www.williams-sonoma.com

This "superior-quality" chain – for some the "standard-bearer" of kitchenware shops – "makes you think NYers actually cook" with its "tempting" "high-end" displays of pots and pans, cutlery and small appliances, as well as "preppy" color-coordinated utensils and cleaning supplies, not to mention baking supplies, specialty oils, vinegars, sauces and cookbooks; "tasting demos", "free samples" and "fab service" mean it's always "fun to shop", despite prices that some say verge on the "ridiculous."

Windfall Farms 🖼 *Produce* — 27 | 21 | 21 | E

See Greenmarket; for more information, call 845-457-5988 | www.windfallfarms.com

Fanciers of arugula and "unique" greens "found nowhere else" count on this Montgomery, NY, producer's year-round Greenmarket stall in Union Square to supply them with "amazingly fresh, flavorful" "specialty" lettuces and edible leaves of all sorts; "they care for their lettuces" and other goods "as if they came from Tiffany's" – and "the price reflects this", which makes some surveyors wonder just who's reaping a windfall, but to the majority it's well "worth it."

Windsor Florist 🖃 *Flowers* — ▽ 24 | 19 | 19 | E

E 70s | 1118 Lexington Ave. (78th St.) | 6 to 77th St. | 212-734-4540

E 70s | 1382 Second Ave. (71st St.) | 6 to 68th St. | 212-734-4524 800-234-3761 | www.thewindsorflorist.com

With two locations on the Upper East Side, this veteran florist (in business since 1936) emphasizes fresh, handpicked flowers over mod, sculptural blooms; although some surveyors suggest the simple style is "boring", most appreciate them as "good neighborhood florists" adept at handling events, weddings and home arrangements too.

W.I.N.E. ❶ *Wine/Liquor* — ▽ 21 | 16 | 19 | E

E 80s | Eli's Manhattan | 1415 Third Ave. (80th St.) | 6 to 77th St. | 212-717-1999 | www.elizabar.com

Prices are "far more gentle" than "the rest of Eli Zabar's empire" at this petite annex to Eli's Manhattan on the Upper East Side, which carries a "small selection" of boutique wines chosen in part for affordability; the "first-rate" staffers "know their stock" well enough to dispense "valuable" tips (show up at 5 PM for daily tastings), and even those who find it "underwhelming" acknowledge it's "convenient" in this underserved neighborhood.

	QUALITY	DISPLAY	SERVICE	COST

Wine & Spirit Co. of Forest Hills ◐ *Wine/Liquor*

▽ 22 | 15 | 19 | M

Forest Hills | 72-09 Austin St. (71st Ave.) | Queens | R/V to 67th Ave. | 718-575-2700

The always "friendly atmosphere" is certain to elevate spirits at this largish "local store" on a "bustling" Forest Hills thorough-fare, known in the neighborhood for a broad selection of grape and grain that features "some unusual finds" and $15–$25 "bargains" in its 2,000-label vino department; also specializing in kosher vintages, it has a resilient rep as "the only good wine shop" in the vicinity.

Winesby.com ▣ *Wine/Liquor*

- | - | - | M

G Village | 23 Jones St. (bet. Bleecker & W. 4th Sts.) | A/B/C/D/E/F/V to W. 4th St. | 212-242-5144 | www.winesby.com

This tiny Greenwich Village shop "makes it easy to try wines" without venturing far from home since better than half of its trade is online or by phone (with Manhattan delivery within two hours); focused on Italian and French labels in the $10–$100 range, the inventory is limited but lovingly chosen by the "super-friendly" owner; N.B. they'll arrange next-day delivery for bottles they don't have on hand.

Wine Therapy ◐◑▣ *Wine/Liquor*

- | - | - | M

NoLita | 171 Elizabeth St. (Spring St.) | 6 to Spring St. | 212-625-2999

Providing "just the sort of therapy NYers should have", this NoLita vintner-in-miniature is run by a couple who spun it off from the adjacent hair salon, using their "wine smarts" to show-case boutique labels from small European vineyards; given its "strong nose" for style, those who attend the Saturday tastings should be in fashionable company.

Winfield-Flynn Ltd. ◐▣ *Wine/Liquor*

▽ 23 | 18 | 21 | M

Murray Hill | 558 Third Ave. (37th St.) | 6 to 33rd St. | 212-679-4455 | 800-364-8918 | www.winfieldflynn.com

"A cut above" "your average wine shop", this longtime Murray Hill entry wins over the "neighborhood" with its "fair prices" and willing-ness to embellish its global lineup with "lesser-known" labels; with savvy staffers to offer "pretty dead-on" recommendations, it's "a good compromise" between low- and high-end venues that loyalists come back to "constantly."

Wizard Events, Inc. *Party Rentals*

- | - | - | M

Jefferson Valley | 3663 Lee Blvd. (E. Main St.), NY | 914-777-0900 | 800-400-3836 | www.wizardevents.com

Going far beyond typical party rental work, this Westchester-based event planner sees to all phases of over-the-top functions, from bringing in Broadway singers, circus acts, wine experts and celebrity look-alikes to dreaming up party themes and designing entire sets and backdrops to match; just remember that putting on the party to end all parties doesn't come cheap.

	QUALITY	DISPLAY	SERVICE	COST

WK Trading Inc. ⌘ *Produce*
(fka WK Vegetable Co.)

	−	−	−	I

Chinatown | 124-126 Mott St. (bet. Grand & Hester Sts.) | 6/J/M/N/Q/R/W/Z to Canal St. | 212-334-4603

Authentic Asian produce, including a few "hard-to-find" offerings, is the mainstay of this inexpensive greengrocer on Mott Street; while it's hardly the only Chinatown storefront with "superior Chinese vegetables" and fruits, it has the added bonus of a "knowledgeable, English-speaking owner."

Wong Bakery ⌘ *Baked Goods*
(fka Maria's Bakery)

	−	−	−	I

Chinatown | 42 Mott St. (bet. Bayard & Pell Sts.) | 6/J/M/N/Q/R/W/Z to Canal St. | 212-732-3888

Just "like you'd expect from a classic", this old-school Chinatown fixture (fka Maria's Bakery) is an ever-"dependable" outlet for fresh "Chinese pastry" with the spotlight on faves like custard tarts, rice balls and stuffed buns; it's nothing fancy, but anyone out for "great value" can't go wong here; N.B. a new branch at 53 East Broadway is expected to open in 2007.

World of Nuts & Chocolates ● *Candy/Nuts*

	15	14	14	M

E 40s | 847 Second Ave. (45th St.) | 4/5/6/7/S to 42nd St./Grand Central | 212-490-7112

E 60s | 1293 First Ave. (bet. 69th & 70th Sts.) | 6 to 68th St. | 212-717-5393

E 70s | 1113 Lexington Ave. (bet. 77th & 78th Sts.) | 6 to 77th St. | 212-717-5622

G Village | 9 E. Eighth St. (bet. 5th Ave. & Univeristy Pl.) | R/W to 8th St. | 212-375-9004

Murray Hill | 529 Third Ave. (35th St.) | 6 to 33rd St. | 212-696-9264

W 50s | 1363 Sixth Ave. (55th St.) | B/D/F/V to 47-50th Sts./Rockefeller Ctr. | 212-956-9322

W 50s | 352 W. 57th St. (bet. 8th & 9th Aves.) | 1/A/B/C/D to 59th St./Columbus Circle | 212-262-4220

W 70s | 2194 Broadway (bet. 77th & 78th Sts.) | 1 to 79th St. | 212-769-1006

Seemingly everywhere, these "handy, reliable" bulk candy stores offer sugar addicts an "adequate" "chocolate or nut fix" for "not a lot of money"; "convenience" and "selection" are the "selling points" here – more so than quality, which respondents say "varies", citing occasional encounters with "stale" product.

Yoghurt Place, The ⌘ *Cheese/Dairy*

	▽ 23	19	21	M

SoHo | 71 Sullivan St. (bet. Broome & Spring Sts.) | C/E to Spring St. | 212-219-3500

Elmhurst | 77-20 21st Ave. (77th St.) | Queens | N/W to Astoria/Ditmars Blvd. | 718-777-5303

The "Greek-style" Kesso yogurt churned out by Vea Kessissoglou's Elmhurst milk plant and retailer is likened to a "delicious" "gift from the Olympian gods", and its SoHo "snack" shack adds smoothies, desserts and savory pastries to the lineup; Hellenists insist anything so tasty for "only a few bucks" qualifies as a "must-try."

Yonah Schimmel
Knish Bakery 🖾 *Baked Goods*

23 | 11 | 16 | I

LES | 137 E. Houston St. (bet. 1st & 2nd Aves.) | F/V to Lower East Side/ 2nd Ave. | 212-477-2858 | www.yonahschimmel.com

A "one-of-a-kind" "old-world noshery", this Lower East Side bakery has "been around since Jonah" (well, since 1910) and "still holds its own" with "perfectly textured" "handmade knishes" in 20 "knock-out" variations – not to mention "killer" kugel and blintzes – chased with egg creams and lime rickeys; the "grumpy service" and "time-warp" setup are "the real thing", and both loyalists and moviegoers at the nearby Sunshine Cinemas "hope they last forever."

Yorkshire
Wines & Spirits 🌑🖾 *Wine/Liquor*

23 | 18 | 22 | M

E 80s | 1646 First Ave. (85th St.) | 4/5/6 to 86th St. | 212-717-5100 | www.yorkshirewines.com

"Wines for all budgets and tastes" are the hallmark of this 25-year Yorkville vet, where the "wide selection" concentrates on California, France and Italy and provides those on "moderate" budgets with plenty to choose from; enthusiasts are equally impressed with a floor team that "goes out of its way to be helpful"; P.S. tastings are held on weekends.

Yorkville Meat Emporium *Meat/Poultry*

∇ 23 | 16 | 18 | M

E 80s | 1560 Second Ave. (81st St.) | 4/5/6 to 86th St. | 212-628-5147 | www.hungarianmeatmarket.com

At this "last bastion" of the "Magyar butchers" on the Upper East Side, you can expect to find "great Hungarian sausages", pork products of all kinds and, of course, "paprika galore" – not to mention take-home portions of authentic goulash, Eastern European breads (and beers), and house-baked strudels, linzertortes and the like.

Yuno's Farm 🖾 *Produce*

29 | 27 | 28 | M

See Greenmarket; for more information, call 609-723-3753

"If Martha Stewart had a farm stand" it wouldn't be any more "gorgeous" than this Bordentown, NJ, grower's Greenmarket stall where the "top-quality" lettuces and greens and other "impeccably fresh, top-notch" produce are so "beautifully displayed", "people take pictures"; among the offerings are some unusual vegetable ("amaze your friends with the latest before they're in expensive shops"), all of which happily "taste as good as they look."

🔲 Zabar's 🖾 *Major Gourmet Mkt.*

27 | 21 | 20 | M

W 80s | 2245 Broadway (bet. 80th & 81st Sts.) | 1 to 79th St. | 212-787-2000 | www.zabars.com

"The one and only" – voted NYC's No. 1 Major Gourmet Market this "thriving" Upper West Side "landmark" is a "multipurpose" "gourmet's delight" renowned as a "quintessential" source of "absolutely the best" smoked fish ("a line worth waiting in") that also boasts "delectable" baked goods "galore", an "exhaustive cheese counter", "yummy prepared foods", a "gold-standard" deli, a "amazing selection" of specialty items, "fab coffee", candy and nut and "great deals" upstairs on "a jumble" of cookware "you never knew you wanted"; the "gruff" salespeople and "chaotic" conditions "are all part of the charm" for "savvy" shoppers who also commend the "very competitive" pricing – so "accept no substitutes", and try to avoid getting hit by the customers using carts as bumper cars.

Zaitzeff ● Prepared Food

∇ 28 | 18 | 22 | M

Financial Dist | 72 Nassau St. (John St.) | J/M/Z to Fulton St. | 212-571-7272 | www.zaitzeffnyc.com

An "undiscovered killer burger joint down among Wall Street's towers", this eat-in/take-out shop specializes in "fresh", hormone-free ground sirloin and Kobe beef patties served on "the best Portuguese muffin rolls" with skillet-cooked fries and organic coffee on the side; for some, "the eats can't be beat" – ditto the "cool, fun staff."

Zarela Catering   Caterer/Events

∇ 24 | 20 | 23 | E

E 50s | 953 Second Ave. (bet. 50th & 51st Sts.) | 6 to 51st St. | 212-644-6740 | www.zarela.com

Amigos affirm the catering arm of Zarela Martinez's East Side cantina "does the best job" around at supplying all the fixings "for a fun Mexican event", with "awesome" regional cuisine laid out as lavishly or casually as you like; their crew can either set up at the restaurant or convert any corporate or private locale into an "authentic" fiesta.

Zaro's Bread Basket ▣ Baked Goods

17 | 17 | 15 | M

E 40s | Grand Central Mkt. | Lexington Ave. (43rd St.) | 4/5/6/7/S to 42nd St./Grand Central | 212-292-0160 ●
Garment Dist | Penn Station | 501 Seventh Ave. (32nd St.) | 1/2/3/A/C/E to 34th St./Penn Station | 212-575-7031
W 40s | Port Authority | 625 Eighth Ave. (bet. 40th & 41st Sts.) | A/C/E to 42nd St./Port Authority | 212-292-0185 ●
877-692-2531 | www.zaro.com

These "mass-market" bakery franchises supply the "transit hubs" with a "large selection" of breads, bagels, cookies and such, making for a "quick and easy" "commuters' crutch"; the goods are just "decent" and the "mall-ish" setups get "a bit frenetic", but they're "always there" when you're "making a dash" and "convenience is key."

Zeytuna ●▣ Major Gourmet Mkt.

∇ 23 | 21 | 16 | M

Financial Dist | 59 Maiden Ln. (William St.) | J/M/Z to Fulton St. | 212-742-2436

Locals and lunchers are attuned to this Financial District gourmet market as their "best choice" for "tasty" sandwiches and Turkish-accented prepared foods (with ample seating to enjoy them in), along with "excellent produce", a "wide variety of cheeses", "delicious" baked goods and a "decent range" of meats; paupers protest the "Wall Street prices", but it remains "one of the few" options in the area.

☒ Zezé Flowers

29 | 28 | 28 | VE

E 50s | 938 First Ave. (bet. 51st & 52nd Sts.) | 6 to 51st St. | 212-753-7767 | www.zezeflowers.com

"Whatever the season, whatever the flowers, you're the winner" at this East 50s "florist to the stars" – rated Best Overall in this Survey –

where the "low-key shop" is a dramatic contrast to the "spectacular arrangements" made from "unusual" blooms (including lots of orchids "so exquisite" they would please "Persephone herself"); the staff even "takes the time to talk with you about the recipient to try to capture the perfect mood", and although perfection "will cost you", it's "worth every last penny."

NEW **Zibetto Espresso Bar** 𝒫 *Coffee/Tea*   ▽ 26 | 21 | 24 | M

W 50s | 1385 Sixth Ave. (bet. 56th & 57th Sts.) | F to 57th St.
Maybe it's "no longer a secret", but this connoisseur's espresso stop still "seems undiscovered somehow", pulling "wow"-quality shots ("with some charming foam art to boot") in its unlikely West 50s location; its "caffeinated wonderfulness" comes in a sliver of a space that feels "perfectly European in every way" from the stand-up marble counter to the Italian sodas and biscotti to the "chic barista who remembers you with a sly, knowing nod the minute you walk in."

ZuZu's Petals *Flowers*   ▽ 26 | 27 | 24 | M

Park Slope | 158A Berkeley Pl. (bet. 6th & 7th Aves.) | Brooklyn | B/Q to 7th Ave. | 718-636-2022
Park Slope | 374 Fifth Ave. (bet. 5th & 6th Sts.) | Brooklyn | F/M/R to 4th Ave./9th St. | 718-638-0918
This "longtime favorite" has been offering "personalized service" at its two Park Slope locations for over 30 years, creating "beautiful arrangements" from "unusual, high-quality flowers, plants and ceramics"; the always-fresh stock (they don't even use refrigeration) is accompanied by a selection of linens, pottery, soaps and other gift items; N.B. in summer, purchase your annuals and perennials from Fifth Avenue's back garden.

Party Sites

The capacity (cap) figures below are only guidelines; for multi-room spaces we show the maximum capacity (max cap) of the largest space. Call ahead for pricing, and remember that most sites will negotiate.

Museums & Other Spaces

Alger House | *rooms: 1 | cap: 125*
G Village | Downing St. (bet. Bedford & 7th Ave. S.) | 212-627-8838 | www.algerhouse.com

Altman Building | *rooms: 2 | max cap: 700*
Chelsea | 135 W. 18th St. (bet. 6th & 7th Aves.) | 212-741-3400 | www.altmanbldg.com

American Museum of Natural History | *rooms: 45 | max cap: 3000*
W 70s | 79th St. & CPW | 212-769-5350 | www.amnh.org/hostanevent

Americas Society | *rooms: 3 | max cap: 120*
E 60s | 680 Park Ave. (68th St.) | 212-249-8950 | www.americas-society.org

Angel Orensanz Foundation | *rooms: 1 | cap: 550*
LES | 172 Norfolk St. (bet. E. Houston & Stanton Sts.) | 212-529-7194 | www.orensanz.org

Art Farm, The | *rooms: 1 | cap: 35*
E 90s | 419 E. 91st St. (bet. 1st & York Aves.) | 212-410-3117 | www.theartfarms.org

Astra | *rooms: 1 | cap: 300*
E 50s | 979 Third Ave., 14th fl. (bet. 58th & 59th Sts.) | 212-644-9394 | www.charliepalmer.com

Bateaux New York | *rooms: 2 | max cap: 300*
Chelsea | Chelsea Piers | Pier 61 (West Side Hwy.) | 212-352-1366 | www.bateauxnewyork.com

Boylan Studios | *rooms: 3 | max cap: 850*
Chelsea | 601 W. 26th St. (11th Ave.) | 212-924-7550 | www.boylanstudios.com

Bridgewaters | *rooms: 3 | max cap: 3000*
Seaport | 11 Fulton St. (bet. East River Piers & Seaport Plaza) | 212-608-7400 | www.theglaziergroup.com

Bronx Zoo | *rooms: 4 | max cap: 750*
Bronx | 2300 Southern Blvd. (Fordham Rd.) | 718-220-5076 | www.bronxzoo.com

Brooklyn Botanic Garden, Palm House | *rooms: 1 | cap: 300*
Prospect Heights | 1000 Washington Ave. (Montgomery St.) | Brooklyn | 718-398-2400 | www.palmhouse.com

Brooklyn Museum of Art | *rooms: 6 | max cap: 1000*
Prospect Heights | 200 Eastern Pkwy. (Washington Ave.) | Brooklyn | 718-638-5000 | www.brooklynmuseum.org

vote at zagat.com   225

Carnegie Hall Dining Rooms | *rooms: 4 | max cap: 600*
W 50s | 154 W. 57th St. (bet. 6th & 7th Aves.) | 212-903-9770 | www.carnegiehall.org

Center for Architecture | *rooms: 3 | max cap: 500*
G Village | 536 LaGuardia Pl. (Bleecker St.) | 212-683-0023 | www.aiany.org

Central Park Wildlife Center | *rooms: 4 | max cap: 1200*
E 60s | 830 Fifth Ave. (bet. 64th & 65th Sts.) | 212-439-6509 | www.wcs.org

Central Park Zoo | *rooms: 5 | max cap: 1200*
E 60s | 830 Fifth Ave. (64th St.) | 212-439-6509 | www.centralparkzoo.com

Chef's Table @ Lotus Space | *rooms: 1 | cap: 400*
E 60s | 122 W. 26th St. (bet. 6th & 7th Aves.) | 212-206-6399 | www.chefstableltd.com

Chelsea Piers Lighthouse | *rooms: 1 | cap: 800*
Chelsea | Chelsea Piers | Pier 61 (bet. 23rd St. & West Side Hwy.) | 212-336-6144 | www.piersixty.com

Chelsea Piers, Pier 60 | *rooms: 1 | cap: 2000*
Chelsea | Chelsea Piers | Pier 60 (bet. 23rd St. & West Side Hwy.) | 212-336-6144 | www.piersixty.com

Children's Museum of Manhattan | *rooms: 7 | max cap: 1200*
W 80s | 212 W. 83rd St. (bet. Amsterdam Ave. & B'way) | 212-721-1223 | www.cmom.org

Cooper Classics Collection, The | *rooms: 2 | max cap: 400*
G Village | 137 Perry St. (bet. Greenwich & Washington Sts.) | 212-929-3909 | www.cooperclassicscars.com

Council on Foreign Relations: Peterson Hall/ Harold Pratt House | *rooms: 6 | max cap: 300*
E 60s | 58 E. 68th St. (bet. Madison & Park Aves.) | 212-434-9576 | www.cfr.org

Culinary Loft | *rooms: 1 | cap: 70*
SoHo | 515 Broadway, 5th fl. (bet. Broome & Spring Sts.) | 212-431-7425 | www.culinaryloft.com

Dance New Amsterdam | *rooms: 6 | max cap: 500*
TriBeCa | 280 Broadway, 2nd fl. (bet. Chambers & Reade Sts.) | 212-625-8369 | www.dnadance.org

Delegates Dining Room | *rooms: 6 | max cap: 800*
E 40s | United Nations | 1st Ave. & 46th St. | 212-963-7625 | www.aramark-un.com

Dia Art Foundation | *rooms: 1 | cap: 450*
Chelsea | 535 W. 22nd St. (bet. 10th & 11th Aves.) | 212-989-5566 | www.diaart.org

Downtown Community Television Center | *rooms: 2 | max cap: 280*
Financial Dist | 87 Lafayette St. (bet. Walker & White Sts.) | 212-966-4510 | www.dctvny.org

Drawing Center | *rooms: 1 | cap: 250*
SoHo | 35 Wooster St. (bet. Broome & Grand Sts.) | 212-219-2166 |
www.drawingcenter.org

Drive In Studios | *rooms: 3 | max cap: 1200*
Chelsea | 443 W. 18th St. (bet. 9th & 10th Aves.) | 212-645-2244 |
www.driveinstudios.com

Elevated Acre | *rooms: 1 | cap: 1000*
Financial Dist | 55 Water St. (bet. Coenties Slip E. & Hanover Sq.) |
212-963-7099 | www.elevatedacre.com

Ellis Island
Immigration Museum | *rooms: 5 | max cap: 2000*
Ellis Island | 212-344-0996 | www.ellisisland.com

Explorers Club | *rooms: 3 | max cap: 300*
E 70s | 46 E. 70th St. (bet. Madison & Park Aves.) | 212-628-8383 |
www.manhattaneventsny.com

Eyebeam | *rooms: 1 | cap: 624*
Chelsea | 540 W. 21st St. (bet. 10th & 11th Aves.) | 212-937-6581 |
www.eyebeam.org

40/40 Club | *rooms: 6 | max cap: 730*
Chelsea | 6 W. 25th St. (bet. B'way & 5th Ave.) | 212-989-0040 |
www.the4040club.com

Foundry, The | *rooms: 1 | cap: 250*
LIC | 42-38 Ninth St. (bet. 43rd Ave. & Queens Plaza S.) | Queens |
718-786-7776 | www.thefoundry.info

Frick Collection | *rooms: 3 | max cap: 350*
E 70s | 1 E. 70th St. (5th Ave.) | 212-288-0700 | www.frick.org

Frying Pan | *rooms: 1 | cap: 270*
Chelsea | Chelsea Piers | Pier 66 (26th St. & West Side Hwy.) |
212-989-6363 | www.fryingpan.com

Georgian Suite | *rooms: 1 | cap: 150*
E 70s | 1A E. 77th St. (5th Ave.) | 212-734-1468

Glorious Food | *rooms: 1 | cap: 125*
E 70s | 522 E. 74th St. (bet. FDR Dr. & York Ave.) | 212-628-2320

Grand Central Terminal,
Northeast Balcony | *rooms: 1 | cap: 200*
E 40s | 42nd St. & Park Ave. | 212-340-3404 |
www.grandcentralterminal.com

Grand Central Terminal,
Vanderbilt Hall | *rooms: 1 | cap: 1300*
E 40s | 42nd St. & Park Ave. | 212-340-3404 |
www.grandcentralterminal.com

House of the Redeemer | *rooms: 3 | max cap: 100*
E 90s | 7 E. 95th St. (bet. 5th & Madison Aves.) | 212-289-0399 |
www.houseoftheredeemer.org

Hudson Yards Catering | *rooms: 2 | max cap: 1500*
Chelsea | Hudson Yards | 640 W. 28th St., 8th fl. (bet. 11th Ave. &
West Side Hwy.) | 212-488-1500 | www.hycnyc.com

Industria | *rooms: 9* | *max cap: 1000*
G Village | 775 Washington St. (bet. Jane & W. 12th Sts.) |
212-366-1114 | www.industrianyc.com

Institute of Culinary Education, The | *rooms: 4* | *max cap: 90*
Chelsea | 50 W. 23rd St. (bet. 5th & 6th Aves.) | 212-847-0707 |
www.iceculinary.com

Intrepid Sea-Air-Space Museum | *rooms: 10* | *max cap: 5000*
Chelsea | Pier 86 (46th St. & 12th Ave.) | 212-957-7342 |
www.intrepidmuseum.org

Italian Wine Merchants | *rooms: 2* | *max cap: 125*
Union Sq | 108 E. 16th St. (bet. Irving Pl. & Union Sq. E.) |
212-473-2323 | www.italianwinemerchant.com

Landmark on the Park | *rooms: 11* | *max cap: 600*
W 70s | 160 Central Park W. (bet. 75th & 76th Sts.) | 212-595-8410 |
www.landmarkonthepark.org

Loft 11 | *rooms: 1* | *cap: 300*
Garment Dist | 336 W. 37th St. (bet. 8th & 9th Aves.) |
212-871-0940 | www.loft11.com

Lotus Space | *rooms: 1* | *cap: 500*
Chelsea | 122 W. 26th St. (bet. 6th & 7th Aves.) | 212-463-9961 |
www.lotusspacenyc.com

Lower East Side Tenement Museum | *rooms: 2* | *max cap: 75*
LES | 91 Orchard St. (Broome St.) | 212-431-0233 |
www.tenement.org

Madame Tussaud's | *rooms: 3* | *max cap: 1000*
W 40s | 234 W. 42nd St. (bet. 7th & 8th Aves.) | 212-512-9611 |
www.madame-tussauds.com

Manhattan Center Studios | *rooms: 3* | *max cap: 3600*
Garment Dist | 311 W. 34th St. (bet. 8th & 9th Aves.) |
212-279-7740 | www.mcstudios.com

Manhattan Penthouse on Fifth Avenue | *rooms: 1* | *cap: 250*
Flatiron | 80 Fifth Ave., 17th fl. (bet. 13th & 14th Sts.) |
212-627-8838 | www.manhattanpentouse.com

Merchant's House Museum | *rooms: 2* | *max cap: 100*
G Village | 29 E. Fourth St. (bet. Bowery & Lafayette St.) |
212-777-1089 | www.merchantshouse.org

Metropolitan Museum of Art | *rooms: 4* | *max cap: 800*
E 80s | 1000 Fifth Ave. (82nd St.) | 212-570-3773 |
www.metmuseum.org

Metropolitan Pavilion | *rooms: 4* | *max cap: 1500*
Flatiron | 125 W. 18th St. (bet. 6th & 7th Aves.) | 212-463-0071 |
www.metropolitanevents.com

Michelson Studio | *rooms: 1* | *cap: 200*
G Village | 163 Bank St. (bet. Washington St. & West Side Hwy.) |
212-633-1111 | www.michelsonstudio.com

Milk Studios | *rooms: 3* | *max cap: 650*
Chelsea | 450 W. 15th St., 1st fl. (bet. 9th & 10th Aves.) |
212-645-2797 | www.milkstudios.com

Morgan Library & Museum | *rooms: 8 | max cap: 800*
Murray Hill | 225 Madison Ave. (bet. 36th & 37th Sts.) |
212-685-0008 | www.morganlibrary.org

Morrell Tasting Room | *rooms: 1 | cap: 60*
E 60s | Morell & Co. | 729 Seventh Ave. (bet. 48th & 49th Sts.) |
212-688-9370 | www.morrellwine.com

Morris-Jumel Mansion | *rooms: 3 | max cap: 35*
Harlem | 65 Jumel Terrace (bet. 160th & 162nd Sts.) | 212-923-8008 |
www.morrisjumel.org

**Mount Vernon Hotel, Museum & Garden and the
Abigail Adams Smith Auditorium** | *rooms: 5 | max cap: 250*
E 60s | 417-421 E. 61st St. (bet. 1st & York Aves.) | 212-838-7225 |
www.mvhm.org

Museum of Arts & Design | *rooms: 1 | cap: 500*
W 50s | 40 W. 53rd St. (bet. 5th & 6th Aves.) | 212-956-3535 |
www.americancraftmuseum.org

Museum of Jewish Heritage | *rooms: 2 | max cap: 1000*
Financial Dist | Battery Park City | 36 Battery Pl. (Little West St.) |
646-437-4206 | www.mjhnyc.org

Museum of the City of New York | *rooms: 3 | max cap: 500*
E 90s | 1220 Fifth Ave. (103rd St.) | 212-534-1672, ext. 3309 |
www.mcny.org

Nansen Park/A Taste of Honey | *rooms: 3 | max cap: 910*
Staten Island | 3465 Victory Blvd. (Signs Rd.) | 718-983-0464 |
www.tasteofhoney.com

National Academy Museum | *rooms: 3 | max cap: 225*
E 80s | 1083 Fifth Ave. (bet. 89th & 90th Sts.) | 212-369-4880 |
www.nationalacademy.org

**National Museum
of the American Indian** | *rooms: 9 | max cap: 1500*
Financial Dist | 1 Bowling Green (State St.) | 212-514-3820 |
www.americanindian.si.edu

NBC Experience Store | *rooms: 1 | cap: 500*
W 40s | 30 Rockefeller Plaza (bet. 49th & 50th Sts.) | 212-664-6452 |
www.nbcuniversalstore.com

New York Academy of Sciences | *rooms: 4 | max cap: 300*
Financial Dist | 7 World Trade Center | 250 Greenwich St.
(bet. Barclay & Vesey Sts.) | 212-838-0230 | www.nyas.org/
hostanevent

New York Aquarium | *rooms: 7 | max cap: 5000*
Coney Island | 602 Surf Ave. (W. 8th St.) | Brooklyn | 718-265-3427 |
www.nyaquarium.com

New York Botanical Garden | *rooms: 2 | max cap: 470*
Bronx | Southern Blvd. & 200th St. | 718-220-0300 |
www.abigailkirsch.com

New York City Bar Association | *rooms: 12 | max cap: 900*
W 40s | 42 W. 44th St. (bet. 5th & 6th Aves.) | 212-382-6637 |
www.nycbar.org

New York City Fire Museum | *rooms: 1* | *cap: 300*
SoHo | 278 Spring St. (bet. Hudson & Varick Sts.) | 212-691-1303 |
www.nycfiremuseum.org

New-York Historical Society | *rooms: 1* | *cap: 500*
W 70s | 2 W. 77th St. (CPW) | 212-873-3466 |
www.nyhistory.org

New York Public Library | *rooms: 4* | *max cap: 750*
E 40s | Fifth Ave. & 42nd St. | 212-930-0730 | www.nypl.org/spacerental

New York State Theater | *rooms: 1* | *cap: 1000*
W 60s | 20 Lincoln Ctr. (62nd St.) | 212-870-5567

91 – The Upper Crust | *rooms: 1* | *cap: 150*
G Village | 91 Horatio St. (bet. Washington St. & West Side Hwy.) |
212-691-4570 | www.tucnyc.com

Party Loft | *rooms: 1* | *cap: 100*
Flatiron | 73 Fifth Ave. (15th St.) | 212-620-0622 |
www.thepartyloft.com

Pasanella & Son, Vintners | *rooms: 1* | *cap: 250*
Seaport | 115 South St. (bet. Beekman St. & Peck Slip) |
212-233-8383 | www.pasanellaandson.com

Penthouse 15 | *rooms: 1* | *cap: 250*
Garment Dist | 336 W. 37th St. (bet. 8th & 9th Aves.) |
212-871-0940 | www.penthouse15.com

Picnic House in Prospect Park | *rooms: 1* | *cap: 250*
Park Slope | 95 Prospect Park W. (5th St.) | Brooklyn | 718-287-6215 |
www.prospectpark.org

Pratt Mansions | *rooms: 2* | *max cap: 150*
E 80s | 1027 Fifth Ave. (bet. 83rd & 84th Sts.) | 212-744-4486, ext. 173 |
www.prattmansions.org

Primal Light Studios | *rooms: 1* | *cap: 125*
Chelsea | 64 Wooster (Broome St.) | 212-741-8000 |
www.primallight.com

Puck Building | *rooms: 2* | *max cap: 1400*
SoHo | 295 Lafayette St. (Houston St.) | 212-274-8900 |
www.thepuckbuilding.com

Radio City Music Hall | *rooms: 15* | *max cap: 5900*
W 50s | 1260 Sixth Ave. (bet. 50th & 51st Sts.) | 212-465-6106 |
www.radiocity.com

Reception House | *rooms: 3* | *max cap: 250*
Flushing | 167-17 Northern Blvd. (167th St.) | Queens |
718-463-1600 | www.receptionhouse.com

Scandinavia House | *rooms: 6* | *max cap: 175*
Murray Hill | 58 Park Ave. (bet. 37th & 38th Sts.) | 212-879-9779 |
www.scandinaviahouse.org

632 on Hudson | *rooms: 1* | *cap: 175*
W Village | 632 Hudson St. (Horatio St.) | 212-620-7631 |
www.632onhudson.com

PARTY SITES – MUSEUMS & OTHER SPACES

Skylight | *rooms: 1* | *cap: 1000*
G Village | 275 Hudson St. (Spring St.) | 212-367-3730 |
www.skylightnyc.com

Sky Studios | *rooms: 2* | *max cap: 300*
G Village | 704A Broadway (bet. 4th St. & Washington Pl.) |
212-533-3030 | www.skystudios.com

South Oxford Space | *rooms: 1* | *cap: 74*
Brooklyn Heights | 138 S. Oxford St. (bet. Atlantic Ave. & Fulton St.) |
Brooklyn | 718-398-3078 | www.offbroadwayonline.com

Spirit Cruises | *rooms: 1* | *cap: 600*
Chelsea | Chelsea Piers | Pier 61 (23rd St. & West Side Hwy.) |
212-727-2789 | www.spiritcruises.com

Splashlight Studios | *rooms: 1* | *cap: 500*
Garment Dist | 529-535 W. 35th St. (bet. 10th & 11th Aves.) |
212-268-7247 | www.splashlightstudios.com

St. Bartholomew's Church | *rooms: 5* | *max cap: 350*
E 50s | 109 E. 50th St. (Park Ave.) | 212-378-0254 |
www.stbarts.org

Studio 450 | *rooms: 1* | *cap: 400*
Garment Dist | 450 W. 31st St. (bet. 9th & 10th Aves.) |
212-290-1400 | www.studio450.com

Sun Factory | *rooms: 1* | *cap: 200*
TriBeCa | 394 Broadway (Walker St.) | 212-965-1213 |
www.sunfactory.com

Toys "R" Us Times Square | *rooms: 2* | *max cap: 300*
W 40s | 1514 Broadway (44th St.) | 646-366-8800 |
www.toysrustimessquare.com

Tribeca Rooftop | *rooms: 1* | *cap: 400*
TriBeCa | 2 Desbrosses St. (bet. Greenwich & Hudson Sts.) |
212-625-2600 | www.tribec.com

Ukrainian Institute of America | *rooms: 3* | *max cap: 250*
E 70s | 2 E. 79th St. (bet. 5th & Madison Aves.) | 212-288-8660 |
www.ukrainianinstitute.org

Union Ballroom | *rooms: 1* | *cap: 200*
W 100s | 3041 Broadway (121st St.) | 212-280-1345 |
www.showstoppersny.com

Union Square Ballroom | *rooms: 2* | *max cap: 475*
Union Sq | 27 Union Sq. W. (bet. 15th & 16th Sts.) | 212-645-1802 |
www.unionsquareballroom.com

Union Square Wines & Spirits | *rooms: 1* | *cap: 60*
Union Sq | 140 Fourth Ave. (13th St.) | 212-675-8100 |
www.unionsquarewines.com

Villa Barone | *rooms: 2* | *max cap: 600*
Bronx | 737 Throgs Neck Expwy. (bet. Philip & Randall Aves.) |
718-892-3500 | www.villabaronemanor.com

Vintage New York | *rooms: 2* | *max cap: 85*
SoHo | 482 Broome St. (Wooster St.) | 212-226-9463 |
www.vintagenewyork.com

Wave Hill | *rooms: 1* | *cap: 180*
Bronx | 675 W. 252nd St. (enter on W. 249th St. at Independence Ave.) |
718-549-3200 | www.wavehill.org

Westside Loft | *rooms: 1* | *cap: 450*
Garment Dist | 336 W. 37th St., 6th fl. (bet. 8th & 9th Aves.) |
212-871-0940 | www.thewestsideloft.com

Whitney Museum | *rooms: 5* | *max cap: 500*
E 70s | 945 Madison Ave. (bet. 74th & 75th Sts.) |
212-570-3600, ext. 388 | www.whitney.org

World Financial Center:
Winter Garden & Plaza | *rooms: 2* | *max cap: 1800*
Financial Dist | 250 Vesey St. (North End Ave.) | 212-417-7143 |
www.rentals.worldfinancialcenter.com

World Yacht | *rooms: 3* | *max cap: 500*
W 40s | Pier 81 (41st St. & West Side Hwy.) | 212-630-8800 |
www.worldyacht.com

Hotels

Alex Hotel | *rooms: 1* | *cap: 50*
E 40s | 205 E. 45th St. (3rd Ave.) | 212-850-6302 |
www.thealexhotel.com

Algonquin | *rooms: 4* | *max cap: 200*
W 40s | 59 W. 44th St. (bet. 5th & 6th Aves.) | 212-840-6800 |
www.algonquinhotel.com

Beekman Tower | *rooms: 1* | *cap: 125*
E 40s | 3 Mitchell Pl. (49th St.) | 212-355-7300 |
www.affinia.com

Bryant Park | *rooms: 2* | *max cap: 300*
W 40s | 40 W. 40th St. (bet. 5th & 6th Aves.) | 212-869-0100 |
www.bryantparkhotel.com

Carlton | *rooms: 7* | *max cap: 175*
Gramercy | 88 Madison Ave. (bet. 28th & 29th Sts.) | 212-532-4100 |
www.carltonhotelny.com

Carlyle | *rooms: 2* | *max cap: 500*
E 70s | 35 E. 76th St. (Madison Ave.) | 212-570-7106 |
www.thecarlyle.com

Crowne Plaza Manhattan | *rooms: 34* | *max cap: 700*
W 50s | 1605 Broadway (bet. 48th & 49th Sts.) | 212-977-4000 |
www.manhattan.crowneplaza.com

DoubleTree Guest Suites | *rooms: 6* | *max cap: 200*
W 40s | 1568 Broadway (47th St.) | 212-719-1600 |
www.nyc.doubletreehotels.com

Dream Hotel | *rooms: 4* | *max cap: 300*
W 50s | 210 W. 55th St. (bet. B'way & 7th Ave.) | 212-974-1934 |
www.dreamny.com

Flatotel | *rooms: 4* | *max cap: 400*
W 50s | 135 W. 52nd St. (bet. 6th & 7th Aves.) | 212-887-9515 |
www.flatotel.com

Gansevoort | *rooms: 4* | *max cap: 250*
Meatpacking | 18 Ninth Ave. (13th St.) | 212-206-6700 |
www.hotelgansevoort.com

Giraffe | *rooms: 1* | *cap: 60*
Gramercy | 365 Park Ave. S. (26th St.) | 212-685-7700 |
www.hotelgiraffe.com

Grand Hyatt New York | *rooms: 25* | *max cap: 1700*
E 40s | 109 E. 42nd St. (Park Ave.) | 646-213-6640 |
www.hyatt.com

Helmsley Park Lane | *rooms: 10* | *max cap: 400*
W 50s | 36 Central Park S. (bet. 5th & 6th Aves.) | 212-521-6203 |
www.helmsleyparklane.com

**Hilton New York
and Towers** | *rooms: 53* | *max cap: 3300*
W 50s | 1335 Sixth Ave. (bet. 53rd & 54th Sts.) | 212-261-5790 |
www.hilton.com

Hotel on Rivington, The | *rooms: 4* | *max cap: 125*
LES | 107 Rivington St. (bet. Essex & Ludlow Sts.) | 212-475-2600 |
www.hotelonrivington.com

Hudson Hotel | *rooms: 8* | *max cap: 300*
W 50s | 356 W. 58th St. (bet. 8th & 9th Aves.) | 212-554-6309 |
www.morganshotelgroup.com

Inn at Irving Place | *rooms: 3* | *max cap: 55*
(aka Lady Mendl's)
Union Sq | 56 Irving Pl. (bet. 17th & 18th Sts.) | 212-533-4466 |
www.innatirving.com

**Inter-Continental,
Barclay NY** | *rooms: 18* | *max cap: 320*
E 40s | 111 E. 48th St. (bet. Lexington & Park Aves.) | 212-906-3124 |
www.interconti.com

Jumeirah Essex House | *rooms: 12* | *max cap: 500*
W 50s | 160 Central Park S. (bet. 6th & 7th Aves.) | 212-484-5144 |
www.jumeirahessexhouse.com

Kitano New York, The | *rooms: 1* | *cap: 146*
Murray Hill | 66 Park Ave. (38th St.) | 212-885-7017 |
www.kitano.com

Le Parker Meridien | *rooms: 9* | *max cap: 800*
W 50s | 118 W. 57th St. (bet. 6th & 7th Aves.) | 212-708-7450 |
www.parkermeridien.com

Library Hotel | *rooms: 1* | *cap: 100*
E 40s | 299 Madison Ave. (41st St.) | 212-983-4500 |
www.libraryhotel.com

Lowell, The | *rooms: 1* | *cap: 75*
E 60s | 28 E. 63rd St. (bet. Madison & Park Aves.) | 212-605-6825 |
www.lowellhotel.com

Mandarin Oriental | *rooms: 3* | *max cap: 900*
W 60s | Time Warner Ctr. | 80 Columbus Circle (60th St.) |
212-805-8800 | www.mandarinoriental.com

Maritime Hotel, The | *rooms: 9* | *max cap: 2475*
Chelsea | 363 W. 16th St. (bet. 8th & 9th Aves.) | 212-242-4300 | www.themaritimehotel.com

Marriott Financial Center | *rooms: 13* | *max cap: 450*
Financial Dist | 85 West St. (Carlisle St.) | 212-266-6145 | www.nymarriottfinancialcenter.com

Millennium Broadway | *rooms: 15* | *max cap: 730*
W 40s | 145 W. 44th St. (bet. B'way & 6th Ave.) | 212-789-7546 | www.millenniumhotels.com

Millennium UN Plaza | *rooms: 7* | *max cap: 300*
E 40s | 1 United Nations Plaza (1st Ave. & 44th St.) | 212-758-1234 | www.millenniumhotels.com/unplaza

Morgans | *rooms: 3* | *max cap: 75*
Murray Hill | 237 Madison Ave. (bet. 37th & 38th Aves.) | 212-686-0300 | www.morganshotelgroup.com

Muse, The | *rooms: 4* | *max cap: 100*
W 40s | 130 W. 46th St. (bet. 6th & 7th Aves.) | 212-485-2400 | www.themusehotel.com

New York Marriott Marquis | *rooms: 58* | *max cap: 2800*
W 40s | 1535 Broadway (bet. 45th & 46th Sts.) | 212-398-1900 | www.marriott.com

New York Palace | *rooms: 13* | *max cap: 300*
E 50s | 455 Madison Ave. (bet. 50th & 51st Sts.) | 212-303-7766 | www.newyorkpalace.com

Night Hotel | *rooms: 1* | *cap: 150*
W 40s | 132 W. 45th St. (bet. 6th & 7th Aves.) | 212-835-9600 | www.nighthotelny.com

Omni Berkshire Place | *rooms: 10* | *max cap: 120*
E 50s | 21 E. 52nd St. (bet. 5th & Madison Aves.) | 212-754-5090 | www.omnihotels.com

Paramount | *rooms: 1* | *cap: 75*
W 40s | 235 W. 46th St. (bet. B'way & 8th Ave.) | 212-764-5500 | www.nycparamount.com

Peninsula, The | *rooms: 6* | *max cap: 200*
E 50s | 700 Fifth Ave. (55th St.) | 212-903-3072 | www.peninsula.com

Pierre, The | *rooms: 6* | *max cap: 1200*
E 60s | 2 E. 61st St. (5th Ave.) | 212-940-8111 | www.fourseasons.com

Plaza Athénée | *rooms: 4* | *max cap: 150*
E 60s | 37 E. 64th St. (bet. Madison & Park Aves.) | 212-606-4663 | www.plaza-athenee.com

Regency | *rooms: 3* | *max cap: 200*
E 60s | 540 Park Ave. (61st St.) | 212-759-4100 | www.loewsregency.com

Ritz-Carlton, Battery Park | *rooms: 10* | *max cap: 500*
Financial Dist | 2 West St. (bet. Battery Pl. & South St.) | 917-790-2400 | www.ritzcarlton.com

PARTY SITES – NIGHTCLUBS/BARS

Ritz-Carlton, Central Park | *rooms: 3* | *max cap: 155*
W 50s | 50 Central Park S. (bet. 5th & 6th Aves.) | 212-308-9100 |
www.ritzcarlton.com

70 Park Avenue | *rooms: 3* | *max cap: 100*
Murray Hill | 70 Park Ave. (38th St.) | 212-973-2400 |
www.70parkave.com

60 Thompson | *rooms: 3* | *max cap: 150*
SoHo | 60 Thompson St. (bet. Broome & Spring Sts.) | 212-431-0400 |
www.60thompson.com

Soho Grand | *rooms: 7* | *max cap: 350*
SoHo | 310 W. Broadway (bet. Canal & Grand Sts.) | 212-519-6666 |
www.sohogrand.com

St. Regis | *rooms: 15* | *max cap: 220*
E 50s | 2 E. 55th St. (bet. 5th & Madison Aves.) | 212-339-6776 |
www.stregis.com

Tribeca Grand | *rooms: 6* | *max cap: 400*
TriBeCa | 2 Sixth Ave. (Church St.) | 212-519-6666 |
www.tribecagrand.com

Waldorf-Astoria | *rooms: 40* | *max cap: 1500*
E 40s | 301 Park Ave. (bet. 49th & 50th Sts.) | 212-872-4700 |
www.waldorf.com

Westin Times Square | *rooms: 40* | *max cap: 330*
W 40s | 270 W. 43rd St. (8th Ave.) | 212-201-2700 |
www.westinny.com

W New York | *rooms: 12* | *max cap: 500*
E 50s | 541 Lexington Ave. (bet. 49th & 50th Sts.) | 212-755-1200 |
www.whotels.com

W The Court | *rooms: 9* | *max cap: 130*
Murray Hill | 130 E. 39th St. (Lexington Ave.) | 212-592-8820 |
www.whotels.com

W Times Square | *rooms: 6* | *max cap: 150*
W 40s | 1567 Broadway (47th St.) | 212-930-7404 |
www.whotels.com

W Union Square | *rooms: 6* | *max cap: 500*
Union Sq | 201 Park Ave. S. (17th St.) | 917-534-5900 |
www.whotels.com

Nightclubs/Bars

For additional listings, see Zagat NYC Nightlife.

APT | *rooms: 2* | *max cap: 300*
Meatpacking | 419 W. 13th St. (bet. 9th Ave. & Washington St.) |
212-414-4245 | www.aptwebsite.com

Aspen | *rooms: 3* | *max cap: 350*
Flatiron | 30 W. 22nd St. (bet. 5th & 6th Aves.) | 212-645-5040 |
www.aspen-nyc.com

Avalon | *rooms: 3* | *max cap: 1557*
Chelsea | 660 Sixth Ave. (bet. 20th & 21st Sts.) | 212-807-7780 |
www.nyavalon.com

Blue Owl | *rooms: 3* | *max cap: 120*
E Village | 196 Second Ave. (bet. 12th & 13th Sts.) | 212-505-2583 |
www.blueowlnyc.com

BLVD | *rooms: 4* | *max cap: 1500*
SoHo | 199 Bowery St. (Spring St.) | 212-982-7767 |
www.blvdnyc.com

Bowlmor | *rooms: 1* | *cap: 600*
G Village | 110 University Pl. (bet. 12th & 13th Sts.) | 212-255-8188 |
www.bowlmor.com

Bubble Lounge | *rooms: 2* | *max cap: 300*
TriBeCa | 228 W. Broadway (bet. Franklin & White Sts.) |
212-431-3433 | www.bubblelounge.com

Buddha Bar | *rooms: 1* | *cap: 1000*
Meatpacking | 25 Little W. 12th St. (bet. 9th Ave. & Washington St.) |
212-647-7315 | www.buddhabarnyc.com

Butter | *rooms: 2* | *max cap: 300*
G Village | 415 Lafayette St. (bet. Astor Pl. & 4th St.) | 212-253-2828 |
www.butterrestaurant.com

Campbell Apartment, The | *rooms: 1* | *cap: 125*
E 40s | Grand Central Terminal | 15 Vanderbilt Ave. (bet. 42nd &
43rd Sts.) | 212-980-9476 | www.hospitalityholdings.com

Canal Room | *rooms: 1* | *cap: 450*
SoHo | 285 W. Broadway (Canal St.) | 212-941-8100, ext. 104 |
www.canalroom.com

Capitale | *rooms: 3* | *max cap: 1500*
SoHo | 130 Bowery (bet. Broome & Grand Sts.) | 212-334-5500 |
www.capitaleny.com

Carnegie Club | *rooms: 2* | *max cap: 150*
W 50s | 156 W. 56th St. (bet. 6th & 7th Aves.) | 212-957-9676 |
www.hospitalityholdings.com

China Club and The Jade Terrace | *rooms: 3* | *max cap: 1200*
W 40s | 268 W. 47th St. (bet. B'way & 8th Ave.) | 212-398-3800 |
www.chinaclubnyc.com

Cotton Club | *rooms: 1* | *cap: 175*
Harlem | 656 W. 125th St. (12th Ave.) | 212-663-7980 |
www.cottonclub-newyork.com

Delancey, The | *rooms: 5* | *max cap: 700*
LES | 168 Delancey St. (bet. Attorney & Clinton Sts.) | 212-254-9920 |
www.thedelancey.com

Duvet | *rooms: 2* | *max cap: 1275*
Flatiron | 45 W. 21st St. (bet. 5th & 6th Aves.) | 212-989-2121 |
www.duvetny.com

Flûte
rooms: 2 | *max cap: 125*
Gramercy | 40 E. 20th St. (bet. B'way & Park Ave. S.) | 212-529-7870
rooms: 1 | *cap: 100*
W 50s | 205 W. 54th St. (bet. B'way & 7th Ave.) | 212-265-5169
www.flutebar.com

Galapagos | *rooms: 1 | cap: 300*
Williamsburg | 70 N. Sixth St. (bet. Kent & Wythe Aves.) | Brooklyn | 718-384-4577 | www.galapagosartspace.com

Glass | *rooms: 1 | cap: 150*
Chelsea | 287 10th Ave. (bet. 26th & 27th Sts.) | 212-904-1580 | www.glassloungenyc.com

Happy Ending | *rooms: 2 | max cap: 250*
E Village | 302 Broome St. (bet. Eldridge & Forsythe Sts.) | 212-334-9676 | www.happyendinglounge.com

Latitude | *rooms: 4 | max cap: 300*
W 40s | 783 Eighth Ave. (bet. 47th & 48th Sts.) | 212-245-3034 | www.latitudebarnyc.com

Madame X | *rooms: 2 | max cap: 150*
G Village | 94 W. Houston St. (bet. La Guardia Pl. & Thompson St.) | 917-568-9069 | www.madamex.com

Mercury Lounge | *rooms: 1 | cap: 250*
LES | 217 E. Houston St. (bet. Essex & Ludlow Sts.) | 212-260-4700 | www.mercuryloungenyc.com

Nikki Midtown | *rooms: 2 | max cap: 468*
E 50s | 151 E. 50th St. (bet. Lexington & 3rd Aves.) | 212-753-1144 | www.nikkibeach.com

Pink Elephant | *rooms: 1 | cap: 360*
Chelsea | 527 W. 27th St. (bet. 10th & 11th Aves.) | 212-463-0000 | www.pinkelephantclub.com

PM | *rooms: 1 | cap: 490*
G Village | 50 Gansevoort St. (bet. Greenwich & Washington Sts.) | 212-255-6676 | www.pmloungenyc.com

Pressure | *rooms: 6 | max cap: 600*
G Village | 110 University Pl., 5th fl. (bet. 12th & 13th Sts.) | 212-255-8188 | www.pressurenyc.com

Providence/Triumph Room | *rooms: 3 | max cap: 1200*
W 50s | 311 W. 57th St. (bet. 8th & 9th Aves.) | 212-505-7400 | www.providencenyc.com

PS 450 | *rooms: 3 | max cap: 350*
Murray Hill | 450 Park Ave. S. (bet. 30th & 31st Sts.) | 212-532-7474 | www.ps450.com

Roseland Ballroom | *rooms: 1 | cap: 2500*
W 50s | 239 W. 52nd St. (bet. B'way & 8th Ave.) | 212-489-8350 | www.roselandballroom.com

S.O.B.'s | *rooms: 2 | max cap: 400*
SoHo | 204 Varick St. (Houston St.) | 212-645-2577 | www.sobs.com

Spice Market | *rooms: 4 | max cap: 222*
Meatpacking | 403 W. 13th St. (9th Ave.) | 212-675-2322 | www.jean-georges.com

Spy Bar | *rooms: 2 | max cap: 700*
Flatiron | 17 W. 19th St. (bet. 5th & 6th Aves.) | 212-352-2001 | www.spyclubnyc.com

Stone Rose | *rooms: 2* | *max cap: 500*
W 50s | Time Warner Ctr. | 10 Columbus Circle, 4th fl. (59th St.) | 212-750-6361 | www.mocbars.com

T New York | *rooms: 3* | *max cap: 750*
W 50s | 240 W. 52nd St. (bet. B'way & 8th Ave.) | 212-489-7656 | www.tnewyorkcity.com

Tonic Times Square | *rooms: 3* | *max cap: 500*
W 40s | 727 Seventh Ave. (bet. 48th & 49th Sts.) | 212-382-1059 | www.thetonicbar.com

230 Fifth | *rooms: 5* | *max cap: 1200*
Chelsea | 230 Fifth Ave., penthouse (bet. 26th & 27th Sts.) | 212-725-4300 | www.230fifthave.com

Via | *rooms: 1* | *cap: 100*
Flatiron | 16 W. 21st St. (bet. 5th & 6th Aves.) | 212-645-5032 | www.viarestaurantnyc.com

Webster Hall | *rooms: 5* | *max cap: 3000*
E Village | 125 E. 11th St. (bet. 3rd & 4th Aves.) | 212-353-1600 | www.websterhall.com

World Bar, The | *rooms: 1* | *cap: 125*
E 40s | Trump World Tower | 845 United Nations Plaza (48th St.) | 212-980-9476 | www.hospitalityholdings.com

Private Clubs

Members only, or nonmembers with sponsorship

Branch | *rooms: 1* | *cap: 450*
E 50s | 226 E. 54th St. (3rd Ave.) | 212-688-5577 | www.branchny.com

National Arts Club, The | *rooms: 7* | *max cap: 300*
Gramercy | 15 Gramercy Park S. (Irving Pl.) | 212-475-3424 | www.nationalartsclub.org

Players Club | *rooms: 4* | *max cap: 350*
Union Sq | 16 Gramercy Park S. (Irving Pl.) | 212-475-6116 | www.theplayersnyc.org

Williams Club | *rooms: 9* | *max cap: 200*
Murray Hill | 24 E. 39th St. (Madison Ave.) | 212-697-5300 | www.williamsclub.org

Yale Club | *rooms: 11* | *max cap: 400*
E 40s | 50 Vanderbilt Ave. (bet. 44th & 45th Sts.) | 212-716-2122 | www.yaleclubnyc.org

Restaurants

For additional listings, see Zagat NYC Restaurants.

Alto | *rooms: 2* | *max cap: 24*
E 50s | 11 E. 53rd St. (bet. 5th & Madison Aves.) | 212-308-1099 | www.altorestaurant.com | Northern Italian

American Girl Place Café | *rooms: 2* | *max cap: 40*
E 40s | 609 Fifth Ave. (49th St.) | 212-371-2220 | www.americangirlplace.com | American

PARTY SITES – RESTAURANTS

Arium | *rooms: 1* | *cap: 65*
Meatpacking | 31 Little W. 12th St. (bet. 9th & Washington Sts.) | 212-463-8630 | www.ariumnyc.com | British

Bar Americain | *rooms: 1* | *cap: 50*
W 50s | 152 W. 52nd St. (bet. 6th & 7th Aves.) | 212-265-9700 | www.baramericain.com | American

Barbetta | *rooms: 4* | *max cap: 140*
W 40s | 321 W. 46th St. (bet. 8th & 9th Aves.) | 212-246-9171 | www.barbettarestaurant.com | Italian

Battery Gardens | *rooms: 2* | *max cap: 250*
Financial Dist | Battery Park (opp. 17 State St.) | 212-809-5508 | www.batterygardens.com | American/Continental

Bayard's | *rooms: 9* | *max cap: 1000*
Financial Dist | 1 Hanover Sq. (bet. Pearl & Stone Sts.) | 212-514-9454 | www.bayards.com | American/French

Beacon | *rooms: 1* | *cap: 200*
W 50s | 25 W. 56th St. (bet. 5th & 6th Aves.) | 212-332-0500 | www.beaconnyc.com | New American

Becco | *rooms: 3* | *max cap: 110*
W 40s | 355 W. 46th St. (bet. 8th & 9th Aves.) | 212-397-7597 | www.becconyc.com | Northern Italian

Bill's Gay '90s | *rooms: 2* | *max cap: 100*
E 50s | 57 E. 54th St. (bet. Madison & Park Aves.) | 212-355-0243 | www.billsnyc.com | American

BLT Fish | *rooms: 1* | *cap: 65*
Flatiron | 21 W. 17th St. (bet. 5th & 6th Aves.) | 212-691-8888 | www.bltfish.com | Seafood

BLT Prime | *rooms: 2* | *max cap: 250*
Gramercy | 111 E. 22nd St. (bet. Lexington Ave. & Park Ave. S.) | 212-995-8500 | www.bltprime.com | New American

BLT Steak | *rooms: 1* | *cap: 32*
E 50s | 106 E. 57th St. (Park Ave.) | 212-752-7470 | www.bltsteak.com | New American/Steakhouse

Blue Fin | *rooms: 3* | *max cap: 195*
W 40s | 1567 Broadway (bet. 47th & 48th Sts.) | 212-918-1400 | www.brguestrestaurants.com | Seafood

Blue Hill | *rooms: 2* | *max cap: 65*
G Village | 75 Washington Pl. (bet. 6th Ave. & Washington Sq. W.) | 212-539-1776 | www.bluehillnyc.com | New American

Blue Smoke | *rooms: 2* | *max cap: 480*
Gramercy | 116 E. 27th St. (bet. Lexington & Park Aves.) | 212-447-7733 | www.bluesmoke.com | BBQ

Blue Water Grill | *rooms: 3* | *max cap: 300*
Union Sq | 31 Union Sq. W. (16th St.) | 212-675-9500 | www.brguestrestaurants.com | Seafood

Bottega del Vino | *rooms: 3* | *max cap: 255*
E 50s | 7 E. 59th St. (bet. 5th & Madison Aves.) | 212-223-3028 | www.bottegadelvinonyc.com | Italian

Brasserie Julien | *rooms: 1* | *cap: 120*
E 80s | 1422 Third Ave. (bet. 80th & 81st Sts.) | 212-744-6327 |
www.brasseriejulien.com | French Brasserie

Brasserie Ruhlmann | *rooms: 1* | *cap: 280*
W 50s | 45 Rockefeller Plaza (bet. 5th & 6th Aves.) | 212-974-2020 |
www.brasserieruhlmann.com | French Brasserie

Bryant Park Grill/Cafe | *rooms: 4* | *max cap: 1500*
W 40s | 25 W. 40th St. (bet. 5th & 6th Aves.) | 212-206-8815 |
www.arkrestaurants.com | American

Bubba Gump Shrimp Co. | *rooms: 1* | *cap: 360*
W 40s | 1501 Broadway (44th St.) | 212-391-7100 |
www.bubbagump.com | Seafood

Buddakan | *rooms: 4* | *max cap: 700*
Chelsea | 75 Ninth Ave. (bet. 15th & 16th Sts.) | 212-989-6699 |
www.buddakannyc.com | Asian Fusion/Chinese

Butterfield 8 | *rooms: 2* | *max cap: 250*
Murray Hill | 5 E. 38th St. (bet. 5th & Madison Aves.) | 212-679-0646 |
www.butterfield8nyc.com | American

Cafe Fiorello | *rooms: 2* | *max cap: 235*
W 60s | 1900 Broadway (63rd St.) | 212-265-0100 |
www.thefiremangroup.com | Italian

Café Gray | *rooms: 3* | *max cap: 300*
W 50s | Time Warner Ctr. | 10 Columbus Circle, 3rd fl.
(60th St.) | 212-823-6338 | www.cafegray.com | French
Brasserie

Calle Ocho | *rooms: 1* | *cap: 350*
W 80s | 446 Columbus Ave. (bet. 81st & 82nd Sts.) | 212-873-5025 |
www.calleochonyc.com | Pan-Latin

Cellini | *rooms: 2* | *max cap: 100*
E 50s | 65 E. 54th St. (bet. Madison & Park Aves.) | 212-751-1555 |
www.cellinirestaurant.com | Northern Italian

Central Park Boathouse | *rooms: 1* | *cap: 1500*
E 70s | Central Park | E. 72nd St. (Central Park Dr. N.) |
212-517-2233 | www.thecentralparkboathouse.com |
New American

Chinatown Brasserie | *rooms: 2* | *max cap: 168*
NoHo | 380 Lafayette St. (Great Jones St.) | 212-533-7000 |
www.chinatownbrasserie.com | Chinese

Chin Chin | *rooms: 2* | *max cap: 80*
SoHo | 216 E. 49th St. (bet. 2nd & 3rd Aves.) | 212-888-4555 |
Chinese

Cipriani Dolci | *rooms: 1* | *cap: 850*
E 40s | 110 E. 42nd St. (bet. Lexington & Park Aves.) |
212-499-0599 | www.cipriani.com | Italian

City Hall | *rooms: 3* | *max cap: 415*
TriBeCa | 131 Duane St. (bet. Church St. & W. B'way) |
212-964-4118 | www.cityhallnewyork.com | American

PARTY SITES - RESTAURANTS

Compass | *rooms: 3* | *max cap: 165*
W 50s | 208 W. 70th St. (bet. Amsterdam & West End Aves.) |
212-875-8600 | www.compassrestaurant.com | New American

Cowgirl | *rooms: 3* | *max cap: 135*
G Village | 519 Hudson St. (10th St.) | 212-633-1133 |
www.cowgirlnyc.com | Southwestern

Craftsteak | *rooms: 1* | *cap: 300*
Chelsea | 85 10th Ave. (bet. 15th & 16th Sts.) | 212-400-6699 |
www.craftsteaknyc.com | Seafood/Steakhouse

Cub Room | *rooms: 3* | *max cap: 168*
SoHo | 131 Sullivan St. (Prince St.) | 212-677-4100 |
www.cubroom.com | New American

Daniel | *rooms: 2* | *max cap: 290*
E 50s | 60 E. 65th St. (bet. Madison & Park Aves.) | 212-933-5261 |
www.danielnyc.com | French

davidburke & donatella | *rooms: 1* | *cap: 110*
E 60s | 133 E. 61st St. (bet. Lexington & Park Aves.) |
212-813-2121 | www.dbdrestaurant.com | New American

Del Frisco's | *rooms: 5* | *max cap: 75*
W 40s | 1221 Sixth Ave. (49th St.) | 212-575-5129 |
www.delfriscos.com | Steakhouse

Del Posto | *rooms: 5* | *max cap: 1200*
Chelsea | 85 10th Ave. (bet. 15th & 16th Sts.) | 646-278-0800 |
Italian

Dos Caminos
rooms: 1 | *cap: 50*
E 50s | 825 Third Ave. (50th St.) | 212-336-5400
rooms: 3 | *max cap: 300*
Gramercy | 373 Park Ave. S. (bet. 26th & 27th Sts.) | 212-294-1000
rooms: 1 | *cap: 110*
G Village | 475 W. Broadway (Houston St.) | 212-277-4300
www.brguestrestaurants.com
Mexican

Eleven Madison Park | *rooms: 2* | *max cap: 50*
Gramercy | 11 Madison Ave. (24th St.) | 212-889-0905 |
www.elevenmadisonpark.com | New French

Eli's Vinegar Factory | *rooms: 1* | *cap: 180*
E 90s | 431 E. 91st St. (bet. 1st & York Aves.) | 212-987-0885 |
www.elizabar.com | American

Elmo | *rooms: 1* | *cap: 100*
Chelsea | 156 Seventh Ave. (bet. 19th & 20th Sts.) | 212-337-8000 |
www.elmorestaurant.com | New American

EN Japanese Brasserie | *rooms: 2* | *max cap: 300*
W Village | 435 Hudson St. (Leroy St.) | 212-647-9196 |
www.enjb.com | Japanese

ESPN Zone | *rooms: 6* | *max cap: 1070*
W 40s | 1472 Broadway (42nd St.) | 212-921-3776 |
www.espnzone.com | American

Felidia | *rooms: 1* | *cap: 65*
E 50s | 243 E. 58th St. (bet. 2nd & 3rd Aves.) | 212-758-1479 |
www.lidiasitaly.com | Italian

Fiamma Osteria | *rooms: 1* | *cap: 80*
SoHo | 206 Spring St. (bet. 6th Ave. & Sullivan St.) | 212-653-0100 |
www.brguestrestaurants.com | Italian

FireBird | *rooms: 6* | *max cap: 350*
W 40s | 365 W. 46th St. (bet. 8th & 9th Aves.) | 212-586-0244 |
www.firebirdrestaurant.com | Russian

5 Ninth | *rooms: 1* | *cap: 250*
G Village | 5 Ninth Ave. (bet. Gansevoort & Little W. 12th Sts.) |
212-929-9460 | www.fiveninth.com | Eclectic

Four Seasons | *rooms: 3* | *max cap: 390*
E 50s | 99 E. 52nd St. (bet. Lexington & Park Aves.) | 212-754-9494 |
www.fourseasonsrestaurant.com | Continental

Fraunces Tavern | *rooms: 3* | *max cap: 350*
Financial Dist | 54 Pearl St. (Broad St.) | 212-968-9689 |
www.frauncestavern.com | American

Fred's at Barneys NY | *rooms: 2* | *max cap: 60*
E 60s | 660 Madison Ave., 9th fl. (bet. 60th & 61st Sts.) |
212-833-2207 | Northern Italian

Freemans | *rooms: 1* | *cap: 150*
LES | Freeman Alley (off Rivington St., bet. Bowery & Chrystie St.) |
212-420-0012 | www.freemansrestaurant.com | New American

Fresco by Scotto | *rooms: 2* | *max cap: 45*
E 50s | 34 E. 52nd St. (bet. Madison & Park Aves.) | 212-935-3434 |
www.frescobyscotto.com | Italian

FR.OG | *rooms: 1* | *cap: 110*
SoHo | 71 Spring St. (bet. Crosby & Lafayette Sts.) | 212-966-5050 |
www.frognyc.com | French

Gabriel's | *rooms: 2* | *max cap: 45*
W 60s | 11 W. 60th St. (B'way) | 212-956-4600 |
www.gabrielsbarandrest.com | Northern Italian

Geisha | *rooms: 2* | *max cap: 40*
E 60s | 33 E. 61st St. (bet. Madison & Park Aves.) | 212-813-1113 |
www.geisharestaurant.com | Japanese/Seafood

Giovanni's Atrium | *rooms: 3* | *max cap: 300*
Financial Dist | 100 Washington St. (Rector St.) | 212-513-4133 |
www.giovannisatriumnyc.com | Italian

Girasole | *rooms: 1* | *cap: 40*
E 80s | 151 E. 82nd St. (bet. Lexington & 3rd Aves.) |
212-772-6690 | Italian

Golden Unicorn | *rooms: 3* | *max cap: 300*
Chinatown | 18 E. Broadway (Catherine St.) | 212-941-0911 |
Chinese

Gramercy Tavern | *rooms: 1* | *cap: 22*
Flatiron | 42 E. 20th St. (bet. B'way & Park Ave. S.) | 212-477-0777 |
www.gramercytavern.com | American

PARTY SITES – RESTAURANTS

Guastavino's | *rooms: 1* | *cap: 1200*
E 50s | 409 E. 59th St. (bet. 1st & York Aves.) | 212-980-2711 |
www.guastavinos.com | New American

Harrison, The | *rooms: 2* | *max cap: 40*
TriBeCa | 355 Greenwich St. (Harrison St.) | 212-274-9310 |
www.theharrison.com | American

Highline | *rooms: 3* | *max cap: 390*
Meatpacking | 835 Washington St. (Little W. 12th St.) |
212-243-3339 | www.nychighline.com | Thai

Ici | *rooms: 3* | *max cap: 140*
Fort Greene | 246 DeKalb Ave. (bet. Clermont & Vanderbilt Aves.) |
Brooklyn | 718-789-2778 | www.icirestaurant.com | American

Il Buco | *rooms: 2* | *max cap: 100*
NoHo | 47 Bond St. (bet. Bowery & Lafayette St.) | 212-533-1932 |
www.ilbuco.com | Italian/Mediterranean

Insieme | *rooms: 1* | *cap: 32*
W 50s | Michelangelo Hotel, The | 777 Seventh Ave. (bet. 50th &
51st Sts.) | 212-582-1310 | www.restaurantinsieme.com | Italian

I Trulli | *rooms: 4* | *max cap: 160*
Gramercy | 122 E. 27th St. (bet. Lexington Ave. & Park Ave. S.) |
212-481-7372 | www.itrulli.com | Southern Italian

Jean Georges | *rooms: 1* | *cap: 35*
W 60s | Trump Int'l Hotel | 1 Central Park W. (bet. 60th & 61st Sts.) |
212-299-3900 | www.jean-georges.com | New French

Keens Steakhouse | *rooms: 4* | *max cap: 500*
Garment Dist | 72 W. 36th St. (bet. 5th & 6th Aves.) | 212-268-5056 |
www.keenssteakhouse.com | Steakhouse

La Esquina | *rooms: 2* | *max cap: 120*
Little Italy | 106 Kenmare St. (bet. Cleveland Pl. & Lafayette St.) |
646-613-7100 | www.esquinanyc.com | Mexican

La Grenouille | *rooms: 1* | *cap: 110*
E 50s | 3 E. 52nd St. (bet. 5th & Madison Aves.) | 212-752-0652 |
www.la-grenouille.com | French

Landmarc | *rooms: 2* | *max cap: 125*
W 60s | 10 Columbus Circle, 3rd fl. (60th St.) | 212-823-6123 |
www.landmarc-restaurant.com | French Bistro

Le Bernardin | *rooms: 2* | *max cap: 200*
W 50s | 155 W. 51st St. (bet. 6th & 7th Aves.) | 212-554-1108 |
www.le-bernardin.com | French/Seafood

Le Cirque | *rooms: 2* | *max cap: 240*
E 50s | One Beacon Court | 151 E. 58th St. (bet. Lexington & 3rd Aves.) |
212-405-5094 | www.lecirque.com | French

Lenox Room | *rooms: 2* | *max cap: 120*
E 70s | 1278 Third Ave. (bet. 73rd & 74th Sts.) | 212-772-0404 |
www.lenoxroom.com | New American

Le Perigord | *rooms: 1* | *cap: 140*
E 50s | 405 E. 52nd St. (bet. FDR Dr. & 1st Ave.) | 212-755-6244 |
www.leperigord.com | French

Lotus | *rooms: 4* | *max cap: 550*
Meatpacking | 409 W. 14th St. (bet. 9th Ave. & Washington St.) |
212-255-8060 | www.lotusnewyork.com | Asian

Lupa | *rooms: 1* | *cap: 30*
G Village | 170 Thompson St. (bet. Bleecker & Houston Sts.) |
212-982-5089 | www.luparestaurant.com | Italian

Megu | *rooms: 3* | *max cap: 600*
TriBeCa | 62 Thomas St. (bet. Church St. & W. B'way) |
212-964-7777 | www.megunyc.com | Japanese

Megu Midtown | *rooms: 1* | *cap: 175*
E 40s | Trump World Tower | 845 United Nations Plaza (1st Ave. &
47th St.) | 212-644-0777 | www.megunyc.com | Japanese

Metrazur | *rooms: 1* | *cap: 600*
E 40s | Grand Central Terminal | East Balcony (42nd St. & Park Ave.) |
212-687-4750 | www.metrazur.com | New American

**Michael Jordan's
The Steak House NYC** | *rooms: 1* | *cap: 500*
E 50s | Grand Central Terminal | West Balcony (42nd St. & Vanderbilt Ave.) |
212-608-7400 | www.theglaziergroup.com | Steakhouse

Mickey Mantle's | *rooms: 3* | *max cap: 300*
W 50s | 42 Central Park S. (bet. 5th & 6th Aves.) | 212-688-7777 |
www.mickeymantles.com | American

Modern, The | *rooms: 1* | *cap: 80*
W 50s | Museum of Modern Art | 9 W. 53rd St. (bet. 5th & 6th Aves.) |
212-408-6641 | www.themodernnyc.com | New American/
New French

Monkey Bar | *rooms: 1* | *cap: 200*
E 50s | 60 E. 54th St. (bet. Madison & Park Aves.) | 212-608-7400 |
www.theglaziergroup.com | American

Moran's Chelsea | *rooms: 4* | *max cap: 500*
Chelsea | 146 10th Ave. (19th St.) | 212-627-3030 |
www.moranschelsea.com | Seafood/Steakhouse

Morimoto | *rooms: 2* | *max cap: 350*
Chelsea | 88 10th Ave. (16th St.) | 212-989-8883 |
www.morimotonyc.com | Japanese

Mr. Chow Tribeca | *rooms: 1* | *cap: 250*
TriBeCa | 121 Hudson St. (N. Moore St.) | 212-965-9500 |
www.mrchow.com | Chinese

Nicole's | *rooms: 1* | *cap: 300*
E 60s | 10 E. 60th St. (bet. 5th & Madison Aves.) | 212-223-2288 |
www.nicolefarhi.com | Continental

Nobu | *rooms: 1* | *cap: 220*
TriBeCa | 105 Hudson St. (Franklin St.) | 212-219-8095 |
www.myriadrestaurantgroup.com | Japanese/Peruvian

Nobu 57 | *rooms: 1* | *cap: 300*
W 50s | 40 W. 57th St. (bet. 5th & 6th Aves.) | 212-757-3000 |
www.myriadrestaurantgroup.com | Japanese/Peruvian

PARTY SITES – RESTAURANTS

Oceana | *rooms: 2* | *max cap: 60*
E 50s | 55 E. 54th St. (bet. Madison & Park Aves.) | 212-759-5941 |
www.oceanarestaurant.com | Seafood

Ocean Grill | *rooms: 2* | *max cap: 175*
W 70s | 384 Columbus Ave. (bet. 78th & 79th Sts.) | 212-579-2300 |
www.brguestrestaurants.com | Seafood

One | *rooms: 1* | *cap: 50*
Meatpacking | 1 Little W. 12th St. (Gansevoort St.) | 212-255-9717 |
www.onelw12.com | Eclectic

One if by Land, Two if by Sea | *rooms: 2* | *max cap: 140*
G Village | 17 Barrow St. (bet. 7th Ave. S. & W. 4th St.) |
212-255-8649 | www.oneifbyland.com | New American

Opia | *rooms: 3* | *max cap: 400*
E 50s | 130 E. 57th St. (Lexington Ave.) | 212-688-3939 |
www.opiarestaurant.com | French

Park, The | *rooms: 5* | *max cap: 1200*
Chelsea | 118 10th Ave. (bet. 17th & 18th Sts.) | 212-352-3313 |
www.theparknyc.com | Mediterranean

Patroon | *rooms: 7* | *max cap: 100*
E 40s | 160 E. 46th St. (bet. Lexington & 3rd Aves.) | 212-883-7373 |
www.patroonrestaurant.com | American

Periyali | *rooms: 2* | *max cap: 21*
Flatiron | 35 W. 20th St. (bet. 5th & 6th Aves.) | 212-463-7890 |
www.periyali.com | Greek

Per Se | *rooms: 2* | *max cap: 60*
W 60s | Time Warner Ctr. | 10 Columbus Circle, 4th fl. (60th St.) |
212-823-9335 | www.perseny.com | French/New American

Picholine | *rooms: 2* | *max cap: 24*
W 60s | 35 W. 64th St. (bet. B'way & CPW) | 212-724-8585 |
www.picholinenyc.com | French/Mediterranean

Pop Burger | *rooms: 1* | *cap: 250*
Meatpacking | 58-60 Ninth Ave. (bet. 14th & 15th Sts.) |
212-414-8686 | American

Primavera | *rooms: 1* | *cap: 50*
E 80s | 1578 First Ave. (82nd St.) | 212-861-8608 |
www.primaveranyc.com | Northern Italian

Provence | *rooms: 2* | *max cap: 120*
SoHo | 38 MacDougal St. (Prince St.) | 212-475-7500 |
www.provencenyc.com | French

Prune | *rooms: 1* | *cap: 30*
E Village | 54 E. First St. (bet. 1st & 2nd Aves.) | 212-677-6221 |
www.prunerestaurant.com | New American

Public | *rooms: 1* | *cap: 120*
NoLita | 210 Elizabeth St. (bet. Prince & Spring Sts.) | 212-343-7011 |
www.public-nyc.com | Eclectic

Quality Meats | *rooms: 1* | *cap: 40*
W 50s | 57 W. 58th St. (bet. 5th & 6th Aves.) | 212-371-7777 |
www.qualitymeatsnyc.com | New American/Steakhouse

Rain | rooms: 1 | cap: 250
W 80s | 100 W. 82nd St. (Columbus Ave.) | 212-501-0776 | www.rainrestaurant.com | Pan-Asian

Rainbow Room | rooms: 7 | max cap: 600
E 40s | 30 Rockefeller Plaza (bet. 49th & 50th Sts.) | 212-632-5000 | www.rainbowroom.com | Continental/Italian

Redeye Grill | rooms: 3 | max cap: 400
W 50s | 890 Seventh Ave. (bet. 56th & 57th Sts.) | 212-265-0100 | www.thefiremangroup.com | New American/Seafood

Remi | rooms: 3 | max cap: 1000
W 50s | 145 W. 53rd St. (bet. 6th & 7th Aves.) | 212-581-4242 | Northern Italian

River Café | rooms: 1 | cap: 125
Dumbo | 1 Water St. (bet. Furman & Old Fulton Sts.) | Brooklyn | 718-522-5200 | www.rivercafe.com | American

Rosa Mexicano | rooms: 2 | max cap: 300
W 60s | 61 Columbus Ave. (62nd St.) | 212-977-7700 | www.rosamexicano.com | Mexican

Rosie O'Grady's
Manhattan Club | rooms: 4 | max cap: 300
W 50s | 800 Seventh Ave. (52nd St.) | 212-582-2975 | www.rosieogradys.com | Italian/Steakhouse

Ruby Foo's
rooms: 1 | cap: 300
W 40s | 1626 Broadway (49th St.) | 212-489-5600
rooms: 2 | max cap: 350
W 70s | 2182 Broadway (77th St.) | 212-724-6700
www.brguestrestaurants.com
Asian

San Domenico | rooms: 2 | max cap: 125
W 50s | 240 Central Park S. (bet. B'way & 7th Ave.) | 212-265-5959 | www.sandomeniconewyork.com | Italian

Shun Lee Palace | rooms: 1 | cap: 30
E 50s | 155 E. 55th St. (bet. Lexington & 3rd Aves.) | 212-371-8844 | www.shunleepalace.com | Chinese

Smith & Wollensky | rooms: 4 | max cap: 200
E 40s | 201 E. 49th St. (3rd Ave.) | 212-753-1530 | www.smithandwollensky.com | Steakhouse

Spotted Pig | rooms: 1 | cap: 100
W Village | 314 W. 11th St. (Greenwich St.) | 212-620-0393 | www.thespottedpig.com | British/Modern European

Stanton Social | rooms: 1 | cap: 120
LES | 99 Stanton St. (bet. Ludlow & Orchard Sts.) | 212-995-0099 | www.thestantonsocial.com | Eclectic

Supper Club, The | rooms: 2 | max cap: 1200
W 40s | 240 W. 47th St. (bet. B'way & 8th Ave.) | 212-921-1940 | www.thesupperclub.com | American

SushiSamba
rooms: 3 | max cap: 189
Flatiron | 245 Park Ave. S. (bet. 19th & 20th Sts.) | 212-475-9377
rooms: 3 | max cap: 270
G Village | 87 Seventh Ave. S. (bet. Bleecker & W. 4th Sts.) |
212-691-7885
www.sushisamba.com
Brazilian/Japanese

Tabla | *rooms: 2 | max cap: 210*
Gramercy | 11 Madison Ave. (25th St.) | 212-889-0667 |
www.tablany.com | American/Indian

Taj | *rooms: 2 | max cap: 350*
Flatiron | 48 W. 21st St. (bet. 5th & 6th Aves.) | 212-620-3033 |
www.tajlounge.com | Indian

Tao | *rooms: 4 | max cap: 500*
E 50s | 42 E. 58th St. (bet. Madison & Park Aves.) | 212-888-2288 |
www.taorestaurant.com | Pan-Asian

Tavern on the Green | *rooms: 7 | max cap: 2500*
W 60s | Central Park W. (bet. 66th & 67th Sts.) | 212-873-4111 |
www.tavernonthegreen.com | American

Terrace in the Sky | *rooms: 2 | max cap: 450*
W 100s | 400 W. 119th St. (bet. Amsterdam Ave. & Morningside Dr.) |
212-666-9490 | www.terraceinthesky.com | French/Mediterranean

Thalassa | *rooms: 3 | max cap: 450*
TriBeCa | 179 Franklin St. (bet. Greenwich & Hudson Sts.) |
212-941-7661 | www.thalassanyc.com | Greek/Seafood

Tocqueville | *rooms: 2 | max cap: 250*
Union Sq | 1 E. 15th St. (bet. 5th Ave. & Union Sq. W.) |
212-647-1515 | www.tocquevillerestaurant.com | New American/
New French

Trattoria Dell'Arte | *rooms: 5 | max cap: 275*
W 50s | 900 Seventh Ave. (bet. 56th & 57th Sts.) | 212-245-9800 |
www.trattoriadellarte.com | Northern Italian

Tribeca Grill | *rooms: 2 | max cap: 160*
TriBeCa | 375 Greenwich St. (Franklin St.) | 212-941-3905 |
www.myriadrestaurantgroup.com | New American

Tuscan Square | *rooms: 3 | max cap: 470*
W 50s | 16 W. 51st St. (bet. 5th & 6th Aves.) | 212-977-7777 |
Northern Italian

Twenty Four Fifth | *rooms: 1 | cap: 500*
G Village | 24 Fifth Ave. (bet. 9th & 10th Sts.) | 212-505-8000 |
www.theglaziergroup.com | French

21 Club | *rooms: 10 | max cap: 150*
W 50s | 21 W. 52nd St. (bet. 5th & 6th Aves.) | 212-582-1400 |
www.21club.com | American

Wallsé | *rooms: 2 | max cap: 115*
G Village | 344 W. 11th St. (Washington St.) | 212-352-2300 |
www.wallse.com | Austrian

PARTY SITES – RESTAURANTS

Water Club | *rooms: 3* | *max cap: 1000*
Murray Hill | 500 E. 30th St. (East River, enter via E. 23rd St.) | 212-545-1155 | www.thewaterclub.com | American

Water's Edge | *rooms: 3* | *max cap: 400*
LIC | 44th Dr. (East River & Vernon Blvd.) | Queens | 718-482-0033 | www.watersedgenyc.com | New American/Seafood

Zarela | *rooms: 2* | *max cap: 160*
E 50s | 953 Second Ave. (bet. 50th & 51st Sts.) | 212-644-6740 | www.zarela.com | Mexican

NYC SOURCES INDEXES

Special Features

Listings cover the best in each category and include source names, locations and Quality ratings. ☒ indicates places with the highest ratings, popularity and importance.

BAGELS & BIALYS

☒ Absolute Bagels | **W 100s**	26
Bagel Bob's | **multi. loc.**	22
Bagel Buffet | **G Vill**	17
Bagel Hole | **Park Slope**	22
Bagel Oasis | **Fresh Meadows**	26
Bagelry | **Murray Hill**	19
Bagels & Co. | **multi. loc.**	22
Bagels on Sq. | **G Vill**	21
Bagelworks | **E 60s**	23
Bagel Zone | **E Vill**	17
☒ Barney Greengrass | **W 80s**	27
Corner Bagel | **E 80s**	22
Corrado | **multi. loc.**	21
Daniel's Bagels | **Murray Hill**	24
David's Bagels | **multi. loc.**	23
East Side Bagel | **E 70s**	21
☒ Eli's Manhattan | **E 80s**	25
Eli's Vinegar | **E 90s**	25
Ess-a-Bagel | **multi. loc.**	26
Good & Plenty | **W 40s**	22
Gourmet Garage | **multi. loc.**	20
H & H Bagels | **multi. loc.**	26
☒ Kossar's | **LES**	28
La Bagel | **multi. loc.**	23
Lenny's | **W 90s**	23
Montague St. | **Bklyn Hts**	22
Murray's Bagels | **multi. loc.**	26
Murray's Sturgeon | **W 80s**	27
Oren's/Roast | **E 50s**	24
Pick a Bagel | **multi. loc.**	20
Tal Bagels | **multi. loc.**	23
Terrace Bagels | **Windsor Terr**	25
Times Sq. Bagels | **W 40s**	19
Yonah Schimmel | **LES**	23
☒ Zabar's | **W 80s**	27

BAKED GOODS

(See also Bagels & Bialys, Cakes & Cupcakes, Cookies, Pies/Tarts)

Addeo's | **Bronx**	27
☒ Agata/Valentina | **E 70s**	26
Amish Market | **multi. loc.**	23
☒ Amy's Bread | **multi. loc.**	26
Andrew & Alan's | **Staten Is**	22

Arte/Corner | **W 70s**	24
Artuso Pastry | **Bronx**	26
Au Bon Pain | **multi. loc.**	16
Baked Ideas | **SoHo**	-
☒ Balducci's | **W 60s**	25
Balthazar Bakery | **SoHo**	27
NEW Barbarini | **Financial**	-
Baskin-Robbins | **multi. loc.**	17
Bay Ridge | **Bay Ridge**	25
☒ Bazzini | **TriBeCa**	27
Beard Papa | **multi. loc.**	24
☒ Bedford Cheese | **W'burg**	27
NEW Betty Bakery | **Boerum Hill**	-
☒ Bierkraft | **Park Slope**	28
Bijoux Doux | **multi. loc.**	-
Billy's Bakery | **Chelsea**	25
Bird Bath | **multi. loc.**	-
☒ Black Hound | **E Vill**	26
☒ Blue Apron | **Park Slope**	27
☒ Blue Ribbon | **G Vill**	28
Boerum Hill Food | **Boerum Hill**	-
Bonsignour | **W Vill**	26
☒ Bouchon Bakery | **W 60s**	27
☒ Bouley Bakery | **TriBeCa**	27
Brasil Coffee | **LIC**	21
Bread Alone | **Boiceville**	27
Bread Stuy | **Bed-Stuy**	-
Bruno Bakery | **G Vill**	23
Bruno/Ravioli | **multi. loc.**	24
Buttercup | **multi. loc.**	23
Café Indulge | **Murray Hill**	23
Cafe Scaramouche | **Carroll Gdns**	-
Caffé Roma | **Little Italy**	23
Caffe' Simpatico/Ruthy's | **multi. loc.**	15
Cake Chef | **Staten Is**	22
Cakeline | **Rockaway Bch**	-
☒ Cake Man | **Ft Greene**	26
Caputo Bakery | **Carroll Gdns**	23
Carrot Top | **Wash. Hts**	23
Carry On Tea | **W Vill**	23
CBK Cookies | **E 80s**	23

Ceci-Cela | **multi. loc.**	24
NEW Cheeks | **W'burg**	–
Cheryl Kleinman | **Boerum Hill**	28
Chez Laurence | **Murray Hill**	23
Chocolate Bar | **multi. loc.**	26
Chocolate Room | **Park Slope**	25
NEW Choice Mkt. | **Clinton Hill**	–
Cipriani | **E 40s**	26
Z Citarella | **multi. loc.**	26
Z City Bakery | **Flatiron**	25
Clinton St. | **LES**	26
NEW Cobblestone | **Carroll Gdns**	–
Z Colette's | **W Vill**	29
NEW Colson | **Park Slope**	25
Columbus | **W 80s**	21
Confetti | **W 80s**	–
Conn. Muffin | **multi. loc.**	17
NEW Corner Bakery | **E 90s**	–
Corrado | **multi. loc.**	21
Così | **multi. loc.**	18
Court | **Carroll Gdns**	25
Creative Cakes | **E 70s**	–
Crumbs | **multi. loc.**	22
Damascus Bread | **Bklyn Hts**	25
Z Dean/DeLuca | **multi. loc.**	27
Delillo Pastry | **Bronx**	26
DeRobertis | **E Vill**	22
Z Dessert Delivery | **E 50s**	28
DiFiore | **G Vill**	–
Z Doughnut Plant | **LES**	26
Downtown Atlantic | **Boerum Hill**	–
Duane Pk. | **TriBeCa**	26
Z E.A.T. | **E 80s**	25
Egg Custard King | **Chinatown**	–
Egidio Pastry | **Bronx**	24
Eileen's Cheesecake | **NoLita**	26
Eleni's Cookies | **Chelsea**	22
Z Eli's Manhattan | **E 80s**	25
Eli's Vinegar | **E 90s**	25
Fabiane's | **W'burg**	–
Z Fairway | **multi. loc.**	26
Fat Witch | **Chelsea**	25
Fay Da | **multi. loc.**	19
Ferrara Cafe | **Little Italy**	22
Financier | **Financial**	27
Fortunato Bros. | **W'burg**	25
Fraser-Morris | **Carroll Gdns**	–
Z Fresh Direct | **LIC**	23

Friend/Farmer | **Gramercy**	21
Gail Watson | **Garment**	–
Garden of Eden | **multi. loc.**	24
Glaser's Bake | **E 80s**	21
Golden Fung | **Chinatown**	18
Good & Plenty | **W 40s**	22
Gourmet Garage | **multi. loc.**	20
Grab Specialty | **Park Slope**	–
Grace's Mktpl. | **E 70s**	24
NEW Z Grandaisy Bakery | **SoHo**	29
Z Greenmarket | **multi. loc.**	26
Güllüoglu | **Sheepshead Bay**	–
Hot/Crusty | **multi. loc.**	15
Hungarian Pastry | **W 100s**	22
Junior's | **multi. loc.**	23
NEW Kidfresh | **E 80s**	–
La Bergamote | **Chelsea**	26
Ladybird Bakery | **Park Slope**	–
Lafayette | **G Vill**	21
La Guli | **Astoria**	24
NEW Le Petit | **Astoria**	–
L'Epicerie | **Ft Greene**	–
Leske's | **Bay Ridge**	23
Z Levain Bakery | **W 70s**	28
Little Pie | **multi. loc.**	24
Lorenzo/Maria's | **E 80s**	25
Lung Moon | **Chinatown**	19
NEW Madison | **E 90s**	–
Z Madonia Bakery | **Bronx**	28
Z Magnolia Bakery | **W Vill**	23
Make My Cake | **Harlem**	25
Mangia | **Flatiron**	24
Mansoura | **Midwood**	–
Margaret Braun | **W Vill**	–
Margaret Palca | **Carroll Gdns**	–
Margot Pâtisserie | **W 70s**	27
Marquet Patisserie | **multi. loc.**	24
Martha's Bakery | **Astoria**	–
Martin's Pretzels | **Theresa**	27
Masturbakers | **E Vill**	22
NEW Max Brenner | **multi. loc.**	22
Z May May | **Chinatown**	23
Mazzola Bakery | **Carroll Gdns**	25
Milk & Cookies | **W Vill**	24
Morrone Bakery | **Harlem**	–
Mother Mousse | **Staten Is**	26
Mother's Bake | **Bronx**	21
Mrs. Field's | **multi. loc.**	18
My Most/Food | **W 40s**	21

Napoli Bakery | **W'burg**	–
Nusbaum & Wu | **W 100s**	18
Once Upon/Tart | **SoHo**	25
One Girl | **Cobble Hill**	24
Orwasher's | **E 70s**	26
Our Daily Bread | **Chatham**	26
Paneantico | **Bay Ridge**	26
Pane d'Italia | **Whitestone**	–
Panya Bakery | **E Vill**	22
Parisi Bakery | **NoLita**	23
☑ Patisserie Claude | **G Vill**	27
☑ Payard | **E 70s**	28
☑ Petrossian | **W 50s**	28
Poseidon | **W 40s**	26
Pozzo Pastry | **W 40s**	21
Puff & Pao | **G Vill**	–
Pumpkins | **Park Slope**	26
☑ Rice/Riches | **NoLita**	23
Rocco's Pastry | **G Vill**	25
Ron Ben-Israel | **SoHo**	25
☑ Royal Crown | **multi. loc.**	26
Ruby/Violette | **W 50s**	26
Sal & Dom's | **Bronx**	28
S&S Cheesecake | **Bronx**	27
Sarabeth's | **multi. loc.**	24
Schick's Bakery | **Borough Pk**	20
Settepani | **multi. loc.**	23
Shakoor's Sweet | **Bed-Stuy**	–
Silver Moon | **W 100s**	26
Something Sweet | **E Vill**	23
☑ Soutine | **W 70s**	27
Steve's/Pies | **Red Hook**	25
☑ Stork's Pastry | **Whitestone**	27
Streit's Matzo | **LES**	25
☑ Sugar Sweet | **LES**	27
☑ Sullivan St. Bakery | **W 40s**	28
Sweet Atelier | **E 80s**	–
Sweet Melissa | **multi. loc.**	24
☑ Sylvia Weinstock | **TriBeCa**	26
Tai Pan Bakery | **multi. loc.**	19
Tazza | **Bklyn Hts**	–
Tempo Presto | **Park Slope**	23
Terranova | **Bronx**	26
NEW Three Tarts | **Chelsea**	22
NEW Tisserie | **Union Sq**	20
☑ Titan Foods | **Astoria**	26
Todaro Bros. | **Murray Hill**	24
NEW Tribeca Treats | **TriBeCa**	27
NEW Trois Pommes | **Park Slope**	–
☑ Two Little Red | **E 80s**	26

Umanoff/Parsons | **TriBeCa**	24
Union Mkt. | **Park Slope**	26
Veniero's | **E Vill**	25
Vesuvio | **SoHo**	23
☑ Villabate | **Bensonhurst**	28
☑ Vosges Haut | **SoHo**	26
Whole Earth | **E Vill**	–
☑ Whole Foods | **multi. loc.**	26
William Greenberg | **E 80s**	25
Wong Bakery | **Chinatown**	–
Yonah Schimmel | **LES**	23
☑ Zabar's | **W 80s**	27
Zaro's Bread | **multi. loc.**	17
Zeytuna | **Financial**	23

BEER SPECIALISTS

American Beer | **Cobble Hill**	26
B & E Beverage | **Woodside**	–
☑ Bierkraft | **Park Slope**	28
BJ's Wholesale | **multi. loc.**	17
Dual Specialty | **E Vill**	–
Eagle Provisions | **Park Slope**	24
East Coast Beer | **Sunset Pk**	–
☑ Fresh Direct | **LIC**	23
Garden | **Greenpt**	24
Gourmet Garage | **multi. loc.**	20
Grace's Mktpl. | **E 70s**	24
New York Bev. | **Bronx**	–
☑ Whole Foods | **Chelsea**	26

BREAD

Addeo's | **Bronx**	27
☑ Amy's Bread | **multi. loc.**	26
Balthazar Bakery | **SoHo**	27
☑ Bedford Cheese | **W'burg**	27
☑ Blue Apron | **Park Slope**	27
☑ Blue Ribbon | **G Vill**	28
☑ Bouchon Bakery | **W 60s**	27
☑ Bouley Bakery | **TriBeCa**	27
Bread Alone | **Boiceville**	27
Bread Stuy | **Bed-Stuy**	–
NEW Cheeks | **W'burg**	–
Corrado | **multi. loc.**	21
Damascus Bread | **Bklyn Hts**	25
☑ Dean/DeLuca | **multi. loc.**	27
☑ E.A.T. | **E 80s**	25
☑ Eli's Manhattan | **E 80s**	25
Eli's Vinegar | **E 90s**	25
NEW ☑ Grandaisy Bakery | **SoHo**	29

Rocco's Pastry | **G Vill**	25
Ron Ben-Israel | **SoHo**	25
☑ Royal Crown | **multi. loc.**	26
Sal & Dom's | **Bronx**	28
S&S Cheesecake | **Bronx**	27
Sarabeth's | **multi. loc.**	24
Schick's Bakery | **Borough Pk**	20
Settepani | **multi. loc.**	23
Shakoor's Sweet | **Bed-Stuy**	–
Silver Moon | **W 100s**	26
Something Sweet | **E Vill**	23
☑ Soutine | **W 70s**	27
☑ Stork's Pastry | **Whitestone**	27
☑ Sugar Sweet | **LES**	27
Sweet Atelier | **E 80s**	–
Sweet Melissa | **multi. loc.**	24
☑ Sylvia Weinstock | **TriBeCa**	26
Tai Pan Bakery | **multi. loc.**	19
Tempo Presto | **Park Slope**	23
NEW Tisserie | **Union Sq**	20
NEW Tribeca Treats | **TriBeCa**	27
☑ Two Little Red | **E 80s**	26
Veniero's | **E Vill**	25
☑ Villabate | **Bensonhurst**	28
☑ Vosges Haut | **SoHo**	26
Whole Earth | **E Vill**	–
☑ Whole Foods | **multi. loc.**	26
William Greenberg | **E 80s**	25
Wong Bakery | **Chinatown**	–
☑ Zabar's | **W 80s**	27

CANDY & NUTS

Aji Ichiban | **multi. loc.**	21
Andrew & Alan's | **Staten Is**	22
Australian Home. | **E Vill**	23
☑ Balducci's | **W 60s**	25
☑ Bazzini | **TriBeCa**	27
☑ Bierkraft | **Park Slope**	28
☑ Black Hound | **E Vill**	26
☑ Blue Apron | **Park Slope**	27
Bruno Bakery | **G Vill**	23
Charbonnel/Walker | **E 40s**	22
Chelsea Baskets | **Chelsea**	24
Choc-Oh! | **Bay Ridge**	–
Chocolate Bar | **multi. loc.**	26
Chocolate Room | **Park Slope**	25
Chocolat Michel | **Gramercy**	25
Chocolat Moderne | **Chelsea**	–
Christopher Norman | **Financial**	23
☑ Citarella | **multi. loc.**	26

Cocoa Bar | **multi. loc.**	26
☑ Dean/DeLuca | **multi. loc.**	27
Debauve/Gallais | **E 60s**	27
☑ Dylan's Candy | **E 60s**	21
Economy Candy | **LES**	24
Eggers Ice Cream | **Staten Is**	25
☑ Eli's Manhattan | **E 80s**	25
Eli's Vinegar | **E 90s**	25
Evelyn's Choc. | **Financial**	25
Fifth Ave. Choc. | **multi. loc.**	20
☑ Fresh Direct | **LIC**	23
Godiva | **multi. loc.**	22
Grab Specialty | **Park Slope**	–
Hershey's Times Sq. | **W 40s**	–
Hinsch's | **Bay Ridge**	22
☑ Jacques Torres | **Dumbo**	28
Jinil/Chocolat | **Midwood**	–
JoMart Choc. | **Marine Pk**	24
☑ Kalustyan's | **Gramercy**	27
☑ Kee's Choc. | **SoHo**	29
☑ La Maison/Choc. | **multi. loc.**	29
Lee Sims Choc. | **Staten Is**	–
Leonidas | **multi. loc.**	26
L'Epicerie | **Ft Greene**	–
Li-Lac Choc. | **multi. loc.**	26
Lindt | **multi. loc.**	–
☑ Manhattan Fruitier | **Gramercy**	27
☑ MarieBelle's | **SoHo**	26
☑ Martine's Choc. | **multi. loc.**	29
☑ Minamoto | **W 40s**	28
Mondel Choc. | **W 100s**	22
m2m | **E Vill**	18
Neuchatel Choc. | **E 50s**	24
Neuhaus Choc. | **multi. loc.**	25
☑ Payard | **E 70s**	28
☑ Petrossian | **W 50s**	28
Philip's Candy | **Staten Is**	–
☑ Pierre Marcolini | **E 50s**	28
☑ Richart Design | **E 50s**	28
☑ Russ & Daughters | **LES**	28
☑ Sahadi's | **Bklyn Hts**	27
Scharffen Berger | **W 80s**	26
☑ Stork's Pastry | **Whitestone**	27
Superior Confections | **Staten Is**	–
Sweet Melissa | **multi. loc.**	24
☑ Teuscher Choc. | **E 40s**	27
NEW Tribeca Treats | **TriBeCa**	27
Varsano's | **G Vill**	–
Vere | **Flatiron**	–
☑ Vosges Haut | **SoHo**	26

subscribe to zagat.com

☑ Whole Foods | **multi. loc.**	26		
World of Nuts | **multi. loc.**	15		
☑ Zabar's | **W 80s**	27		

CARRIAGE TRADE

☑ Abigail Kirsch | **multi. loc.**	26
Acker Merrall | **W 70s**	26
☑ Agata/Valentina | **E 70s**	26
NEW ☑ Alessi | **SoHo**	27
☑ Balducci's | **W 60s**	25
☑ Belle Fleur | **Flatiron**	28
Butterfield Mkt. | **E 70s**	23
Cakeline | **Rockaway Bch**	–
Castle/Pierpont | **Garment**	24
Caviar Russe | **E 50s**	26
CBK Cookies | **E 80s**	23
☑ Citarella | **multi. loc.**	26
☑ Dean/DeLuca | **multi. loc.**	27
Debauve/Gallais | **E 60s**	27
☑ Eli's Manhattan | **E 80s**	25
Eli's Vinegar | **E 90s**	25
Feast/Fêtes | **E 60s**	27
Fellan Florist | **E 60s**	24
☑ Glorious Food | **E 70s**	25
Grace's Mktpl. | **E 70s**	24
Holland Court | **E 90s**	24
☑ Ito En | **E 60s**	28
☑ Lady M | **E 70s**	28
☑ La Maison/Choc. | **multi. loc.**	29
☑ Lobel's Meats | **E 80s**	29
L'Olivier | **E 70s**	29
Lorenzo/Maria's | **E 80s**	25
☑ Manhattan Fruitier | **Gramercy**	27
Marché Madison | **multi. loc.**	20
Margaret Braun | **W Vill**	–
☑ MarieBelle's | **SoHo**	26
Miho Kosuda | **E 40s**	–
☑ Morrell & Co. | **W 40s**	27
New York/Warehse. | **LIC**	–
O&CO. | **multi. loc.**	25
☑ Payard | **E 70s**	28
☑ Petrossian | **W 50s**	28
☑ Pierre Marcolini | **E 50s**	28
Renny/Reed | **E 50s**	–
Richard Salome | **E 70s**	–
Robert Isabell | **Meatpacking**	27
Ronaldo Maia | **E 90s**	–
Ron Ben-Israel | **SoHo**	25
☑ Sherry-Lehmann | **E 60s**	29
Susan Holland | **Flatiron**	–

☑ Sylvia Weinstock | **TriBeCa**	26
☑ Takashimaya | **E 50s**	28
Tea Box | **E 50s**	27
Tentation Potel | **Garment**	22
☑ Teuscher Choc. | **multi. loc.**	27
☑ Vosges Haut | **SoHo**	26
Wild Edibles | **E 40s**	26
William Greenberg | **E 80s**	25
☑ William Poll | **E 70s**	26

CATERERS

(See also Event Planners and Office Catering)

☑ Abigail Kirsch | **multi. loc.**	26
☑ Agata/Valentina | **E 70s**	26
Areo Rist. | **Bay Ridge**	21
Artie's Deli | **W 80s**	21
Ben's Kosher | **multi. loc.**	21
Between/Bread | **W 50s**	21
Blue Smoke | **Chelsea**	25
Boerum Hill Food | **Boerum Hill**	–
Bottega/Via | **E 70s**	25
Cafe Scaramouche | **Carroll Gdns**	–
Caffe' Simpatico/Ruthy's | **Chelsea**	15
Callahan | **Garment**	–
Call Cuisine | **E 50s**	24
☑ Carnegie Deli | **W 50s**	23
Carol's Cuisine | **Staten Is**	–
Carve | **W 40s**	23
Catering/Rest. Assoc. | **Garment**	20
Catering Co. | **Chelsea**	–
Ceriello | **multi. loc.**	24
Certé | **W 50s**	–
Charles/Sally/Charles | **Park Slope**	–
Chef & Co. | **Flatiron**	25
☑ Citarella | **multi. loc.**	26
☑ City Bakery | **Flatiron**	25
☑ Cleaver Co. | **Chelsea**	25
Creative Edge | **W Vill**	–
Cucina | **E 40s**	21
Cucina Vivolo | **E 70s**	23
David Burke | **E 50s**	23
David Ziff | **E 90s**	–
☑ Dean/DeLuca | **multi. loc.**	27
Deli Masters | **Fresh Meadows**	21
Delmonico | **multi. loc.**	21
Devon/Blakely | **multi. loc.**	22
Dishes | **E 40s**	24

☑ Dom's | **SoHo**	27
Durso's Pasta | **Flushing**	26
☑ E.A.T. | **E 80s**	25
Eli's Vinegar | **E 90s**	25
Family Store | **Bay Ridge**	-
F&B | **Chelsea**	20
Feast/Fêtes | **E 60s**	27
Financier | **Financial**	27
Fine/Schapiro | **W 70s**	20
Fireman Hospitality | **W 50s**	-
Food/Thought | **Chelsea**	-
Fresco/Scotto | **E 50s**	24
Garden of Eden | **multi. loc.**	24
Good & Plenty | **W 40s**	22
Grace's Mktpl. | **E 70s**	24
Great Performances | **SoHo**	24
Iavarone Bros. | **Maspeth**	25
Indiana Mkt. | **W 80s**	26
Italian Food | **Little Italy**	22
Jeffrey's | **LES**	-
☑ Katz's Deli | **LES**	24
Lassen/Hennigs | **Bklyn Hts**	22
Lorenzo/Maria's | **E 80s**	25
Luscious Food | **Park Slope**	-
Manganaro Foods | **Garment**	24
Mangia | **multi. loc.**	24
Mazur's Marketpl. | **Douglaston**	20
Movable Feast | **Park Slope**	23
Naturally Delicious | **Carroll Gdns**	-
Nordic Delicacies | **Bay Ridge**	28
Olivier Cheng | **TriBeCa**	22
☑ Payard | **E 70s**	28
Petak's | **E 80s**	23
Peter's Mkt. | **Bayside**	-
Pret A Manger | **multi. loc.**	21
Ready to Eat | **W Vill**	21
Remi | **W 50s**	26
Risotteria | **G Vill**	23
Robbins Wolfe | **Meatpacking**	26
Salsa | **Bronx**	-
Sandwich Planet | **Garment**	25
Sebastians | **E 50s**	-
Second Helpings | **Park Slope**	-
Serena Bass | **Meatpacking**	-
Snack | **SoHo**	27
Special Attention | **LES**	-
Spoonbread | **Harlem**	23
Starwich | **multi. loc.**	23
Susan Holland | **Flatiron**	-
Taste Caterers | **W Vill**	22

Tastings/Payard | **E 70s**	27
Tentation Potel | **Garment**	22
Thomas Preti | **LIC**	23
Trunzo Bros. | **Bensonhurst**	25
☑ Whole Foods | **multi. loc.**	26
Wild Edibles | **multi. loc.**	26
☑ William Poll | **E 70s**	26
Williamson Calvert | **Prospect Hts**	-
Zeytuna | **Financial**	23

CAVIAR & SMOKED FISH

Acme Fish | **Greenpt**	24
☑ Agata/Valentina | **E 70s**	26
☑ Balducci's | **W 60s**	25
☑ Barney Greengrass | **W 80s**	27
☑ Blue Apron | **Park Slope**	27
Blue Moon Fish | **Mattituck**	29
Caviar Russe | **E 50s**	26
☑ Citarella | **multi. loc.**	26
☑ Dean/DeLuca | **multi. loc.**	27
☑ E.A.T. | **E 80s**	25
☑ Eli's Manhattan | **E 80s**	25
Eli's Vinegar | **E 90s**	25
☑ Fairway | **multi. loc.**	26
☑ Fresh Direct | **LIC**	23
Grace's Mktpl. | **E 70s**	24
Leonard's | **E 70s**	26
M & I Foods | **Brighton Bch**	24
Murray's Sturgeon | **W 80s**	27
Paramount Caviar | **LIC**	-
☑ Petrossian | **W 50s**	28
☑ Russ & Daughters | **LES**	28
Sable's Smoked | **E 70s**	27
Todaro Bros. | **Murray Hill**	24
Truffette | **E Vill**	-
☑ Whole Foods | **multi. loc.**	26
Wild Edibles | **multi. loc.**	26
☑ William Poll | **E 70s**	26
☑ Zabar's | **W 80s**	27
Zeytuna | **Financial**	23

CHARCUTERIE

☑ Agata/Valentina | **E 70s**	26
☑ Balducci's | **W 60s**	25
B & B Meat | **W'burg**	-
Bari Pork | **multi. loc.**	24
☑ Bedford Cheese | **W'burg**	27
Belfiore Meats | **Staten Is**	25
☑ Blue Apron | **Park Slope**	27

L'Epicerie | **Ft Greene**	-]
Lioni Latticini | **Bensonhurst**	29]
Maya Schaper | **W 60s**	22]
Mediterranean | **Astoria**	26]
☑ Murray's Cheese | **multi. loc.**	28]
Ninth Ave. Int'l | **W 40s**	23]
☑ Pastosa Ravioli | **multi. loc.**	26]
Peter's Mkt. | **Bayside**	-]
Piazza Mercato | **Bay Ridge**	-]
Pumpkins | **Park Slope**	26]
☑ Ronnybrook | **Chelsea**	28]
Russo Mozzarella | **multi. loc.**	26]
☑ Sahadi's | **Bklyn Hts**	27]
Saxelby Cheese | **LES**	28]
☑ Staubitz Mkt. | **Cobble Hill**	29]
Stinky Bklyn | **Cobble Hill**	28]
3-Corner Farm | **Shushan**	27]
☑ Titan Foods | **Astoria**	26]
Todaro Bros. | **Murray Hill**	24]
☑ Trader Joe's | **Union Sq**	24]
Westside Mkt. | **multi. loc.**	21]
☑ Whole Foods | **multi. loc.**	26]
Yoghurt Place | **multi. loc.**	23]
☑ Zabar's | **W 80s**	27]
Zeytuna | **Financial**	23]

CLASSES

(Call for details)

NEW ☑ Alessi | **SoHo**	27]
☑ Artisanal | **multi. loc.**	28]
Astor Wines | **NoHo**	25]
☑ Balducci's | **Chelsea**	25]
Bloomingdale's | **E 50s**	24]
NEW Brooklyn Kitchen | **W'burg**	-]
Bruno Bakery | **G Vill**	23]
Carol's Cuisine | **Staten Is**	-]
CBK Cookies | **E 80s**	23]
Chocolat Michel | **Gramercy**	25]
☑ Colette's | **W Vill**	29]
Confetti | **W 80s**	-]
Garden of Eden | **Bklyn Hts**	24]
Gourmet Garage | **W 90s**	20]
JoMart Choc. | **Marine Pk**	24]
NEW Kidfresh | **E 80s**	-]
Make My Cake | **Harlem**	25]
Margaret Palca | **Carroll Gdns**	-]
☑ Moore Bros. | **Flatiron**	29]
One Girl | **Cobble Hill**	24]
Pumpkins | **Park Slope**	26]
Stinky Bklyn | **Cobble Hill**	28]

☑ Sullivan St. Bakery | **W 40s**	28]
Sur La Table | **SoHo**	26]
Sweet Atelier | **E 80s**	-]
T Salon | **Chelsea**	26]

COFFEE & TEA

☑ Agata/Valentina | **E 70s**	26]
NEW ☑ Alessi | **SoHo**	27]
Alice's Tea | **multi. loc.**	24]
Amish Market | **multi. loc.**	23]
☑ Balducci's | **W 60s**	25]
☑ Bazzini | **TriBeCa**	27]
Bell Bates | **TriBeCa**	24]
☑ Blue Apron | **Park Slope**	27]
Bodum | **Meatpacking**	24]
☑ Bouchon Bakery | **W 60s**	27]
Brasil Coffee | **multi. loc.**	21]
BuonItalia | **Chelsea**	26]
NEW Café Grumpy | **multi. loc.**	26]
Carry On Tea | **W Vill**	23]
Chelsea Baskets | **Chelsea**	24]
Chocolate Bar | **multi. loc.**	26]
☑ Citarella | **multi. loc.**	26]
Cocoa Bar | **multi. loc.**	26]
☑ D'Amico | **Carroll Gdns**	27]
☑ Dean/DeLuca | **multi. loc.**	27]
Dual Specialty | **E Vill**	-]
Dynasty Supermkt. | **Chinatown**	19]
☑ Eli's Manhattan | **E 80s**	25]
Eli's Vinegar | **E 90s**	25]
Empire Coffee | **W 40s**	23]
☑ Fairway | **multi. loc.**	26]
Family Store | **Bay Ridge**	-]
NEW Fika | **W 50s**	22]
Franchia | **Murray Hill**	24]
☑ Fresh Direct | **LIC**	23]
Gimme! Coffee | **W'burg**	27]
Giorgione | **G Vill**	-]
Gorilla Coffee | **Park Slope**	24]
Gourmet Garage | **multi. loc.**	20]
Guy/Gallard | **multi. loc.**	20]
Harlem Tea | **Harlem**	25]
Hungarian Pastry | **W 100s**	22]
Iavarone Bros. | **Middle Vill**	25]
☑ Ito En | **E 60s**	28]
☑ Jack's Stir Brew | **G Vill**	27]
Java Girl | **E 60s**	24]
Jefferson Mkt. | **G Vill**	26]
Joe | **multi. loc.**	26]
Juan Valdez | **multi. loc.**	22]

Kalustyan's | **Gramercy**	27
Katagiri | **E 50s**	23
Klatch Coffee | **Financial**	-
Leaf/Bean | **Park Slope**	23
Le Pain Quotidien | **W 70s**	24
L'Epicerie | **Ft Greene**	-
Manhattan Espresso | **E 40s**	21
McNulty's Tea | **W Vill**	27
Mudspot | **E Vill**	26
Mule | **Park Slope**	-
Myers/Keswick | **W Vill**	23
Naidre's | **multi. loc.**	22
NEW Nespresso | **E 60s**	25
Ninth Ave. Int'l | **W 40s**	23
Ninth St. Espresso | **multi. loc.**	28
Oslo Coffee | **W'burg**	-
Ozzie's Coffee | **Park Slope**	19
Paneantico | **Bay Ridge**	26
Porto Rico | **multi. loc.**	26
Puff & Pao | **G Vill**	-
Rohrs | **E 80s**	24
Sahadi's | **Bklyn Hts**	27
Sensuous Bean | **W 70s**	25
71 Irving Pl. | **Gramercy**	22
Starbucks | **multi. loc.**	18
NEW Subtle Tea | **Murray Hill**	-
SugarHill Java | **Harlem**	-
Tamarind Tea | **Flatiron**	-
Tarallucci e Vino | **multi. loc.**	24
Tea Box | **E 50s**	27
Tea Lounge | **multi. loc.**	21
Ten Ren Tea | **multi. loc.**	25
Todaro Bros. | **Murray Hill**	24
T Salon | **multi. loc.**	26
Two for the Pot | **Bklyn Hts**	27
202 to Go | **Chelsea**	22
Union Mkt. | **Park Slope**	26
Whole Foods | **multi. loc.**	26
Zabar's | **W 80s**	27
Zeytuna | **Financial**	23
NEW Zibetto Espresso | **W 50s**	26

COOKIES

Agata/Valentina | **E 70s**	26
Amy's Bread | **multi. loc.**	26
Andrew & Alan's | **Staten Is**	22
Baked Ideas | **SoHo**	-
Balducci's | **W 60s**	25
Balthazar Bakery | **SoHo**	27
NEW Betty Bakery | **Boerum Hill**	-
Bijoux Doux | **multi. loc.**	-
Black Hound | **E Vill**	26
Bouchon Bakery | **W 60s**	27
Bread Alone | **Boiceville**	27
Bruno Bakery | **G Vill**	23
Café Indulge | **Murray Hill**	23
Cafe Scaramouche | **Carroll Gdns**	-
Caffé Roma | **Little Italy**	23
Caffe' Simpatico/Ruthy's | **multi. loc.**	15
Cake Chef | **Staten Is**	22
Cake Man | **Ft Greene**	26
Carry On Tea | **W Vill**	23
CBK Cookies | **E 80s**	23
Ceci-Cela | **multi. loc.**	24
Citarella | **multi. loc.**	26
City Bakery | **Flatiron**	25
Columbus | **W 80s**	21
Court | **Carroll Gdns**	25
Crumbs | **multi. loc.**	22
Dean/DeLuca | **multi. loc.**	27
Delillo Pastry | **Bronx**	26
DeRobertis | **E Vill**	22
Dessert Delivery | **E 50s**	28
Duane Pk. | **TriBeCa**	26
E.A.T. | **E 80s**	25
Eleni's Cookies | **Chelsea**	22
Eli's Manhattan | **E 80s**	25
Eli's Vinegar | **E 90s**	25
Ferrara Cafe | **Little Italy**	22
Financier | **Financial**	27
Good & Plenty | **W 40s**	22
Grace's Mktpl. | **E 70s**	24
Hungarian Pastry | **W 100s**	22
La Bergamote | **Chelsea**	26
Ladybird Bakery | **Park Slope**	-
Leske's | **Bay Ridge**	23
Levain Bakery | **W 70s**	28
Little Pie | **multi. loc.**	24
Madonia Bakery | **Bronx**	28
Magnolia Bakery | **W Vill**	23
Mansoura | **Midwood**	-
Margaret Palca | **Carroll Gdns**	-
Margot Pâtisserie | **W 70s**	27
Milk & Cookies | **W Vill**	24
Mother Mousse | **Staten Is**	26
Mother's Bake | **Bronx**	21
Mrs. Field's | **multi. loc.**	18
My Most/Food | **W 40s**	21

Nusbaum & Wu | **W 100s**	18
One Girl | **Cobble Hill**	24
Panya Bakery | **E Vill**	22
☑ Patisserie Claude | **G Vill**	27
☑ Payard | **E 70s**	28
Pozzo Pastry | **W 40s**	21
Rocco's Pastry | **G Vill**	25
Ruby/Violette | **W 50s**	26
Sal & Dom's | **Bronx**	28
Sarabeth's | **multi. loc.**	24
Schick's Bakery | **Borough Pk**	20
Settepani | **multi. loc.**	23
Silver Moon | **W 100s**	26
Something Sweet | **E Vill**	23
☑ Soutine | **W 70s**	27
☑ Stork's Pastry | **Whitestone**	27
Sweet Melissa | **multi. loc.**	24
Todaro Bros. | **Murray Hill**	24
☑ Two Little Red | **E 80s**	26
Veniero's | **E Vill**	25
Whole Earth | **E Vill**	-
☑ Whole Foods | **multi. loc.**	26
William Greenberg | **E 80s**	25

COOKWARE & SUPPLIES

NEW ☑ Alessi | **SoHo**	27
Art of Cooking | **W Vill**	23
Bed Bath/Beyond | **multi. loc.**	20
BJ's Wholesale | **multi. loc.**	17
Bloomingdale's | **E 50s**	24
Bodum | **Meatpacking**	24
Bowery Kitchen | **Chelsea**	22
☑ Bridge Kitchen. | **E 40s**	28
Broadway Pan. | **G Vill**	26
NEW Brooklyn Kitchen | **W'burg**	-
Choc-Oh! | **Bay Ridge**	-
Cook's Companion | **Bklyn Hts**	26
Costco | **Sunset Pk**	21
Crate/Barrel | **multi. loc.**	22
☑ Dean/DeLuca | **SoHo**	27
Gracious Home | **multi. loc.**	25
Hung Chong | **Chinatown**	19
Kam Man | **Chinatown**	21
☑ Korin Jap. | **TriBeCa**	28
Macy's Cellar | **Garment**	21
Maya Schaper | **W 60s**	22
O&CO. | **G Vill**	25
S. Feldman | **E 90s**	23
Sunrise Mart | **E Vill**	23
Sur La Table | **SoHo**	26

Target | **multi. loc.**	17
Tarzian West | **Park Slope**	22
☑ Terence Conran | **E 50s**	25
☑ Williams-Sonoma | **multi. loc.**	27

DELIS & SANDWICHES

☑ Agata/Valentina | **E 70s**	26
☑ Amy's Bread | **multi. loc.**	26
Artie's Deli | **W 80s**	21
☑ Balducci's | **W 60s**	25
Bánh Mì Saigon | **Chinatown**	25
NEW Barbarini | **Financial**	-
Belfiore Meats | **Staten Is**	25
Bell Bates | **TriBeCa**	24
Ben's Kosher | **multi. loc.**	21
Berger's | **Murray Hill**	21
Between/Bread | **W 50s**	21
Bottega/Via | **E 70s**	25
Bottino | **Chelsea**	22
☑ Bouchon Bakery | **W 60s**	27
☑ Bouley Bakery | **TriBeCa**	27
Bread Stuy | **Bed-Stuy**	-
BuonItalia | **Chelsea**	26
Butterfield Mkt. | **E 70s**	23
Café Habana | **NoLita**	24
Cafe Scaramouche | **Carroll Gdns**	-
Call Cuisine | **E 50s**	24
☑ Carnegie Deli | **W 50s**	23
Carve | **W 40s**	23
NEW Chicory Bklyn. | **Cobble Hill**	-
NEW Colson | **Park Slope**	25
Così | **multi. loc.**	18
Deli Masters | **Fresh Meadows**	21
Delmonico | **multi. loc.**	21
☑ Dom's | **SoHo**	27
☑ D'Vine | **Park Slope**	25
Eagle Provisions | **Park Slope**	24
☑ E.A.T. | **E 80s**	25
Eisenberg's Sandwich | **Flatiron**	20
☑ Eli's Manhattan | **E 80s**	25
Eli's Vinegar | **E 90s**	25
NEW Fika | **W 50s**	22
Financier | **Financial**	27
Fine/Schapiro | **W 70s**	20
Fraser-Morris | **Carroll Gdns**	-
Fresco/Scotto | **E 50s**	24
Garden of Eden | **multi. loc.**	24

Giorgione	G Vill	–
Good & Plenty	W 40s	22
Grace's Mktpl.	E 70s	24
NEW Z Grandaisy Bakery	SoHo	29
Guy/Gallard	multi. loc.	20
Health Nuts	multi. loc.	21
Iavarone Bros.	Maspeth	25
Italian Food	Little Italy	22
Z Kalustyan's	Gramercy	27
Z Katz's Deli	LES	24
Lassen/Hennigs	Bklyn Hts	22
Le Pain Quotidien	multi. loc.	24
L'Epicerie	Ft Greene	–
Lioni Latticini	Bensonhurst	29
Manganaro Foods	Garment	24
Manganaro's Hero	Garment	21
Mangia	multi. loc.	24
Milano Gourmet	multi. loc.	25
Z Murray's Cheese	G Vill	28
Naidre's	multi. loc.	22
Nicky's Viet.	multi. loc.	24
Z Olive's	SoHo	25
Paneantico	Bay Ridge	26
Parisi Bakery	NoLita	23
Pastrami Factory	Gramercy	22
Pastrami Queen	E 70s	21
Petak's	E 80s	23
Peter's Mkt.	Bayside	–
P.J. Bernstein	E 70s	19
Press 195	multi. loc.	25
Pret A Manger	multi. loc.	21
Russo Mozzarella	Park Slope	26
Z Salumeria	Chelsea	29
Sandwich Planet	Garment	25
Sarge's Deli	Murray Hill	21
Silver Moon	W 100s	26
Starwich	multi. loc.	23
NEW Swich	Chelsea	23
Tazza	Bklyn Hts	–
Tempo Presto	Park Slope	23
Todaro Bros.	Murray Hill	24
Trunzo Bros.	Bensonhurst	25
Tuscan Sq.	W 50s	22
Viet-Nam Bánh	Chinatown	23
Z Whole Foods	LES	26
'wichcraft	multi. loc.	24
Z William Poll	E 70s	26
Z Zabar's	W 80s	27
Zeytuna	Financial	23

DRIED FRUIT

Aji Ichiban	multi. loc.	21
Z Balducci's	W 60s	25
Z Bazzini	TriBeCa	27
Bell Bates	TriBeCa	24
Z Citarella	multi. loc.	26
Commodities	E Vill	25
Z Dean/DeLuca	multi. loc.	27
Dual Specialty	E Vill	–
Economy Candy	LES	24
Z Eli's Manhattan	E 80s	25
Eli's Vinegar	E 90s	25
Gourmet Garage	multi. loc.	20
Greenwich Produce	E 40s	25
Z Kalustyan's	Gramercy	27
Manhattan Fruit Ex.	Chelsea	24
Patel Bros.	Jackson Hts	23
Z Russ & Daughters	LES	28
Z Sahadi's	Bklyn Hts	27
Sweet Life	LES	23
Truffette	E Vill	–
Z Zabar's	W 80s	27

EVENT PLANNERS

Banchet Flowers	Meatpacking	–
Callahan	Garment	–
Castle/Pierpont	Garment	24
Chestnuts	TriBeCa	–
Z Cleaver Co.	Chelsea	25
Colin Cowie	Flatiron	28
NEW David Stark	Carroll Gdns	–
Gracious Thyme	Harlem	–
jesGORDON	Garment	–
Jonathan Flowers	W 50s	–
L'Olivier	multi. loc.	29
Miho Kosuda	E 40s	–
Movable Feast	Park Slope	23
Naturally Delicious	Carroll Gdns	–
Olivier Cheng	TriBeCa	22
Renny/Reed	E 50s	–
Robert Isabell	Meatpacking	27
Salsa	Bronx	–
Serena Bass	Meatpacking	–
Susan Holland	Flatiron	–
TableToppers	Stamford	–
Taste Caterers	W Vill	22
Tempo Presto	Park Slope	23
Tentation Potel	Garment	22
Wizard Events	Jeff Valley	–

EXOTIC PRODUCE

☑ Agata/Valentina | **E 70s**	26
☑ Dean/DeLuca | **E 80s**	27
☑ Eli's Manhattan | **E 80s**	25
Eli's Vinegar | **E 90s**	25
☑ Fairway | **multi. loc.**	26
Garden of Eden | **multi. loc.**	24
Grace's Mktpl. | **E 70s**	24
Greenwich Produce | **E 40s**	25
Hong Kong | **multi. loc.**	20
Jim/Andy's | **Cobble Hill**	-
Katagiri | **E 50s**	23
Keith's Farm | **Westtown**	28
Likitsakos | **E 80s**	22
Manhattan Fruit Ex. | **Chelsea**	24
Marché Madison | **E 70s**	20
Perelandra | **Bklyn Hts**	24
3 Guys/Brooklyn | **Bay Ridge**	23
Truffette | **E Vill**	-
Zeytuna | **Financial**	23

FLOWERS

Academy Floral | **W 100s**	23
Anthony Gdn. | **E 70s**	-
Antony Todd | **E Vill**	-
Ariston | **multi. loc.**	27
Banchet Flowers | **Meatpacking**	-
☑ Belle Fleur | **Flatiron**	28
Big Apple Florist | **E 40s**	24
☑ Bloom | **E 50s**	27
Blue Water | **SoHo**	-
Castle/Pierpont | **Garment**	24
Chelsea Wholesale | **Chelsea**	25
Chestnuts | **TriBeCa**	-
Dahlia | **multi. loc.**	26
☑ Dean/DeLuca | **multi. loc.**	27
☑ Eli's Manhattan | **E 80s**	25
Eli's Vinegar | **E 90s**	25
Elizabeth Ryan | **E Vill**	28
Fellan Florist | **E 60s**	24
Floralies | **E 50s**	26
Flowers/Reuven | **Garment**	-
Flowers/World | **multi. loc.**	28
Gotham Gardens | **W 70s**	24
☑ Greenmarket | **multi. loc.**	26
Jonathan Flowers | **W 50s**	-
Katrina Parris | **Harlem**	-
LMD Floral | **E Vill**	-
L'Olivier | **E 70s**	29
Magnolia Flowers | **W Vill**	26

Michael George | **E 40s**	25
Miho Kosuda | **E 40s**	-
Mille Fiori | **Chelsea**	-
Ovando | **W Vill**	-
Plaza Flowers | **E 60s**	-
Polux Fleuriste | **NoLita**	-
Renny/Reed | **E 50s**	-
Richard Salome | **E 70s**	-
Robert Isabell | **Meatpacking**	27
Ronaldo Maia | **E 90s**	-
Rootstock/Quade | **Park Slope**	-
Rosa Rosa | **E 60s**	21
Seaport Flowers | **Bklyn Hts**	-
Stonekelly | **W 50s**	25
Surroundings | **W 70s**	25
☑ Takashimaya | **E 50s**	28
VSF | **W Vill**	29
☑ Whole Foods | **multi. loc.**	26
Windsor Florist | **E 70s**	24
☑ Zezé | **E 50s**	29
ZuZu's Petals | **Park Slope**	26

GAME

(May need prior notice)

☑ Agata/Valentina | **E 70s**	26
Albert's Meats | **E 60s**	26
☑ Balducci's | **W 60s**	25
Biancardi Meats | **Bronx**	27
☑ Citarella | **multi. loc.**	26
☑ Dean/DeLuca | **multi. loc.**	27
☑ Dom's | **SoHo**	27
Eagle Provisions | **Park Slope**	24
☑ Eli's Manhattan | **E 80s**	25
Eli's Vinegar | **E 90s**	25
Empire Market | **College Pt**	-
Esposito Meat | **Garment**	25
☑ Florence Meat | **G Vill**	29
Frank's | **Chelsea**	24
Grace's Mktpl. | **E 70s**	24
Heights Meats | **Bklyn Hts**	24
Holland Court | **E 90s**	24
Iavarone Bros. | **Maspeth**	25
Le Marais | **W 40s**	26
Leonard's | **E 70s**	26
Les Halles | **Gramercy**	24
☑ Lobel's Meats | **E 80s**	29
Mazur's Marketpl. | **Douglaston**	20
Oppenheimer | **W 90s**	26
☑ Ottomanelli & Sons | **multi. loc.**	27
Ottomanelli Bros. | **multi. loc.**	24

☑ Ottomanelli's Meats | **Flushing** 27	Grace's Mktpl. | **E 70s** 24
Peter's Mkt. | **Bayside** –	Iavarone Bros. | **multi. loc.** 25
Pino Meats | **SoHo** 27	Italian Food | **Little Italy** 22
Quattro's | **Pleasant Valley** 26	☑ Ito En | **E 60s** 28
☑ Schaller & Weber | **E 80s** 27	☑ Jacques Torres | **Dumbo** 28
Schatzie's Meats | **E 80s** 25	Java Girl | **E 60s** 24
☑ Simchick | **E 50s** 28	Jinil/Chocolat | **Midwood** –
Vincent's Meat | **Bronx** 27	K & D Wines | **E 90s** 24
☑ Whole Foods | **multi. loc.** 26	Leaf/Bean | **Park Slope** 23
	Le Pain Quotidien | **SoHo** 24
GIFT BASKETS	Magnolia Flowers | **W Vill** 26
(All Mail Order index entries as well	☑ Manhattan Fruitier | **Gramercy** 27
as most candy and flower shops,	☑ MarieBelle's | **SoHo** 26
plus the following standouts)	Marquet Patisserie | **Boerum Hill** 24
Acker Merrall | **W 70s** 26	Maya Schaper | **W 60s** 22
☑ Agata/Valentina | **E 70s** 26	☑ Minamoto | **W 40s** 28
Antony Todd | **E Vill** –	☑ Morrell & Co. | **W 40s** 27
☑ Artisanal | **multi. loc.** 28	☑ Murray's Cheese | **G Vill** 28
Australian Home. | **E Vill** 23	Myers/Keswick | **W Vill** 23
☑ Balducci's | **W 60s** 25	Nordic Delicacies | **Bay Ridge** 28
☑ Bazzini | **TriBeCa** 27	O&CO. | **multi. loc.** 25
Beth's Kitchen | **Stuyvesant Falls** 27	Once Upon/Tart | **SoHo** 25
☑ Black Hound | **E Vill** 26	One Girl | **Cobble Hill** 24
☑ Bloom | **E 50s** 27	Orchard | **Midwood** 27
Butterfield Mkt. | **E 70s** 23	Oren's/Roast | **multi. loc.** 24
Cafe Scaramouche | **Carroll Gdns** –	Pane d'Italia | **Whitestone** –
Caviar Russe | **E 50s** 26	Paramount Caviar | **LIC** –
CBK Cookies | **E 80s** 23	☑ Petrossian | **W 50s** 28
Chelsea Baskets | **Chelsea** 24	Red Jacket | **Geneva** 27
Chelsea Wine | **Chelsea** 23	Richard Salome | **E 70s** –
Chocolate Bar | **W Vill** 26	Ruby/Violette | **W 50s** 26
Christopher Norman | **Financial** 23	☑ Russ & Daughters | **LES** 28
☑ Citarella | **multi. loc.** 26	☑ Sahadi's | **Bklyn Hts** 27
Dale & Thomas | **W 70s** 23	Sarabeth's | **multi. loc.** 24
☑ Dean/DeLuca | **multi. loc.** 27	Scharffen Berger | **W 80s** 26
☑ Dessert Delivery | **E 50s** 28	Sea Grape | **W Vill** 23
☑ Dylan's Candy | **E 60s** 21	☑ Sherry-Lehmann | **E 60s** 29
☑ E.A.T. | **E 80s** 25	☑ Soutine | **W 70s** 27
Economy Candy | **LES** 24	Surroundings | **W 70s** 25
☑ Eli's Manhattan | **E 80s** 25	☑ Takashimaya | **E 50s** 28
Eli's Vinegar | **E 90s** 25	**NEW** Tribeca Treats | **TriBeCa** 27
Family Store | **Bay Ridge** –	Truffette | **E Vill** –
Fat Witch | **Chelsea** 25	Trunzo Bros. | **Bensonhurst** 25
Fellan Florist | **E 60s** 24	T Salon | **Chelsea** 26
Fifth Ave. Choc. | **multi. loc.** 20	Vintage NY | **multi. loc.** 23
Financier | **Financial** 27	☑ Vosges Haut | **SoHo** 26
Fraser-Morris | **Carroll Gdns** –	☑ Whole Foods | **multi. loc.** 26
Garden of Eden | **multi. loc.** 24	Wild Edibles | **multi. loc.** 26
Gotham Gardens | **W 70s** 24	William Greenberg | **E 80s** 25
Grab Specialty | **Park Slope** –	

☑ William Poll | **E 70s**	26
☑ Zabar's | **W 80s**	27
Zeytuna | **Financial**	23
☑ Zezé | **E 50s**	29

GIFT IDEAS

(See also Gift Baskets)

NEW ☑ Alessi | **SoHo**	27
Alice's Tea | **W 70s**	24
Art of Cooking | **W Vill**	23
☑ Bazzini | **TriBeCa**	27
Bloomingdale's | **E 50s**	24
Bodum | **Meatpacking**	24
☑ Bridge Kitchen. | **E 40s**	28
Broadway Pan. | **G Vill**	26
☑ Dean/DeLuca | **SoHo**	27
☑ Ito En | **E 60s**	28
☑ Korin Jap. | **TriBeCa**	28
Leaf/Bean | **Park Slope**	23
☑ MarieBelle's | **SoHo**	26
Maya Schaper | **W 60s**	22
☑ Minamoto | **W 40s**	28
Nordic Delicacies | **Bay Ridge**	28
Ronaldo Maia | **E 90s**	-
☑ Takashimaya | **E 50s**	28
Tea Box | **E 50s**	27
☑ Terence Conran | **E 50s**	25
☑ Williams-Sonoma | **multi. loc.**	27

GINGERBREAD HOUSES

Amish Market | **W 40s**	23
☑ Bazzini | **TriBeCa**	27
Bruno Bakery | **G Vill**	23
Caffe' Simpatico/Ruthy's | **multi. loc.**	15
Chez Laurence | **Murray Hill**	23
☑ Citarella | **multi. loc.**	26
☑ Dean/DeLuca | **multi. loc.**	27
Egidio Pastry | **Bronx**	24
Garden of Eden | **multi. loc.**	24
Ladybird Bakery | **Park Slope**	-
Todaro Bros. | **Murray Hill**	24
☑ Two Little Red | **E 80s**	26

GREENMARKET

(See p. 108 for locations)

Berkshire Berries	27
Berried Treasures	28
Beth's Kitchen	27
Blue Moon Fish	29
Bread Alone	27
Bulich Mushroom	29
Cato Farm	27
Cherry Ln.	28
Coach Dairy	28
DiPaola Turkey	27
Eckerton Hill	26
Flying Pigs	28
Gorzynski/Farm	27
☑ Greenmarket	26
Hawthorne Farm	28
Keith's Farm	28
Martin's Pretzels	27
Migliorelli Farm	26
Our Daily Bread	26
Paffenroth	28
PE & DD	28
Quattro's	26
Red Jacket	27
☑ Ronnybrook	28
Samascott	27
Stokes Farm	27
Terhune Orchards	27
3-Corner Farm	27
Violet Hill	29
Windfall Farms	27
Yuno's Farm	29

HARD-TO-FIND INGREDIENTS

☑ Agata/Valentina | **E 70s**	26
Angelica's Herbs | **E Vill**	23
Aphrodisia | **G Vill**	26
Asia Market | **Chinatown**	21
☑ Balducci's | **W 60s**	25
☑ Bangkok Grocery | **Chinatown**	27
☑ Citarella | **multi. loc.**	26
☑ Dean/DeLuca | **multi. loc.**	27
Dual Specialty | **E Vill**	-
☑ Eli's Manhattan | **E 80s**	25
Eli's Vinegar | **E 90s**	25
☑ Fairway | **multi. loc.**	26
Foods/India | **Murray Hill**	23
Grace's Mktpl. | **E 70s**	24
☑ Greenmarket | **Financial**	26
Han Ah Reum | **multi. loc.**	22
Hong Keung | **Chinatown**	22
JAS Mart | **W 100s**	21
☑ Kalustyan's | **Gramercy**	27
Kam Man | **Chinatown**	21
Katagiri | **E 50s**	23

m2m	**multi. loc.**	18
Ninth Ave. Int'l	**W 40s**	23
Nordic Delicacies	**Bay Ridge**	28
Patel Bros.	**multi. loc.**	23
✏ Sahadi's	**Bklyn Hts**	27
Spice Corner	**Gramercy**	24
Sunrise Mart	**E Vill**	23
Teitel Bros.	**Bronx**	26
✏ Titan Foods	**Astoria**	26
Truffette	**E Vill**	–
✏ Two for the Pot	**Bklyn Hts**	27
✏ Whole Foods	**Chelsea**	26
✏ Zabar's	**W 80s**	27

HEALTH & NATURAL FOODS

(See also Organic)

A Matter/Health	**E 70s**	21
BabyCakes	**LES**	24
Back/Land	**Park Slope**	23
Bell Bates	**TriBeCa**	24
Better Burger	**Murray Hill**	19
Bird Bath	**E Vill**	–
Commodities	**E Vill**	25
✏ Fairway	**multi. loc.**	26
Foragers Mkt.	**Dumbo**	–
✏ Fresh Direct	**LIC**	23
Gary Null's	**W 80s**	25
Health/Harmony	**W Vill**	26
Health Nuts	**multi. loc.**	21
Integral Yoga	**W Vill**	24
Le Pain Quotidien	**E 60s**	24
LifeThyme Mkt.	**G Vill**	24
Natural Frontier	**multi. loc.**	24
Nature's Gifts	**E 80s**	21
Park Natural	**Carroll Gdns**	–
Perelandra	**Bklyn Hts**	24
Pumpkins	**Park Slope**	26
Second Helpings	**Park Slope**	–
Tastebud's	**Staten Is**	–
✏ Westerly Natural	**W 50s**	25
Whole Earth	**E Vill**	–
✏ Whole Foods	**multi. loc.**	26

HERBS & SPICES

Angelica's Herbs	**E Vill**	23
Aphrodisia	**G Vill**	26
Asia Market	**Chinatown**	21
Bell Bates	**TriBeCa**	24
Commodities	**E Vill**	25
✏ Dean/DeLuca	**multi. loc.**	27

Dual Specialty	**E Vill**	–
Dynasty Supermkt.	**Chinatown**	19
Family Store	**Bay Ridge**	–
Foods/India	**Murray Hill**	23
✏ Kalustyan's	**Gramercy**	27
Ninth Ave. Int'l	**W 40s**	23
Patel Bros.	**Jackson Hts**	23
✏ Penzeys Spices	**E 40s**	27
✏ Sahadi's	**Bklyn Hts**	27
Spice Corner	**Gramercy**	24
Truffette	**E Vill**	–
✏ Two for the Pot	**Bklyn Hts**	27
✏ Zabar's	**W 80s**	27

HISTORIC INTEREST

(Year opened)

1820	Acker Merrall	**W 70s**	26
1886	Bazzini	**TriBeCa**	27
1888	Katz's Deli	**LES**	24
1890	Esposito Meat	**Garment**	25
1890	Yonah Schimmel	**LES**	23
1892	Alleva Dairy	**Little Italy**	27
1892	Ferrara Cafe	**Little Italy**	22
1893	Manganaro Foods	**Garment**	24
1894	Veniero's	**E Vill**	25
1895	McNulty's Tea	**W Vill**	27
1896	Rohrs	**E 80s**	24
1897	Jahn's Ice Cream	**Richmond Hill**	20
1898	Sahadi's	**Bklyn Hts**	27
1900	Faicco's Pork	**multi. loc.**	28
1900	Ottomanelli Bros.	**E 80s**	24
1900	Samascott	**Kinderhook**	27
1900	Sea Breeze	**W 40s**	23
1902	Glaser's Bake	**E 80s**	21
1904	Caputo Bakery	**Carroll Gdns**	23
1906	Raffetto's	**G Vill**	28
1907	Katagiri	**E 50s**	23
1908	Barney Greengrass	**W 80s**	27
1908	Empire Coffee	**W 40s**	23
1908	Russo Mozzarella	**E Vill**	26
1910	Academy Floral	**W 100s**	23
1910	Eddie's Sweet	**Forest Hills**	25
1910	Leonard's	**E 70s**	26
1910	Parisi Bakery	**NoLita**	23
1910	Pisacane	**E 50s**	28
1912	Egidio Pastry	**Bronx**	24
1914	Russ & Daughters	**LES**	28

1915 | Butterfield Mkt. | **E 70s** 23
1915 | Consenza's | **Bronx** 27
1915 | Teitel Bros. | **Bronx** 26
1916 | Orwasher's | **E 70s** 26
1917 | Staubitz Mkt. | **Cobble Hill** 29
1917 | Todaro Bros. | **Murray Hill** 24
1918 | Caffé Roma | **Little Italy** 23
1918 | Madonia Bakery | **Bronx** 28
1920 | Piemonte Ravioli | **Little Italy** 27
1920 | Slavin | **Brownsville** 23
1920 | Vesuvio | **SoHo** 23
1921 | Empire Market | **College Pt** –
1921 | William Poll | **E 70s** 26
1922 | Casa Della | **Bronx** 29
1922 | Esposito's Pork | **Carroll Gdns** 26
1923 | Jeffrey's | **LES** –
1923 | Poseidon | **W 40s** 26
1924 | Hinsch's | **Bay Ridge** 22
1925 | County Chair | **Mt. Vernon** –
1925 | Delillo Pastry | **Bronx** 26
1925 | DiPalo Dairy | **Little Italy** 29
1925 | Joe's Dairy | **SoHo** 28
1925 | Randazzo's | **Bronx** 28
1925 | Salumeria | **Chelsea** 29
1925 | Streit's Matzo | **LES** 25
1927 | Fellan Florist | **E 60s** 24
1927 | Mazzola Bakery | **Carroll Gdns** 25
1929 | Addeo's | **Bronx** 27
1929 | Eisenberg's Sandwich | **Flatiron** 20
1929 | Jefferson Mkt. | **G Vill** 26
1929 | Lafayette | **G Vill** 21
1929 | S. Feldman | **E 90s** 23
1930 | Bruno Bakery | **G Vill** 23
1930 | Damascus Bread | **Bklyn Hts** 25
1930 | Philip's Candy | **Staten Is** –
1931 | Zabar's | **W 80s** 27
1932 | Biancardi Meats | **Bronx** 27
1932 | Quality Hse. | **Murray Hill** 27
1933 | Eggers Ice Cream | **Staten Is** 25
1933 | In Vino | **E 70s** 25
1933 | Sutton Wine | **E 50s** 22
1934 | Carnegie Deli | **W 50s** 23
1934 | Economy Candy | **LES** 24
1935 | Borgatti's | **Bronx** 29
1935 | Kossar's | **LES** 28

1935 | McAdam | **Gramercy** 22
1935 | Mount Carmel | **Bronx** 26
1935 | Ottomanelli & Sons | **G Vill** 27
1936 | Florence Meat | **G Vill** 29
1937 | La Guli | **Astoria** 24
1937 | Schaller & Weber | **E 80s** 27
1937 | Stage Deli | **W 50s** 21
1938 | Jordan's Lobster | **Sheepshead Bay** 23
1940 | Beekman Mktpl. | **E 40s** 22
1940 | Holland Court | **E 90s** 24
1941 | Italian Food | **Little Italy** 22
1943 | Mondel Choc. | **W 100s** 22
1943 | Schick's Bakery | **Borough Pk** 20
1944 | Lemon Ice | **Corona** 27
1946 | Artuso Pastry | **Bronx** 26
1946 | JoMart Choc. | **Marine Pk** 24
1946 | Murray's Sturgeon | **W 80s** 27
1946 | William Greenberg | **E 80s** 25
1948 | Court | **Carroll Gdns** 25
1948 | D'Amico | **Carroll Gdns** 27
1948 | Frank's Gourmet | **Wash. Hts** 21
1948 | Yorkville Meat | **E 80s** 23
1949 | Fischer Bros. | **W 70s** 27
1949 | Lassen/Hennigs | **Bklyn Hts** 22
1950 | Leske's | **Bay Ridge** 23
1950 | Stork's Pastry | **Whitestone** 27
1951 | DiPaola Turkey | **Hamilton** 27
1952 | Calandra Cheese | **Bronx** 26
1952 | Cheese/World | **Forest Hills** 25
1952 | Pozzo Pastry | **W 40s** 21
1954 | Acme Fish | **Greenpt** 24
1954 | Ideal Cheese | **E 50s** 27
1954 | Lobel's Meats | **E 80s** 29
1954 | Mother's Bake | **Bronx** 21
1954 | Oppenheimer | **W 90s** 26
1954 | Vincent's Meat | **Bronx** 27
1956 | Manganaro's Hero | **Garment** 21
1956 | Sal & Dom's | **Bronx** 28

HORS D'OEUVRES

Ⓩ Agata/Valentina | **E 70s** 26
Ⓩ Balducci's | **W 60s** 25
Between/Bread | **W 50s** 21
BJ's Wholesale | **multi. loc.** 17

Butterfield Mkt.	**E 70s**	23	🅩 Colson	**Park Slope**	25
Call Cuisine	**E 50s**	24	Cones	**G Vill**	26
🅩 Carnegie Deli	**W 50s**	23	🅩 Dylan's Candy	**E 60s**	21
Ceriello	**multi. loc.**	24	🆕 East Village Ice Cream	**E Vill**	–
Certé	**W 50s**	–		
Chez Laurence	**Murray Hill**	23	Eddie's Sweet	**Forest Hills**	25
🅩 Citarella	**multi. loc.**	26	Eggers Ice Cream	**Staten Is**	25
🅩 Dean/DeLuca	**multi. loc.**	27	Emack/Bolio	**multi. loc.**	25
Dishes	**E 40s**	24	Ferrara Cafe	**Little Italy**	22
Dumpling Man	**E Vill**	20	Financier	**Financial**	27
🅩 E.A.T.	**E 80s**	25	🆕 Grom	**W 70s**	–
Eli's Vinegar	**E 90s**	25	Häagen Dazs	**multi. loc.**	24
🅩 Fairway	**multi. loc.**	26	Hinsch's	**Bay Ridge**	22
Family Store	**Bay Ridge**	–	🅩 Il Laboratorio	**LES**	28
Gourmet Garage	**multi. loc.**	20	Jahn's Ice Cream	**Richmond Hill**	20
Grace's Mktpl.	**E 70s**	24	La Guli	**Astoria**	24
Italian Food	**Little Italy**	22	L'Arte/Gelato	**Chelsea**	27
Likitsakos	**E 80s**	22	🅩 Lemon Ice	**Corona**	27
Mangia	**multi. loc.**	24	Maggie Moo's	**multi. loc.**	21
Mansoura	**Midwood**	–	Mary's Dairy	**multi. loc.**	24
Marché Madison	**E 70s**	20	Max & Mina's	**Flushing**	25
🅩 May May	**Chinatown**	23	🅩 Payard	**E 70s**	28
Nordic Delicacies	**Bay Ridge**	28	pinkberry	**multi. loc.**	–
Once Upon/Tart	**SoHo**	25	Piu Bello	**Forest Hills**	21
Petak's	**E 80s**	23	Ralph's/Ices	**multi. loc.**	24
Peter's Mkt.	**Bayside**	–	Rita's Ices	**Staten Is**	21
🅩 Petrossian	**W 50s**	28	Rocco's Pastry	**G Vill**	25
Piazza Mercato	**Bay Ridge**	–	🅩 Ronnybrook	**Chelsea**	28
Remi	**W 50s**	26	Sant Ambroeus	**multi. loc.**	26
🅩 Soutine	**W 70s**	27	Sedutto's	**multi. loc.**	24
Special Attention	**LES**	–	Shake Shack	**Flatiron**	25
Todaro Bros.	**Murray Hill**	24	Sundaes & Cones	**E Vill**	25
🅩 Trader Joe's	**Union Sq**	24	Tarallucci e Vino	**Flatiron**	24
Wild Edibles	**E 40s**	26	Tempo Presto	**Park Slope**	23
🅩 William Poll	**E 70s**	26	Uncle Louie	**multi. loc.**	20
🅩 Zabar's	**W 80s**	27	🅩 Villabate	**Bensonhurst**	28
			🅩 Vosges Haut	**SoHo**	26

ICE CREAM

Anopoli Ice Cream	**Bay Ridge**	–	**KOSHER**		
Australian Home.	**E Vill**	23	Bagels & Co.	**multi. loc.**	22
Baskin-Robbins	**multi. loc.**	17	Ben's Kosher	**multi. loc.**	21
🅩 Bazzini	**TriBeCa**	27	Brasil Coffee	**Murray Hill**	21
Ben & Jerry's	**multi. loc.**	24	Buttercup	**W 70s**	23
🆕 Blue Pig	**Bklyn Hts**	–	Crumbs	**multi. loc.**	22
Bottega/Via	**multi. loc.**	25	Deli Masters	**Fresh Meadows**	21
Brooklyn Ice Cream	**multi. loc.**	25	🅩 Dessert Delivery	**E 50s**	28
Bruno Bakery	**G Vill**	23	Dimple	**multi. loc.**	22
Chinatown Ice Cream	**Chinatown**	25	Fifth Ave. Choc.	**multi. loc.**	20
Ciao Bella	**multi. loc.**	25	Fine/Schapiro	**W 70s**	20
Cold Stone	**multi. loc.**	20	Fischer Bros.	**W 70s**	27

Foremost Caterers	**Moonachie**	24
H & H Bagels	**multi. loc.**	26
H & H Midtown	**E 80s**	25
Jinil/Chocolat	**Midwood**	–
⚡ Kossar's	**LES**	28
Le Marais	**W 40s**	26
Maggie Moo's	**Park Slope**	21
Manna Catering	**TriBeCa**	–
Mansoura	**Midwood**	–
Mauzone	**Flushing**	22
Max & Mina's	**Flushing**	25
Mazur's Marketpl.	**Douglaston**	20
Mother's Bake	**Bronx**	21
My Most/Food	**W 40s**	21
Newman/Leventhal	**W 80s**	–
Orchard	**Midwood**	27
Orwasher's	**E 70s**	26
Park E. Kosher	**E 80s**	26
Pastrami Queen	**E 70s**	21
⚡ Pickle Guys	**LES**	27
Schick's Bakery	**Borough Pk**	20
Streit's Matzo	**LES**	25
William Greenberg	**E 80s**	25

MAJOR GOURMET MARKETS

⚡ Agata/Valentina	**E 70s**	26
Amish Market	**multi. loc.**	23
⚡ Balducci's	**multi. loc.**	25
BJ's Wholesale	**Starrett City**	17
⚡ Citarella	**multi. loc.**	26
Costco	**multi. loc.**	21
⚡ Dean/DeLuca	**multi. loc.**	27
⚡ Dom's	**SoHo**	27
⚡ Eli's Manhattan	**E 80s**	25
Eli's Vinegar	**E 90s**	25
⚡ Fairway	**multi. loc.**	26
Food Emporium	**multi. loc.**	16
⚡ Fresh Direct	**LIC**	23
Garden of Eden	**multi. loc.**	24
Gourmet Garage	**multi. loc.**	20
Grace's Mktpl.	**E 70s**	24
Jefferson Mkt.	**G Vill**	26
Jubilee	**Financial**	21
⚡ Trader Joe's	**Union Sq**	24
Union Mkt.	**Park Slope**	26
⚡ Whole Foods	**Chelsea**	26
⚡ Zabar's	**W 80s**	27
Zeytuna	**Financial**	23

MEAT & POULTRY

⚡ Agata/Valentina	**E 70s**	26
Albert's Meats	**E 60s**	26
Astoria Meat	**Astoria**	25
⚡ Balducci's	**W 60s**	25
B & B Meat	**W'burg**	–
Bari Pork	**multi. loc.**	24
Bayard St.	**multi. loc.**	23
⚡ Bazzini	**TriBeCa**	27
Beekman Mktpl.	**E 40s**	22
Belfiore Meats	**Staten Is**	25
Biancardi Meats	**Bronx**	27
⚡ Calabria Pork	**Bronx**	28
Ceriello	**multi. loc.**	24
Christos Steak	**Astoria**	–
⚡ Citarella	**multi. loc.**	26
Costco	**multi. loc.**	21
⚡ Dean/DeLuca	**multi. loc.**	27
Deluxe Food	**Chinatown**	21
⚡ Dom's	**SoHo**	27
Dynasty Supermkt.	**Chinatown**	19
Eagle Provisions	**Park Slope**	24
⚡ East Village Meat	**E Vill**	28
⚡ Eli's Manhattan	**E 80s**	25
Eli's Vinegar	**E 90s**	25
Empire Market	**College Pt**	–
Esposito Meat	**Garment**	25
Esposito's Pork	**Carroll Gdns**	26
⚡ Faicco's Pork	**multi. loc.**	28
⚡ Fairway	**multi. loc.**	26
Fischer Bros.	**W 70s**	27
⚡ Florence Meat	**G Vill**	29
Frank's	**Chelsea**	24
⚡ Fresh Direct	**LIC**	23
Garden	**Greenpt**	24
Garden of Eden	**multi. loc.**	24
Grace's Mktpl.	**E 70s**	24
⚡ Greenmarket	**multi. loc.**	26
G.S. Food	**Chinatown**	19
Hawthorne Farm	**Ghent**	28
Heights Meats	**Bklyn Hts**	24
Holland Court	**E 90s**	24
Iavarone Bros.	**Maspeth**	25
Jeffrey's	**LES**	–
Jubilee	**multi. loc.**	21
Koglin Hams	**E 40s**	24
Le Marais	**W 40s**	26
Leonard's	**E 70s**	26
L'Epicerie	**Ft Greene**	–
Les Halles	**Gramercy**	26

NYC SOURCES

SPECIAL FEATURES

⚡ Amy's Bread	**G Vill**	26
Arte/Corner	**W 70s**	24
Arthur Ave.	**Bronx**	24
⚡ Balducci's	**Chelsea**	25
Balthazar Bakery	**SoHo**	27
NEW Barbarini	**Financial**	-
Bari Pork	**multi. loc.**	24
⚡ Barney Greengrass	**W 80s**	27
⚡ Bazzini	**TriBeCa**	27
Beekman Mktpl.	**E 40s**	22
Belfiore Meats	**Staten Is**	25
Between/Bread	**W 50s**	21
Boerum Hill Food	**Boerum Hill**	-
Bonsignour	**W Vill**	26
Bottega/Via	**E 70s**	25
Bottino	**Chelsea**	22
⚡ Bouchon Bakery	**W 60s**	27
⚡ Bouley Bakery	**TriBeCa**	27
BuonItalia	**Chelsea**	26
Butterfield Mkt.	**E 70s**	23
Call Cuisine	**E 50s**	24
Carmine's	**multi. loc.**	23
Carve	**W 40s**	23
Certé	**W 50s**	-
NEW Chicory Bklyn.	**Cobble Hill**	-
Cipriani	**E 40s**	26
⚡ Citarella	**multi. loc.**	26
⚡ City Bakery	**Flatiron**	25
Clinton St.	**LES**	26
NEW Cobblestone	**Carroll Gdns**	-
Cucina	**multi. loc.**	21
Cucina Vivolo	**multi. loc.**	23
⚡ Dean/DeLuca	**multi. loc.**	27
Delmonico	**multi. loc.**	21
Dishes	**multi. loc.**	24
⚡ Dom's	**SoHo**	27
⚡ E.A.T.	**E 80s**	25
⚡ Eli's Manhattan	**E 80s**	25
Eli's Vinegar	**E 90s**	25
⚡ Fairway	**multi. loc.**	26
Fresco/Scotto	**E 50s**	24
Giorgione	**G Vill**	-
Good & Plenty	**W 40s**	22
Grace's Mktpl.	**E 70s**	24
Hale/Hearty	**multi. loc.**	22
Indian Bread	**G Vill**	21
Italian Food	**Little Italy**	22
⚡ Katz's Deli	**LES**	24

Le Pain Quotidien	**multi. loc.**	24
Lorenzo/Maria's	**E 80s**	25
Luscious Food	**Park Slope**	-
NEW Madison	**E 90s**	-
Mangia	**multi. loc.**	24
Mansoura	**Midwood**	-
Marché Madison	**E 70s**	20
Melange	**E 60s**	21
Milano Gourmet	**multi. loc.**	25
Out/Kitchen	**W Vill**	-
⚡ Payard	**E 70s**	28
Petak's	**E 80s**	23
Petite Abeille	**multi. loc.**	22
Pret A Manger	**multi. loc.**	21
Ready to Eat	**W Vill**	21
Remi	**W 50s**	26
⚡ Salumeria	**Chelsea**	29
Sandwich Planet	**Garment**	25
Starwich	**multi. loc.**	23
NEW Swich	**Chelsea**	23
Tempo Presto	**Park Slope**	23
Todaro Bros.	**Murray Hill**	24
Tuscan Sq.	**W 50s**	22
⚡ Whole Foods	**multi. loc.**	26
⚡ Zabar's	**W 80s**	27
Zeytuna	**Financial**	23

ONE-STOP SHOPPING

⚡ Agata/Valentina	**E 70s**	26
Amish Market	**multi. loc.**	23
⚡ Balducci's	**W 60s**	25
⚡ Bazzini	**TriBeCa**	27
BJ's Wholesale	**multi. loc.**	17
⚡ Citarella	**multi. loc.**	26
Costco	**multi. loc.**	21
⚡ Dean/DeLuca	**multi. loc.**	27
Delmonico	**multi. loc.**	21
⚡ Eli's Manhattan	**E 80s**	25
Eli's Vinegar	**E 90s**	25
⚡ Fairway	**multi. loc.**	26
Food Emporium	**multi. loc.**	16
⚡ Fresh Direct	**LIC**	23
Garden	**Greenpt**	24
Garden of Eden	**multi. loc.**	24
Gary Null's	**W 80s**	25
Gourmet Garage	**multi. loc.**	20
Grace's Mktpl.	**E 70s**	24
Hong Keung	**Chinatown**	22
Jefferson Mkt.	**G Vill**	26
Jubilee	**Financial**	21

Kam Man | **Chinatown** — 21
LifeThyme Mkt. | **G Vill** — 24
M & I Foods | **Brighton Bch** — 24
Patel Bros. | **multi. loc.** — 23
Perelandra | **Bklyn Hts** — 24
Sunrise Mart | **E Vill** — 23
☑ Titan Foods | **Astoria** — 26
Todaro Bros. | **Murray Hill** — 24
☑ Trader Joe's | **Union Sq** — 24
Union Mkt. | **Park Slope** — 26
☑ Whole Foods | **multi. loc.** — 26
☑ Zabar's | **W 80s** — 27
Zeytuna | **Financial** — 23

OPEN LATE

BAGELS & BIALYS
☑ Absolute Bagels | **W 100s** — 26
Daniel's Bagels | **Murray Hill** — 24
East Side Bagel | **E 70s** — 21
Ess-a-Bagel | **multi. loc.** — 26
H & H Bagels | **multi. loc.** — 26
H & H Midtown | **E 80s** — 25
Murray's Bagels | **G Vill** — 26
Pick a Bagel | **multi. loc.** — 20
Tal Bagels | **multi. loc.** — 23
Times Sq. Bagels | **W 40s** — 19

BAKED GOODS
☑ Amy's Bread | **multi. loc.** — 26
Artuso Pastry | **Bronx** — 26
Au Bon Pain | **multi. loc.** — 16
Balthazar Bakery | **SoHo** — 27
Billy's Bakery | **Chelsea** — 25
☑ Black Hound | **E Vill** — 26
Bruno Bakery | **G Vill** — 23
Buttercup | **E 50s** — 23
Carrot Top | **Wash. Hts** — 23
Clinton St. | **LES** — 26
Columbus | **W 80s** — 21
Court | **Carroll Gdns** — 25
Crumbs | **multi. loc.** — 22
Eileen's Cheesecake | **NoLita** — 26
Fabiane's | **W'burg** — -
Ferrara Cafe | **Little Italy** — 22
Financier | **Financial** — 27
Hungarian Pastry | **W 100s** — 22
Junior's | **multi. loc.** — 23
Little Pie | **E 40s** — 24
Mrs. Field's | **Seaport** — 18
Nusbaum & Wu | **W 100s** — 18

☑ Payard | **E 70s** — 28
☑ Rice/Riches | **NoLita** — 23
Rocco's Pastry | **G Vill** — 25
Sarabeth's | **multi. loc.** — 24
☑ Sugar Sweet | **LES** — 27
Sweet Melissa | **Cobble Hill** — 24
Tai Pan Bakery | **Chinatown** — 19
Veniero's | **E Vill** — 25

CANDY & NUTS
Chocolate Bar | **W Vill** — 26
☑ Dylan's Candy | **E 60s** — 21
Godiva | **Financial** — 22
World of Nuts | **multi. loc.** — 15

CHEESE & DAIRY
☑ Artisanal | **Murray Hill** — 28
☑ Bedford Cheese | **W'burg** — 27

COFFEE & TEA
Brasil Coffee | **LIC** — 21
Carry On Tea | **W Vill** — 23
Doma | **W Vill** — 25
Franchia | **Murray Hill** — 24
Gorilla Coffee | **Park Slope** — 24
Juan Valdez | **W 40s** — 22
Mudspot | **E Vill** — 26
Naidre's | **multi. loc.** — 22
Ozzie's Coffee | **Park Slope** — 19
☑ Tavalon Tea | **Union Sq** — 24
Tea Lounge | **Park Slope** — 21

DELIS & SANDWICHES
☑ Carnegie Deli | **W 50s** — 23
Così | **multi. loc.** — 18
☑ Katz's Deli | **LES** — 24
Nicky's Viet. | **E Vill** — 24
Tiny's Giant | **LES** — 22

HEALTH & NATURAL FOODS
Gary Null's | **W 80s** — 25
Health/Harmony | **W Vill** — 26
Health Nuts | **multi. loc.** — 21
Integral Yoga | **W Vill** — 24
LifeThyme Mkt. | **G Vill** — 24

ICE CREAM
Australian Home. | **E Vill** — 23
Baskin-Robbins | **multi. loc.** — 17
Ben & Jerry's | **multi. loc.** — 24
Brooklyn Ice Cream | **Dumbo** — 25
Chinatown Ice Cream | **Chinatown** — 25
Cold Stone | **multi. loc.** — 20

Cones	**G Vill**	26
Emack/Bolio	**W 70s**	25
Häagen Dazs	**multi. loc.**	24
☑ Lemon Ice	**Corona**	27
Maggie Moo's	**multi. loc.**	21
Sant Ambroeus	**multi. loc.**	26
Sedutto's	**multi. loc.**	24

MEAT, POULTRY & GAME

Christos Steak	**Astoria**	-

PREPARED FOODS

A Salt/Battery	**W Vill**	22
Better Burger	**multi. loc.**	19
Café Habana	**NoLita**	24
Cafe Spice	**E 40s**	19
Carmine's	**multi. loc.**	23
Cozy Soup	**G Vill**	17
F&B	**Chelsea**	20
Hampton Chutney	**SoHo**	23
Mandler's	**Union Sq**	22
Milano Gourmet	**W 100s**	25
Otafuku	**E Vill**	19
Petite Abeille	**multi. loc.**	22
Pie/Pound	**E Vill**	20
Risotteria	**G Vill**	23
Snack	**SoHo**	27
Starwich	**Financial**	23
Tuck Shop	**E Vill**	-
Zaitzeff	**Financial**	28

PRODUCE

Annie's	**E 80s**	21
Likitsakos	**E 80s**	22
#1 Farmers Mkt.	**multi. loc.**	23

SOUPS

☑ Original SoupMan	**multi. loc.**	23

SPECIALTY SHOPS

Ceriello	**E 40s**	24
Dale & Thomas	**multi. loc.**	23
Delmonico	**multi. loc.**	21
Han Ah Reum	**multi. loc.**	22
JAS Mart	**multi. loc.**	21
Kam Man	**Chinatown**	21
Marlow	**W'burg**	-
m2m	**W 100s**	18
Patel Bros.	**multi. loc.**	23
Sunrise Mart	**multi. loc.**	23
Todaro Bros.	**Murray Hill**	24

WINES, BEER & LIQUOR

Astor Wines	**NoHo**	25
Beacon Wines	**W 70s**	21
☑ Bierkraft	**Park Slope**	28
De Vino	**LES**	25
Greene Grape	**Financial**	24
Is Wine	**G Vill**	-
☑ Le Dû's Wines	**W Vill**	27
Manley's Wines	**W Vill**	22
Nancy's-Wines	**W 70s**	24
New York/Exchange	**Financial**	23
Pasanella	**Seaport**	-
Sea Grape	**W Vill**	23
Sept. Wines	**LES**	-
Wine Therapy	**NoLita**	-
Winfield-Flynn	**Murray Hill**	23

OPEN SUNDAY

(Except for liquor stores, butchers and fish markets, most places are open Sunday; here are some sources in those hard-to-find categories)

Acker Merrall	**W 70s**	26
Ambassador Wine	**E 50s**	24
Astor Wines	**NoHo**	25
Bacchus Wine	**W 70s**	19
Bari Pork	**multi. loc.**	24
Bayard St.	**multi. loc.**	23
Beacon Wines	**W 70s**	21
Belfiore Meats	**Staten Is**	25
Best Cellars	**multi. loc.**	21
☑ Bierkraft	**Park Slope**	28
Blanc & Rouge	**Dumbo**	-
Brooklyn Liquors	**Sunset Pk**	23
Chambers Wines	**TriBeCa**	26
Chelsea Wine	**Chelsea**	23
Christos Steak	**Astoria**	-
Columbus Wine	**W 50s**	22
Crossroads	**Union Sq**	25
☑ Crush Wine	**E 50s**	26
De Vino	**LES**	25
Discovery Wines	**E Vill**	22
Eagle Provisions	**Park Slope**	24
Embassy Wines	**E 60s**	19
Empire Market	**College Pt**	-
Esposito's Pork	**Carroll Gdns**	26
☑ Faicco's Pork	**multi. loc.**	28
Frank's	**Chelsea**	24
Garnet Wines	**E 60s**	24
Gotham Wines	**W 90s**	22
Gramercy Fish	**Gramercy**	24

Grande Harvest	**E 40s**	23
Greene Grape	**multi. loc.**	24
G.S. Food	**Chinatown**	19
Harlem Vintage	**Harlem**	28
Hong Keung	**Chinatown**	22
Iavarone Bros.	**multi. loc.**	25
Is Wine	**G Vill**	-
Jordan's Lobster	**Sheepshead Bay**	23
Koglin Hams	**E 40s**	24
Le Marais	**W 40s**	26
⚡ LeNell's	**Red Hook**	27
Leonard's	**E 70s**	26
Les Halles	**Gramercy**	26
Lobster Pl.	**Chelsea**	26
Manley's Wines	**W Vill**	22
Mazur's Marketpl.	**Douglaston**	20
McAdam	**Gramercy**	22
McCabe's Wines	**E 70s**	19
Mister Wright	**E 80s**	24
⚡ Morrell & Co.	**E 60s**	26
Mount Carmel	**Bronx**	26
Nancy's-Wines	**W 70s**	24
New Beef	**Chinatown**	-
Ottomanelli Bros.	**multi. loc.**	24
Park E. Kosher	**E 80s**	26
Pescatore	**E 40s**	25
Piazza Mercato	**Bay Ridge**	-
Premier Cru	**E 80s**	24
⚡ Prospect Wine	**Park Slope**	26
Quattro's	**Pleasant Valley**	26
⚡ Red/White	**Park Slope**	26
Sea Grape	**W Vill**	23
67 Wines	**W 60s**	25
Slavin	**Brownsville**	23
Slope Cellars	**Park Slope**	24
Smith & Vine	**Cobble Hill**	23
Sui Cheong Meat	**Chinatown**	20
Sutton Wine	**E 50s**	22
Union Sq. Wines	**Union Sq**	25
Uva	**W'burg**	-
⚡ Vino	**Gramercy**	28
Vintage NY	**multi. loc.**	23
Warehouse Wines	**G Vill**	22
Wild Edibles	**multi. loc.**	26
W.I.N.E.	**E 80s**	21
Winfield-Flynn	**Murray Hill**	23
Yorkshire Wines	**E 80s**	23
Yorkville Meat	**E 80s**	23

ORGANIC

Albert's Meats	**E 60s**	26
A Matter/Health	**E 70s**	21
Amish Market	**multi. loc.**	23
⚡ Amy's Bread	**W 40s**	26
Aphrodisia	**G Vill**	26
Appellation	**Chelsea**	25
Arte/Corner	**W 70s**	24
BabyCakes	**LES**	24
Back/Land	**Park Slope**	23
Beekman Mktpl.	**E 40s**	22
Bell Bates	**TriBeCa**	24
⚡ Bierkraft	**Park Slope**	28
Bird Bath	**multi. loc.**	-
Boerum Hill Food	**Boerum Hill**	-
⚡ Bouchon Bakery	**W 60s**	27
Bread Alone	**Boiceville**	27
⚡ City Bakery	**Flatiron**	25
⚡ Cleaver Co.	**Chelsea**	25
Columbus	**W 80s**	21
Commodities	**E Vill**	25
Discovery Wines	**E Vill**	22
Earthmatters	**LES**	21
Empire Market	**College Pt**	-
⚡ Fairway	**multi. loc.**	26
Foragers Mkt.	**Dumbo**	-
Frank's Gourmet	**Wash. Hts**	21
⚡ Fresh Direct	**LIC**	23
Garden	**Greenpt**	24
Gary Null's	**W 80s**	25
Gorilla Coffee	**Park Slope**	24
Gourmet Garage	**multi. loc.**	20
Hawthorne Farm	**Ghent**	28
Health/Harmony	**W Vill**	26
Health Nuts	**multi. loc.**	21
Holland Court	**E 90s**	24
Integral Yoga	**W Vill**	24
⚡ Jack's Stir Brew	**multi. loc.**	27
Jubilee	**SoHo**	21
Keith's Farm	**Westtown**	28
NEW Kidfresh	**E 80s**	-
Leaf/Bean	**Park Slope**	23
Le Pain Quotidien	**multi. loc.**	24
L'Epicerie	**Ft Greene**	-
LifeThyme Mkt.	**G Vill**	24
Liqueteria	**E Vill**	19
Marlow	**W'burg**	-
Milk & Cookies	**W Vill**	24
Mule	**Park Slope**	-
Natural Frontier	**multi. loc.**	24

Nordic Delicacies | **Bay Ridge**	28
Oppenheimer | **W 90s**	26
Orchard | **Midwood**	27
☑ Ottomanelli & Sons | **G Vill**	27
Ottomanelli Bros. | **E 80s**	24
Ozzie's Coffee | **Park Slope**	19
Park Natural | **Carroll Gdns**	–
Pino Meats | **SoHo**	27
Pumpkins | **Park Slope**	26
Really Cool | **E 60s**	21
☑ Ronnybrook | **Chelsea**	28
Second Helpings | **Park Slope**	–
Sensuous Bean | **W 70s**	25
Starwich | **multi. loc.**	23
Tastebud's | **Staten Is**	–
Tea Lounge | **multi. loc.**	21
Tempo Presto | **Park Slope**	23
202 to Go | **Chelsea**	22
Union Mkt. | **Park Slope**	26
Urban Organic | **Park Slope**	22
Uva | **W'burg**	–
☑ Westerly Natural | **W 50s**	25
Whole Earth | **E Vill**	–
☑ Whole Foods | **multi. loc.**	26
Zeytuna | **Financial**	23

PARTY RENTALS

Abbey Rent | **Bayside**	–
☑ Atlas Party | **Mt. Vernon**	23
Broadway Famous | **multi. loc.**	19
County Chair | **Mt. Vernon**	–
Metro Party | **Paterson**	–
Party Rental | **multi. loc.**	22
Party Time | **Elmhurst**	20
Props/Today | **Garment**	20
Something Different | **Paterson**	–
TableToppers | **Stamford**	–
☑ TriServe | **E 60s**	24
Wizard Events | **Jeff Valley**	–

PASTAS

☑ Agata/Valentina | **E 70s**	26
Arte/Corner | **W 70s**	24
☑ Balducci's | **W 60s**	25
☑ Bazzini | **TriBeCa**	27
☑ Borgatti's | **Bronx**	29
Bruno/Ravioli | **multi. loc.**	24
Cassinelli Food | **Astoria**	25
Ceriello | **multi. loc.**	24
☑ Citarella | **multi. loc.**	26

☑ Coluccio/Sons | **Borough Pk**	28
☑ Dean/DeLuca | **multi. loc.**	27
☑ DiPalo Dairy | **Little Italy**	29
☑ Dom's | **SoHo**	27
Durso's Pasta | **Flushing**	26
☑ Eli's Manhattan | **E 80s**	25
Eli's Vinegar | **E 90s**	25
☑ Fairway | **multi. loc.**	26
☑ Fresh Direct | **LIC**	23
Gourmet Garage | **multi. loc.**	20
Grace's Mktpl. | **E 70s**	24
Iavarone Bros. | **multi. loc.**	25
Italian Food | **Little Italy**	22
Lioni Latticini | **Bensonhurst**	29
☑ Murray's Cheese | **G Vill**	28
Papa Pasquale | **Bensonhurst**	26
☑ Pastosa Ravioli | **multi. loc.**	26
Peter's Mkt. | **Bayside**	–
Piemonte Ravioli | **Little Italy**	27
Queen Ann | **Bensonhurst**	27
☑ Raffetto's | **G Vill**	28
Ravioli | **SoHo**	25
Russo Mozzarella | **multi. loc.**	26
Savino's Pasta | **W'burg**	–
Todaro Bros. | **Murray Hill**	24
☑ Whole Foods | **multi. loc.**	26
☑ Zabar's | **W 80s**	27

PICNICS

Between/Bread | **W 50s**	21
Cafe Scaramouche | **Carroll Gdns**	–
☑ Citarella | **multi. loc.**	26
☑ Dean/DeLuca | **multi. loc.**	27
☑ Eli's Manhattan | **E 80s**	25
Eli's Vinegar | **E 90s**	25
Garden of Eden | **multi. loc.**	24
Good & Plenty | **W 40s**	22
Grace's Mktpl. | **E 70s**	24
Great Performances | **SoHo**	24
Lassen/Hennigs | **Bklyn Hts**	22
Movable Feast | **Park Slope**	23
Todaro Bros. | **Murray Hill**	24
Wild Edibles | **Murray Hill**	26

PIES/TARTS

Balthazar Bakery | **SoHo**	27
☑ Black Hound | **E Vill**	26
☑ Bouchon Bakery | **W 60s**	27
Bread Alone | **Boiceville**	27
Buttercup | **E 50s**	23

Café Indulge | **Murray Hill**	23	William Greenberg | **E 80s**	25
Cafe Scaramouche | **Carroll Gdns**	–	Wong Bakery | **Chinatown**	–

PREPARED FOODS

(See also Delis & Sandwiches and Soups)

Caffe' Simpatico/Ruthy's | **Chelsea**	15	☑ Agata/Valentina | **E 70s**	26
Cake Chef | **Staten Is**	22	Arte/Corner | **W 70s**	24
Ceci-Cela | **multi. loc.**	24	A Salt/Battery | **W Vill**	22
☑ Citarella | **multi. loc.**	26	☑ Balducci's | **W 60s**	25
☑ City Bakery | **Flatiron**	25	NEW Barbarini | **Financial**	–
☑ Dean/DeLuca | **multi. loc.**	27	Bari Pork | **multi. loc.**	24
Delillo Pastry | **Bronx**	26	☑ Bazzini | **TriBeCa**	27
☑ Dessert Delivery | **E 50s**	28	Belfiore Meats | **Staten Is**	25
Duane Pk. | **TriBeCa**	26	Bell Bates | **TriBeCa**	24
Egidio Pastry | **Bronx**	24	Better Burger | **multi. loc.**	19
Fabiane's | **W'burg**	–	Between/Bread | **W 50s**	21
☑ Fairway | **multi. loc.**	26	Bonsignour | **W Vill**	26
Financier | **Financial**	27	Bottega/Via | **E 70s**	25
Friend/Farmer | **Gramercy**	21	☑ Bouchon Bakery | **W 60s**	27
Glaser's Bake | **E 80s**	21	BuonItalia | **Chelsea**	26
Grace's Mktpl. | **E 70s**	24	Butterfield Mkt. | **E 70s**	23
Hungarian Pastry | **W 100s**	22	Café Habana | **NoLita**	24
La Bergamote | **Chelsea**	26	Café Indulge | **Murray Hill**	23
Ladybird Bakery | **Park Slope**	–	Cafe Spice | **E 40s**	19
La Guli | **Astoria**	24	Call Cuisine | **E 50s**	24
Little Pie | **multi. loc.**	24	Carmine's | **multi. loc.**	23
☑ Magnolia Bakery | **W Vill**	23	Carry On Tea | **W Vill**	23
Margaret Palca | **Carroll Gdns**	–	Chickpea | **E Vill**	23
Margot Pâtisserie | **W 70s**	27	NEW Chicory Bklyn. | **Cobble Hill**	–
Marquet Patisserie | **multi. loc.**	24	NEW Choice Mkt. | **Clinton Hill**	–
Martha's Bakery | **Astoria**	–	NEW Christie's | **Prospect Hts**	21
My Most/Food | **W 40s**	21	☑ Citarella | **multi. loc.**	26
Once Upon/Tart | **SoHo**	25	☑ City Bakery | **Flatiron**	25
Panya Bakery | **E Vill**	22	☑ Cleaver Co. | **Chelsea**	25
☑ Patisserie Claude | **G Vill**	27	Clinton St. | **LES**	26
☑ Payard | **E 70s**	28	NEW Cobblestone | **Carroll Gdns**	–
☑ Petrossian | **W 50s**	28	Commodities | **E Vill**	25
Sarabeth's | **multi. loc.**	24	NEW Corner Bakery | **E 90s**	–
Settepani | **multi. loc.**	23	Così | **multi. loc.**	18
Shakoor's Sweet | **Bed-Stuy**	–	Costco | **Sunset Pk**	21
Silver Moon | **W 100s**	26	Cozy Soup | **G Vill**	17
☑ Soutine | **W 70s**	27	Cucina | **multi. loc.**	21
Steve's/Pies | **Red Hook**	25	Daisy May's | **W 40s**	24
☑ Stork's Pastry | **Whitestone**	27	☑ Dean/DeLuca | **multi. loc.**	27
☑ Sugar Sweet | **LES**	27	Delmonico | **multi. loc.**	21
Sweet Melissa | **multi. loc.**	24	Devon/Blakely | **multi. loc.**	22
NEW Three Tarts | **Chelsea**	22	DiFiore | **G Vill**	–
☑ Two Little Red | **E 80s**	26	Dimple | **multi. loc.**	22
Umanoff/Parsons | **TriBeCa**	24		
Veniero's | **E Vill**	25		

Dirty Bird | **W Vill**	20
Dishes | **multi. loc.**	24
⊠ Dom's | **SoHo**	27
DUB Pies | **Carroll Gdns**	24
Dumpling Man | **E Vill**	20
Durso's Pasta | **Flushing**	26
⊠ D'Vine | **Park Slope**	25
⊠ E.A.T. | **E 80s**	25
Egg Custard King | **Chinatown**	–
⊠ Eli's Manhattan | **E 80s**	25
Eli's Vinegar | **E 90s**	25
⊠ Faicco's Pork | **multi. loc.**	28
⊠ Fairway | **multi. loc.**	26
Family Store | **Bay Ridge**	–
F&B | **Chelsea**	20
Fifth Ave. Epicure | **Flatiron**	19
Financier | **Financial**	27
First Ave. Pierogi | **E Vill**	25
Flor/Mayo | **multi. loc.**	23
Fresco/Scotto | **E 50s**	24
Fresh Bites | **W 50s**	–
Garden of Eden | **multi. loc.**	24
Gary Null's | **W 80s**	25
Gauchas | **E 90s**	25
Good & Plenty | **W 40s**	22
Gourmet Garage | **multi. loc.**	20
Grace's Mktpl. | **E 70s**	24
Gramercy Fish | **Gramercy**	24
Hampton Chutney | **multi. loc.**	23
Health Nuts | **multi. loc.**	21
Iavarone Bros. | **Maspeth**	25
Indian Bread | **G Vill**	21
Integral Yoga | **W Vill**	24
Int'l Poultry | **E 50s**	–
Italian Food | **Little Italy**	22
JAS Mart | **multi. loc.**	21
Jefferson Mkt. | **G Vill**	26
Jubilee | **multi. loc.**	21
⊠ Kalustyan's | **Gramercy**	27
Kam Man | **Chinatown**	21
Katagiri | **E 50s**	23
NEW Kidfresh | **E 80s**	–
Leonard's | **E 70s**	26
Le Pain Quotidien | **W 70s**	24
LifeThyme Mkt. | **G Vill**	24
Likitsakos | **E 80s**	22
⊠ Lobel's Meats | **E 80s**	29
Lobster Pl. | **Chelsea**	26
Lorenzo/Maria's | **E 80s**	25
Luscious Food | **Park Slope**	–
NEW Madison | **E 90s**	–
M & I Foods | **Brighton Bch**	24
Mandler's | **multi. loc.**	22
Manganaro Foods | **Garment**	24
Mangia | **multi. loc.**	24
Marché Madison | **E 50s**	20
Mauzone | **Flushing**	22
NEW Max Brenner | **multi. loc.**	22
⊠ May May | **Chinatown**	23
Mazur's Marketpl. | **Douglaston**	20
Melange | **E 60s**	21
Michelle's Kitchen | **E 90s**	18
Milano Gourmet | **multi. loc.**	25
Myers/Keswick | **W Vill**	23
Natural Frontier | **multi. loc.**	24
Ninth Ave. Int'l | **W 40s**	23
⊠ Olive's | **SoHo**	25
Ottomanelli Bros. | **multi. loc.**	24
⊠ Ottomanelli's Meats | **Flushing**	27
Paneantico | **Bay Ridge**	26
Park E. Kosher | **E 80s**	26
Pepe | **multi. loc.**	26
Perelandra | **Bklyn Hts**	24
Pescatore | **E 40s**	25
Petak's | **E 80s**	23
Peter's Mkt. | **Bayside**	–
Petite Abeille | **multi. loc.**	22
Piazza Mercato | **Bay Ridge**	–
Pie/Pound | **E Vill**	20
Press 195 | **multi. loc.**	25
Pret A Manger | **multi. loc.**	21
Puff & Pao | **G Vill**	–
Ready to Eat | **W Vill**	21
Remi | **W 50s**	26
Risotteria | **G Vill**	23
Ruben's | **multi. loc.**	20
Russo Mozzarella | **Park Slope**	26
⊠ Sahadi's | **Bklyn Hts**	27
Sandwich Planet | **Garment**	25
⊠ Schaller & Weber | **E 80s**	27
Second Helpings | **Park Slope**	–
Shake Shack | **Flatiron**	25
Snack | **multi. loc.**	27
Sunrise Mart | **multi. loc.**	23
Sweet Melissa | **multi. loc.**	24
Tanoreen | **Bay Ridge**	–
Tastebud's | **Staten Is**	–
Tazza | **Bklyn Hts**	–
Thalia Kitchen | **W 50s**	21
Tiny's Giant | **LES**	22

NEW Tisserie | **Union Sq**	20
Todaro Bros. | **Murray Hill**	24
Tuck Shop | **multi. loc.**	–
Tuscan Sq. | **W 50s**	22
Union Mkt. | **Park Slope**	26
United Meat | **Windsor Terr**	–
Westside Mkt. | **multi. loc.**	21
☑ Whole Foods | **multi. loc.**	26
Wild Edibles | **multi. loc.**	26
☑ William Poll | **E 70s**	26
Yonah Schimmel | **LES**	23
☑ Zabar's | **W 80s**	27
Zaitzeff | **Financial**	28
Zeytuna | **Financial**	23

PRODUCE

☑ Agata/Valentina | **E 70s**	26
Amish Market | **multi. loc.**	23
Annie's | **E 80s**	21
Asia Market | **Chinatown**	21
☑ Balducci's | **W 60s**	25
☑ Bazzini | **TriBeCa**	27
Bell Bates | **TriBeCa**	24
Berried Treasures | **Roscoe**	28
Bulich Mushroom | **Catskill**	29
Butterfield Mkt. | **E 70s**	23
Cherry Ln. | **Bridgeton**	28
☑ Citarella | **multi. loc.**	26
Commodities | **E Vill**	25
Costco | **multi. loc.**	21
☑ Dean/DeLuca | **E 80s**	27
Dynasty Supermkt. | **Chinatown**	19
☑ E.A.T. | **E 80s**	25
Eckerton Hill | **Hamburg**	26
☑ Eli's Manhattan | **E 80s**	25
Eli's Vinegar | **E 90s**	25
☑ Fairway | **multi. loc.**	26
☑ Fresh Direct | **LIC**	23
Garden | **Greenpt**	24
Garden of Eden | **multi. loc.**	24
Gary Null's | **W 80s**	25
Gourmet Garage | **multi. loc.**	20
Grace's Mktpl. | **E 70s**	24
☑ Greenmarket | **multi. loc.**	26
Greenwich Produce | **E 40s**	25
Hawthorne Farm | **Ghent**	28
Health/Harmony | **W Vill**	26
Health Nuts | **multi. loc.**	21
Hong Kong | **multi. loc.**	20
Integral Yoga | **W Vill**	24

Jefferson Mkt. | **G Vill**	26
Jim/Andy's | **Cobble Hill**	–
Katagiri | **E 50s**	23
Keith's Farm | **Westtown**	28
LifeThyme Mkt. | **G Vill**	24
Likitsakos | **E 80s**	22
Manhattan Fruit Ex. | **Chelsea**	24
☑ Manhattan Fruitier | **Gramercy**	27
Marché Madison | **E 70s**	20
Migliorelli Farm | **Tivoli**	26
Natural Frontier | **multi. loc.**	24
Nature's Gifts | **E 80s**	21
New Green Pea | **Bklyn Hts**	23
#1 Farmers Mkt. | **multi. loc.**	23
Paffenroth | **Warwick**	28
Park Natural | **Carroll Gdns**	–
Perelandra | **Bklyn Hts**	24
Pumpkins | **Park Slope**	26
Red Jacket | **Geneva**	27
Samascott | **Kinderhook**	27
Tan My My | **Chinatown**	22
Terhune Orchards | **Salt Pt**	27
3 Guys/Brooklyn | **Bay Ridge**	23
☑ Trader Joe's | **Union Sq**	24
Truffette | **E Vill**	–
Urban Organic | **Park Slope**	22
Westside Mkt. | **multi. loc.**	21
☑ Whole Foods | **multi. loc.**	26
Windfall Farms | **Montgomery**	27
WK Trading | **Chinatown**	–
Yuno's Farm | **Bordentown**	29
☑ Zabar's | **W 80s**	27
Zeytuna | **Financial**	23

SEAFOOD

☑ Agata/Valentina | **E 70s**	26
Amish Market | **multi. loc.**	23
Asia Market | **Chinatown**	21
☑ Balducci's | **W 60s**	25
Blue Moon Fish | **Mattituck**	29
☑ Citarella | **multi. loc.**	26
Consenza's | **Bronx**	27
Costco | **multi. loc.**	21
☑ Dean/DeLuca | **multi. loc.**	27
☑ Dorian's Seafood | **E 80s**	25
Dynasty Supermkt. | **Chinatown**	19
☑ Eli's Manhattan | **E 80s**	25
Eli's Vinegar | **E 90s**	25
☑ Fairway | **multi. loc.**	26
Fish Tales | **Cobble Hill**	25

🅵 Fresh Direct | **LIC**	23
Garden of Eden | **multi. loc.**	24
Gourmet Garage | **multi. loc.**	20
Grace's Mktpl. | **E 70s**	24
Gramercy Fish | **Gramercy**	24
🅵 Greenmarket | **multi. loc.**	26
G.S. Food | **Chinatown**	19
Holland Court | **E 90s**	24
Hong Kong | **multi. loc.**	20
Jefferson Mkt. | **G Vill**	26
Jubilee | **multi. loc.**	21
Leonard's | **E 70s**	26
Lobster Pl. | **multi. loc.**	26
New Star Fish | **LES**	–
131 Fish Market | **Chinatown**	24
Pescatore | **E 40s**	25
🅵 Pisacane | **E 50s**	28
Rainbo's Fish | **LES**	–
🅵 Randazzo's | **Bronx**	28
Sea Breeze | **W 40s**	23
Slavin | **Brownsville**	23
Sunrise Mart | **multi. loc.**	23
Tan My My | **Chinatown**	22
Todaro Bros. | **Murray Hill**	24
Union Mkt. | **Park Slope**	26
🅵 Whole Foods | **multi. loc.**	26
Wild Edibles | **multi. loc.**	26
Zeytuna | **Financial**	23

SOUPS

🅵 Agata/Valentina | **E 70s**	26
🅵 Balducci's | **W 60s**	25
🅵 Bazzini | **TriBeCa**	27
Cafe Scaramouche | **Carroll Gdns**	–
Caffe' Simpatico/Ruthy's | **W 50s**	15
Cipriani | **E 40s**	26
🅵 Citarella | **multi. loc.**	26
Cozy Soup | **G Vill**	17
🅵 Dean/DeLuca | **multi. loc.**	27
Dishes | **multi. loc.**	24
🅵 Dom's | **SoHo**	27
🅵 Eli's Manhattan | **E 80s**	25
Fabiane's | **W'burg**	–
🅵 Fairway | **multi. loc.**	26
Fifth Ave. Epicure | **Flatiron**	19
Financier | **Financial**	27
Good & Plenty | **W 40s**	22
Grace's Mktpl. | **E 70s**	24

Hale/Hearty | **multi. loc.**	22
Iavarone Bros. | **Maspeth**	25
Jefferson Mkt. | **G Vill**	26
Le Pain Quotidien | **multi. loc.**	24
Likitsakos | **E 80s**	22
Liqueteria | **E Vill**	19
Marquet Patisserie | **Ft Greene**	24
🅵 Olive's | **SoHo**	25
🅵 Original SoupMan | **multi. loc.**	23
🅵 Pisacane | **E 50s**	28
Todaro Bros. | **Murray Hill**	24
Tuscan Sq. | **W 50s**	22
🅵 Westerly Natural | **W 50s**	25
🅵 Whole Foods | **multi. loc.**	26
🅵 Zabar's | **W 80s**	27

SPECIALTY SHOPS

Asia Market | **Chinatown**	21
🅵 Bangkok Grocery | **Chinatown**	27
Beth's Kitchen | **Stuyvesant Falls**	27
🅵 Blue Apron | **Park Slope**	27
BuonItalia | **Chelsea**	26
Butterfield Mkt. | **E 70s**	23
Ceriello | **multi. loc.**	24
Chelsea Baskets | **Chelsea**	24
NEW Cobblestone | **Carroll Gdns**	–
🅵 Coluccio/Sons | **Borough Pk**	28
Dale & Thomas | **multi. loc.**	23
Delmonico | **multi. loc.**	21
Deluxe Food | **Chinatown**	21
🅵 Despaña | **multi. loc.**	27
🅵 Dom's | **SoHo**	27
🅵 D'Vine | **Park Slope**	25
Dynasty Supermkt. | **Chinatown**	19
Family Store | **Bay Ridge**	–
Fong Inn | **Chinatown**	–
Foragers Mkt. | **Dumbo**	–
Frank's Gourmet | **Wash. Hts**	21
Garden | **Greenpt**	24
Grab Specialty | **Park Slope**	–
Han Ah Reum | **multi. loc.**	22
Hong Kong | **multi. loc.**	20
Italian Food | **Little Italy**	22
JAS Mart | **multi. loc.**	21
Jubilee | **multi. loc.**	21
🅵 Kalustyan's | **Gramercy**	27
Kam Man | **Chinatown**	21
Katagiri | **E 50s**	23
NEW Kidfresh | **E 80s**	–

L'Epicerie | **Ft Greene**	–
M & I Foods | **Brighton Bch**	24
☑ Manhattan Fruitier | **Gramercy**	27
Marlow | **W'burg**	–
☑ May May | **Chinatown**	23
Mediterranean | **Astoria**	26
m2m | **multi. loc.**	18
Myers/Keswick | **W Vill**	23
Ninth Ave. Int'l | **W 40s**	23
Nordic Delicacies | **Bay Ridge**	28
O&CO. | **multi. loc.**	25
Orchard | **Midwood**	27
Patel Bros. | **multi. loc.**	23
Peter's Mkt. | **Bayside**	–
☑ Pickle Guys | **LES**	27
Pickles/Olives | **E 80s**	23
Pumpkins | **Park Slope**	26
☑ Sahadi's | **Bklyn Hts**	27
NEW ☑ Stonehouse | **E Vill**	27
Sunrise Mart | **multi. loc.**	23
Teitel Bros. | **Bronx**	26
☑ Titan Foods | **Astoria**	26
Todaro Bros. | **Murray Hill**	24
Truffette | **E Vill**	–
Trunzo Bros. | **Bensonhurst**	25

TRENDY

NEW ☑ Alessi | **SoHo**	27
☑ Artisanal | **Murray Hill**	28
Baked | **Red Hook**	25
Balthazar Bakery | **SoHo**	27
Billy's Bakery | **Chelsea**	25
☑ Bouchon Bakery | **W 60s**	27
Centovini | **SoHo**	20
NEW Cheeks | **W'burg**	–
Chocolate Room | **Park Slope**	25
☑ City Bakery | **Flatiron**	25
NEW Colson | **Park Slope**	26
Cones | **G Vill**	21
☑ Dylan's Candy | **E 60s**	21
Falai Panetteria | **LES**	27
☑ Fresh Direct | **LIC**	23
Gimme! Coffee | **W'burg**	27
Gorilla Coffee | **Park Slope**	24
NEW Grom | **W 70s**	–
☑ Il Laboratorio | **LES**	28
☑ Jacques Torres | **Dumbo**	28
Le Pain Quotidien | **multi. loc.**	24
☑ Magnolia Bakery | **W Vill**	23
☑ MarieBelle's | **SoHo**	26

Marlow | **W'burg**	–
☑ Moore Bros. | **Flatiron**	29
Mudspot | **E Vill**	26
☑ Murray's Cheese | **multi. loc.**	28
Ovando | **W Vill**	–
Pasanella | **Seaport**	–
☑ Pierre Marcolini | **E 50s**	28
pinkberry | **multi. loc.**	–
☑ Red/White | **Park Slope**	26
Shake Shack | **Flatiron**	25
☑ Sullivan St. Bakery | **W 40s**	28
Sweet Melissa | **Cobble Hill**	24
☑ Terence Conran | **E 50s**	25
☑ Trader Joe's | **Union Sq**	24
☑ Vosges Haut | **SoHo**	26
☑ Whole Foods | **multi. loc.**	26

WEDDING CAKES

Andrew & Alan's | **Staten Is**	22
Artuso Pastry | **Bronx**	26
Balthazar Bakery | **SoHo**	27
NEW Betty Bakery | **Boerum Hill**	–
Bijoux Doux | **Boerum Hill**	–
Buttercup | **E 50s**	23
Cafe Scaramouche | **Carroll Gdns**	–
Caffé Roma | **Little Italy**	23
Cake Chef | **Staten Is**	22
Cakeline | **Rockaway Bch**	–
☑ Cake Man | **Ft Greene**	26
Ceci-Cela | **multi. loc.**	24
Cheryl Kleinman | **Boerum Hill**	28
Chez Laurence | **Murray Hill**	23
☑ Citarella | **multi. loc.**	26
☑ Colette's | **W Vill**	29
Confetti | **W 80s**	–
Creative Cakes | **E 70s**	–
Delillo Pastry | **Bronx**	26
☑ Dessert Delivery | **E 50s**	28
Fabiane's | **W'burg**	–
Financier | **Financial**	27
Gail Watson | **Garment**	–
Hungarian Pastry | **W 100s**	22
La Bergamote | **Chelsea**	26
Ladybird Bakery | **Park Slope**	–
Lafayette | **G Vill**	21
Margaret Braun | **W Vill**	–
Margot Pâtisserie | **W 70s**	27
Mother Mousse | **Staten Is**	26
My Most/Food | **W 40s**	21

Paneantico | **Bay Ridge**	26
Panya Bakery | **E Vill**	22
∅ Patisserie Claude | **G Vill**	27
∅ Payard | **E 70s**	28
Rocco's Pastry | **G Vill**	25
Ron Ben-Israel | **SoHo**	25
∅ Royal Crown | **multi. loc.**	26
Sal & Dom's | **Bronx**	28
Schick's Bakery | **Borough Pk**	20
Settepani | **multi. loc.**	23
Silver Moon | **W 100s**	26
Something Sweet | **E Vill**	23
∅ Soutine | **W 70s**	27
∅ Stork's Pastry | **Whitestone**	27
Sweet Atelier | **E 80s**	–
Sweet Melissa | **multi. loc.**	24
∅ Sylvia Weinstock | **TriBeCa**	26
NEW Tribeca Treats | **TriBeCa**	27
∅ Two Little Red | **E 80s**	26
Veniero's | **E Vill**	25
∅ Villabate | **Bensonhurst**	28
∅ Vosges Haut | **SoHo**	26
Whole Earth | **E Vill**	–
William Greenberg | **E 80s**	25

WINES & LIQUOR

(* Open Sunday)

Acker Merrall* | **W 70s**	26
Ambassador Wine* | **E 50s**	24
Appellation | **Chelsea**	25
Astor Wines* | **NoHo**	25
Bacchus Wine* | **W 70s**	19
Beacon Wines* | **W 70s**	21
Beekman Liquors | **E 40s**	24
Best Cellars* | **multi. loc.**	21
Big Nose | **Park Slope**	24
Blanc & Rouge* | **Dumbo**	–
∅ Bottlerocket | **Flatiron**	26
Bottle Shoppe | **W'burg**	–
Brooklyn Liquors* | **Sunset Pk**	23
∅ Burgundy | **Chelsea**	29
Cellar 72 | **E 70s**	26
Chambers Wines* | **TriBeCa**	26
Chelsea Wine* | **Chelsea**	23
Columbus Wine* | **W 50s**	22
Crossroads* | **Union Sq**	25
∅ Crush Wine* | **E 50s**	26
Discovery Wines* | **E Vill**	22
Embassy Wines* | **E 60s**	19
Famous Wines | **Financial**	22

First Ave. Wines | **Gramercy**	23
∅ Fresh Direct* | **LIC**	23
Garnet Wines* | **E 60s**	24
Gotham Wines* | **W 90s**	22
Grande Harvest* | **E 40s**	23
Grand Wine | **Astoria**	25
Greene Grape* | **multi. loc.**	24
Harlem Vintage* | **Harlem**	28
Heights Chateau | **Bklyn Hts**	25
Hendricks Wine | **Bay Ridge**	–
In Vino | **E 70s**	25
Is Wine* | **G Vill**	–
∅ Italian Wine | **Union Sq**	27
K & D Wines | **E 90s**	24
Landmark Wine | **Chelsea**	25
∅ Le Dû's Wines | **W Vill**	27
∅ LeNell's* | **Red Hook**	27
Manley's Wines* | **W Vill**	22
Martin Bros. | **W 100s**	21
McAdam* | **Gramercy**	22
McCabe's Wines* | **E 70s**	19
Michael-Towne | **Bklyn Hts**	24
Mister Wright* | **E 80s**	24
∅ Moore Bros. | **Flatiron**	29
∅ Morrell & Co. | **W 40s**	27
Mount Carmel* | **Bronx**	26
Nancy's–Wines* | **W 70s**	24
New York/Exchange | **Financial**	23
New York/Warehse. | **LIC**	–
Olivino Wines | **Ft Greene**	–
Park Ave. Liquor | **E 40s**	26
Pasanella | **Seaport**	–
Pete Milano's | **Staten Is**	–
PJ Wine | **Inwood**	27
NEW Pour | **W 70s**	21
Premier Cru* | **E 80s**	24
∅ Prospect Wine* | **Park Slope**	26
Quality Hse. | **Murray Hill**	27
∅ Red/White* | **Park Slope**	26
Rosenthal Wine | **E 80s**	28
Royal Wine | **Gramercy**	–
Sea Grape* | **W Vill**	23
Sept. Wines | **LES**	–
7th Ave. Wine | **Park Slope**	20
∅ Sherry-Lehmann | **E 60s**	29
NEW Sip | **Park Slope**	27
67 Wines* | **W 60s**	25
Skyview Wines | **Bronx**	26
Slope Cellars* | **Park Slope**	24
Smith & Vine* | **Cobble Hill**	23

NYC SOURCES

SPECIAL FEATURES

Ethnic Focus

Listings cover the best in each category and include source names, categories and Quality ratings. ⚡ indicates places with the highest ratings, popularity and importance.

AMERICAN

Andrew & Alan's | *Baked Gds.*	22
Better Burger | *Prepared*	19
Between/Bread | *Caterer*	21
⚡ Blue Apron | *Spec. Shop*	27
Bread Alone | *Baked Gds.*	27
Buttercup | *Baked Gds.*	23
Carrot Top | *Baked Gds.*	23
Chocolate Room | *Candy/Nuts*	25
⚡ City Bakery | *Baked Gds.*	25
Cousin John's | *Baked Gds.*	21
Cozy Soup | *Prepared*	17
David Burke | *Caterer/Events*	23
Devon/Blakely | *Prepared*	22
Eddie's Sweet | *Ice Cream*	25
Emack/Bolio | *Ice Cream*	25
Fraser-Morris | *Prepared*	-
Friend/Farmer | *Baked Gds.*	21
Good & Plenty | *Prepared*	22
Gracious Thyme | *Caterer*	-
Great Performances | *Caterer*	24
Hinsch's | *Ice Cream*	22
Indiana Mkt. | *Caterer*	26
⚡ Jacques Torres | *Candy/Nuts*	28
Jahn's Ice Cream | *Ice Cream*	20
Junior's | *Baked Gds.*	23
Ladybird Bakery | *Baked Gds.*	-
Little Pie | *Baked Gds.*	24
Luscious Food | *Prepared*	-
Maggie Moo's | *Ice Cream*	21
⚡ Magnolia Bakery | *Baked Gds.*	23
Martha's Bakery | *Baked Gds.*	-
Mondel Choc. | *Candy/Nuts*	22
Naidre's | *Coffee/Tea*	22
Neuman's | *Caterer*	25
⚡ Olive's | *Deli/Sandwich*	25
One Girl | *Baked Gds.*	24
Out/Kitchen | *Prepared*	-
⚡ Ronnybrook | *Cheese/Dairy*	28
Sandwich Planet | *Deli/Sandwich*	25
Sarabeth's | *Baked Gds.*	24
Saxelby Cheese | *Cheese/Dairy*	28
Shake Shack | *Prepared*	25
Starwich | *Deli/Sandwich*	23

Sweet Melissa | *Baked Gds.*	24
Tempo Presto | *Deli/Sandwich*	23
Thalia Kitchen | *Prepared*	21
NEW Trois Pommes | *Baked Gds.*	-
⚡ Two Little Red | *Baked Gds.*	26
Vintage NY | *Wine/Liquor*	23
'wichcraft | *Deli/Sandwich*	24
Williamson Calvert | *Caterer*	-
Zaitzeff | *Prepared*	28

ARGENTINEAN

Cafe Scaramouche | *Baked Gds.*	-
Gauchas | *Prepared*	25
Ruben's | *Prepared*	20

ASIAN

(See also Chinese, Japanese, Korean, Thai and Vietnamese)

Aji Ichiban | *Candy/Nuts*	21
Cafe Spice | *Prepared*	19
Chinatown Ice Cream | *Ice Cream*	25
Dimple | *Prepared*	22
Dual Specialty | *Herbs/Spices*	-
Foods/India | *Herbs/Spices*	23
Franchia | *Coffee/Tea*	24
Hampton Chutney | *Prepared*	23
Indian Bread | *Prepared*	21
⚡ Kalustyan's | *Spec. Shop*	27
⚡ Kee's Choc. | *Candy/Nuts*	29
Lassi | *Prepared*	21
Patel Bros. | *Spec. Shop*	23
Spice Corner | *Herbs/Spices*	24
Tamarind Tea | *Coffee/Tea*	-

AUSTRALIAN

DUB Pies | *Prepared*	24
Tuck Shop | *Prepared*	-

BELGIAN

NEW Colson | *Baked Gds.*	25
Leonidas | *Candy/Nuts*	26
Le Pain Quotidien | *Baked Gds.*	24
⚡ Martine's Choc. | *Candy/Nuts*	29
Michelle's Kitchen | *Prepared*	18
Neuhaus Choc. | *Candy/Nuts*	25
Petite Abeille | *Prepared*	22
⚡ Pierre Marcolini | *Candy/Nuts*	28

BRAZILIAN

Brasil Coffee | *Coffee/Tea* — 21
Puff & Pao | *Coffee/Tea* — -

CARIBBEAN

🆕 Christie's | *Prepared* — 21
Salsa | *Caterer/Events* — -

CHINESE

Asia Market | *Spec. Shop* — 21
Bayard St. | *Meat/Poultry* — 23
Deluxe Food | *Spec. Shop* — 21
Dumpling Man | *Prepared* — 20
Dynasty Supermkt. | *Spec. Shop* — 19
Egg Custard King | *Baked Gds.* — -
Fay Da | *Baked Gds.* — 19
Flor/Mayo | *Prepared* — 23
Fong Inn | *Spec. Shop* — -
Golden Fung | *Baked Gds.* — 18
Hong Keung | *Seafood* — 22
Hong Kong | *Spec. Shop* — 20
🅩 Ito En | *Coffee/Tea* — 28
Kam Man | *Spec. Shop* — 21
Lung Moon | *Baked Gds.* — 19
🅩 May May | *Spec. Shop* — 23
New Beef | *Meat/Poultry* — -
Sui Cheong Meat | *Meat/Poultry* — 20
Tai Pan Bakery | *Baked Gds.* — 19
🅩 Ten Ren Tea | *Coffee/Tea* — 25
Wong Bakery | *Baked Gds.* — -

CUBAN

Café Habana | *Prepared* — 24

ECLECTIC

(Most caterers and prepared food shops offer a variety of cuisines)

🅩 Abigail Kirsch | *Caterer* — 26
🅩 Artisanal | *Cheese/Dairy* — 28
🅩 Balducci's | *Maj. Gourmet* — 25
🅩 Bottlerocket | *Wine/Liquor* — 26
Butterfield Mkt. | *Spec. Shop* — 23
Call Cuisine | *Prepared* — 24
Certé | *Caterer/Events* — -
Cheese/World | *Cheese/Dairy* — 25
Chocolate Bar | *Candy/Nuts* — 26
Chocolate Room | *Candy/Nuts* — 25
🅩 Citarella | *Maj. Gourmet* — 26
Consenza's | *Seafood* — 27
David Ziff | *Caterer* — -
Delmonico | *Spec. Shop* — 21

Dishes | *Prepared* — 24
🅩 D'Vine | *Spec. Shop* — 25
🅩 Dylan's Candy | *Candy/Nuts* — 21
East Coast Beer | *Beer* — -
East Village Cheese | *Cheese/Dairy* — 22
Elizabeth Ryan | *Flowers* — 28
Fabiane's | *Baked Gds.* — -
🅩 Fairway | *Maj. Gourmet* — 26
F&B | *Prepared* — 20
Fish Tales | *Seafood* — 25
Floralies | *Flowers* — 26
Flowers/World | *Flowers* — 28
Food Emporium | *Maj. Gourmet* — 16
Food/Thought | *Prepared* — -
Foragers Mkt. | *Spec. Shop* — -
Frank's Gourmet | *Spec. Shop* — 21
🅩 Fresh Direct | *Maj. Gourmet* — 23
Garden of Eden | *Maj. Gourmet* — 24
Giorgione | *Deli/Sandwich* — -
Good & Plenty | *Prepared* — 22
Gotham Gardens | *Flowers* — 24
Gracious Thyme | *Caterer* — -
Ideal Cheese | *Cheese/Dairy* — 27
Jeffrey's | *Meat/Poultry* — -
Jubilee | *Maj. Gourmet* — 21
🅩 Kalustyan's | *Spec. Shop* — 27
Klatch Coffee | *Coffee/Tea* — -
Lassen/Hennigs | *Caterer* — 22
Luscious Food | *Prepared* — -
Manna Catering | *Caterer* — -
🆕 Max Brenner | *Candy/Nuts* — 22
Maya Schaper | *Cheese/Dairy* — 22
Mille Fiori | *Flowers* — -
Movable Feast | *Caterer* — 23
Myzel Choc. | *Candy/Nuts* — -
Natural Frontier | *Health* — 24
🆕🅩 Nespresso | *Coffee/Tea* — 25
Neuman's | *Caterer* — 25
Once Upon/Tart | *Baked Gds.* — 25
Orchard | *Spec. Shop* — 27
Paneantico | *Baked Gds.* — 26
Porto Rico | *Coffee/Tea* — 26
Puff & Pao | *Coffee/Tea* — -
Pumpkins | *Spec. Shop* — 26
Ready to Eat | *Prepared* — 21
Really Cool | *Prepared* — 21
Robbins Wolfe | *Caterer* — 26
Rootstock/Quade | *Flowers* — -
Second Helpings | *Prepared* — -
SugarHill Java | *Coffee/Tea* — -

Susan Holland	*Caterer*	–
Sweet Life	*Candy/Nuts*	23
NEW Swich	*Deli/Sandwich*	23
Taste Caterers	*Caterer*	22
Z Tavalon Tea	*Coffee/Tea*	24
Tea Lounge	*Coffee/Tea*	21
Tentation Potel	*Caterer/Events*	22
Thomas Preti	*Caterer*	23
Truffette	*Spec. Shop*	–
T Salon	*Coffee/Tea*	26

ENGLISH

A Salt/Battery	*Prepared*	22
Carry On Tea	*Coffee/Tea*	23
Charbonnel/Walker	*Candy/Nuts*	22
Myers/Keswick	*Spec. Shop*	23
Pret A Manger	*Deli/Sandwich*	21

FRENCH

Balthazar Bakery	*Baked Gds.*	27
Bonsignour	*Prepared*	26
Z Bouchon Bakery	*Baked Gds.*	27
Z Bouley Bakery	*Baked Gds.*	27
Z Burgundy	*Wine/Liquor*	29
Caputo Bakery	*Baked Gds.*	23
Ceci-Cela	*Baked Gds.*	24
Chez Laurence	*Baked Gds.*	23
Chocolat Michel	*Candy/Nuts*	25
NEW Colson	*Baked Gds.*	25
Columbus	*Baked Gds.*	21
Debauve/Gallais	*Candy/Nuts*	27
Duane Pk.	*Baked Gds.*	26
Feast/Fêtes	*Caterer*	27
Financier	*Baked Gds.*	27
Z Jacques Torres	*Candy/Nuts*	28
La Bergamote	*Baked Gds.*	26
Lafayette	*Baked Gds.*	21
Z La Maison/Choc.	*Candy/Nuts*	29
La Tropezienne	*Baked Gds.*	–
Le Marais	*Meat/Poultry*	26
Le Pain Quotidien	*Baked Gds.*	24
NEW Le Petit	*Baked Gds.*	–
L'Epicerie	*Spec. Shop*	–
Les Halles	*Meat/Poultry*	26
Margot Pâtisserie	*Baked Gds.*	27
Marquet Patisserie	*Baked Gds.*	24
Michelle's Kitchen	*Prepared*	18
Z Patisserie Claude	*Baked Gds.*	27
Z Payard	*Baked Gds.*	28

Z Petrossian	*Caviar/Smoked Fish*	28
Polux Fleuriste	*Flowers*	–
Z Richart Design	*Candy/Nuts*	28
Royal Wine	*Wine/Liquor*	–
Silver Moon	*Baked Gds.*	26
Sweet Melissa	*Baked Gds.*	24
Tastings/Payard	*Caterer/Events*	27
NEW Tisserie	*Baked Gds.*	20
NEW Trois Pommes	*Baked Gds.*	–
Williamson Calvert	*Caterer*	–

GERMAN/AUSTRIAN

Andrew & Alan's	*Baked Gds.*	22
Duane Pk.	*Baked Gds.*	26
Empire Market	*Meat/Poultry*	–
Koglin Hams	*Meat/Poultry*	24
Oppenheimer	*Meat/Poultry*	26
Z Schaller & Weber	*Meat/Poultry*	27
Z Stork's Pastry	*Baked Gds.*	27

GREEK

Z Artopolis	*Baked Gds.*	28
Christos Steak	*Meat/Poultry*	–
Likitsakos	*Produce*	22
Mediterranean	*Spec. Shop*	26
Nature's Gifts	*Health*	21
Ninth Ave. Int'l	*Spec. Shop*	23
Poseidon	*Baked Gds.*	26
Snack	*Prepared*	27
Z Titan Foods	*Spec. Shop*	26

HUNGARIAN

Hungarian Pastry	*Baked Gds.*	22
Yorkville Meat	*Meat/Poultry*	23

INDIAN

Cafe Spice	*Prepared*	19
Dimple	*Prepared*	22
Dual Specialty	*Herbs/Spices*	–
Foods/India	*Herbs/Spices*	23
Hampton Chutney	*Prepared*	23
Indian Bread	*Prepared*	21
Z Ito En	*Coffee/Tea*	28
Z Kalustyan's	*Spec. Shop*	27
Lassi	*Prepared*	21
Patel Bros.	*Spec. Shop*	23
Spice Corner	*Herbs/Spices*	24
Tamarind Tea	*Coffee/Tea*	–

ITALIAN

Addeo's | *Baked Gds.* — 27
☑ Agata/Valentina | *Maj. Gourmet* — 26
NEW ☑ Alessi | *Cookware* — 27
Alidoro | *Deli/Sandwich* — 27
Alleva Dairy | *Cheese/Dairy* — 27
Andrew & Alan's | *Baked Gds.* — 22
Areo Rist. | *Caterer* — 21
Arte/Corner | *Baked Gds.* — 24
Arthur Ave. | *Caterer* — 24
Artuso Pastry | *Baked Gds.* — 26
☑ Balducci's | *Maj. Gourmet* — 25
NEW Barbarini | *Prepared* — –
Bari Pork | *Meat/Poultry* — 24
Belfiore Meats | *Meat/Poultry* — 25
Biancardi Meats | *Meat/Poultry* — 27
☑ Borgatti's | *Pasta* — 29
Bottega/Via | *Prepared* — 25
Bottino | *Prepared* — 22
Bruno Bakery | *Baked Gds.* — 23
Bruno/Ravioli | *Pasta* — 24
BuonItalia | *Spec. Shop* — 26
Caffè Roma | *Baked Gds.* — 23
☑ Calabria Pork | *Meat/Poultry* — 28
Calandra Cheese | *Cheese/Dairy* — 26
Caputo Bakery | *Baked Gds.* — 23
Carmine's | *Prepared* — 23
Carol's Cuisine | *Caterer* — –
Casa Della | *Cheese/Dairy* — 29
Cassinelli Food | *Pasta* — 25
Centovini | *Wine/Liquor* — 20
Ceriello | *Spec. Shop* — 24
Ciao Bella | *Ice Cream* — 25
Cipriani | *Baked Gds.* — 26
☑ Coluccio/Sons | *Spec. Shop* — 28
Consenza's | *Seafood* — 27
Court | *Baked Gds.* — 25
Cucina Vivolo | *Prepared* — 23
☑ D'Amico | *Coffee/Tea* — 27
Delillo Pastry | *Baked Gds.* — 26
DeRobertis | *Baked Gds.* — 22
☑ DiPalo Dairy | *Cheese/Dairy* — 29
☑ Dom's | *Spec. Shop* — 27
Durso's Pasta | *Pasta* — 26
Egidio Pastry | *Baked Gds.* — 24
Esposito Meat | *Meat/Poultry* — 25
Esposito's Pork | *Meat/Poultry* — 26
☑ Faicco's Pork | *Meat/Poultry* — 28
Falai Panetteria | *Baked Gds.* — 27

Fay Da | *Baked Gds.* — 19
Ferrara Cafe | *Baked Gds.* — 22
☑ Florence Meat | *Meat/Poultry* — 29
Fortunato Bros. | *Baked Gds.* — 25
Fresco/Scotto | *Prepared* — 24
Giorgione | *Deli/Sandwich* — –
NEW ☑ Grandaisy Bakery | *Baked Gds.* — 29
NEW Grom | *Ice Cream* — –
Iavarone Bros. | *Prepared* — 25
☑ Il Laboratorio | *Ice Cream* — 28
Italian Food | *Spec. Shop* — 22
☑ Italian Wine | *Wine/Liquor* — 27
☑ Joe's Dairy | *Cheese/Dairy* — 28
La Guli | *Baked Gds.* — 24
Lamarca | *Cheese/Dairy* — 26
L'Arte/Gelato | *Ice Cream* — 27
☑ Lemon Ice | *Ice Cream* — 27
Lioni Latticini | *Cheese/Dairy* — 29
NEW Lorimer St. Meat | *Meat/Poultry* — –
☑ Madonia Bakery | *Baked Gds.* — 28
Manganaro Foods | *Deli/Sandwich* — 24
Manganaro's Hero | *Deli/Sandwich* — 21
Mangia | *Prepared* — 24
Mazzola Bakery | *Baked Gds.* — 25
Milano Gourmet | *Prepared* — 25
Morrone Bakery | *Baked Gds.* — –
Mount Carmel | *Wine/Liquor* — 26
Mule | *Coffee/Tea* — –
Napoli Bakery | *Baked Gds.* — –
☑ Ottomanelli & Sons | *Meat/Poultry* — 27
Ottomanelli Bros. | *Meat/Poultry* — 24
☑ Ottomanelli's Meats | *Meat/Poultry* — 27
Paneantico | *Baked Gds.* — 26
Pane d'Italia | *Baked Gds.* — –
Papa Pasquale | *Pasta* — 26
Parisi Bakery | *Baked Gds.* — 23
☑ Pastosa Ravioli | *Pasta* — 26
Pepe | *Prepared* — 26
Peter's Mkt. | *Spec. Shop* — –
Piazza Mercato | *Meat/Poultry* — –
Pie/Pound | *Prepared* — 20
Piemonte Ravioli | *Pasta* — 27
Pino Meats | *Meat/Poultry* — 27
Piu Bello | *Ice Cream* — 21
Porto Rico | *Coffee/Tea* — 26
Queen Ann | *Pasta* — 27

☑ Raffetto's | *Pasta*	28
Ralph's/Ices | *Ice Cream*	24
☑ Randazzo's | *Seafood*	28
Ravioli | *Pasta*	25
Remi | *Prepared*	26
Risotteria | *Prepared*	23
Rita's Ices | *Ice Cream*	21
Rocco's Pastry | *Baked Gds.*	25
☑ Royal Crown | *Baked Gds.*	26
Royal Wine | *Wine/Liquor*	–
Russo Mozzarella | *Cheese/Dairy*	26
Sal & Dom's | *Baked Gds.*	28
☑ Salumeria | *Meat/Poultry*	29
Sant Ambroeus | *Ice Cream*	26
Savino's Pasta | *Pasta*	–
Settepani | *Baked Gds.*	23
☑ Sullivan St. Bakery | *Baked Gds.*	28
Tarallucci e Vino | *Baked Gds.*	24
Tazza | *Baked Gds.*	–
Teitel Bros. | *Spec. Shop*	26
Tempo Presto | *Deli/Sandwich*	23
Terrace Bagels | *Bagels*	25
Terranova | *Baked Gds.*	26
Todaro Bros. | *Spec. Shop*	24
Trunzo Bros. | *Spec. Shop*	25
Tuscan Sq. | *Prepared*	22
United Meat | *Meat/Poultry*	–
Veniero's | *Baked Gds.*	25
Vesuvio | *Prepared*	23
☑ Villabate | *Baked Gds.*	28
Vincent's Meat | *Meat/Poultry*	27
☑ Vino | *Wine/Liquor*	28
NEW Zibetto Espresso | *Coffee/Tea*	26

JAPANESE

Beard Papa | *Baked Gds.*	24
Han Ah Reum | *Spec. Shop*	22
☑ Ito En | *Coffee/Tea*	28
JAS Mart | *Spec. Shop*	21
Katagiri | *Spec. Shop*	23
Landmark Wine | *Wine/Liquor*	25
☑ Minamoto | *Candy/Nuts*	28
m2m | *Spec. Shop*	18
Otafuku | *Prepared*	19
Panya Bakery | *Baked Gds.*	22
Sunrise Mart | *Spec. Shop*	23
☑ Takashimaya | *Flowers*	28
Tea Box | *Coffee/Tea*	27

JEWISH

Acme Fish | *Caviar/Smoked Fish*	24
Artie's Deli | *Deli/Sandwich*	21
Bagels & Co. | *Bagels*	22
☑ Barney Greengrass | *Caviar/Smoked Fish*	27
Ben's Kosher | *Deli/Sandwich*	21
Berger's | *Deli/Sandwich*	21
☑ Carnegie Deli | *Deli/Sandwich*	23
Deli Masters | *Deli/Sandwich*	21
Eisenberg's Sandwich | *Deli/Sandwich*	20
Fine/Schapiro | *Deli/Sandwich*	20
Fischer Bros. | *Meat/Poultry*	27
Foremost Caterers | *Caterer*	24
☑ Katz's Deli | *Deli/Sandwich*	24
☑ Kossar's | *Bagels*	28
Mansoura | *Baked Gds.*	–
Mauzone | *Prepared*	22
Mazur's Marketpl. | *Meat/Poultry*	20
Mother's Bake | *Baked Gds.*	21
Murray's Sturgeon | *Caviar/Smoked Fish*	27
#1 Farmers Mkt. | *Produce*	23
Oppenheimer | *Meat/Poultry*	26
Orwasher's | *Baked Gds.*	26
Park E. Kosher | *Meat/Poultry*	26
Pastrami Queen | *Deli/Sandwich*	21
☑ Pickle Guys | *Spec. Shop*	27
P.J. Bernstein | *Deli/Sandwich*	19
☑ Russ & Daughters | *Smoked Fish*	28
Sarge's Deli | *Deli/Sandwich*	21
Schick's Bakery | *Baked Gds.*	20
Stage Deli | *Deli/Sandwich*	21
Streit's Matzo | *Baked Gds.*	25
William Greenberg | *Baked Gds.*	25
Yonah Schimmel | *Baked Gds.*	23

KOREAN

Han Ah Reum | *Spec. Shop*	22
m2m | *Spec. Shop*	18

MEDITERRANEAN

☑ Artopolis | *Baked Gds.*	28
Caffe' Simpatico/Ruthy's | *Baked Gds.*	15
Cucina | *Prepared*	21
Good & Plenty | *Prepared*	22
Mangia | *Prepared*	24
Melange | *Prepared*	21

Ninth Ave. Int'l | *Spec. Shop*	23
O&CO. | *Spec. Shop*	25
Tanoreen | *Prepared*	–
Tempo Presto | *Deli/Sandwich*	23
Todaro Bros. | *Spec. Shop*	24
Zeytuna | *Maj. Gourmet*	23

MEXICAN/TEX-MEX

Café Habana | *Prepared*	24
✓ Kalustyan's | *Spec. Shop*	27
Zarela | *Caterer/Events*	24

MIDDLE EASTERN

Chickpea | *Prepared*	23
Damascus Bread | *Baked Gds.*	25
✓ D'Vine | *Spec. Shop*	25
Family Store | *Spec. Shop*	–
✓ Kalustyan's | *Spec. Shop*	27
Mansoura | *Baked Gds.*	–
Melange | *Prepared*	21
#1 Farmers Mkt. | *Produce*	23
✓ Sahadi's | *Spec. Shop*	27
Snack | *Prepared*	27
Spice Corner | *Herbs/Spices*	24
Tanoreen | *Prepared*	–
Yoghurt Place | *Cheese/Dairy*	23

POLISH

B & B Meat | *Meat/Poultry*	–
Eagle Provisions | *Meat/Poultry*	24
✓ East Village Meat | *Meat/ Poultry*	28

RUSSIAN

Caviar Russe | *Caviar*	26
M & I Foods | *Spec. Shop*	24
✓ Petrossian | *Caviar/Smoked Fish*	28

SCANDINAVIAN

NEW Fika | *Coffee/Tea*	22
Leske's | *Baked Gds.*	23
Nordic Delicacies | *Spec. Shop*	28

SOUTH AMERICAN

Brasil Coffee | *Coffee/Tea*	21
Flor/Mayo | *Prepared*	23
Juan Valdez | *Coffee/Tea*	22
Ruben's | *Prepared*	20

SOUTHERN/SOUL FOOD

Blue Smoke | *Caterer*	25
✓ Cake Man | *Baked Gds.*	26
Daisy May's | *Prepared*	24
Dirty Bird | *Prepared*	20
Make My Cake | *Baked Gds.*	25
Salsa | *Caterer/Events*	–
Shakoor's Sweet | *Baked Gds.*	–
Spoonbread | *Caterer*	23

SPANISH

✓ Despaña | *Spec. Shop*	27
NEW Tinto Fino | *Wine/Liquor*	–

SWISS

Lindt | *Candy/Nuts*	–
Neuchatel Choc. | *Candy/Nuts*	24
✓ Teuscher Choc. | *Candy/Nuts*	27

THAI

Asia Market | *Spec. Shop*	21
✓ Bangkok Grocery | *Spec. Shop*	27

TURKISH

Güllüoglu | *Baked Gds.*	–
Zeytuna | *Maj. Gourmet*	23

UKRAINIAN

Astoria Meat | *Meat/Poultry*	25
✓ East Village Meat | *Meat/ Poultry*	28
First Ave. Pierogi | *Prepared*	25

VEGETARIAN

(Most prepared food shops and health food stores offer vegetarian options, including these standouts)

A Matter/Health | *Health*	21
Back/Land | *Health*	23
Bell Bates | *Health*	24
✓ City Bakery | *Baked Gds.*	25
Dimple | *Prepared*	22
✓ Fairway | *Maj. Gourmet*	26
Gary Null's | *Health*	25
Health Nuts | *Health*	21
Integral Yoga | *Health*	24
LifeThyme Mkt. | *Health*	24
Second Helpings | *Prepared*	–
Silver Moon | *Baked Gds.*	26
Tastebud's | *Health*	–
Urban Organic | *Produce*	22
Whole Earth | *Baked Gds.*	–

VIETNAMESE

Bánh Mì Saigon | *Deli/Sandwich*	25
Nicky's Viet. | *Deli/Sandwich*	24
Viet-Nam Bánh | *Deli/Sandwich*	23

Locations

Includes source names, categories and Quality ratings. ☑ indicates places with the highest ratings, popularity and importance.

Manhattan

CHELSEA

(24th to 30th Sts., west of 5th; 14th to 24th Sts., west of 6th)

☑ Abigail Kirsch	*Caterer*	26
☑ Amy's Bread	*Baked Gds.*	26
Appellation	*Wine/Liquor*	25
Ariston	*Flowers*	27
☑ Balducci's	*Maj. Gourmet*	25
Baskin-Robbins	*Ice Cream*	17
Bed Bath/Beyond	*Cookware*	20
Better Burger	*Prepared*	19
Billy's Bakery	*Baked Gds.*	25
Blue Smoke	*Caterer*	25
Bottino	*Prepared*	22
Bowery Kitchen	*Cookware*	22
BuonItalia	*Spec. Shop*	26
☑ Burgundy	*Wine/Liquor*	29
NEW Café Grumpy	*Coffee/Tea*	26
Caffe' Simpatico/Ruthy's	*Baked Gds.*	15
Catering Co.	*Events*	–
Chelsea Baskets	*Spec. Shop*	24
Chelsea Wholesale	*Flowers*	25
Chelsea Wine	*Wine/Liquor*	23
Chocolat Moderne	*Candy/Nuts*	–
Choux Factory	*Baked Gds.*	23
☑ Cleaver Co.	*Caterer/Events*	25
Corrado	*Baked Gds.*	21
David Beahm	*Flowers*	–
Eleni's Cookies	*Baked Gds.*	22
F&B	*Prepared*	20
Fat Witch	*Baked Gds.*	25
Food/Thought	*Prepared*	–
Frank's	*Meat/Poultry*	24
Garden of Eden	*Maj. Gourmet*	24
Haas Co.	*Cookware*	–
Hale/Hearty	*Soup*	22
Hudson Yards	*Caterer/Events*	24
La Bergamote	*Baked Gds.*	26
Landmark Wine	*Wine/Liquor*	25
L'Arte/Gelato	*Ice Cream*	27
Lobster Pl.	*Seafood*	26
L'Olivier	*Flowers*	29
Manhattan Fruit Ex.	*Produce*	24

Mille Fiori	*Flowers*	–
Murray's Bagels	*Bagels*	26
Party Rental	*Party Rent.*	22
Pepe	*Prepared*	26
pinkberry	*Ice Cream*	–
☑ Ronnybrook	*Cheese/Dairy*	28
☑ Salumeria	*Meat/Poultry*	29
Sarabeth's	*Baked Gds.*	24
Spruce	*Flowers*	27
NEW Swich	*Deli/Sandwich*	23
NEW Three Tarts	*Baked Gds.*	22
T Salon	*Coffee/Tea*	26
202 to Go	*Baked Gds.*	22
Westside Mkt.	*Maj. Gourmet*	21
☑ Whole Foods	*Maj. Gourmet*	26
'wichcraft	*Deli/Sandwich*	24
☑ Williams-Sonoma	*Cookware*	27

CHINATOWN

(Canal to Pearl Sts., west of B'way)

Aji Ichiban	*Candy/Nuts*	21
Asia Market	*Spec. Shop*	21
☑ Bangkok Grocery	*Spec. Shop*	27
Bánh Mì Saigon	*Deli/Sandwich*	25
Bayard St.	*Meat/Poultry*	23
Chinatown Ice Cream	*Ice Cream*	25
Deluxe Food	*Spec. Shop*	21
Dynasty Supermkt.	*Spec. Shop*	19
Egg Custard King	*Baked Gds.*	–
Fay Da	*Baked Gds.*	19
Fong Inn	*Spec. Shop*	–
Golden Fung	*Baked Gds.*	18
G.S. Food	*Seafood*	19
Häagen Dazs	*Ice Cream*	24
Hong Keung	*Seafood*	22
Hong Kong	*Spec. Shop*	20
Hung Chong	*Cookware*	19
Kam Man	*Spec. Shop*	21
Lung Moon	*Baked Gds.*	19
☑ May May	*Spec. Shop*	23
New Beef	*Meat/Poultry*	–
131 Fish Market	*Seafood*	24
Starbucks	*Coffee/Tea*	18
Sui Cheong Meat	*Meat/Poultry*	20
Tai Pan Bakery	*Baked Gds.*	19
Tan My My	*Seafood*	22

⊡ Ten Ren Tea	*Coffee/Tea*	25
Viet-Nam Bánh	*Deli/Sandwich*	23
WK Trading	*Produce*	–
Wong Bakery	*Baked Gds.*	–

EAST 40S

Amish Market	*Maj. Gourmet*	23
Ariston	*Flowers*	27
Au Bon Pain	*Baked Gds.*	16
Beard Papa	*Baked Gds.*	24
Beekman Liquors	*Wine/Liquor*	24
Beekman Mktpl.	*Meat/Poultry*	22
Ben & Jerry's	*Ice Cream*	24
Big Apple Florist	*Flowers*	24
⊡ Bridge Kitchen.	*Cookware*	28
Cafe Spice	*Prepared*	19
Ceriello	*Spec. Shop*	24
Charbonnel/Walker	*Candy/Nuts*	22
Choux Factory	*Baked Gds.*	23
Ciao Bella	*Ice Cream*	25
Cipriani	*Baked Gds.*	26
Corrado	*Baked Gds.*	21
Cucina	*Prepared*	21
Dahlia	*Flowers*	26
Delmonico	*Spec. Shop*	21
Devon/Blakely	*Prepared*	22
Dishes	*Prepared*	24
Fifth Ave. Choc.	*Candy/Nuts*	20
Godiva	*Candy/Nuts*	22
Grande Harvest	*Wine/Liquor*	23
Greenwich Produce	*Produce*	25
Hale/Hearty	*Soup*	22
Health Nuts	*Health*	21
Hot/Crusty	*Baked Gds.*	15
Juan Valdez	*Coffee/Tea*	22
Junior's	*Baked Gds.*	23
Koglin Hams	*Meat/Poultry*	24
Li-Lac Choc.	*Candy/Nuts*	26
Lindt	*Candy/Nuts*	–
Little Pie	*Baked Gds.*	24
Mangia	*Prepared*	24
Manhattan Espresso	*Coffee/Tea*	21
Michael George	*Flowers*	25
Miho Kosuda	*Flowers*	–
⊡ Murray's Cheese	*Cheese/Dairy*	28
Neuhaus Choc.	*Candy/Nuts*	25
O&CO.	*Spec. Shop*	25
Oren's/Roast	*Coffee/Tea*	24
⊡ Original SoupMan	*Soup*	23
Park Ave. Liquor	*Wine/Liquor*	26

⊡ Penzeys Spices	*Herbs/Spices*	27
Pepe	*Prepared*	26
Pescatore	*Seafood*	25
Pret A Manger	*Deli/Sandwich*	21
⊡ Teuscher Choc.	*Candy/Nuts*	27
UN Wine	*Wine/Liquor*	–
'wichcraft	*Deli/Sandwich*	24
Wild Edibles	*Seafood*	26
World of Nuts	*Candy/Nuts*	15
Zaro's Bread	*Baked Gds.*	17

EAST 50S

Ambassador Wine	*Wine/Liquor*	24
⊡ Bloom	*Flowers*	27
Bloomingdale's	*Cookware*	24
Bottega/Via	*Prepared*	25
Buttercup	*Baked Gds.*	23
Call Cuisine	*Prepared*	24
Caviar Russe	*Caviar*	26
Così	*Deli/Sandwich*	18
Crate/Barrel	*Cookware*	22
⊡ Crush Wine	*Wine/Liquor*	26
Cucina Vivolo	*Prepared*	23
David Burke	*Caterer/Events*	23
Delmonico	*Spec. Shop*	21
⊡ Dessert Delivery	*Baked Gds.*	28
Devon/Blakely	*Prepared*	22
Dishes	*Prepared*	24
Ess-a-Bagel	*Bagels*	26
F&B	*Prepared*	20
Fifth Ave. Choc.	*Candy/Nuts*	20
Floralies	*Flowers*	26
Food Emporium	*Maj. Gourmet*	16
Fresco/Scotto	*Prepared*	24
Godiva	*Candy/Nuts*	22
Ideal Cheese	*Cheese/Dairy*	27
Int'l Poultry	*Prepared*	–
Juan Valdez	*Coffee/Tea*	22
Katagiri	*Spec. Shop*	23
Leonidas	*Candy/Nuts*	26
Marché Madison	*Prepared*	20
⊡ Martine's Choc.	*Candy/Nuts*	29
Neuchatel Choc.	*Candy/Nuts*	24
Neuhaus Choc.	*Candy/Nuts*	25
#1 Farmers Mkt.	*Produce*	23
Oren's/Roast	*Coffee/Tea*	24
⊡ Original SoupMan	*Soup*	23
⊡ Pierre Marcolini	*Candy/Nuts*	28
⊡ Pisacane	*Seafood*	28
Pret A Manger	*Deli/Sandwich*	21

Renny/Reed	*Flowers*	▬
🔲 Richart Design	*Candy/Nuts*	28
Sebastians	*Caterer*	▬
🔲 Simchick	*Meat/Poultry*	28
Starwich	*Deli/Sandwich*	23
Sutton Wine	*Wine/Liquor*	22
🔲 Takashimaya	*Flowers*	28
Tal Bagels	*Bagels*	23
Tea Box	*Coffee/Tea*	27
🔲 Terence Conran	*Cookware*	25
🔲 Williams-Sonoma	*Cookware*	27
Zarela	*Caterer/Events*	24
🔲 Zezé	*Flowers*	29

EAST 60S

Albert's Meats	*Meat/Poultry*	26
Alice's Tea	*Coffee/Tea*	24
Bagelworks	*Bagels*	23
Baskin-Robbins	*Ice Cream*	17
Bed Bath/Beyond	*Cookware*	20
Debauve/Gallais	*Candy/Nuts*	27
🔲 Dylan's Candy	*Candy/Nuts*	21
Embassy Wines	*Wine/Liquor*	19
Feast/Fêtes	*Caterer*	27
Fellan Florist	*Flowers*	24
Food Emporium	*Maj. Gourmet*	16
Garnet Wines	*Wine/Liquor*	24
Godiva	*Candy/Nuts*	22
Gourmet Garage	*Maj. Gourmet*	20
Häagen Dazs	*Ice Cream*	24
Hale/Hearty	*Soup*	22
Health Nuts	*Health*	21
Hot/Crusty	*Baked Gds.*	15
🔲 Ito En	*Coffee/Tea*	28
Java Girl	*Coffee/Tea*	24
Le Pain Quotidien	*Baked Gds.*	24
Melange	*Prepared*	21
🔲 Morrell & Co.	*Wine/Liquor*	26
NEW 🔲 Nespresso	*Coffee/Tea*	25
Plaza Flowers	*Flowers*	▬
Really Cool	*Prepared*	21
Rosa Rosa	*Flowers*	21
🔲 Sherry-Lehmann	*Wine/Liquor*	29
🔲 Teuscher Choc.	*Candy/Nuts*	27
🔲 TriServe	*Party Rent.*	24
World of Nuts	*Candy/Nuts*	15

EAST 70S

🔲 Agata/Valentina	*Maj. Gourmet*	26
A Matter/Health	*Health*	21

Anthony Gdn.	*Flowers*	▬
Bagels & Co.	*Bagels*	22
Bottega/Via	*Prepared*	25
Butterfield Mkt.	*Spec. Shop*	23
Cellar 72	*Wine/Liquor*	26
🔲 Citarella	*Maj. Gourmet*	26
Corrado	*Baked Gds.*	21
Creative Cakes	*Baked Gds.*	▬
Crumbs	*Baked Gds.*	22
Cucina Vivolo	*Prepared*	23
East Side Bagel	*Bagels*	21
🔲 Glorious Food	*Caterer*	25
Grace's Mktpl.	*Maj. Gourmet*	24
Gracious Home	*Cookware*	25
In Vino	*Wine/Liquor*	25
🔲 Lady M	*Baked Gds.*	28
🔲 La Maison/Choc.	*Candy/Nuts*	29
Leonard's	*Seafood*	26
Le Pain Quotidien	*Baked Gds.*	24
L'Olivier	*Flowers*	29
Maggie Moo's	*Ice Cream*	21
Marché Madison	*Prepared*	20
McCabe's Wines	*Wine/Liquor*	19
#1 Farmers Mkt.	*Produce*	23
Oren's/Roast	*Coffee/Tea*	24
🔲 Original SoupMan	*Soup*	23
Orwasher's	*Baked Gds.*	26
Pastrami Queen	*Deli/Sandwich*	21
🔲 Payard	*Baked Gds.*	28
Pick a Bagel	*Bagels*	20
P.J. Bernstein	*Deli/Sandwich*	19
Richard Salome	*Flowers*	▬
Sable's Smoked	*Caviar/Smoked Fish*	27
Sant Ambroeus	*Ice Cream*	26
Sarabeth's	*Baked Gds.*	24
Sedutto's	*Ice Cream*	24
Starbucks	*Coffee/Tea*	18
Starwich	*Deli/Sandwich*	23
Tastings/Payard	*Caterer/Events*	27
🔲 William Poll	*Prepared*	26
Windsor Florist	*Flowers*	24
World of Nuts	*Candy/Nuts*	15

EAST 80S

Alice's Tea	*Coffee/Tea*	24
Annie's	*Produce*	21
Bagel Bob's	*Bagels*	22
Best Cellars	*Wine/Liquor*	21
CBK Cookies	*Baked Gds.*	23

Choux Factory	*Baked Gds.*	23
Cold Stone	*Ice Cream*	20
Corner Bagel	*Bagels*	22
☑ Dean/DeLuca	*Maj. Gourmet*	27
☑ Dorian's Seafood	*Seafood*	25
☑ E.A.T.	*Prepared*	25
☑ Eli's Manhattan	*Maj. Gourmet*	25
Emack/Bolio	*Ice Cream*	25
Food Emporium	*Maj. Gourmet*	16
Glaser's Bake	*Baked Gds.*	21
H & H Midtown	*Bagels*	25
Hot/Crusty	*Baked Gds.*	15
NEW Kidfresh	*Spec. Shop*	-
Krispy Kreme	*Baked Gds.*	19
Le Pain Quotidien	*Baked Gds.*	24
Likitsakos	*Produce*	22
☑ Lobel's Meats	*Meat/Poultry*	29
Lorenzo/Maria's	*Prepared*	25
☑ Martine's Choc.	*Candy/Nuts*	29
Milano Gourmet	*Prepared*	25
Mister Wright	*Wine/Liquor*	24
Natural Frontier	*Health*	24
Nature's Gifts	*Health*	21
Oren's/Roast	*Coffee/Tea*	24
Ottomanelli Bros.	*Meat/Poultry*	24
Park E. Kosher	*Meat/Poultry*	26
Petak's	*Prepared*	23
Pickles/Olives	*Spec. Shop*	23
Pie/Pound	*Prepared*	20
pinkberry	*Ice Cream*	-
Premier Cru	*Wine/Liquor*	24
Rohrs	*Coffee/Tea*	24
Rosenthal Wine	*Wine/Liquor*	28
☑ Schaller & Weber	*Meat/Poultry*	27
Schatzie's Meats	*Meat/Poultry*	25
Sweet Atelier	*Baked Gds.*	-
Tal Bagels	*Bagels*	23
☑ Two Little Red	*Baked Gds.*	26
William Greenberg	*Baked Gds.*	25
☑ Williams-Sonoma	*Cookware*	27
W.I.N.E.	*Wine/Liquor*	21
Yorkshire Wines	*Wine/Liquor*	23
Yorkville Meat	*Meat/Poultry*	23

EAST 90S & 100S

(90th to 110th Sts.)

Ciao Bella	*Ice Cream*	25
NEW Corner Bakery	*Deli/ Sandwich*	-

David Ziff	*Caterer*	-
Eli's Vinegar	*Maj. Gourmet*	25
Gauchas	*Prepared*	25
Gourmet Garage	*Maj. Gourmet*	20
Holland Court	*Meat/Seafood*	24
K & D Wines	*Wine/Liquor*	24
NEW Madison	*Baked Gds.*	-
Michelle's Kitchen	*Prepared*	18
Ronaldo Maia	*Flowers*	-
Sarabeth's	*Baked Gds.*	24
S. Feldman	*Cookware*	23
Starbucks	*Coffee/Tea*	18

EAST VILLAGE

(14th to Houston Sts., east of B'way)

Angelica's Herbs	*Herbs/Spices*	23
Antony Todd	*Flowers*	-
Australian Home.	*Ice Cream*	23
Bagel Zone	*Bagels*	17
Beard Papa	*Baked Gds.*	24
Ben & Jerry's	*Ice Cream*	24
Bird Bath	*Baked Gds.*	-
☑ Black Hound	*Baked Gds.*	26
Blue Meadow	*Flowers*	-
Chickpea	*Prepared*	23
Commodities	*Health*	25
David's Bagels	*Bagels*	23
DeRobertis	*Baked Gds.*	22
Discovery Wines	*Wine/Liquor*	22
Dual Specialty	*Herbs/Spices*	-
Dumpling Man	*Prepared*	20
East Village Cheese	*Cheese/Dairy*	22
NEW East Village Ice Cream	*Ice Cream*	-
☑ East Village Meat	*Meat/ Poultry*	28
Elizabeth Ryan	*Flowers*	28
First Ave. Pierogi	*Prepared*	25
JAS Mart	*Spec. Shop*	21
Joe	*Coffee/Tea*	26
Liqueteria	*Soup*	19
LMD Floral	*Flowers*	-
Mary's Dairy	*Ice Cream*	24
Masturbakers	*Baked Gds.*	22
NEW Max Brenner	*Candy/Nuts*	22
m2m	*Spec. Shop*	18
Mudspot	*Coffee/Tea*	26
Nicky's Viet.	*Deli/Sandwich*	24
Ninth St. Espresso	*Coffee/Tea*	28
Otafuku	*Prepared*	19

Panya Bakery	*Baked Gds.*	22
Pepe	*Prepared*	26
Pie/Pound	*Prepared*	20
Porto Rico	*Coffee/Tea*	26
Ruben's	*Prepared*	20
Russo Mozzarella	*Cheese/Dairy*	26
Something Sweet	*Baked Gds.*	23
Starbucks	*Coffee/Tea*	18
NEW Z Stonehouse	*Spec. Shop*	27
Sundaes & Cones	*Ice Cream*	25
Sunrise Mart	*Spec. Shop*	23
Sympathy	*Coffee/Tea*	27
Tarallucci e Vino	*Baked Gds.*	24
NEW Tinto Fino	*Wine/Liquor*	–
Truffette	*Spec. Shop*	–
Tuck Shop	*Prepared*	–
Veniero's	*Baked Gds.*	25
Whole Earth	*Baked Gds.*	–

FINANCIAL DISTRICT

(South of Murray St.)

Amish Market	*Maj. Gourmet*	23
Au Bon Pain	*Baked Gds.*	16
NEW Barbarini	*Prepared*	–
Christopher Norman	*Candy/Nuts*	23
Ciao Bella	*Ice Cream*	25
Così	*Deli/Sandwich*	18
Z Dean/DeLuca	*Maj. Gourmet*	27
Evelyn's Choc.	*Candy/Nuts*	25
Famous Wines	*Wine/Liquor*	22
Fifth Ave. Choc.	*Candy/Nuts*	20
Financier	*Baked Gds.*	27
Flowers/World	*Flowers*	28
Godiva	*Candy/Nuts*	22
Greene Grape	*Wine/Liquor*	24
Jubilee	*Maj. Gourmet*	21
Klatch Coffee	*Coffee/Tea*	–
Leonidas	*Candy/Nuts*	26
Mangia	*Prepared*	24
New York/Exchange	*Wine/Liquor*	23
Z Original SoupMan	*Soup*	23
Pick a Bagel	*Bagels*	20
Pret A Manger	*Deli/Sandwich*	21
Ruben's	*Prepared*	20
Starwich	*Deli/Sandwich*	23
Zaitzeff	*Prepared*	28
Zeytuna	*Maj. Gourmet*	23

FLATIRON DISTRICT

(14th to 24th Sts., 6th Ave. to Park Ave. S., excluding Union Sq.)

Baskin-Robbins	*Ice Cream*	17
Z Belle Fleur	*Flowers*	28
Z Bottlerocket	*Wine/Liquor*	26
Chef & Co.	*Caterer/Events*	25
Z City Bakery	*Baked Gds.*	25
Colin Cowie	*Events*	28
Casa/Cupcake	*Baked Gds.*	22
Eisenberg's Sandwich	*Deli/Sandwich*	20
Fifth Ave. Epicure	*Prepared*	19
JAS Mart	*Spec. Shop*	21
NEW Leapfrog Caterers	*Caterer*	–
Mangia	*Prepared*	24
Z Moore Bros.	*Wine/Liquor*	29
New York Cake	*Cookware*	24
Petite Abeille	*Prepared*	22
Shake Shack	*Prepared*	25
Susan Holland	*Caterer*	–
Tamarind Tea	*Coffee/Tea*	–
Tarallucci e Vino	*Baked Gds.*	24
Vere	*Candy/Nuts*	–
'wichcraft	*Deli/Sandwich*	24

GARMENT DISTRICT

(30th to 40th Sts., west of 5th)

Z Artisanal	*Cheese/Dairy*	28
Au Bon Pain	*Baked Gds.*	16
Ben & Jerry's	*Ice Cream*	24
Ben's Kosher	*Deli/Sandwich*	21
Callahan	*Caterer/Events*	–
Castle/Pierpont	*Flowers*	24
Catering/Rest. Assoc.	*Caterer*	20
Cucina	*Prepared*	21
Dimple	*Prepared*	22
Esposito Meat	*Meat/Poultry*	25
Flowers/Reuven	*Flowers*	–
Gail Watson	*Baked Gds.*	–
Guy/Gallard	*Coffee/Tea*	20
Häagen Dazs	*Ice Cream*	24
Hale/Hearty	*Soup*	22
Han Ah Reum	*Spec. Shop*	22
Hot/Crusty	*Baked Gds.*	15
jesGORDON	*Flowers*	–
Krispy Kreme	*Baked Gds.*	19
Macy's Cellar	*Cookware*	21
Mandler's	*Prepared*	22
Manganaro Foods	*Deli/Sandwich*	24

Manganaro's Hero | *Deli/Sandwich* — 21

Mrs. Field's | *Baked Gds.* — 18

pinkberry | *Ice Cream* — -

Pret A Manger | *Deli/Sandwich* — 21

Props/Today | *Party Rent.* — 20

Rebecca Cole | *Flowers* — -

Sandwich Planet | *Deli/Sandwich* — 25

Starwich | *Deli/Sandwich* — 23

Tentation Potel | *Caterer/Events* — 22

Zaro's Bread | *Baked Gds.* — 17

GRAMERCY PARK

(24th to 30th Sts., east of 5th; 14th to 24th Sts., east of Park)

Baskin-Robbins | *Ice Cream* — 17

Bruno/Ravioli | *Pasta* — 24

Chocolat Michel | *Candy/Nuts* — 25

Così | *Deli/Sandwich* — 18

David's Bagels | *Bagels* — 23

Ess-a-Bagel | *Bagels* — 26

First Ave. Wines | *Wine/Liquor* — 23

Friend/Farmer | *Baked Gds.* — 21

Gramercy Fish | *Seafood* — 24

🔲 Kalustyan's | *Spec. Shop* — 27

Lamarca | *Cheese/Dairy* — 26

Les Halles | *Meat/Poultry* — 26

🔲 Manhattan Fruitier | *Spec. Shop* — 27

McAdam | *Wine/Liquor* — 22

Natural Frontier | *Health* — 24

Pastrami Factory | *Deli/Sandwich* — 22

Petite Abeille | *Prepared* — 22

Pick a Bagel | *Bagels* — 20

Royal Wine | *Wine/Liquor* — -

71 Irving Pl. | *Coffee/Tea* — 22

Spice Corner | *Herbs/Spices* — 24

🔲 Vino | *Wine/Liquor* — 28

GREENMARKET

(See p. 108 for locations)

Berkshire Berries | *Produce* — 27

Berried Treasures | *Produce* — 28

Beth's Kitchen | *Spec. Shop* — 27

Blue Moon Fish | *Seafood* — 29

Bread Alone | *Baked Gds.* — 27

Bulich Mushroom | *Produce* — 29

Cato Farm | *Cheese/Dairy* — 27

Cherry Ln. | *Produce* — 28

Coach Dairy | *Cheese/Dairy* — 28

DiPaola Turkey | *Meat/Poultry* — 27

Eckerton Hill | *Produce* — 26

Flying Pigs | *Meat/Poultry* — 28

Gorzynski/Farm | *Produce* — 27

Hawthorne Farm | *Produce* — 28

Keith's Farm | *Produce* — 28

Martin's Pretzels | *Baked Gds.* — 27

Migliorelli Farm | *Produce* — 26

Our Daily Bread | *Baked Gds.* — 26

Paffenroth | *Produce* — 28

PE & DD | *Seafood* — 28

Quattro's | *Meat/Poultry* — 26

Red Jacket | *Produce* — 27

Samascott | *Produce* — 27

Stokes Farm | *Produce* — 27

Terhune Orchards | *Produce* — 27

3-Corner Farm | *Cheese/Dairy* — 27

Violet Hill | *Meat/Poultry* — 29

Windfall Farms | *Produce* — 27

Yuno's Farm | *Produce* — 29

GREENWICH VILLAGE

(Houston to 14th Sts., west of B'way, east of 7th Ave. S., excluding NoHo)

🔲 Amy's Bread | *Baked Gds.* — 26

Anstice Carroll | *Caterer/Events* — 26

Aphrodisia | *Herbs/Spices* — 26

Bagel Bob's | *Bagels* — 22

Bagel Buffet | *Bagels* — 17

Bagels on Sq. | *Bagels* — 21

Bijoux Doux | *Baked Gds.* — -

🔲 Blue Ribbon | *Baked Gds.* — 28

Broadway Pan. | *Cookware* — 26

Bruno Bakery | *Baked Gds.* — 23

🔲 Citarella | *Maj. Gourmet* — 26

Cold Stone | *Ice Cream* — 20

Cones | *Ice Cream* — 26

Così | *Deli/Sandwich* — 18

Cozy Soup | *Prepared* — 17

Crumbs | *Baked Gds.* — 22

🔲 Dean/DeLuca | *Maj. Gourmet* — 27

DiFiore | *Baked Gds.* — -

🔲 Faicco's Pork | *Meat/Poultry* — 28

🔲 Florence Meat | *Meat/Poultry* — 29

Giorgione | *Deli/Sandwich* — -

Glazier Group | *Caterer* — -

Gourmet Garage | *Maj. Gourmet* — 20

Indian Bread | *Prepared* — 21

Is Wine | *Wine/Liquor* — -

🔲 Jack's Stir Brew | *Coffee/Tea* — 27

Jefferson Mkt. | *Maj. Gourmet* — 26

Joe | *Coffee/Tea* — 26

Lafayette | *Baked Gds.* — 21

Lassi | *Prepared* | 21
Le Pain Quotidien | *Baked Gds.* | 24
LifeThyme Mkt. | *Health* | 24
Lobster Pl. | *Seafood* | 26
Mary's Dairy | *Ice Cream* | 24
Murray's Bagels | *Bagels* | 26
☑ Murray's Cheese | *Cheese/Dairy* | 28
O&CO. | *Spec. Shop* | 25
Oren's/Roast | *Coffee/Tea* | 24
☑ Ottomanelli & Sons | *Meat/Poultry* | 27
☑ Patisserie Claude | *Baked Gds.* | 27
Porto Rico | *Coffee/Tea* | 26
Puff & Pao | *Coffee/Tea* | -
☑ Raffetto's | *Pasta* | 28
Risotteria | *Prepared* | 23
Rocco's Pastry | *Baked Gds.* | 25
Varsano's | *Candy/Nuts* | -
Warehouse Wines | *Wine/Liquor* | 22
'wichcraft | *Deli/Sandwich* | 24
Winesby | *Wine/Liquor* | -
World of Nuts | *Candy/Nuts* | 15

HARLEM/EAST HARLEM

(110th to 157th Sts., excluding Columbia U. area)

☑ Citarella | *Maj. Gourmet* | 26
☑ Fairway | *Maj. Gourmet* | 26
Gracious Thyme | *Caterer* | -
Harlem Tea | *Coffee/Tea* | 25
Harlem Vintage | *Wine/Liquor* | 28
Katrina Parris | *Flowers* | -
La Tropezienne | *Baked Gds.* | -
Make My Cake | *Baked Gds.* | 25
Morrone Bakery | *Baked Gds.* | -
☑ Original SoupMan | *Soup* | 23
Settepani | *Baked Gds.* | 23
Spoonbread | *Caterer* | 23
Starbucks | *Coffee/Tea* | 18
SugarHill Java | *Coffee/Tea* | -

LITTLE ITALY

(Canal to Kenmare Sts., Bowery to Lafayette St.)

Aji Ichiban | *Candy/Nuts* | 21
Alleva Dairy | *Cheese/Dairy* | 27
Bayard St. | *Meat/Poultry* | 23
Caffè Roma | *Baked Gds.* | 23
Ceci-Cela | *Baked Gds.* | 24
☑ Despaña | *Spec. Shop* | 27
☑ DiPalo Dairy | *Cheese/Dairy* | 29

Ferrara Cafe | *Baked Gds.* | 22
Italian Food | *Spec. Shop* | 22
Piemonte Ravioli | *Pasta* | 27

LOWER EAST SIDE

(Houston to Canal Sts., east of Bowery)

BabyCakes | *Baked Gds.* | 24
Bari Equipment | *Cookware* | 24
Bowery Kitchen | *Cookware* | 22
Clinton St. | *Baked Gds.* | 26
Cocoa Bar | *Candy/Nuts* | 26
De Vino | *Wine/Liquor* | 25
☑ Doughnut Plant | *Baked Gds.* | 26
Earthmatters | *Health* | 21
Economy Candy | *Candy/Nuts* | 24
Falai Panetteria | *Baked Gds.* | 27
NEW Formaggio Essex | *Cheese/Dairy* | 26
☑ Il Laboratorio | *Ice Cream* | 28
Jeffrey's | *Meat/Poultry* | -
☑ Katz's Deli | *Deli/Sandwich* | 24
☑ Kossar's | *Bagels* | 28
Neuman's | *Caterer* | 25
New Star Fish | *Seafood* | -
☑ Pickle Guys | *Spec. Shop* | 27
Rainbo's Fish | *Seafood* | -
☑ Russ & Daughters | *Smoked Fish* | 28
Saxelby Cheese | *Cheese/Dairy* | 28
Sept. Wines | *Wine/Liquor* | -
Special Attention | *Caterer* | -
Streit's Matzo | *Baked Gds.* | 25
☑ Sugar Sweet | *Baked Gds.* | 27
Sweet Life | *Candy/Nuts* | 23
Tiny's Giant | *Deli/Sandwich* | 22
☑ Whole Foods | *Maj. Gourmet* | 26
Yonah Schimmel | *Baked Gds.* | 23

MEATPACKING DISTRICT

(Gansevoort to 15th Sts., west of 9th Ave.)

Banchet Flowers | *Flowers* | -
Bodum | *Coffee/Tea* | 24
Little Pie | *Baked Gds.* | 24
Robbins Wolfe | *Caterer* | 26
Robert Isabell | *Flowers* | 27
Serena Bass | *Caterer* | -

MURRAY HILL

(30th to 40th Sts., east of 5th)

☑ Artisanal | *Cheese/Dairy* | 28
Bagelry | *Bagels* | 19

Baskin-Robbins	Ice Cream	17
Berger's	Deli/Sandwich	21
Better Burger	Prepared	19
Brasil Coffee	Coffee/Tea	21
Café Indulge	Prepared	23
Chez Laurence	Baked Gds.	23
Così	Deli/Sandwich	18
Daniel's Bagels	Bagels	24
☑ Dean/DeLuca	Maj. Gourmet	27
Food Emporium	Maj. Gourmet	16
Foods/India	Herbs/Spices	23
Franchia	Coffee/Tea	24
Guy/Gallard	Coffee/Tea	20
Milano Gourmet	Prepared	25
Oren's/Roast	Coffee/Tea	24
Quality Hse.	Wine/Liquor	27
Sarge's Deli	Deli/Sandwich	21
Starbucks	Coffee/Tea	18
NEW Subtle Tea	Coffee/Tea	-
Todaro Bros.	Spec. Shop	24
'wichcraft	Deli/Sandwich	24
Wild Edibles	Seafood	26
Winfield-Flynn	Wine/Liquor	23
World of Nuts	Candy/Nuts	15

NOHO

(Houston to 4th Sts., Bowery to B'way)

Astor Wines	Wine/Liquor	25
Au Bon Pain	Baked Gds.	16
Crate/Barrel	Cookware	22
Häagen Dazs	Ice Cream	24

NOLITA

(Houston to Kenmare Sts., Bowery to Lafayette St.)

Café Habana	Prepared	24
Ciao Bella	Ice Cream	25
Conn. Muffin	Baked Gds.	17
Eileen's Cheesecake	Baked Gds.	26
Parisi Bakery	Baked Gds.	23
Polux Fleuriste	Flowers	-
☑ Rice/Riches	Baked Gds.	23
Wine Therapy	Wine/Liquor	-

SOHO

(Canal to Houston Sts., west of Lafayette St.)

NEW ☑ Alessi	Cookware	27
Alidoro	Deli/Sandwich	27
Baked Ideas	Baked Gds.	-
Balthazar Bakery	Baked Gds.	27
Blue Water	Flowers	-
Centovini	Wine/Liquor	20
☑ Dean/DeLuca	Maj. Gourmet	27
☑ Dom's	Spec. Shop	27
Emack/Bolio	Ice Cream	25
Gourmet Garage	Maj. Gourmet	20
NEW ☑ Grandaisy Bakery	Baked Gds.	29
Great Performances	Caterer	24
Hampton Chutney	Prepared	23
☑ Jacques Torres	Candy/Nuts	28
Joe	Coffee/Tea	26
☑ Joe's Dairy	Cheese/Dairy	28
Jubilee	Maj. Gourmet	21
☑ Kee's Choc.	Candy/Nuts	29
Le Pain Quotidien	Baked Gds.	24
☑ MarieBelle's	Candy/Nuts	26
☑ Olive's	Deli/Sandwich	25
Once Upon/Tart	Baked Gds.	25
Pepe	Prepared	26
Pino Meats	Meat/Poultry	27
Porto Rico	Coffee/Tea	26
Ravioli	Pasta	25
Ron Ben-Israel	Baked Gds.	25
Ruben's	Prepared	20
Snack	Prepared	27
SoHo Wines	Wine/Liquor	21
Starbucks	Coffee/Tea	18
Sunrise Mart	Spec. Shop	23
Sur La Table	Cookware	26
☑ Ten Ren Tea	Coffee/Tea	25
T Salon	Coffee/Tea	26
Vesuvio	Prepared	23
Vintage NY	Wine/Liquor	23
☑ Vosges Haut	Candy/Nuts	26
'wichcraft	Deli/Sandwich	24
Yoghurt Place	Cheese/Dairy	23

SOUTH STREET SEAPORT

Glazier Group	Caterer	-
Häagen Dazs	Ice Cream	24
☑ Jack's Stir Brew	Coffee/Tea	27
Mrs. Field's	Baked Gds.	18
Pasanella	Wine/Liquor	-
Ruben's	Prepared	20

TRIBECA

(Canal to Murray Sts., west of B'way)

Baskin-Robbins	Ice Cream	17
☑ Bazzini	Maj. Gourmet	27
Bell Bates	Health	24

☑ Bouley Bakery	*Baked Gds.*	27
Ceci-Cela	*Baked Gds.*	24
Chambers Wines	*Wine/Liquor*	26
Chestnuts	*Flowers*	-
Duane Pk.	*Baked Gds.*	26
Food Emporium	*Maj. Gourmet*	16
☑ Korin Jap.	*Cookware*	28
Manna Catering	*Caterer*	-
Olivier Cheng	*Caterer*	22
Petite Abeille	*Prepared*	22
☑ Sylvia Weinstock	*Baked Gds.*	26
NEW Tribeca Treats	*Baked Gds.*	27
Tribeca Wine	*Wine/Liquor*	23
Umanoff/Parsons	*Baked Gds.*	24
NEW Vestry Wines	*Wine/Liquor*	-
VinoVino	*Wine/Liquor*	25
'wichcraft	*Deli/Sandwich*	24

UNION SQUARE

(14th to 17th Sts., 5th Ave. to Union Sq. E.)

Au Bon Pain	*Baked Gds.*	16
Broadway Famous	*Party Rent.*	19
Crossroads	*Wine/Liquor*	25
Food Emporium	*Maj. Gourmet*	16
Garden of Eden	*Maj. Gourmet*	24
☑ Italian Wine	*Wine/Liquor*	27
Le Pain Quotidien	*Baked Gds.*	24
Mandler's	*Prepared*	22
NEW Max Brenner	*Candy/Nuts*	22
Ninth St. Espresso	*Coffee/Tea*	28
☑ Tavalon Tea	*Coffee/Tea*	24
NEW Tisserie	*Baked Gds.*	20
☑ Trader Joe's	*Maj. Gourmet*	24
Trader Joe's Wine	*Wine/Liquor*	19
Union Sq. Wines	*Wine/Liquor*	25
☑ Whole Foods	*Maj. Gourmet*	26

WASHINGTON HTS./ INWOOD

(North of W. 157th St.)

Carrot Top	*Baked Gds.*	23
Frank's Gourmet	*Spec. Shop*	21
PJ Wine	*Wine/Liquor*	27

WEST 40S

Amish Market	*Maj. Gourmet*	23
☑ Amy's Bread	*Baked Gds.*	26
Au Bon Pain	*Baked Gds.*	16
Ben & Jerry's	*Ice Cream*	24
Better Burger	*Prepared*	19

Carmine's	*Prepared*	23
Carve	*Deli/Sandwich*	23
Casa/Cupcake	*Baked Gds.*	22
Cold Stone	*Ice Cream*	20
Così	*Deli/Sandwich*	18
Crumbs	*Baked Gds.*	22
Cucina	*Prepared*	21
Dahlia	*Flowers*	26
Daisy May's	*Prepared*	24
Dale & Thomas	*Spec. Shop*	23
☑ Dean/DeLuca	*Maj. Gourmet*	27
Empire Coffee	*Coffee/Tea*	23
Food Emporium	*Maj. Gourmet*	16
Godiva	*Candy/Nuts*	22
Good & Plenty	*Prepared*	22
Hale/Hearty	*Soup*	22
H & H Bagels	*Bagels*	26
Hershey's Times Sq.	*Candy/Nuts*	-
Juan Valdez	*Coffee/Tea*	22
Junior's	*Baked Gds.*	23
☑ La Maison/Choc.	*Candy/Nuts*	29
Le Marais	*Meat/Poultry*	26
Little Pie	*Baked Gds.*	24
☑ Minamoto	*Candy/Nuts*	28
☑ Morrell & Co.	*Wine/Liquor*	27
Mrs. Field's	*Baked Gds.*	18
My Most/Food	*Baked Gds.*	21
Ninth Ave. Int'l	*Spec. Shop*	23
Poseidon	*Baked Gds.*	26
Pozzo Pastry	*Baked Gds.*	21
Pret A Manger	*Deli/Sandwich*	21
Sea Breeze	*Seafood*	23
Starbucks	*Coffee/Tea*	18
Starwich	*Deli/Sandwich*	23
☑ Sullivan St. Bakery	*Baked Gds.*	28
Times Sq. Bagels	*Bagels*	19
Tuck Shop	*Prepared*	-
'wichcraft	*Deli/Sandwich*	24
Zaro's Bread	*Baked Gds.*	17

WEST 50S

Au Bon Pain	*Baked Gds.*	16
Between/Bread	*Caterer*	21
Caffe' Simpatico/Ruthy's	*Baked Gds.*	15
☑ Carnegie Deli	*Deli/Sandwich*	23
Certé	*Caterer/Events*	-
Chocolate Bar	*Candy/Nuts*	26
Columbus Wine	*Wine/Liquor*	22
Così	*Deli/Sandwich*	18

☑ Dean/DeLuca | *Maj. Gourmet*	27
NEW Fika | *Coffee/Tea*	22
Fireman Hospitality | *Caterer*	–
Flowers/World | *Flowers*	28
Fresh Bites | *Prepared*	–
Godiva | *Candy/Nuts*	22
Hale/Hearty | *Soup*	22
Jonathan Flowers | *Flowers*	–
Le Pain Quotidien | *Baked Gds.*	24
Lindt | *Candy/Nuts*	–
Mangia | *Prepared*	24
Myzel Choc. | *Candy/Nuts*	–
☑ Original SoupMan | *Soup*	23
☑ Petrossian | *Caviar/Smoked Fish*	28
Pick a Bagel | *Bagels*	20
Pret A Manger | *Deli/Sandwich*	21
Remi | *Prepared*	26
Ruby/Violette | *Baked Gds.*	26
Stage Deli | *Deli/Sandwich*	21
Stonekelly | *Flowers*	25
Thalia Kitchen | *Prepared*	21
Tuscan Sq. | *Prepared*	22
☑ Westerly Natural | *Health*	25
☑ Whole Foods | *Maj. Gourmet*	26
☑ Williams-Sonoma | *Cookware*	27
World of Nuts | *Candy/Nuts*	15
NEW Zibetto Espresso | *Coffee/Tea*	26

WEST 60S

☑ Balducci's | *Maj. Gourmet*	25
Bed Bath/Beyond | *Cookware*	20
☑ Bouchon Bakery | *Baked Gds.*	27
Food Emporium | *Maj. Gourmet*	16
Gracious Home | *Cookware*	25
Häagen Dazs | *Ice Cream*	24
Jubilee | *Maj. Gourmet*	21
Le Pain Quotidien | *Baked Gds.*	24
Maya Schaper | *Cheese/Dairy*	22
67 Wines | *Wine/Liquor*	25
Starbucks | *Coffee/Tea*	18

WEST 70S

Acker Merrall | *Wine/Liquor*	26
Alice's Tea | *Coffee/Tea*	24
Arte/Corner | *Baked Gds.*	24
Bacchus Wine | *Wine/Liquor*	19
Bagels & Co. | *Bagels*	22
Beacon Wines | *Wine/Liquor*	21
Beard Papa | *Baked Gds.*	24

Bruno/Ravioli | *Pasta*	24
Buttercup | *Baked Gds.*	23
☑ Citarella | *Maj. Gourmet*	26
Così | *Deli/Sandwich*	18
Crumbs | *Baked Gds.*	22
Dale & Thomas | *Spec. Shop*	23
Emack/Bolio | *Ice Cream*	25
☑ Fairway | *Maj. Gourmet*	26
Fine/Schapiro | *Deli/Sandwich*	20
Fischer Bros. | *Meat/Poultry*	27
Godiva | *Candy/Nuts*	22
Gotham Gardens | *Flowers*	24
NEW Grom | *Ice Cream*	–
Häagen Dazs | *Ice Cream*	24
Health Nuts | *Health*	21
Le Pain Quotidien | *Baked Gds.*	24
☑ Levain Bakery | *Baked Gds.*	28
Margot Pâtisserie | *Baked Gds.*	27
Nancy's-Wines | *Wine/Liquor*	24
Neuhaus Choc. | *Candy/Nuts*	25
Ottomanelli Bros. | *Meat/Poultry*	24
NEW Pour | *Wine/Liquor*	21
Sensuous Bean | *Coffee/Tea*	25
☑ Soutine | *Baked Gds.*	27
Surroundings | *Flowers*	25
Westside Mkt. | *Maj. Gourmet*	21
World of Nuts | *Candy/Nuts*	15

WEST 80S

Artie's Deli | *Deli/Sandwich*	21
☑ Barney Greengrass | *Caviar/Smoked Fish*	27
Best Cellars | *Wine/Liquor*	21
Columbus | *Baked Gds.*	21
Confetti | *Baked Gds.*	–
Flor/Mayo | *Prepared*	23
Gary Null's | *Health*	25
Hampton Chutney | *Prepared*	23
H & H Bagels | *Bagels*	26
Hot/Crusty | *Baked Gds.*	15
Indiana Mkt. | *Caterer*	26
Le Pain Quotidien | *Baked Gds.*	24
Murray's Sturgeon | *Caviar/Smoked Fish*	27
Newman/Leventhal | *Caterer*	–
Sarabeth's | *Baked Gds.*	24
Scharffen Berger | *Candy/Nuts*	26
Uncle Louie | *Ice Cream*	20
West Side Wine | *Wine/Liquor*	24
☑ Zabar's | *Maj. Gourmet*	27

WEST 90S

Carmine's | *Prepared*	23
Food Emporium | *Maj. Gourmet*	16
Gotham Wines | *Wine/Liquor*	22
Gourmet Garage | *Maj. Gourmet*	20
Health Nuts | *Health*	21
Lenny's | *Bagels*	23
Oppenheimer | *Meat/Poultry*	26
Tal Bagels | *Bagels*	23
Vintage NY | *Wine/Liquor*	23

WEST 100S

(See also Harlem/East Harlem)

☑ Absolute Bagels | *Bagels*	26
Academy Floral | *Flowers*	23
Ben & Jerry's | *Ice Cream*	24
Flor/Mayo | *Prepared*	23
Garden of Eden | *Maj. Gourmet*	24
Häagen Dazs | *Ice Cream*	24
Hot/Crusty | *Baked Gds.*	15
Hungarian Pastry | *Baked Gds.*	22
JAS Mart | *Spec. Shop*	21
Martin Bros. | *Wine/Liquor*	21
Milano Gourmet | *Prepared*	25
Mondel Choc. | *Candy/Nuts*	22
m2m | *Spec. Shop*	18
Nusbaum & Wu | *Baked Gds.*	18
Oren's/Roast | *Coffee/Tea*	24
Silver Moon | *Baked Gds.*	26

WEST VILLAGE

(Houston to 14th Sts., west of 7th Ave. S., excluding Meatpacking District)

Art of Cooking | *Cookware*	23
A Salt/Battery | *Prepared*	22
Beard Papa | *Baked Gds.*	24
Bird Bath | *Baked Gds.*	–
Bonsignour | *Prepared*	26
Carry On Tea | *Coffee/Tea*	23
Chocolate Bar | *Candy/Nuts*	26
☑ Colette's | *Baked Gds.*	29
Creative Edge | *Caterer*	–
Dirty Bird | *Prepared*	20
Doma | *Coffee/Tea*	25
Health/Harmony | *Health*	26
Integral Yoga | *Health*	24
☑ Le Dû's Wines | *Wine/Liquor*	27
Li-Lac Choc. | *Candy/Nuts*	26
☑ Magnolia Bakery | *Baked Gds.*	23
Magnolia Flowers | *Flowers*	26
Manley's Wines | *Wine/Liquor*	22

Margaret Braun | *Baked Gds.*	–
McNulty's Tea | *Coffee/Tea*	27
Milk & Cookies | *Baked Gds.*	24
Myers/Keswick | *Spec. Shop*	23
Out/Kitchen | *Prepared*	–
Ovando | *Flowers*	–
Pepe | *Prepared*	26
Petite Abeille | *Prepared*	22
Ready to Eat | *Prepared*	21
Sant Ambroeus | *Ice Cream*	26
Sea Grape | *Wine/Liquor*	23
Snack | *Prepared*	27
Taste Caterers | *Caterer*	22
VSF | *Flowers*	29

Bronx

☑ Abigail Kirsch | *Caterer*	26
Addeo's | *Baked Gds.*	27
Arthur Ave. | *Caterer*	24
Artuso Pastry | *Baked Gds.*	26
Biancardi Meats | *Meat/Poultry*	27
☑ Borgatti's | *Pasta*	29
☑ Calabria Pork | *Meat/Poultry*	28
Calandra Cheese | *Cheese/Dairy*	26
Casa Della | *Cheese/Dairy*	29
Consenza's | *Seafood*	27
Delillo Pastry | *Baked Gds.*	26
Egidio Pastry | *Baked Gds.*	24
☑ Madonia Bakery | *Baked Gds.*	28
Mother's Bake | *Baked Gds.*	21
Mount Carmel | *Wine/Liquor*	26
New York Bev. | *Beer*	–
☑ Pastosa Ravioli | *Pasta*	26
☑ Randazzo's | *Seafood*	28
Sal & Dom's | *Baked Gds.*	28
Salsa | *Caterer/Events*	–
S&S Cheesecake | *Baked Gds.*	27
Skyview Wines | *Wine/Liquor*	26
Target | *Cookware*	17
Teitel Bros. | *Spec. Shop*	26
Terranova | *Baked Gds.*	26
Uncle Louie | *Ice Cream*	20
Vincent's Meat | *Meat/Poultry*	27

Brooklyn

BAY RIDGE

Anopoli Ice Cream | *Ice Cream*	–
Areo Rist. | *Caterer*	21
Bay Ridge | *Baked Gds.*	25
Choc-Oh! | *Candy/Nuts*	–

☑ Faicco's Pork | *Meat/Poultry* — 28
Family Store | *Spec. Shop* — –
Hendricks Wine | *Wine/Liquor* — –
Hinsch's | *Ice Cream* — 22
Leske's | *Baked Gds.* — 23
Nordic Delicacies | *Spec. Shop* — 28
Paneantico | *Baked Gds.* — 26
Piazza Mercato | *Meat/Poultry* — –
Tanoreen | *Prepared* — –
3 Guys/Brooklyn | *Produce* — 23

BEDFORD-STUYVESANT

Bread Stuy | *Baked Gds.* — –
Shakoor's Sweet | *Baked Gds.* — –

BENSONHURST

Bari Pork | *Meat/Poultry* — 24
Cold Stone | *Ice Cream* — 20
Lioni Latticini | *Cheese/Dairy* — 29
Papa Pasquale | *Pasta* — 26
☑ Pastosa Ravioli | *Pasta* — 26
Queen Ann | *Pasta* — 27
☑ Royal Crown | *Baked Gds.* — 26
Trunzo Bros. | *Spec. Shop* — 25
☑ Villabate | *Baked Gds.* — 28

BOERUM HILL

NEW Betty Bakery | *Baked Gds.* — –
Bijoux Doux | *Baked Gds.* — –
Boerum Hill Food | *Prepared* — –
Cheryl Kleinman | *Baked Gds.* — 28
Downtown Atlantic | *Prepared* — –
Marquet Patisserie | *Baked Gds.* — 24
Nicky's Viet. | *Deli/Sandwich* — 24

BOROUGH PARK

Bari Pork | *Meat/Poultry* — 24
☑ Coluccio/Sons | *Spec. Shop* — 28
Schick's Bakery | *Baked Gds.* — 20

BRIGHTON BEACH

M & I Foods | *Spec. Shop* — 24

BROOKLYN HEIGHTS

NEW Blue Pig | *Ice Cream* — –
Conn. Muffin | *Baked Gds.* — 17
Cook's Companion | *Cookware* — 26
Damascus Bread | *Baked Gds.* — 25
Garden of Eden | *Maj. Gourmet* — 24
Hale/Hearty | *Soup* — 22
Heights Chateau | *Wine/Liquor* — 25
Heights Meats | *Meat/Poultry* — 24
La Bagel | *Bagels* — 23

Lassen/Hennigs | *Caterer* — 22
Michael-Towne | *Wine/Liquor* — 24
Montague St. | *Bagels* — 22
New Green Pea | *Produce* — 23
Perelandra | *Health* — 24
☑ Sahadi's | *Spec. Shop* — 27
Seaport Flowers | *Flowers* — –
Tazza | *Baked Gds.* — –
☑ Two for the Pot | *Coffee/Tea* — 27

BROWNSVILLLE

Slavin | *Seafood* — 23

CANARSIE

Bed Bath/Beyond | *Cookware* — 20

CARROLL GARDENS

Cafe Scaramouche | *Baked Gds.* — –
Caputo Bakery | *Baked Gds.* — 23
NEW Cobblestone | *Spec. Shop* — –
Court | *Baked Gds.* — 25
☑ D'Amico | *Coffee/Tea* — 27
NEW David Stark | *Caterer/Events* — –
DUB Pies | *Prepared* — 24
Esposito's Pork | *Meat/Poultry* — 26
Fraser-Morris | *Prepared* — –
Margaret Palca | *Baked Gds.* — –
Mazzola Bakery | *Baked Gds.* — 25
Naidre's | *Coffee/Tea* — 22
Naturally Delicious | *Caterer/Events* — –
Park Natural | *Health* — –

CLINTON HILL

NEW Choice Mkt. | *Prepared* — –
Jive Turkey | *Prepared* — 23

COBBLE HILL

American Beer | *Beer* — 26
NEW Chicory Bklyn. | *Prepared* — –
Fish Tales | *Seafood* — 25
Jim/Andy's | *Produce* — –
One Girl | *Baked Gds.* — 24
Smith & Vine | *Wine/Liquor* — 23
☑ Staubitz Mkt. | *Meat/Poultry* — 29
Stinky Bklyn | *Cheese/Dairy* — 28
Sweet Melissa | *Baked Gds.* — 24
Tea Lounge | *Coffee/Tea* — 21

DITMAS PARK

NEW Ackerson, T.B. | *Wine/Liquor* — –

DOWNTOWN

Au Bon Pain	Baked Gds.	16
Cold Stone	Ice Cream	20
Junior's	Baked Gds.	23

DUMBO

☑ Almondine	Baked Gds.	28
Blanc & Rouge	Wine/Liquor	–
Brooklyn Ice Cream	Ice Cream	25
Ciao Bella	Ice Cream	25
Foragers Mkt.	Spec. Shop	–
☑ Jacques Torres	Candy/Nuts	28
La Bagel	Bagels	23

FORT GREENE

☑ Cake Man	Baked Gds.	26
Conn. Muffin	Baked Gds.	17
Greene Grape	Wine/Liquor	24
L'Epicerie	Spec. Shop	–
Marquet Patisserie	Baked Gds.	24
Olivino Wines	Wine/Liquor	–

GRAVESEND

Bari Pork	Meat/Poultry	24

GREENPOINT

Acme Fish	Caviar/Smoked Fish	24
Baskin-Robbins	Ice Cream	17
Brooklyn Ice Cream	Ice Cream	25
NEW Café Grumpy	Coffee/Tea	26
Garden	Spec. Shop	24

KINGS PLAZA/ MARINE PARK

JoMart Choc.	Candy/Nuts	24
Tops Wines	Wine/Liquor	23

MIDWOOD

Jinil/Chocolat	Candy/Nuts	–
Mansoura	Baked Gds.	–
Orchard	Spec. Shop	27

MILL BASIN

☑ Pastosa Ravioli	Pasta	26

PARK SLOPE

Back/Land	Health	23
Bagel Hole	Bagels	22
☑ Bierkraft	Beer	28
Big Nose	Wine/Liquor	24
☑ Blue Apron	Spec. Shop	27
Café Regular	Coffee/Tea	–
Charles/Sally/Charles	Caterer/Events	–
Chocolate Room	Candy/Nuts	25
Cocoa Bar	Candy/Nuts	26
NEW Colson	Baked Gds.	25
Conn. Muffin	Baked Gds.	17
Cousin John's	Baked Gds.	21
☑ D'Vine	Spec. Shop	25
Eagle Provisions	Meat/Poultry	24
Gorilla Coffee	Coffee/Tea	24
Grab Specialty	Spec. Shop	–
La Bagel	Bagels	23
Ladybird Bakery	Baked Gds.	–
Leaf/Bean	Coffee/Tea	23
Luscious Food	Prepared	–
Maggie Moo's	Ice Cream	21
Movable Feast	Caterer	23
Mule	Coffee/Tea	–
Naidre's	Coffee/Tea	22
Ozzie's Coffee	Coffee/Tea	19
Press 195	Deli/Sandwich	25
☑ Prospect Wine	Wine/Liquor	26
Pumpkins	Spec. Shop	26
☑ Red/White	Wine/Liquor	26
Rootstock/Quade	Flowers	–
Russo Mozzarella	Cheese/Dairy	26
Second Helpings	Prepared	–
7th Ave. Wine	Wine/Liquor	20
Shawn's Wines	Wine/Liquor	24
NEW Sip	Wine/Liquor	27
Slope Cellars	Wine/Liquor	24
Sweet Melissa	Baked Gds.	24
Tarzian West	Cookware	22
Tea Lounge	Coffee/Tea	21
Tempo Presto	Deli/Sandwich	23
NEW Trois Pommes	Baked Gds.	–
Uncle Louie	Ice Cream	20
Union Mkt.	Maj. Gourmet	26
Urban Organic	Produce	22
ZuZu's Petals	Flowers	26

PROSPECT HEIGHTS

NEW Christie's	Prepared	21
Fermented	Wine/Liquor	22
Target	Cookware	17
Uncle Louie	Ice Cream	20
Williamson Calvert	Caterer	–

RED HOOK

Baked	Baked Gds.	25
☑ Fairway	Maj. Gourmet	26
☑ LeNell's	Wine/Liquor	27
Steve's/Pies	Baked Gds.	25

SHEEPSHEAD BAY

Güllüoglu	Baked Gds.	–
Jordan's Lobster	Seafood	23

STARRETT CITY

BJ's Wholesale	Maj. Gourmet	17
Target	Cookware	17

SUNSET PARK

Brooklyn Liquors	Wine/Liquor	23
Costco	Maj. Gourmet	21
East Coast Beer	Beer	–
Hong Kong	Spec. Shop	20
Z Ten Ren Tea	Coffee/Tea	25

WILLIAMSBURG

B & B Meat	Meat/Poultry	–
Z Bedford Cheese	Cheese/Dairy	27
Bottle Shoppe	Wine/Liquor	–
Broadway Famous	Party Rent.	19
NEW Brooklyn Kitchen	Cookware	–
NEW Cheeks	Baked Gds.	–
Fabiane's	Baked Gds.	–
Fortunato Bros.	Baked Gds.	25
Gimme! Coffee	Coffee/Tea	27
NEW Lorimer St. Meat	Meat/Poultry	–
Marlow	Spec. Shop	–
Napoli Bakery	Baked Gds.	–
Oslo Coffee	Coffee/Tea	–
Savino's Pasta	Pasta	–
Settepani	Baked Gds.	23
Uva	Wine/Liquor	–

WINDSOR TERRACE

Terrace Bagels	Bagels	25
United Meat	Meat/Poultry	–

Queens

ASTORIA

Z Artopolis	Baked Gds.	28
Astoria Meat	Meat/Poultry	25
Cassinelli Food	Pasta	25
Christos Steak	Meat/Poultry	–
Cold Stone	Ice Cream	20
Costco	Maj. Gourmet	21
Grand Wine	Wine/Liquor	25
La Guli	Baked Gds.	24
NEW Le Petit	Baked Gds.	–
Martha's Bakery	Baked Gds.	–
Mediterranean	Spec. Shop	26

Z Titan Foods	Spec. Shop	26
Uncle Louie	Ice Cream	20

BAYSIDE

Abbey Rent	Party Rent.	–
Ben's Kosher	Deli/Sandwich	21
Health Nuts	Health	21
Maggie Moo's	Ice Cream	21
Peter's Mkt.	Spec. Shop	–
Press 195	Deli/Sandwich	25
Ralph's/Ices	Ice Cream	24

COLLEGE POINT

BJ's Wholesale	Maj. Gourmet	17
Empire Market	Meat/Poultry	–
Target	Cookware	17

CORONA

Z Lemon Ice	Ice Cream	27

DOUGLASTON

Ceriello	Spec. Shop	24
Mazur's Marketpl.	Meat/Poultry	20

ELMHURST

Bed Bath/Beyond	Cookware	20
Cold Stone	Ice Cream	20
Fay Da	Baked Gds.	19
Hong Kong	Spec. Shop	20
Mrs. Field's	Baked Gds.	18
Party Time	Party Rent.	20
Target	Cookware	17
Z Ten Ren Tea	Coffee/Tea	25
Yoghurt Place	Cheese/Dairy	23

FLORAL PARK

Ralph's/Ices	Ice Cream	24

FLUSHING

Durso's Pasta	Pasta	26
Fay Da	Baked Gds.	19
Han Ah Reum	Spec. Shop	22
Hong Kong	Spec. Shop	20
Mauzone	Prepared	22
Max & Mina's	Ice Cream	25
Z Ottomanelli's Meats	Meat/Poultry	27
Patel Bros.	Spec. Shop	23
Tai Pan Bakery	Baked Gds.	19
Z Ten Ren Tea	Coffee/Tea	25

FOREST HILLS

Cheese/World	Cheese/Dairy	25
Eddie's Sweet	Ice Cream	25

Piu Bello	*Ice Cream*	21
Ralph's/Ices	*Ice Cream*	24
Uncle Louie	*Ice Cream*	20
Wine & Spirit	*Wine/Liquor*	22

FRESH MEADOWS

Bagel Oasis	*Bagels*	26
Cold Stone	*Ice Cream*	20
Deli Masters	*Deli/Sandwich*	21

GLENDALE

Amish Market	*Maj. Gourmet*	23

HILLCREST

Bagels & Co.	*Bagels*	22

HOWARD BEACH

Uncle Louie	*Ice Cream*	20

JACKSON HEIGHTS

☑ Despaña	*Spec. Shop*	27
Dimple	*Prepared*	22
Patel Bros.	*Spec. Shop*	23

KEW GARDENS

Hot Bialys	*Bagels*	25
Uncle Louie	*Ice Cream*	20

LONG ISLAND CITY

Brasil Coffee	*Coffee/Tea*	21
☑ Fresh Direct	*Maj. Gourmet*	23
New York/Warehse.	*Wine/Liquor*	-
Paramount Caviar	*Caviar*	-
Thomas Preti	*Caterer*	23

MASPETH

Iavarone Bros.	*Prepared*	25

MIDDLE VILLAGE

BJ's Wholesale	*Maj. Gourmet*	17
Iavarone Bros.	*Prepared*	25

OZONE PARK

☑ Pastosa Ravioli	*Pasta*	26

REGO PARK

Bed Bath/Beyond	*Cookware*	20

RICHMOND HILL

Jahn's Ice Cream	*Ice Cream*	20

ROCKAWAY BEACH

Cakeline	*Baked Gds.*	-

WHITESTONE

Pane d'Italia	*Baked Gds.*	-
Ralph's/Ices	*Ice Cream*	24
☑ Stork's Pastry	*Baked Gds.*	27

WOODSIDE

B & E Beverage	*Beer*	-
☑ Ottomanelli & Sons	*Meat/Poultry*	27

Staten Island

Andrew & Alan's	*Baked Gds.*	22
Bari Pork	*Meat/Poultry*	24
Bed Bath/Beyond	*Cookware*	20
Belfiore Meats	*Meat/Poultry*	25
Cake Chef	*Baked Gds.*	22
Carol's Cuisine	*Caterer*	-
Costco	*Maj. Gourmet*	21
Eggers Ice Cream	*Ice Cream*	25
Lee Sims Choc.	*Candy/Nuts*	-
Mother Mousse	*Baked Gds.*	26
☑ Original SoupMan	*Soup*	23
☑ Pastosa Ravioli	*Pasta*	26
Pete Milano's	*Wine/Liquor*	-
Philip's Candy	*Candy/Nuts*	-
Ralph's/Ices	*Ice Cream*	24
Rita's Ices	*Ice Cream*	21
☑ Royal Crown	*Baked Gds.*	26
Sedutto's	*Ice Cream*	24
Superior Confections	*Candy/Nuts*	-
Tastebud's	*Health*	-
Uncle Louie	*Ice Cream*	20

Out of Town

☑ Abigail Kirsch	*Caterer*	26
☑ Atlas Party	*Party Rent.*	23
County Chair	*Party Rent.*	-
Foremost Caterers	*Caterer*	24
Metro Party	*Party Rent.*	-
Party Rental	*Party Rent.*	22
Something Different	*Party Rent.*	-
TableToppers	*Party Rent.*	-
Wizard Events	*Party Rent.*	-

Mail Order

Listings cover the best in each category and include source names and Quality ratings. ☑ indicates places with the highest ratings, popularity and importance.

BAGELS & BIALYS

Bagel Oasis	26
Bagels & Co.	22
Ess-a-Bagel	26
H & H Midtown	25
☑ Kossar's	28
Montague St.	22

BAKED GOODS

Addeo's	27
Andrew & Alan's	22
BabyCakes	24
Baked	25
Baked Ideas	-
Bijoux Doux	-
☑ Black Hound	26
Bread Alone	27
Bruno Bakery	23
Cafe Scaramouche	-
Caffe' Simpatico/Ruthy's	15
Caputo Bakery	23
CBK Cookies	23
Cipriani	26
Damascus Bread	25
Delillo Pastry	26
DeRobertis	22
☑ Dessert Delivery	28
☑ Doughnut Plant	26
Egidio Pastry	24
Eileen's Cheesecake	26
Eleni's Cookies	22
Falai Panetteria	27
Fat Witch	25
Ferrara Cafe	22
Fortunato Bros.	25
Gail Watson	-
NEW☑ Grandaisy Bakery	29
Güllüoglu	-
Junior's	23
☑ Lady M	28
La Guli	24
La Tropezienne	-
☑ Levain Bakery	28
Little Pie	24

Mansoura	-
Martin's Pretzels	27
Milk & Cookies	24
Mother Mousse	26
Mrs. Field's	18
My Most/Food	21
Once Upon/Tart	25
One Girl	24
Orwasher's	26
Pane d'Italia	-
☑ Payard	28
☑ Rice/Riches	23
Rocco's Pastry	25
S&S Cheesecake	27
Sarabeth's	24
Schick's Bakery	20
Settepani	23
☑ Sylvia Weinstock	26
NEW Three Tarts	22
NEW Tisserie	20
NEW Tribeca Treats	27
Umanoff/Parsons	24
Veniero's	25
William Greenberg	25
Yonah Schimmel	23
Zaro's Bread	17

CANDY & NUTS

Aji Ichiban	21
Chocolate Bar	26
Chocolate Room	25
Chocolat Michel	25
Chocolat Moderne	-
Christopher Norman	23
Debauve/Gallais	27
☑ Dylan's Candy	21
Economy Candy	24
Evelyn's Choc.	25
Fifth Ave. Choc.	20
Godiva	22
Hershey's Times Sq.	-
☑ Jacques Torres	28
Jinil/Chocolat	-
JoMart Choc.	24
☑ La Maison/Choc.	29

Lee Sims Choc.	–	McNulty's Tea	27
Leonidas	26	Mudspot	26
Li-Lac Choc.	26	Oren's/Roast	24
Lindt	–	Ozzie's Coffee	19
Z MarieBelle's	26	Porto Rico	26
Z Martine's Choc.	29	Rohrs	24
NEW Max Brenner	22	Sensuous Bean	25
Z Minamoto	28	Starbucks	18
Mondel Choc.	22	NEW Subtle Tea	–
Myzel Choc.	–	Sympathy	27
Neuchatel Choc.	24	Z Ten Ren Tea	25
Neuhaus Choc.	25	T Salon	26
Z Pierre Marcolini	28	Z Two for the Pot	27
Z Richart Design	28		

COOKWARE & SUPPLIES

Scharffen Berger	26	NEW Z Alessi	27
Superior Confections	–	Art of Cooking	23
Sweet Life	23	Bed Bath/Beyond	20
Z Teuscher Choc.	27	Bloomingdale's	24
Varsano's	–	Bowery Kitchen	22
Vere	–	Z Bridge Kitchen.	28
Z Vosges Haut	26	Broadway Pan.	26
		NEW Brooklyn Kitchen	–

CAVIAR & SMOKED FISH

Z Barney Greengrass	27	Crate/Barrel	22
Caviar Russe	26	Gracious Home	25
Murray's Sturgeon	27	Haas Co.	–
Paramount Caviar	–	Z Korin Jap.	28
Z Petrossian	28	Macy's Cellar	21
Z Russ & Daughters	28	New York Cake	24
Sable's Smoked	27	S. Feldman	23
		Sur La Table	26

CHEESE & DAIRY

Alleva Dairy	27	Target	17
Z Artisanal	28	Z Terence Conran	25
Z Bedford Cheese	27	Z Williams-Sonoma	27

DRIED FRUIT

Ideal Cheese	27	Aji Ichiban	21
Maya Schaper	22	Z Balducci's	25
Z Murray's Cheese	28	Z Bazzini	27
		Z Citarella	26

COFFEE & TEA

Bodum	24	Z Dean/DeLuca	27
Brasil Coffee	21	Economy Candy	24
Carry On Tea	23	Z Eli's Manhattan	25
Z D'Amico	27	Eli's Vinegar	25
Empire Coffee	23	Z Kalustyan's	27
Gimme! Coffee	27	Patel Bros.	23
Gorilla Coffee	24	Z Russ & Daughters	28
Z Ito En	28	Sweet Life	23
Z Jack's Stir Brew	27	Truffette	–
Leaf/Bean	23	Z Zabar's	27

FLOWERS

Academy Floral	23
Ariston	27
Banchet Flowers	-
Big Apple Florist	24
Castle/Pierpont	24
Chelsea Wholesale	25
Fellan Florist	24
Flowers/World	28
Gotham Gardens	24
Katrina Parris	-
L'Olivier	29
Polux Fleuriste	-
Richard Salome	-
Spruce	27
Surroundings	25
Z Takashimaya	28
Windsor Florist	24

HEALTH & NATURAL FOODS

A Matter/Health	21
Health/Harmony	26
Health Nuts	21
Z Westerly Natural	25

HERBS & SPICES

Z Penzeys Spices	27

MEAT, POULTRY & GAME

Albert's Meats	26
Beekman Mktpl.	22
Z Calabria Pork	28
Z East Village Meat	28
Fischer Bros.	27
Z Florence Meat	29
Iavarone Bros.	25
Koglin Hams	24
Le Marais	26
Z Lobel's Meats	29
New Beef	-
Oppenheimer	26
Z Ottomanelli & Sons	27
Ottomanelli Bros.	24
Z Ottomanelli's Meats	27
Park E. Kosher	26
Piazza Mercato	-
Quattro's	26
Z Salumeria	29
Z Schaller & Weber	27
Vincent's Meat	27

PARTY RENTALS

TableToppers	-
Z TriServe	24

PASTAS

Durso's Pasta	26
Iavarone Bros.	25
Z Pastosa Ravioli	26
Ravioli	25

PRODUCE

Berkshire Berries	27
Red Jacket	27

SEAFOOD

Z Dorian's Seafood	25
Gramercy Fish	24
Leonard's	26
Lobster Pl.	26
Pescatore	25
Wild Edibles	26

SPECIALTY SHOPS

Beth's Kitchen	27
BuonItalia	26
Butterfield Mkt.	23
Ceriello	24
Chelsea Baskets	24
Dale & Thomas	23
Z Despaña	27
Foragers Mkt.	-
Han Ah Reum	22
Z Kalustyan's	27
Kam Man	21
Katagiri	23
Z Manhattan Fruitier	27
Z May May	23
Mediterranean	26
Myers/Keswick	23
Ninth Ave. Int'l	23
Nordic Delicacies	28
O&CO.	25
Patel Bros.	23
Peter's Mkt.	-
Z Pickle Guys	27
Pickles/Olives	23
NEW Z Stonehouse	27
Teitel Bros.	26
Z Titan Foods	26
Todaro Bros.	24
Truffette	-
Trunzo Bros.	25

WINES & LIQUOR

Acker Merrall	26	McAdam	22
Appellation	25	ⓩ Moore Bros.	29
Astor Wines	25	ⓩ Morrell & Co.	27
Bacchus Wine	19	Mount Carmel	26
Beacon Wines	21	Nancy's-Wines	24
Beekman Liquors	24	New York/Exchange	23
Best Cellars	21	New York/Warehse.	-
Big Nose	24	Park Ave. Liquor	26
Blanc & Rouge	-	PJ Wine	27
ⓩ Burgundy	29	ⓩ Prospect Wine	26
Cellar 72	26	Quality Hse.	27
Chambers Wines	26	ⓩ Red/White	26
Chelsea Wine	23	Royal Wine	-
Columbus Wine	22	Sea Grape	23
Crossroads	25	ⓩ Sherry-Lehmann	29
ⓩ Crush Wine	26	67 Wines	25
Embassy Wines	19	Skyview Wines	26
Famous Wines	22	Sutton Wine	22
Garnet Wines	24	Tribeca Wine	23
Gotham Wines	22	Union Sq. Wines	25
Grand Wine	25	NEW Vestry Wines	-
Harlem Vintage	28	ⓩ Vino	28
ⓩ Italian Wine	27	Vintage NY	23
K & D Wines	24	Winesby	-
ⓩ Le Dû's Wines	27	Wine Therapy	-
ⓩ LeNell's	27	Winfield-Flynn	23
Martin Bros.	21	Yorkshire Wines	23

subscribe to zagat.com

ONLINE SOURCES

Best Overall

Averaging Quality, Display & Service ratings.

26 Recchiuti Confections
Browne Trading
Zingerman's
Burdick, L.A.
Cheese/Beverly Hills

25 Upton Tea Imports
Fine Stationery
King Arthur Flour
Cowgirl Creamery
American Spoon

Top Quality Ratings

Ratings are to the left of names.

29 Enstrom's
Hudson/Foie Gras
Upton Tea Imports

28 La Colombe
Cowgirl Creamery

Mighty Leaf
Salumi Armandino
Fante's Kitchen
Zingerman's
Fran's Chocolates

BY CATEGORY

BAKED GOODS

28 Zingerman's
27 Burdick, L.A.
26 Dancing Deer Baking
25 Big Island Candies
24 Boudin Bakery

CANDY

29 Enstrom's
28 Fran's Chocolates
Recchiuti Confections
Fran's Chocolates
27 Burdick, L.A.
25 Bridgewater Chocolate

CAVIAR/SMOKED FISH

28 Browne Trading
Pike Place Fish
26 Di Bruno Bros.
igourmet.com
24 Tsar Nicoulai

CHARCUTERIE

28 Salumi Armandino
Zingerman's
D'Artagnan
26 Di Bruno Bros.
Ferrari, A.G.

CHEESE/DAIRY

28 Cowgirl Creamery
Zingerman's
Cheese/Beverly Hills

26 Di Bruno Bros.
25 Artisan Made-NE

COFFEE/TEA

29 Upton Tea Imports
28 La Colombe
Mighty Leaf
Fortnum & Mason
27 Illy

COOKWARE/SUPPLIES

28 Fante's Kitchen
King Arthur Flour
27 CutleryAndMore
26 Surfas
Cooking Enthusiast

FLOWERS

25 Calyx & Corolla
23 MarthaStewartFlowers
22 Hallmark
ProFlowers

GIFT BASKETS

28 Zingerman's
Fran's Chocolates
Cheese/Beverly Hills
Fortnum & Mason
27 American Spoon

HERBS/SPICES

27 Spice House
26 La Tienda

Surfas
Adriana's Caravan
24 ChefShop

MEAT, POULTRY & GAME
29 Hudson/Foie Gras
28 Niman Ranch
D'Artagnan
27 Neuske's
Allen Brothers

PARTY ACCESSORIES
26 Fine Stationery
25 Paper Source
24 Amazon.com
22 Hallmark
21 Illuminations

PASTAS, GRAINS & BEANS
28 King Arthur Flour
27 Bob's Red Mill
26 Surfas
Ferrari, A.G.
24 Amazon.com
ChefShop.com

PRODUCE, NUTS & DRIED FRUIT
27 Bob's Red Mill
24 Cushman Fruit
NapaStyle
ChefShop
Hadley Fruit

SEAFOOD
28 Browne Trading
Pike Place Fish
26 igourmet.com
23 Lobster Gram
Sea Bear

SPECIALTY ITEMS
28 Zingerman's
27 American Spoon
Stonewall Kitchen
La Tienda
26 Ferrari, A.G.

WINES/LIQUOR
28 D. Sokolin
27 Wally's Wine
26 K&L Wine
Zachy's
Wine Library

Top Display Ratings

Ratings are to the left of names.

26 Fine Stationery
Burdick, L.A.
25 Recchiuti Confections
Calyx & Corolla
Stonewall Kitchen

24 NapaStyle
Cookies By Design
Plum Party
Browne Trading
Di Bruno Bros.

Top Service Ratings

Ratings are to the left of names.

26 La Tienda
Zingerman's
Browne Trading
Recchiuti Confections
25 Upton Tea Imports

Niman Ranch
Cheese/Beverly Hills
King Arthur Flour
Fante's Kitchen
American Spoon

ONLINE SOURCES
DIRECTORY

	QUALITY	DISPLAY	SERVICE	COST

Adriana's Caravan *Herbs/Spices*

26 | 20 | 21 | M

www.adrianascaravan.com | 800-316-0820

A "virtual magic blanket" of seasonings, this purveyor – still "missed" as a former inhabitant of Grand Central – proffers a "terrific" selection of herbs and spices, from everyday staples to "obscure finds", as well as a cornucopia of condiments (e.g. more than 30 hot sauces, organized by zing); "helpful descriptions" of the products are handy, especially in the absence of photos, and "excellent customer service" is also available via e-mail or phone; P.S. rated one of the "best values around", it really becomes a bargain when you buy in bulk (discounts apply for orders by the case as well as those over $200).

Allen Brothers *Meat/Poultry*

27 | 23 | 24 | VE

www.allenbrothers.com | 800-957-0111

"Other steaks pale in comparison" to the "first-rate", "perfectly trimmed" prime specimens from this online arm of a circa-1893 Chicago butcher and supplier to "top steakhouses", whose "memorable" meats include Wagyu beef, pork, lamb, sausages and burgers, and there's also game, seafood and prepared foods; its goods are considered by most to be "worth every cent" of their "way-expensive" prices, not least because they arrive "on time" and "in excellent shape"; P.S. its many gift assortments "blow recipients away."

Amazon.com *Cookware/Specialty Shop*

24 | 21 | 23 | M

www.amazon.com

This "clearinghouse for vendors of all shapes and sizes" has become the site to "check before buying" anywhere else due to "highly competitive pricing" (especially with "free shipping" on many items), an "easy-to-use" setup and the "convenience" of shopping a "gigantic selection" of "cook's gear" as well as "gourmet wares" like coffee, tea, chocolates, meat, seafood, cheese, pasta, caviar and charcuterie; sure, delivery's "not flawless", "top-quality products" aren't always available and customer service is "hard to reach" (good luck "trying to find an 800 number" if you need it), but "if you know what you want" you'll most likely get "a deal."

American Spoon Foods *Specialty Shop*

27 | 24 | 25 | E

www.spoon.com | 800-222-5886

Find "heaven in a jar" at this online home of Michigan's "favorite" condiment specialist, where "sour cherry"-lovers and others shop for "top-of-the-heap" artisanal jams, preserves and fruit spreads, as well as "simple", "delicious" savories including salsas, dressings and sauces, all ordered from an easy-to-browse list; its sweet gift boxes are "pricey but special" ideas for food enthusiasts, particularly since voters assure you can "count on the quality."

Artisan Made-Northeast *Cheese/Dairy*

25 | 18 | 21 | E

www.artisanmade-ne.com

Say "cheese" – this site carries the best of Northeastern-produced handcrafted foods, including 80-plus varieties of "delicious" farmstead fromages, some "undiscovered" gems among them, that are as "fresh" as they are "expensive", and there are also other Yankee-made offerings like "delicious" chocolates, jams and sauces; though aesthetes pan its overall look as "one-dimensional", all appreciate the "ease of ordering" and navigation, as well as special services like pairing advice from sommelier Sally Camm, which make this "the place" for artisanal treats.

Big Island Candies *Candy/Nuts*
25 | 21 | 22 | M

www.bigislandcandies.com | 800-935-5510

It's easy to get "hooked on" the "delicious" candies, cookies and such produced by "Hawaii's premier" confectioner, according to "big fans" of its "decadent" signatures like macadamia-studded nut clusters and "divine chocolate-dipped shortbread", as well as newer offerings including truffles with exotic flavorings (hibiscus, yuzu); factor in "beautiful" packaging and numerous gift basket options and you've got the makings of a "wonderful" present; N.B. the altar-bound can work with a wedding specialist to create perfectly packaged favors.

Bob's Red Mill *Grains/Beans*
27 | 21 | 22 | M

www.bobsredmill.com | 800-349-2173

This "old-time company" has "made the jump to the Internet" with aplomb according to surveyors "impressed" with its "marvelous" selection of some 400 "natural" whole grains, flours, beans, nuts, dried fruit, baking mixes, hot cereals and more (many of them organic); its Web site allows for browsing in several ways, has fun features like a short video in which founder Bob Moore takes viewers through the production process as well as recipes and other useful items; P.S. insiders suggest "buy in bulk" as "shipping can be expensive."

Boudin Bakery *Baked Goods*
24 | 20 | 20 | M

www.boudinbakery.com | 800-992-1849

For a slice of San Francisco "delivered right to your door", it's hard to beat the online adjunct of this historic (since 1849) bakery whose selection of the "best sourdough" maybe "isn't tremendous", but it's "tremendous-quality" according to aficionados of its specialty breads and accompaniments, including seasonal ones (e.g. bunny shaped-loaves for Easter); there are also basket and club options for gift-givers, all baked-to-order and sent out the same day, though some say such special handling can add up to a lot of dough ("shipping costs are high").

Bridgewater Chocolate *Candy/Nuts*
25 | 24 | 22 | VE

www.bridgewaterchocolate.com | 800-888-8742

"Wow", this tony confectioner's "fabulous" classic American sweets like toffee, caramels, truffles and turtles are "habit"-forming, and packaged prettily enough to make them "perfect for gift-giving"; its Web site is a pleasure to browse thanks to mouthwatering photographs showing each item as it will look upon arrival, and though it's seriously pricey, surveyors say if you're in the mood to "splurge" – "go for it."

	QUALITY	DISPLAY	SERVICE	COST

Browne Trading Co. *Caviar*

| 28 | 24 | 26 | E |

www.brownetrading.com | 800-944-7848

"When only the best will do" fish finatics turn to this Maine-based, family-run company that's been supplying high-end restaurants (e.g. NYC's Le Bernardin) with impeccable fresh catch, as well as smoked seafood and caviar "to die for", for generations; sure, it's "expensive", but to loyalists it's "worth every penny", especially when you factor in the "unparalleled service" and a Web site that's "great to shop" and boasts detailed product explanations, serving guidelines and recipes; N.B. it also vends a select assortment of oils, vinegars, salts and such.

Burdick, L.A., Handmade Chocolates *Candy/Nuts*

| 27 | 26 | 24 | E |

www.burdickchocolate.com | 800-229-2419

Gift-givers looking to "spoil someone they love" turn to this online arm of a veteran New Hampshire "chocolate heaven", whose "tiny treasures" are "expensive" but deemed "worth every darn penny" since they're "handmade in the European style" with "quality" ingredients; among the "ethereal confections" are ganache-filled bonbons, trademark "adorable chocolate mice" ("how can you resist?") and a line of Swiss pastries, available in numerous favor and gift assortments; "very good service" and reliable delivery that has everything "arriving fresh and lovely" are icing on the cake.

Calyx & Corolla *Flowers*

| 25 | 25 | 23 | VE |

www.calyxandcorolla.com | 800-800-7788

This petal peddler's cut flowers, arrangements and plants are "fresh" and "gorgeous" enough to make "the giver look good", while its "reliable" speedy delivery can allow even "guys with the worst foresight" to come off like a "Casanova"; the "quality" is voted better and the "designs more exotic" and "upscale-feeling" than the "other big online" players, and while it can be hard to choose among its "impressive" array of options, customers can always look to the "top-notch customer service" for guidance, but just keep in mind that "beauty doesn't come cheap" here.

Cheese Store of Beverly Hills *Cheese/Dairy*

| 28 | 24 | 25 | E |

www.cheesestorebh.com | 800-547-1515

Fromage fans "bow to" this online extension of a Los Angeles "mecca" for "top-notch" artisanal cheeses, citing a "wonderful" 600-strong lactic inventory boasting "fabulous freshness and variety" – from "stinky to smooth and sweet" – and there are also wine, oils, vinegars, salts, caviar and truffles (in season); "fabulous gift baskets" are a strong suit, as is "excellent service", so never mind if a few detect a slight, well, "cheesy" feel to this somewhat basic site.

Chefs *Cookware*

| 25 | 21 | 21 | M |

www.chefscatalog.com | 800-884-2433

A "toque above" many online cookware stores, this mega-site purveys all the "kitchen tools" that "serious cooks" and "wannabe

QUALITY DISPLAY SERVICE COST

chefs" could ever want, plus lots of fun "not-so-essential" gadgets, offered in an "attractive" format that makes shopping simple (search by brand or category, or check out the recipe section for inspiration); the service is generally considered solid and prices "reasonable", though the savvy suggest "hold out for sales" and "free shipping offers" and you really "can get some deals"; N.B. it offers wedding registry services too.

ChefShop.com *Specialty Shop*

24 | 20 | 22 | E

www.chefshop.com | 800-596-0885

"Half the fun is exploring" the somewhat "weird" assortment of culinary "treats" (prawn chutney, anyone?) available at this online specialty store whose "fabulous, quality products" include everything from fresh meat, salami, seafood and produce to herbs and spices, grains, beans, pastas and baking supplies; shopping is generally an "excellent experience" due to "fast, accurate service" and a wealth of "information" and recipes provided on the site, though a befuddled few feel its convoluted layout is "in need of simplification."

Chef's Resource *Cookware*

25 | 21 | 22 | E

www.chefsresource.com | 866-765-2433

"Most everything you need for your kitchen" can be found through this "easy-to-deal-with" online cookware specialist, whose "amazing", well-laid-out selection spans cookware, cutlery, small appliances and every imaginable tool and gadget, plus grilling equipment, kitchen furniture and a smattering of gourmet foodstuffs like condiments, vinegars and oils; though perspectives differ on the prices ("good" vs. "there are better elsewhere"), no one complains about the "outstanding" variety of offerings that are seemingly "never on backorder."

Cookies By Design *Baked Goods*

21 | 24 | 22 | E

www.cookiesbydesign.com | 888-882-6654

"Cookies that get noticed" are the forte of this online outfit whose "cute" "colorful" signature baked treat comes in "all shapes and designs" imaginable, making for "pretty arrangements" that are "fun to send as gifts" – and "easy" too considering that the options are organized by occasion (baby shower, anniversary, housewarming, recital, etc.) and can also be "customized"; yes, it'll cost you "a lot of dough", but "people just love getting them."

Cooking.com *Cookware*

24 | 21 | 21 | M

www.cooking.com | 800-663-8810

"If they don't have it, it might not exist" say worshipers of this online mecca" of "all things kitchen-related" vending "name-brand" consumer goods at "a fraction of the cost of department stores" – and sending out "frequent free-shipping offers" that can make for real bargains"; shoppers appreciate its "helpful" customer-written product reviews and the fact that it "redirects you to other sources if it doesn't stock an item"; other pluses like "discussion boards", recipes, "fantastic customer service" and "prompt shipping" have most praising it as an all-around "reliable resource."

	QUALITY	DISPLAY	SERVICE	COST

Cooking Enthusiast *Cookware*

26 | 20 | 23 | E

www.cutlery.com | 800-792-6650

"Real chefs and wannabes" alike "love" this "first stop for kitchen supplies", which is known foremost for its "excellent selection of knives", but also offers a range of high-end cookware, "hard-to-find gadgets", tableware and a selection of specialty foods (oils and vinegars, condiments, etc.); wallet-watchers note it's "sometimes higher-priced than its competitors", but its overall "quality", including "excellent service" and an easy-to-navigate site featuring "nice notes on equipment", tip the scales in its favor.

Cowgirl Creamery *Cheese/Dairy*

28 | 23 | 24 | E

www.cowgirlcreamery.com | 866-433-7834

Founded a decade ago by a pair of former chefs, this Point Reyes Station, CA, "cheese heaven" is now recognized as "one of America's finest" producers of "distinctive, delicious" artisanal fromages, but it also imports "wonderful" varieties from France and around the world, adding up to an overall "fantastic" (if "expensive") lineup; "online ordering is easy" thanks to the helpful info provided in its 'library of cheese', as well as by its "sharp customer service reps", and since "they know how to ship" it's sure to arrive as fresh as when it left the cave.

Cushman Fruit Co. *Produce*

24 | 19 | 24 | M

www.honeybell.com | 800-776-7575

"Get your bib ready" for the "drippy" goodness of this longtime family-run Florida fruit seller's signature offering: "sweet, super juicy, utterly delicious" honeybells, a tangerine-grapefruit hybrid available for only a few weeks in January ("you haven't lived until you've had" one); though few find fault with the "premium" goods including various kinds of citrus and other fruits, plus sweets and gift baskets – surveyors say these "courteous" folks "stand behind their product" and will "replace it if it's not satisfactory."

CutleryAndMore *Cookware*

27 | 22 | 23 | M

www.cutleryandmore.com | 800-650-9866

Not surprisingly, this "well-organized", no-nonsense Web "favorite" is particularly "great for its namesake" product, offering "good deals" on hundreds of "high-quality" knives, cleavers, shears, scissors and sharpeners, though it also stocks a vast array of cookware and tools, as well as tough-to-find small appliance replacement parts; users report a "good shopping experience" overall, with "prompt service", low shipping costs and "well-packaged" products that "arrive in a timely fashion."

Dancing Deer Baking Co. *Baked Goods*

26 | 22 | 22 | E

www.dancingdeer.com | 888-699-3337

"Wonderful" baked goods "worth violating your diet" over ("particularly the cookies") are on offer via the "user-friendly" site of this "Boston institution" known for its "natural", "high-quality" ingredients and "good-looking packages" that make it a "go-to for gifts" "great service" and "fast shipping" are other appeals, and though the "delicious" products are "pricey", "community"-minded customers say it's "worth it" considering that the "company gives back" a portion of its profits to charity.

D'Artagnan *Meat/Poultry*

28 | 22 | 24 | E

www.dartagnan.com | 800-327-8246

The "freshest game you can get without a bird dog" is the word on the "exquisite" products from Ariane Daguin's "wonderful", renowned New Jersey–based site, from signature "to-die-for" foie gras and other "hard-to-find duck specialties" (pâtés, sausages, smoked delicacies) to organic poultry and "delicious" delicacies like truffles and mushrooms, many "from Perigord"; "whatever they do" is "just the best" approve its legions of fans, who appreciate the "hassle-free" service and "terrific" online recipes, and note that while the goods are predictably "expensive", it's "worth the extravagance."

Di Bruno Bros. *Cheese/Dairy*

26 | 24 | 24 | E

www.dibruno.com | 888-322-4337

If you can't shop in person at this circa-1939 "Philly institution" of an Italian market (aka "the house of cheese"), its "great online system" is the next best thing, boasting "some of the best" formaggio around – 500 or so varieties, browsable by type or country of origin – as well as "top-quality" charcuterie, caviar and smoked fish, olives, Boot-centric specialty ingredients, kitchenware and "excellent gift baskets"; reviewers report it can be "less expensive" than other "upscale" members of the genre, though there are a few grumbles about "hefty shipping and handling" fees.

D. Sokolin *Wine/Liquor*

28 | 19 | 23 | E

www.sokolin.com | 800-946-3947

A favorite of collectors and other deep-pocketed oenophiles, this Hamptons-based online wine merchant (the progeny of a NYC shop founded in 1934) boasts an astounding 100,000-label selection, including many "not readily available locally", with an emphasis on Bordeaux, Burgundy and fine and rare vintages; buyers "certainly feel confident" in purchasing, particularly when guided by the "professional, knowledgeable" staff, though naturally they "pay dearly" for the privilege – not to mention the "killer shipping fees"; N.B. it also sells futures and offers private storage services.

Enstrom's *Candy/Nuts*

29 | 21 | 24 | M

www.enstrom.com | 800-367-8766

"World-class toffee" worth "breaking your caps" for is the "unparalleled" signature sweet that has surveyors seranading this Colorado-based confectioner as the "hands-down best" on the Web, though it also produces "love-'em" chocolate truffles, chews, fudge and even sugar-free bonbons; shopping is simple given the "great gift" options and "very helpful" customer service, and though it can get "pricey when shipping is added into the equation", "addicts" "order anyway" because it's "that good."

	QUALITY	DISPLAY	SERVICE	COST

Ethnic Grocer *Specialty Shop* | 23 | 18 | 22 | M |

www.ethnicgrocer.com | 630-860-1733

"Hard-to-find ingredients are now easy to find" thanks to this "unique" Web site that stocks a "wide, international" array of specialty food items that definitely "aren't at the local grocery store"; explore the "accessible and informative" homepage for "inspiration", browsing products organized by country and type, or hit the "terrific" 'cooking school' section supplying "reliable" recipes from "any number of cultures and cuisines" – just "keep this one bookmarked."

Fante's Kitchen *Cookware* | 28 | 20 | 25 | M |

www.fantes.com | 800-443-2683

"This is where to find the kitchen tools you didn't know you needed" say shoppers smitten with this online arm of a circa-1906 Philly cookware store that "has the stock", from basics to more "unusual items", with a particular emphasis on baking equipment and "specialty Italian stuff"; all appreciate the "reasonable prices", pro customer service (they "know more about cooking than some chefs") as well as the "helpful" online product info – now if only they'd give the Web site "a little updating."

Ferrari, A.G., Foods *Specialty Shop* | 26 | 22 | 21 | E |

www.agferrari.com | 877-878-2783

"If you don't live close to an Italian store, don't worry" – there's always this Northern California–based purveyor's "helpful" site offering "well-chosen", "high-quality" (and "costly") artisanal goods from The Boot, including cheeses, charcuterie, pastas, wines and lots of specialty food items; customers can search by product type or region, and there are also "nicely packaged gift baskets" and a lengthy recipes section.

Fine Stationery *Party Accessories* | 26 | 26 | 24 | E |

www.finestationery.com | 888-808-3463

Offering "the biggest selection of the best" paper goods out there, this online stationer is considered a "top-notch" source for "beautiful, unique" custom invitations of all kinds; its easy-to-browse Web site organizes products based on occasion, and orders are "shipped quickly", making it ideal for "weddings, parties and baby announcements", though some feel the personalization process "isn't the most user-friendly" and "prices are higher" than some of the competition.

Fortnum & Mason *Coffee/Tea* | 28 | 23 | 23 | E |

www.fortnumandmason-usa.com | 877-533-2636

The U.S. site for this venerable, nearly 300-year-old Piccadilly Circus purveyor of "fine British teas and coffees" and traditional "English" snacks "never disappoints", supplying anglophiles and expats with "superb" loose leaves and beans, as well as biscuits, jams and other "upscale" tea-time treats, plus "wonderful gift baskets"; maybe "it's not quite like enjoying the store with its coat-and-tails staff" (and it "doesn't have the full selection" either), but admirers

	QUALITY	DISPLAY	SERVICE	COST

appreciate that delivery is "prompt", and as for the "slightly numbing" prices – it's still "cheaper than a trip to London."

Fran's Chocolates *Candy/Nuts*

| 28 | 23 | 23 | E |

www.franschocolates.com | 800-422-3726

Though she's "best known for her salted caramels", it's hard to pass up any of Seattle confectioner Fran Bigelow's "sinfully delicious" confections, given that the "great chocolate" bars and "fantastic" truffles in "luxurious", big-bowed gift boxes tempt anyone browsing her "easy-to-navigate" Web site; happily for the "addicted", delivery is "quick", though "high prices" make its "to-die-for" morsels an expensive "vice."

Hadley Fruit Orchards *Candy/Nuts*

| 24 | 18 | 20 | M |

www.hadleyfruitorchards.com | 800-854-5655

Maybe "it's not as much fun as going there in person" but visits to this online arm of an "old reliable" Banning, CA, fruit grower are rewarded with products that "look good and taste even better", including dates (notably "great" Medjools), dried fruits and nuts; gift-givers can choose from a variety of assortment options, and there are also "yummy" trail mixes, leaving most to marvel "how do you not find something here?"

Hallmark *Flowers*

| 22 | 21 | 21 | M |

www.hallmarkflowers.com | 800-425-5627

This mega-brand known for its "thoughtful" cards adds "better-than-you'd-expect" flowers and plants to its roster of "consistently good products", presenting them on an "easy-to-use" site offering several ways to search arrangements (occasion, type, price), a helpful 'learn about' section full of flower facts and tips, and a "free e-card" area; recipients say its blooms "last a long time", and the "Hallmark card" included with deliveries is "a nice touch"; N.B. party-throwers should note it's also a source for invitations.

Harney & Sons *Coffee/Tea*

| 27 | 24 | 23 | M |

www.harney.com | 888-427-6398

"Tea freaks" frequent this "favorite site" – the online extension of a "family-run" Millerton, NY, shop – for its "wonderful" selection of "very fine, full-flavored teas" that span the spectrum from "staples" to "innovative" blends, and there are also "terrific" accessories; the loose leaves and sachets come "well-packaged" in adorable tins, which lend themselves naturally to a "wide variety" of "great gift" sets, while "reasonable prices" and the company's general "dedication to customers" seal the deal – just "beware the seduction" factor lest you end up with "a cabinetful."

Harry & David *Gift Baskets*

| 23 | 23 | 22 | E |

www.harryanddavid.com | 877-322-1200

"Always appreciated" "offerings for the hard-to-shop-for" have crowned this Oregon-based business the "king of gift baskets", boasting an "easy-to-manage" Web site where "classic" selections that "everyone loves getting" – trademark "amazing, juicy pears best eaten with a bib" or "over-the-top" towers of treats – are easily purchased and "reliably" delivered (but if there's a problem, "customer service bends over backwards" to make it right); there are grumbles about "very costly" prices and "extra fees for everything", but the majority maintains "dependability" is "worth paying for."

Hudson Valley Foie Gras *Meat/Poultry*	29	22	24	VE

www.hudsonvalleyfoiegras.com | 877-289-3643

"*The* source for fresh foie gras" is this "dependable duck" dealer whose products are rated the "best you can get in the U.S.", perhaps because all stages of production, from breeding to packaging, happen on its 20-acre farm in Ferndale, NY; in addition to its signature "to-die-for" whole goose livers, there are terrines, pâtés and fresh duck breasts and more, and its site boasts appealing extras like recipes and travelogues from cofounder Michael Ginor; P.S. naturally it's "expensive", but given the "very-best" quality most maintain it's "worth every penny."

igourmet.com *Gift Baskets*	26	21	23	E

www.igourmet.com | 877-446-8763

"You'll reorder often" say supporters of this "lifesaver" of a site, where you can "make a gift basket out of anything you choose" – or order à la carte just for yourself – selecting from an "astounding" array of "delicacies" "from a wide range of countries", including "*très magnifique* cheeses"; some say the "amazing" number of options can make shopping here a "bit cumbersome" until "you get used to it", but the relatively "moderate prices" given the "luxury" genre make it a "great resource", as do the "helpful service" and "prompt shipping."

Illuminations *Party Accessories*	21	21	19	M

www.illuminations.com | 800-621-2998

Some of the "best scents in the biz" can be found at this "no-hassles" site for "reasonably priced" candles and related "imaginative" accessories and "decorative items", including votives, tealights and tapers perfect for party-throwers; "new items" are added "all the time" and there are "lots of online specials and sales", making it a boon for "bargain-hunters."

Illy *Coffee/Tea*	27	23	21	E

www.illyusa.com | 877-469-4559

"*Bellissimo!*" – bring "real Italian espresso" and other "rich-tasting roasts and blends" "to your home" via this famous Trieste-based purveyor's "modern" U.S. site, which, in addition to its "delicious", "pricey" beans, offers "good espresso machines" and coffeemakers with "top-notch design and function" (and they can be had "cheaply" if you sign up for regular coffee deliveries); if "shipping can be spotty", at least "the quality is consistent"; P.S. "love the limited-edition espresso cup" collections designed by well-known artists.

Intelligentsia Coffee *Coffee/Tea*	27	20	23	M

www.intelligentsiacoffee.com | 888-945-9786

"Deli coffee it ain't" quip patrons of this informative online offshoot of a Chicago-based coffee retailer that offers a reasonably priced

ONLINE SOURCES

QUALITY
DISPLAY
SERVICE
COST

ONLINE SOURCES

"wide variety of Fair Trade coffee and tea", including everything from Charlie Trotter's house blend to "green beans for home-roasters", and it also vends loose leaf and chai teas and all the necessary brewing apparatus; its "consistent" "telephone voicemail system", along with a staff that "fills orders quickly", have many applauding it as "the coffee company to end all arguments."

K&L Wine Merchants *Wine/Liquor* 26 | 19 | 21 | M
www.klwines.com | 877-559-4637

Ok, maybe it "isn't too sexy", but "who needs style when you have substance?" pose partisans of this Web adjunct of a "favorite" San Francisco Bay Area wine purveyor, which imparts seriously "detailed" information about its "terrific selection" strong on California, Bordeaux and Burgundy producers (including "high-end" and hard-to-find vintages); its "competitive prices", "quality" goods "received in pristine condition" and "great e-mail and phone service" have most toasting it as an "Internet sensation"; P.S. "make sure to sign up for" their "amusing, informative" newsletter.

Karl Ehmer *Meat/Poultry* 25 | 19 | 23 | M
www.karlehmer.com | 800-487-5275

"*Sehr gut!*" cry enthusiasts of this unpretentious online market whose "old-world bratwurst and Westphalian and assorted cold cuts" trace their roots back to Mr. Ehmer's first butcher shop in NYC (founded in 1932); since his products are "hard to find in local stores", this Web site is prized for its offerings from *senfgurken* pickles, red cabbage and spaetzle to, of course, those "wondrous sausages" and other "German-style meats" that are simply "the very, very best."

King Arthur Flour/ 28 | 23 | 25 | M
The Baker's Catalogue *Grains/Beans*
www.bakerscatalogue.com | 800-827-6836

This online arm of a 200-year-old New England flour "mecca" offers a "fantastic", "high-quality" selection spanning "everything for your baking needs", from the "best flours", mixes and "fine ingredients" to "hard-to-find accoutrements"; the company is known for its "excellent customer service", which extends to its Web site in the form of "good recipes, advice" and "technical information" about the products, making it "a must if you bake" – and "if you don't, you will after visiting."

La Colombe *Coffee/Tea* 28 | 20 | 22 | E
www.lacolombe.com | 800-563-0860

It's admired as "one of the best roasters in the business", and this favorite of coffee connoisseurs – "Philly's best-known!" – sells its five "rich" blends, poured in many of the country's "finest restaurants" (e.g. Jean-Georges Vongerichten's), via an attractive, easy-to-use Web site; yes, such "superb" products will run you a lot of beans, but at least the flat-rate fee for its "fast delivery" is "reasonable"; N.B. plans are afoot for a NYC retail outlet in late 2007.

	QUALITY	DISPLAY	SERVICE	COST

La Tienda *Specialty Shop* | 26 | 22 | 26 | M |
www.tienda.com | 800-710-4304

"*The* place" on the Web for "authentic Spanish foods", this "excellent" purveyor's "wonderful", "well-displayed, expansive selection" of imports boasts everything from artisanal chorizo, *jamon* and cheeses to olives, nuts, grains, spices, cookware and wine, including many "otherwise hard-to-find" offerings; the crowning touches are "fair prices", top-drawer service and reliable delivery that ensures the goods arrive "in a timely fashion."

Lobster Gram *Seafood* | 23 | 22 | 24 | E |
www.livelob.com | 800-548-3562

"It's the original and still the best" say crustacean-lovers of this Maine monolith offering what may be "the best Internet deal for" live lobsters and frozen tails, as well as shrimp, scallops and clam bakes, not to mention prepared foods like "soups and bisques to-die-for"; its site is "easy to navigate" and the service people are "great to work with", leading connoisseurs to cheer "you can't go wrong"; P.S. those "succulent" bugs make "great gifts", especially as "all the tools down to bibs and wipes" are included.

MarthaStewartFlowers.com *Flowers* | 23 | 23 | 20 | E |
www.marthastewartflowers.com | 800-462-7842

The domestic doyenne herself "must be on the shipping floor" because the "beautiful, fresh", "clever" arrangements from this online florist "all come out" with "that signature Martha touch"; its handy site allowing customers to "upgrade the vase" and "see what it will look like with selected flowers", not to mention "quick service", means most find it "worth" the somewhat "expensive" rates; P.S. many choices are "arrange-it-yourself", so "be sure you know what you're ordering."

Mighty Leaf *Coffee/Tea* | 28 | 23 | 23 | E |
www.mightyleaf.com | 877-698-5323

Though it's the top-"quality" hand-blended teas that win this San Francisco outfit its customers' unflagging loyalty ("Mighty Leaf, I love you"), what draws the most comments are its "wonderful" "netted fabric" teabags that "don't impart extra flavor" to the brew and are "pretty" to boot; the "amazing", largely organic selection spans green, black, white and herbal varieties, including "unusual" blends, arrayed on a site that's "easy-to-navigate" and backed by "great", "knowledgeable" service, which for most offsets the somewhat steep prices; N.B. there are also accessories like teapots as well as gift assortments.

Molinari & Sons *Charcuterie* | 25 | 18 | 20 | M |
www.molinarisalame.com

"Beautiful, authentic salumi" is the specialty of this 100-year-old family-owned San Francisco business that sells its coppa and other dry-cured meats, as well as cooked cold cuts, via a straightforward Web site; prices are happily "reasonable", "ordering is easy" and delivery "on-time", making this the next best thing to living "down the street" from the store – "if you like salami, this is the place."

NapaStyle *Specialty Shop*
| 24 | 24 | 22 | E |

www.napastyle.com | 866-766-1600

Have "a piece of Wine Country delivered to your home" via chef Michael Chiarello's Web site that "really shows off the Napa life-style" while peddling an "extensive" array of "high-quality food products" – cheeses, oils, vinegars, seasonings, chocolates, specialty cookware – plus wine from Chiarello's own vineyard; it's a "great source for gifts", though price-watchers note that aside from its many "unique" offerings, you can "find the same items on other sites cheaper" – or avoid the "dazzling prices" by "waiting for a sale."

Neuske's *Meat/Poultry*
| 27 | 24 | 24 | E |

www.nueskes.com | 800-392-2266

When you're "achin' for bacon" this 75-year-old Wisconsin purveyor's applewood-smoked version is considered by connoisseurs the "absolute best anywhere", and through its no-nonsense Web site it also peddles a range of other "fantastic" "pig"-centric products, as well as beef, chicken, game, cheeses and various gift assortments; while a finicky few object to its site's "mass-market" feel, all appreciate its "great customer service."

Niman Ranch *Meat/Poultry*
| 28 | 22 | 25 | E |

www.nimanranch.com | 866-808-0340

"You can taste the humane treatment in every bite" claim conscientious carnivores partial to this "excellent" purveyor's "top-of-the-line" all-natural meats, including "tender, flavorful" traditionally and sustainably raised pork, beef and lamb from independent family farms; beyond the "can't-go-wrong" quality of its offerings, customers also appreciate the "great Web site", virtually "unequalled service" and "fastest delivery" – "these are good people."

Paper Source *Party Accessories*
| 25 | 22 | 23 | M |

www.paper-source.com | 888-727-3711

Among "the best there is in paper and invites", including "lovely" handmade products "no other store" carries, this Web dealer's "fantastic selection" and many customization options make it ideal for parties and weddings; there's "friendly service if you have questions", "everything comes as-ordered" and delivery is "quick", and savvy shoppers note "if you buy in bulk, it's really cheap."

Peet's Coffee & Tea *Coffee/Tea*
| 26 | 22 | 23 | M |

www.peets.com | 800-999-2132

"Before Starbucks there was" this Bay Area–based chain beloved by legions of "Peetniks" for its "top-notch", "strong", "flavorful" coffees in a variety of "excellent" roasts, available to those who "don't live near a store" via an "easy-to-use" Web site; "addicts" appreciate that its "amazing beans" and "delicious" leaves ("they take their teas as seriously as their coffees") are "reasonable priced", "lovingly shipped" and "delivered on time" – "these people rock!"

Pike Place Fish Market*Seafood*

| 28 | 23 | 24 | E |

www.pikeplacefish.com | 800-542-7732

The next best thing to "going in person", this Web counterpart to Seattle's "famous" Pike Place Market is "the place to go for salmon of any type", as well as other Pacific Northwest specialties including Dungeness crabs, halibut and "incredible" smoked Copper River king salmon; "you can't get any fresher" according to fin fans who appreciate that its well-packed goods "come fast", and though they concede it's "expensive" – "you get what you pay for."

Plum Party*Party Accessories*

| 23 | 24 | 21 | M |

www.plumparty.com | 800-227-0314

"*Très* cute" with "the perfect accessories for all occasions", this stylish site is a "fun, inspirational" place to find "terrific party supplies, decorations and special favors" according to enthusiastic hosts who note it could "save you hours of in-person shopping"; handily it "lets you search by theme or occasion", but just know "it's dangerous" – "everything is so nifty, you want to buy it all."

ProFlowers*Flowers*

| 22 | 20 | 22 | M |

www.proflowers.com | 800-776-3569

"Always on time", this online florist "consistently" provides the "freshest flowers around" according to legions of fanciers who say its "beautiful", "classy arrangements", "long-lasting blooms" and "reasonable prices" add up to solid "bang for your buck"; "excellent customer service" and "reliable" delivery that has the goods "arriving in great shape" are other endearments; P.S. it extends "special offers to regular customers."

Recchiuti Confections*Candy/Nuts*

| 28 | 25 | 26 | VE |

www.recchiuti.com | 800-500-3396, ext. 201

Approaching "chocolate perfection", Michael Recchiuti's "wonderful", "beautifully balanced" bonbons and other confections (including "exquisite fleur de sel caramels") tend toward "inventive and adventurous flavors" and "fantastic" shapes; though a few lament that the "Web site has a slim" lineup compared to Recchiuti's San Francisco store, the majority finds "outstanding quality and selection" that "put other more well-known chocolatiers to shame" – and that are "worth the outrageous cost"; P.S. sign up for the "great monthly newsletter."

Republic of Tea*Coffee/Tea*

| 25 | 23 | 22 | M |

www.republicoftea.com | 800-298-4832

"Tea as a fine art form" is the aspiration of this company run by "people passionate on the subject", whose "huge selection" of "exotic", "high-quality", "wonderfully packaged" leaves are backed by "environmental and health commitments" that "make you feel good buying from them"; though its products are now "widely available in stores", insiders recommend its "beautiful Web site" as "the place" to shop the "full array of wares" (including "pretty accessories"), and say "buying in bulk" will get you the "best value."

	QUALITY	DISPLAY	SERVICE	COST

Salumi Armandino*Charcuterie*

28 | 20 | 23 | E

www.salumicuredmeats.com | 877-223-0813

"Mario's dad is the best cured-meat maker in the world" declare devotees of Armandino Batali and his Seattle salumeria, whose Web site allows the rest of the country a shot at his "crazy-good" Italian-style products showcasing the "pig in all its glory"; the "exquisite, complex" offerings include about a dozen varieties of salami and other cured meats, all made traditionally by hand, so perhaps it's not surprising that the "prices are kind of high" and "they seem to be out of stock of certain things often" – most don't mind because the "quality is unparalled."

SeaBear Wild Salmon*Seafood*

23 | 19 | 23 | E

www.seabear.com | 800-645-3474

"Excellent" Copper River salmon is the mainstay of this Alaskan fishery and its straightforward Web site, but it also provides a "very good selection" of other fresh seafood (halibut, king crab), house-smoked wild salmon (packed with its patented 'gold seal pouch', which requires no refrigeration until opened) as well as prepared dishes like ready-to-eat fish and chowders; some carp about "expensive" prices, but all can appreciate that "shipments are prompt"; N.B. it also offers cedar wraps, planks and other grilling accessories.

See's Candies*Candy/Nuts*

24 | 21 | 23 | M

www.sees.com | 800-347-7337

"You don't have to go to California" to get the "scrumptious" chocolates, peanut brittle, scotch mallows and other "old-fashioned" confections that this "classic West Coast wonder" has long been beloved for, thanks to its "reliable" online counterpart; "the site is very easy to navigate", making it "very simple to purchase items for gifts" while prices "won't break the bank", adding up to "amazing value" – "nothing beats it!"

Spice House, The*Herbs/Spices*

27 | 21 | 23 | M

www.thespicehouse.com | 800-972-8496

Voted "easily the best" spice and herb purveyor – "online and off", this family-owned Chicago merchant boasts an "everything-under-the-sun" lineup of seasonings "from all over the world", which arrive "quick" and "super-fresh"; its site's wealth of product information and features like online forums, not to mention "knowledgeable" service folk who "help you sort through the differences of hundreds" of products, add up to "great shopping experiences", with "good-deal" prices to seal the deal.

Stonewall Kitchen*Specialty Shop*

27 | 25 | 24 | E

www.stonewallkitchen.com | 800-207-5267

"Delicious" jams, jellies, sauces and condiments with a "homey" look and taste are the stock in trade of this New England outfit whose "great Web site" allows easy access to the full line of its "now ubiquitous" array of "high-quality" products, many with "unusual" flavor combinations; it offers many assortments "perfect for gifting", and

QUALITY · DISPLAY · SERVICE · COST

there are also "tasty marinades" and pre-made baking mixtures that allow novice cooks and the pressed-for-time to "fake it" in style, all of which leads lauders to take in stride the "pricey" rates.

Surfas *Cookware*
26 | 18 | 19 | M

www.surfasonline.com | 866-799-4770

When on the hunt for "those harder-to-find items", savvy surfas turn to this moderately priced online annex to "the best kitchen supply store in LA", a "chef's nirvana" of "commercial"-quality cookware and accessories from pots and pans and cutlery to small appliances, "gizmos" and baking supplies, not to mention "interesting foodstuffs" including beans, grains, herbs, spices and more; "if it exists, they have it", however, some say the Web site itself "could use some improvement", and ditto the service.

Tsar Nicoulai *Caviar*
24 | 19 | 21 | VE

www.tsarnicoulai.com | 800-952-2842

"At last, domestic caviar that competes with the imports" cheer connoisseurs of this San Francisco–based purveyor best known for its "fresh, fabulous" farmed Californian Estate Osetra, though it also offers "elegant" eggs from Russia, Romania and Iran; its products are worthy of any "imperial feast", and a guilt-free one too considering that they're all sustainably sourced; N.B. it also offers the requisite accessories (mother-of-pearl spoons, etc.) as well as triple-smoked sturgeon and an array of gift assortments.

Upton Tea Imports *Coffee/Tea*
29 | 23 | 25 | M

www.uptontea.com | 800-234-8927

It "sets the standard for online tea purveyors" rave reviewers of this "fabulous" Massachusetts-based outfit that caters to the "complete fanatic" with its "superb" 400-plus selection of "quality" loose leaves "from all over the world", plus teapots, kettles and other accessories, all at "great prices"; its "easy site" allows browsing by product type (black, green, herbal, etc.) or by country of origin and provides a wealth of info on all things tea, while its "prompt" delivery and "reliable" service cinch its standing as "the best of the best."

Wally's Wine & Spirits *Wine/Liquor*
27 | 23 | 23 | E

www.wallywine.com | 888-992-5597

It's "easy in Wally world" according to devotees of this LA wine store and its nimble site allowing shoppers access to its "vast" (9,000 labels) "well-considered selection" of wines and spirits – "rare and hard-to-find items are no problem for them" – and its extensive "gourmet food" offerings including cheeses and charcuterie; its "helpful" customer service and delivery that gets it there "well-packed and quick" win kudos, though even "loyal Wallyites" note that while "some great prices can be had", it's "generally on the expensive side."

Whole Latte Love *Coffee/Tea*
24 | 21 | 24 | M

www.wholelattelove.com | 888-411-5282

"These guys are serious about their coffee!" rave reviewers of this connoisseur's source covering the "whole gamut of brewing needs" – from a "wide selection" of high-quality beans to "top-of-the-line espresso machines" and every imaginable tool and accessory in between; its "very competitive prices" and "exceptional" "personalized" service are other virtues, while the "easily navigable" site itself wins praise for its "helpful and objective pre-purchase advice" (including "in-depth product reviews") and "video demonstrations"; N.B. it also stocks tea and related accoutrements.

Wine.com *Wine/Liquor*

21 | 20 | 20 | M

www.wine.com | 800-592-5870

It's known as "the original" online wine store and it's "still one of the best" say admirers of this "easy-to-use" site whose 10,000-strong selection tends toward "mass-market" labels but includes "some harder-to-find" bottlings too; "fair prices" (augmented with frequent "shipping promotions") and a convenient array of gift options are points in its favor, but nonetheless a critical contingent claiming that it succeeds "by name alone" dismisses its offerings as "serviceable, but not memorable."

Wine Library *Wine/Liquor*

26 | 22 | 24 | M

www.winelibrary.com | 888-980-9463

An oenophile "could get lost for hours" browsing this "wacky" "wine-lover's heaven" of a site, the online counterpart of a legendary New Jersey store, whose "wide", "well-rounded" selection, "good prices" and "fast delivery" make it one of the "best on the Web" – "if you can't find something to your liking here, give up!"; it's also appreciated for its "informative format" with features like the "must-see" Wine TV daily video blog hosted by the owner (he's "a nut").

Zachy's *Wine/Liquor*

26 | 21 | 23 | E

www.zachys.com | 866-922-4971

This "exemplary" Westchester wine store and its "amazing Web site" boast a "huge" (5,000 labels) selection in "all price brackets", though it's particularly known for its "high-end" vintages (especially Bordeaux, Californian and Italian producers), as well as for its "excellent" futures and online auctions; it's a "pleasure to order from them" say surveyors who appreciate that the inventory is "well-displayed" and easy to browse, while the service is "efficient and helpful", and though there are complaints about "costly" prices, connoisseurs shrug "you get what you pay for."

Zingerman's *Specialty Shop*

28 | 23 | 26 | E

www.zingermans.com | 888-636-8162

The "personality and flair" of Ann Arbor's beloved landmark, widely considered the "best deli outside of NYC", extend to its "terrific Web site", whose "entertaining writing" and "cute illustrations" help "make you feel like you're in the store" browsing its "zingy" array of artisanal products including "unbeatable" breads, olive oils, cheeses, charcuterie and myriad "unique treats"; also a forte are "fun" gift baskets perfect "for the foodie", which most say "arrive in great shape", but "if there's a problem", the "nice" staff will "cheerfully solve it" – "who could want more?"

ONLINE SOURCES
INDEXES

Special Features

Listings cover the best in each category and include Quality ratings.

BAKED GOODS

Big Island Candies	25
Boudin Bakery	24
Burdick, L.A.	27
Cookies By Design	21
Cooking.com	24
Dancing Deer Baking	26
Ethnic Grocer	23
igourmet.com	26
Zingerman's	28

CANDY

Amazon.com	24
Artisan Made-NE	25
Big Island Candies	25
Bridgewater Chocolate	25
Burdick, L.A.	27
ChefShop.com	24
Cooking.com	24
Enstrom's	29
Ethnic Grocer	23
Fortnum & Mason	28
Fran's Chocolates	28
Hadley Fruit	24
igourmet.com	26
La Tienda	26
NapaStyle	24
Recchiuti Confections	28
Republic of Tea	25
See's Candies	24
Surfas	26
Zingerman's	28

CAVIAR & SMOKED FISH

Amazon.com	24
Browne Trading	28
Cooking.com	24
Di Bruno Bros.	26
igourmet.com	26
Pike Place Fish	28
SeaBear Wild Salmon	23
Tsar Nicoulai	24
Wally's Wine	27

CHARCUTERIE

Amazon.com	24
ChefShop.com	24
D'Artagnan	28

Di Bruno Bros.	26
Ferrari, A.G.	26
igourmet.com	26
Karl Ehmer	25
Molinari & Sons	25
NapaStyle	24
Salumi Armandino	28
Wally's Wine	27
Zingerman's	28

CHEESE & DAIRY

Amazon.com	24
Artisan Made-NE	25
Cheese/Beverly Hills	28
Cooking.com	24
Cowgirl Creamery	28
Di Bruno Bros.	26
Ferrari, A.G.	26
igourmet.com	26
La Tienda	26
NapaStyle	24
Wally's Wine	27
Zingerman's	28

COFFEE & TEA

Amazon.com	24
Cooking Enthusiast	26
Di Bruno Bros.	26
Ethnic Grocer	23
Ferrari, A.G.	26
Fortnum & Mason	28
Harney & Sons	27
igourmet.com	26
Illy	27
Intelligentsia Coffee	27
La Colombe	28
Mighty Leaf	28
Peet's Coffee	26
Republic of Tea	25
Upton Tea Imports	29
Whole Latte Love	24

COOKWARE & SUPPLIES

Amazon.com	24
Chefs	25
Chef's Resource	25
Cooking.com	24
Cooking Enthusiast	26

ONLINE SOURCES

SPECIAL FEATURES